AN EXPLANATION OF CONSTRAINED OPTIMIZATION
FOR ECONOMISTS

In a constrained optimization problem, the decisionmaker wants to select the "optimal" choice – the one most valuable to him or her – that meets all of the constraints imposed by the problem. Such problems are at the heart of modern economics, where the typical behavioral postulate is that a decisionmaker behaves "rationally"; that is, chooses optimally from a set of constrained choices.

Most books on constrained optimization are technical and full of jargon that makes it hard for the inexperienced reader to gain an holistic understanding of the topic. Peter B. Morgan's *Explanation of Constrained Optimization for Economists* solves this problem by emphasizing explanations, both written and visual, of the manner in which many constrained optimization problems can be solved. Suitable as a textbook or a reference for advanced undergraduate and graduate students familiar with the basics of one-variable calculus and linear algebra, this book is an accessible, user-friendly guide to this key concept.

PETER B. MORGAN is an associate professor in the Department of Economics at the University at Buffalo.

An Explanation of Constrained Optimization for Economists

PETER B. MORGAN

UNIVERSITY OF TORONTO PRESS
Toronto Buffalo London

© University of Toronto Press 2015

Toronto Buffalo London

www.utpublishing.com

Printed in the U.S.A.

ISBN 978-1-4426-4278-2 (cloth)
ISBN 978-1-4426-7777-4 (paper)

Printed on acid-free paper.

Library and Archives Canada Cataloguing in Publication

Morgan, Peter B., 1949–, author
An Explanation of Constrained Optimization for Economists / Peter B. Morgan

Includes bibliographical references and index.
ISBN 978-1-4426-4653-7 (bound). ISBN 978-1-4426-1446-8 (pbk.)

1. Constrained optimization. 2. Economics, Mathematical. I. Title.

QA323.M67 2015   519.6   C2015-900428-4

University of Toronto acknowledges the financial assistance to its publishing program of the Canada Council for the Arts and the Ontario Arts Council, an agency of the Government of Ontario.

  Canada Council **Conseil des Arts**
                      for the Arts   **du Canada**

 ONTARIO ARTS COUNCIL
                      CONSEIL DES ARTS DE L'ONTARIO
                      an Ontario government agency
                      un organisme du gouvernement de l'Ontario

University of Toronto Press acknowledges the financial support of the Government of Canada through the Canada Book Fund for its publishing activities.

To my grandmother, Phoebe Powley, for giving up so much to care for me.

To my mother, June Powley, for fiercely emphasizing education.

To my wife, Bea, with my love.

ACKNOWLEDGMENTS

Thanks are due to Professor Carl Simon for allowing my classes at the University at Buffalo to use a mathematical economics coursepack that he authored. The genesis of this book is in part a result of questions asked by students who sought to complete their understanding of Professor Simon's fine coursepack.

I sincerely thank Song Wei for pointing out various errors in an early draft of this manuscript. Thanks are also due to the many classes that have allowed me to practice upon them and, especially, for their insistence upon having clear explanations provided to them. Special thanks are due to Nicole Hunter for her tireless checking of this manuscript and her discovery of many potential embarrassments.

Several reviewers provided helpful suggestions and criticisms. I thank each for their time and efforts, and for their perspectives.

Full responsibility for any remaining errors, omissions, ambiguities, eccentricities, and the like remain with the author.

Contents

List of Figures

List of Tables

Chapter 1

Introduction

Hi there. Let's start by stating what this book is not. It is not a book about mathematics. It is instead a book about economics. Particularly, it is a book about economics spoken using the formal language of mathematics. What is the point? Why not just speak about economics in a language such as English or Spanish and maybe draw some pictures to help with a verbal analysis of the economic issue that interests you? The problem is the lack of precision inherent in a verbal argument. Mathematics is a precise language. Of course this precision comes with the cost that every little detail must be treated precisely. This is usually what drives economics students crazy and sometimes scares them. Then, on top of this agony there is the language and symbolism of mathematics itself. Who wants to worry about the meanings of squiggles such as ∇, $\otimes$, $\gg$, and $\uplus$? Actually, *you* should. These squiggles are nothing more than convenient short forms of longer phrases. ∇, for example, denotes an important something called a gradient vector. Surely it is easier to write down ∇ than it is to write the words "gradient vector," especially if you have to do this repeatedly. So here is the good news – the language is easy to learn and the ideas expressed by it are simple, practical, and usually rather obvious. There is nothing to fear. You and I have a lot to talk over and I think you will find it both valuable and fun – yes, fun! More than that, you will be able to protect yourself from those who will seek to challenge your arguments. Oftentimes an economist will have a strong intuitive hunch about the solution to a problem, but that is not enough. I should know – too often I have had a "strong intuition" about the answer to a problem only to discover eventually that I was wrong. Intuition is helpful, but nothing more than that. A precise answer is the outcome of a logical analysis, and there are few better ways to communicate logically than to use the language we call mathematics.

You may be one of the walking wounded who have studied mathematics or mathematical economics and have found it to be confusing. Perhaps you have found yourself wondering if you are not as clever as you hoped. Perhaps you have been reduced to mindless memorization of mathematical arguments, having given up on ever properly understanding them. I know what that is like. I also know that memorization is useless since it teaches no understanding, and, in the end, understanding is all that matters. So I want you to know at the outset that I am sympathetic to your needs and that we are going to work together to get it all straight.

Where is the right place to start? I'm sure that you already have quite a substantial knowledge of the basic ideas, such as sets, derivatives, vectors, and things like maxima and minima. The trouble is that quite often students are taught the meaning of important ideas in only special contexts. Since this is all they know, trouble arises whenever the student is asked to use an idea outside the special context in which it was "taught." Here is an example. Let me ask you, "What is an open set?" Now I'm serious about this. Stop reading. Pick up a pencil and on a piece of paper write down your answer(s) to this question. Go on. Go no further until you have done this.

Done it?

Maybe you wrote something like, "A set is open if and only if its complement is a closed set." If you did so then you are correct, but now I must ask you, "What is a closed set?" Don't tell me that a set is closed if and only if its complement is an open set, because then you have just gone around in a circle and said nothing useful.

Perhaps instead you wrote words like, "A set is open if and only if it consists only of interior points" or "A set is open if and only if it does not contain any of its boundary points." Of course, I now have to ask you what "interior" or "boundary" means. More important, even if I did, you would still be thinking about an open set in a rather special way. Now that's OK, in that special context. The trouble is, economists sometimes have to think about problems outside that context, and then you won't have a clue about the true, general meaning of "open set."

I don't want to worry you. My point is that your understanding of basic ideas may have been distorted by presentations of special cases of them that suggested to you that these special instances were more general. This can lead to a lot of confusion and distress. I would like my sometimes unpleasant experiences to help you to avoid that suffering. We are going to be alert to these possibilities as needed, so please don't fret. These issues will get sorted out one at a time as and when we need to sort them out.

So here's the plan. We economists constantly talk about a "rational choice" or an "optimal solution." When we do so we have in mind a problem in which a decisionmaker wants as much payoff (utility, profit, or whatever) as is possible. Often the decisionmaker's choices are restricted by one or more constraints (a budget or a technology, for instance). This book is aimed at making sense of this rational choice idea that is at the very heart of modern economics. By making sense I mean constructing a completely logical and precise *understanding* of the idea. If you have less than this, then how can you call yourself a properly educated economist? I like to visualize ideas. I spend a lot of time drawing pictures that display to me the essence of an economics problem. I use the picture to help me to write down the mathematical description of the problem. I work out the solution and then (this is important) I go back to the picture and see what the mathematics has told me. I need to convince myself that the information given to me by the mathematics is completely consistent with what the picture shows me. I need to *see* the solution and to understand it in a very basic and elementary way that lets me explain it with complete clarity to myself and to anyone else interested in my discovery. You should have the same goals. Half an understanding is a dangerous outcome.

I hope that you can now see why I say that this is not a book *about* mathematics. We will talk about economics in this book, and we will do so with coherent logic and precision. We will *use* mathematics, draw lots of pictures, and make sense of all of it as a cohesive whole, not as a bunch of disjointed bits and pieces. Trust me, this is going to be a good experience. I will need something from you, however, and that is a commitment from you to *think*. Understanding comes from patient contemplation and logical reasoning – these are your tools.

How should you use this book? That depends upon who you are. The core chapters are Chapters 8 and 10, which explain in some detail the ways in which we can solve rational choice problems, also known as *constrained optimization problems*. These two chapters make extensive use of ideas that are developed in Chapters 5, 6, and 7. These chapters in turn rely upon ideas developed in Chapters 2, 3, and 4. So if you already have a good understanding of the contents of Chapters 2, 3, 4, 5, 6, and 7, then you should proceed directly to Chapters 8 and 10. Otherwise, use the listing of chapter contents to decide when and how to use parts of the earlier chapters so that you can understand Chapters 8 and 10. No one book can hope to present everything you need to know about mathematics as it is applied to economics, so you might need also to have accessible to you another book that presents more basic materials. Three, of many, widely used such books are Simon and Blume 1994, Hoy et al. 2011, and Chiang and Wainwright 2005.

I did not intend to write this book. It "just happened." The blame lies with the many students who pressured me for clear explanations of mathematical ideas that their studies forced them to examine. My first reaction was to look for accessible, not too technical, accurate explanatory references that would meet their needs. I soon found that for the most part these references did not exist. The best available was a fine coursepack prepared by Professor Carl Simon at the University of Michigan. Professor Simon graciously allowed me to use his coursepack to instruct students trying to complete their Ph.D. in Economics degrees at the University at Buffalo. Even so, the requests did not cease. I found myself spending many long evenings preparing handouts on one topic after another. After several years of doing this I had unintentionally written about two-thirds of a book. For several years I resisted completing the task. I noticed that as time passed ever more blurry photocopies of my handouts were being passed from older to newer cohorts of students. There appeared requests for more materials, updates, and so on. So I finally decided to finish the job. I suspect that many books get written this way. In the end, the deciding factor is that the materials are wasted if they are not made accessible. Here it is, at last. I hope it is of value to you.

This book is not overly concerned with statements of theorems and their detailed proofs. Yes, there are theorems and there are proofs. But the emphasis of this book is on *explanation*. The question "Why?" is not a request for a proof. It is a request for understanding, and conveying understanding often requires a less than completely rigorous story so that small details do not distract from the essentials of an argument. I have tried always to remember this when writing. Where detailed proofs are provided, I have tried to explain their arguments.

I have found over the years that I can usually divide a group of students into two distinct sets. One set I usually label as the "techies," meaning the students who concentrate upon mathematics and find satisfaction in deriving formulae and memorizing proofs. But ask a typical techie to draw a picture illustrating the economic content of his or her work, or ask for an economist's explanation of what he or she has done, and you usually get a look back that suggests the student is wondering if you are insane. "Why would I ever want to do that?" seems to be the implied question. The answer is that economics merely uses mathematics, where appropriate, to understand more about economics. Mathematics itself is never the goal. The other set I think of as the "hand wavers." These students will happily draw a diagram, usually a little vaguely, and mutter in an imprecise way about what the solution to a problem "should look like." Asking for precise logic seems for many of these students to be a cruel and unreasonable request. So it will not surprise you to learn that most of my classes start out disgruntled when they learn that I insist both upon logic and upon an economist's understanding of what the logic yields. Usually, by about the middle of the semester, both groups have improved upon the deficient skill and the class becomes more homogeneous and better humored.

Let's get started!

Chapter 2

Basics

This book is not intended to be a substitute for the many others that already explain well the basics of the calculus and of linear algebra. But for your convenience this chapter provides a review of the mathematical ideas that are used in various places in the following chapters. If you are familiar with all of these ideas, then skip this chapter. Otherwise, select from within this chapter the appropriate reading. The discussions herein are less complete than in books that explain in detail the mathematical methods typically used by economists because the discussions provided here are tailored only to their uses in later parts of this book.

2.1 Space

Mathematicians are always talking about "spaces." They talk of metric spaces, vector spaces, and all sorts of such stuff, and we too will often use the word "space," so what does it mean? A space is a set. Not just any old set though. A space is a set that contains elements that all satisfy the same collection of properties. For example, we might be considering a set of elements all of which have the property that we can measure the distance between any pair of these elements. Such a set is called a *metric space* (the word metric means that distances between points are measurable). Or it might be that each element is a real number, and so we call such a set a real number space (a name that usually is abbreviated to *real space*). You will get the idea as we go along, so don't be alarmed by the word "space."

2.2 Real Vector Space

A real vector space is a set that is a space for two reasons. First, the set contains only real numbers (hence, a real space). Second, the real numbers in a real vector space form *ordered lists* of numbers that are called *vectors* because they possess a particular common collection of arithmetic properties. What are these properties? What is a vector?

First, think of an integer $n \geq 1$ that is the common length of every list of real numbers that we will consider. Symbols like x_i and y_i will denote the real numbers in the ith positions in these lists, for $i = 1, \ldots, n$. Consider, for example, the (vertically) ordered lists of real numbers

$$x = \begin{pmatrix} 1 \\ -7 \\ 0 \\ 6 \cdot 55 \end{pmatrix} \quad \text{and} \quad y = \begin{pmatrix} -3 \\ 16/7 \\ 9/2 \end{pmatrix}.$$

The number of positions in a list is the *dimension n* of the list. So the list x has dimension $n = 4$ and the elements of this list are $x_1 = 1$, $x_2 = -7$, $x_3 = 0$, and $x_4 = 6 \cdot 55$ (real numbers don't have to be integers, right?). The list y has dimension $n = 3$ and the elements of this list are $y_1 = -3$, $y_2 = 16/7$, and $y_3 = 9/2$.

Now let's insist that every ordered list of real numbers has the same dimension n, so that typical lists are written as

$$x = \begin{pmatrix} x_1 \\ x_2 \\ \vdots \\ x_{n-1} \\ x_n \end{pmatrix}, \quad y = \begin{pmatrix} y_1 \\ y_2 \\ \vdots \\ y_{n-1} \\ y_n \end{pmatrix}, \quad \text{or} \quad z = \begin{pmatrix} z_1 \\ z_2 \\ \vdots \\ z_{n-1} \\ z_n \end{pmatrix}.$$

A set X of such n-dimensional ordered lists of real numbers is a set of n-dimensional real vectors, an *n-dimensional real vector space*, when all of the lists in X possess a variety of obvious arithmetic properties.

Definition 2.1 (Real Vector Space). *A set X of n-dimensional ordered lists of real numbers is an n-dimensional real vector space if and only if:*

   1. *Addition. $x, y \in X$ implies that $z = x + y \in X$. So, for example, if $n = 3$ and $\begin{pmatrix} 1 \\ -4 \\ 6 \end{pmatrix} \in X$ and $\begin{pmatrix} 2 \\ 0 \\ -2 \end{pmatrix} \in X$, then $\begin{pmatrix} 3 \\ -4 \\ 4 \end{pmatrix} \in X$ also.*

2. Commutativity. *For every $x, y \in X$, $x + y = y + x$; i.e. the order of addition does not matter.*

3. Associativity. *$x, y, z \in X$ implies that $(x + y) + z = x + (y + z)$; i.e. how you pair up vectors when adding them does not matter.*

4. Zero Vector. *There is an ordered list $\underline{0} \in X$ such that for every $x \in X$, $x + \underline{0} = \underline{0} + x = x$. The zero vector is the n-dimensional list in which every element is the number zero; e.g. $\underline{0} = \left(\begin{smallmatrix} 0 \\ 0 \\ 0 \end{smallmatrix}\right)$ is the three-dimensional zero vector.*

5. Inverse Vector. *For each $x \in X$, there is $-x \in X$ such that $x + (-x) = (-x) + x = \underline{0}$; e.g. if $x = \left(\begin{smallmatrix} 1 \\ -4 \\ 6 \end{smallmatrix}\right) \in X$, then $-x = \left(\begin{smallmatrix} -1 \\ 4 \\ -6 \end{smallmatrix}\right) \in X$ and $x + (-x) = \left(\begin{smallmatrix} 1 \\ -4 \\ 6 \end{smallmatrix}\right) + \left(\begin{smallmatrix} -1 \\ 4 \\ -6 \end{smallmatrix}\right) = \left(\begin{smallmatrix} 0 \\ 0 \\ 0 \end{smallmatrix}\right)$. $-x$ is the inverse of x, and x is the inverse of $-x$.*

6. Scalar Multiplication. *Given all of the above properties, if λ and μ are scalar real numbers, then X also possesses the property of scalar multiplication if*

   (a) *for every $x, y \in X$, $\lambda(x + y) = \lambda x + \lambda y$,*

   (b) *for every $x \in X$, $(\lambda + \mu)x = \lambda x + \mu x$, and*

   (c) *for every $x \in X$, $(\lambda\mu)x = \lambda(\mu x)$.*

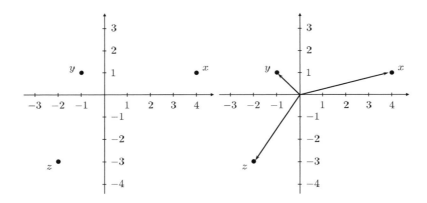

Figure 2.1: Vectors are points, not arrows.

The left-side panel of Figure 2.1 displays the two-dimensional vectors $x = \left(\begin{smallmatrix} 4 \\ 1 \end{smallmatrix}\right)$, $y = \left(\begin{smallmatrix} -1 \\ 1 \end{smallmatrix}\right)$, and $z = \left(\begin{smallmatrix} -2 \\ -3 \end{smallmatrix}\right)$. The *points* displayed in the panel are the vectors. In the right-side panel of the figure you again see the three vectors along with an arrow from the origin to each point. A common error for beginners is to believe that these arrows are the vectors, but they are not. The arrows depict how distant each vector (point) is from the origin, and the directions of the vectors from the origin. Sometimes, then, it is visually more informative to use an arrow to indicate a vector than it is to draw the (dot) vector itself. This will often be done in later chapters.

2.3 Some Linear Algebra

Several important results to do with constrained optimization amount to asking if a particular set of linear equations has a particular type of solution. So let us think of a simple pair of linear equations;

$$\begin{aligned} 2x_1 + x_2 &= 5 \\ x_2 + 4x_2 &= 13. \end{aligned} \qquad (2.1)$$

The unique solution is $x_1 = 1$ and $x_2 = 3$. Now look at the vector equation

$$x_1 \begin{pmatrix} 2 \\ 1 \end{pmatrix} + x_2 \begin{pmatrix} 1 \\ 4 \end{pmatrix} = \begin{pmatrix} 5 \\ 13 \end{pmatrix}. \qquad (2.2)$$

(2.2) and (2.1) are equivalent and have the same solution. They are equivalent because

$$\begin{aligned} x_1 \begin{pmatrix} 2 \\ 1 \end{pmatrix} + x_2 \begin{pmatrix} 1 \\ 4 \end{pmatrix} &= \begin{pmatrix} 2x_1 \\ x_1 \end{pmatrix} + \begin{pmatrix} x_2 \\ 4x_2 \end{pmatrix} \quad \text{(scalar multiplication property of vectors)} \\ &= \begin{pmatrix} 2x_1 + x_2 \\ x_1 + 4x_2 \end{pmatrix} \quad \text{(addition property of vectors)} \\ &= \begin{pmatrix} 5 \\ 13 \end{pmatrix}. \end{aligned}$$

Any set of linear simultaneous equations like (2.1) is the same as a vector equation like (2.2). That is, a system of m linear equations in n unknowns $x_1, \ldots, x_n$

$$\begin{aligned} a_{11}x_1 + a_{12}x_2 + \cdots + a_{1n}x_n &= b_1 \\ a_{21}x_1 + a_{22}x_2 + \cdots + a_{2n}x_n &= b_2 \\ \vdots \qquad \vdots \qquad\quad \vdots \qquad \vdots \\ a_{m1}x_1 + a_{m2}x_2 + \cdots + a_{mn}x_n &= b_m \end{aligned} \qquad (2.3)$$

is equivalent to the vector equation

$$x_1 \begin{pmatrix} a_{11} \\ a_{21} \\ \vdots \\ a_{m1} \end{pmatrix} + x_2 \begin{pmatrix} a_{12} \\ a_{22} \\ \vdots \\ a_{m2} \end{pmatrix} + \cdots + x_n \begin{pmatrix} a_{1n} \\ a_{2n} \\ \vdots \\ a_{mn} \end{pmatrix} = \begin{pmatrix} b_1 \\ b_2 \\ \vdots \\ b_m \end{pmatrix}. \tag{2.4}$$

The left side of (2.2) is a weighted sum of the vectors $\binom{2}{1}$ and $\binom{1}{4}$. The weights are x_1 and x_2. A weighted sum of vectors is called a *linear combination* of the vectors. Thus the left side of (2.2) is a linear combination of $\binom{2}{1}$ and $\binom{1}{4}$, and this linear combination creates, or *generates*, the vector $\binom{5}{13}$ when the weights used in the linear combination are $x_1 = 1$ and $x_2 = 3$. This means that the equations (2.1) have a solution if and only if there are values for the weights x_1 and x_2 that create a linear combination of $\binom{2}{1}$ and $\binom{1}{4}$ that generates $\binom{5}{13}$. This is true in general. That is,

the simultaneous linear equation system (2.3) *has a solution if and only if there exist weights* $x_1, \ldots, x_n$ *satisfying* (2.4).

This is why we should now spend some time thinking about when vectors can be, or cannot be, generated as linear combinations of other vectors.

Take a given set V of vectors v and let $L(V)$ be the set of all of the vectors that can be created (generated) by linear combinations of the vectors $v \in V$. A basic example is the set

$$V = \{e^1, e^2\}, \text{ where } e^1 = \begin{pmatrix} 1 \\ 0 \end{pmatrix} \text{ and } e^2 = \begin{pmatrix} 0 \\ 1 \end{pmatrix}.$$

Think of any two-dimensional vector at all, say, $\binom{x_1}{x_2}$. This vector is generated from e^1 and e^2 by the linear combination

$$x_1 e^1 + x_2 e^2 = x_1 \begin{pmatrix} 1 \\ 0 \end{pmatrix} + x_2 \begin{pmatrix} 0 \\ 1 \end{pmatrix} = \begin{pmatrix} x_1 \\ x_2 \end{pmatrix},$$

so $\{e^1, e^2\}$ is a set of vectors that, by linear combination, can generate every vector in the two-dimensional real vector space $L(\{e^1, e^2\}) = \Re^2$ (see Figure 2.2).

For another example consider the set

$$V = \{v^1, v^2\}, \text{ where } v^1 = \begin{pmatrix} 1 \\ 1 \end{pmatrix} \text{ and } v^2 = \begin{pmatrix} -1 \\ -1 \end{pmatrix}.$$

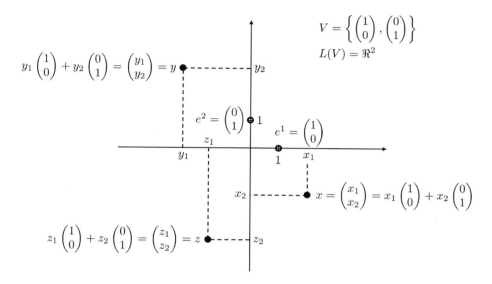

Figure 2.2: Linear combinations of $e^1 = \begin{pmatrix} 1 \\ 0 \end{pmatrix}$ and $e^2 = \begin{pmatrix} 0 \\ 1 \end{pmatrix}$ generate all of $\Re^2$.

A linear combination of v^1 and v^2 is a vector

$$v = x_1 v^1 + x_2 v^2 = x_1 \begin{pmatrix} 1 \\ 1 \end{pmatrix} + x_2 \begin{pmatrix} -1 \\ -1 \end{pmatrix} = \begin{pmatrix} x_1 - x_2 \\ x_1 - x_2 \end{pmatrix}$$

consisting of the same element in both positions. All such vectors are contained in the $45°$ straight line $L(V)$ through the origin that contains both v^1 and v^2; see Figure 2.3. This straight line is only a tiny part of $\Re^2$. A vector not in the line $L(V)$, such as $\begin{pmatrix} 3 \\ 2 \end{pmatrix}$ for example, cannot be generated by v^1 and v^2. Equivalently, then, the simultaneous linear equation system

$$1 \times x_1 + (-1) \times x_2 = 3$$
$$1 \times x_1 + (-1) \times x_2 = 2$$

(2.5)

does not have a solution.

The set $L(V)$ of vectors generated by linear combinations of the vectors in V is called the set of vectors *spanned* by V and the set V is called a *basis* for $L(V)$. In our examples, $\{\begin{pmatrix} 1 \\ 0 \end{pmatrix}, \begin{pmatrix} 0 \\ 1 \end{pmatrix}\}$ spans all of $\Re^2$ and is a basis for $\Re^2$, and $\{\begin{pmatrix} 1 \\ 1 \end{pmatrix}, \begin{pmatrix} -1 \\ -1 \end{pmatrix}\}$ spans the $45°$ line $\{(x, x) \mid -\infty < x < \infty\}$ and is a basis for this line.

Why does the set $\{e^1, e^2\}$ generate all of $\Re^2$ while the set $\{v^1, v^2\}$ generates only the $45°$ line in Figure 2.3? The answer is that neither of the vectors e^1 and e^2 can be written as a multiple of the other; *i.e.* there is no number λ such that $\begin{pmatrix} 1 \\ 0 \end{pmatrix} = \lambda \begin{pmatrix} 0 \\ 1 \end{pmatrix}$.

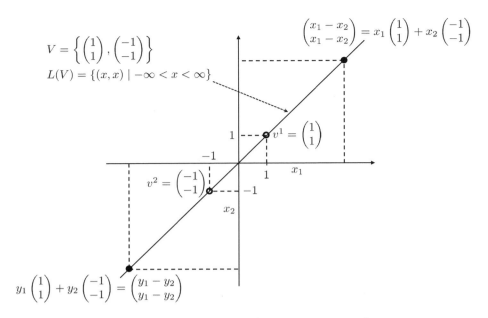

Figure 2.3: Linear combinations of $v^1 = \begin{pmatrix} 1 \\ 1 \end{pmatrix}$ and $v^2 = \begin{pmatrix} -1 \\ -1 \end{pmatrix}$ generate only vectors $\begin{pmatrix} x \\ x \end{pmatrix}$.

We say that the vectors e^1 and e^2 are *linearly independent*. In contrast, the vectors v^1 and v^2 are multiples of each other; *i.e.* $\begin{pmatrix} 1 \\ 1 \end{pmatrix} = (-1) \begin{pmatrix} -1 \\ -1 \end{pmatrix}$. Such vectors v^1 and v^2 are *linearly dependent*. To make further progress we need to formally define the ideas of linear independence and linear dependence.

Definition 2.2 (Linear Dependence, Linear Independence). *A set of n-dimensional vectors is* linearly independent *if and only if none of the vectors can be generated as a linear combination of other vectors in the set. The set of vectors is* linearly dependent *if and only if the set is not linearly independent.*

A spanned vector space often has more than one basis. For example, $\{\begin{pmatrix} 1 \\ 1 \end{pmatrix}, \begin{pmatrix} -1 \\ 0 \end{pmatrix}\}$ is another basis for $\Re^2$. The result that tells us this is called the Spanning Theorem. It is one of the most basic results in linear algebra.

Theorem 2.1 (Spanning Theorem). *Any set of n linearly independent real vectors of dimension n is a basis for the real vector space $\Re^n$.*

An Exercise. Show that the set $\{\begin{pmatrix} 1 \\ 1 \end{pmatrix}, \begin{pmatrix} -1 \\ 0 \end{pmatrix}\}$ is a basis for $\Re^2$.

Answer. We need to show that any vector in $\Re^2$, say, $\begin{pmatrix} b_1 \\ b_2 \end{pmatrix}$, can be generated as a linear combination of the vectors $\begin{pmatrix} 1 \\ 1 \end{pmatrix}$ and $\begin{pmatrix} -1 \\ 0 \end{pmatrix}$. That is, we need to show that, for any arbitrary but given values b_1 and b_2, there exist values x_1 and x_2 such that

$$x_1 \begin{pmatrix} 1 \\ 1 \end{pmatrix} + x_2 \begin{pmatrix} -1 \\ 0 \end{pmatrix} = \begin{pmatrix} b_1 \\ b_2 \end{pmatrix}.$$

It is easy to see that this is true when

$$x_1 = b_2 \quad \text{and} \quad x_2 = b_2 - b_1. \qquad \square$$

An immediate and important implication of the Spanning Theorem is

Theorem 2.2. *Any set of m real vectors of dimension n is a linearly dependent set if $m > n$.*

Another Exercise. Use the Spanning Theorem to prove Theorem 2.2.

Answer. Consider any subset V of n of the m vectors. Either this subset is a linearly dependent set or it is not. If the subset V is linearly dependent, then so is the set of all m vectors. If the subset V is linearly independent, then, by Theorem 2.1, it is a basis for $\Re^n$ and so each of the other $m - n$ vectors may be written as linear combinations of the vectors in V, making the set of all m vectors linearly dependent. $\qquad \square$

One of the most famous of the theorems to do with solving constrained optimization problems asks if there exists a nonzero and nonnegative solution to some particular linear equations. For now we don't need to worry about why this matters, but this is the right place to see what such a solution looks like. So have a look at Figure 2.4. The figure displays two linearly independent vectors: $v^1 = \begin{pmatrix} 2 \\ 1 \end{pmatrix}$ and $v^2 = \begin{pmatrix} 1 \\ 3 \end{pmatrix}$. The set consisting of v^1 and v^2 is a basis for all of $\Re^2$, so we can write any vector $\begin{pmatrix} b_1 \\ b_2 \end{pmatrix}$ as a unique linear combination of v^1 and v^2. That is, for any given values of b_1 and b_2, there always exist unique values for x_1 and x_2, solving

$$x_1 \begin{pmatrix} 2 \\ 1 \end{pmatrix} + x_2 \begin{pmatrix} 1 \\ 3 \end{pmatrix} = \begin{pmatrix} b_1 \\ b_2 \end{pmatrix}.$$

The question is "Are the values of x_1 and x_2 positive or negative?" The answer depends upon the values of b_1 and b_2. For example, if $(b_1, b_2) = (3, 4)$, then $(x_1, x_2) = (1, 1)$; if $(b_1, b_2) = (3, -1)$, then $(x_1, x_2) = (2, -1,)$; and if $(b_1, b_2) = (-5, -5)$, then $(x_1, x_2) = (-2, -1)$. The dotted line in Figure 2.4 that contains both the origin and v^1 is the line containing all multiples (positive, zero, and negative) $x_1 v^1$ of v^1. The dotted line containing both the origin and v^2 is the line containing all multiples $x_2 v^2$ of v^2. These two dotted lines partition $\Re^2$ into four parts, labeled Regions 1, 2, 3,

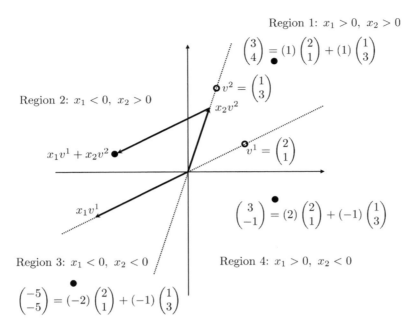

Figure 2.4: Various linear combinations of the basis vectors $v^1 = \begin{pmatrix} 2 \\ 1 \end{pmatrix}$ and $v^2 = \begin{pmatrix} 1 \\ 3 \end{pmatrix}$.

and 4 in Figure 2.4. The figure displays a vector in Region 2 that is created by a linear combination $x_1 v^1 + x_2 v^2$ in which $x_1 < 0$ and $x_2 > 0$. It will turn out that Region 1 is of great interest to us. This is the region consisting of vectors that are generated by positive (both $x_1 > 0$ and $x_2 > 0$) linear combinations of the two linearly independent vectors v^1 and v^2. Such regions are called *convex cones* and are crucial in computing solutions to constrained optimization problems.

It is time to introduce a new, more brief notation. Let us write the list of vectors used in (2.4) as the *matrix* A, the list of linear combination weights as the column vector x, and the list of right-side values as the column vector b:

$$
A \equiv \begin{pmatrix} a_{11} & a_{12} & \cdots & a_{1n} \\ a_{21} & a_{22} & \cdots & a_{2n} \\ \vdots & \vdots & \vdots & \vdots \\ a_{m1} & a_{m2} & \cdots & a_{mn} \end{pmatrix}, \quad x \equiv \begin{pmatrix} x_1 \\ x_2 \\ \vdots \\ x_n \end{pmatrix}, \quad \text{and} \quad b \equiv \begin{pmatrix} b_1 \\ b_2 \\ \vdots \\ b_n \end{pmatrix}.
$$

The matrix A is just a space-saving way of writing down an ordered list of column vectors all of the same dimension. Because A has m rows and n columns, we call A an $m \times n$ matrix (always write the number of rows first and the number of columns second). Next, again for brevity, we write

$$
Ax \equiv
\begin{pmatrix}
a_{11} & a_{12} & \cdots & a_{1n} \\
a_{21} & a_{22} & \cdots & a_{2n} \\
\vdots & \vdots & \vdots & \vdots \\
a_{m1} & a_{m2} & \cdots & a_{mn}
\end{pmatrix}
\begin{pmatrix}
x_1 \\
x_2 \\
\vdots \\
x_n
\end{pmatrix}
$$

$$
\equiv x_1
\begin{pmatrix}
a_{11} \\
a_{21} \\
\vdots \\
a_{m1}
\end{pmatrix}
+ x_2
\begin{pmatrix}
a_{12} \\
a_{22} \\
\vdots \\
a_{m2}
\end{pmatrix}
+ \cdots + x_n
\begin{pmatrix}
a_{1n} \\
a_{2n} \\
\vdots \\
a_{mn}
\end{pmatrix}
=
\begin{pmatrix}
b_1 \\
b_2 \\
\vdots \\
b_m
\end{pmatrix}
= b.
$$

(2.6)

Statement (2.6) defines what is meant by the symbol Ax, called the multiplication of an $m \times n$ matrix A and an n-dimensional vector x. Such a multiplication is a convenient brief way of writing down a linear combination of the column vectors that make up the matrix A. $Ax = b$ is the same statement as (2.3) and (2.4). It says that the vector b can be written as a linear combination of the vectors that make up the columns of the matrix A and that, therefore, b belongs to the set of vectors that are spanned by the set of vectors that are the columns of the matrix A. We have arrived at another important result in linear algebra.

Theorem 2.3. *The simultaneous linear equation system $Ax = b$ has at least one solution if and only if b is a member of the set of vectors that is spanned by the column vectors of the matrix A.*

An Exercise. If the simultaneous linear equation system $Ax = b$ has a solution, then must the set of vectors

$$
\begin{pmatrix}
a_{11} \\
a_{21} \\
\vdots \\
a_{m1}
\end{pmatrix},
\begin{pmatrix}
a_{12} \\
a_{22} \\
\vdots \\
a_{m2}
\end{pmatrix},
\cdots,
\begin{pmatrix}
a_{1n} \\
a_{2n} \\
\vdots \\
a_{mn}
\end{pmatrix},
\begin{pmatrix}
b_1 \\
b_2 \\
\vdots \\
b_m
\end{pmatrix}
$$

(2.7)

(i) be linearly dependent?
(ii) If this set of vectors is linearly dependent, then must $Ax = b$ have a solution?

Answer.

(i) Yes. If $Ax = b$, then b is linearly dependent upon the column vectors making up the matrix A.

(ii) No. (2.5) is a counterexample. $Ax = b$ has a solution if and only if the vector b is linearly dependent upon the column vectors of A. The set (2.7) can be linearly dependent because of linear dependence among the column vectors of A irrespective of whether or not b is linearly dependent upon the column vectors of A. □

Now let's think about how many solutions there can be to an equation system such as (2.1). Reconsider our earlier examples of

$$2x_1 + x_2 = 5 \quad \text{and} \quad x_1 - x_2 = 3.$$
$$x_2 + 4x_2 = 13$$

The first of these possesses just one solution, $(x_1, x_2) = (1, 3)$. The second possesses infinitely many solutions $(x_1, x_2) = (x_1, x_1 - 3)$, one for each value of $x_1 \in \Re$. What causes these differences? Probably you are saying to yourself something like "The first example has two independent equations in two unknowns while the second example has only one equation in two unknowns." I agree. But think about this from another point of view. In the first example, the left sides of the two equations are the linear combination

$$Ax = \begin{pmatrix} 2 & 1 \\ 1 & 4 \end{pmatrix} \begin{pmatrix} x_1 \\ x_2 \end{pmatrix} = x_1 \begin{pmatrix} 2 \\ 1 \end{pmatrix} + x_2 \begin{pmatrix} 1 \\ 4 \end{pmatrix}$$

of two linearly independent vectors of dimension 2; neither $\begin{pmatrix} 2 \\ 1 \end{pmatrix}$ nor $\begin{pmatrix} 1 \\ 4 \end{pmatrix}$ is a multiple of the other. This is actually what you mean when you say "independent equations." In the second example, the left side of the equation is the linear combination

$$Bx = \begin{pmatrix} 1 & -1 \end{pmatrix} \begin{pmatrix} x_1 \\ x_2 \end{pmatrix} = x_1(1) + x_2(-1)$$

of two linearly dependent vectors of dimension 1; (1) and (−1) are multiples of each other. Observe that the row vectors $(2, 1)$ and $(1, 4)$ in the matrix A are linearly independent of each other since neither is a multiple of the other, and that there is just a single row vector $(1, -1)$ in the matrix B. The number of linearly independent *row* vectors in a matrix is called the *rank* of the matrix, so the rank of A is $r(A) = 2$ and the rank of B is $r(B) = 1$. You can think of the rank of a matrix as the number of "linearly independent equations" implied by the matrix.

An Exercise. What are the ranks of the matrices

$$A = \begin{pmatrix} 2 & 1 & 1 \\ 0 & -1 & 2 \\ 5 & 3 & 0 \end{pmatrix}, \quad B = \begin{pmatrix} 2 & 1 \\ 0 & -1 \\ 5 & 3 \end{pmatrix}, \quad \text{and} \quad C = \begin{pmatrix} 2 & 1 & 5 \\ 1 & 4 & 13 \end{pmatrix}?$$

Answer. $r(A) = 3$ because none of the row vectors $(2, 1, 1)$, $(0, -1, 2)$ or $(5, 3, 0)$ can be generated as a linear combination of the other two row vectors. $r(B) = 2$ because any one of the row vectors $(2, 1)$, $(0, -1)$, or $(5, 3)$ can be generated as a linear combination of the other two. For example, $(5, 3) = \frac{5}{2}(2, 1) - \frac{1}{2}(0, -1)$. $r(C) = 2$ because neither of the row vectors $(2, 1, 5)$ and $(1, 4, 13)$ is a multiple of the other. □

Simply put, if the linear simultaneous equation system $Ax = b$ displayed in (2.6) has a solution, then it has exactly one solution if the rank of the matrix A is the same as the number of unknowns, n. This amounts to saying that the equation system has the same number of linearly independent equations as there are unknowns. Fortunately for us, in most applications of these ideas to constrained optimization problems the number of equations, m, and the number of unknowns, n, is the same. When $m = n$ we can make simpler statements about when a linear simultaneous equation system $Ax = b$ has a solution, has a unique solution, or has more than one solution. In such cases the number of rows and the number of columns of the matrix A are both n, making the matrix A an $n \times n$ matrix. We call such a matrix a *square matrix* of *order n*.

Theorem 2.4. *If the linear simultaneous equation system (2.6) $Ax = b$ has at least one solution and $m = n$, then the system has a unique solution if the rank of A is n, and infinitely many solutions if the rank of A is less than n.*

So now we need a way of figuring out if the rank of an order n square matrix A is n, or is less than n. Fortunately there is a relatively easy way to do this. Let me introduce you to the *determinant* of a square matrix (nonsquare matrices, where $m \neq n$, do not have determinants). We will use $\det(A)$ to denote the determinant of a matrix A. The determinant of a matrix is just a number. It can be zero, or positive, or negative. Let's start with an order 1 matrix and an order 2 matrix. The determinant of a 1×1 matrix $A = (a_{11})$ is just a_{11}; $\det(a_{11}) = a_{11}$. The determinant of a 2×2 matrix $A = \begin{pmatrix} a & b \\ c & d \end{pmatrix}$ is

$$\det \begin{pmatrix} a & b \\ c & d \end{pmatrix} = ad - bc. \tag{2.8}$$

For example, $\det\left(\begin{smallmatrix} 1 & 6 \\ 2 & 3 \end{smallmatrix}\right) = -9$ and $\det\left(\begin{smallmatrix} -1 & 4 \\ -3 & -7 \end{smallmatrix}\right) = 19$. Once we get to square matrices of orders greater than 2 we have to work harder. There is more than one way to compute the determinant of a matrix. I will explain only one, the "expansion by cofactors" method. Consider the 3×3 matrix

$$A = \begin{pmatrix} -3 & 1 & -2 \\ 2 & -5 & 1 \\ 7 & 2 & 3 \end{pmatrix}. \tag{2.9}$$

For any $i = 1, 2, 3$ and for any $j = 1, 2, 3$, the ij^{th} *minor* of the matrix A, denoted by M_{ij}, is the determinant of the matrix obtained from A after we exclude both the ith row and the jth column of A. Thus, the minors of the matrix A above are

$$M_{11} = \det\begin{pmatrix} -5 & 1 \\ 2 & 3 \end{pmatrix} = -17, \ M_{12} = \det\begin{pmatrix} 2 & 1 \\ 7 & 3 \end{pmatrix} = -1, \quad M_{13} = \det\begin{pmatrix} 2 & -5 \\ 7 & 2 \end{pmatrix} = 39$$

$$M_{21} = \det\begin{pmatrix} 1 & -2 \\ 2 & 3 \end{pmatrix} = 7, \quad M_{22} = \det\begin{pmatrix} -3 & -2 \\ 7 & 3 \end{pmatrix} = 5, \ M_{23} = \det\begin{pmatrix} -3 & 1 \\ 7 & 2 \end{pmatrix} = -13$$

$$M_{31} = \det\begin{pmatrix} 1 & -2 \\ -5 & 1 \end{pmatrix} = -9, \ M_{32} = \det\begin{pmatrix} -3 & -2 \\ 2 & 1 \end{pmatrix} = 1, \ M_{33} = \det\begin{pmatrix} -3 & 1 \\ 2 & -5 \end{pmatrix} = 13.$$

When we multiply the ij^{th} minor of the matrix A by $(-1)^{i+j}$, we obtain the ij^{th} *cofactor* of the matrix A, denoted by C_{ij}; i.e. $C_{ij} = (-1)^{i+j} M_{ij}$. So for our matrix the cofactors are

$$C_{11} = (-1)^{1+1} M_{11} = -17, \ C_{12} = (-1)^{1+2} M_{12} = 1, \quad C_{13} = (-1)^{1+3} M_{13} = 39,$$
$$C_{21} = (-1)^{2+1} M_{21} = -7, \quad C_{22} = (-1)^{2+2} M_{22} = 5, \quad C_{23} = (-1)^{2+3} M_{23} = 13,$$
$$C_{31} = (-1)^{3+1} M_{31} = -9, \quad C_{32} = (-1)^{3+2} M_{32} = -1, C_{33} = (-1)^{3+3} M_{33} = 13.$$

The "expansion by cofactors" method of evaluating a determinant is simple. All you do is choose any row or any column and then, for each element in that row or column, add up the values of the element multiplied by its cofactor. Let's pick the third column, so $j = 3$. The sum of the elements in the third column of (2.9), each multiplied by its cofactor, is

$$a_{13}C_{13} + a_{23}C_{23} + a_{33}C_{33} = -2 \times 39 + 1 \times 13 + 3 \times 13 = -26.$$

Now let's instead pick the second row, so $i = 2$. The sum of the elements in the second row, each multiplied by its cofactor, is

$$a_{21}C_{21} + a_{22}C_{22} + a_{23}C_{23} = 2 \times (-7) + (-5) \times 5 + 1 \times 13 = -26.$$

Give it a try. Pick a row or a column and use the expansion by cofactors. No matter which row or column you choose, you will compute the same number, -26. This is the value of the determinant of the matrix. So, if you like shortcuts, you will look at a matrix to see which row or column contains the most zero elements (if any) and then expand along that row or column to minimize the amount of boring arithmetic.

An Exercise. Compute the determinants of the matrices below.

$$A = \begin{pmatrix} 4 & -1 \\ -8 & 6 \end{pmatrix}, \quad B = \begin{pmatrix} 3 & 0 & -4 \\ 5 & 1 & -2 \\ 1 & -1 & 6 \end{pmatrix}, \quad \text{and } C = \begin{pmatrix} 4 & -3 & 5 \\ -2 & 1 & -3 \\ -3 & 4 & -2 \end{pmatrix}. \tag{2.10}$$

Answer. $\det(A) = 24 - 8 = 16$. To minimize the work needed to compute the determinant of B, expand along either the first row or the second column. Let's choose the second column. Then,

$$\det(B) = (-1)^{2+2}(1)M_{22} + (-1)^{3+2}(-1)M_{32} = M_{22} + M_{32}$$

$$= \det \begin{pmatrix} 3 & -4 \\ 1 & 6 \end{pmatrix} + \det \begin{pmatrix} 3 & -4 \\ 5 & -2 \end{pmatrix} = (18 + 4) + (-6 + 20) = 36.$$

Let's expand along the second row of C. Then,

$$\det(C) = (-1)^{2+1}(-2)M_{21} + (-1)^{2+2}(1)M_{22} + (-1)^{2+3}(-3)M_{23}$$

$$= 2M_{21} + M_{22} + 3M_{23} = 2 \begin{pmatrix} -3 & 5 \\ 4 & -2 \end{pmatrix} + \begin{pmatrix} 4 & 5 \\ -3 & -2 \end{pmatrix} + 3 \begin{pmatrix} 4 & -3 \\ -3 & 4 \end{pmatrix}$$

$$= 2(6 - 20) + (-8 + 15) + 3(16 - 9) = 0. \qquad \square$$

For square matrices of orders $n \geq 4$, the expansion by cofactors method of computing a determinant is similar to the computations we have already performed, but the method quickly becomes very tedious as n increases. Once n is 5 or higher you probably should use a computer to do the job for you. To evaluate the determinant of an order n matrix A, you again start by choosing any row i or any column j and then expand along that row or column, giving

$$\det(A) = \underbrace{\sum_{j=1}^{n} (-1)^{i+j} a_{ij} M_{ij}}_{\text{row expansion}} = \underbrace{\sum_{i=1}^{n} (-1)^{i+j} a_{ij} M_{ij}}_{\text{column expansion}}. \tag{2.11}$$

Each of the minors M_{ij} is a determinant of an order $n-1$ square matrix. Each of these determinants must be evaluated, so, for each in turn, write the determinant as a sum like (2.11) of minors that are determinants of order $n - 2$ matrices. Keep going until you end up with only order 2 minors and use (2.8) to evaluate them. Problem 2.1 asks you to evaluate the determinant of a 4×4 matrix to give you an idea of what all of this involves.

Why are we computing determinants? Here is why.

Theorem 2.5. *Let A be an order n square matrix. Then* $\det (A) \neq 0$ *if and only if* $r(A) = n$.

Combine this statement with Theorem 2.4 and we learn that a system $Ax = b$ of n linear simultaneous equations in n unknowns with at least one solution has only a unique solution if the determinant of A is not zero, since this ensures that the columns of A are a linearly independent set of vectors. In other words, the rank of the order n matrix A is n. We say that such a matrix has *full rank*. Let's look again at the matrices in (2.10). There we see that $\det (A) = 16 \neq 0$, so A has full rank, $r(A) = 2$, telling us that the columns of A are a linearly independent set of vectors. Similarly, $\det (B) = 36 \neq 0$, so B is a full rank matrix, $r(B) = 3$, again meaning that the columns of B are a linearly independent set of vectors. $\det (C) = 0$, so C is not a full rank matrix. $r(C) < 3$ tells us that at least one of the columns of C is a linear combination of one or both of the other two columns. In fact, $\begin{pmatrix} 5 \\ -3 \\ -2 \end{pmatrix} = 2 \begin{pmatrix} 4 \\ -2 \\ -3 \end{pmatrix} + \begin{pmatrix} -3 \\ 1 \\ 4 \end{pmatrix}$.

This section presents only a few topics in linear algebra, each of which is used later in this book. Indeed, several of the important results in constrained optimization theory are applications of topics introduced here. Comprehensive introductions to linear algebra are available in many other books.

2.4   Direct Products of Sets

Suppose we have two sets, possibly containing quite different sorts of elements. Let's say that the sets are

$$S_1 = \{1, 2, 3\} \quad \text{and} \quad S_2 = \{\text{frog}, \text{toad}, \text{newt}, \text{salamander}\}.$$

We want to construct all possible *ordered* pairings of the elements of the first set with elements of the second set. Particularly, we want the first element in each pair to be from the first set and the second element in each pair to be from the second set. The collection of all such pairs is called the *direct product of S_1 with S_2* and is denoted by $S_1 \times S_2$. Thus,

$$S_1 \times S_2 = \{(1, \text{frog}), (1, \text{toad}), (1, \text{newt}), (1, \text{salamander}), (2, \text{frog}), (2, \text{toad}), (2, \text{newt}),$$
$$(2, \text{salamander}), (3, \text{frog}), (3, \text{toad}), (3, \text{newt}), (3, \text{salamander})\}.$$

By writing S_1 first and S_2 second in the symbol $S_1 \times S_2$, we state that in each pair the first element is from S_1 and the second element is from S_2.

So, what is the direct product $S_2 \times S_1$? Go ahead. Write it down before you read further.

The answer is the collection of pairs

$$S_2 \times S_1 = \{(\text{frog}, 1), (\text{frog}, 2), (\text{frog}, 3), (\text{toad}, 1), (\text{toad}, 2), (\text{toad}, 3), (\text{newt}, 1),$$
$$(\text{newt}, 2), (\text{newt}, 3), (\text{salamander}, 1), (\text{salamander}, 2), (\text{salamander}, 3)\}.$$

Notice that $S_1 \times S_2 \neq S_2 \times S_1$; the order of the direct product matters.

Briefly put, then, the direct product

$$S_1 \times S_2 = \{(x, y) \mid x \in S_1, \ y \in S_2\}$$

and the direct product

$$S_2 \times S_1 = \{(y, x) \mid x \in S_1, \ y \in S_2\}.$$

For a second example, suppose that $S_1 = [0, 1]$ and that $S_2 = [1, 3]$. Then the direct products $S_1 \times S_2$ and $S_2 \times S_1$ are as displayed in Figure 2.5.

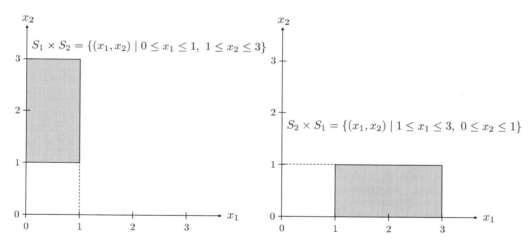

Figure 2.5: The direct products of the sets $S_1 = [0, 1]$ and $S_2 = [1, 3]$.

Ordered lists, such as the above pairs, can be of any length. For example, we can think of a triple (x, y, z), where x is an element of some set X, y is an element of some set Y, and z is an element of some set Z; *i.e.* $(x, y, z) \in X \times Y \times Z$. Or we can think of a list $(x_1, \ldots, x_n)$ of some arbitrary length n in which each element x_i belongs to some set X_i, for $i = 1, \ldots, n$. We write that

$$(x_1, \ldots, x_n) \in X_1 \times \cdots \times X_n = \times_{i=1}^{n} X_i.$$

For economists the usual such lists are n-dimensional vectors of real numbers.

Definition 2.3 (Direct Product of Sets). *The* direct product *of the sets* $S_1, \ldots, S_n$ *is*

$$\times_{i=1}^{n} S_i = S_1 \times \cdots \times S_n = \{(x_1, \ldots, x_n) \mid x_1 \in S_1, \ldots, x_n \in S_n\}.$$

When the sets $S_1, \ldots, S_n$ are the same set, S, the symbol $\underbrace{S \times \cdots \times S}_{n \text{ times}}$ is often abbreviated to S^n. For most of us, the most common example of this is to write

$$\Re^n \equiv \underbrace{\Re \times \cdots \times \Re}_{n \text{ times}} = \{(x_1, \ldots, x_n) \mid x_1 \in \Re, \ldots, x_n \in \Re\}.$$

2.5   Addition of Sets

Here are two simple sets, $S_1 = \{1 \text{ toaster}, 3 \text{ toasters}\}$ and $S_2 = \{4 \text{ toasters}, 6 \text{ toasters}\}$. Notice that all of the elements in both sets are measured in the same unit. This is important because we are about to add together elements from the two sets and for this to have meaning we require that the elements being added are measured in the same unit. The addition of these two sets is simply the collection of the sums of all of the possible pairings of the elements of the two sets. This is

$$S_1 + S_2 = \{1 \text{ toaster} + 4 \text{ toasters}, \ 1 \text{ toaster} + 6 \text{ toasters}, \ 3 \text{ toasters} + 4 \text{ toasters},$$
$$3 \text{ toasters} + 6 \text{ toasters}, \}$$
$$= \{5 \text{ toasters}, \ 7 \text{ toasters}, \ 9 \text{ toasters}\}.$$

The order in which we add the elements of the sets does not matter so it follows that $S_1 + S_2 = S_2 + S_1$.

It should be obvious that we can add together as many sets as we want, so long as the elements in all of the sets have the same unit of measurement. Convince yourself that, if $S_3 = \{0 \text{ toasters}, 2 \text{ toasters}\}$, then

$$S_1 + S_2 + S_3 = \{5 \text{ toasters}, \ 7 \text{ toasters}, \ 9 \text{ toasters}, \ 11 \text{ toasters}\}$$

and

$$S_1 + S_2 + S_3 = S_1 + S_3 + S_2 = S_2 + S_1 + S_3 = S_2 + S_3 + S_1 = S_3 + S_1 + S_2 = S_3 + S_2 + S_1.$$

Definition 2.4 (Addition of Sets). *Let X be a set for which the operation of addition, $+$, is defined. Let $S_i \subseteq X$ for $i = 1, \ldots, n$. Then,*

$$\sum_{i=1}^{n} S_i = S_1 + \cdots + S_n = \{x \mid x = \sum_{i=1}^{n} x_i, \ x_i \in S_i \text{ for } i = 1, \ldots, n\}.$$

An alternative, equivalent, way of writing this sum of sets is

$$S_1 + \cdots + S_n = \cup_{\substack{x_1 \in S_1 \\ \vdots \\ x_n \in S_n}} \left\{ \sum_{i=1}^{n} x_i \right\}.$$

This too is the statement that the set $S_1 + \cdots + S_n$ consists of all of the sums $x_1 + \cdots + x_n$ that can be constructed from the elements of the sets $S_1, \ldots, S_n$.

An Exercise. $S_1 = \{-4, 2, 5\}$. $S_2 = \{1, 2\}$. What is the set $S_1 + S_2$?

Answer. $S_1 + S_2 = \{-3, -2, 3, 4, 6, 7\}$. $\square$

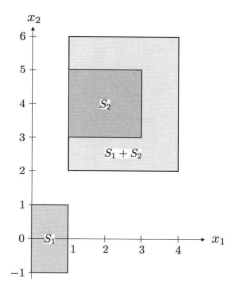

Figure 2.6: $S_1 + S_2 = ([0, 1] \times [-1, 1]) + ([1, 3] \times [3, 5]) = [1, 4] \times [2, 6]$.

An Exercise. The *negative of a set* S is denoted by $-S$ and is the set that contains the negatives of all of the elements of S. For example, if $S = \{-3, 0, 2\}$, then $-S = \{-2, 0, 3\}$. Is it true that adding a set S to its negative $-S$ creates the singleton set $\{0\}$; *i.e.* must $S + (-S) = \{0\}$?

Answer. No, in general. If the set S is a singleton, say $S = \{5\}$, then the set $-S = \{-5\}$ and then $S + (-S) = \{0\}$. But if, say, $S = \{-4, -1, 5\}$, then $-S = \{-5, 1, 4\}$ and so $S + (-S) = \{-9, -6, -3, 0, 3, 6, 9\} \neq \{0\}$. $\square$

An Exercise. What is the set $S = S_1 + S_2 = S_2 + S_1$ when $S_1 = \{(x_1, x_2) \mid 0 \leq x_1 \leq 1,\ -1 \leq x_2 \leq 1\}$ and $S_2 = \{(x_1, x_2) \mid 1 \leq x_1 \leq 3,\ 3 \leq x_2 \leq 5\}$?

Answer. $S = \{(x_1, x_2) \mid 1 \leq x_1 \leq 4,\ 2 \leq x_2 \leq 6\}$; see Figure 2.6. $\square$

If you had some trouble getting this answer, then here is an easy way to do it. Think of adding the set S_1 to each point in turn of the set S_2. Let's start by taking the left-bottom corner point $(1, 3)$ of S_2 and then adding the entire set S_1 to this point. Then take the next point just a tiny bit directly above $(1, 3)$ and again add the entire set S_1 to this point. Keep doing this until you reach the left-upper point $(1, 5)$ of S_2. You now have the "ribbon" displayed in the left-side panel of Figure 2.7 of vertically aligned, overlapping rectangles that in union are the rectangle $\{(x_1, x_2) \mid 1 \leq x_1 \leq 2,\ 2 \leq x_2 \leq 6\}$.

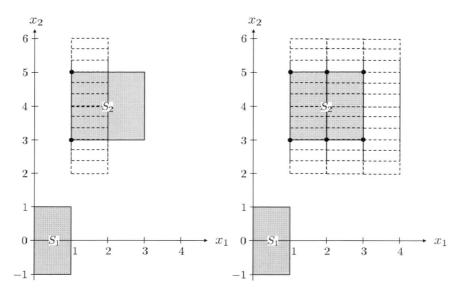

Figure 2.7: Constructing $S_1 + S_2 = ([0, 1] \times [-1, 1]) + ([1, 3] \times [3, 5]) = [1, 4] \times [2, 6]$.

If we do the same thing but start, say, at the point $(2, 3)$ in S_2 and then continue up to the point $(2, 5)$ in S_2, then we will create another ribbon of vertically aligned, overlapping rectangles that in union are the rectangle $\{(x_1, x_2) \mid 2 \leq x_1 \leq 3,\ 2 \leq x_2 \leq 6\}$ (see the right-side panel of Figure 2.7). We do this for every vertical line in S_2, finally creating the ribbon of vertically aligned, overlapping rectangles that in union are the rectangle $\{(x_1, x_2) \mid 3 \le x_1 \le 4,\ 2 \le x_2 \le 6\}$; see the right-side panel of Figure 2.7. Now we take the union of all of these rectangles and we see that the sum of the sets S_1 and S_2 is the rectangle $\{(x_1, x_2) \mid 1 \le x_1 \le 4,\ 2 \le x_2 \le 6\}$ that is displayed in Figure 2.6.

Another Exercise. Let $S_1 = \{(x_1, x_2) \mid 1 \le x_1 \le 3,\ 3 \le x_2 \le 5\}$ and let $-S_1 = \{(x_1, x_2) \mid -3 \le x_1 \le -1,\ -5 \le x_2 \le -3\}$. What is the set $S = S_1 + (-S_1)$?

Answer. $S = \{(x_1, x_2) \mid -2 \le x_1 \le 2,\ -2 \le x_2 \le 2\}$; see Figure 2.8. $\qquad\square$

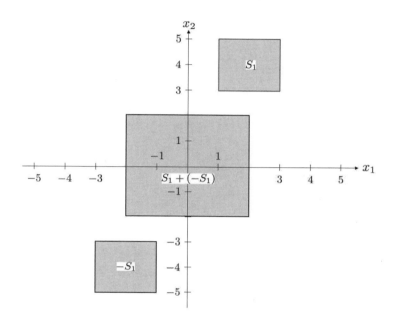

Figure 2.8: $S_1 + S_2 = ([1, 3] \times [3, 5]) + ([-3, -1] \times [-5, -3]) = [-2, 2] \times [-2, 2]$.

One More Exercise. Let $S_1, S_2 \subset \Re^2$ with $S_1 = \{(x_1, x_2) \mid x_1 - x_2 = 0\}$ and $S_2 = \{(x_1, x_2) \mid x_1 + x_2 = 0\}$. What is the set $S_1 + S_2$?

Answer. All of $\Re^2$. $\qquad\square$

Now let's see how good you have become. Try this next exercise. Let $S_1 = \{(x_1, x_2) \mid 0 \le x_1 \le 2,\ 0 \le x_2 \le 1\}$ and S_2 be the triangle with vertices at $(0, 0)$, $(1, 0)$, and $(\frac{1}{2}, 1)$ along with all of the points inside the triangle. These two sets are displayed in Figure 2.9. What is the sum $S_1 + S_2$ of these two sets? This is problem 2.9. Try it and then check your answer.

Before we leave this discussion of adding sets, there is one caution that I need to emphasize to you. When we say that some element $x \in X$, we often mean that

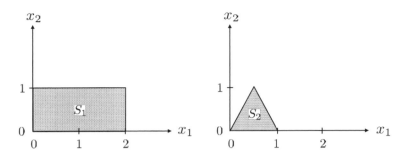

Figure 2.9: The sets S_1 and S_2.

X is a reference set; *i.e.* X is the set of all of the elements x that we are allowed to consider. So suppose that we are allowed to consider only values for x satisfying $0 \leq x \leq 4$, meaning that the reference set is $X = [0,4]$. Now consider the subsets S_1 and S_2 of X that are $S_1 = [0,2]$ and $S_2 = [1,3]$. What do you mean by $S_1 + S_2$? Is $S_1 + S_2 = [1,5]$? If you intend that $S_1 + S_2$ must be a subset of the reference set $X = [0,4]$, then the answer must be that $S_1 + S_2 = [1,4]$ only, since we are not permitted to consider any values outside of $[0,4]$. If instead you intend that $S_1 + S_2$ is a subset of $X + X = [0,8]$, then indeed $S_1 + S_2 = [1,5]$. So be careful. When you add a set $S_1 \subset X$ to another subset $S_2 \subset X$, you need to consider whether or not you intend that $S_1 + S_2 \subset X$ also. Sometimes there is no need to pay attention to this detail. For example, if $X = \Re$ and $S_1, S_2 \subset \Re$, then $S_1 + S_2 \subset \Re$ always. When adding sets, always remember what is the reference set.

2.6   Convex Sets

Simply put, a set is convex if, for every pair of elements in the set, every point in the "straight line" joining the two elements is a member of the set. Consider the subsets of $\Re^2$ that are displayed in Figure 2.10. The subsets S_1, S_2, and S_3 are all convex sets because any straight line that runs from any arbitrarily chosen point in the set to any other arbitrarily chosen point in the same set is entirely contained within the set. The subsets S_4, S_5, and S_6 are not convex since for each set there is at least one pair of points in the set such that the straight line connecting the points is not everywhere within the set.

The "straight line" between two members x' and x'' of some set is the set of *convex combinations* of x' and x''. Each of these convex combinations is just a weighted average of x' and x'' in which the weights are θ and $1 - \theta$ with $0 \leq \theta \leq 1$. More

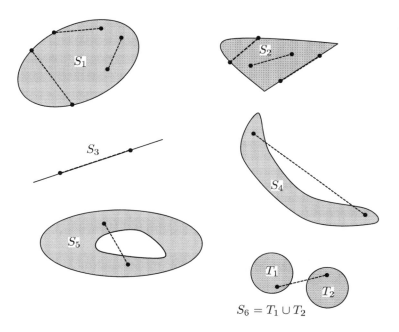

Figure 2.10: Some convex and nonconvex subsets of $\Re^2$.

formally, for a given value of $\theta \in [0, 1]$, the θ-weighted convex combination of x' and x'' is

$$x(\theta) = (1 - \theta)x' + \theta x''.$$

If $\theta = 0$, then the value of the convex combination is $x(0) = x'$. $x(1) = x''$. $x\left(\frac{1}{2}\right)$ is the point halfway along the straight line connecting x' and x'' or, if you prefer, it is the simple arithmetic average of x' and x''.

Definition 2.5 (Convex Set). *A set S is* convex *if it is empty or if, for every $x', x'' \in S$ and for every $\theta \in [0, 1]$, $x(\theta) = (1 - \theta)x' + \theta x'' \in S$.*

The above discussion and Figure 2.10 use the term "straight line" to describe when a set is convex or not. This is well enough for sets in which straight lines are well-defined geometric objects, such as in the real spaces $\Re^n$. But the ideas of convex combinations and convex sets are much more general than Figure 2.10 suggests. Consider the set of all of the real-valued and continuous functions $f : X \mapsto \Re$ that are defined on some set X. Any convex combination of such functions is also a real-valued and continuous function defined on X, so this set of functions is convex even though it cannot be depicted using a diagram as simple as Figure 2.10. Consider any two quadratic functions $a_1x^2 + b_1x + c_1$ and $a_2x^2 + b_2x + c_2$ mapping from the real line $\Re$. The convex combination of these quadratics is

$$\underbrace{((1-\theta)a_1 + \theta a_2)}_{a}\, x^2 + \underbrace{((1-\theta)b_1 + \theta b_2)}_{b}\, x + \underbrace{(1-\theta)c_1 + \theta c_2}_{c}\,,$$

which is another quadratic. Thus the set of all quadratics mapping from the real line is a convex set. There are endless other examples, but the main point here is that convexity of sets is an idea that is used for much more than just subsets of real number vector spaces.

It is often necessary to distinguish between sets such as S_1 and S_2 in Figure 2.10. Both sets are convex. But notice that the boundary of S_1 is everywhere "curved" while the boundary of S_2 has a "straight" segment. Because the boundary of S_1 is everywhere curved, any line connecting two points in S_1, excluding its end points, lies entirely in the *interior* of S_1; *i.e.* with its end points removed, such a line never intersects the boundary of S_1. In contrast, in set S_2 it is possible to find two points such that the straight line connecting them, with its end points removed, does intersect with the set's boundary – see the right-most of the three dashed lines in S_2. A set such as S_1 is called *strictly convex*. A set such as S_2 is just convex, although we should call it *weakly convex* whenever we wish to emphasize that it is not strictly convex. By the way, the interior of a set S is usually denoted by the symbol Int S.

Definition 2.6 (Strictly Convex Set). *A set S is* strictly convex *if, for all $x', x'' \in S$ with $x' \neq x''$, $x(\theta) = (1-\theta)x' + \theta x'' \in$ Int S for all $\theta \in (0,1)$.*

Notice that we consider only $0 < \theta < 1$. By not considering either $\theta = 0$ or $\theta = 1$, we are "chopping off" the endpoints x' and x'' from the line connecting x' and x''. Notice also that for a set to be strictly convex it must contain at least two different points; we are not allowed to consider $x' = x''$.

It is important to note that a set must have a nonempty interior to be strictly convex. Consider, for example, the set S_3 in Figure 2.10. S_3 is (weakly) convex; because the set does not have an interior (Int $S_3 = \emptyset$), it cannot be strictly convex.

Is a singleton set, such as, say, $S = \{3\}$, a convex set? Is a singleton set a strictly convex set? Consider your answers before proceeding to the next paragraph.

Look again at Definition 2.6 and recollect that a strictly convex set S must have at least two *distinct* points, x' and x'' with $x' \neq x''$, in it. Obviously this is not so for a singleton set, which is, therefore, not a strictly convex set. Why so? For a set to have a nonempty interior, it must contain more than one point, right? A singleton set has no interior and so cannot be strictly convex. Even so, is a singleton set a convex set? Look again at Definition 2.5 and notice that there is no requirement that the points x' and x'' be distinct; *i.e.* $x' = x''$ is allowed. So suppose S is the singleton set $\{x'\}$. Take $x'' = x'$ and the convex combination $x(\theta) = (1 - \theta)x' + \theta x'' = x'$ for all $\theta \in [0, 1]$, so $x(\theta) = x' \in S$ for all $\theta \in [0, 1]$. Thus a singleton set is always a weakly convex set and is never a strictly convex set.

Is the empty set $\emptyset$ a convex set? Definition 2.5 simply asserts that the empty set is convex. Is the empty set a strictly convex set? Definition 2.6 requires that a strictly convex set contain at least two distinct points. Obviously this is not so for the empty set, so the empty set is only weakly convex by definition.

For economists, common examples of convex sets are the budget set $B(p_1, p_2, m) = \{(x_1, x_2) \mid x_1 \geq 0, \ x_2 \geq 0, \ p_1 x_1 + p_2 x_2 \leq m\}$ with $p_1 > 0$, $p_2 > 0$ and $m \geq 0$, the set of bundles $\mathrm{WP}(x_1', x_2') = \{(x_1, x_2) \mid (x_1, x_2) \succeq (x_1', x_2')\}$ that a consumer with convex preferences prefers at least as much as a given bundle (x_1', x_2'), and the technology set $T = \{(x, y) \mid x \geq 0, \ 0 \leq y \leq f(x)\}$ of a firm with a production function $f(x)$ that exhibits decreasing returns to scale and uses a quantity x of a single input to produce a quantity y of a single product. All three sets are displayed in Figure 2.11. As drawn, the budget set $B(p_1, p_2, m)$ and the technology set T are weakly convex while the weakly preferred set $\mathrm{WP}(x_1', x_2')$ is strictly convex.

Convex sets have a variety of useful properties. Included in these are that the intersection of convex sets is a convex set, the addition of convex sets is a convex set and the direct product of convex sets is a convex set.

Theorem 2.6 (Intersection of Convex Sets). *Let $S_1, \ldots, S_n$ be convex subsets of a set X. Then the set $S = S_1 \cap \cdots \cap S_n$ is a convex subset of X.*

Figure 2.12 illustrates the result by displaying six intersections of convex sets. S_1 and S_2 are both strictly convex sets. Their intersection, $S_1 \cap S_2$, is also a strictly convex set. So is it always the case that the intersection of two strictly convex sets is a strictly convex set? Have a good look at Figure 2.12 before you answer.

The answer is "No." For example, S_7 and S_8 are both strictly convex sets, but their intersection is only a singleton set, and a singleton set is always weakly convex. Again, both S_9 and S_{10} are strictly convex sets, but their intersection is the empty set, which is a weakly convex set. But there is an important case in which the intersection of two strictly convex sets is a strictly convex set. What is it? Hint: Look again at Figure 2.12 and note what is different about $S_1 \cap S_2$ and either of $S_7 \cap S_8$ or $S_9 \cap S_{10}$.

The crucial difference is that $S_1 \cap S_2$ has a nonempty interior, while both $S_7 \cap S_8$ and $S_9 \cap S_{10}$ have empty interiors. The theorem is that, "if S_1 and S_2 are both strictly convex subsets of X, then $S_1 \cap S_2$ is a strictly convex subset of X if and only if the interior of $S_1 \cap S_2$ is not empty."

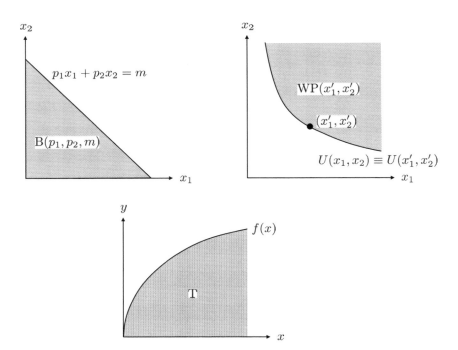

Figure 2.11: A weakly convex budget set, a strictly convex set of weakly preferred consumption bundles, and a weakly convex technology set.

Can the intersection of weakly convex sets be a strictly convex set? Once again, have a good look at Figure 2.12 before you answer.

The answer is "Yes." In Figure 2.12 the sets S_5 and S_6 are only weakly convex. Yet their intersection $S_5 \cap S_6$ is a strictly convex set. Even so, as is illustrated by $S_{11} \cap S_{12}$, the intersection of two weakly convex sets can be a weakly convex set. And $S_3 \cap S_4 = S_4$ illustrates that the intersection of a strictly convex set with a weakly convex set can be a weakly convex set. It should take you only a moment to think of some examples in which the intersection of a strictly convex set and a weakly convex set is a strictly convex set.

Theorem 2.7 (Addition of Convex Sets). *Let $S_1, \ldots, S_n$ be convex subsets of a set X. Then the set $S = S_1 + \cdots + S_n$ is a convex subset of $\underbrace{X + \cdots + X}_{n \text{ times}}$.*

Figure 2.7, Figure 2.8, and, together, Figures 2.9 and Figure 2.34 all illustrate the result. Problems 2.16 and 2.17 ask you for proofs.

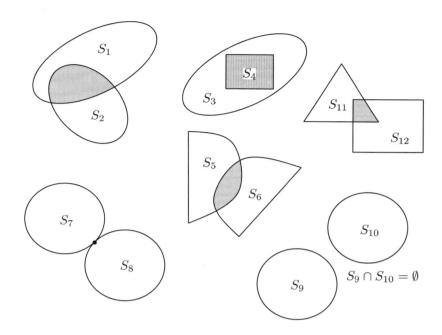

Figure 2.12: Six intersections of convex sets.

Theorem 2.8 (Direct Product of Convex Sets). *For $i = 1, \ldots, n$ let S_i be a convex subset of a set X_i. Then the set $S = S_1 \times \cdots \times S_n$ is a convex subset of the set $X = X_1 \times \cdots \times X_n$.*

Figure 2.13 provides some examples of the result. In the top panel, $S_1 = \{x \mid 1 \leq x \leq 3\}$ and $S_2 = \{x \mid 3 \leq x \leq 4\}$ are both intervals in the real line $\Re^1$. Their direct product is the rectangle in $\Re^1 \times \Re^1 = \Re^2$ that is $[1, 3] \times [3, 4] = \{(x_1, x_2) \mid 1 \leq x_1 \leq 3,\ 3 \leq x_2 \leq 4\}$. Notice that both S_1 and S_2 are *strictly* convex subsets of $\Re^1$ and yet their direct product is a *weakly* convex subset of $\Re^2$.

In the middle panel of Figure 2.13, $S_1 = \{(x_1, x_2) \mid (x_1 - 2)^2 + (x_2 - 2)^2 = 4\}$ is the subset of $\Re^2$ that is the circle of radius 2 centered at the point $(x_1, x_2) = (2, 2)$. The set $S_2 = \{2\}$ is the singleton set of $\Re^1$ that contains only the number 2. Their direct product is the circle of radius 2 centered at the point $(x_1, x_2, x_3) = (2, 2, 2)$ that lies only in the "horizontal" plane $x_3 \equiv 2$. The set S_1 is not a convex set since it consists only of the circumference of the circle. As a consequence the set $S_1 \times S_2$ is not convex. However, if we change S_1 by also including all of the points inside the circle, then we have changed S_1 into the disk with radius 2 centered at $(x_1, x_2) = (2, 2)$ in $\Re^2$; *i.e.* now $S_1 = \{(x_1, x_2) \mid (x_1 - 2)^2 + (x_2 - 2)^2 \leq 4\}$. S_1 is now a strictly convex subset of $\Re^2$. S_2 is a weakly convex subset of R_1. The direct product $S_1 \times S_2$ then

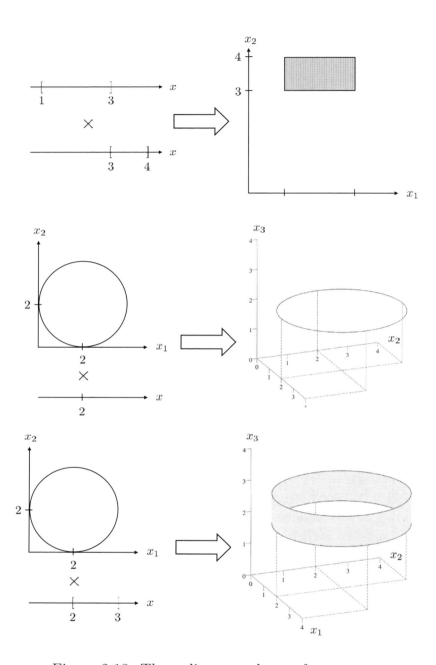

Figure 2.13: Three direct products of convex sets.

becomes the disk of radius 2 centered at $(x_1, x_2, x_3) = (2, 2, 2)$ that lies only in the plane $x_3 \equiv 2$; *i.e.* now $S_1 \times S_2 = \{(x_1, x_2, 2) \mid (x_1 - 2)^2 + (x_2 - 2)^2 \leq 4\}$. This is a weakly convex subset of $\Re^3$.

In the bottom panel of Figure 2.13 S_1 is again the subset of $\Re_2$ that is the circle of radius 2 centered at $(x_1, x_2) = (2, 2)$. S_2 is the interval $[2, 3]$ in $\Re^1$. The direct product $S_1 \times S_2$ is the "hollow vertical cylinder" made up of all of the circles of radius 2 and centered at $(x_1, x_2, x_3) = (2, 2, x_3)$ with "heights" $2 \leq x_3 \leq 3$; *i.e.* $S_1 \times S_2 = \{(x_1, x_2, x_3) \mid (x_1 - 2)^2 + (x_2 - 2)^2 = 4, \ 2 \leq x_3 \leq 4\}$. The circular set S_1 is not a convex set, so the hollow cylindrical direct product $S_1 \times S_2$ is not a convex set either. If, again, we alter S_1 to the disk in $\Re^2$ that has radius 2 and center $(x_1, x_2) = (2, 2)$, then the direct product $S_1 \times S_2$ becomes the "solid" version of the cylinder seen in the bottom panel of Figure 2.13. That is, $S_1 \times S_2$ is composed of all of the disks of radius 2 that are centered at $(x_1, x_2, x_3) = (2, 2, x_3)$ with "heights" $2 \leq x_3 \leq 3$; $S_1 \times S_2 = \{(x_1, x_2, x_3) \mid (x_1 - 2)^2 + (x_2 - 2)^2 \leq 4, \ 2 \leq x_3 \leq 3\}$. This solid cylinder is only a weakly convex set of $\Re^3$ even though S_1 is a strictly convex subset of $\Re^2$ and S_2 is a strictly convex subset of $\Re^1$.

2.7 Partial Derivatives

We all know that a derivative of a function $f(x)$ at, say, $x = 6$, is a slope. Put in other words, it is, at the point $x = 6$, the rate at which the value of f changes as x increases. What I want to emphasize is that any derivative is a *directional* quantity. To repeat myself with only a slight rewording, at $x = 6$ the value of the derivative of the function $f(x)$ with respect to x is the rate of change at $x = 6$ of the value of f in the *direction of increasing x*. We scarcely take notice of this when thinking about functions of a single variable, $f(x)$, because there is only one direction in which x can be increased. But we have to be more careful when we think about the slope of a function of more than a single variable. So suppose we have a function $f(x_1, x_2)$ of two variables, x_1 and x_2. What do we mean now by the "slope of f"? Do we mean the slope of f in the direction of increasing x_1? Do we mean the slope of f in the direction of increasing x_2? Or do we mean the slope of f in some other direction? Unless we say exactly which direction interests us, the phrase "slope of f" has no meaning. An example will help us to think about this.

Consider the function $f(x_1, x_2) = x_1^{1/2} x_2^{1/2}$. Two graphs of this function are provided in Figure 2.14, both plotted only for $0 \leq x_1 \leq 9$ and $0 \leq x_2 \leq 9$. In the left-side of Figure 2.14 the graph shows lines drawn on the surface that form a rectangular grid. Each one of these lines corresponds either to a fixed x_1 value or to a fixed x_2 value. The graph in the right-side panel of Figure 2.14 shows various constant height lines (contours) drawn on the surface. Each depiction of the graph has its distinct uses, as we shall see.

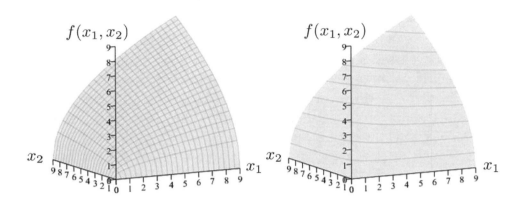

Figure 2.14: Two plots of $f(x_1, x_2) = x_1^{1/2} x_2^{1/2}$.

Before we go further, I wish to introduce a useful notational device. When I write $f(x_1, x_2)$ with a comma between x_1 and x_2, I mean that both x_1 and x_2 are variables; both can change in value. But when I write $f(x_1; x_2)$ with a semi-colon between x_1 and x_2, I mean that x_1 is a variable but the value of x_2 is fixed. Similarly, writing $f(x_2; x_1)$ means that x_2 is variable but the value of x_1 is fixed. Again, for example, if we had a function g of x_1, x_2, x_3, x_4, and x_5 and I write $g(x_1, x_2, x_3, x_4, x_5)$, then I mean that all of $x_1, \ldots, x_5$ are variable, but if I write $g(x_2, x_4; x_1, x_3, x_5)$, then I mean that only the values of x_2 and x_4 are variable and that the values of x_1, x_3, and x_5 are all fixed. Simply put, anything to the left of a semi-colon is variable and anything to the right of a semi-colon is fixed.

The graph displayed in the left-side panel of Figure 2.15 is the same as the graph in the left-side panel of Figure 2.14 except that all but two of the grid lines have been removed. These are the lines, parallel to the x_1-axis, along which the values of x_2 are fixed at $x_2 = 4$ and $x_2 = 9$. The diagram in the right-side panel of Figure 2.15 is the same as in the left-side panel except that because we view the graph by looking directly along the x_2-axis we see only the x_1-axis and the vertical axis. This gives the graph a two-dimensional perspective. It appears that we are looking only at the graphs of the functions $f(x_1; x_2 = 4) = 2x_1^{1/2}$ and $f(x_1; x_2 = 9) = 3x_1^{1/2}$.

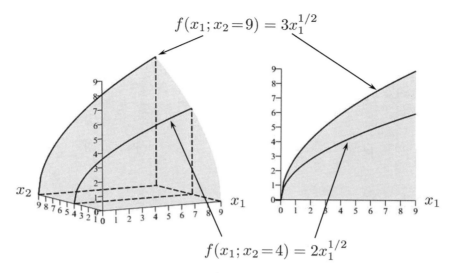

$$f(x_1; x_2 = 9) = 3x_1^{1/2}$$

$$f(x_1; x_2 = 4) = 2x_1^{1/2}$$

Figure 2.15: Plots of $f(x_1; x_2) = x_1^{1/2} x_2^{1/2}$ with x_2 fixed at values of 4 and 9.

The derivative of f with respect to x_1 evaluated at some point (x_1', x_2') is the slope of f at that point in the *direction* of x_1. This is the value of the slope of the curve that is $f(x_1; x_2 = x_2')$ at the point $x_1 = x_1'$ when x_2 is fixed at the value x_2'. For example, suppose we choose $x_2' = 4$ and ask what is the slope at the point $x_1 = 3$ of the curve that is $f(x_1; x_2 = 4) = 2x_1^{1/2}$? The slope of the curve (in the x_1-direction since this is the curve's only direction) is

$$\frac{\mathrm{d}f(x_1; x_2 = 4)}{\mathrm{d}x_1} = \frac{\mathrm{d}}{\mathrm{d}x_1}\left(2x_1^{1/2}\right) = x_1^{-1/2} = \frac{1}{\sqrt{x_1}} \;.$$

Thus the value at the point $(x_1, x_2) = (3, 4)$ of the slope in the x_1-direction of the curve $f(x_1, x_2)$ is

$$\frac{\mathrm{d}f(x_1; x_2 = 4)}{\mathrm{d}x_1}\Big|_{x_1=3} = \frac{1}{\sqrt{x_1}}\Big|_{x_1=3} = \frac{1}{\sqrt{3}} \;.$$

To make it clear that we are evaluating the slope of a function of more than one variable, the notation changes from using a "d" to using a "∂" symbol (pronounced as "dell") to denote *directional* differentiation of functions of more than a single variable, usually known as *partial* differentiation. Thus we may write

$$\frac{\mathrm{d}f(x_1; x_2 = 4)}{\mathrm{d}x_1} = \frac{\mathrm{d}}{\mathrm{d}x_1}\left(2x_1^{1/2}\right) = x_1^{-1/2} = \frac{1}{\sqrt{x_1}}$$

to denote the rate of change of $f(x_1, x_2)$ with respect to x_1 when x_2 is fixed at $x_2 = 4$ or, alternatively, write the slope of $f(x_1, x_2)$ in the x_1-direction when x_2 is fixed at $x_2 = 4$ as

$$\frac{\partial f(x_1, x_2)}{\partial x_1}\bigg|_{x_2=4} = \frac{1}{2\sqrt{x_1}} \times x_2^{1/2}\bigg|_{x_2=4} = \frac{1}{2\sqrt{x_1}} \times 4^{1/2} = \frac{1}{\sqrt{x_1}} .$$

Thus the value at the point $(x_1, x_2) = (3, 4)$ of the slope in the x_1-direction of the curve $f(x_1, x_2)$ is

$$\frac{\partial f(x_1, x_2)}{\partial x_1}\bigg|_{\substack{x_1=3 \\ x_2=4}} = \frac{1}{2\sqrt{x_1}} \times x_2^{1/2}\bigg|_{\substack{x_1=3 \\ x_2=4}} = \frac{1}{2\sqrt{3}} \times 4^{1/2} = \frac{1}{\sqrt{3}} .$$

Similarly, if x_2 is instead fixed at $x_2 = 9$, then we are considering only the curve along which $x_2 = 9$. This is the curve $f(x_1; x_2 = 9) = x_1^{1/2} \times 9^{1/2} = 3x_1^{1/2}$. The slope of this curve in the x_1-direction is

$$\frac{\mathrm{d}f(x_1; x_2 = 9)}{\mathrm{d}x_1} = \frac{\mathrm{d}}{\mathrm{d}x_1}\left(3x_1^{1/2}\right) = \frac{3}{2\sqrt{x_1}} .$$

Thus the value at the point $(x_1, x_2) = (3, 9)$ of the slope in the x_1-direction of the curve $f(x_1, x_2)$ is

$$\frac{\mathrm{d}f(x_1; x_2 = 9)}{\mathrm{d}x_1}\bigg|_{x_1=3} = \frac{3}{2\sqrt{x_1}}\bigg|_{x_1=3} = \frac{3}{2\sqrt{3}} = \frac{\sqrt{3}}{2} .$$

Alternatively, we may write the value at the point $(x_1, x_2) = (3, 9)$ of the slope of $f(x_1, x_2)$ in the x_1-direction when x_2 is fixed at $x_2 = 9$ as

$$\frac{\partial f(x_1, x_2)}{\partial x_1}\bigg|_{\substack{x_1=3 \\ x_2=9}} = \frac{1}{2\sqrt{x_1}} \times x_2^{1/2}\bigg|_{\substack{x_1=3 \\ x_2=9}} = \frac{1}{2\sqrt{3}} \times 9^{1/2} = \frac{\sqrt{3}}{2} .$$

I hope it is now clear that a partial derivative is just a derivative with respect to a single variable. A partial derivative is the rate of change, or slope of the graph, of a function in the direction of only that single variable, so that, in effect, the values of any other variables are constant.

An Exercise.

(i) Discover the equations that are the partial derivatives of $f(x_1, x_2) = x_1^{1/2}x_2^{1/2}$ with respect to x_2, when $x_1 = 3$, and then when $x_1 = 9$. What are the values of these

The slope of $f(x_1, x_2) = x_1^{1/2} x_2^{1/2}$ at $(x_1, x_2) = (3, 9)$ in the x_1-direction is the slope of $f(x_1; x_2 = 9) = 3x_1^{1/2}$ at $(x_1, x_2) = (3, 9)$, which is $\sqrt{3}/2$.

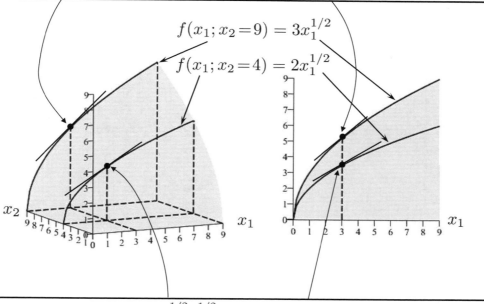

The slope of $f(x_1, x_2) = x_1^{1/2} x_2^{1/2}$ at $(x_1, x_2) = (3, 4)$ in the x_1-direction is the slope of $f(x_1; x_2 = 4) = 2x_1^{1/2}$ at $(x_1, x_2) = (3, 4)$, which is $1/\sqrt{3}$.

Figure 2.16: The slopes at $x_1 = 3$ of $f(x_1, x_2) = x_1^{1/2} x_2^{1/2}$ in the x_1-direction, when $x_2 = 4$, and when $x_2 = 9$.

derivatives when $x_2 = 4$? Use the above diagrams to visualize what you have just computed.

(ii) Discover the equation that is the partial derivative of $f(x_1, x_2) = x_1^{1/2} x_2^{1/2}$ with respect to x_2 for any arbitrary value of x_1.

Answer to (i). When x_1 is fixed at $x_1 = 3$, the function is $f(x_2; x_1 = 3) = \sqrt{3}\, x_2^{1/2}$. The derivative of this function (*i.e.* the slope of $f(x_2; x_1 = 3)$ in the x_2-direction) is

$$\frac{\mathrm{d}f(x_2; x_1 = 3)}{\mathrm{d}x_2} = \frac{\sqrt{3}}{2\sqrt{x_2}}.$$

The value of this derivative for $x_2 = 4$ is

$$\frac{\mathrm{d}f(x_2; x_1 = 3)}{\mathrm{d}x_2}\bigg|_{x_2=4} = \frac{\sqrt{3}}{2\sqrt{x_2}}\bigg|_{x_2=4} = \frac{\sqrt{3}}{4}.$$

When x_1 is fixed at $x_1 = 9$, the function is $f(x_2; x_1 = 9) = 3x_2^{1/2}$. The derivative of this function (*i.e.* the slope of $f(x_2; x_1 = 9)$ in the x_2-direction) is

$$\frac{\mathrm{d}f(x_2; x_1 = 9)}{\mathrm{d}x_2} = \frac{3}{2\sqrt{x_2}}.$$

The value of this derivative for $x_2 = 4$ is

$$\frac{\mathrm{d}f(x_2; x_1 = 9)}{\mathrm{d}x_2}\Big|_{x_2=4} = \frac{3}{2\sqrt{x_2}}\Big|_{x_2=4} = \frac{3}{4}.$$

Answer to (ii). The partial derivative of $f(x_1, x_2) = x_1^{1/2} x_2^{1/2}$ with respect to x_2 for any arbitrary value of x_1 is

$$\frac{\partial f(x_1, x_2)}{\partial x_2} = \frac{\partial}{\partial x_2}\left(x_1^{1/2} x_2^{1/2}\right) = x_1^{1/2} \times \frac{1}{2x_2^{1/2}} = \frac{1}{2}\left(\frac{x_1}{x_2}\right)^{1/2}. \qquad \square$$

2.8   Total Derivatives

Again consider the function $f(x_1, x_2) = x_1^{1/2} x_2^{1/2}$. The graph of this function that is displayed in the left-side panel of Figure 2.17 is the same as that displayed in the left-side panel of Figure 2.14 except that all but four of the "grid" lines have been removed.

Two of these four "grid" lines are paths along the graph for fixed values of x_1. Specifically, for one line x_1 is fixed at the value $x_1 = 3$ and for the other line x_1 is fixed at the larger value $x_1 = 3 + \Delta x_1$. The other two "grid" lines are paths along the graph for fixed values of x_2. Specifically, for one line x_2 is fixed at the value $x_2 = 4$ and for the other line x_2 is fixed at the larger value $x_2 = 4 + \Delta x_2$.

We have already discovered that the x_1-directional rate of change of $f(x_1, x_2) = x_1^{1/2} x_2^{1/2}$ evaluated at some specific point $(x_1, x_2) = (x_1', x_2')$, known as the value at (x_1', x_2') of the partial derivative of f with respect to x_1, is

$$\frac{\partial f(x_1, x_2)}{\partial x_1}\Big|_{\substack{x_1=x_1' \\ x_2=x_2'}} = \frac{1}{2}\left(\frac{x_2}{x_1}\right)^{1/2}\Big|_{\substack{x_1=x_1' \\ x_2=x_2'}} = \frac{1}{2}\left(\frac{x_2'}{x_1'}\right)^{1/2}.$$

We also discovered that the x_2-directional rate of change of $f(x_1, x_2) = x_1^{1/2} x_2^{1/2}$ evaluated at some specific point $(x_1, x_2) = (x_1', x_2')$, known as the value at (x_1', x_2') of the partial derivative of f with respect to x_2, is

$$\frac{\partial f(x_1, x_2)}{\partial x_2}\Big|_{\substack{x_1=x_1' \\ x_2=x_2'}} = \frac{1}{2}\left(\frac{x_1}{x_2}\right)^{1/2}\Big|_{\substack{x_1=x_1' \\ x_2=x_2'}} = \frac{1}{2}\left(\frac{x_1'}{x_2'}\right)^{1/2}.$$

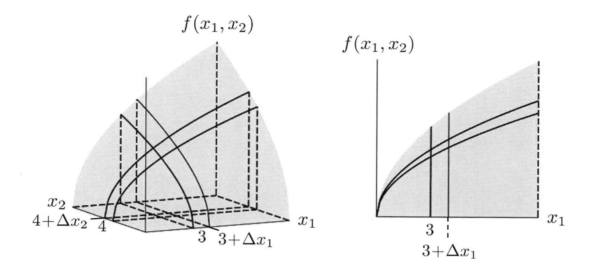

Figure 2.17: $f(x_1; x_2 = 4)$, $f(x_1; x_2 = 4 + \Delta x_2)$, $f(x_2; x_1 = 3)$, and $f(x_2; x_1 = 3 + \Delta x_1)$.

At the particular point $(x_1, x_2) = (3, 4)$, these directional rates of change have the values

$$\frac{\partial f(x_1, x_2)}{\partial x_1}\Big|_{\substack{x_1=3 \\ x_2=4}} = \frac{1}{2}\left(\frac{4}{3}\right)^{1/2} \approx 0{\cdot}577 \quad \text{and} \quad \frac{\partial f(x_1, x_2)}{\partial x_2}\Big|_{\substack{x_1=3 \\ x_2=4}} = \frac{1}{2}\left(\frac{3}{4}\right)^{1/2} \approx 0{\cdot}433.$$

Given that the value of x_2 is fixed at $x_2 = 4$, the change in the value of f that is caused by changing the value of x_1 from $x_1 = 3$ to $x_1 = 3 + \Delta x_1$ is

$$\begin{aligned} \Delta^{\text{true}} f &\equiv f(3 + \Delta x_1, 4) - f(3, 4) \\ &= (3 + \Delta x_1)^{1/2} \times 4^{1/2} - 3^{1/2} \times 4^{1/2} \\ &= 2\left((3 + \Delta x_1)^{1/2} - 3^{1/2}\right). \end{aligned}$$

We can construct a first-order, or "linear," approximation to this change by supposing, incorrectly, that the function $f(x_1; x_2 = 4)$ is linear over the interval $3 \le x_1 \le 3 + \Delta x_1$ with a constant slope equal to that of f at the point $(x_1, x_2) = (3, 4)$. This approximation is

$$\Delta^{\text{approx}} f \equiv f(3,4) + \frac{\partial f(x_1, x_2)}{\partial x_1}\Big|_{\substack{x_1=3 \\ x_2=4}} \times \Delta x_1 - f(3,4)$$

$$= \frac{1}{2}\left(\frac{4}{3}\right)^{1/2} \times \Delta x_1$$

$$= \frac{\Delta x_1}{\sqrt{3}}.$$

Figure 2.18 displays the graph of $f(x_1; x_2 = 4) = 2x_1^{1/2}$ and the graph of the linear approximation that is

$$f(3,4) + \frac{\partial f(x_1, x_2)}{\partial x_1}\Big|_{\substack{x_1=3 \\ x_2=4}} \times \Delta x_1 = 2\sqrt{3} + \frac{\Delta x_1}{\sqrt{3}}.$$

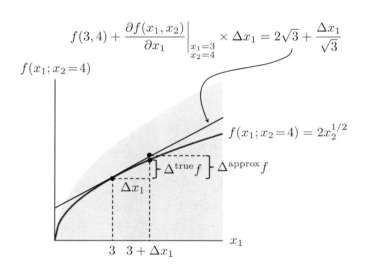

Figure 2.18: The true difference $f(3 + \Delta x_1; 4) - f(3; 4)$ and its first-order approximation.

Clearly the approximate difference $\Delta^{\text{approx}} f$ is not the same as the true difference $\Delta^{\text{true}} f$. But are they "almost the same"? Table 2.1 presents values for $\Delta^{\text{true}} f$ and $\Delta^{\text{approx}} f$ for some values of Δx_1 between 0 and 6. For this example, so long as Δx_1 is not "too big" the approximate difference $\Delta^{\text{approx}} f$ has values that are quite close to the true difference $\Delta^{\text{true}} f$, meaning that the first-order approximation for f works

Table 2.1: True and first-order approximate values of $f(3 + \Delta x_1; x_2 = 4) - f(3, 4)$.

Δx_1	0	0·1	0·5	1	2	4	6
$\Delta^{\text{true}} f$	0	0·006	0·029	0·536	1·008	1·827	2·536
$\Delta^{\text{approx}} f$	0	0·006	0·029	0·577	1·155	2·309	3·464

well for small enough values of Δx_1. Particularly, then, *for extremely small values of Δx_1 (i.e. for $\Delta x_1 \approx 0$) the first-order approximate difference and the true difference are indistinguishable from each other.* We say that such extremely small values of Δx_1 are *infinitesimally small*, and denote them by $\mathrm{d}x_1$ rather than by Δx_1. The *true* infinitesimal change to the value of f that is caused by an infinitesimal change from $(x_1, x_2) = (3, 4)$ to $(x_1, x_2) = (3 + \mathrm{d}x_1, 4)$ is therefore

$$\mathrm{d}f = \frac{\partial f(x_1, x_2)}{\partial x_1}\Big|_{\substack{x_1=3 \\ x_2=4}} \times \mathrm{d}x_1 = \frac{1}{2}\left(\frac{4}{3}\right)^{1/2} \times \mathrm{d}x_1 = \frac{\mathrm{d}x_1}{\sqrt{3}}.$$

Now consider a change to the values of both x_1 and x_2. Particularly, consider a change from $(x_1, x_2) = (3, 4)$ to $(x_1, x_2) = (3 + \Delta x_1, 4 + \Delta x_2)$. The difference so caused to the value of f is

$$\Delta^{\text{true}} f = f(3 + \Delta x_1, 4 + \Delta x_2) - f(3, 4).$$

Look at Figure 2.19. The change from $(x_1, x_2) = (3, 4)$ to $(x_1, x_2) = (3 + \Delta x_1, 4 + \Delta x_2)$ can be thought of as a "two-step" change, being a change first from $(x_1, x_2) = (3, 4)$ to $(x_1, x_2) = (3 + \Delta x_1, 4)$, followed by a second change from $(x_1, x_2) = (3 + \Delta x_1, 4)$ to $(x_1, x_2) = (3 + \Delta x_1, 4 + \Delta x_2)$. This "path" is indicated in Figure 2.19 by the dark arrows on the base plane of the figure. With each step, the value of f changes. Particularly, the change from $(x_1, x_2) = (3, 4)$ to $(x_1, x_2) = (3 + \Delta x_1, 4)$ causes the value of f to change by

$$\Delta^{\text{true}} f_1 = f(3 + \Delta x_1, 4) - f(3, 4).$$

Then, the change from $(x_1, x_2) = (3 + \Delta x_1, 4)$ to $(x_1, x_2) = (3 + \Delta x_1, 4 + \Delta x_2)$ causes a further change of

$$\Delta^{\text{true}} f_2 = f(3 + \Delta x_1, 4 + \Delta x_2) - f(3 + \Delta x_1, 4)$$

to the value of f. The overall change to the value of f caused by the change from $(x_1, x_2) = (3, 4)$ to $(x_1, x_2) = (3 + \Delta x_1, 4 + \Delta x_2)$ is thus

$$\Delta^{\text{true}} f = \Delta^{\text{true}} f_1 + \Delta^{\text{true}} f_2.$$

This decomposition of the overall change $\Delta^{\text{true}}f$ into its two components $\Delta^{\text{true}}f_1$ and $\Delta^{\text{true}}f_2$ is displayed in Figure 2.19.

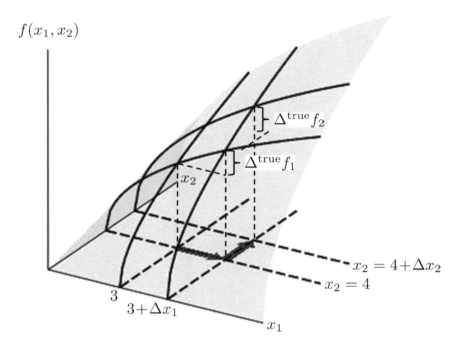

Figure 2.19: Decomposing $\Delta^{\text{true}}f$ into its two components, $\Delta^{\text{true}}f_1$ and $\Delta^{\text{true}}f_2$.

Just as was done earlier for a change to only a single variable, the value of the true change caused to the value of f can be approximated using first-order (*i.e.* linear) approximations. We do this by separately approximating each of $\Delta^{\text{true}}f_1$ and $\Delta^{\text{true}}f_2$. Figure 2.20 illustrates how this is done by magnifying the part of Figure 2.19 for $3 \leq x_1 \leq 3 + \Delta x_1$ and $4 \leq x_2 \leq 4 + \Delta x_2$ and by adding two tangent lines. The change $\Delta^{\text{true}}f_1$ caused by the change from $(x_1, x_2) = (3, 4)$ to $(x_1, x_2) = (3 + \Delta x_1, 4)$ is approximated by using the tangent to f at $(x_1, x_2) = (3, 4)$ in the x_1 direction. This is the straight line starting at $f(3, 4)$ with the constant slope $\partial f(x_1, x_2)/\partial x_1$ evaluated at $(x_1, x_2) = (3, 4)$. The change in the height of this straight line due to the change from $(x_1, x_2) = (3, 4)$ to $(x_1, x_2) = (3 + \Delta x_1, 4)$ is

$$\Delta^{\text{approx}}f_1 = \frac{\partial f(x_1, x_2)}{\partial x_1}\Big|_{\substack{x_1=3 \\ x_2=4}} \times \Delta x_1 = \frac{1}{2}\left(\frac{4}{3}\right)^{1/2} \times \Delta x_1 = \frac{\Delta x_1}{\sqrt{3}}.$$

Similarly, the change $\Delta^{\text{true}}f_2$ caused by the change from $(x_1, x_2) = (3 + \Delta x_1, 4)$ to $(x_1, x_2) = (3 + \Delta x_1, 4 + \Delta x_2)$ is approximated by using the tangent to f at $(x_1, x_2) =$

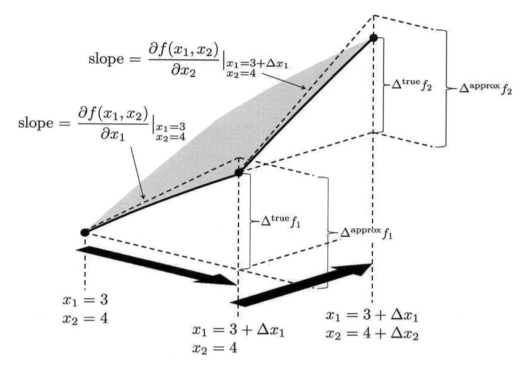

$$\text{slope} = \frac{\partial f(x_1, x_2)}{\partial x_2}\Big|_{\substack{x_1=3+\Delta x_1 \\ x_2=4}}$$

$$\text{slope} = \frac{\partial f(x_1, x_2)}{\partial x_1}\Big|_{\substack{x_1=3 \\ x_2=4}}$$

$\Delta^{\text{true}} f_2$ $\Delta^{\text{approx}} f_2$

$\Delta^{\text{true}} f_1$ $\Delta^{\text{approx}} f_1$

$$x_1 = 3$$
$$x_2 = 4$$

$$x_1 = 3 + \Delta x_1$$
$$x_2 = 4$$

$$x_1 = 3 + \Delta x_1$$
$$x_2 = 4 + \Delta x_2$$

Figure 2.20: The first-order approximations of $\Delta^{\text{true}} f_1$ and $\Delta^{\text{true}} f_2$.

$(3+\Delta x_1, 4)$ in the x_2 direction. This is the straight line starting at $f(3+\Delta x_1, 4)$ with the constant slope $\partial f(x_1, x_2)/\partial x_2$ evaluated at $(x_1, x_2) = (3 + \Delta x_1, 4)$. The change in the height of this straight line due to the change from $(x_1, x_2) = (3 + \Delta x_1, 4)$ to $(x_1, x_2) = (3 + \Delta x_1, 4 + \Delta x_2)$ is

$$\Delta^{\text{approx}} f_2 = \frac{\partial f(x_1, x_2)}{\partial x_2}\Big|_{\substack{x_1=3+\Delta x_1 \\ x_2=4}} \times \Delta x_2 = \frac{1}{2}\left(\frac{3+\Delta x_1}{4}\right)^{1/2} \times \Delta x_2.$$

The sum of these two first-order approximations is our approximation for the true value of the overall change to the value of f; *i.e.* our approximation for $\Delta^{\text{true}} f$ is

$$\Delta^{\text{approx}} f = \Delta^{\text{approx}} f_1 + \Delta^{\text{approx}} f_2$$

$$= \frac{\partial f(x_1, x_2)}{\partial x_1}\Big|_{\substack{x_1=3 \\ x_2=4}} \times \Delta x_1 + \frac{\partial f(x_1, x_2)}{\partial x_2}\Big|_{\substack{x_1=3+\Delta x_1 \\ x_2=4}} \times \Delta x_2.$$

Just as we saw above, the approximation $\Delta^{\text{approx}} f_1$ becomes very close to the true value $\Delta^{\text{true}} f_1$ as Δx_1 becomes small, and the approximation $\Delta^{\text{approx}} f_2$ becomes very close to the true value $\Delta^{\text{true}} f_2$ as Δx_2 becomes small. Therefore, the approximation $\Delta^{\text{approx}} f$ becomes very close to the true value $\Delta^{\text{true}} f$ as *both* Δx_1 and Δx_2 become small. When both Δx_1 and Δx_2 become infinitesimally small, we write the infinitesimal change to the value of f that is caused by the infinitesimal change from $(x_1, x_2) = (3, 4)$ to $(x_1, x_2) = (3 + \mathrm{d}x_1, 4 + \mathrm{d}x_2)$ as

$$\mathrm{d}f = \frac{\partial f(x_1, x_2)}{\partial x_1}\Big|_{\substack{x_1=3 \\ x_2=4}} \times \mathrm{d}x_1 + \frac{\partial f(x_1, x_2)}{\partial x_2}\Big|_{\substack{x_1=3 \\ x_2=4}} \times \mathrm{d}x_2$$
$$= \frac{1}{2}\left[\left(\frac{4}{3}\right)^{1/2} \mathrm{d}x_1 + \left(\frac{3}{4}\right)^{1/2} \mathrm{d}x_2\right].$$

This expression is called the *total differential of f* evaluated at $(x_1, x_2) = (3, 4)$. The idea extends naturally to functions $f(x_1, \ldots, x_n)$ of any finite number $n \geq 1$ of variables.

Definition 2.7 (Total Differential). *Let $f : \Re^n \mapsto \Re$ be a differentiable function. The total differential of f evaluated at $(x_1, \ldots, x_n) = (x_1', \ldots, x_n')$ is*

$$\mathrm{d}f = \frac{\partial f(x_1, \ldots, x_n)}{\partial x_1}\Big|_{\substack{x_1=x_1' \\ \vdots \\ x_n=x_n'}} \times \mathrm{d}x_1 + \cdots + \frac{\partial f(x_1, \ldots, x_n)}{\partial x_n}\Big|_{\substack{x_1=x_1' \\ \vdots \\ x_n=x_n'}} \times \mathrm{d}x_n.$$

2.9   Continuous Differentiability

Sometimes we will consider functions that are *continuously differentiable* to some order. What does this mean? Let's start with just *differentiability* to some order. For example, a function is differentiable to order 2 if and only if all of the function's first-order and second-order derivatives exist. Thus a function $f(x_1, x_2)$ is differentiable to order 2 if and only if all of the derivatives $\partial f(x_1, x_2)/\partial x_1$, $\partial f(x_1, x_2)/\partial x_2$, $\partial^2 f(x_1, x_2)/\partial x_1^2$, $\partial^2 f(x_1, x_2)/\partial x_1 \partial x_2$, $\partial^2 f(x_1, x_2)/\partial x_2 \partial x_1$, and $\partial^2 f(x_1, x_2)/\partial x_2^2$ are all well-defined functions. More generally we speak of functions that are differentiable to order r, where r is some integer; $r = 1, 2, 3, \ldots$.

Definition 2.8 (Differentiability to Order r). *Let S be a nonempty subset of $\Re^n$ that is open with respect to the Euclidean topology on $\Re^n$. A function $f : \Re^n \to \Re$ is differentiable to order r at a point in S if and only if the function possesses every derivative of all orders 1 to r at that point. If the function is differentiable to order r at every point in S, then the function is differentiable to order r on S.*

Suppose that S is the interval $(0, 1)$. Then, a function f is differentiable to order 3 on $(0, 1)$ if and only if at each point in $(0, 1)$ all of the first-, second-, and third-order derivatives of the function exist. If, as well, every one of these derivative functions is itself a continuous function at every point in $(0, 1)$, then we say that the function f is *continuously* differentiable to order 3 on $(0, 1)$. Thus adding the word "continuously" means that every derivative function to order 3 is a continuous function.

Definition 2.9 (Continuous Differentiability to Order r). *Let f be a function that is differentiable to order r on a set S. If every one of the derivatives of f from order 1 to order r is a continuous function at a particular point in S, then f is* continuously *differentiable to order r at that point. If f is continuously differentiable to order r at every point in S, then f is continuously differentiable on S.*

Usually the symbol $C^r(S)$ denotes the set of all functions that are continuously differentiable to order r on a set S.

It is easy to think of functions that are continuously differentiable to any order. For example, the quadratic $f(x) = ax^2 + bx + c$ is continuously differentiable on $\Re$ to any order; *i.e.* to infinite order. In such a case, we write $f \in C^\infty(\Re)$.

Now, think of the function $g : \Re \mapsto \Re$ that is defined by

$$g(x) = \begin{cases} x + \frac{1}{2} & , \ -\infty < x < 0 \\ \frac{1}{2}(x+1)^2 & , \ 0 \le x < \infty. \end{cases}$$

The first-order derivative of this function is the continuous function

$$\frac{\mathrm{d}g(x)}{\mathrm{d}x} = \begin{cases} 1 & , \ -\infty < x < 0 \\ x + 1 & , \ 0 \le x < \infty. \end{cases}$$

The second-order derivative is the function

$$\frac{\mathrm{d}^2 g(x)}{\mathrm{d}x^2} = \begin{cases} 0 & , \ -\infty < x < 0 \\ 1 & , \ 0 \le x < \infty \end{cases}$$

that is discontinuous at $x = 0$ and so is not everywhere differentiable on $\Re$. g is thus a function that is continuously differentiable to order 1 on $\Re$, differentiable but not continuously differentiable to order 2 on $\Re$, and is not differentiable to any order $r \ge 3$.

2.10   Contour Sets

Think again of the function $f(x_1, x_2) = x_1^{1/2} x_2^{1/2}$ defined for $x_1 \geq 0$ and $x_2 \geq 0$. This function has the same value, 6, at each of the points $(x_1, x_2) = (1, 36)$, $(6, 6)$, $(12, 3)$, and many others. The set of all such points is

$$C_f(6) = \{(x_1, x_2) \mid x_1 \geq 0, \ x_2 \geq 0, \ f(x_1, x_2) = 6\}.$$

This is called the *contour set of f with level 6* or the *level set of f with isovalue 6*. Both names, level set and contour set, are in common usage. To avoid confusion, I will use only the name "contour set." Notice that the above contour set is a collection of pairs (x_1, x_2) and is, therefore, a subset of the domain of the function. I mention this because it is common to use the label "contours" for horizontal lines on the graph of a function, such as those in the right-side panel of Figure 2.14. Such contours are not contour sets since they are sets of points of the form (x_1, x_2, y), where y is the constant "height" of the graph for these points (*i.e.* points in a contour line on a graph have a "height" dimension y that points in contour sets do not possess). For example, some of the points in the contour of the graph of $f(x_1, x_2) = x_1^{1/2} x_2^{1/2}$ with height or level 6 are $(3, 12, 6)$, $(36, 1, 6)$, and $(6, 6, 6)$. The corresponding points in the contour set of f with level 6 are $(3, 12)$, $(36, 1)$, and $(6, 6)$.

An Exercise.   Consider the function $f : \Re^2 \mapsto \Re$ that is defined by $f(x, y) = 40 - (x - 2)^2 - (y - 3)^2$. What is the contour set with level 36 for f? What is the contour set with level 40 for f? What is the contour set with level 41 for f?

Answer.   The contour set with level 36 for f is

$$C_f(36) = \{(x, y) \mid 40 - (x - 2)^2 - (y - 3)^2 = 36\} = \{(x, y) \mid (x - 2)^2 + (y - 3)^2 = 4\}.$$

This set is the circle of radius 2 centered at the point $(x, y) = (2, 3)$.

The contour set with level 40 for f is

$$C_f(40) = \{(x, y) \mid 40 - (x - 2)^2 - (y - 3)^2 = 40\} = \{(x, y) \mid (x - 2)^2 + (y - 3)^2 = 0\}$$
$$= \{(2, 3)\}.$$

This is the singleton set containing only the point $(x, y) = (2, 3)$. A contour set does not have to be a curve.

The contour set with level 41 for f is

$$C_f(41) = \{(x, y) \mid 41 - (x-2)^2 - (y-3)^2 = 40\} = \{(x, y) \mid (x-2)^2 + (y-3)^2 = -1\} = \emptyset.$$

A contour set for a function f is empty whenever the level for the set is not contained in the image of f.   □

2.11 Marginal Rates of Substitution

Consider the function $g(x_1, x_2) = x_1^{1/3} x_2^{2/3}$. The contour set with level 4 for g contains the point $(x_1, x_2) = (1, 8)$. Now consider another point $(1 + \Delta x_1, 8 + \Delta x_2)$ that belongs to the same contour set as $(1, 8)$. Then,

$$g(1, 8) = 1^{1/3} 8^{2/3} = 4 = g(1 + \Delta x_1, 8 + \Delta x_2) = (1 + \Delta x_1)^{1/3} (8 + \Delta x_2)^{2/3}. \quad (2.12)$$

What is the relationship between Δx_1 and Δx_2? That is, if we change the value of x_2, from 8 to $8 + \Delta x_2$, then by what amount Δx_1 must we change the value of x_1, from 1 to $1 + \Delta x_1$, so as to keep the value of g constant at 4?

One way to answer this question is to try to solve for Δx_1 in terms of Δx_2. Often this is not possible, but our example is simple enough that we can obtain such an equation. From (2.12),

$$4 = (1 + \Delta x_1)^{1/3} (8 + \Delta x_2)^{2/3} \quad \Rightarrow \quad 4^3 = 64 = (1 + \Delta x_1)(8 + \Delta x_2)^2.$$

Therefore,

$$\Delta x_1 = -1 + \frac{64}{(8 + \Delta x_2)^2} \quad (2.13)$$

is the equation that tells us by how much, Δx_1, to change the value of x_1 when the value of x_2 changes by Δx_2 in order to remain in the level 4 contour set of g.

If, as happens in most cases, it is not possible to obtain an equation that explicitly states Δx_1 in terms of Δx_2, then what can we do? The answer is that, so long as we consider only infinitesimally small changes $\mathrm{d}x_1$ and $\mathrm{d}x_2$ to the values of x_1 and x_2, then we can obtain expressions for the *rate* at which x_1 must change as x_2 changes in order to keep the value of the function g unchanged. These rate-of-change expressions between x_1 and x_2 while keeping the value of g constant are called *marginal rates of substitution between x_1 and x_2*.

Remember that the total derivative of a function $g(x_1, x_2)$ is

$$\mathrm{d}g = \frac{\partial g(x_1, x_2)}{\partial x_1} \, \mathrm{d}x_1 + \frac{\partial g(x_1, x_2)}{\partial x_2} \, \mathrm{d}x_2.$$

The partial derivatives of $g(x_1, x_2) = x_1^{1/3} x_2^{2/3}$ are

$$\frac{\partial g(x_1, x_2)}{\partial x_1} = \frac{1}{3} \left(\frac{x_2}{x_1} \right)^{2/3} \quad \text{and} \quad \frac{\partial g(x_1, x_2)}{\partial x_2} = \frac{2}{3} \left(\frac{x_1}{x_2} \right)^{1/3}.$$

The values of these partial derivatives at $(x_1, x_2) = (1, 8)$ are

$$\frac{\partial g(x_1, x_2)}{\partial x_1}\Big|_{\substack{x_1=1 \\ x_2=8}} = \frac{1}{3}\left(\frac{8}{1}\right)^{2/3} = \frac{4}{3} \quad \text{and} \quad \frac{\partial g(x_1, x_2)}{\partial x_2}\Big|_{\substack{x_1=1 \\ x_2=8}} = \frac{2}{3}\left(\frac{1}{8}\right)^{1/3} = \frac{1}{3}.$$

Thus, evaluated at $(x_1, x_2) = (1, 8)$, the total derivative of g is

$$dg = \frac{4}{3} \, dx_1 + \frac{1}{3} \, dx_2.$$

But $dg = 0$ because the point $(x_1, x_2) = (1 + dx_1, 8 + dx_2)$, like the point $(x_1, x_2) = (1, 8)$, is a member of the level 4 contour of g. Accordingly we write

$$dg = 0 = \frac{4}{3} \, dx_1 + \frac{1}{3} \, dx_2, \tag{2.14}$$

and then write that

$$\frac{dx_1}{dx_2}\Big|_{\substack{g\equiv4 \\ x_1=1 \\ x_2=8}} = -\frac{1}{4}. \tag{2.15}$$

This is a statement that a very small change in the value of x_2 from $x_2 = 8$ to $x_2 = 8 + dx_2$ must be accompanied by a very small change in the value of x_1 from $x_1 = 1$ to $x_1 + dx_1$, where the change dx_1 must be of the opposite sign to dx_2 and one-quarter as large as dx_2. (Note: It looks like (2.15) was obtained by rearranging (2.14) but this is not so – it is obtained by using the Implicit Function Theorem.)

Let's check (2.15) by using (2.13) to evaluate at the point $(x_1, x_2) = (1, 8)$ the rate at which Δx_1 must change as Δx_2 changes if we are to keep the value of g constant at 4. This rate is the derivative of Δx_1 with respect to Δx_2 which, from (2.13), is

$$\frac{d(\Delta x_1)}{d(\Delta x_2)} = -\frac{2 \times 64}{(8 + \Delta x_2)^3}.$$

If we make Δx_2 extremely small (*i.e.* $\Delta x_2 \approx 0$), then this rate-of-change is indistinguishable from

$$\frac{d(\Delta x_1)}{d(\Delta x_2)} = -\frac{2 \times 64}{8^3} = -\frac{1}{4},$$

which is the marginal rate of substitution value that we obtained in (2.15).

What we have done so far for functions of two variables generalizes without any additional work to functions of as many variables as you like. For differentiable functions $f(x_1, \ldots, x_n)$, the total derivative of f is

$$df = \frac{\partial f(x_1, \ldots, x_n)}{\partial x_1} \, dx_1 + \frac{\partial f(x_1, \ldots, x_n)}{\partial x_2} \, dx_2 + \cdots + \frac{\partial f(x_1, \ldots, x_n)}{\partial x_n} \, dx_n.$$

Suppose that a point $(x'_1, \ldots, x'_n)$ and a very nearby point $(x'_1 + dx_1, \ldots, x'_n + dx_n)$ are both members of the function's level α contour set; *i.e.* $f(x'_1, \ldots, x'_n) = \alpha$ and $f(x'_1 + dx_1, \ldots, x'_n + dx_n) = \alpha$. Then

$$df = 0 = \frac{\partial f(x_1, \ldots, x_n)}{\partial x_1}\Big|_{\substack{x_1 = x'_1 \\ \vdots \\ x_n = x'_n}} dx_1 + \frac{\partial f(x_1, \ldots, x_n)}{\partial x_2}\Big|_{\substack{x_1 = x'_1 \\ \vdots \\ x_n = x'_n}} dx_2$$

$$+ \cdots + \frac{\partial f(x_1, \ldots, x_n)}{\partial x_n}\Big|_{\substack{x_1 = x'_1 \\ \vdots \\ x_n = x'_n}} dx_n. \tag{2.16}$$

This makes it easy to obtain the marginal rate of substitution between any *pair* of the variables $x_1, \ldots, x_n$ at some point in the function's level-α contour set. For example, suppose you want the marginal rate of substitution between x_1 and x_2 at the point $(x_1, \ldots, x_n) = (x'_1, \ldots, x'_n)$. Only x_1 and x_2 are being substituted for each other, meaning that the values of all of the other variables $x_3, \ldots, x_n$ are being held fixed at $x'_3, \ldots, x'_n$, so $dx_3 = \cdots = dx_n = 0$ and (2.16) becomes only

$$df = 0 = \frac{\partial f(x_1, \ldots, x_n)}{\partial x_1}\Big|_{\substack{x_1 = x'_1 \\ \vdots \\ x_n = x'_n}} dx_1 + \frac{\partial f(x_1, \ldots, x_n)}{\partial x_2}\Big|_{\substack{x_1 = x'_1 \\ \vdots \\ x_n = x'_n}} dx_2.$$

Thus the marginal rate of substitution between x_1 and x_2 at the point $(x_1, \ldots, x_n) = (x'_1, \ldots, x'_n)$ is

$$\frac{dx_2}{dx_1}\Big|_{\substack{df=0 \\ x_1=x'_1 \\ \vdots \\ x_n=x'_n}} = -\frac{\partial f(x_1, \ldots, x_n)/\partial x_1}{\partial f(x_1, \ldots, x_n)/\partial x_2}\Big|_{\substack{x_1=x'_1 \\ \vdots \\ x_n=x'_n}}.$$

Similarly, suppose you want the marginal rate of substitution between x_3 and x_5 at the point $(x_1, \ldots, x_n) = (x'_1, \ldots, x'_n)$. Only x_3 and x_5 are being substituted for each other, meaning that the values of all the other variables $x_1, x_2, x_4, x_6, \ldots, x_n$ are being held fixed at $x'_1, x'_2, x'_4, x'_6, \ldots, x'_n$, so $dx_1 = dx_2 = dx_4 = dx_6 = \cdots = dx_n = 0$ and (2.16) becomes only

$$df = 0 = \frac{\partial f(x_1, \ldots, x_n)}{\partial x_3}\Big|_{\substack{x_1=x'_1 \\ \vdots \\ x_n=x'_n}} dx_3 + \frac{\partial f(x_1, \ldots, x_n)}{\partial x_5}\Big|_{\substack{x_1=x'_1 \\ \vdots \\ x_n=x'_n}} dx_5.$$

The marginal rate of substitution between x_3 and x_5 at $(x_1, \ldots, x_n) = (x_1', \ldots, x_n')$ is

$$\left.\frac{\mathrm{d}x_3}{\mathrm{d}x_5}\right|_{\substack{\mathrm{d}f=0 \\ x_1=x_1' \\ \vdots \\ x_n=x_n'}} = - \left.\frac{\partial f(x_1, \ldots, x_n)/\partial x_5}{\partial f(x_1, \ldots, x_n)/\partial x_3}\right|_{\substack{x_1=x_1' \\ \vdots \\ x_n=x_n'}}.$$

2.12   Gradient Vectors

In our review of partial derivatives, we emphasized that any derivative is a slope in a specified direction. With a function $f(x_1, x_2)$ of just two variables, the directions that typically are emphasized are the x_1 direction and the x_2 direction. This is quite natural since the rate of change of f in the x_1 direction is the rate of change of the value of f as the value of only x_1 is altered; *i.e.* the partial derivative of f with respect to x_1. Similarly, the rate of change of f in the x_2 direction is the rate of change of the value of f as the value of only x_2 is altered; *i.e.* the partial derivative of f with respect to x_2. The ordered list of these two partial derivatives is called the *gradient vector of f*, and is denoted by

$$\nabla f(x_1, x_2) \equiv \left(\frac{\partial f(x_1, x_2)}{\partial x_1}, \; \frac{\partial f(x_1, x_2)}{\partial x_2} \right).$$

Notice that by default a gradient vector is a row vector; *i.e.* a vector in which the elements are written as a horizontal list. I mention this because most other vectors are by default column vectors; *i.e.* vectors in which the elements are written as vertical lists.

The idea of a gradient vector extends naturally to functions $f(x_1, \ldots, x_n)$ of $n \geq 1$ variables. For such a function, the gradient vector is

$$\nabla f(x_1, \ldots, x_n) = \left(\frac{\partial f(x_1, \ldots, x_n)}{\partial x_1}, \; \ldots \;, \frac{\partial f(x_1, \ldots, x_n)}{\partial x_n} \right)$$

and, for brevity, is often denoted by just $\nabla f(x)$.

An Exercise.

(i) What is the gradient vector of the function $f(x, y) = 40 - (x - 2)^2 - (y - 3)^2$?

(ii) What is the gradient vector of the function $g(x_1, x_2) = x_1^{1/2} x_2^{1/2}$?

Answer to (i). The gradient vector of f is the row vector

$$\nabla f(x, y) = \left(\frac{\partial f(x, y)}{\partial x}, \; \frac{\partial f(x, y)}{\partial y} \right) = (-2(x - 2), \; -2(y - 3)).$$

Answer to (ii). The gradient vector of g is the row vector

$$\nabla g(x_1, x_2) = \left(\frac{\partial g(x_1, x_2)}{\partial x_1}, \frac{\partial g(x_1, x_2)}{\partial x_2} \right) = \left(\frac{1}{2} \left(\frac{x_2}{x_1} \right)^{1/2}, \frac{1}{2} \left(\frac{x_1}{x_2} \right)^{1/2} \right). \qquad \square$$

2.13 Inner Products

There are all sorts of inner products, but the particular inner product that economists most frequently encounter is the *Euclidean inner product*. Because of its common use, the Euclidean inner product of two vectors x and x' has been given a special, brief notation and is usually written as $x \cdot x'$. This is why the Euclidean inner product of x and x' is often called the *dot product* of x and x' or the *scalar product* of x and x'.

Definition 2.10 (Euclidean Inner Product). *The* Euclidean inner product *on $\Re^n$ is the function $f : \Re^n \times \Re^n \to \Re$ that, for $x, x' \in \Re^n$, is the multiplicative product of the vectors x and x':*

$$f(x, x') \equiv x \cdot x' \equiv (x_1, \ldots, x_n) \begin{pmatrix} x'_1 \\ \vdots \\ x'_n \end{pmatrix} \equiv x_1 x'_1 + \cdots + x_n x'_n.$$

Notice that the Euclidean inner product of the vector x and the vector x' is the same as the Euclidean inner product of the vector x' and the vector x; *i.e.* the order of multiplication does not matter.

$$x \cdot x' = (x_1, \ldots, x_n) \begin{pmatrix} x'_1 \\ \vdots \\ x'_n \end{pmatrix} = x_1 x'_1 + \cdots + x_n x'_n$$

$$= x'_1 x_1 + \cdots + x'_n x_n = (x'_1, \ldots, x'_n) \begin{pmatrix} x_1 \\ \vdots \\ x_n \end{pmatrix} = x' \cdot x.$$

An Exercise. What is the value of the Euclidean inner product for each of the following pairs of vectors?

$a = (6, 2)$ and $a' = (-3, 3)$, $b = (3, 24, -18)$ and $b' = (-1, -8, 6)$, $c = (6, 12)$ and $c' = (-4, 2)$, and $d = (6, 2, 0)$ and $d' = (3, 0, 1)$.

Answer.

$$a{\cdot}a' = (6,2)\begin{pmatrix} -3 \\ 3 \end{pmatrix} = -18 + 6 = -12.$$

$$b{\cdot}b' = (3,24,-18)\begin{pmatrix} -1 \\ -8 \\ 6 \end{pmatrix} = -3 - 192 - 108 = -303.$$

$$c{\cdot}c' = (6,12)\begin{pmatrix} -4 \\ 2 \end{pmatrix} = -24 + 24 = 0.$$

$$d{\cdot}d' = (6,2,0)\begin{pmatrix} 3 \\ 0 \\ 1 \end{pmatrix} = 18.$$

Euclidean inner products can thus be zero, positive, or negative numbers. □

The Euclidean inner product of any vector x with itself is the sum of the squares of the vector's elements;

$$x{\cdot}x = (x_1,\ldots,x_n)\begin{pmatrix} x_1 \\ \vdots \\ x_n \end{pmatrix} = x_1^2 + \cdots + x_n^2 \geq 0.$$

Thus the Euclidean inner product of any vector x with itself is strictly positive unless the vector is the zero vector, in which case the inner product is zero.

The *Euclidean norm* of a vector $x \in \Re^n$ is a common way of measuring the distance of the vector x from the origin. The usual notation for the Euclidean norm of x is $\|x\|_E$.

Definition 2.11 (Euclidean Norm). *Let $x \in \Re^n$. The* Euclidean norm *of x is*

$$\|x\|_E \equiv \sqrt{x_1^2 + \cdots + x_n^2}.$$

It is easy to see that the square of the Euclidean norm of x is the same as the Euclidean inner product of x with itself:

$$x{\cdot}x = (x_1,\ldots,x_n)\begin{pmatrix} x_1 \\ \vdots \\ x_n \end{pmatrix} = x_1^2 + \cdots + x_n^2 = \left(\sqrt{x_1^2 + \cdots + x_n^2}\right)^2 = \|x\|_E^2.$$

Less obvious is the following very useful result. For a proof, see Simon and Blume 1994, pp. 215–16.

Theorem 2.9. *Let $x, x' \in \Re^n$ and let θ be the angle between x and x'. Then,*

$$x{\cdot}x' = \|x\|_E \times \|x'\|_E \times \cos\theta. \tag{2.17}$$

You may have forgotten the properties of the cosine function. If so, then consider Figure 2.21, where you will observe that

$$\cos\theta \begin{cases} = 1 & , \text{ if } \theta = 0° \text{ or } \theta = 360° \\ = -1 & , \text{ if } \theta = 180° \\ = 0 & , \text{ if } \theta = 90° \text{ or } \theta = 270° \\ \in (0,1) & , \text{ if } 0° < \theta < 90° \text{ or } 270° < \theta < 360° \\ \in (-1,0) & , \text{ if } 90° < \theta < 270°. \end{cases}$$

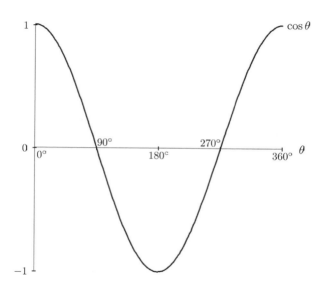

Figure 2.21: The graph of cosine(θ) for $0° \le \theta \le 360°$.

It follows, then, that if two vectors x and x'

- are positively collinear (the vectors point in exactly the same direction; $\theta = 0°$ or $\theta = 360°$), then their Euclidean inner product is the product of their distances from the origin (norms) because $\cos 0° = \cos 360° = 1$; $x'{\cdot}x'' = \|x'\|_E\|x''\|_E$;

- are negatively collinear (the vectors point in exactly opposite directions; $\theta = 180°$), then their Euclidean inner product is the negative of the product of their distances from the origin because $\cos 180° = -1$; $x'{\cdot}x'' = -\|x'\|_E\|x''\|_E$;

- are orthogonal ($\theta = 90°$ or $\theta = 270°$; the vectors point in directions that are right-angled with respect to each other), then their Euclidean inner product is zero because $\cos 90° = \cos 270° = 0$; $x'{\cdot}x'' = 0$;

- have an acute angle between them ($0° < \theta < 90°$), then their Euclidean inner product is positive and is smaller in size than the product of their distances from the origin because $0 < \cos\theta < 1$ for $0° < \theta < 90°$; $\|x'\|_E\|x''\|_E > x'{\cdot}x'' > 0$;

- have an obtuse angle between them ($90° < \theta < 180°$), then their Euclidean inner product is negative and is smaller in size than the product of their distances from the origin because $-1 < \cos\theta < 0$ for $90° < \theta < 180°$; $-\|x'\|_E\|x''\|_E < x'{\cdot}x'' < 0$.

An Exercise. For each of the four pairs of vectors of the previous exercise, determine if the two vectors are collinear, negatively collinear, separated by an acute angle, or separated by an obtuse angle.

Answer. $a{\cdot}a' = -12 < 0$, so the angle θ between a and a' is obtuse. From (2.17),

$$a{\cdot}a' = -12 = \|a\|_E\|a'\|_E \cos\theta.$$

The Euclidean norms of a and a' are

$$\|a\|_E = \sqrt{6^2 + 2^2} = \sqrt{40} \text{ and } \|a'\|_E = \sqrt{(-3)^2 + 3^2} = \sqrt{18},$$

so

$$\cos\theta = -\frac{12}{\sqrt{40} \times \sqrt{18}} = -\frac{1}{\sqrt{5}} \quad\Rightarrow\quad \theta \approx \cos^{-1}(-0{\cdot}447) \approx 116{\cdot}6°.$$

Draw a and a' to confirm visually that they are separated by an obtuse angle.

The vectors b and b' are negatively collinear. Notice that the Euclidean norm (*i.e.* the Euclidean distance from the origin) of b is $\|b\|_E = \sqrt{3^2 + 24^2 + (-18)^2} = \sqrt{909} = 3\sqrt{101}$ and that the Euclidean norm of b' is $\|b'\|_E = \sqrt{(-1)^2 + (-8)^2 + 6^2} = \sqrt{101}$. Let θ be the angle between b and b'. Then,

$$b{\cdot}b' = -303 = \|b\|_E\|b'\|_E \cos\theta = 3\sqrt{101} \times \sqrt{101} \cos\theta = 303 \cos\theta.$$

Thus $\cos\theta = -1$, which implies that $\theta = 180°$ and, therefore, that the vectors b and b' are collinear and point in exactly opposite directions. Draw b and b' to confirm visually that they are negatively collinear.

$c{\cdot}c' = 0$, so c and c' are orthogonal. Draw c and c' to confirm visually that they are orthogonal.

$d{\cdot}d' = 18 > 0$, so the angle θ between d and d' is acute. From (2.17),

$$d{\cdot}d' = 18 = \|d\|_E \|d'\|_E \cos\theta.$$

The Euclidean norms of d and d' are

$$\|d\|_E = \sqrt{6^2 + 2^2 + 0^2} = \sqrt{40} \text{ and } \|d'\|_E = \sqrt{3^2 + 0^2 + 1^2} = \sqrt{10},$$

so

$$\cos\theta = \frac{18}{\sqrt{40} \times \sqrt{10}} = \frac{9}{10} \quad\Rightarrow\quad \theta = \cos^{-1}(0{\cdot}9) \approx 25{\cdot}8°.$$

Draw d and d' to confirm visually that they are separated by an acute angle. $\qquad\square$

2.14 Gradients, Rates of Substitution, and Inner Products

These three ideas are related to each other in ways that are crucial to understanding rational choice making, the main topic of this book. So let us take a little time to be sure that these connections are recognized and understood. An example will help, so again consider the function $f(x,y) = 40 - (x-2)^2 - (y-3)^2$. The gradient vector for this function is

$$\nabla f(x,y) = \left(\frac{\partial f(x,y)}{\partial x},\ \frac{\partial f(x,y)}{\partial y}\right) = (-2(x-2), -2(y-3)).$$

The marginal rate of substitution at any point (x,y) other than those with $y = 3$ is

$$\mathrm{MRS}_f(x,y) = \left.\frac{dy}{dx}\right|_{df=0} = -\left.\frac{\partial f(x,y)/\partial x}{\partial f(x,y)/\partial y}\right|_{df=0} = -\frac{x-2}{y-3}.$$

Now let's consider a contour set for f. The level-36 contour set for f, considered earlier, is as good as any, and is

$$C_f(36) = \{(x,y) \mid 40 - (x-2)^2 - (y-3)^2 = 36\} = \{(x,y) \mid (x-2)^2 + (y-3)^2 = 4\}.$$

This set is the circle of radius 2 centered at the point $(x,y) = (2,3)$, and is displayed in Figure 2.22. $(x,y) = (1, 3-\sqrt{3}) \approx (1, 1{\cdot}27)$ and $(x,y) = (1, 3+\sqrt{3}) \approx (1, 4{\cdot}73)$ are two of the points in the contour set $C_f(36)$.

At the point $(x, y) = \left(1, 3 - \sqrt{3}\right)$, the values of the function's gradient vector and marginal rate of substitution are

$$\nabla f \left(1, 3 - \sqrt{3}\right) = \left(2, 2\sqrt{3}\right) \quad \text{and} \quad \text{MRS}_f \left(1, 3 - \sqrt{3}\right) = \left.\frac{dy}{dx}\right|_{\substack{f \equiv 36 \\ x=1 \\ y=3-\sqrt{3}}} = -\frac{1}{\sqrt{3}}.$$

Consider a small shift from the point $\left(1, 3 - \sqrt{3}\right)$ to a point $\left(1 + dx, 3 - \sqrt{3} + dy\right)$ that too is contained in $C_f(36)$. The changes dx and dy to the values of x and y are *perturbations* from the initial point $\left(1, 3 - \sqrt{3}\right)$. The value of the marginal rate of substitution, $-1/\sqrt{3}$, says that the point $\left(1 + dx, 3 - \sqrt{3} + dy\right)$ that is very near to $\left(1, 3 - \sqrt{3}\right)$ lies in the $C_f(36)$ contour set only if

$$\left.\frac{dy}{dx}\right|_{\substack{f \equiv 36 \\ x=1 \\ y=3-\sqrt{3}}} = -\frac{1}{\sqrt{3}} \quad \Rightarrow \quad dy = -\frac{dx}{\sqrt{3}}. \tag{2.18}$$

In Figure 2.22 the short bold, dashed line through the point $\left(1, 3 - \sqrt{3}\right)$ displays the points $(1 + dx, 3 - \sqrt{3} + dy)$ that are very near to the point $\left(1, 3 - \sqrt{3}\right)$, and obey (2.18). The line containing the small perturbations (dx, dy) is displayed as another short bold, dashed line drawn through the origin in the right-side region of Figure 2.22 that is surrounded by a finely dotted line. Also displayed is the value of f's gradient vector at $\left(1, 3 - \sqrt{3}\right)$. The arrow depicting the direction of the vector and the short bold, dashed line depicting the perturbation(dx, dy) satisfying (2.18) are orthogonal to each another. Why? Well, the marginal rate of substitution equation (2.18) is

$$
\begin{aligned}
0 = \frac{1}{\sqrt{3}}\, dx + dy \quad &\Rightarrow \quad 0 = 2\sqrt{3}\left(\frac{1}{\sqrt{3}}\, dx + dy\right) \\
&\Rightarrow \quad 0 = \left(2dx, 2\sqrt{3}\, dy\right) \\
&\Rightarrow \quad 0 = \left(2, 2\sqrt{3}\right)\begin{pmatrix} dx \\ dy \end{pmatrix} \\
&\Rightarrow \quad 0 = \nabla f\left(1, 3 - \sqrt{3}\right) \cdot \begin{pmatrix} dx \\ dy \end{pmatrix}.
\end{aligned}
\tag{2.19}
$$

The Euclidean inner product of two vectors is zero if the vectors are orthogonal to each other, so at the point $\left(1, 3 - \sqrt{3}\right)$ the function's gradient vector and the small perturbation vector (dx, dy) are orthogonal. Re-expressed, (2.19) is just the

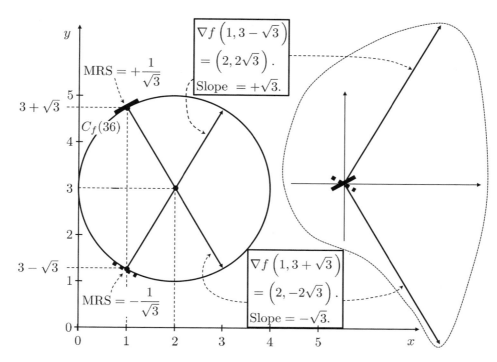

Figure 2.22: The level-36 contour set $C_f(36)$ and the gradient vectors of f evaluated at the points $\left(1, 3 - \sqrt{3}\right)$ and $\left(1, 3 + \sqrt{3}\right)$.

statement made earlier that at any point in a contour set a small movement $(\mathrm{d}x, \mathrm{d}y)$ to another very nearby point in the same contour set must give a total differential value of zero.

Figure 2.22 displays the function's marginal rate of substitution and its gradient vector at the point $\left(1, 3 + \sqrt{3}\right)$ also. To check how well you have understood the reasoning above, try to repeat the reasoning at this other point. You should conclude that at the point $\left(1, 3 + \sqrt{3}\right)$ the gradient vector $\nabla f\left(1, 3 + \sqrt{3}\right)$ is orthogonal to the vector $(\mathrm{d}x, \mathrm{d}y)$ of small perturbations between the point $\left(1, 3 + \sqrt{3}\right)$ and any other very nearby point $\left(1 + \mathrm{d}x, 3 + \sqrt{3} + \mathrm{d}y\right)$ that is also a member of the function's level-36 contour set.

Is it true in general that at any point in a contour set of a differentiable function the gradient vector of the function and the vector of small perturbations that move only to other nearby points within the contour set are orthogonal to each other? Yes, it is. Moreover, this simple idea is at the heart of the Karush-Kuhn-Tucker Necessity Theorem, one of the most useful results in all of constrained optimization theory.

An Exercise. The points $(x, y) = \left(3, 3 - \sqrt{3}\right) \approx (3, 1{\cdot}27)$ and $\left(3, 3 + \sqrt{3}\right) \approx (3, 4{\cdot}73)$ are also members of the $C_f(36)$ contour set described above. For each point in turn, evaluate the function's gradient vector and the short line containing the small perturbations $(\mathrm{d}x, \mathrm{d}y)$ that satisfy the marginal rate of substitution condition at the point. Plot the short line and the gradient vector on Figure 2.22, and then confirm that the gradient vector and the vector of perturbations $(\mathrm{d}x, \mathrm{d}y)$ are orthogonal to each other by showing that the value of their Euclidean inner product is zero.

Answer. For the point $(x, y) = \left(3, 3 - \sqrt{3}\right)$, the values of the function's gradient vector and marginal rate of substitution are

$$\nabla f\left(3, 3 - \sqrt{3}\right) = \left(-2, 2\sqrt{3}\right) \quad \text{and} \quad \mathrm{MRS}_f\left(3, 3 - \sqrt{3}\right) = \left.\frac{\mathrm{d}y}{\mathrm{d}x}\right|_{\substack{f \equiv 36 \\ x = 3 \\ y = 3 - \sqrt{3}}} = +\frac{1}{\sqrt{3}}.$$

The value of the marginal rate of substitution asserts that the vector of small perturbations $(\mathrm{d}x, \mathrm{d}y)$ is

$$(\mathrm{d}x, \mathrm{d}y) \text{ with } \left.\frac{\mathrm{d}y}{\mathrm{d}x}\right|_{\substack{f \equiv 36 \\ x = 3 \\ y = 3 - \sqrt{3}}} = +\frac{1}{\sqrt{3}} \quad \Rightarrow \quad \mathrm{d}y = +\frac{1}{\sqrt{3}}\,\mathrm{d}x.$$

The Euclidean inner product of the gradient vector ∇f and the perturbation vector $(\mathrm{d}x, \mathrm{d}y)$ is

$$\nabla f\left(3, 3 - \sqrt{3}\right) \cdot \begin{pmatrix} \mathrm{d}x \\ \mathrm{d}y \end{pmatrix} = \left(-2, 2\sqrt{3}\right)\begin{pmatrix} \mathrm{d}x \\ \mathrm{d}y \end{pmatrix} = \left(-2, 2\sqrt{3}\right)\begin{pmatrix} \mathrm{d}x \\ \mathrm{d}x/\sqrt{3} \end{pmatrix} = 0.$$

For the point $(x, y) = \left(3, 3 + \sqrt{3}\right)$, the values of the function's gradient vector and marginal rate of substitution are

$$\nabla f\left(3, 3 + \sqrt{3}\right) = \left(-2, -2\sqrt{3}\right) \quad \text{and} \quad \mathrm{MRS}_f\left(3, 3 + \sqrt{3}\right) = -\frac{1}{\sqrt{3}}.$$

The value of the marginal rate of substitution asserts that the vector of small perturbations $(\mathrm{d}x, \mathrm{d}y)$ is

$$(\mathrm{d}x, \mathrm{d}y) \text{ with } \left.\frac{\mathrm{d}y}{\mathrm{d}x}\right|_{\substack{f \equiv 36 \\ x = 3 \\ y = 3 + \sqrt{3}}} = -\frac{1}{\sqrt{3}} \quad \Rightarrow \quad \mathrm{d}y = -\frac{1}{\sqrt{3}}\,\mathrm{d}x.$$

The Euclidean inner product of the gradient vector ∇f and the perturbation vector $(\mathrm{d}x, \mathrm{d}y)$ is

$$\nabla f\left(3, 3 + \sqrt{3}\right) \cdot \begin{pmatrix} \mathrm{d}x \\ \mathrm{d}y \end{pmatrix} = \left(-2, -2\sqrt{3}\right)\begin{pmatrix} \mathrm{d}x \\ \mathrm{d}y \end{pmatrix} = \left(-2, -2\sqrt{3}\right)\begin{pmatrix} \mathrm{d}x \\ -\mathrm{d}x/\sqrt{3} \end{pmatrix} = 0. \quad \square$$

Another Exercise. Consider the function $f(x_1, x_2) = x_1^{1/2} x_2^{1/2}$.

(i) What is the gradient vector for this function?

(ii) The points $(x_1, x_2) = (1, 16)$, $(x_1, x_2) = (4, 4)$, and $(x_1, x_2) = (16, 1)$ all belong to the level-4 contour set of f. For each point in turn, compute the value of the function's gradient vector and the marginal rate of substitution between x_1 and x_2. Then compute the line containing the small perturbations $dx = (dx_1, dx_2)$ that satisfy the marginal rate of substitution condition at the point. Finally, show that the gradient vector and the perturbation vector dx are orthogonal at the point.

Answer to (i). The gradient vector for f is the row vector

$$\nabla f(x_1, x_2) = \left(\frac{\partial f(x_1, x_2)}{\partial x_1}, \frac{\partial f(x_1, x_2)}{\partial x_2} \right) = \left(\frac{1}{2} \left(\frac{x_2}{x_1} \right)^{1/2}, \frac{1}{2} \left(\frac{x_1}{x_2} \right)^{1/2} \right).$$

Answer to (ii). Along the $f \equiv 4$ contour set, the marginal rate of substitution between x_1 and x_2 is

$$\frac{dx_2}{dx_1}\bigg|_{f \equiv 4} = - \frac{\partial f(x_1, x_2)/\partial x_1}{\partial f(x_1, x_2)/\partial x_2} = - \frac{(1/2)(x_2/x_1)^{1/2}}{(1/2)(x_1/x_2)^{1/2}} = - \frac{x_2}{x_1}$$

for x_1 and x_2 satisfying $x_1^{1/2} x_2^{1/2} = 4$.

See Figure 2.23. At the point $(x_1, x_2) = (1, 16)$, the value of the function's gradient vector is

$$\nabla f(1, 16) = \left(\frac{1}{2} \left(\frac{16}{1} \right)^{1/2}, \frac{1}{2} \left(\frac{1}{16} \right)^{1/2} \right) = \left(2, \frac{1}{8} \right).$$

This vector is displayed in Bubble 1 in Figure 2.23. The value of the function's marginal rate of substitution is

$$\frac{dx_2}{dx_1}\bigg|_{\substack{df=0 \\ x_1=1 \\ x_2=16}} = - \frac{16}{1} = -16. \tag{2.20}$$

Therefore the perturbation vector is $dx = (dx_1, dx_2)$, where $dx_2 = -16 dx_1$. Such perturbation vectors are displayed in Bubble 1 as a short thick line containing the origin. The Euclidean inner product of any such perturbation vector and the gradient vector at $(x_1, x_2) = (1, 16)$ is

$$\nabla f(1, 16) \cdot (dx_1, dx_2) = \left(2, \frac{1}{8} \right) \left(\begin{matrix} dx_1 \\ -16 dx_1 \end{matrix} \right) = 0.$$

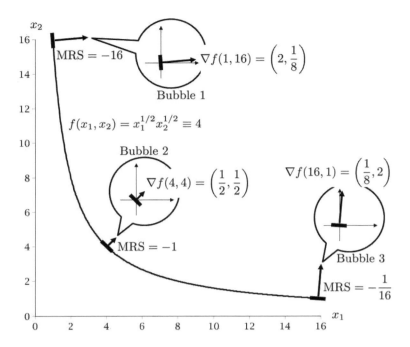

Figure 2.23: Gradients and marginal rates of substitution for $f(x_1, x_2) = x_1^{1/2} x_2^{1/2}$.

The two vectors are therefore orthogonal.

At the point $(x_1, x_2) = (4, 4)$, the value of the function's gradient vector is

$$\nabla f(4,4) = \left(\frac{1}{2} \left(\frac{4}{4} \right)^{1/2}, \frac{1}{2} \left(\frac{4}{4} \right)^{1/2} \right) = \left(\frac{1}{2}, \frac{1}{2} \right).$$

The value of the function's marginal rate of substitution is

$$\left. \frac{\mathrm{d}x_2}{\mathrm{d}x_1} \right|_{\substack{\mathrm{d}f=0 \\ x_1=4 \\ x_2=4}} = -\frac{4}{4} = -1. \tag{2.21}$$

Therefore the perturbation vector is $\mathrm{d}x = (\mathrm{d}x_1, \mathrm{d}x_2)$, where $\mathrm{d}x_2 = -\mathrm{d}x_1$. Such perturbation vectors are displayed in Bubble 2 as a short thick line containing the origin. The Euclidean inner product of any such perturbation vector and the gradient vector at $(x_1, x_2) = (4, 4)$ is

$$\nabla f(1, 16) \cdot (\mathrm{d}x_1, \mathrm{d}x_2) = \left(\frac{1}{2}, \frac{1}{2} \right) \left(\begin{matrix} \mathrm{d}x_1 \\ -\mathrm{d}x_1 \end{matrix} \right) = 0.$$

The two vectors are therefore orthogonal.

At the point $(x_1, x_2) = (16, 1)$, the value of the function's gradient vector is

$$\nabla f(16, 1) = \left(\frac{1}{2} \left(\frac{1}{16} \right)^{1/2}, \frac{1}{2} \left(\frac{16}{1} \right)^{1/2} \right) = \left(\frac{1}{8}, 2 \right).$$

The value of the function's marginal rate of substitution is

$$\frac{\mathrm{d}x_2}{\mathrm{d}x_1} \bigg|_{\substack{\mathrm{d}f=0 \\ x_1=16 \\ x_2=1}} = -\frac{1}{16}. \tag{2.22}$$

Therefore the perturbation vector is $\mathrm{d}x = (\mathrm{d}x_1, \mathrm{d}x_2)$, where $-16\mathrm{d}x_2 = \mathrm{d}x_1$. Such perturbation vectors are displayed in Bubble 3 as a short thick line containing the origin. The Euclidean inner product of any such perturbation vector and the gradient vector at $(x_1, x_2) = (16, 1)$ is

$$\nabla f(16, 1){\cdot}(\mathrm{d}x_1, \mathrm{d}x_2) = \left(\frac{1}{8}, 2 \right) \left(\begin{array}{c} -16\,\mathrm{d}x_2 \\ \mathrm{d}x_2 \end{array} \right) = 0.$$

The two vectors are therefore orthogonal.   □

2.15   Quadratic Forms

A *quadratic form* is just a special type of order 2 polynomial in n variables $x_1, \ldots, x_n$.

If $n = 1$, then the only possible quadratic form is

$$Q(x) = ax^2 \text{ where } a \in \Re.$$

Examples are $Q(x) = x^2$ (*i.e.* $a = 1$), $Q(x) = -7x^2$ (*i.e.* $a = -7$) and $Q(x) \equiv 0$ (*i.e.* $a = 0$).

If $n = 2$, then the quadratic form is

$$\begin{aligned} Q(x_1, x_2) &= a_{11}x_1^2 + a_{12}x_1x_2 + a_{21}x_2x_1 + a_{22}x_2^2 \\ &= a_{11}x_1^2 + (a_{12} + a_{21})x_1x_2 + a_{22}x_2^2, \end{aligned}$$

where all of a_{11}, a_{12}, a_{21} and a_{22} are real numbers.

The general quadratic form is

$$\begin{aligned} Q(x_1, \ldots, x_n) = {} & a_{11}x_1^2 + a_{12}x_1x_2 + \cdots + a_{1n}x_1x_n + \\ & a_{21}x_2x_1 + a_{22}x_2^2 + \cdots + a_{2n}x_2x_n + \\ & \cdots \ + \\ & a_{n1}x_nx_1 + a_{n2}x_nx_2 + \cdots + a_{nn}x_n^2, \end{aligned} \tag{2.23}$$

where each coefficient a_{ij} is a real number, for $i, j = 1, \ldots, n$.

All of the terms in a quadratic form are of order 2 in $x_1, \ldots, x_n$. That is, every term is either a square, x_i^2 for $i = 1, \ldots, n$, or it is a cross-product, $x_i x_j$ for $i, j = 1, \ldots, n$ with $i \neq j$. There are no linear terms and there are no constants.

(2.23) is the product

$$x^T A x = (x_1, \ldots, x_n) \begin{pmatrix} a_{11} & a_{12} & \cdots & a_{1n} \\ a_{21} & a_{22} & \cdots & a_{2n} \\ \vdots & \vdots & \ddots & \vdots \\ a_{n1} & a_{n2} & \cdots & a_{nn} \end{pmatrix} \begin{pmatrix} x_1 \\ \vdots \\ x_n \end{pmatrix}, \tag{2.24}$$

and so the two identical statements (2.23) and (2.24) are called the *quadratic form of the matrix A*. Hopefully it is clear that only square matrices possess quadratic forms.

Notice that the quadratic form (2.23) contains two cross-product terms $x_i x_j$ for each $i, j = 1, \ldots, n$ with $i \neq j$. For example, there is a term $a_{12} x_1 x_2$ and a term $a_{21} x_2 x_1$, which can be collected together to write $(a_{12} + a_{21}) x_1 x_2$. Similarly, there is a term $a_{1n} x_1 x_n$ and a term $a_{n1} x_n x_1$. Their sum is $(a_{1n} + a_{n1}) x_1 x_n$. Halving each sum lets us rewrite the quadratic form (2.23) as

$$\begin{aligned} Q(x_1, \ldots, x_n) = a_{11} x_1^2 + \frac{a_{12} + a_{21}}{2} x_1 x_2 + \cdots + \frac{a_{1n} + a_{n1}}{2} x_1 x_n + \\ \frac{a_{12} + a_{21}}{2} x_2 x_1 + a_{22} x_2^2 + \cdots + \frac{a_{2n} + a_{n2}}{2} x_2 x_n + \\ \cdots + \\ \frac{a_{1n} + a_{n1}}{2} x_n x_1 + \frac{a_{2n} + a_{n2}}{2} x_n x_2 + \cdots + a_{nn} x_n^2. \end{aligned} \tag{2.25}$$

(2.25) is the same as the product

$$x^T B x = (x_1, \ldots, x_n) \begin{pmatrix} a_{11} & (a_{12} + a_{21})/2 & \cdots & (a_{1n} + a_{n1})/2 \\ (a_{12} + a_{21})/2 & a_{22} & \cdots & (a_{2n} + a_{n2})/2 \\ \vdots & \vdots & \ddots & \vdots \\ (a_{1n} + a_{n1})/2 & (a_{2n} + a_{n2})/2 & \cdots & a_{nn} \end{pmatrix} \begin{pmatrix} x_1 \\ \vdots \\ x_n \end{pmatrix}.$$

The matrix A is typically asymmetric while the matrix B, constructed from the elements of the matrix A, is symmetric. Thus *the quadratic form of any asymmetric matrix is also the quadratic form of a symmetric matrix*. This fact can be a great algebraic convenience.

An Exercise. Write each of the quadratic forms listed below in the matrix form $x^T A x$ and then in the form $x^T B x$, where A is an asymmetric matrix and B is a symmetric matrix.

(i) $x_1^2 - 8x_1 x_2 + x_2^2$;

(ii) $3x_1^2 - 8x_1 x_2 - 5x_2^2$; and

(iii) $2x_1^2 + x_2^2 + 5x_3^2 + 3x_1 x_2 - 6x_1 x_3 + 10x_2 x_3$.

Answer.

(i) The quadratic form is $Q(x_1, x_2) = a_{11}x_1^2 + (a_{12} + a_{21})x_1 x_2 + a_{22}x_2^2$, where $a_{11} = 1$, $a_{12} + a_{21} = -8$ and $a_{22} = 1$. A is therefore any asymmetric matrix in which $a_{11} = 1$, $a_{12} + a_{21} = -8$ and $a_{22} = 1$. One of the infinitely many such matrices is

$$A = \begin{pmatrix} 1 & -462 \\ 454 & 1 \end{pmatrix}.$$

The only symmetric matrix, B, has elements $b_{11} = 1$, $b_{12} = b_{21} = -4$ and $b_{22} = 1$; *i.e.*

$$B = \begin{pmatrix} 1 & -4 \\ -4 & 1 \end{pmatrix}.$$

(ii) The quadratic form is $Q(x_1, x_2) = a_{11}x_1^2 + (a_{12} + a_{21})x_1 x_2 + a_{22}x_2^2$, where $a_{11} = 3$, $a_{12} + a_{21} = -8$ and $a_{22} = -5$. A is therefore any asymmetric matrix in which $a_{11} = 3$, $a_{12} + a_{21} = -8$ and $a_{22} = -5$. One of the infinitely many such matrices is

$$A = \begin{pmatrix} 3 & 34 \\ -42 & -5 \end{pmatrix}.$$

The only symmetric matrix, B, has elements $b_{11} = 3$, $b_{12} = b_{21} = -4$ and $b_{22} = -5$; *i.e.*

$$B = \begin{pmatrix} 3 & -4 \\ -4 & -5 \end{pmatrix}.$$

(iii) The quadratic form is $Q(x_1, x_2, x_3) = a_{11}x_1^2 + (a_{12} + a_{21})x_1 x_2 + (a_{13} + a_{31})x_1 x_3 + a_{22}x_2^2 + (a_{23} + a_{32})x_2 x_3 + a_{33}x_3^2$, where $a_{11} = 2$, $a_{22} = 1$, $a_{33} = 5$, $a_{12} + a_{21} = 3$, $a_{13} + a_{31} = -6$ and $a_{23} + a_{32} = 10$. A is therefore any asymmetric matrix in which $a_{11} = 2$, $a_{22} = 1$, $a_{33} = 5$, $a_{12} + a_{21} = 3$, $a_{13} + a_{31} = -6$ and $a_{23} + a_{32} = 10$. One of the infinitely many such matrices is

$$A = \begin{pmatrix} 2 & 7 & -3 \\ -4 & 1 & 17 \\ -3 & -7 & 5 \end{pmatrix}.$$

The only symmetric matrix, B, has elements $b_{11} = 2$, $b_{22} = 1$, $b_{33} = 5$, $b_{12} = b_{21} = 3/2$, $b_{13} = b_{31} = -3$ and $b_{23} = b_{32} = 5$; *i.e.*

$$B = \begin{pmatrix} 2 & 3/2 & -3 \\ 3/2 & 1 & 5 \\ -3 & 5 & 5 \end{pmatrix}. \qquad \square$$

All quadratic forms fall into at least one of five categories. These are as follows.

Definition 2.12 (Definiteness of Quadratic Forms). *A quadratic form* $Q(x_1, \ldots, x_n)$ *is*
(i) positive-definite if and only if $Q(x_1, \ldots, x_n) > 0$ *for all* $x \in \Re^n$, $x \neq \underline{0}$;
(ii) positive-semi-definite if and only if $Q(x_1, \ldots, x_n) \geq 0$ *for all* $x \in \Re^n$;
(iii) negative-semi-definite if and only if $Q(x_1, \ldots, x_n) \leq 0$ *for all* $x \in \Re^n$;
(iv) negative-definite if and only if $Q(x_1, \ldots, x_n) < 0$ *for all* $x \in \Re^n$, $x \neq \underline{0}$;
(v) indefinite if and only if there is at least one point $(x'_1, \ldots, x'_n) \in \Re^n$ *and at least one other point* $(x''_1, \ldots, x''_n) \in \Re^n$ *for which* $Q(x'_1, \ldots, x'_n) > 0$ *and* $Q(x''_1, \ldots, x''_n) < 0$.

$$Q(x_1, x_2)$$

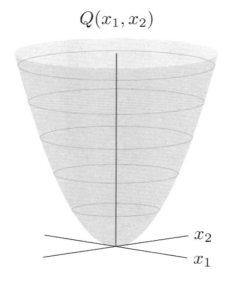

Figure 2.24: The graph of the positive-definite quadratic form $Q(x_1, x_2) = x_1^2 - x_1 x_2 + 2x_2^2$.

If $x = \underline{0}$, then $Q(x) = 0$, so every quadratic form, no matter its definiteness type, has the origin as a point in its graph.

Let's take $n = 2$ and ask "What does the graph of a positive-definite quadratic form look like?" By its definition (see (i) above), for any (x_1, x_2) other than $(0, 0)$,

$$a_{11}x_1^2 + (a_{12} + a_{21})x_1x_2 + a_{22}x_2^2 > 0.$$

We are allowed to choose $x_2 = 0$ (so long as we do not choose $x_1 = 0$ at the same time). Then we have $a_{11}x_1^2 > 0$, so, necessarily, $a_{11} > 0$. Similarly, we are allowed to choose $x_1 = 0$ (so long as we do not choose $x_2 = 0$ at the same time), in which case we have $a_{22}x_2^2 > 0$, so, necessarily, $a_{22} > 0$. So when the quadratic form is positive-definite, it is a sum of two squares $a_{11}x_1^2$ and $a_{22}x_2^2$ in which the coefficients a_{11} and a_{22} are both strictly positive. The graphs of such functions are "positive parabolas" like the one displayed in Figure 2.24 in which $a_{11} = 1$, $a_{12} + a_{21} = -1$ and $a_{22} = 2$. This quadratic form is

$$Q(x_1, x_2) = x_1^2 - x_1x_2 + 2x_2^2 = x_1^2 - x_1x_2 + \frac{x_2^2}{4} + \frac{7x_2^2}{4}$$

$$= \left(x_1 - \frac{x_2}{2}\right)^2 + \frac{7x_2^2}{4} > 0 \text{ for all } (x_1, x_2) \neq (0, 0).$$

Notice that a positive-definite quadratic form has value zero only at the origin.

Now let's ask "What does a positive-semi-definite quadratic form look like?" By its definition (see (ii) above), for any (x_1, x_2),

$$a_{11}x_1^2 + (a_{12} + a_{21})x_1x_2 + a_{22}x_2^2 \geq 0.$$

Choosing $x_2 = 0$ gives $a_{11}x_1^2 \geq 0$, so, necessarily, $a_{11} \geq 0$. Similarly, necessarily, $a_{22} \geq 0$. So when the quadratic form is positive-semi-definite, it is a sum of two squares $a_{11}x_1^2$ and $a_{22}x_2^2$ in which the coefficients a_{11} and a_{22} are both nonnegative (either one or both could be zero). The graphs of such functions typically are again "positive parabolas" but may also include a line at a height of zero, as is displayed in Figure 2.25 for $a_{11} = 1$, $a_{12} + a_{21} = -2$ and $a_{22} = 1$. In this case the quadratic form is $Q(x_1, x_2) = x_1^2 - 2x_1x_2 + x_2^2 = (x_1 - x_2)^2$ and so has value zero at any point (x_1, x_2) with $x_1 = x_2$, not just at $(0, 0)$.

It should be clear by now that if a quadratic form is negative-definite, then, necessarily, $a_{11} < 0$ and $a_{22} < 0$, and that if a quadratic form is negative-semi-definite, then, necessarily, $a_{11} \leq 0$ and $a_{22} \leq 0$. The typical graph of a negative-definite quadratic form is like the graph in Figure 2.24 turned upside down. The typical graph of a negative-semi-definite quadratic form looks like the graph in Figure 2.25 turned upside down.

Figure 2.26 displays the graph of the quadratic form $Q(x_1, x_2) = x_1^2 - x_2^2$. This quadratic form takes both positive and negative values, so it is indefinite.

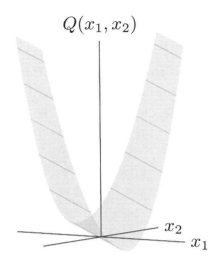

Figure 2.25: The graph of the positive-semi-definite quadratic form $Q(x_1, x_2) = x_1^2 - 2x_1x_2 + x_2^2 = (x_1 - x_2)^2$.

Theorem 2.10. *The quadratic form of an $n \times n$ matrix A is* $\left\{ \begin{array}{c} \textit{positive-definite} \\ \textit{positive-semi-definite} \\ \textit{negative-semi-definite} \\ \textit{negative-definite} \end{array} \right\}$

only if a_{ii} $\left\{ \begin{array}{c} > 0 \\ \geq 0 \\ \leq 0 \\ < 0 \end{array} \right\}$ *for all $i = 1, \ldots, n$.*

Be clear that this theorem applies to asymmetric as well as to symmetric matrices.

An Exercise. A and B are both $n \times n$ matrices. If A is negative-semi-definite and B is negative-definite, then must the matrix $A + B$ be negative-definite?

Answer. For every vector $x \in \Re^n$, $x \neq \underline{0}$, $x^T A x \leq 0$ and $x^T B x < 0$. Therefore,

$$x^T (A + B)x = x^T A x + x^T B x < 0 \; \forall \; x \in \Re^n, \; x \neq \underline{0}.$$

That is, $A + B$ is a negative-definite matrix.   □

So long as the order n of a square matrix is not large, then it may be possible without too much effort to determine algebraically to which of the five above definiteness categories a matrix belongs. But for many cases such an approach is much too

$$Q(x_1, x_2)$$

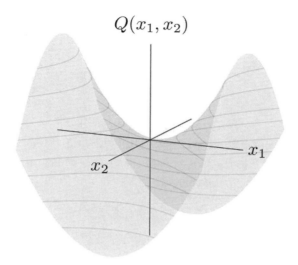

Figure 2.26: The graph of the indefinite quadratic form $Q(x_1, x_2) = x_1^2 - x_2^2$.

tedious. Is there an easier way to make this determination? There are two sensible alternative approaches. One involves the computation of the *eigenroots* (also called *characteristic roots*) of the matrix. I will not discuss this approach, but the interested reader will find it explained in many other texts. The second approach uses the *successive principal minors* of a square matrix.

Consider the 3×3 matrix

$$A = \begin{pmatrix} a_{11} & a_{12} & a_{13} \\ a_{21} & a_{22} & a_{23} \\ a_{31} & a_{32} & a_{33} \end{pmatrix}.$$

Now consider the square submatrices contained in A that all contain the top-left element a_{11} and that expand down along the main, or principal, diagonal of A. These are the submatrices

$$A_1 = \begin{pmatrix} a_{11} \end{pmatrix}, \ A_2 = \begin{pmatrix} a_{11} & a_{12} \\ a_{21} & a_{22} \end{pmatrix} \text{ and } A_3 = A = \begin{pmatrix} a_{11} & a_{12} & a_{13} \\ a_{21} & a_{22} & a_{23} \\ a_{31} & a_{32} & a_{33} \end{pmatrix}.$$

These submatrices are the *leading principal submatrices of A*. The determinants of these leading principal submatrices of A are called the *leading principal minors of A*:

$$\det A_1 = \det \begin{pmatrix} a_{11} \end{pmatrix}, \ \det A_2 = \det \begin{pmatrix} a_{11} & a_{12} \\ a_{21} & a_{22} \end{pmatrix}$$

$$\text{and } \ \det A_3 = \det A = \det \begin{pmatrix} a_{11} & a_{12} & a_{13} \\ a_{21} & a_{22} & a_{23} \\ a_{31} & a_{32} & a_{33} \end{pmatrix}. \tag{2.26}$$

Definition 2.13 (Leading Principal Submatrix). *Let A be an $n \times n$ matrix. For $k = 1, \ldots, n$, the kth leading principal submatrix of A is the matrix formed by deleting from A the last $n - k$ rows and columns.*

Definition 2.14 (Leading Principal Minor). *Let A be an $n \times n$ matrix. For $k = 1, \ldots, n$, the kth leading principal minor of A is the determinant of the kth leading principal submatrix of A.*

Odd though it may seem, for a *symmetric* matrix the *strict* definiteness (or not) of the matrix can be deduced by the signs of the matrix's leading principal minors. Theorem 2.11 states how this is done. Notice that the theorem applies only to matrices that are, first, symmetric and, second, have quadratic forms that are either positive-definite, negative-definite, or indefinite. Particularly, the theorem does not apply to semi-definite matrices. The theorem also does not apply to asymmetric matrices, but I earlier noted that the quadratic form of any asymmetric matrix is the same as the quadratic form of a symmetric matrix that is constructed from the asymmetric matrix. The theorem can, therefore, be applied to any square asymmetric matrix by first constructing the symmetric matrix with the same quadratic form, and then applying the theorem to the symmetric matrix.

Theorem 2.11 (Leading Principal Minors and Definiteness). *Let A be a symmetric $n \times n$ matrix. Then the quadratic form of A is*
(i) positive-definite if and only if all of the leading principal minors of A are positive;
(ii) negative-definite if and only if all of the leading principal minors of A are nonzero and alternate in sign, with the sign of the kth leading principal minor being $(-1)^k$; and
(iii) if any one of the leading principal minors of A is not zero and has a sign inconsistent with either (i) or (ii) then the quadratic form of A is indefinite.

Statements (i) and (ii) are equivalency statements. Statement (iii) is only a sufficiency statement.

To see more clearly how Theorem 2.11 is used, let's rewrite the above 3×3 matrix A as a symmetric matrix:

$$A = \begin{pmatrix} a_{11} & a_{12} & a_{13} \\ a_{12} & a_{22} & a_{23} \\ a_{13} & a_{23} & a_{33} \end{pmatrix}.$$

The leading principal submatrices of A are now

$$A_1 = (a_{11}), \quad A_2 = \begin{pmatrix} a_{11} & a_{12} \\ a_{12} & a_{22} \end{pmatrix}, \quad \text{and } A_3 = A = \begin{pmatrix} a_{11} & a_{12} & a_{13} \\ a_{12} & a_{22} & a_{23} \\ a_{13} & a_{23} & a_{33} \end{pmatrix},$$

and the leading principal minors of A are

$$\det A_1 = \det (a_{11}), \quad \det A_2 = \det \begin{pmatrix} a_{11} & a_{12} \\ a_{12} & a_{22} \end{pmatrix}, \quad \det A_3 = \det A = \det \begin{pmatrix} a_{11} & a_{12} & a_{13} \\ a_{12} & a_{22} & a_{23} \\ a_{13} & a_{23} & a_{33} \end{pmatrix}.$$

Theorem 2.11 states that the quadratic form of A is positive-definite if and only if

$$\det A_1 = \det (a_{11}) = a_{11} > 0, \tag{2.27}$$

$$\det A_2 = \det \begin{pmatrix} a_{11} & a_{12} \\ a_{12} & a_{22} \end{pmatrix} = a_{11}a_{22} - a_{12}^2 > 0, \tag{2.28}$$

$$\text{and } \det A_3 = \det A = \det \begin{pmatrix} a_{11} & a_{12} & a_{13} \\ a_{12} & a_{22} & a_{23} \\ a_{13} & a_{23} & a_{33} \end{pmatrix} > 0. \tag{2.29}$$

These conditions restrict the values that the matrix's elements a_{ij} may have. For example, (2.27) requires that $a_{11} > 0$. Next, (2.28) requires that $a_{11}a_{22} > a_{12}^2 \geq 0$, which, with $a_{11} > 0$, requires that $a_{22} > 0$. Together, the leading principal minor statements (2.27), (2.28), and (2.29) provide all of the restrictions on the elements of A that ensure that the quadratic form of A is positive-definite.

Theorem 2.11 also states that the quadratic form of the symmetric matrix A is negative-definite if and only if

$$\det A_1 = \det \begin{pmatrix} a_{11} \end{pmatrix} = a_{11} < 0 \text{ (nonzero and has the sign } (-1)^1), \tag{2.30}$$

$$\det A_2 = \det \begin{pmatrix} a_{11} & a_{12} \\ a_{12} & a_{22} \end{pmatrix} = a_{11}a_{22} - a_{12}^2 > 0 \text{ (nonzero and has the sign } (-1)^2), \tag{2.31}$$

$$\text{and } \det A_3 = \det A = \det \begin{pmatrix} a_{11} & a_{12} & a_{13} \\ a_{12} & a_{22} & a_{23} \\ a_{13} & a_{23} & a_{33} \end{pmatrix} < 0 \text{ (nonzero and has the sign } (-1)^3). \tag{2.32}$$

These conditions restrict the values that the matrix's elements a_{ij} may have. (2.30) requires that $a_{11} < 0$. (2.31) requires that $a_{11}a_{22} > a_{12}^2 \geq 0$, which, with $a_{11} < 0$, requires that $a_{22} < 0$. Together, the leading principal minor statements (2.30), (2.31) and (2.32) provide all of the restrictions on the elements of A that ensure that the quadratic form of A is negative-definite.

2.16   Critical Points

A critical point for a real-valued and differentiable function $f(x_1, \ldots, x_n)$ is a point at which the function's slope is zero in all of the $x_1, \ldots, x_n$ directions.

Definition 2.15 (Critical Point). *Let O be a nonempty open subset of $\Re^n$ and let $f : \Re^n \mapsto \Re$ be a function that is differentiable on O. Then $x^* \in O$ is a critical point of f if the gradient of f is the n-dimensional zero vector at $x = x^*$; i.e. if $\partial f(x)/\partial x_i = 0$ at $x = x^*$ for all $i = 1, \ldots, n$.*

Any (interior to the domain) local maximum for f is a critical point, as is any interior local minimum or point of inflexion at which the gradient of f is the zero vector. Another type of critical point that will turn out to be of great interest to us is a saddle-point.

2.17   Hessian Matrices

The *Hessian matrix* of a twice-differentiable function is a matrix array of all of the function's second-order derivatives. Specifically, if $f(x_1, \ldots, x_n)$ is a function that is differentiable to order 2, then the function's Hessian matrix is the array of functions

$$H_f(x) = \begin{pmatrix} \dfrac{\partial^2 f}{\partial x_1^2} & \dfrac{\partial^2 f}{\partial x_1 \partial x_2} & \cdots & \dfrac{\partial^2 f}{\partial x_1 \partial x_n} \\[2ex] \dfrac{\partial^2 f}{\partial x_2 \partial x_1} & \dfrac{\partial^2 f}{\partial x_2^2} & \cdots & \dfrac{\partial^2 f}{\partial x_2 \partial x_n} \\[2ex] \vdots & \vdots & \ddots & \vdots \\[2ex] \dfrac{\partial^2 f}{\partial x_n \partial x_1} & \dfrac{\partial^2 f}{\partial x_n \partial x_2} & \cdots & \dfrac{\partial^2 f}{\partial x_n^2} \end{pmatrix}.$$

If the function f is continuously differentiable to order 2, then the order of differentiation does not matter: $\partial^2 f / \partial x_i \partial x_j = \partial^2 f / \partial x_j \partial x_i$ for all $i, j = 1, \ldots, n$. For order 2 continuously differentiable functions, then, the Hessian matrices are symmetric.

2.18   Quadratic Approximations of Functions

Why would you want to use a quadratic function to approximate another function? Once you achieve a clear understanding of how to solve constrained optimization problems in which the constraint and objective functions are all differentiable, you will realize that it is all about using quadratic functions as local approximations of differentiable functions, so it is important that you understand this section clearly. Whether you realize it or not, you have already done this many times before. A large part of the chapter on constrained optimization is concerned with helping you to realize this and then to understand why it makes sense to do it. The central idea, used repeatedly in later chapters, is a special case of the famous "Taylor's Theorem" published in 1715 by Brook Taylor. Oddly enough, this important result was ignored for another 57 years until the French mathematician Joseph Lagrange drew attention to it in 1772. Taylor did not give a complete proof of his result; that was provided in 1841 by another famous French mathematician, Augustin Cauchy. Another point of interest is that various special cases of Taylor's result were known well before Taylor's publication of his more general statement.

I will give you an example that I hope will make clear why quadratic approximations are so useful for solving differentiable constrained optimization problems. Here is a simple function:

$$f(x) = -50x + x^3 + 100 \ln (1 + x) \text{ for } x \in [0, 4]. \tag{2.33}$$

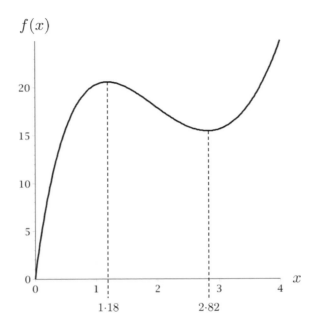

Figure 2.27: The graph of $f(x) = -50x + x^3 + 100 \ln(1 + x)$ for $0 \leq x \leq 4$.

This function is not even close to being a quadratic, which is why I chose it. Figure 2.27 displays the graph of the function for $0 \leq x \leq 4$. The function has a local maximum at $x \approx 1 \cdot 18350342$. Taylor's Theorem tells us that a particular quadratic function is a good approximation to $f(1 \cdot 18350342 + \Delta x)$ for values of Δx that are close to zero; *i.e.* for points close to $x = 1 \cdot 18350342$. The quadratic is $g(\Delta x) = a(\Delta x)^2 + b\Delta x + c$, where c is the value of f at $x = 1 \cdot 18350342$, b is the value of the first-order derivative of f at $x = 1 \cdot 18350342$, and a is one-half of the value of the second-order derivative of f at $x = 1 \cdot 18350342$. That is,

$$c = f(x = 1 \cdot 18350342) \approx 20 \cdot 575605,$$

$$b = \frac{\mathrm{d}f(x)}{\mathrm{d}x}\Big|_{x=1 \cdot 18350342} = \left(-50 + 3x^2 + \frac{100}{1+x}\right)\Big|_{x=1 \cdot 183503419} \approx 0,$$

$$\text{and} \quad a = \frac{1}{2}\frac{\mathrm{d}^2 f(x)}{\mathrm{d}x^2}\Big|_{x=1 \cdot 18350342} = \frac{1}{2}\left(6x - \frac{100}{(1+x)^2}\right)\Big|_{x=1 \cdot 183503419} \approx -6 \cdot 936754975.$$

So the approximating quadratic is

$$g(\Delta x) = 20 \cdot 575605 - 6 \cdot 936754975(\Delta x)^2$$

for small values, both positive and negative, of Δx that are close to zero.

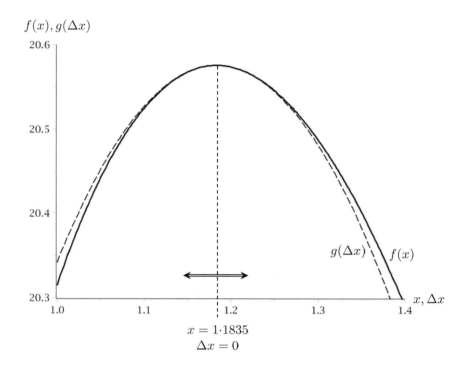

Figure 2.28: The function f and the approximating quadratic g near to $x = 1{\cdot}1835$.

Figure 2.28 shows the graphs of f and g for values of x in a small neighborhood about $x = 1{\cdot}18350342$. For any small enough neighborhood about $x = 1{\cdot}18350342$, such as that indicated by the double-ended arrow, the two graphs are almost the same; the quadratic g is a close approximation to the function f. Following the same procedure will give us a close quadratic approximation to f at any value of $x \in [0, 4]$, not just at a local maximum. So if, for example, we selected $x = 2$, a point that is neither a local maximum nor a local minimum for f (see Figure 2.27), then we can use the above procedure to construct a new quadratic function that is a close approximation to the function f for values of x that are close to $x = 2$. The point to grasp, then, is that at *any point* in the domain of *any twice-continuously differentiable function* f there exists a quadratic function that is almost exactly the same as the differentiable function f over a small enough neighborhood of domain values around the chosen point. This is the result that is the second-order version of Taylor's Theorem.

So let's see the second-order version of Taylor's Theorem. I will introduce it in two steps. The first time around, we will consider only functions that map from the real line. The second pass will consider functions that map from $\Re^n$. (There are many other books in which you can read the general version of the theorem and see it in its full glory.)

Theorem 2.12 (Second-Order Taylor's Theorem for Functions Mapping from $\Re$ to $\Re$). *Let $S \subseteq \Re$ be a nonempty set that is open with respect to the Euclidean topology on $\Re$. Let $f : S \mapsto \Re$ be a $C^2(S)$ function. Let $x', x' + \Delta x \in S$. Then there exists a function $R_2(x', \Delta x) \in \mathcal{C}^2(S)$ such that*

$$f(x' + \Delta x) = f(x') + \frac{\mathrm{d}f(x)}{\mathrm{d}x}|_{x=x'}\Delta x + \frac{1}{2}\frac{\mathrm{d}^2 f(x)}{\mathrm{d}x^2}|_{x=x'} (\Delta x)^2 + R_2(x', \Delta x), \quad (2.34)$$

where

$$\frac{R_2(x', \Delta x)}{(\Delta x)^2} \to 0 \ as \ \Delta x \to 0. \quad (2.35)$$

The first three terms on the right-hand side of (2.34) are the *Taylor quadratic*

$$Q(x', \Delta x) = f(x') + \frac{\mathrm{d}f(x)}{\mathrm{d}x}|_{x=x'}\Delta x + \frac{1}{2}\frac{\mathrm{d}^2 f(x)}{\mathrm{d}x^2}|_{x=x'} (\Delta x)^2 \quad (2.36)$$

that is the quadratic approximation to the function f at and nearby to $x = x'$. The approximation error at a point $x = x' + \Delta x$ is the difference in the values at $x = x' + \Delta x$ of f and the approximation $Q(x', \Delta x)$. This error is the second-order Taylor's series *remainder term $R_2(x', \Delta x)$*. (2.35) states that as $\Delta x \to 0$ the remainder term's contribution to the right-hand side of (2.34) becomes negligibly small, making the Taylor quadratic an evermore accurate approximation to the function f at values $x = x' + \Delta x$ that are ever closer to $x = x'$. This is what we discovered in our above example.

Now let's see Taylor's Theorem for functions that map from $\Re^n$ to $\Re$.

Theorem 2.13 (Second-Order Taylor's Theorem for Functions Mapping from $\Re^n$ to $\Re$). *Let $S \subseteq \Re^n$ be a nonempty set that is open with respect to the Euclidean metric topology on $\Re^n$. Let $f : S \mapsto \Re$ be a $C^2(S)$ function. Let $x' \in S$. Let $B(x', \varepsilon)$ be an open ball centered at x' with radius $\varepsilon > 0$ in S. Let $x' + \Delta x \in B(x', \varepsilon)$. Then there exists a function $R_2(x', \Delta x) \in \mathcal{C}^2(S)$ such that, for every $x' + \Delta x \in B(x', \varepsilon)$,*

$$f(x' + \Delta x) = f(x') + \nabla f(x)|_{x=x'} \cdot \Delta x + \frac{1}{2}\Delta x^T H_f(x)|_{x=x'}\Delta x + R_2(x', \Delta x), \quad (2.37)$$

where

$$\frac{R_2(x', \Delta x)}{\|\Delta x\|_E^2} \to 0 \ as \ \|\Delta x\|_E \to 0. \tag{2.38}$$

The sum of the first three terms of (2.37) is again the Taylor quadratic function of $\Delta x = (\Delta x_1, \ldots, \Delta x_n)$ that more and more accurately approximates the function f on the ball centered at $x = x'$ with radius ε as Δx approaches the zero vector.

Let's have a look at (2.37) for the function $f(x_1, x_2) = x_1^{1/2} + x_1 x_2 + \ln(1 + x_1 + x_2)$. The gradient of f is the row vector

$$\nabla f(x_1, x_2) = \left(\frac{\partial f(x_1, x_2)}{\partial x_1} , \frac{\partial f(x_1, x_2)}{\partial x_2} \right)$$

$$= \left(\frac{1}{2} x_1^{-1/2} + x_2 + \frac{1}{1 + x_1 + x_2} , x_1 + \frac{1}{1 + x_1 + x_2} \right),$$

and the Hessian matrix of f is

$$H_f(x_1, x_2) = \begin{pmatrix} -\frac{1}{4} x_1^{-3/2} - \dfrac{1}{(1 + x_1 + x_2)^2} & 1 - \dfrac{1}{(1 + x_1 + x_2)^2} \\ 1 - \dfrac{1}{(1 + x_1 + x_2)^2} & -\dfrac{1}{(1 + x_1 + x_2)^2} \end{pmatrix}.$$

Now let's pick a particular point (x_1, x_2), say $(x_1, x_2) = (1, 1)$. At this point the values of the function, its gradient vector, and its Hessian matrix are

$$f(1, 1) = 2 + \ln 3 \approx 3 \cdot 099, \quad \nabla f(1, 1) = \left(\frac{11}{6} , \frac{4}{3} \right) \text{ and } H_f(1, 1) = \begin{pmatrix} -\dfrac{13}{36} & \dfrac{8}{9} \\ \dfrac{8}{9} & -\dfrac{1}{9} \end{pmatrix}.$$

So, evaluated at the point $(x_1, x_2) = (1, 1)$, the Taylor quadratic is

$$Q(\Delta x_1, \Delta x_2) = f(1, 1) + \nabla f(1, 1) \cdot (\Delta x_1, \Delta x_2) + \frac{1}{2} (\Delta x_1, \Delta x_2) H_f(1, 1) \begin{pmatrix} \Delta x_1 \\ \Delta x_2 \end{pmatrix}$$

$$= 2 + \ln 3 + \left(\frac{11}{6} , \frac{4}{3} \right) \begin{pmatrix} \Delta x_1 \\ \Delta x_2 \end{pmatrix} + \frac{1}{2} (\Delta x_1, \Delta x_2) \begin{pmatrix} -\dfrac{13}{36} & \dfrac{8}{9} \\ \dfrac{8}{9} & -\dfrac{1}{9} \end{pmatrix} \begin{pmatrix} \Delta x_1 \\ \Delta x_2 \end{pmatrix}$$

$$= 2 + \ln 3 + \frac{11}{6} \Delta x_1 + \frac{4}{3} \Delta x_2 - \frac{13}{72} (\Delta x_1)^2 + \frac{8}{9} \Delta x_1 \Delta x_2 - \frac{1}{18} (\Delta x_2)^2$$

Table 2.2: Various evaluations of f and Q about $(x_1, x_2) = (1, 1)$.

(x_1, x_2)	$(\Delta x_1, \Delta x_2)$	$f(x_1, x_2)$	$Q(\Delta x_1, \Delta x_2)$	$|f(x_1, x_2) - Q(\Delta x_1, \Delta x_2)|$
$(1{\cdot}00, 1{\cdot}00)$	$(0{\cdot}00, 0{\cdot}00)$	$3{\cdot}09861$	$3{\cdot}09861$	$0{\cdot}00000$
$(1{\cdot}00, 0{\cdot}98)$	$(0{\cdot}00, -0{\cdot}02)$	$3{\cdot}07192$	$3{\cdot}07192$	$0{\cdot}00000$
$(0{\cdot}98, 0{\cdot}98)$	$(-0{\cdot}02, -0{\cdot}02)$	$3{\cdot}03554$	$3{\cdot}03554$	$0{\cdot}00000$
$(1{\cdot}02, 1{\cdot}02)$	$(0{\cdot}02, 0{\cdot}02)$	$3{\cdot}16221$	$3{\cdot}16221$	$0{\cdot}00000$
$(1{\cdot}05, 0{\cdot}95)$	$(0{\cdot}05, -0{\cdot}05)$	$3{\cdot}12081$	$3{\cdot}12080$	$0{\cdot}00001$
$(1{\cdot}05, 1{\cdot}05)$	$(0{\cdot}05, 0{\cdot}05)$	$3{\cdot}25860$	$3{\cdot}25858$	$0{\cdot}00002$
$(0{\cdot}90, 0{\cdot}90)$	$(-0{\cdot}10, -0{\cdot}10)$	$2{\cdot}78830$	$2{\cdot}78847$	$0{\cdot}00017$
$(1{\cdot}10, 1{\cdot}10)$	$(0{\cdot}10, 0{\cdot}10)$	$3{\cdot}42196$	$3{\cdot}42181$	$0{\cdot}00015$
$(0{\cdot}50, 1{\cdot}50)$	$(-0{\cdot}50, 0{\cdot}50)$	$2{\cdot}55572$	$2{\cdot}56736$	$0{\cdot}01164$
$(1{\cdot}50, 1{\cdot}50)$	$(0{\cdot}50, 0{\cdot}50)$	$4{\cdot}86104$	$4{\cdot}84514$	$0{\cdot}01590$
$(0{\cdot}00, 3{\cdot}00)$	$(-1{\cdot}00, 2{\cdot}00)$	$1{\cdot}38629$	$1{\cdot}75139$	$0{\cdot}36510$
$(3{\cdot}00, 3{\cdot}00)$	$(2{\cdot}00, 2{\cdot}00)$	$12{\cdot}67796$	$12{\cdot}04306$	$0{\cdot}63490$

where Δx_1 and Δx_2 are deviations from the values $x_1 = 1$ and $x_2 = 1$, respectively. Table 2.2 displays the values of the function f and the Taylor quadratic for various points $(x_1, x_2) = (1 + \Delta x_1, 1 + \Delta x_2)$ around the point $(x_1, x_2) = (1, 1)$. The quadratic approximation is accurate for values of (x_1, x_2) that are close to $(x_1, x_2) = (1, 1)$.

2.19   Saddle-Points

A *saddle-point* is a particular type of critical point for a function of more than one variable. A saddle-point is a point in the domain of the function that is a blend of a local maximum and a local minimum in that, in some x_i direction(s), the function is locally maximized at the saddle-point, while in all of the other x_j direction(s) the function is locally minimized at the saddle-point. It is easiest to get the idea of a saddle-point if we first consider a function $f(x_1, x_2)$ of just two variables.

Let $S \subset \Re^2$ be some nonempty neighborhood. A point $(x_1, x_2) = (x_1', x_2')$ is a saddle-point in S for a function $f(x_1, x_2)$ if

$$f(x_1'; x_2') = \max_{(x_1, x_2') \in S} f(x_1; x_2') \text{ and } f(x_2'; x_1') = \min_{(x_1', x_2) \in S} f(x_2; x_1').$$

That is,

$$f(x_1; x_2') \leq f(x_1'; x_2') \text{ for all } (x_1, x_2') \in S \text{ and } f(x_2'; x_1') \leq f(x_2; x_1') \text{ for all } (x_1', x_2) \in S.$$

Let's read this carefully. The most important thing to notice is that two different restricted versions of the function $f(x_1, x_2)$ are being considered. One of these is the function of x_1 only that is $f(x_1; x_2')$; *i.e.* the function $f(x_1, x_2)$ in which the value of x_2 is fixed at $x_2 = x_2'$. The other restricted function is $f(x_2; x_1')$; *i.e.* the function $f(x_1, x_2)$ in which the value of x_1 is fixed at $x_1 = x_1'$. The point (x_1', x_2') is a saddle-point for the unrestricted function $f(x_1, x_2)$ if the restricted function $f(x_1; x_2')$ is maximized at $x_1 = x_1'$ and, also, the restricted function $f(x_2; x_1')$ is minimized at $x_2 = x_2'$. The usual example of a function with a saddle-point is $f(x_1, x_2) = x_1^2 - x_2^2$. This function has only one critical point, at $(x_1, x_2) = (0, 0)$, and it is a saddle-point, as may be seen in Figure 2.29. The function $f(x_1, x_2) = x_1^2 - x_2^2$ restricted by $x_2 = 0$ is $f(x_1; x_2 = 0) = x_1^2$. This function is minimized at $x_1 = 0$. The function $f(x_1, x_2) = x_1^2 - x_2^2$ restricted by $x_1 = 0$ is $f(x_2; x_1 = 0) = -x_2^2$. This function is maximized at $x_2 = 0$. Thus,

$$f(x_2; x_1 = 0) = -x_2^2 \leq f(x_1 = 0, x_2 = 0) = 0 \leq f(x_1; x_2 = 0) = x_1^2 \ \forall \ (x_1, x_2) \in \Re^2$$

and so $(x_1, x_2) = (0, 0)$ is a saddle-point for $f(x_1, x_2) = x_1^2 - x_2^2$.

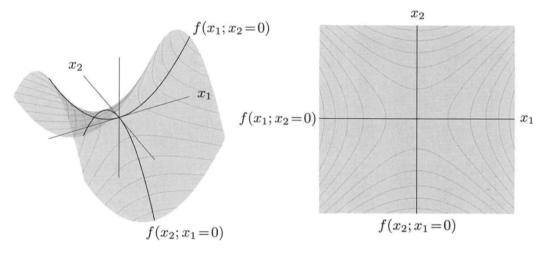

Figure 2.29: $f(x_1, x_2) = x_1^2 - x_2^2$ has a saddle-point at $(x_1, x_2) = (0, 0)$.

Once we consider functions of more than two variables, the number of possible types of saddle-points increases rather rapidly. Nevertheless, the essential characteristic of any saddle-point possessed by some function is that at the saddle-point the function is locally maximized with respect to some of its variables and is locally minimized with respect to the rest of its variables.

Definition 2.16 (Saddle-point). *Let $X \subset \Re^n$ and $Y \subset \Re^m$. Let the function $f : X \times Y \mapsto \Re$. Then $(x', y') \in X \times Y$ is a* saddle-point *for f on $X \times Y$ if*

$$f(x; y') \leq f(x', y') \ \forall \ x \in X \ and \ f(x', y') \leq f(y; x') \ \forall \ y \in Y.$$

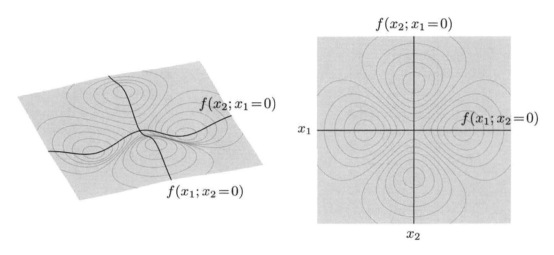

Figure 2.30: $f(x_1, x_2) = (x^2 - y^2)/e^{x^2+y^2}$ has a saddle-point at $(x_1, x_2) = (0, 0)$, and also two local minima and two local maxima in the set $[-2, 2] \times [-2, 2]$.

If the function is differentiable and if the saddle-point is in the interior of the function's domain, then, necessarily, the value at the saddle-point of the gradient vector of the function is a zero vector, making the saddle-point a critical point. We already know that a function can possess more than one critical point, so it should not surprise you that a function may have one or more saddle-points along with other types of critical points, such as local minima or local maxima. Figure 2.30 displays the graph of a function with five critical points, one of which is a saddle-point, two of which are local minima, and two of which are local maxima. As the right-side panels of Figures 2.29 and 2.30 show, it is sometimes easier graphically to locate a function's saddle-point by examining a contour plot of the function. A local maximum or local minimum displays as a point in the "middle" of concentric contours. A saddle-point displays as a point towards which the contours "bulge."

2.20 Metrics

How often have you measured the distance between two points? Have you ever needed to cut a cookie exactly in half? Have you ever wanted to know how high something is above the ground? The thing common to these activities is *distance*. You want your knife to cut at half of the distance across the cookie. You want to know the distance of the something from the ground. Metric spaces are sets of points with the property that you can measure how distant any point in the set is from any other point in the set. You have used this idea each day since you were a child. In economics, we use metric spaces all the time. Most times the space is the familiar set of real points with distances between points measured by Pythagoras's Theorem. But there are other metric spaces that are much less familiar and yet are important to economists, and others. So let us explore the ideas of a metric function and a metric space. You will quickly see their practical values.

It's very simple. A metric is a function that measures distances between points. For example, the straight-line distance, measured in, say, kilometers, between Town A and Town B might be called the "as the crow flies" distance between the towns. The distance is positive, and it is the same whether we measure it from Town A to Town B or from Town B to Town A. The number of kilometers covered when driving a car between the same two towns might be called the "driving distance" between the towns. Once again the distance is positive, and is the same whether we measure it from Town A to Town B or in the reverse direction. But the "as the crow flies" distance and the "driving distance" between the towns will not be the same unless the road between them is exactly straight. This is a simple example of the fact that there is often more than one reasonable way to measure a distance.

Although these are familiar examples for all of us, the idea of measuring distances between points is an idea of wide applicability. We can, for example, measure distances between colors, between sounds, or between quadratics. Let's start by defining the term *metric*. The usual symbol for a metric function is d, short for *distance*.

Definition 2.17 (Metric). *A metric defined on a set X is a function $d : X \times X \mapsto \Re_+$ with the following properties:*

(i) nonnegativity: for all $x', x'' \in X$, $d(x', x'') \geq 0$ with $d(x', x'') = 0$ if and only if $x' = x''$;

(ii) symmetry: for all $x', x'' \in X$, $d(x', x'') = d(x'', x')$;

(iii) triangular inequality: for all $x', x'', x''' \in X$, $d(x', x''') \leq d(x', x'') + d(x'', x''')$.

(i) says that distance is never negative, that the distance of any point from itself is zero, and that the distance between any two different points is strictly positive. (ii) says that the direction in which distance is measured does not matter; the distance from x' to x'' is the same as the distance from x'' to x'. (iii) says that the "direct" distance between any two points x' and x''' is never larger than the distance between x' and any other point x'' added to the distance between x'' and x'''. For example, it is never a shorter trip from Town A to Town B via Town C than it is to travel directly from Town A to Town B.

Let's look at ways of measuring the distances between points in the real line, $\Re$. The obvious, and certainly the most commonly used, metric is the *Euclidean distance function* d_E defined on $\Re \times \Re$:

$$\forall \; x', x'' \in \Re, \; d_E(x', x'') = |x' - x''|. \tag{2.39}$$

Now let's think about measuring distances between points in the real plane, $\Re^2$. Once again, the most commonly used metric is the Euclidean distance function d_E, which, defined on $\Re^2 \times \Re^2$, is

$$\forall \; x', x'' \in \Re^2, \; d_E(x', x'') = +\sqrt{(x'_1 - x''_1)^2 + (x'_2 - x''_2)^2}. \tag{2.40}$$

This is the famous distance measure devised by Pythagoras. But there are reasonable alternative ways of measuring distances between points in $\Re^2$. One of these alternatives is the metric function

$$d_0(x', x'') = |x'_1 - x''_1| + |x'_2 - x''_2|. \tag{2.41}$$

Yet another is the metric function

$$d_1(x', x'') = \max \left\{ |x'_1 - x''_1|, \; |x'_2 - x''_2| \right\}. \tag{2.42}$$

All of the metrics (2.40), (2.41), and (2.42) may be adapted to measure distances between points in $\Re^n$ for any $n \geq 1$. Notice that for $n = 1$ all three metrics are the same function.

How can we use metrics to measure distances between sounds and colors? That's easy. Just measure the distance between the wave frequencies of two sounds or of two colors.

How might we measure the distance between two continuous real-valued functions defined on an interval $[a, b]$? Two possibilities are displayed in Figure 2.31. One is

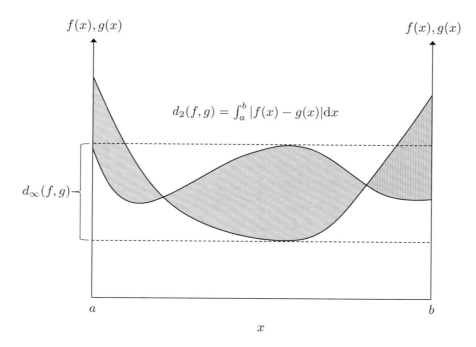

Figure 2.31: Two metrics that measure the distance between the functions f and g.

the function known as the *sup metric*:

$$d_\infty(f, g) = \sup_{x \in [a,b]} |f(x) - g(x)|. \qquad (2.43)$$

This, the least upper bound of the differences $|f(x) - g(x)|$ over all of $[a, b]$, is displayed on the left-hand axis of Figure 2.31. The other distance measure is the (shaded) area between the graphs of the functions f and g:

$$d_2(f, g) = \int_a^b |f(x) - g(x)| \, \mathrm{d}x. \qquad (2.44)$$

In both cases the distance between f and g is zero if and only if the two continuous functions are identical on $[a, b]$. If f and g are continuous but not identical, then both metrics show a strictly positive distance between the functions. Both metrics have the symmetry property. Both also have the triangular property (prove this as an exercise – it's simple to do).

The primary uses that we shall make of metrics are, first, in determining when sequences converge or not, and, second, to define small neighborhoods around points of interest to us. These neighborhoods are called *balls*. You have often used them.

For example, whenever you have said something like "consider a small open interval $(x - \varepsilon, x + \varepsilon)$ centered at a point x" you have in fact been talking of the ball of radius ε that is centered at the point x.

The pair (X, d) that consists of a set X, together with a metric function d defined on $X \times X$, is called a *metric space*. I'm sure that you already comprehend that there are lots of metrics and lots of metric spaces.

For economists the most useful metric spaces are the *Euclidean metric spaces*. The pair $(\Re, d_E)$, consisting of the real line $\Re$ together with the Euclidean metric function (2.39) defined on $\Re \times \Re$, is the one-dimensional Euclidean metric space and is denoted by $E^1 \equiv (\Re, d_E)$. The pair $(\Re^2, d_E)$, consisting of the two-dimensional real space $\Re^2$ together with the Euclidean metric function (2.40) defined on $\Re^2 \times \Re^2$, is the two-dimensional Euclidean metric space and is denoted by $E^2 \equiv (\Re^2, d_E)$. The n-dimensional Euclidean space is $E^n \equiv (\Re^n, d_E)$, where the Euclidean metric function defined on $\Re^n \times \Re^n$ is

$$d_E(x', x'') = +\sqrt{(x_1' - x_1'')^2 + \cdots + (x_n' - x_n'')^2} \ \ \forall \ x', x'' \in \Re^n.$$

2.21   Norms

A norm is a function that measures the distances of points in a space from the particular point that is the "origin" of the space. A norm is usually denoted by the symbol $\|\cdot\|$. The origin on the real line is the number zero, so the *Euclidean norm* on the real line is, from (2.39),

$$\|x\|_E = d_E(x, 0) = |x - 0| = |x|. \tag{2.45}$$

The origin in $\Re^2$ is the point $(0, 0)$, so the Euclidean norm in $\Re^2$ is, from (2.40),

$$\|x\|_E = d_E(x, 0) = \sqrt{(x_1 - 0)^2 + (x_2 - 0)^2} = \sqrt{x_1^2 + x_2^2}. \tag{2.46}$$

The origin in the space of all real-valued continuous functions defined on $[a, b]$ is the function $o(x) \equiv 0$, so we can use (2.44) to define the distance of a function f defined on $[a, b]$ from the origin function o as

$$\|f\| = d_2(f, o) = \int_a^b |f(x) - o(x)| \, dx = \int_a^b |f(x)| \, dx.$$

I hope it is clear that, if we have a metric space (X, d) and the space X has an "origin" element, then we can define a norm function $\|\cdot\|$ on this space just by using the metric function d to measure distances from only the origin element in X. The pair $(X, \|\cdot\|)$ that consists of the set X together with the norm $\|\cdot\|$ defined on X is called a *normed space*. For example, the n-dimensional Euclidean normed space is $(\Re^n, \|\cdot\|_E)$, where

$$\|x\|_E = +\sqrt{x_1^2 + \cdots + x_n^2} \ \ \forall \ x \in \Re^n.$$

2.22 How to Proceed from Here

Chapter 8 is the first chapter that directly deals with solving constrained optimization problems. Its explanations rely upon your having a reasonable understanding of the contents of Chapters 6 and 7. Chapter 6 introduces hyperplanes and how they may be used to separate certain types of sets from one another. This material is geometrically quite obvious and you may skip to this chapter directly if you are willing to forgo the ability to follow some of the more detailed arguments and proofs. Chapter 7 introduces cones and convex cones. These are simple but very useful types of sets. Sometimes we can use a hyperplane to separate a convex cone from another convex cone, and sometimes not. When we can, and cannot, is at the very heart of constrained optimization theory. Understanding Chapter 7 thus requires a reasonable prior understanding of Chapter 6. So, in short, one reasonable strategy for proceeding from this point is to study just Chapters 6 and 7 prior to studying Chapter 8. You will get a useful, but somewhat incomplete, understanding of the basics of constrained optimization theory. You will also be able to proceed through Chapter 9 and a lot, but not all, of Chapter 10. For many readers, this may be a satisfactory outcome.

A second reasonable strategy for proceeding from this point is to jump to Chapter 6 and read until you encounter an idea that is new to you and that you wish to understand. You can then go to the appropriate part of an earlier chapter, gain the knowledge you need, and then return to where you were originally reading.

If you want to understand everything in detail, then simply read on. Enjoy.

2.23   Problems

Problem 2.1.

$$A = \begin{pmatrix} 2 & 0 & -2 & 3 \\ -5 & 3 & -1 & 5 \\ 1 & 0 & 7 & -3 \\ 6 & -2 & 3 & 3 \end{pmatrix}.$$

(i) What is the value of the determinant of the matrix A?

(ii)

$$S = \left\{ \begin{pmatrix} 2 \\ -5 \\ 1 \\ 6 \end{pmatrix}, \begin{pmatrix} 0 \\ 3 \\ 0 \\ -2 \end{pmatrix}, \begin{pmatrix} -2 \\ -1 \\ 7 \\ 3 \end{pmatrix}, \begin{pmatrix} 3 \\ 5 \\ -3 \\ 3 \end{pmatrix} \right\}.$$

Is S a set of linearly independent vectors?

(iii) Can the vector $\begin{pmatrix} 307 \\ -651 \\ 999 \\ -712 \end{pmatrix}$ be generated as a linear combination of the vectors in S?

(iv) Does the equation system

$$2x_1 - 2x_3 + 3x_4 = b_1$$
$$-5x_1 + 3x_2 - x_3 + 5x_4 = b_2$$
$$x_1 + 7x_3 - 3x_4 = b_3$$
$$6x_1 - 2x_2 + 3x_3 + 3x_4 = b_4$$

have a solution for any values for b_1, b_2, b_3, and b_4? If not, then why not? If so, then how many solutions are there?

Problem 2.2.

$$B = \begin{pmatrix} 2 & 0 & -2 \\ -10 & 6 & -17 \\ 6 & -2 & 3 \end{pmatrix}.$$

(i) What is the value of the determinant of the matrix B?

(ii)

$$V = \left\{ \begin{pmatrix} 2 \\ -10 \\ 6 \end{pmatrix}, \begin{pmatrix} 0 \\ 6 \\ -2 \end{pmatrix}, \begin{pmatrix} -2 \\ -17 \\ 3 \end{pmatrix} \right\}.$$

Is V a set of linearly independent vectors?

(iii) What is the set $L(V)$ of vectors in $\Re^3$ that is spanned by V?

(iv) Does either of the equation systems

$$2x_1 - 2x_3 = 2 \qquad\qquad\qquad 2x_1 - 2x_3 = 2$$
$$-10x_1 + 6x_2 - 17x_3 = 2 \quad \text{and} \quad -10x_1 + 6x_2 - 17x_3 = -2$$
$$6x_1 - 2x_2 + 3x_3 = 2 \qquad\qquad 6x_1 - 2x_2 + 3x_3 = 2$$

have a solution? If not, why not? If so, how many solutions are there?

Problem 2.3. Draw a diagram that displays the vectors $v^1 = \left(\begin{smallmatrix} 4 \\ 1 \end{smallmatrix}\right)$ and $v^2 = \left(\begin{smallmatrix} -4 \\ 3 \end{smallmatrix}\right)$. Then, for any $x_1 \geq 0$ and for any $x_2 \geq 0$, display the vectors $x_1 v^1$ and $x_2 v^2$. Next, display the vector $x_1 v^1 + x_2 v^2$. On your diagram, where is the region that contains all of the vectors that are linear combinations $x_1 v^1 + x_2 v^2$ with $x_1 \geq 0$ and $x_2 \geq 0$?

Use a similar method to discover the region that contains all of the vectors that are linear combinations $y_1 v^1 + y_2 v^2$ with $y_1 \leq 0$ and $y_2 \leq 0$.

Problem 2.4. Review Section 2.2 to remind yourself of what is meant by the term "vector space." You know already that the real space $\Re^n$ is a vector space, but what about some other spaces?
(i) Let $\mathcal{P}$ be the space of all polynomial functions defined on $\Re$. For example, all quadratic and cubic functions defined on $\Re$ belong to this space. Is $\mathcal{P}$ a vector space?
(ii) Let $\mathcal{W}$ be the space of all functions defined on $\Re$ that are bounded by the constant $M > 0$; *i.e.* a function $f \in \mathcal{W}$ only if $-M \leq f(x) \leq +M$ for every $x \in \Re$. Is $\mathcal{W}$ a vector space?

Problem 2.5. A function $f : \Re^n \to \Re$ of the form $f(x) = a_1 x_1 + \cdots + a_n x_n + b$, where $a_1, \ldots, a_n, b \in \Re$, is an *affine* function defined on $\Re^n$. A function $g : \Re^n \to \Re$ of the form $g(x) = a_1 x_1 + \cdots a_n x_n$, where $a_1, \ldots, a_n \in \Re$, is a *linear* function defined on $\Re^n$. Let $\mathcal{A}(\Re^n)$ be the space of all affine functions defined on $\Re^n$. Let $\mathcal{L}(\Re^n)$ be the space of all linear functions defined on $\Re^n$.
(i) Is $\mathcal{A}(\Re^n)$ a vector space?
(ii) Is $\mathcal{L}(\Re^n)$ a vector space?
(iii) Consider the singleton subset $S = \{\underline{0}\} \subset \Re^n$. Is S a vector space?

Definition 2.18 (Subspace). *A set V' is a subspace of a vector space V if and only if*

(a) $V' \subseteq V$, and
(b) $x, y \in V'$ implies that $ax + by \in V'$ for all $a, b \in \Re$.

A subspace of a vector space V is often called a *linear manifold* of V. If V' is a subspace of V and V' is *strictly* contained in V, then V' is a *proper subspace* of V.

(iv) Is the vector space V a subspace of itself? Is it a proper subspace of itself?

(v) Is $\mathcal{L}(\Re^n)$ a proper subspace of $\mathcal{A}(\Re^n)$?

Problem 2.6. S is a proper subspace of $\Re^n$. What type of set must S be, other than merely the singleton set consisting of only the origin?

Problem 2.7. $X = \{-3, -2, -1, 0, 1, 2, 3\}$. $S_1 = \{1, 2, 3\}$. $S_2 = \{-3, -2, -1\}$. True or false: $S_1 + S_2 = \{0\}$?

Problem 2.8. $X = \Re^2$. $S_1 = \{(x_1, x_2) \in \Re^2 \mid 1 \leq x_1 \leq 3, x_2 = 6\}$. $S_2 = \{(2, 3), (4, 1)\}$. What is the set $S_1 + S_2$?

Problem 2.9. Sum the two sets displayed in Figure 2.9.

Problem 2.10. $X = \Re^2$. $S_1 = \{(x_1, x_2) \in \Re^2 \mid x_2 = -x_1, -1 \leq x_1 \leq 0\}$. $S_2 = \{(x_1, x_2) \in \Re^2 \mid x_2 = -x_1, 0 \leq x_1 \leq 1\}$. What is the set $S_1 + S_2$?

Problem 2.11. $X = \Re^2$. $S_1 = \{(x_1, x_2) \in \Re^2 \mid x_2 = -x_1\}$. $S_2 = \{(x_1, x_2) \in \Re^2 \mid x_2 = x_1\}$. What is the set $S_1 + S_2$?

Problem 2.12. $S_1 = \{(x_1, x_2) \in \Re^2 \mid x_2 = -x_1, -1 \leq x_1 \leq 0\}$. $S_2 = \{x \in \Re \mid 0 \leq x \leq 1\}$. What are the sets $S_1 \times S_2$ and $S_2 \times S_1$?

Problem 2.13. Prove that if S_1 and S_2 are convex subsets of a set X, then $S_1 \cap S_2$ is a convex subset of X.

Problem 2.14. Use the result proved in problem 2.13, together with forward induction, to prove that, if, for any finite $k \geq 2$, $S_1, \ldots, S_k$ are all convex subsets of X, then $S_1 \cap \cdots \cap S_k$ is a convex subset of X.

Problem 2.15. Suppose that $S_1, \ldots, S_n$ are all *strictly* convex subsets of a set X. Then as you have seen in the above theorem the intersection of these subsets is a set that must be convex in X. Give two examples to show that this intersection need not be *strictly* convex in X.

Problem 2.16. Let S_1 and S_2 be convex subsets of $\Re^n$. Prove that $S_1 + S_2$ is a convex subset of $\Re^n$.

Problem 2.17. Let $S_1, \ldots, S_k$ be convex subsets of $\Re^n$, for finite $k \geq 2$. Use the result obtained in problem 2.16 together with forward induction to prove that $S_1 + \cdots + S_k$ is a convex subset of $\Re^n$.

Problem 2.18. Prove the following theorem.

Theorem. Let $S_1, \ldots, S_n$ be any finite collection of convex subsets of a set X. Then $S_1 \times \cdots \times S_n$ is a convex subset of $X^n = \underbrace{X \times \cdots \times X}_{n \text{ times}}$.

Problem 2.19. Let S_1 and S_2 be strictly convex subsets of $\Re^n$. Prove that $S_1 + S_2$ is a strictly convex subset of $\Re^n$. Use this result to prove the more general result that, if $S_1, \ldots, S_k$ for $k \geq 2$ are all strictly convex subsets of $\Re^n$, then $S_1 + \cdots + S_k$ is a strictly convex subset of $\Re^n$.

Problem 2.20. In Section 2.6 we encountered examples in which the direct products of two strictly convex sets are sets that are only weakly convex. This may have instilled the impression that the direct product of two convex sets is never a strictly convex set. But, in fact, the direct product of two convex sets can be (does not have to be) a strictly convex set. Provide an example in which the direct product of two strictly convex sets is a strictly convex set.

Problem 2.21. Consider the function $f(x_1, x_2) = x_1(1 + x_2)$ defined on $\Re^2$.
(i) What is the value of the gradient vector of f at the point $(1, 9)$?
(ii) What is the contour set for $f \equiv 10$?
(iii) Consider the $f \equiv 10$ contour set at the point $(1, 9)$. Define the marginal rate of substitution of x_1 for x_2, $\mathrm{MRS}(x_1, x_2)$, as the differential rate of change of x_2 with respect to x_1 along the contour set at the point (x_1, x_2). What is the value of this marginal rate of substitution at the point $(1, 9)$?
(iv) Construct the tangent to the $f \equiv 10$ contour set at the point $(1, 9)$.
(v) What is the gradient vector of this tangent?
(vi) Show that the tangent and the gradient vector of the $f \equiv 10$ contour set at the point $(1, 9)$ are orthogonal.

Problem 2.22. Consider the following matrices:

$$A = \begin{pmatrix} 4 & 12 \\ -16 & 1 \end{pmatrix}, \quad B = \begin{pmatrix} 7 & -2 \\ -4 & 1 \end{pmatrix}, \quad C = \begin{pmatrix} 0 & a \\ a & 0 \end{pmatrix}, \quad D = \begin{pmatrix} 1 & -a & b \\ a & 1 & -c \\ -b & c & 1 \end{pmatrix},$$

where a, b, and c are arbitrary real numbers.
(i) Write out the quadratic form of the matrix A as a quadratic equation in x_1 and x_2. Then use the method of "completion of squares" to determine from this equation if the matrix A has a particular definiteness property.

(ii) Write out the quadratic form of the matrix B as a quadratic equation in x_1 and x_2. Then use the method of "completion of squares" to determine from this equation if the matrix B has a particular definiteness property.

(iii) Does the matrix C have a particular definiteness property?

(iv) Does the matrix D have a particular definiteness property?

Problem 2.23. Consider the function $f : \Re \times \Re \to \Re$ that is

$$f(x, y) = \begin{cases} 0 & , \text{ if } x = y \\ 1 & , \text{ if } x \neq y \end{cases} \quad \text{for all } x, y \in \Re.$$

Is f a metric on $\Re \times \Re$?

Problem 2.24. Let the function $d : X \times X \to \Re$ be a metric on $X \times X$.

(i) Let the function $f : X \times X \to \Re$ be defined by $f(x, y) = ad(x, y) + b$, where $a, b \in \Re$ with $a > 0$. Is f a metric on $X \times X$?

(ii) Let $g : X \times X \to \Re$ be defined by $g(x, y) = d(x, y)^2$. Is g a metric on $X \times X$?

(iii) Let $h : X \times X \to \Re$ be defined by $h(x, y) = +\sqrt{d(x, y)}$. Is h a metric on $X \times X$?

Problem 2.25. Consider the function $f(x_1, x_2) = 2 + x_1 - x_2$ defined on $[0, 1]^2$. Does this function have a saddle-point? If so, is the saddle-point a critical point for the function?

Problem 2.26. Consider the function $f(x_1, x_2) = (x_1^2 - x_2^2)e^{-(x_1^2 + x_2^2)}$ defined on $\Re^2$. Use the restricted functions $f(x_1; x_2)$ and $f(x_2; x_1)$ to prove that $(x_1, x_2) = (0, 0)$ is a saddle-point for f. Is this saddle-point also a critical point for f?

Problem 2.27. Let $f(x_1, x_2) = x_1^3 - x_1^2 x_2 + x_2^3$. Construct the Taylor quadratic $Q(2 + \Delta x_1, 1 + \Delta x_2)$ approximation to the function f at the point $(x_1, x_2) = (2, 1)$. Then evaluate the function f and the quadratic for the points $(x_1, x_2) = (2, 1)$, $(x_1, x_2) = (2 \cdot 1, 1 \cdot 1)$, $(x_1, x_2) = (1 \cdot 9, 0 \cdot 9)$ $(x_1, x_2) = (2 \cdot 5, 1 \cdot 5)$, $(x_1, x_2) = (3, 2)$, and $(x_1, x_2) = (1, 3)$ to get an idea of how well, or poorly, the quadratic approximates f.

2.24 Answers

Answer to Problem 2.1.
(i) It is easiest if we expand down the second column of A. Doing so gives

$$\det(A) = (-1)^{2+2}(3)M_{22} + (-1)^{4+2}(-2)M_{42} = 3M_{22} - 2M_{42}.$$

$$M_{22} = \det \begin{pmatrix} 2 & -2 & 3 \\ 1 & 7 & -3 \\ 6 & 3 & 3 \end{pmatrix}$$

$$= (-1)^{1+1}(2)\det \begin{pmatrix} 7 & -3 \\ 3 & 3 \end{pmatrix} + (-1)^{2+1}(1)\det \begin{pmatrix} -2 & 3 \\ 3 & 3 \end{pmatrix} + (-1)^{3+1}(6)\det \begin{pmatrix} -2 & 3 \\ 7 & -3 \end{pmatrix}$$

$$= 2(21+9) - (-6-9) + 6(6-21) = -15.$$

$$M_{42} = \det \begin{pmatrix} 2 & -2 & 3 \\ -5 & -1 & 5 \\ 1 & 7 & -3 \end{pmatrix}$$

$$= (-1)^{1+1}(2)\det \begin{pmatrix} -1 & 5 \\ 7 & -3 \end{pmatrix} + (-1)^{2+1}(-5)\det \begin{pmatrix} -2 & 3 \\ 7 & -3 \end{pmatrix} + (-1)^{3+1}(1)\det \begin{pmatrix} -2 & 3 \\ -1 & 5 \end{pmatrix}$$

$$= 2(3-35) + 5(6-21) + (-10+3) = -146.$$

So,

$$\det(A) = 3 \times (-15) - 2 \times (-146) = 247.$$

(ii) Yes. $\det(A) \neq 0$ only if S is a set of linearly independent vectors.
(iii) Yes. S is a set of four linearly independent vectors of dimension 4, so S is a basis for all of $\Re^4$. That is, any vector in $\Re^4$ can be generated as a linear combination of the vectors in S.
(iv) Asking if the equation system has a solution is equivalent to asking if the vector $\begin{pmatrix} b_1 \\ b_2 \\ b_3 \\ b_4 \end{pmatrix}$ can be generated as a linear combination of the vectors in S. We already know this to be true, so the equation system has at least one solution. Since the rank of the matrix A is 4 (thus, A has full rank), there is only a unique solution. $\quad\square$

Answer to Problem 2.2.
(i) The arithmetic required is least if we expand across the first row of B. Doing so gives

$$\det(B) = (-1)^{1+1}(2)M_{11} + (-1)^{1+3}(-2)M_{13} = 2M_{11} - 2M_{13}$$

$$= 2\det \begin{pmatrix} 6 & -17 \\ -2 & 3 \end{pmatrix} - 2\det \begin{pmatrix} -10 & 6 \\ 6 & -2 \end{pmatrix} = 2(18-34) - 2(20-36) = 0.$$

(ii) No. $\det(B) = 0$ only if V is a set of linearly dependent vectors. For example,

$$-\begin{pmatrix} 2 \\ -10 \\ 6 \end{pmatrix} - \frac{9}{2} \begin{pmatrix} 0 \\ 6 \\ -2 \end{pmatrix} = \begin{pmatrix} -2 \\ -17 \\ 3 \end{pmatrix}.$$

(iii) V is a set of three linearly dependent vectors of dimension 3, so V is not a basis for all of $\Re^3$. Any vector $\begin{pmatrix} b_1 \\ b_2 \\ b_3 \end{pmatrix}$ contained in $L(V)$ can be generated as a linear combination of any two of the vectors in V, so let us consider all of the linear combinations of the vectors $\begin{pmatrix} 2 \\ -10 \\ 6 \end{pmatrix}$ and $\begin{pmatrix} 0 \\ 6 \\ -2 \end{pmatrix}$. Thus a vector $\begin{pmatrix} b_1 \\ b_2 \\ b_3 \end{pmatrix}$ is contained in $L(V)$ if and only if there are weights x_1 and x_2 for which

$$x_1 \begin{pmatrix} 2 \\ -10 \\ 6 \end{pmatrix} + x_2 \begin{pmatrix} 0 \\ 6 \\ -2 \end{pmatrix} = \begin{pmatrix} 2x_1 \\ -10x_1 + 6x_2 \\ 6x_1 - 2x_2 \end{pmatrix} = \begin{pmatrix} b_1 \\ b_2 \\ b_3 \end{pmatrix}.$$

This requires

$$x_1 = \frac{b_1}{2}, \quad -10x_1 + 6x_2 = -5b_1 + 6x_2 = b_2 \;\Rightarrow\; x_2 = \frac{1}{6}(5b_1 + b_2)$$

$$\text{and } 6x_1 - 2x_2 = 3b_1 - \frac{1}{3}(5b_1 + b_2) = \frac{1}{3}(4b_1 - b_2) = b_3.$$

Thus the vectors in $L(V)$, the vectors $\begin{pmatrix} b_1 \\ b_2 \\ b_3 \end{pmatrix}$ that can be generated as linear combinations of $\begin{pmatrix} 2 \\ -10 \\ 6 \end{pmatrix}$ and $\begin{pmatrix} 0 \\ 6 \\ -2 \end{pmatrix}$, are the vectors in which the elements b_1, b_2, and b_3 satisfy the restriction $4b_1 - b_2 - 3b_3 = 0$. This is the equation of only a plane in $\Re^3$. For example, the vector $\begin{pmatrix} 2 \\ 2 \\ 2 \end{pmatrix} \in L(V)$, while the vector $\begin{pmatrix} 2 \\ -2 \\ 2 \end{pmatrix} \notin L(V)$.

(iv) The equation system

$$2x_1 - 2x_3 = 2$$
$$-10x_1 + 6x_2 - 17x_3 = 2$$
$$6x_1 - 2x_2 + 3x_3 = 2$$

has a solution if and only if the vector $\begin{pmatrix} 2 \\ 2 \\ 2 \end{pmatrix}$ can be generated as a linear combination of the vectors $\begin{pmatrix} 2 \\ -10 \\ 6 \end{pmatrix}$ and $\begin{pmatrix} 0 \\ 6 \\ -2 \end{pmatrix}$. We showed this to be true in part (iii), so the equation system has at least one solution. We also know, from part (i), that the matrix B has less than full rank, $r(B) = 2 < 3$, so the equation system has infinitely many solutions. Check for yourself that the complete set of solutions is $\{(x_1, x_2, x_3) \mid x_1 = 1 + x_3,\ x_2 = 2 + 9x_3/2,\ -\infty < x_3 < \infty\}$.

The equation system

$$2x_1 - 2x_3 = 2$$
$$-10x_1 + 6x_2 - 17x_3 = -2$$
$$6x_1 - 2x_2 + 3x_3 = 2$$

has a solution if and only if the vector $\begin{pmatrix} 2 \\ -2 \\ 2 \end{pmatrix}$ can be generated as a linear combination

of the vectors $\begin{pmatrix} 2 \\ -10 \\ 6 \end{pmatrix}$ and $\begin{pmatrix} 0 \\ 6 \\ -2 \end{pmatrix}$. In part (iii) we showed this is not so. Trying to solve the system produces two inconsistent equations. $\qquad\square$

Answer to Problem 2.3. Look at Figure 2.32. The figure displays the vectors $v^1 = \begin{pmatrix} 4 \\ 1 \end{pmatrix}$, $v_2 = \begin{pmatrix} -4 \\ 3 \end{pmatrix}$, the finely dotted line from the origin (a ray) containing nonnegative multiples $x_1 v^1$ of v^1 and the finely dotted ray containing nonnegative multiples $x_2 v^2$ of v^2. The sum of a nonnegative multiple $x_1 v^1$ of v^1 and a nonnegative multiple $x_2 v^2$ of v^2 necessarily lies within the region in Figure 2.32 that is bounded by the ray containing v^1 and the ray containing v^2. If $x_1 = x_2 = 0$, then the sum $x_1 v^1 + x_2 v^2$ is the origin vector $\begin{pmatrix} 0 \\ 0 \end{pmatrix}$. If $x_1 = 0$ and $x_2 > 0$, then the sum $x^1 v^1 + x^2 v^2 = x_2 v^2$, a vector in the ray containing v^2. If $x_1 > 0$ and $x_2 = 0$, then the sum $x_1 v^1 + x_2 v^2 = x_1 v^1$, a vector in the ray containing v^1. If $x_1 > 0$ and $x_2 > 0$, then the sum $x_1 v^1 + x_2 v^2$ is a vector that lies strictly inside the region bounded by the rays containing v^1 and v^2. Thus the region containing all of the sums $x_1 v^1 + x_2 v^2$ with $x_1 \geq 0$ and $x_2 \geq 0$ is the upper shaded region in Figure 2.32, including its edges.

The ray containing nonpositive multiples $y_1 v^1$ of v^1 is the dot-dashed line from the origin that is opposite the ray containing v^1. The ray containing nonpositive multiples $y_2 v^2$ of v^2 is the dot-dashed line from the origin that is opposite the ray containing v^2. The region containing all sums $y_1 v^1 + y_2 v^2$ with $y_1 \leq 0$ and $y_2 \leq 0$ is the region consisting of these two dot-dashed lines from the origin together with all of the points between them. This is the lower dot-filled region in Figure 2.32, including its edges. $\qquad\square$

Answer to Problem 2.4.

(i) $\mathcal{P}$ is a vector space. Since the sum of polynomials on $\Re$ is a polynomial on $\Re$ and since the scalar multiple of any polynomial on $\Re$ is a polynomial on $\Re$, it is easy to see that $\mathcal{P}$ possesses properties 1, 2, 3, and 6 of Definition 2.1. The zero

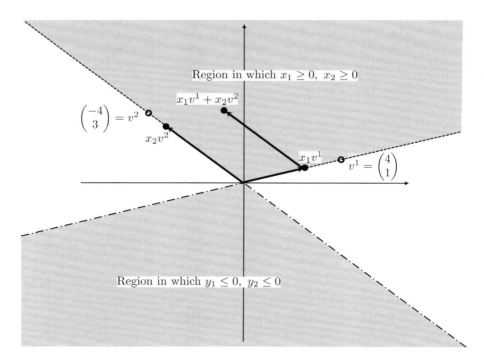

Figure 2.32: The region containing the vectors that are linear combinations $x_1v^1 + x_2v^2$ with $x_1 \geq 0$ and $x_2 \geq 0$, and the region containing the vectors that are linear combinations $y_1v^1 + y_2v^2$ with $y_1 \leq 0$ and $y_2 \leq 0$.

polynomial, $o(x) \equiv 0$, is the zero element of $\mathcal{P}$, since $g(x) + o(x) = g(x) + 0 = g(x)$ for any $g \in \mathcal{P}$. Thus $\mathcal{P}$ possesses property 4 of Definition 2.1. If $g \in \mathcal{P}$, then $(-g) \in \mathcal{P}$ (*i.e.* the negative of a polynomial on $\Re$ is a polynomial on $\Re$), and then $g(x) + (-g(x)) = o(x) \equiv 0$, so $\mathcal{P}$ possesses property 5 of Definition 2.1.

(ii) $\mathcal{W}$ is not a vector space. Consider the functions $f, g \in \mathcal{W}$ that are $f(x) \equiv 3M/4$ and $g(x) \equiv M/2$ for all $x \in \Re$. Then $f(x) + g(x) \equiv 5M/4 \notin \mathcal{W}$, so $\mathcal{W}$ does not have the addition property that $af(x) + bg(x) \in \mathcal{W}$ for any $a, b \in \Re$. As well, $2f(x) \equiv 3M/2 \notin \mathcal{W}$, so $\mathcal{W}$ also does not satisfy the scalar multiplication property that $af(x) \in \mathcal{W}$ for all $a \in \Re$.   □

Answer to Problem 2.5.

(i) Consider any $f, g \in \mathcal{A}(\Re^n)$. Then, there are scalars $a_1, \ldots, a_n, b \in \Re$ and scalars $a'_1, \ldots, a'_n, b' \in \Re$ for which $f(x_1, \ldots, x_n) = a_1 x_1 + \cdots + a_n x_n + b$ and $g(x_1, \ldots, x_n) = a'_1 x_1 + \cdots + a'_n x_n + b'$ for $(x_1, \ldots, x_n) \in \Re^n$.

For any $\alpha, \beta \in \Re$, the function $h = \alpha f + \beta g$ is

$$h(x_1, \ldots, x_n) = (\alpha a_1 + \beta a_1')x_1 + \cdots + (\alpha a_n + \beta a_n')x_n + \alpha b + \beta b' = a_1'' x_1 + \cdots + a_n'' x_n + b'',$$

where $a_i'' = \alpha a_i + \beta a_i'$ for $i = 1, \ldots, n$ and $b'' = \alpha b + \beta b'$. Thus $\alpha f + \beta g \in \mathcal{A}(\Re^n)$.

$f \in \mathcal{A}(\Re^n)$ implies $-f \in \mathcal{A}(\Re^n)$, where $(-f)(x_1, \ldots, x_n) = (-a_1)x_1 + \cdots + (-a_n)x_n + (-b)$.

The zero element of $\mathcal{A}(\Re^n)$ is the function $o(x_1, \ldots x_n) = 0 \times x_1 + \cdots 0 \times x_n + 0$. For any $\alpha \in \Re$ the function $h = \alpha f$ is

$$h(x_1, \ldots, x_n) = \alpha a_1 x_1 + \cdots + \alpha a_n x_n + \alpha b = a_1'' x_1 + \cdots a_n'' x_n + b'',$$

where $a_i'' = \alpha a_i$ for $i = 1, \ldots, n$ and $b'' = \alpha b$. Thus $\alpha f \in \mathcal{A}(\Re^n)$.

(ii) Repeating the argument given in part (i) shows that $\mathcal{L}(\Re^n)$ is a vector space – do it.

(iii) Yes. It is called the *trivial vector space.* □

Answer to Problem 2.6. S is any (hyper)plane in $\Re^n$ that includes the origin. That is,

$$S = \{x \in \Re^n \mid p{\cdot}x = 0\}$$

is a proper subspace of $\Re^n$ for any vector $p \in \Re^n$ such that $p \neq \underline{0}$ and $\|p\|_E < \infty$. Why? First, $S \subset \Re^n$ (property (a) in Definition 2.18). Second, take any $x', x'' \in S$. Then $p{\cdot}x' = 0$ and $p{\cdot}x'' = 0$, so for any $a, b \in \Re$, $p{\cdot}ax' = ap{\cdot}x' = 0$ and $p{\cdot}bx'' = bp{\cdot}x'' = 0$. Thus $p{\cdot}(ax' + bx'') = 0$, implying that $ax' + bx'' \in S$ (property (b) in Definition 2.18). □

Answer to Problem 2.7. False. $S_1 + S_2 = \{-2, -1, 0, 1, 2\}$. □

Answer to Problem 2.8. See Figure 2.33.

$$S_1 + S_2 = \{\{(2,3)\} + S_1\} \cup \{\{(4,1)\} + S_1\}$$
$$= \{(x_1, x_2) \mid 3 \leq x_1 \leq 5, x_2 = 9\} \cup \{(x_1, x_2) \mid 5 \leq x_1 \leq 7, x_2 = 7\}. \quad □$$

Answer to Problem 2.9. See Figure 2.34. □

Answer to Problem 2.10. $S_1 + S_2 = \{(x_1, x_2) \mid x_2 = -x_1, \ -1 \leq x_1 \leq 1\}$. □

Answer to Problem 2.11. $S_1 + S_2 = \Re^2$. □

Answer to Problem 2.12.

$$S_1 \times S_2 = \{(x_1, x_2, x_3) \in \Re^3 \mid x_2 = -x_1 \text{ for } -1 \leq x_1 \leq 0, \ 0 \leq x_3 \leq 1\}.$$

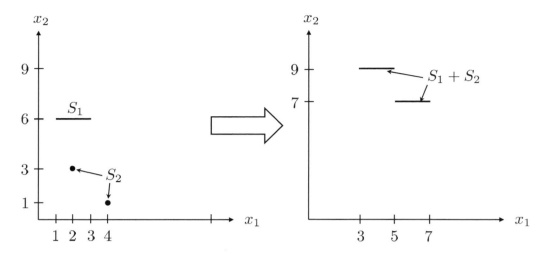

Figure 2.33: $\{(x_1, x_2) \mid 1 \leq x_1 \leq 3, x_2 = 6\} + \{(2,3), (4,1)\}$.

See the top panel of Figure 2.35.

$$S_2 \times S_1 = \{(x_1, x_2, x_3) \in \Re^3 \mid 0 \leq x_1 \leq 1, \ x_3 = -x_2 \text{ for } -1 \leq x_2 \leq 0\}.$$

See the bottom panel of Figure 2.35.   □

Answer to Problem 2.13. There are three possibilities. First, $S_1 \cap S_2$ is empty, in which case the result is true by definition (see Definition 2.5). Second, $S_1 \cap S_2$ is a singleton, in which case the result is again (trivially) true. The third possibility is that $S_1 \cap S_2$ contains at least two elements, so suppose that this is so.

We start by arbitrarily choosing any two elements $x', x'' \in S_1 \cap S_2$. What we now have to show is that the convex combination $\theta x' + (1-\theta)x'' \in S_1 \cap S_2$ for every value of $\theta \in [0, 1]$.

x' and x'' belong to the intersection of S_1 and S_2, so we know that x' and x'' both belong to S_1 and, also, that x' and x'' both belong to S_2. S_1 is a convex set, so $\theta x' + (1-\theta)x'' \in S_1$ for all $\theta \in [0, 1]$. Similarly, S_2 is a convex set, so $\theta x' + (1-\theta)x'' \in S_2$ also, for all $\theta \in [0, 1]$. Since $\theta x' + (1-\theta)x''$ belongs to both S_1 and S_2 for all $\theta \in [0, 1]$, it belongs to their intersection $S_1 \cap S_2$. This establishes the result.   □

Answer to Problem 2.14. The argument given in problem 2.13 establishes the result for a pair of subsets of X. Thus we have already proved the result for $k = 2$.

The forward-induction argument works as follows. We assume that the result is true for some value of k, and then prove that the result must be true for $k + 1$. Then, since the result is proved already for $k = 2$, we know that the result is also true for $k = 3$, which then tells us that the result is true for $k = 4$ and so on.

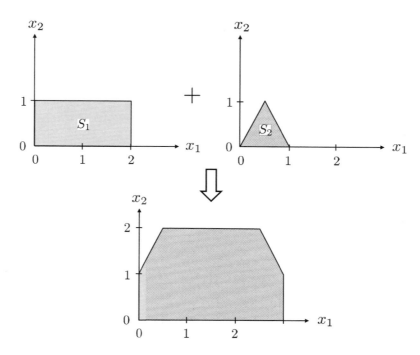

Figure 2.34: Summing a rectangle and a triangle.

So, choose some value for $k \geq 2$. We start with the convex subsets $S_1, \ldots, S_k$ of X and assume that their intersection $S_1 \cap \cdots \cap S_k$ is a convex subset of X. Now we add S_{k+1}, an additional convex subset of X. But the intersection $S_1 \cap \cdots \cap S_k \cap S_{k+1}$ is the intersection of just two convex subsets of X, being the subset $S_1 \cap \cdots \cap S_k$ and the subset S_{k+1}. We have already proved that the intersection of two convex sets is a convex set, so it follows that $S_1 \cap \cdots \cap S_k \cap S_{k+1}$ is a convex subset of X.

Now we apply forward induction starting at $k = 2$, and the result is proved. □

Answer to Problem 2.15. If the intersection is either the empty set or a singleton set then it is convex, but only weakly convex in X. If, however, the intersection is a set with a nonempty interior, then the intersection must be a strictly convex subset of X. You should try to prove this since it is only a small extension of the proof of problem 2.13. Remember, a strictly convex set must have a nonempty interior. □

Answer to Problem 2.16. We have to show that the convex combination of any two elements chosen from the subset $S_1 + S_2$ is entirely contained in $S_1 + S_2$. So, start by selecting arbitrarily any two elements $x', x'' \in S_1 + S_2$. Any element in $S_1 + S_2$ is the sum of an element in S_1 with an element in S_2. So, there are elements $y' \in S_1$ and $z' \in S_2$ that sum to x' (*i.e.* $x' = y' + z'$) and there are elements $y'' \in S_1$ and

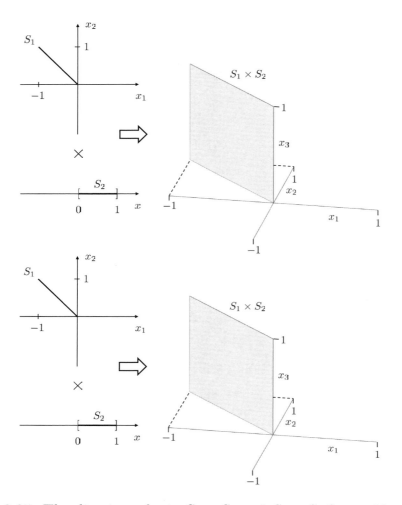

Figure 2.35: The direct products $S_1 \times S_2$ and $S_2 \times S_1$ for problem 2.12.

$z'' \in S_2$ that sum to x'' (*i.e.* $x'' = y'' + z''$).

The next step is to note that, since S_1 is a convex subset of $\Re^n$ and $y', y'' \in S_1$, any convex combination of y' and y'' is contained in S_1; *i.e.*

$$\theta y' + (1 - \theta)y'' \in S_1 \text{ for } 0 \le \theta \le 1.$$

Similarly, since S_2 is a convex subset of $\Re^n$ and $z', z'' \in S_2$, any convex combination of z' and z'' is contained in S_2; *i.e.*

$$\theta z' + (1 - \theta)z'' \in S_2 \text{ for } 0 \le \theta \le 1.$$

Since $\theta y' + (1 - \theta)y'' \in S_1$ and $\theta z' + (1 - \theta)z'' \in S_2$, the sum of these elements must be an element of $S_1 + S_2$; *i.e.*

$$\theta y' + (1-\theta)y'' + \theta z' + (1-\theta)z'' = \theta(y' + z') + (1-\theta)(y'' + z'') = \theta x' + (1-\theta)x'' \in S_1 + S_2.$$

This establishes the result. $\qquad\square$

Answer to Problem 2.17. The argument given in problem 2.16 establishes the result for a pair of subsets of $\Re^n$. Thus we have already proved the result for $k = 2$.

So, assume, for some $k \geq 2$, that, if $S_1, \dots, S_k$ are all convex subsets of $\Re^n$, then $S_1 + \cdots + S_k$ is a convex subset of $\Re^n$. Now, we introduce the set S_{k+1} which, too, is a convex subset of $\Re^n$. But in fact all we have here are two convex subsets of $\Re^n$, being the subset $S_1 + \cdots + S_k$ and the subset S_{k+1}. We have proved already that the sum of two convex subsets of $\Re^n$ is a convex subset of $\Re^n$, so applying this result tells us that $S_1 + \cdots + S_k + S_{k+1}$ is also a convex subset of $\Re^n$. Now, we apply forward induction starting from $k = 2$ and the result is proved. $\qquad\square$

Answer to Problem 2.18. Let $S = S_1 \times \cdots \times S_n$. Choose any two elements $x'_0, x''_0 \in S$. Then, there are elements $x'_i, x''_i \in S_i$ for each $i = 1, \dots, n$ such that $x'_0 = (x'_1, \dots, x'_n)$ and $x''_0 = (x''_1, \dots, x''_n)$. Since each S_i is a convex subset of X, for any number θ where $0 \leq \theta \leq 1$ the element $\theta x'_i + (1 - \theta)x''_i \in S_i$. But then $(\theta x'_1 + (1 - \theta)x''_1, \dots, \theta x'_n + (1 - \theta)x''_n \in S_1 \times \cdots \times S_n$. That is, $\theta x'_0 + (1 - \theta)x''_0 \in S$, so S is a convex subset of $\times_{i=1}^n X = X^n$. $\qquad\square$

Answer to Problem 2.19. We are given that both of the sets S_1 and S_2 are strictly convex sets. Therefore both sets have nonempty interiors (see Definition 2.6). The sum of a point from the interior of S_1 and a point from the interior of S_2 must be a point in the interior of $S_1 + S_2$, so the set $S_1 + S_2$ also has a nonempty interior.

Our purpose is to select arbitrarily any two points x' and x'' with $x' \neq x''$ from the interior of $S_1 + S_2$. We must then show that the *strict* convex combination of x' and x'', which is $\theta x' + (1 - \theta)x''$ for $0 < \theta < 1$ (note: not $\theta = 0$ and not $\theta = 1$), lies entirely within the interior of $S_1 + S_2$.

Now that we have chosen the distinct points x' and x'' from $S_1 + S_2$, we note that both x' and x'' are the sums of pairs of elements from S_1 and S_2. That is, there are points y' and y'' in S_1 and points z' and z'' in S_2 for which $x' = y' + z'$ and $x'' = y'' + z''$. S_1 is a strictly convex set, so the strict convex combination that is $\theta y' + (1 - \theta)y''$ for $0 < \theta < 1$ is everywhere contained in the interior of S_1. Similarly, since S_2 is a strictly convex set, the strict convex combination $\theta z' + (1 - \theta)z''$ for $0 < \theta < 1$ is everywhere contained in the interior of S_2. Summing these two points in the interiors of S_1 and S_2 must give us a point in the interior of $S_1 + S_2$. That is, for $0 < \theta < 1$,

$$\theta y' + (1-\theta)y'' + \theta z' + (1-\theta)z'' = \theta(y'+z') + (1-\theta)(y''+z'') = \theta x' + (1-\theta)x''$$

is a point in the interior of $S_1 + S_2$. This establishes the result for summing a pair of sets.

Now consider a sum $S_1 + \cdots + S_k$ of $k \geq 2$ strictly convex subsets. Assume that this sum is a strictly convex subset. Now introduce another strictly convex subset S_{k+1}. The sum $S_1 + \cdots + S_k + S_{k+1}$ is the sum of two strictly convex sets, being the set $S_1 + \cdots + S_k$ and the set S_{k+1}. Since we have already proved that the sum of a pair of strictly convex sets is a strictly convex set, we can assert that $S_1 + \cdots + S_k + S_{k+1}$ is a strictly convex set. Now we apply forward induction starting from $k \geq 2$ and the result is proved.   □

Answer to Problem 2.20.   Consider the sets $S_1 \subset \mathfrak{R}^2$ and $S_2 \subset \mathfrak{R}^1$ that are $S_1 = \{(x_1, x_2) \mid x_1^2 + x_2^2 \leq r^2\}$ and $S_2 = \{r \mid r \geq 0\}$. If $r = 0$ then S_1 is the singleton set $\{(0,0)\}$ and so is a weakly convex subset of $\mathfrak{R}^2$. If $r > 0$ then S_1 is a strictly convex subset of $\mathfrak{R}^2$. S_2 is a strictly convex subset of $\mathfrak{R}^1$. S_1 and S_2 are displayed in the left-side panel of Figure 2.36. The direct product $S_1 \times S_2$ of these two convex sets is $S_1 \times S_2 = \{(x_1, x_2, r) \in \mathfrak{R}^3 \mid x_1^2 + x_2^2 \leq r^2, \; r \geq 0\}$. This strictly convex subset of $\mathfrak{R}^3$ is the solid version of the parabola that is displayed in the right-side panel of Figure 2.36 and continued for all $r \geq 0$.   □

Answer to Problem 2.21. See Figure 2.37.
(i) The gradient vector function is

$$\nabla f(x_1, x_2) = (1 + x_2, x_1).$$

The value at the point $(1,9)$ of the gradient vector is $\nabla f(1,9) = (10, 1)$.
(ii) The $f \equiv 10$ contour set is the set $S = \{(x_1, x_2) \in \mathfrak{R}^2 \mid x_1(1 + x_2) = 10\}$.
(iii) The total derivative of f is

$$\mathrm{d}f = \frac{\partial f(x_1, x_2)}{\partial x_1}\,\mathrm{d}x_1 + \frac{\partial f(x_1, x_2)}{\partial x_2}\,\mathrm{d}x_2.$$

When the perturbations $\mathrm{d}x_1$ and $\mathrm{d}x_2$ are constrained to the $f \equiv 10$ contour set, we have $\mathrm{d}f = 0$. The total differential then gives the marginal rate of substitution at any point (x_1, x_2) on the $f \equiv 10$ contour set as

$$\mathrm{MRS}(x_1, x_2) = \frac{\mathrm{d}x_2}{\mathrm{d}x_1}\Big|_{f \equiv 10} = -\frac{\partial f(x_1, x_2)/\partial x_1}{\partial f(x_1, x_2)/\partial x_2}\Big|_{f \equiv 10} = -\frac{1 + x_2}{x_1}\Big|_{f \equiv 10}.$$

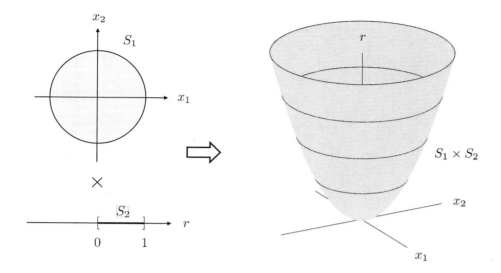

Figure 2.36: A direct product of strictly convex sets that is a strictly convex set.

The value at $(1, 9)$ of the marginal rate of substitution is $\mathrm{MRS}(1, 9) = -10$.

(iv) The tangent is a straight line with slope -10, so the equation of the tangent is $x_2 = -10x_1 + b$ for some intercept b. Since the point $(1, 9)$ lies in this tangent, $9 = -10 + b \quad \Rightarrow \quad b = 19$. The equation of the tangent is therefore

$$x_2 = -10x_1 + 19 \quad \text{or} \quad g(x_1, x_2) = 10x_1 + x_2 \equiv 19.$$

(v) $\nabla g(x_1, x_2) = (10, 1)$.

(vi) From part (i), the value at $(1, 9)$ of the gradient vector of the $f \equiv 10$ contour set is $\nabla f(1, 9) = (10, 1)$. This is the same as the gradient vector of the tangent, $\nabla g(x_1, x_2) = (10, 1)$. Since these two vectors are collinear, the tangent and the gradient vector of the $f \equiv 10$ contour set at the point $(1, 9)$ must be orthogonal. $\square$

Answer to Problem 2.22.

(i) The quadratic form of the matrix A is

$$Q_A(x_1, x_2) = (x_1, x_2) \begin{pmatrix} 4 & 12 \\ -16 & 1 \end{pmatrix} \begin{pmatrix} x_1 \\ x_2 \end{pmatrix} = 4x_1^2 - 4x_1x_2 + x_2^2 = (2x_1 - x_2)^2 \geq 0.$$

A is therefore a positive-semi-definite matrix.

(ii) The quadratic form of the matrix B is

$$Q_B(x_1, x_2) = (x_1, x_2) \begin{pmatrix} 7 & -2 \\ -4 & 1 \end{pmatrix} \begin{pmatrix} x_1 \\ x_2 \end{pmatrix} = 7x_1^2 - 6x_1x_2 + x_2^2 = -2x_1^2 + (3x_1 - x_2)^2.$$

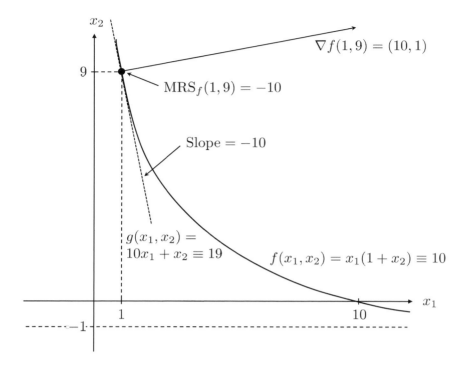

Figure 2.37: Diagram for Problem 2.21.

This quadratic takes both positive and negative values, so B is an indefinite matrix.
(iii) The quadratic form of the matrix C is

$$Q_C(x_1, x_2) = (x_1, x_2) \begin{pmatrix} 0 & a \\ a & 0 \end{pmatrix} \begin{pmatrix} x_1 \\ x_2 \end{pmatrix} = 2ax_1x_2.$$

If $a = 0$, then this quadratic is identically zero, so C is then both a positive-semi-definite and a negative-semi-definite matrix. If $a \neq 0$, then the quadratic takes both positive and negative values, so C is then an indefinite matrix.
(iv) The quadratic form of the matrix D is the same as the quadratic form of the order-3 identity matrix; *i.e.*

$$Q_D(x_1, x_2, x_3) = (x_1, x_2, x_3) \begin{pmatrix} 1 & -a & b \\ a & 1 & -c \\ -b & c & 1 \end{pmatrix} \begin{pmatrix} x_1 \\ x_2 \\ x_3 \end{pmatrix} = (x_1, x_2, x_3) \begin{pmatrix} 1 & 0 & 0 \\ 0 & 1 & 0 \\ 0 & 0 & 1 \end{pmatrix} \begin{pmatrix} x_1 \\ x_2 \\ x_3 \end{pmatrix}$$

$$= x_1^2 + x_2^2 + x_3^2 > 0 \; \forall \; (x_1, x_2, x_3) \neq (0, 0, 0)$$

so D is a positive-definite matrix for all a, b and c in $\Re$. $\qquad\qquad\qquad\qquad\qquad\square$

Answer to Problem 2.23. Take a moment to review the definition of a metric (see Definition 2.17).

f possesses the nonnegativity property, since $f(x, y) = 0$ if and only if $x = y$ and $f(x, y) = 1 > 0$ otherwise.

f also possesses the symmetry property, since, for any $x, y \in \Re$ with $x \neq y$, $f(x, y) = 1 = f(y, x)$.

Take any $x, y, z \in \Re$. If $x = y = z$ then $f(x, z) = 0 = 0 + 0 = f(x, y) + f(y, z)$. If $x = y \neq z$ then $f(x, z) = 0 + f(y, z) = f(x, y) + f(y, z)$. If $x \neq y \neq z$ then $f(x, z) = 1 < f(x, y) + f(y, z) = 2$. Thus f satisfies the triangular inequality and so is a metric on $\Re^2$. $\qquad\square$

Answer to Problem 2.24.

(i) The function f is a metric only if $f(x, x) = ad(x, x) + b = b = 0$ for any $x \in X$. So now we need consider only $f(x', x'') = ad(x', x'')$ for all $x', x'' \in X$. It is clear that f possesses the nonnegativity property of a metric (since $a > 0$) and, also, the symmetry property. Does f satisfy the triangular inequality? Take any $x', x'', x''' \in X$. Since d is a metric, $d(x', x''') \leq d(x', x'') + d(x'', x''')$. Consequently,

$$f(x', x''') = ad(x', x''') \leq a(d(x', x'') + d(x'', x''')) = f(x', x'') + f(x'', x''').$$

Thus f is a metric if $b = 0$.

(ii) g is not a metric. For example, let d be the Euclidean metric on the real line. Then $d(1, 5) = 4 = 1 + 3 = d(1, 2) + d(2, 5)$ (thus satisfying the triangular inequality), but $g(1, 5) = d(1, 5)^2 = 16 \nleq g(1, 2) + g(2, 5) = d(1, 2)^2 + d(2, 5)^2 = 1^2 + 3^2 = 10$. More generally, take $x' < x'' < x''' \in \Re$. Then,

$$\begin{aligned} g(x', x''') &= (x' - x''')^2 = (x' - x'' + x'' - x''')^2 \\ &= (x' - x'')^2 + 2(x' - x'')(x'' - x''') + (x'' - x''')^2 \\ &\nleq (x' - x'')^2 + (x'' - x''')^2 \\ &= g(x', x'') + g(x'', x'''). \end{aligned}$$

(iii) h is a metric. First, for any $x \in \Re$, $h(x, x) = +\sqrt{d(x, x)} = +\sqrt{0} = 0$. Second, for any $x', x'' \in \Re$ with $x' \neq x''$, $h(x', x'') = +\sqrt{d(x', x'')} > 0$ since $d(x', x'') > 0$. Next, h possesses the symmetry property because d possesses the symmetry property:

$$h(x', x'') = +\sqrt{d(x', x'')} = +\sqrt{d(x'', x')} = h(x'', x').$$

It remains to show that for any $x', x'', x''' \in \Re$, $h(x', x''') \le h(x', x'') + h(x'', x''')$.

$$h(x', x''') = +\sqrt{d(x', x''')} \le +\sqrt{d(x', x'') + d(x'', x''')} \quad \text{(because } d \text{ is a metric)}$$

$$\le +\sqrt{d(x', x'') + 2\sqrt{d(x', x'')} \times \sqrt{d(x'', x''')} + d(x'', x''')}$$

$$= \sqrt{\left(+\sqrt{d(x', x'')} + \sqrt{d(x'', x''')} \right)^2}$$

$$= +\sqrt{d(x', x'')} + \sqrt{d(x'', x''')}$$

$$= h(x', x'') + h(x'', x''').$$ □

Answer to Problem 2.25. When defined on $[0,1] \times [0,1]$, $f(x_1, x_2) = 2 + x_1 - x_2$ has a saddle-point at $(x_1, x_2) = (0,0)$. The restricted function $f(x_1; x_2{=}0) = 2 + x_1$ is minimized at $x_1 = 0$ and the restricted function $f(x_2; x_1{=}0) = 2 - x_2$ is maximized at $x_2 = 0$. However, the point $(0,0)$ is not a critical point for the function. This demonstrates that a saddle-point for a function need not be a critical point for the function if the saddle-point is not in the interior of the function's domain.   □

Answer to Problem 2.26. The function $f(x_1, x_2) = (x_1^2 - x_2^2)e^{-(x_1^2 + x_2^2)}$ has five critical points. $(x_1, x_2) = (1, 0)$ and $(x_1, x_2) = (-1, 0)$ are global maxima. $(x_1, x_2) = (0, 1)$ and $(x_1, x_2) = (0, -1)$ are global minima. $(x_1, x_2) = (0, 0)$ is a saddle-point.

The gradient vector of f is

$$\nabla f(x_1, x_2) = \left(2x_1 \left(1 - x_1^2 + x_2^2\right) e^{-x_1^2 - x_2^2}, \; -2x_2 \left(1 + x_1^2 - x_2^2\right) e^{-x_1^2 - x_2^2} \right).$$

The solutions to $\nabla f(x_1, x_2) = (0, 0)$ are the critical points of f, listed above.

The first-order derivative of the restricted function $f(x_1; x_2{=}0) = x_1^2 e^{-x_1^2}$ is

$$\frac{\mathrm{d}f(x_1; x_2{=}0)}{\mathrm{d}x_1} = 2x_1(1 - x_1^2)e^{-x_1^2} = 0$$

at $x_1 = -1, 0, +1$. The restricted function's second-order derivative is

$$\frac{\mathrm{d}^2 f(x_1; x_2{=}0)}{\mathrm{d}x_1^2} = 2(1 - 5x_1^2 + 2x_1^4)e^{-x_1^2}.$$

The values of this second-order derivative at $x_1 = -1, 0 + 1$ are negative, positive, and negative, respectively. The function $f(x_1; x_2{=}0)$ is locally minimized at $x_1 = 0$.

The first-order derivative of the restricted function $f(x_2; x_1{=}0) = -x_2^2 e^{-x_2^2}$ is

$$\frac{\mathrm{d}f(x_2; x_1{=}0)}{\mathrm{d}x_2} = -2x_2(1 - x_2^2)e^{-x_2^2} = 0$$

at $x_2 = -1, 0, +1$. The restricted function's second-order derivative is

$$\frac{\mathrm{d}^2 f(x_2; x_1{=}0)}{\mathrm{d}x_2^2} = -2(1 - 5x_2^2 + 2x_2^4)e^{-x_2^2}.$$

The values of this second-order derivative at $x_2 = -1, 0 + 1$ are positive, negative, and positive, respectively. The function $f(x_2; x_1{=}0)$ is locally maximized at $x_2 = 0$. This and above the paragraph together show that $(x_1, x_2) = (0, 0)$ is a saddle-point for the function f. □

Table 2.3: The values of f and Q at the requested points.

(x_1, x_2)	$(\Delta x_1, \Delta x_2)$	$f(x_1, x_2)$	$Q(2 + \Delta x_1, 1 + \Delta x_2)$
$(2, 1)$	$(0, 0)$	5	5
$(2{\cdot}1, 1{\cdot}1)$	$(0{\cdot}1, 0{\cdot}1)$	5·741	5·740
$(1{\cdot}9, 0{\cdot}9)$	$(-0{\cdot}1, -0{\cdot}1)$	4·339	4·340
$(2{\cdot}5, 1{\cdot}5)$	$(+0{\cdot}5, +0{\cdot}5)$	9·625	9·50
$(3, 2)$	$(+1, +1)$	17	16
$(1, 3)$	$(-1, +2)$	25	20

Answer to Problem 2.27. The gradient vector for $f(x_1, x_2) = x_1^3 - x_1^2 x_2 + x_2^3$ is

$$\nabla f(x_1, x_2) = (3x_1^2 - 2x_1 x_2, -x_1^2 + 3x_2^2) = (8, -1)$$

when evaluated at $(x_1, x_2) = (2, 1)$. The function's Hessian matrix is

$$H_f(x_1, x_2) = \begin{pmatrix} 6x_1 - 2x_2 & -2x_1 \\ -2x_1 & 6x_2 \end{pmatrix} = \begin{pmatrix} 10 & -4 \\ -4 & 6 \end{pmatrix}$$

when evaluated at $(x_1, x_2) = (2, 1)$. Last, $f(2, 1) = 5$, so the Taylor quadratic is

$$Q(2 + \Delta x_1, 1 + \Delta x_2) = 5 + (8, -1)\begin{pmatrix} \Delta x_1 \\ \Delta x_2 \end{pmatrix} + \frac{1}{2}(\Delta x_1, \Delta x_2)\begin{pmatrix} 10 & -4 \\ -4 & 6 \end{pmatrix}\begin{pmatrix} \Delta x_1 \\ \Delta x_2 \end{pmatrix}$$
$$= 5 + 8\Delta x_1 - \Delta x_2 + 5(\Delta x_1)^2 - 4\Delta x_1 \Delta x_2 + 3(\Delta x_2)^2. \qquad \square$$

Chapter 3

Basics of Topology

Obtaining a clear understanding of the essentials of constrained optimization theory requires repeated use of ideas that depend upon the properties of sets. Examples are ideas as basic and important as an "open set" and "continuity of a mapping." So we must start by examining basic properties of sets. The name of the branch of mathematics that studies the properties of sets that are preserved by mappings is *topology*. I used to think that topology was a subject that mattered only for serious mathematicians, and my heart would sink whenever a research paper said something ominous like "Let $\mathcal{T}(X)$ denote the something-or-other topology on X ..." Help! I surrender! The truth is that the basics of topology are easy. Yes, easy. Of course some sets and mappings can be rather complicated, and that is when topology gets complicated. But the topological ideas that economists typically use are pretty simple. Do not be afraid.

3.1 Topology

The most basic of basics, the foundation upon which all will be built, is the *reference set*. I will typically denote such a set by X. What the reference set contains will depend upon the problem we are working on. For example, if it is a problem of choosing a color, then the reference set will be the set containing all possible colors. But if the problem is choosing which house to buy, then the reference set will be the set of all houses. The reference set X is the complete collection of elements relevant to the problem we are thinking about. The typical label we will use to denote any element in the set X is x, so you will often see the statement $x \in X$, meaning that x is an element of, or belongs to, or is contained in the set X.

You already know that the basic operations used on sets are union $\cup$ and intersection $\cap$. We use these operations to construct new subsets of X from some original collection of subsets of X. A topology on a reference set X is merely a collection of subsets of X that are formed by particular uses of the union and intersection operations. It is a simple idea.

Definition 3.1 (Topology). *A topology $\mathcal{T}(X)$ on a reference set X is a collection of subsets of X such that*

(i) $\emptyset \in \mathcal{T}(X)$,
(ii) $X \in \mathcal{T}(X)$,
(iii) any union of any members of $\mathcal{T}(X)$ is a member of $\mathcal{T}(X)$, and
(iv) any intersection of any finite collection of members of $\mathcal{T}(X)$ is a member of $\mathcal{T}(X)$.

A few examples will help make you comfortable with the idea of a topology. For the first example, take any reference set X you like and then consider the collection of sets $\mathcal{C} = \{\emptyset, X\}$. Is $\mathcal{C}$ a topology with respect to X? Think about it before you proceed to the next paragraph.

$\mathcal{C}$ is indeed a topology with respect to X. It is obvious that $\mathcal{C}$ possesses properties (i) and (ii). What about property (iii)? Let $S_1, S_2, \ldots$ be any sequence of subsets in $\mathcal{C}$. Then either $S_i = \emptyset$ for all i, or it does not. If $S_i = \emptyset$ for all i, then $S = \cup_{i=1}^{\infty} = \emptyset \in \mathcal{C}$. If not, then $S_i = X$ for at least one i so $S = \cup_{i=1}^{\infty} S_i = X \in \mathcal{C}$. $\mathcal{C}$ therefore possesses property (iii). What about property (iv)? This time we consider only a *finite* sequence $S_1, \ldots, S_n$ of subsets in $\mathcal{C}$. Either $S_i = X$ for all $i = 1, \ldots, n$ or it does not. If $S_i = X$ for all $i = 1, \ldots, n$, then $S = \cap_{i=1}^{n} = X \in \mathcal{C}$. If not, then $S_i = \emptyset$ for at least one i, so $S = \cap_{i=1}^{n} S_i = \emptyset \in \mathcal{C}$. Hence $\mathcal{C}$ possesses all of properties (i), (ii), (iii), and (iv) and is a topology with respect to the reference set X. What we have described here is in fact the simplest (the "coarsest," in the parlance of topology) of all topologies in that it is the smallest of all of the topologies that can be constructed from any given reference set. This two-element topology is called the *indiscrete topology* on X.

Here is a second example. The reference set is $X = \{1, 2, 3\}$. The collection $\mathcal{C}$ of subsets of X is now

$$\mathcal{C} = \{\emptyset, \{1\}, \{1, 3\}, \{1, 2, 3\}\}.$$

Work out for yourself if $\mathcal{C}$ is a topology with respect to X before continuing to the next paragraph.

Yes, it is. For a third example, again take $X = \{1, 2, 3\}$. Consider the collection

$$\mathcal{C} = \{\emptyset, \{1\}, \{2\}, \{1, 3\}, \{1, 2, 3\}\}.$$

Is $\mathcal{C}$ a topology with respect to X? Come to a conclusion before proceeding to the next paragraph.

No, it is not. Why not? Because $\{1\} \cup \{2\} = \{1, 2\} \notin \mathcal{C}$.

For a fourth example, consider the collection

$$\mathcal{C} = \{\emptyset, \{1\}, \{1, 3\}, \{2, 3\}, \{1, 2, 3\}\}.$$

Is $\mathcal{C}$ a topology with respect to $X = \{1, 2, 3\}$?

No, because $\{1, 3\} \cap \{2, 3\} = \{3\} \notin \mathcal{C}$. By now you should have realized that it is possible to form more than one topology from the same reference set X. Confirm for yourself that each of the following collections of subsets is a topology with respect to $X = \{1, 2, 3\}$:

$$
\begin{aligned}
\mathcal{C}' &= \{\emptyset, \{1\}, \{1, 2, 3\}\}. \\
\mathcal{C}'' &= \{\emptyset, \{2\}, \{1, 3\}, \{1, 2, 3\}\}. \\
\mathcal{C}''' &= \{\emptyset, \{1\}, \{2\}, \{3\}, \{1, 2\}, \{1, 3\}, \{2, 3\}, \{1, 2, 3\}\}.
\end{aligned}
$$

If one topology on X contains all of the subsets contained in a second topology on X, then the first topology is said to be at least as *refined* as (or "no more coarse than") the second topology.

Definition 3.2 (Refined Topology). *Let $\mathcal{T}'(X)$ and $\mathcal{T}''(X)$ be topologies on X. If $S \in \mathcal{T}'(X)$ for every $S \in \mathcal{T}''(X)$, but $\mathcal{T}'(X) \neq \mathcal{T}''(X)$ (i.e. $\mathcal{T}''(X) \subset \mathcal{T}'(X)$), then the topology $\mathcal{T}'(X)$ is strictly more refined, or strictly finer, or strictly less coarse than, or is a strict refinement of the topology $\mathcal{T}''(X)$, and the topology $\mathcal{T}''(X)$ is strictly less refined, or strictly coarser, or strictly more coarse than the topology $\mathcal{T}''(X)$.*

In our above examples, $\mathcal{C}'$ and $\mathcal{C}''$ are not refinements of each other, because $\mathcal{C}' \not\subset \mathcal{C}''$ and $\mathcal{C}'' \not\subset \mathcal{C}'$. $\mathcal{C}'''$ is a strict refinement of $\mathcal{C}'$ because $\mathcal{C}'''$ contains all of the subsets in $\mathcal{C}'$ ($\mathcal{C}' \subset \mathcal{C}'''$) and has at least one more subset of X as well ($\mathcal{C}' \neq \mathcal{C}'''$). $\mathcal{C}'''$ is also a strict refinement of $\mathcal{C}''$. For any reference set X, the coarsest, or least refined, topology on X is always the indiscrete topology.

What is the most refined of all of the possible topologies on a set X? It must be the collection of *all* of the possible subsets of X, including $\emptyset$ and X. This is called the *power set* of X and is denoted by $\mathcal{P}(X)$. The power set of X is always a topology on X. Why? Clearly $\emptyset \in \mathcal{P}(X)$ and $X \in \mathcal{P}(X)$. Also, since $\mathcal{P}(X)$ contains all of the subsets of X, it must contain all of the subsets of X that can be created by all possible unions and all possible finite intersections of the subsets of X. Hence $\mathcal{P}(X)$

must be a topology on X. It is easy to see that $\mathcal{P}(X)$ is the most refined of all of the topologies on X. (Think of a quick, easy proof.) For this reason it is given a special name. $\mathcal{P}(X)$ is called the *discrete topology on X*. Check for yourself that the above example $\mathcal{C}'''$ is the discrete topology on $X = \{1, 2, 3\}$.

3.2 Topological Bases

The next basic ideas in topology are a *basis of a topology* and *generating a topology from a basis*. Simply put, here they are. From a given reference set X, we take a collection $\mathcal{B}$ of subsets of X. If this collection satisfies two particular properties, then we call it a *basis in X*. We then generate another collection $\mathcal{C}$ of subsets of X by taking all of the possible unions of the subsets in $\mathcal{B}$ and then, if need be, adding the empty set into $\mathcal{C}$. $\mathcal{C}$ will be a topology on X, and we say that $\mathcal{C}$ is the *topology generated by the basis $\mathcal{B}$*. The practical value of a basis is that it allows us a simple way of constructing a topology. You will see a little later that you have already used this idea, even if you are not yet aware of having done so.

Definition 3.3 (Basis of a Topology). *Let $\mathcal{B}$ be a collection of subsets of X. $\mathcal{B}$ is a basis for a topology on X if*

(i) for every $x \in X$ there is a $B \in \mathcal{B}$ with $x \in B$, and

(ii) for any $x \in B_1 \cap B_2$, where $B_1, B_2 \in \mathcal{B}$, there exists $B_3 \in \mathcal{B}$ with $B_3 \subseteq B_1 \cap B_2$ and $x \in B_3$.

What does all this mean? Requirement (i) just says that every element of X must be contained in at least one of the subsets in $\mathcal{B}$. If this is not so, then we cannot generate X by taking the union of all of the subsets in $\mathcal{B}$ and so we cannot generate a topology on X. But what is the purpose of requirement (ii) – it seems to be a bit mysterious, doesn't it? Remember that, for a collection of subsets of X to be a topology, any finite intersection of these subsets must be a subset contained in the topology. Requirement (ii) ensures that this is so. Some examples will make this easier for you to see.

Again take $X = \{1, 2, 3\}$. Start with the collection of subsets of X that is

$$\mathcal{B}_1 = \{\{1\}, \{2, 3\}\}.$$

Is B_1 a basis?

Yes, it is. Each of the elements 1, 2, and 3 in X is contained in at least one of the subsets contained in $\mathcal{B}_1$. Requirement (ii) does not apply since all of the subsets in $\mathcal{B}_1$ have only an empty intersection with each other. What, then, is the topology on X that is generated by taking all possible unions of the subsets in $\mathcal{B}_1$ and then including the empty set also? It is

$$\mathcal{T}_1(X) = \{\emptyset, \{1\}, \{2, 3\}, \{1, 2, 3\}\}.$$

Take a moment to check that $\mathcal{T}_1(X)$ really is a topology on $X = \{1, 2, 3\}$.

Is

$$\mathcal{B}_2 = \{\emptyset, \{1, 2\}, \{2, 3\}\}$$

a basis?

No. Why not? Because $2 \in \{1, 2\} \cap \{2, 3\}$ and there is no subset in $\mathcal{B}_2$ that is a subset of $\{1, 2\} \cap \{2, 3\}$ and contains 2. So what happens if we take the union of all of the subsets in $\mathcal{B}_2$? Do we generate a topology on X? The collection of subsets of X that is generated is

$$\mathcal{C}_2 = \{\emptyset, \{1, 2\}, \{2, 3\}, \{1, 2, 3\}\}.$$

But $\mathcal{C}_2$ is not a topology on X because $\{1, 2\} \cap \{2, 3\} = \{2\} \notin \mathcal{C}_2$. This would not have happened had $\mathcal{B}_2$ satisfied requirement (ii).

Is

$$\mathcal{B}_3 = \{\{1, 3\}, \{2\}, \{3\}\}$$

a basis?

Yes, it is. Notice that $3 \in \{3\} \subseteq \{1, 3\} \cap \{3\}$. The topology generated on X by taking all possible unions of the members of $\mathcal{B}_3$ and then also including the empty set is

$$\mathcal{T}_3(X) = \{\emptyset, \{2\}, \{3\}, \{1, 3\}, \{2, 3\}, \{1, 2, 3\}\}.$$

Check for yourself that this really is a topology on $X = \{1, 2, 3\}$.

As a last example, consider

$$\mathcal{B}_4 = \{\emptyset, \{1\}, \{2\}, \{3\}\}.$$

Confirm for yourself that this is a basis and that it generates the discrete topology on $X = \{1, 2, 3\}$.

A moment of thought should make it clear to you that, if we have two different bases, $\mathcal{B}'$ and $\mathcal{B}''$, for X with $\mathcal{B}' \subset \mathcal{B}''$ and $\mathcal{B}' \neq \mathcal{B}''$ (*i.e.* the basis $\mathcal{B}''$ contains all of the subsets in the basis $\mathcal{B}'$ and at least one more subset of X), then the topology generated by $\mathcal{B}''$ must be at least as refined as the topology generated by $\mathcal{B}'$.

By the way, the term *topological space* means a reference set X paired up with a topology defined on X.

Definition 3.4 (Topological Space). *If $\mathcal{T}(X)$ is a topology on a reference set X, then the ordered pair $(X, \mathcal{T}(X))$ is called a* topological space.

We have covered the basic ideas of topologies. The next thing to do is to examine the meanings of two of the most important ideas in mathematics. These are open sets and closed sets.

3.3 Open and Closed Sets

You might be used to saying something like the following: A set is open if and only if every point in the set is interior to the set, and that a point is interior to a set if and only if the point can be surrounded by an open ball of finite radius with that ball entirely contained in the interior of the set. Whew! What a mouthful. Not only that, such statements are special and are not to be used as a general definition of an open set. As you will see in a moment, you should never say that a set is open, or closed for that matter, unless you also say from which topology the set is taken. Yes, openness of a set is a topological idea. So for now I want you to forget entirely any notions you may have that sets are open only if they are something like sets with only interior points, or some such. Please, put them out of your mind. We will get back to these ideas when we are ready to consider the special cases in which such statements are true.

Given a reference set X and a subset $S \subseteq X$, the collection of all elements of X that are not contained in S is called the *complement of S in X* and will be denoted by S^c; $S^c \equiv \{x \in X \mid x \notin S\}$.

The general definitions of open and closed sets are easy to understand. Here they are.

Definition 3.5 (Open Set). *Given a topology $\mathcal{T}(X)$ on a set X, a set $S \subseteq X$ is* open *with respect to $\mathcal{T}(X)$ if and only if $S \in \mathcal{T}(X)$.*

All this says is that a subset S of X is open with respect to some topology $\mathcal{T}(X)$ on X if and only if S is one of the subsets contained in $\mathcal{T}(X)$. That's all there is to it – really!

Definition 3.6 (Closed Set). *Given a topology $\mathcal{T}(X)$ on a set X, a set $S \subseteq X$ is* closed *with respect to $\mathcal{T}(X)$ if and only if $S^c \in \mathcal{T}(X)$; i.e. if and only if S^c is open with respect to $\mathcal{T}(X)$.*

So a subset S of X is closed with respect to some topology $\mathcal{T}(X)$ on X if and only if the complement in X of S is one of the subsets contained in $\mathcal{T}(X)$. Simple, isn't it?

Let's play around with some examples. Start with the simplest of all topologies; *i.e.* the indiscrete topology $\mathcal{T}(X) = \{\emptyset, X\}$. The above definition of an open set says that both sets, $\emptyset$ and X, are open with respect to the indiscrete topology just because they are members of that topology. And since *any* topology on X contains both the empty set $\emptyset$ and the reference set X, these sets are always open sets. What is the complement of the open set X with respect to X? It is the empty set $\emptyset$, so the empty set must be a closed set with respect to that topology. Similarly, the complement with respect to X of the open set $\emptyset$ is the reference set X, so the reference set must be closed with respect to that topology. We have discovered that, no matter what topology you are working with, the empty set $\emptyset$ and the reference set X are always *both open and closed* with respect to that topology.

Reconsider some of our earlier examples for the reference set $X = \{1,2,3\}$. One topology on X is $\mathcal{C}' = \{\emptyset, \{1\}, \{2,3\}, \{1,2,3\}\}$. Therefore the sets $\emptyset$, $\{1\}$, $\{2,3\}$, and $\{1,2,3\}$ are all open with respect to the topology $\mathcal{C}'$. Hence their complements, which are respectively the sets $\{1,2,3\}$, $\{2,3\}$, $\{1\}$, and $\emptyset$ are all sets that are closed with respect to the topology $\mathcal{C}'$. Thus all of the members of this topology happen to be sets that are both open and closed with respect to the topology $\mathcal{C}'$.

Another example we considered is the topology on $X = \{1,2,3\}$ that is $\mathcal{C}'' = \{\emptyset, \{1\}, \{1,2,3\}\}$. Therefore the subset $\{1\}$ is open with respect to $\mathcal{C}''$, and so the subset $\{1\}^c = \{2,3\}$ is closed with respect to the topology $\mathcal{C}''$. What about the subset $\{2\}$? It is not open with respect to $\mathcal{C}''$ since it is not a member of $\mathcal{C}''$. Nor is it closed with respect to $\mathcal{C}''$ since $\{2\}^c = \{1,3\}$ is not open with respect to $\mathcal{C}''$ because $\{1,3\}$ is not a member of $\mathcal{C}''$. Thus whether or not a set is open or closed depends not only on the set but also upon the topology being used. Given a topology on X, some subsets of X are open sets, some are closed sets, some subsets may be both open and closed, and some subsets may be neither open nor closed – it all depends upon the particular topology you are using.

Here is a little teaser for you. Take any reference set X and construct its discrete topology $\mathcal{T}(X)$. Now take any subset S of X. By construction, $S \in \mathcal{T}(X)$ and so S is open with respect to the discrete topology. This establishes that any subset of X is open with respect to the discrete topology on X. *Must S* also be closed with respect to the discrete topology on X? In other words, must every possible subset of X be a set that is both open and closed with respect to the discrete topology on X? Think it over. I'll let you know in a little while.

Typically a lot of topologies are possible for a given reference set X. In economics it is usually the case that X is some subset of $\Re^n$. This will be the case we examine most in this book, but you should always remember that the ideas we have met here are very general. For instance, the reference set can be something like $X = \{$green, butterfly, Fred, Africa, water$\}$, and we can logically talk of topologies on this set and of open and closed subsets of this X.

Did you decide if every member of the discrete topology on X must be both open and closed with respect to that topology, no matter what is the reference set X? The answer is "Yes" and it is easy to see why. The discrete topology on X contains *every* possible subset of X, so every possible subset of X is open with respect to the discrete topology on X. Pick any one of these open subsets. Its complement must also belong to the discrete topology because that topology contains *every possible* subset of X, and so this set must be open with respect to the topology, but it must also be closed since it is the complement of an open set. If this is confusing to you, look back at the discrete topology $\mathcal{C}'''$ used as an example earlier. Every set in $\mathcal{C}'''$ is a subset of the reference set $X = \{1, 2, 3\}$ that is both open and closed with respect to the topology $\mathcal{C}'''$. Try working out an example for yourself.

Now let's move on to some special cases that will look more familiar to you.

3.4 Metric Space Topologies

If you have forgotten, or not yet examined, what is a metric space, then you need to stop reading this section and explore Section 2.20. Come back here once you have understood it.

The idea we are going to use repeatedly in this section is that of a *ball*.

Definition 3.7 (Ball). *Let (X, d) be a metric space. Let $x \in X$. Let $\varepsilon \in \Re_{++}$. The ball centered at x with radius ε is the set*

$$B_d(x, \varepsilon) = \{x' \in X \mid d(x, x') < \varepsilon\}.$$

In simple words, the ball $B_d(x, \varepsilon)$ is the set of elements in X that are distant from x by strictly less than ε. Such a ball is often called an *ε-neighborhood about x*. Notice that every element in the ball belongs to X, so $B_d(x, \varepsilon) \subseteq X$. You have met sets like this before. Simple examples are intervals in the real line such as

$$B_d(x, \varepsilon) = \{x' \in \Re \mid d(x, x') = |x - x'| < \varepsilon\} = (x - \varepsilon, x + \varepsilon),$$

discs in $\Re^2$ such as

$$B_d(x, \varepsilon) = \left\{ x' \in \Re^2 \mid d(x, x') = \sqrt{(x_1 - x'_1)^2 + (x_2 - x'_2)^2} < \varepsilon \right\}, \qquad (3.1)$$

and balls in $\Re^n$ such as

$$B_d(x, \varepsilon) = \left\{ x' \in \Re^n \mid d(x, x') = \sqrt{(x_1 - x'_1)^2 + \cdots + (x_n - x'_n)^2} < \varepsilon \right\}. \qquad (3.2)$$

Some care has to be taken when constructing balls in bounded spaces since, remember, any ball is entirely contained in its reference space. For example, if $X = [0, 4]$ and distance is measured by the Euclidean metric, then

$$B_{d_E}(3, 1) = \{ x \in [0, 4] \mid |x - 3| < 1 \} = (2, 4),$$
$$\text{but} \quad B_{d_E}(3, 2) = \{ x \in [0, 4] \mid |x - 3| < 2 \} = (1, 4].$$

Similarly, if $X = [0, 4] \times [0, 4]$ and distance is again measured by the Euclidean metric, then

$$B_{d_E}((4, 2), 2) = \{ (x_1, x_2) \in [0, 4]^2 \mid \sqrt{(x_1 - 4)^2 + (x_2 - 2)^2} < 2 \}$$

is the *half*-disc centered at $(4, 2)$. Draw it.

Balls do not have to be intervals, discs, or spherical subsets of real numbers. Consider the metric space that is the set $C(X)$ of all functions that are continuous, real-valued, and bounded on a set X, with the distance between any two such functions measured by the sup norm d_∞ (see (2.43)). Then in the metric space $(C(X), d_\infty)$ the ball centered at the function f and with radius $\varepsilon > 0$ is the set

$$B_{d_\infty}(f, \varepsilon) = \left\{ g \in C(X) \mid d_\infty(f, g) = \sup_{x \in X} |f(x) - g(x)| < \varepsilon \right\}.$$

Such a set looks nothing like a nice round Euclidean ball.

Now let's form the collection of all of the balls in a metric space (X, d). This is the collection

$$\mathcal{B}(X) = \{ B_d(x, \varepsilon) \mid \forall \, \varepsilon > 0 \text{ and } \forall \, x \in X \}.$$

For example, if the metric space is the two-dimensional Euclidean metric space $E^2 = (\Re^2, d_E)$, then $\mathcal{B}(\Re^2)$ is the collection of every possible disc (3.1). The claim I want to make here is that, no matter what is the metric space you are considering, $\mathcal{B}(X)$ is a topological basis in that space. Let's see why.

Does $\mathcal{B}(X)$ satisfy the two requirements of a basis? Look again at Definition 3.3. It is easy to see that requirement (i) is satisfied since $\mathcal{B}(X)$ contains at least one ball centered at every $x \in X$. What about requirement (ii)? Choose any two balls you like from $\mathcal{B}(X)$. Call them $B_d(x', \varepsilon')$ and $B_d(x'', \varepsilon'')$. If $B_d(x', \varepsilon') \cap B_d(x'', \varepsilon'') = \emptyset$, then requirement (ii) is irrelevant. Suppose $B_d(x', \varepsilon') \cap B_d(x'', \varepsilon'') \neq \emptyset$. Choose any $\tilde{x} \in B_d(x', \varepsilon') \cap B_d(x'', \varepsilon'')$. $\mathcal{B}(X)$ contains balls $B_d(\tilde{x}, \varepsilon)$ that are centered at $\tilde{x}$. In fact, $\mathcal{B}(X)$ contains such a ball for every possible radius $\varepsilon > 0$. Therefore there is a ball $B_d(\tilde{x}, \varepsilon)$ with a radius ε small enough that the ball is entirely contained in the intersection $B_d(x', \varepsilon') \cap B_d(x'', \varepsilon'')$ and, obviously, $\tilde{x}$ is contained in this ball. Thus requirement (ii) is satisfied and so $\mathcal{B}(X)$ is indeed a basis in (X, d).

Therefore, if we take all of the possible unions of the balls in $\mathcal{B}(X)$, we will generate a topology on (X, d). Any set in this topology is thus the union of some collection of balls and, by definition, every such set is open with respect to the topology so generated.

You have already met this construction, in the special case of the Euclidean spaces. In $E^n = (\Re^n, d_E)$ the balls are perfectly round spheres (see (3.1) and (3.2)) with radii measured by the Euclidean metric, with every point in $\Re^n$ being the center of one such ball for every possible positive radius:

$$\mathcal{B}(\Re^n) = \{B_{d_E}(x, \varepsilon) \; \forall \; \varepsilon > 0 \text{ and } \forall \; x \in \Re^n\}.$$

The topology generated by this basis is called the *Euclidean metric topology on* $\Re^n$ so any set that is open with respect to this topology is a set that is the union of some subset of the ε-balls in $\mathcal{B}(\Re^n)$. I hope it is now clear why we say that a set is open in E^n (*i.e* the set belongs to the topology on $\Re^n$ that is generated by the basis $\mathcal{B}(\Re^n)$ consisting of all possible Euclidean ε-balls in $\Re^n$) if and only if every point in the set is surrounded by an ε-ball that is entirely contained within the set. This "definition" is just a restatement of the manner in which the sets in the Euclidean metric topology on $\Re^n$ are generated by taking unions of ε-balls. I also hope that you now understand that such a statement can be made for any set in *any* metric space topology that is generated from the basis that consists of all of the possible ε-balls in that metric space. It is not a statement that is restricted only to the Euclidean metric spaces. Do understand, though, that the statement is restricted to metric spaces.

Think once more about the topologies $\mathcal{C}'$, $\mathcal{C}''$, and $\mathcal{C}'''$ on $X = \{1, 2, 3\}$ that we have already repeatedly examined. In $\mathcal{C}''$, for example, the subset $\{1, 3\}$ is open with respect to $\mathcal{C}''$, but there are no balls here. Why not? Because there is no metric function defined on $X = \{1, 2, 3\}$. Openness of a set is an idea that does not rely upon being able to measure distances.

Well, that is about all we need to say about bases and about open and closed sets. The next important idea is that of a *bounded* set.

3.5   Bounded Sets

This is an obvious idea. A set is bounded if and only if it is inside a ball with a finite radius. This guarantees that the set does not "go forever" in any direction. For example, think of a peanut inside of a basketball. The peanut is a subset contained inside the larger set that is the basketball. Because the basketball has only a finite radius, the peanut is a bounded set. Notice, then, that to talk about whether a set is or is not bounded we need a distance measure (something that we do not need to decide if a set is open or closed), and so we talk about bounded sets in the context of a metric space.

Definition 3.8 (Bounded Set). *Let (X, d) be a metric space. A set $S \subseteq X$ is bounded in (X, d) if there is a point $x \in X$ and a finite radius $r > 0$ such that $S \subseteq B_d(x, r)$.*

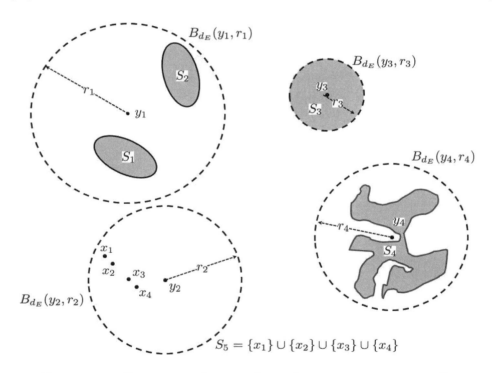

Figure 3.1: Some sets that are bounded with respect to E^2.

All of the sets in Figure 3.1 are bounded with respect to the metric space E^2. For example, each of the sets S_1 and S_2 is contained in the ball $B_{d_E}(y_1, r_1)$ with finite radius r_1, so both sets are bounded. So is the set $S_1 \cup S_2$ and the set S_4. The set S_3 is the same as the ball of finite radius $B_{d_E}(y_3, r_3)$ that contains it, so it too is bounded.

In contrast, each of the three sets displayed in Figure 3.2 is not bounded with respect to E^2. The half-space that is the set $S_7 = \{(x_1, x_2) \mid x_1 + x_2 \geq 2\}$ is not "bounded above" and so cannot be contained inside any ball with only a finite radius. The set of points $S_8 = \{(x_1, x_2) \mid x_2 \leq -x_1^2\}$ is not "bounded below" and so it too cannot be contained inside any ball with only a finite radius. An example of a discrete set that is not bounded is the set S_9 of all of the integers.

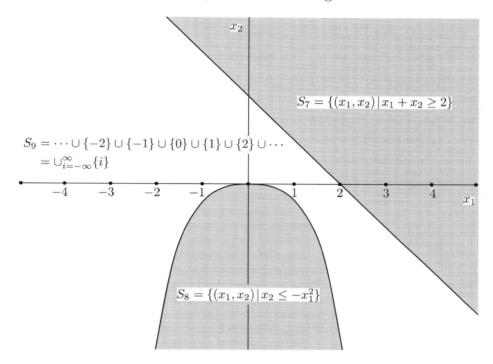

Figure 3.2: Some sets that are not bounded with respect to E^2.

The next important idea is that of a *compact* set.

3.6 Compact Sets

Just think of the word, compact. It seems to suggest something that is not too spread out and with edges to it – isn't that what you mean when you say, for example, that a car or an apartment is compact? With respect to the Euclidean metric topologies, how do we describe a set that does not extend all over the place; *i.e.* a set in which any two points are not "too far" apart? We say that such a set is *bounded*, don't we? And how do we say that a set contains its "edges"? We say that the set is *closed*.

This probably is already familiar to you since you will often have heard the statement that a set is compact if and only if it is both closed and bounded. If at this moment you are nodding to yourself and saying that's right, then *stop!* The statement is not true in general. It is true in a special case that is very important to economists, so let's state the relevant theorem and have a close look at it.

Theorem 3.1 (Heine-Borel). *Let $S \subset \Re^n$. S is compact with respect to the Euclidean metric space $E^n = (R^n, d_E)$ if and only if S is both closed and bounded with respect to this metric space.*

The conditions imposed by this theorem are severe. First, it considers only subsets of real spaces. Second, it considers only one topology on the real spaces – just one! So the Heine-Borel Theorem, while very important and useful, is rather special. Fortunately, the Euclidean metric topology is where we economists do most of our thinking. But there are times when economists have to work in other topological spaces, and then compactness is not the same as closed and bounded. It is true that in any metric-space topology a set is compact only if (note: just "only if," not "if and only if") it is bounded and closed. But in general metric space topologies, the converse is typically not true, so be careful.

3.7   How Do Our Topological Ideas Get Used?

By now you may be wondering why the ideas discussed in this chapter matter. Who cares if some set is compact? So what if a set is open, or not? Isn't constrained optimization really about computing things? If so, then why aren't we getting ready to crunch some numbers? I think we all become a little impatient when trying to understand clearly some body of knowledge. The details never seem to end, and seem to slow up our progress towards the heart of whatever it is we are trying to understand. But experience has taught me the hard way that patient and organized study of a topic is the only way to master it. Nothing that has been presented in this chapter is less than essential to a detailed understanding of the types of constrained optimization problems that confront economists.

Why does it matter whether a set is open or closed? Most constrained optimization problems have two parts to them. The first part is the set of things from which a decisionmaker is allowed to choose. The second part is a function that states the decisionmaker's valuations of these available choices. For the typical economist's problem, if the set of available choices is not closed, then there may not be a solution to the problem. As well, the function that states the decisionmaker's valuations is usually "continuous" (meaning "varies smoothly without sudden jumps"), but a function is continuous only if it is defined over open sets. Continuity of functions is a really basic, important idea that we will use a lot, and for this we will need to know when sets are open or not.

Why should economists care about bounded sets? Well, what is it that makes economics such an important and practical science? The answer is *scarcity*. What is scarcity? It is the fact that in our world resources are available only in finite quantities. Recognizing this is the same as saying that the set consisting of all available resources is bounded. In every economics problem I can think of to do with allocating some resource (a budget or a production input, perhaps), the set of available choices is a bounded set and, typically, a compact (both closed and bounded) set.

So, have patience and proceed to the next necessary ideas, which are sequences and limits. Sequences and, if they converge, their limits are used in Euclidean metric space environments to verify if sets are open or closed, and to verify if functions are continuous or not, so you should view the contents of the next chapter as providing you a means of determining the properties of sets that we have discussed in this chapter. You will find that there are many places in the chapters that follow where we will use sequences to establish results that are crucial for solving constrained optimization problems.

3.8   Problems

Problem 3.1. Let $X = \{1, 2, 3, 4, 5\}$. Consider the following collection of subsets of X:

$$\mathcal{C}_1 = \{\{1, 2\}, \{3, 4, 5\}, \emptyset\}.$$

Generate the collection $\mathcal{D}_1$ of subsets of X by taking all possible unions of the sets in $\mathcal{C}_1$.

(i) Show that $\mathcal{C}_1$ is a topological basis in X. Then show that $\mathcal{D}_1$ is a topology with respect to X.

(ii) Now consider the following collection of subsets of X:

$$\mathcal{C}_2 = \{\{4\}, \{1, 2\}, \{3, 4, 5\}, \emptyset\}.$$

Show that $\mathcal{C}_2$ is a topological basis in X. Then generate the collection $\mathcal{D}_2$ of subsets of X by taking all of the possible unions of the sets in $\mathcal{C}_2$ and show that $\mathcal{D}_2$ is the topology in X that is generated by $\mathcal{C}_2$.

(iii) Notice that $\{4\} \in \mathcal{C}_2$ is a subset of the basis element $\{3, 4, 5\} \in \mathcal{C}_1$. Also notice, by comparing how you generated the topologies $\mathcal{D}_1$ and $\mathcal{D}_2$, that this is why $\mathcal{D}_1$ is strictly contained in $\mathcal{D}_2$; more formally, $\mathcal{D}_2$ is *finer* in X than is $\mathcal{D}_1$. It is a general result. Here is the theorem.

   Theorem. Let $\mathcal{B}_1$ and $\mathcal{B}_2$ be bases in X. Let $\mathcal{T}_1$ be the topology in X that is generated by $\mathcal{B}_1$ and let $\mathcal{T}_2$ be the topology in X that is generated by $\mathcal{B}_2$. Then $\mathcal{T}_2$ is finer in X than is $\mathcal{T}_1$ if and only if, for every $x \in X$ and for every basis element $B \in \mathcal{B}_1$ that contains x, there is a basis element $C \in \mathcal{B}_2$ such that $x \in C \subseteq B$.

Problem 3.2. Let $X = \{1, 2, 3, 4, 5\}$. Let $\mathcal{B} = \{\emptyset, \{1, 2\}, \{3, 4, 5\}\}$. $\mathcal{B}$ is a basis for a topology on X.

(i) What is the topology on X that is generated by $\mathcal{B}$?

(ii) Consider the topology generated in part (i). Is it possible for *all* of the sets in a topology (other than the indiscrete and discrete topologies) to be both open and closed with respect to that topology?

Problem 3.3. It is claimed in the text of this chapter that a particular collection of subsets of $\Re^n$ is a basis for the Euclidean metric topology on $\Re^n$. The collection of sets is

$$\mathcal{B}(\Re^n) = \{B_{d_E}(x, \varepsilon) \ \forall \ x \in \Re^n, \ \forall \ \varepsilon > 0\}.$$

Explain why this claim is true.

Problem 3.4. Prove the following theorem.

Theorem. If $S_1, \ldots, S_n$ is a finite collection of subsets that are bounded with respect to a metric space (X, d), then $S = \cup_{i=1}^{n} S_i$ is bounded with respect to (X, d).

Problem 3.5. Present a counterexample to the assertion that, if $S_1, S_2, \ldots$ is any countable collection of subsets that are bounded with respect to a metric space (X, d), then $S = \cup_{i=1}^{\infty} S_i$ must be bounded with respect to (X, d).

Problem 3.6. Prove the following theorem.

Theorem. Let $S_1, S_2, \ldots$ be any countable collection of subsets that are bounded with respect to a metric space (X, d). Then $S = \cap_{i=1}^{\infty} S_i$ is bounded with respect to (X, d).

Problem 3.7. Present a counterexample to the assertion that $S = \cap_{i=1}^{\infty} S_i$ is bounded with respect to (X, d) only if $S_1, S_2, \ldots$ is a countable collection of subsets that are bounded with respect to a metric space (X, d).

Problem 3.8. Prove the following theorem.

Theorem. Let $S_1, \ldots, S_n$ be any finite collection of subsets that are compact with respect to the metric space E^n. Then $S = \cup_{i=1}^{n} S_i$ is compact with respect to E^n.

Problem 3.9. Present a counterexample to the assertion that, if $S_1, S_2, \ldots$ is a countable collection of subsets that are compact with respect to the metric space E^n, then $S = \cup_{i=1}^{\infty} S_i$ must be compact with respect to E^n.

Problem 3.10. Present a counterexample to the assertion that $S = \cup_{i=1}^{n} S_i$ is compact with respect to E^n only if $S_1, \ldots, S_n$ is a countable collection of subsets that are compact with respect to E^n.

Problem 3.11. Prove the following theorem.

Theorem. Let $S_1, \ldots, S_n$ be any finite collection of subsets that are compact with respect to E^n. Then $S = \cap_{i=1}^{n} S_i$ is compact with respect to E^n.

3.9 Answers

Answer to Problem 3.1.

(i) $\mathcal{C}_1$ is a basis in X if and only if

    (a) $x \in X$ implies $x \in B$ for at least one member B in the collection $\mathcal{C}_1$, and

    (b) if $B_1, B_2 \in \mathcal{C}_1$ and $x \in B_1 \cap B_2$, then there exists $B_3 \in \mathcal{C}_1$ such that $B_3 \subseteq B_1 \cap B_2$ and $x \in B_3$.

It is easily seen that each of the individual elements 1, 2, 3, 4, and 5 belongs to at least one of the members of $\mathcal{C}_1$. Thus (a) is true. (b) is trivially satisfied since there is no $x \in X$ that belongs to the intersection of elements of $\mathcal{C}_1$. Therefore $\mathcal{C}_1$ is a basis. Particularly, $\mathcal{C}_1$ is the basis for the topology that is generated by taking unions of the elements of $\mathcal{C}_1$. This is the collection

$$\mathcal{D}_1 = \{\emptyset, \{1, 2\}, \{3, 4, 5\}, \{1, 2, 3, 4, 5\}\}.$$

Inspection shows that unions of any members of $\mathcal{D}_1$ generate only members of $\mathcal{D}_1$ and that finite intersections of any members of $\mathcal{D}_1$ generate only members of $\mathcal{D}_1$. Also, $\emptyset \in \mathcal{D}_1$ and $X = \{1, 2, 3, 4, 5\} \in \mathcal{D}_1$. Hence $\mathcal{D}_1$ is the topology with respect to X that is generated by the basis $\mathcal{C}_1$. All of the members of $\mathcal{D}_1$ are thus sets that are open with respect to the topology $\mathcal{D}_1$ in $X = \{1, 2, 3, 4, 5\}$.

(ii) $\mathcal{C}_2$ is a basis in X if and only if

(a) $x \in X$ implies $x \in B$ for at least one member B in the collection $\mathcal{C}_2$, and

(b) if $B_1, B_2 \in \mathcal{C}_2$ and $x \in B_1 \cap B_2$, then there exists $B_3 \in \mathcal{C}_2$ such that $B_3 \subseteq B_1 \cap B_2$ and $x \in B_3$.

Again it is easily seen that each of the individual elements 1, 2, 3, 4, and 5 belong to at least one of the members of $\mathcal{C}_2$. Thus (a) is true. The only element of X that belongs to an intersection of elements in $\mathcal{C}_2$ is 4, since $4 \in \{4\} \cap \{3, 4, 5\}$. Notice that $4 \in \{4\} \subseteq \{4\} \cap \{3, 4, 5\}$. Thus (b) is also true and so $\mathcal{C}_2$ is a basis. Particularly, $\mathcal{C}_2$ is the basis for the topology that is generated by taking unions of the elements of $\mathcal{C}_2$. This is the collection

$$\mathcal{D}_2 = \{\emptyset, \{4\}, \{1, 2\}, \{1, 2, 4\}, \{3, 4, 5\}, \{1, 2, 3, 4, 5\}\}.$$

Inspection shows that unions of any members of $\mathcal{D}_2$ generate only members of $\mathcal{D}_2$ and that finite intersections of any members of $\mathcal{D}_2$ generate only members of $\mathcal{D}_2$. Also, $\emptyset \in \mathcal{D}_2$ and $X = \{1, 2, 3, 4, 5\} \in \mathcal{D}_2$, so $\mathcal{D}_2$ is the topology with respect to X that is generated by the basis $\mathcal{C}_2$. All of the members of $\mathcal{D}_2$ are thus sets that are open with respect to the topology $\mathcal{D}_2$ in $X = \{1, 2, 3, 4, 5\}$. $\square$

Answer to Problem 3.2.

(i) The topology is

$$\mathcal{T} = \{\emptyset, \{1, 2\}, \{3, 4, 5\}, \{1, 2, 3, 4, 5\}\}.$$

(ii) Each of the sets in $\mathcal{T}$ is open with respect to $\mathcal{T}$. The complements of each of these sets are thus closed with respect to $\mathcal{T}$. These closed sets are, respectively,

$$\{1, 2, 3, 4, 5\}, \{3, 4, 5\}, \{1, 2\} \text{ and } \emptyset.$$

Therefore every set in $\mathcal{T}$ is both open and closed with respect to $\mathcal{T}$. The answer to the question "Is it possible for *all* of the sets in a topology (other than the indiscrete and discrete topologies) to be both open and closed with respect to that topology?" is "Yes". $\square$

Answer to Problem 3.3. $\mathcal{B}(\Re^n)$ is a basis for a topology on $\Re^n$ if and only if $\mathcal{B}(\Re^n)$ satisfies properties (i) and (ii) in Definition 3.3. It is clear that, by construction,

$$\mathcal{B}(\Re^n) = \{B_{d_E}(x, \varepsilon) \ \forall \ x \in \Re^n, \ \forall \ \varepsilon > 0\}$$

satisfies property (i). What about property (ii)? Take any two members B_1 and B_2 from $\mathcal{B}(\Re^n)$ such that $B_1 \cap B_2 \neq \emptyset$. Let $x \in B_1 \cap B_2$. Notice that $B_1 \cap B_2$ cannot be a singleton set. Why? Well, if it were, then x would be a boundary point for both the ball B_1 and the ball B_2. But, by construction, none of the balls in $\mathcal{B}(\Re^n)$ contains any of its boundary points, so $B_1 \cap B_2$ is not a singleton set. This implies that, for any $x \in B_1 \cap B_2$, there is a small enough $\varepsilon' > 0$ such that the ball $B_3 = B_{d_E}(x, \varepsilon') = \{y \in \Re^n \mid d_E(x, y) < \varepsilon'\} \subset B_1 \cap B_2$. Again, by construction, $B_3 \in \mathcal{B}(\Re^n)$. Thus $\mathcal{B}(\Re^n)$ also satisfies property (ii), establishing that $\mathcal{B}(\Re^n)$ is a basis for a topology on $\Re^n$. $\square$

Answer to Problem 3.4. The result is trivial for $n = 1$. Consider the case of $n = 2$. Since S_1 is a bounded set, there exists a point $x_1 \in X$ and a radius $\varepsilon_1 > 0$ such that $S_1 \subseteq B_d(x_1, \varepsilon_1)$. Similarly, since S_2 is a bounded set, there exists a point $x_2 \in X$ and a radius $\varepsilon_2 > 0$ such that $S_2 \subseteq B_d(x_2, \varepsilon_2)$. Let $x' \in S_1$ and let $x'' \in S_2$. Then, by the triangular inequality property of a metric function,

$$d(x', x'') \leq d(x', x_1) + d(x_1, x_2) + d(x_2, x'') \leq \varepsilon_1 + d(x_1, x_2) + \varepsilon_2.$$

The right-hand-side quantity is a finite and positive number that is independent of both x' and x''. Hence

$$d(x', x'') \leq \varepsilon_1 + d(x_1, x_2) + \varepsilon_2 \equiv \delta \ \forall \ x' \in S_1, \ \forall \ x'' \in S_2.$$

Thus $S_1 \cup S_2 \subseteq B_d(x_1, \delta)$, which establishes that $S_1 \cup S_2$ is a bounded subset of X.

The result is extended to the union of any finite number $n \geq 2$ of sets by induction. For any $n \geq 2$, write the union of the sets $S_1, \ldots, S_n$ as $\cup_{i=1}^{n-1} S_i \cup S_n$. By the induction hypothesis, $\cup_{i=1}^{n-1} S_i$ is a bounded set. Therefore the union of the two bounded subsets $\cup_{i=1}^{n-1} S_i$ and S_n must be bounded in (X, d). Since the result is true for $n = 2$, it is true for all $n \geq 2$. $\square$

Answer to Problem 3.5. Let $X = \Re$ and let d be the Euclidean metric. For $i = 0, 1, 2, \ldots$, let $S_i = [i, i+1] \subset \Re$. Each set S_i is bounded, but

$$S = \cup_{i=0}^{\infty} S_i = \cup_{i=0}^{\infty} [i, i+1] = [0, \infty)$$

is not bounded with respect to E^n. $\square$

Answer to Problem 3.6. S_1 is bounded in (X, d), so there exists $x \in X$ and $\varepsilon_1 > 0$ such that $S_1 \subseteq B_d(x, \varepsilon_1)$. $S = \cap_{i=1}^{\infty} S_i \subseteq S_1$ so $S \subseteq B_d(x, \varepsilon_1)$. That is, S is bounded in (X, d). $\square$

Answer to Problem 3.7. Consider the countable collection S_1 and S_2, where $S_1 = (-\infty, 0]$ and $S_2 = [0, \infty)$. Neither S_1 nor S_2 is bounded with respect to E^1. Yet $S_1 \cap S_2 = \{0\}$ is bounded with respect to E^1. $\square$

Answer to Problem 3.8. Each S_i is closed in E^n and the union of *finitely* many closed sets is a closed set. Thus S is a closed set. From Problem 3.4, S is also bounded and so is compact with respect to E^n. $\square$

Answer to Problem 3.9. The counterexample provided for Problem 3.5 is a counterexample here also. $\square$

Answer to Problem 3.10. Let $S_1 = [0, 1]$ and $S_i = (0, 1)$ for all $i = 2, 3, \ldots$. Obviously all of $S_2, S_3, \ldots$ are open, and thus not compact, with respect to E^1. But $S_1 \cup S_2 \cup S_3 \cup \cdots = [0, 1]$, which is compact with respect to E^1. $\square$

Answer to Problem 3.11. The intersection of any finite collection of subsets that are closed with respect to (X, d) is a subset that is closed with respect to (X, d). The proof given in Problem 3.6 states that S is bounded in (X, d). Then S is both closed and bounded with respect to (X, d). If $X = \Re^n$ and d is the Euclidean metric, then $(X, d) = E^n$ and so S is compact with respect to E^n (by the Heine-Borel Theorem). $\square$

Chapter 4

Sequences and Convergence

4.1 Sequences

This chapter presents only a few of the many ideas and results to do with sequences. Its content is determined solely by what is required to understand discussions in later chapters of this book. There is little value in duplicating the extensive discussions of sequences that are presented in other places, so the interested reader is invited to advance his or her knowledge of sequences beyond the contents of this chapter by perusing any of the many mathematics books that provide more expansive expositions.

We are going to make a lot of use of the set of positive integers because they are the numbers that we most often use as "counters" when constructing a sequence. The positive integers are called the *natural numbers*. This set $\{1, 2, 3, \ldots\}$ is often denoted by N, but N is also used to denote many other quantities so, to avoid ambiguity we will follow mathematicians and use Z_+ to denote the set of natural numbers; $Z_+ = \{1, 2, 3, \ldots\}$.

Definition 4.1 (Sequence). *A sequence of elements from a set X is a surjective function $f : Z_+ \to X$.*

All this means is that we construct a mapping of the form $\{(n_1, x_1), (n_2, x_2), \ldots\}$ that more commonly we write as $\{x_{n_1}, x_{n_2}, \ldots\}$ by using the subscript n_i on x_{n_i} to denote the natural number n_i that is mapped only to the element $x_{n_i} \in X$. That the function is required to be surjective (see Definition 5.7) means every element in the sequence is associated with at least one "counter" index element n. In most cases the indices are $1, 2, 3, \ldots$, so we usually see a sequence written as $x_1, x_2, x_3, \ldots$. When we say that x_1 is the first member of a sequence, we are saying that the number 1 is

123

associated with (*i.e.* the number 1 is mapped to) the first value in the sequence. And, more generally, when we say that x_i is the ith member of a sequence, we are saying that the number i is associated with the ith value in the sequence, for $i = 1, 2, 3, \ldots$. A particular element in a sequence may be associated with more than one index element. For example, it might be that $x_3 = x_{15} = 9$; *i.e.* the third and fifteenth elements of the sequence are both the number 9.

A sequence can be infinite, $x_1, x_2, \ldots, x_i, \ldots$, or it can be finite, $x_1, \ldots, x_m$ for some finite integer $m \geq 1$. There are various notations used for sequences. Some people write a sequence simply as x_n, but this leads to ambiguities so I will not use it. Others use (x_n), $\langle x_n \rangle$ or $\langle x_n \rangle_{n=1}^{\infty}$. Still others use $\{x_n\}$ or $\{x_n\}_{n=1}^{\infty}$. I will use the last of these. $\{x_n\}_{n=1}^{\infty}$ will denote a sequence of infinitely many elements. $\{x_n\}_{n=1}^{m}$ will denote a finite sequence of n elements.

Economics is the science of scarcity. Scarcity imposes bounds upon what is achievable. Consequently many of the sequences that concern economists are *bounded sequences*.

4.2   Bounded Sequences

A sequence is bounded, meaning both bounded above and bounded below, if all of the elements in the sequence are not larger than some finite upper bound and also are not less than some finite lower bound.

Definition 4.2 (Bounded Sequence). *Let $X \subset \Re$ and let $\{x_n\}_{n=1}^{\infty}$ be a sequence of elements from X. $\{x_n\}_{n=1}^{\infty}$ is bounded on X if there exists $B \in X$ such that $|x_n| \leq B$ for all $n = 1, 2, \ldots$.*

Definition 4.2 is the same as saying that the set $\{x_1, x_2, \ldots\}$ is contained in a closed ball centered at zero and with a finite radius of at least B in the range of the function $f : Z_+ \to X$ that defines the sequence $\{x_n\}_{n=1}^{\infty}$.

Bounds are not unique. Consider the sequence $\{2, -1, 2, -1, 2, -1, \ldots\}$. Any number 2 or larger is an upper bound for this sequence. Any number -1 or less is a lower bound. 2 is significant in that it is the least upper bound for the sequence. -1 is significant in that it is the greatest lower bound.

Now consider the sequence $\left\{1 - \frac{1}{n}\right\}_{n=1}^{\infty} = \left\{0, \frac{1}{2}, \frac{2}{3}, \frac{3}{4}, \ldots\right\}$. This sequence is bounded, above and below. The greatest lower bound is zero, and this is a member (the first element) of the sequence. The least upper bound is 1, which is not a member of the sequence. So, a bounded sequence may or may not contain its least upper bound or its greatest lower bound. The least upper bound of a sequence $\{x_n\}_{n=1}^{\infty}$ is the *supremum* of the sequence and is denoted by $\sup x_n$. The greatest lower bound of the sequence is the *infimum* of the sequence and is denoted by $\inf x_n$.

Some sequences are only bounded above, meaning that there is a finite number B such that $x_n \leq B$ for every $n \geq 1$. An example is $S = \{0, -1, -2, -3, \ldots\}$. For this sequence the least upper bound of zero is the supremum: $\sup(S) = 0$. Since the sequence is unbounded below, there is no numerical value for the infimum, and we write $\inf(S) = -\infty$. Other sequences are only bounded below, meaning that there is a finite number B such that $B \leq x_n$ for every $n \geq 1$. An example is $S' = \{0, 1, 2, 3, \ldots\}$. The greatest lower bound for this sequence is zero: $\inf(S') = 0$. There is no numerical value for the supremum of this sequence, so we write $\sup(S') = +\infty$.

Be careful with your terminology. If you say that a sequence is "bounded," then you mean that the sequence is bounded above and bounded below. If you mean only one of these, then say so.

4.3 Convergence

Let's refresh our memories about the idea of convergence of a sequence. We have some set X and we construct a sequence of elements x_n from X. Most sequences are not convergent. But if, as n becomes very large, the elements of the sequence become "arbitrarily close" to some value $x_0 \in X$, then we state that the sequence converges and that x_0 is the limit of the sequence. To state this exactly requires something that gives a precise meaning of "close." The usual tool is a metric function d that allows us to measure the distance $d(x_k, x_0)$ between any element x_k in the sequence and the limiting value x_0. So the idea is that, eventually, when we get far enough along a convergent sequence, the distances $d(x_k, x_0)$ all are very small and continue to get ever closer to zero as k increases; *i.e.* as we continue to go ever further out along the sequence.

Definition 4.3 (Convergent Sequence). *Let (X, d) be a metric space. Let $\{x_n\}_{n=1}^{\infty}$ be a sequence of elements of X. $\{x_n\}_{n=1}^{\infty}$ converges to $x_0 \in X$ with respect to the metric d if and only if, for every $\varepsilon > 0$, there exists an integer $M(\varepsilon)$ such that $d(x_n, x_0) < \varepsilon$ for every $n \geq M(\varepsilon)$.*

Think of the following simple example. Let the reference set $X = [1, 2]$ and let the metric function be the Euclidean metric. Consider the sequence

$$s^* = \left\{1, 1 + \frac{1}{2}, 1 + \frac{2}{3}, 1 + \frac{3}{4}, \ldots, 1 + \frac{n-1}{n}, \ldots\right\}.$$

Is s^* a convergent sequence? If so, then what is its limit? Can you prove it? Don't read on until you have an answer.

s^* *is* convergent on $X = [1, 2]$ with respect to the Euclidean metric. The limit is 2. A proof is that the Euclidean distance of any element $x_n = 1 + (n-1)/n$ from 2 is

$$d_E(x_n, 2) = \sqrt{\left(1 + \frac{n-1}{n} - 2\right)^2} = \frac{1}{n} \to 0 \text{ as } n \to \infty.$$

Thus, as $n \to \infty$ (*i.e.* as we move further and further along the sequence), the distances of elements x_n from 2 become arbitrarily close to zero.

That was easy. Let's modify the example a little by changing the reference set to $X = [1, 2)$. Is s^* still a convergent sequence? If so, then what is its limit? Again, don't read on until you have thought about it and come to a reasoned response.

s^* is *not* convergent. If you said otherwise, then you have made a common but serious error. A sequence cannot be convergent unless there exists a limit for it. So if you want to say that s^* is still convergent then you have to say that its limit exists. But you cannot say that the limit of s^* is 2 because 2 is not an element of the reference set; as far as we are concerned, the number 2 does not exist. And if the limit does not exist, then the sequence is not convergent. Never think about whether a sequence converges or not without taking careful note of the reference set.

It is obvious that a sequence that converges cannot have elements in it that are persistently wildly different from each other. In fact the opposite should occur, at least eventually. So that must mean that all of the elements of a convergent sequence of real numbers should lie between some upper bound and some lower bound; *i.e.* a convergent sequence of real numbers should be bounded. This is indeed so, and it is easy to prove. Before stating the theorem and its proof, however, have a look at the following convergent sequence of real numbers. Let the reference set $X = \Re$ and use the Euclidean metric to measure distances.

$$s^{**} = \{-1000, 2000, -2500, 8200, -10, 8, -4, 3, 0, 2, 2, 2, \ldots, 2, \ldots\}.$$

It is easy to see that this is a convergent sequence with 2 as its limit. You can see that any number at least as large as 8200 is an upper bound on the sequence and that any number less than -2500 is a lower bound, so the sequence is bounded (meaning both bounded above and bounded below). The fact that the early elements of the sequence vary greatly in value affects neither that the sequence converges nor that the sequence is bounded.

Now let's prove our assertion that any sequence that converges is a bounded sequence.

Theorem 4.1 (A Convergent Sequence is Bounded). *Let $X \subset \Re$ and let $\{x_n\}_{n=1}^{\infty}$ be a sequence of elements from X. If $\{x_n\}_{n=1}^{\infty}$ is convergent on X, then $\{x_n\}_{n=1}^{\infty}$ is bounded on X.*

Proof. We are given that the sequence $\{x_n\}_{n=1}^{\infty}$ converges to some limiting value x_0: $x_n \to x_0 \in X$. So pick any distance $\varepsilon > 0$ and there must exist an integer $M(\varepsilon)$ such that, for the part of the sequence $x_{M(\varepsilon)}, x_{M(\varepsilon)+1}, x_{M(\varepsilon)+2}, \ldots$, the distance between each of these elements of the sequence and the limiting value x_0 is less than ε; $d_E(x_n, x_0) = |x_n - x_0| < \varepsilon$ for every $n \geq M(\varepsilon)$. Therefore

$$|x_n| < |x_0| + \varepsilon \; \equiv L_1 \text{ for every } n \geq M(\varepsilon).$$

That is, the part of the sequence that is $x_{M(\varepsilon)}, x_{M(\varepsilon)+1}, x_{M(\varepsilon)+2}, \ldots$ is bounded by the number $L_1 = |x_0| + \varepsilon$.

The rest, the first part, of the sequence is $x_1, x_2, \ldots, x_{M(\varepsilon)-1}$. The distances of these sequence elements from the limiting value x_0 form a finite set of values $d(x_1, x_0) = |x_1 - x_0|, \ldots, d(x_{M(\varepsilon)-1}, x_0) = |x_{M(\varepsilon)-1} - x_0|$. Thus

$$|x_1| < |x_0| + d(x_1, x_0), \ldots, |x_{M(\varepsilon)-1}| < |x_0| + d(x_{M(\varepsilon)-1}, x_0),$$

and so

$$|x_1| < |x_0| + \max\left\{d(x_1, x_0), \ldots, d(x_{M(\varepsilon)-1}, x_0)\right\}$$
$$\vdots \qquad\qquad\qquad\qquad \vdots$$
$$|x_{M(\varepsilon)-1}| < |x_0| + \max\left\{d(x_1, x_0), \ldots, d(x_{M(\varepsilon)-1}, x_0)\right\}.$$

Thus the first part of the sequence is bounded by the number

$$L_2 \equiv |x_0| + \max\left\{d(x_1, x_0), \ldots, d(x_{M(\varepsilon)-1}, x_0)\right\}.$$

Hence the entire sequence is bounded by the larger of the two numbers L_1 and L_2:

$$|x_n| \leq \max\{L_1, L_2\} \text{ for every } n \geq 1. \qquad \square$$

It is easy to see that the converse is not true. That is, a bounded sequence need not be convergent. For example, the sequence $\{0, 1, 0, 1, 0, 1, \ldots\}$ is bounded but it is not convergent. However, there are two simple and important types of sequences of real numbers that are always convergent.

Definition 4.4 (Monotonic Sequence). *Let $X \subset \Re$. Let $\{x_n\}_{n=1}^{\infty}$ be a sequence of elements from X. If $x_n \leq x_{n+1}$ for every $n \geq 1$, then $\{x_n\}_{n=1}^{\infty}$ is a* monotonic increasing *sequence on X. If $x_n < x_{n+1}$ for every $n \geq 1$, then $\{x_n\}_{n=1}^{\infty}$ is a* strictly monotonic increasing *sequence on X. If $x_n \geq x_{n+1}$ for every $n \geq 1$, then $\{x_n\}_{n=1}^{\infty}$ is a* monotonic decreasing *sequence on X. If $x_n > x_{n+1}$ for every $n \geq 1$, then $\{x_n\}_{n=1}^{\infty}$ is a* strictly monotonic decreasing *sequence on X.*

When a sequence is increasing we write $x_n \nearrow$, and when a sequence is decreasing we write $x_n \searrow$. If a sequence is increasing and is convergent to a limit x_0, then we write $x_n \nearrow x_0$. If a sequence is decreasing and is convergent to a limit x_0, then we write $x_n \searrow x_0$.

What if a sequence $\{x_n\}_{n=1}^{\infty}$ is increasing and is bounded above? Well, the elements in the sequence cannot decrease as n increases and neither can they increase past a certain value. Shouldn't such a sequence be convergent? Similarly, shouldn't a decreasing sequence that is bounded below be convergent? Both statements are true and are very useful.

Theorem 4.2 (Monotonic Increasing Sequence Bounded Above Converges). *Let $\{x_n\}_{n=1}^{\infty}$ be a monotonic increasing sequence of real numbers that is bounded above. Then $\{x_n\}_{n=1}^{\infty}$ is convergent.*

Proof. $x_n \nearrow$. Let B be an upper bound for $\{x_n\}_{n=1}^{\infty}$. Then $\overline{x} = \sup x_n \leq B$ and so the least upper bound $\overline{x}$ exists. Since $\overline{x}$ is the least upper bound and since $x_n \nearrow$ for any $\varepsilon > 0$, there must exist an integer $M(\varepsilon)$ such that $|x_n - \overline{x}| < \varepsilon$ for every $n \geq M(\varepsilon)$. Hence the sequence converges to $\overline{x}$. $\qquad\square$

Theorem 4.3 (Monotonic Decreasing Sequence Bounded Below Converges). *Let $\{x_n\}_{n=1}^{\infty}$ be a monotonic decreasing sequence of real numbers that is bounded below. Then $\{x_n\}_{n=1}^{\infty}$ is convergent.*

The proof is almost the same as for Theorem 4.2, so take a few minutes and construct it for yourself.

Here is one last small caution before we move along to the next section. Suppose you have a sequence of real numbers x_n with $x_n < b$ for every $n \geq 1$. Suppose that the sequence converges to some limit x_0. Must $x_0 < b$? Think about it. Write down an example or two. When you are ready, move to the next paragraph.

$x_0 < b$ may not be true. $x_0 \leq b$ is always true. Think of the sequence in which $x_n = 2 - 1/n$. Clearly $x_n < 2$ for every $n \geq 1$. Even so, $x_n \to 2$. Similarly, if $x_n > b$ for every $n \geq 1$ and $x_n \to x_0$, then it is always true that $x_0 \geq b$ but the statement that $x_0 > b$ may be false.

4.4 Subsequences

How common is it to work with monotonic sequences? For economists, the answer is "Quite often." Perhaps more important still is that *any* sequence of real numbers (convergent or not) possesses at least one *subsequence* that is monotonic. In a lot of the cases that matter to economists, this is a really important piece of information. Let's start by understanding what is a subsequence.

Definition 4.5 (Subsequence). *Let $\{x_n\}_{n=1}^{\infty}$ be a sequence in X. Let $\{k_1, k_2, \ldots\}$ be a subset of $\{1, 2, \ldots\}$ with $k_1 < k_2 < \cdots$. Then $\{x_{k_i}\}_{i=1}^{\infty}$ is a subsequence of $\{x_n\}_{n=1}^{\infty}$.*

Put into simple words, a subsequence is a subset of the elements of the parent sequence. The order of the elements in the subsequence is the same as in the parent sequence. For example, the sequence $\{-2, -4, 15\}$ is a subsequence of the sequence $\{3, -2, 7, 0, -4, -8, 9, 15, 2\}$, while the sequence $\{-4, -2, 15\}$ is not.

As the following theorem states, monotonic subsequences of real numbers are commonplace.

Theorem 4.4 (Any Sequence of Real Numbers Contains a Monotonic Subsequence). *Any sequence $\{x_n\}_{n=1}^{\infty}$ of real numbers possesses at least one monotonic subsequence.*

Proof. For each $n \geq 1$ define the subsequence $s_n = \{x_n, x_{n+1}, \ldots\}$. There are two possibilities. Either the parent sequence $\{x_n\}_{n=1}^{\infty}$ possesses a largest element, or it does not.

Suppose that $\{x_n\}_{n=1}^{\infty}$ does not possess a largest element. Then it possesses a monotonically increasing sequence $\{y_k\}_{k=1}^{\infty}$ constructed as follows. Set $y_1 = x_1$. Then set y_2 equal to the first element in s_2 that is larger than y_1 (such an element exists because the original sequence $\{x_n\}_{n=1}^{\infty}$ does not have a maximal element). Denote this element by x_{m_2}. Then set y_3 equal to the first element in s_{m_2+1} that is larger than y_2; call this element x_{m_3}. Continuing in this way constructs a sequence $\{y_1, y_2, y_3, \ldots\} = \{x_1, x_{m_2}, x_{m_3}, \ldots\}$ that is monotonically increasing.

Now suppose instead that $\{x_n\}_{n=1}^{\infty}$ does possess a largest element. Then the sequence possesses a monotonically decreasing sequence $\{z_k\}_{k=1}^{\infty}$ constructed as follows. For each $i \geq 1$ let $\max s_i$ be the largest element in s_i. Set $z_1 = \max s_1$ and denote this element by x_{m_1}. Then set $z_2 = \max s_{m_1}$ and denote this element by x_{m_2}. Clearly $z_1 \geq z_2$. Continue in this manner. The sequence $\{z_k\}_{k=1}^{\infty}$ is monotonically decreasing. $\square$

In the above proof we could equally well have said that the two cases to be considered are, first, that $\{x_n\}_{n=1}^{\infty}$ does not possess a minimal element and, second, that $\{x_n\}_{n=1}^{\infty}$ does possess a minimal element. You might like to "reprove" the theorem for these two cases. The statement of the theorem will not alter.

If we put together what we have learned about sequences of real numbers from Theorems 4.2, 4.3, and 4.4, then we immediately have a tremendously useful and famous theorem. Here it is. Proving it wasn't all that hard, was it?

Theorem 4.5 (Bolzano-Weierstrass). *Every bounded sequence of real numbers possesses at least one convergent subsequence.*

Remember our earlier example of the nonconvergent sequence of real numbers $\{0, 1, 0, 1, 0, 1, \ldots\}$? This is a bounded sequence, so it must possess at least one convergent subsequence. Actually it possesses lots of convergent subsequences. Here are just a few of them:

$$\{0, 0, 0, 0, 0, 0, 0, \ldots, 0, \ldots\} \to 0,$$
$$\{1, 1, 1, 1, 1, 1, 1, \ldots, 1, \ldots\} \to 1,$$
$$\{0, 1, 0, 0, 0, 0, 0, \ldots, 0, \ldots\} \to 0,$$
$$\text{and} \quad \{0, 0, 0, 1, 1, 1, 1, \ldots, 1, \ldots\} \to 1.$$

There are two types of subsequences that are especially useful when deciding if a sequence is, or is not, convergent. They are the *limit superior* subsequence and the *limit inferior* subsequence.

Definition 4.6 (Limit Superior and Limit Inferior). *The* limit superior *of a sequence* $\{x_n\}_{n=1}^{\infty}$ *with* $x_n \in \Re$ *for all* $n \geq 1$ *is*

$$\limsup x_n = \lim_{n \to \infty} \sup_{k \geq n} x_k. \tag{4.1}$$

The limit inferior *of the sequence* $\{x_n\}_{n=1}^{\infty}$ *is*

$$\liminf x_n = \lim_{n \to \infty} \inf_{k \geq n} x_k. \tag{4.2}$$

If the limit superior does not exist, then $\limsup x_n = +\infty$. *If the limit inferior does not exist, then* $\liminf x_n = -\infty$.

These two limits seem a bit odd at a first glance, but there is nothing difficult about either of them. Let's consider the limit superior first. From (4.1) we see that, for any given $n \geq 1$, we are asked to consider the subsequence $\{x_n, x_{n+1}, x_{n+2}, \ldots\}$ and then, for this particular subsequence, to discover its supremum (*i.e.* its least upper bound). So let's call this supremum $\bar{s}_n = \sup \{x_n, x_{n+1}, x_{n+2}, \ldots\}$. Then we do the same thing for the shorter subsequence $\{x_{n+1}, x_{n+2}, \ldots\}$; *i.e.* we discover the supremum $\bar{s}_{n+1} = \sup \{x_{n+1}, x_{n+2}, \ldots\}$. We keep doing this for each $n \geq 1$. As n increases we are evaluating the supremum of an ever smaller collection of elements of the original sequence $\{x_n\}_{n=1}^{\infty}$ so the sequence of these suprema is weakly decreasing: $\bar{s}_n \geq \bar{s}_{n+1}$ for every $n \geq 1$. Figure 4.1 will help you to understand the idea.

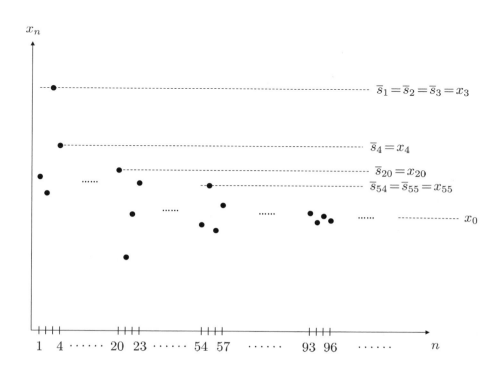

Figure 4.1: The limit superior of a sequence.

In Figure 4.1 you see plotted some of the elements x_n of the original sequence $\{x_n\}_{n=1}^{\infty}$. For $n = 1$ we evaluate $\bar{s}_1$, the supremum of every element of the original sequence. For $n = 2$ we evaluate the supremum $\bar{s}_2$ of a new sequence that is the original sequence without the element x_1. In the figure it happens that $\bar{s}_1 = \bar{s}_2$. We keep doing this for each value of n. By the time we reach $n = 20$, we are evaluating $\bar{s}_{20}$, the least upper bound on the sequence $\{x_{20}, x_{21}, \ldots\}$. In the figure $\bar{s}_{20}$ is smaller than $\bar{s}_1, \ldots, \bar{s}_{19}$ because the elements $x_1, \ldots, x_{19}$ of the original sequence are no longer being considered. As n continues to increase, the suprema $\bar{s}_n$ never increase and, in the figure, gradually fall in value towards a limiting value x_0. This limit of the sequence of suprema is the limit superior of the original sequence $\{x_n\}_{n=1}^{\infty}$; *i.e.* $x_0 = \lim_{n\to\infty} \overline{s}_n = \lim_{n\to\infty} \sup\{x_n, x_{n+1}, \ldots\} = \lim\sup x_n$.

The limit inferior of a sequence is very similar in concept to the limit superior of the sequence. We start by considering the infimum (*i.e.* greatest lower bound) of the subsequence $\{x_n, x_{n+1}, x_{n+2}, \ldots\}$. This is $\underline{s}_n = \inf\{x_n, x_{n+1}, x_{n+2}, \ldots\}$. Then we consider the sequence of these infima as $n \to \infty$. The limit of this sequence of infima is the limit inferior of the original sequence; $\lim_{n\to\infty} \underline{s}_n = \lim_{n\to\infty} \inf\{x_n, x_{n+1}, x_{n+2}, \ldots\} = \lim\inf x_n$.

It is possible, of course, that a particular sequence is not convergent. Even so, such a sequence might possess both a limit superior and a limit inferior. An obvious example is once again the sequence $\{1, -1, 1, -1, 1, -1, \ldots\}$. This is not a convergent sequence. Even so, the limit superior of the sequence is 1 and the limit inferior is -1. The fact that the limit superior and the limit inferior are not the same tells us that the sequence is not convergent.

Now consider again the convergent sequence $\{1, -1, \frac{1}{2}, -\frac{1}{2}, \frac{1}{3}, -\frac{1}{3}, \ldots\}$. I hope it is clear to you that the limit superior of this sequence is the limit of the sequence of suprema that is $\{1, \frac{1}{2}, \frac{1}{2}, \frac{1}{3}, \frac{1}{3}, \ldots\}$ and that the limit inferior of the sequence is the limit of the sequence of infima that is $\{-1, -1, -\frac{1}{2}, -\frac{1}{2}, -\frac{1}{3} \ldots\}$. The limits of both sequences are zero. Clearly the limit of the original sequence too is zero, so for this convergent sequence the limit superior, the limit inferior, and the limit are all the same value. This is, in fact, an alternative way of stating when a sequence is convergent.

Theorem 4.6. *Let (X, d) be a metric space and let $x_n \in X$ for all $n \geq 1$. Then the sequence $\{x_n\}_{n=1}^{\infty}$ is convergent if and only if $\lim\sup x_n = \lim\inf x_n$. The value of the limit of the sequence is $\lim_{n\to\infty} x_n = \lim\sup x_n = \lim\inf x_n$.*

4.5   Cauchy Sequences

According to our earlier definition of convergence of a sequence, you need to know the value of the limit x_0 of the sequence to establish if the sequence is convergent, for, if not, then how will you be able to measure the differences $d(x_k, x_0)$ and decide if these differences eventually shrink to zero as k increases? This is a Catch-22 situation. If I know the limit of a sequence, then I already know it is convergent and to what value. If I don't know the limit of a sequence, then I cannot check that the sequence converges and so I will not be able to discover the limit.

This seems to be most unsatisfactory, and I am sure that you are muttering to yourself that you don't really need to know the limit of a sequence in order to check that it is a convergent sequence. Perhaps you think that all you really need to check is that eventually the neighboring values in the sequence all become almost the same as each other, and get closer and closer in value as we move further and further along the sequence? Unfortunately that's not always true, as we will see, though I sympathize with what you have in mind, but a modification of your idea has proved to be most useful. It was given to us by the great French mathematician Augustin-Louis Cauchy, and now is the time to work it out for ourselves. Let's look at a few examples.

Sequences that are convergent can converge in various ways. Think about the following sequences.

$$s' = \left\{ 1, \frac{1}{2}, \frac{1}{3}, \frac{1}{4}, \frac{1}{5}, \ldots \right\},$$

$$s'' = \left\{ 1, -\frac{1}{2}, \frac{1}{3}, -\frac{1}{4}, \frac{1}{5}, \ldots \right\},$$

$$\text{and } s''' = \left\{ 1, 0, \frac{1}{2}, 0, 0, \frac{1}{3}, 0, 0, 0, \frac{1}{4}, 0, 0, 0, 0, \frac{1}{5}, \ldots \right\}.$$

All three of these sequences converge. All three converge to the same limit, zero. But the convergences occur in different ways. Of them all, the sequence s' can be judged to converge in the "smoothest" manner. As you travel along s', the elements stay positive and the distances $|(1/n) - (1/(n+1))|$ between neighboring elements all monotonically decrease towards zero. The sequence s'' also contains only elements that always get closer to zero, but the differences $|(1/n) + (1/(n+1))|$ between neighboring elements are greater than for s'. Even so, these differences also monotonically shrink towards zero as n increases. The sequence s''' consists of segments commencing with $1/n$ and followed by n zeros. In this case, as n increases there are longer and longer strings of zeros interspersed with smaller and smaller nonzero numbers $1/n$. Notice that the distance between neighboring zeros is zero and that the distance between any nonzero element $1/n$ and its zero neighbors is greater than zero. Thus the distances between neighboring elements of s''' do not monotonically decrease towards zero. But I'm sure that you were able quickly to deduce that each of the sequences converged, and converged to zero, even though I did not tell you that the value of each limit is zero. What was your reasoning? I'm ready to bet that you reasoned that, as you moved further and further along the sequence, the distance between *any* of the remaining elements of the sequence was generally getting smaller and eventually would be arbitrarily close to zero for *all* of the remaining elements. If so, then accept my congratulations because you have discovered the important idea of a *Cauchy sequence*.

Definition 4.7 (Cauchy Sequence). *Let (X, d) be a metric space. Let $\{x_n\}_{n=1}^{\infty}$ be a sequence of elements of X. If, for any positive $\varepsilon > 0$, there exists an integer $M(\varepsilon) \geq 1$ such that $d(x_i, x_j) < \varepsilon$ for all $i, j \geq M(\varepsilon)$, then the sequence is a Cauchy sequence with respect to d.*

What does all this mean? Here's the idea. Choose a value for $\varepsilon > 0$, say, $\varepsilon = \frac{1}{2}$. If a sequence is Cauchy, then there will be an element, the $M\left(\frac{1}{2}\right)^{\text{th}}$ element, in the sequence such that, for *every* pairing of elements selected from the $M\left(\frac{1}{2}\right)^{\text{th}}$ element and its successors, the distance between the pair of elements is *strictly* less than $\frac{1}{2}$. In sequence s', $M\left(\frac{1}{2}\right) = 2$. In sequence s'', $M\left(\frac{1}{2}\right) = 4$. In sequence s''', $M\left(\frac{1}{2}\right) = 4$. Now choose a smaller value for ε, say, $\varepsilon = \frac{1}{10}$. For sequence s', the distance between any pair of elements after the third element is strictly less than $\frac{1}{10}$ so $M\left(\frac{1}{10}\right) = 3$. For sequence s'', $M\left(\frac{1}{10}\right) = 20$. For sequence s''', $M\left(\frac{1}{10}\right) = 56$. The value that you select for ε is an upper bound on the distances that you will accept from all possible pairs of elements in the sequence. As you command ε to become nearer to zero, you are insisting that the elements of the "right-hand end" of the sequence *all* become closer to each other and thus closer to a common value. Typically this will happen only if you consider elements far enough along in the sequence, and so typically the value of $M(\varepsilon)$ rises as the value you impose on ε gets closer to zero. And since you can make the value of ε as close to zero as you like, it should be clear that any Cauchy sequence is a convergent sequence. Let's try a few more examples.

Is the sequence

$$\hat{s} = \{1, -1, 1, -1, 1, -1, \ldots\}$$

Cauchy or not? Think about it and come to a definite conclusion before reading any further.

For the sequence to be Cauchy, you must be able, for *any* $\varepsilon > 0$, to find an $M(\varepsilon)^{\text{th}}$ element such that all pairs of elements further along the sequence are distant by less than the value you chose for ε. Let's choose $\varepsilon = \frac{1}{2}$. Is there in $\hat{s}$ any element such that all later pairs of elements are distant from each other by less than $\frac{1}{2}$? No, there is not. No matter how far you look along the sequence, there will always be elements distant from each other by 2, which is not less than $\varepsilon = \frac{1}{2}$. Therefore $\hat{s}$ is not a Cauchy sequence.

Is the sequence

$$\tilde{s} = \left\{ 1, 1 + \frac{1}{2}, 1 + \frac{1}{2} + \frac{1}{3}, \ldots, \sum_{i=1}^{n} \frac{1}{i}, \ldots \right\}$$

a Cauchy sequence? Don't read on until you have a definite answer – this is an important example.

$\tilde{s}$ is not a Cauchy sequence. It is not even a convergent sequence. The trap (I hope you did not get caught in it) in this example is that the distance $d(x_n, x_{n+1}) = 1/(n+1)$ between an element in the sequence and its *immediate* neighbor monotonically decreases towards zero as n increases, and this might seem to suggest that the sequence is convergent. Not so. Looking at the distances between only neighboring elements does not tell you if a sequence is convergent. You need to look at the distances between *all* pairs of elements, not just neighbors. Suppose you choose $\varepsilon = 1/100$. If you look at, say, the 100th and 101st elements, then indeed the distance between these neighboring elements is $1/101 < 1/100$. But notice that the distance between the 100th and 102nd element is $1/101 + 1/102 = 203/10302 > 1/100$. In fact for any n the distance $d(x_n, x_k) = \sum_{i=n+1}^{k} 1/i$ strictly increases as $k > n$ increases and, moreover, has no upper bound. A sequence is Cauchy if and only if, for any positive bound ε (no matter how close to zero) placed on the distances between *all* pairs of successive elements, there is always an element in the sequence beyond which all of these pairwise distances are strictly less than ε. $\tilde{s}$ is a counterexample to the incorrect assertion that a sequence must converge if the distance between neighboring elements x_n and x_{n+1} goes to zero as $n \to \infty$.

What are the relationships between Cauchy sequences and convergent sequences? It should be reasonably easy to see that a convergent sequence must be a Cauchy sequence, but must every Cauchy sequence be convergent? The following theorem gives the answers. Have a look at the proofs. They are instructive and quite easy to follow.

Theorem 4.7. *Let (X, d) be a metric space. Let $\{x_n\}_{n=1}^{\infty}$ be a sequence of elements drawn from X.*

(i) $\{x_n\}_{n=1}^{\infty}$ is a convergent sequence only if it is a Cauchy sequence.

(ii) If $\{x_n\}_{n=1}^{\infty}$ is a Cauchy sequence, then it may not be convergent in X.

(iii) If $\{x_n\}_{n=1}^{\infty}$ is a Cauchy sequence, then it is a sequence that is bounded in X.

(iv) If $\{x_n\}_{n=1}^{\infty}$ is a Cauchy sequence that contains a subsequence that is convergent in X, then $\{x_n\}_{n=1}^{\infty}$ is also convergent in X and has the same limit as its subsequence.

Proof of (i). Since the sequence $\{x_n\}_{n=1}^{\infty}$ is convergent in X, there is an $x_0 \in X$ that is the limit of the sequence; $x_n \to x_0$. Therefore, for any $\varepsilon > 0$ there is an integer $M(\varepsilon/2)$ such that

$$d(x_n, x_0) < \frac{\varepsilon}{2} \text{ for every } n \geq M(\varepsilon/2).$$

Since d is a metric,

$$d(x_n, x_m) \leq d(x_n, x_0) + d(x_0, x_m) \text{ for every } n, m \geq 1,$$

and so, for $n, m > M(\varepsilon/2)$ in particular,

$$d(x_n, x_m) < \frac{\varepsilon}{2} + \frac{\varepsilon}{2} = \varepsilon.$$

That is, the sequence $\{x_n\}_{n=1}^{\infty}$ is Cauchy. □

Proof of (ii). An example suffices as a proof. Choose $X = [1, 2)$ and consider the sequence $\{x_n\}_{n=1}^{\infty}$, where $x_n = 2 - 1/n$ for $n = 1, 2, \ldots$. It is easily shown that this is a Cauchy sequence, but it does not converge since $2 \notin X$. □

Proof of (iii). $\{x_n\}_{n=1}^{\infty}$ is Cauchy. The task is to show that there is a ball of finite radius that contains every element of the sequence. Choose any $\varepsilon > 0$. Then there exists an integer $M(\varepsilon)$ such that $d(x_n, x_m) < \varepsilon$ for every $n, m \geq M(\varepsilon)$. Hence, for $n = M(\varepsilon)$ in particular,

$$d(x_{M(\varepsilon)}, x_m) < \varepsilon \text{ for every } m \geq M(\varepsilon),$$

and so

$$x_m \in B_d(x_{M(\varepsilon)}, \varepsilon) \text{ for every } m \geq M(\varepsilon).$$

Define

$$\rho \equiv \max \left\{ d(x_1, x_{M(\varepsilon)}), d(x_2, x_{M(\varepsilon)}), \ldots, d(x_{M(\varepsilon)-1}, x_{M(\varepsilon)}) \right\} + \mu,$$

where $\mu > 0$ is any positive real number. Then

$$x_m \in B_d(x_{M(\varepsilon)}, \rho) \text{ for every } m = 1, \ldots, M(\varepsilon) - 1.$$

Therefore

$$x_m \in B_d(x_{M(\varepsilon)}, \max \{\varepsilon, \rho\}) \text{ for every } m \geq 1.$$ □

Proof of (iv). $\{x_n\}_{n=1}^{\infty}$ is Cauchy. $\{x_{m_k}\}_{k=1}^{\infty}$ is a convergent subsequence of $\{x_n\}_{n=1}^{\infty}$. Let x_0 denote the limit of $\{x_{m_k}\}_{k=1}^{\infty}$. Then, for any $\varepsilon > 0$, there exists an integer $M_{x_m}(\varepsilon/2)$ such that

$$d(x_0, x_{m_k}) < \frac{\varepsilon}{2} \text{ for every } k \geq M_{x_m}(\varepsilon/2).$$

The integer $M_{x_m}(\varepsilon/2)$ is the number (position) of an element in $\{x_{m_k}\}_{k=1}^{\infty}$. Because $\{x_{m_k}\}_{k=1}^{\infty}$ is a subsequence of $\{x_n\}_{n=1}^{\infty}$, this element is also a member of $\{x_n\}_{n=1}^{\infty}$. Let

$M_x(\varepsilon/2)$ be the position of this element in $\{x_n\}_{n=1}^{\infty}$. $M_x(\varepsilon/2) \geq M_{x_m}(\varepsilon/2)$ because $\{x_{m_1}, x_{m_2}, \ldots\}$ is a subset of $\{x_1, x_2, \ldots\}$.

Since $\{x_n\}_{n=1}^{\infty}$ is a Cauchy sequence, for the same choice of ε there exists an integer $N_x(\varepsilon/2)$ such that

$$d(x_i, x_j) < \frac{\varepsilon}{2} \text{ for every } i, j \geq N_x(\varepsilon/2).$$

Since d is a metric,

$$d(x_0, x_i) \leq d(x_0, x_{m_k}) + d(x_{m_k}, x_i).$$

Define $M(\varepsilon) = \max\{M_x(\varepsilon/2), N_x(\varepsilon/2)\}$. Then, for every $i \geq M(\varepsilon)$,

$$d(x_0, x_i) < \frac{\varepsilon}{2} + \frac{\varepsilon}{2} = \varepsilon.$$

Therefore x_0 is also the limit of the sequence $\{x_n\}_{n=1}^{\infty}$. $\qquad\square$

Combining (i) and (iv) of the above theorem gives the following more commonly expressed statement.

Corollary 4.1. *Any subsequence of a convergent sequence is convergent and converges to the same limit as the parent sequence.*

In general not every Cauchy sequence in some space will converge to a point in that space – this we have already seen and discussed. However, there are spaces in which every possible Cauchy sequence does converge (to a point in that space). These are called *complete space*.

Definition 4.8 (Complete Metric Space). *Let (X, d) be a metric space. (X, d) is a complete metric space if and only if every Cauchy sequence in X is convergent in X with respect to d.*

You will no doubt be relieved to discover that the Euclidean metric spaces are all complete spaces.

4.6 Remarks

Most of the time economists work in Euclidean spaces where sequences and their limits, if they exist, often are used to establish whether sets are closed and whether functions are continuous. So, in the chapters that follow, which almost always develop ideas in Euclidean spaces, this is how we will use the ideas presented in this chapter, and we will do this a lot. As remarked at the end of Chapter 3, when analyzing constrained optimization problems, it is important to determine the properties of sets of available choices and whether or not the function that reveals a decisionmaker's valuations of available choices is continuous. Convergence of sequences is how we will try to determine when such properties are present.

The next chapter presents an explanation of various ideas of continuity of mappings. What sort of mappings would interest an economist? All sorts, is the answer. For example, economists talk of demand functions. These are mappings that report quantities demanded for given prices and incomes. How does quantity demanded change as, say, a particular price changes? Does quantity demanded change smoothly, for example, or does it jump suddenly? This is a continuity question. Perhaps you are familiar with determining the rate of change of quantity demanded as a price changes. Such rates of change are well defined if the demand function is differentiable and may not be defined otherwise. Differential rates of change do not exist for a function unless the function is continuous. I could make similar remarks for all sorts of functions that are important to economists. The point, then, is that continuity is a really important topic for economists interested in solving constrained optimization problems, and to talk of continuity we will often need to use sequences and limits.

4.7 Problems

Problem 4.1. Consider the sequence $\{x_i\}_{i=1}^\infty = \{1, 1+\frac{1}{2}, 1+\frac{2}{3}, \ldots, 1+\frac{i-1}{i}, \ldots\}$. For each $i = 1, 2, 3, \ldots$, let $\overline{s}_i = \sup\{1 + \frac{i-1}{i}, 1 + \frac{i}{i+1}, 1 + \frac{i+1}{i+2}, \ldots\}$ be the supremum of the elements $x_i, x_{i+1}, \ldots$ and let $\underline{s}_i = \inf\{1 + \frac{i-1}{i}, 1 + \frac{i}{i+1}, 1 + \frac{i+1}{i+2}, \ldots\}$ be their infimum.
(i) Prove that, with respect to the Euclidean metric on $\Re$, the sequence $\{x_i\}_{i=1}^\infty$ converges to 2.
(ii) What is the sequence $\{\overline{s}_i\}_{i=1}^\infty$? Does this sequence converge with respect to the Euclidean metric on $\Re$? If so, then to what limit? What is the value of the $\limsup x_i$?
(iii) What is the sequence $\{\underline{s}_i\}_{i=1}^\infty$? Does this sequence converge with respect to the Euclidean metric on $\Re$? If so, then to what limit? What is the value of the $\liminf x_i$?
(iv) Do the answers to parts (ii) and (iii) confirm that the sequence $\{x_i\}_{i=1}^\infty$ is convergent to 2? Explain.
(v) Prove that $\{x_i\}_{i=1}^\infty$ is a Cauchy sequence.

Problem 4.2. Consider the sequence $\{x_i\}_{i=1}^\infty$, in which $x_i = \sum_{j=1}^i \frac{1}{j}$. This sequence is monotonically increasing and is unbounded above, since $\sum_{j=1}^i \frac{1}{j} \to \infty$ as $i \to \infty$.
(i) Prove that the sequence $\{x_i\}_{i=1}^\infty$ is not convergent with respect to the Euclidean metric on $\Re$.
(ii) Prove that the sequence $\{x_i\}_{i=1}^\infty$ is not a Cauchy sequence with respect to the Euclidean metric on $\Re$.

Problem 4.3. Let $f : \Re \to \Re$ be a function with the property that,

$$\text{for any } x', x'' \in \Re, \ d_E(f(x'), f(x'')) \le \theta d_E(x', x''), \text{ where } 0 \le \theta < 1.$$

Such a mapping is called a *contraction with modulus* θ on $\Re$, with respect to the Euclidean metric, because the Euclidean distance between any two image values, $f(x')$ and $f(x'')$, is never larger than only a fraction θ of the Euclidean distance between the domain values x' and x''. In this sense, then, f "contracts" or "shrinks" distances. A simple example is $f(x) = \frac{1}{2}x$. The distance between any two domain values x' and x'' is $|x' - x''|$. The distance $|\frac{1}{2}x' - \frac{1}{2}x''| = \frac{1}{2}|x' - x''|$ between the image values $\frac{1}{2}x'$ and $\frac{1}{2}x''$ is only one-half of the distance between x' and x''. Thus $f(x) = \frac{1}{2}x$ is a contraction on $\Re$ with modulus $\theta = \frac{1}{2}$.

Start with any $x_1 \in \Re$. Then construct the infinite sequence $\{x_1, x_2, x_3, x_4, \ldots\}$, in which $x_{i+1} = f(x_i)$ for $i = 1, 2, 3, \ldots$. That is,

$$x_2 = f(x_1),$$
$$x_3 = f(x_2) = f(f(x_1)) = f^2(x_1),$$
$$x_4 = f(x_3) = f(f^2(x_1)) = f^3(x_1),$$

and so on. A useful example is the function $f(x) = x^{1/2} + 2$ defined for $x \geq 1$. This is a contraction with modulus $\theta = \frac{1}{2}$ on the interval $[1, \infty)$. So let us take $x_1' = 1$ as a starting value for our sequence. Then the first ten elements in the sequence are

$$x_1' = 1,$$
$$x_2' = f(1) = 1^{1/2} + 2 = 3,$$
$$x_3' = f(3) = 3^{1/2} + 2 \approx 3{\cdot}732050808,$$
$$x_4' = f(3{\cdot}732050808) = 3{\cdot}732050808^{1/2} + 2 \approx 3{\cdot}931851653,$$
$$x_5' = f(3{\cdot}931851653) = 3{\cdot}931851653^{1/2} + 2 \approx 3{\cdot}982889723,$$
$$x_6' = f(3{\cdot}982889723) = 3{\cdot}982889723^{1/2} + 2 \approx 3{\cdot}995717847,$$
$$x_7' = f(3{\cdot}995717847) = 3{\cdot}995717847^{1/2} + 2 \approx 3{\cdot}998929175,$$
$$x_8' = f(3{\cdot}998929175) = 3{\cdot}998929175^{1/2} + 2 \approx 3{\cdot}999732276,$$
$$x_9' = f(3{\cdot}999732276) = 3{\cdot}999732276^{1/2} + 2 \approx 3{\cdot}999933068, \quad \text{and}$$
$$x_{10}' = f(3{\cdot}999933068) = 3{\cdot}999933068^{1/2} + 2 \approx 3{\cdot}999983267.$$

This sequence converges to 4. Now let's try generating a new sequence, using the same function f, but from a quite different starting value $x_1'' = 300$. The first ten elements in this new sequence are

$$x_1'' = 300,$$
$$x_2'' = f(300) = 300^{1/2} + 2 \approx 19{\cdot}32050808,$$
$$x_3'' = f(19{\cdot}32050808) = 19{\cdot}32050808^{1/2} + 2 \approx 6{\cdot}395509991,$$
$$x_4'' = f(6{\cdot}395509991) = 6{\cdot}395509991^{1/2} + 2 \approx 4{\cdot}528934556,$$
$$x_5'' = f(4{\cdot}528934556) = 4{\cdot}528934556^{1/2} + 2 \approx 4{\cdot}128129356,$$
$$x_6'' = f(4{\cdot}128129356) = 4{\cdot}128129356^{1/2} + 2 \approx 4{\cdot}031779849,$$
$$x_7'' = f(4{\cdot}031779849) = 4{\cdot}031779849^{1/2} + 2 \approx 4{\cdot}007929244,$$
$$x_8'' = f(4{\cdot}007929244) = 4{\cdot}007929244^{1/2} + 2 \approx 4{\cdot}001981330,$$
$$x_9'' = f(4{\cdot}001981330) = 4{\cdot}001981330^{1/2} + 2 \approx 4{\cdot}000495271, \quad \text{and}$$
$$x_{10}'' = f(4{\cdot}000495271) = 4{\cdot}000495271^{1/2} + 2 \approx 4{\cdot}000123814.$$

This new sequence also converges to 4. In fact, no matter what starting value you take for x_1 from the set $[1, \infty)$, you will, using the above procedure, always create a sequence that converges to 4. Try it for yourself. We will explore why this is so a little later. For now it is enough to observe that the two sequences we have created are both convergent.

The examples we have just worked through are a special case of a much more general and very useful result. In the following parts of this question, we will establish that, if $f : \Re \mapsto \Re$ is a function that is a contraction with modulus θ, then the sequence $\{x_i\}_{i=1}^{\infty}$ that is generated by the algorithm $x_{i+1} = f(x_i)$ for $i \geq 1$ is a Cauchy sequence that converges to a limit $x_0 \in \Re$. This limit is the solution to the equation $x = f(x)$.

(i) Let $f : \Re \to \Re$ be a function that is a contraction with modulus θ on $\Re$ with respect to the Euclidean metric. $0 \leq \theta < 1$. Prove that the sequence $\{x_i\}_{i=1}^{\infty}$ is a Cauchy sequence.

(ii) Review the statements of Theorem 4.5 and parts (iii) and (iv) of Theorem 4.7. Then prove that the sequence $\{x_i\}_{i=1}^{\infty}$, in which $x_{i+1} = f(x_i)$ for $i \geq 1$, is convergent. Use x_0 to denote the limit of the sequence.

(iii) Prove that the limit x_0 of the sequence $\{x_i\}_{i=1}^{\infty}$ is the solution to the equation $x = f(x)$.

4.8   Answers

Answer to Problem 4.1.

(i) The Euclidean distance between any element x_i of the sequence and the number 2 is

$$d_E(x_i, 2) = |x_i - 2| = 2 - x_i = 1 - \frac{i-1}{i} = \frac{1}{i} \ .$$

Choose any $\varepsilon > 0$. Then,

$$d_E(x_i, 2) = \frac{1}{i} < \varepsilon \quad \text{if} \quad i > \frac{1}{\varepsilon} = M(\varepsilon).$$

Thus, for any value $\varepsilon > 0$, no matter how small, there is a finite number $M(\varepsilon) = 1/\varepsilon$ such that, for every $i > M(\varepsilon)$, every element x_i of the sequence is distant from 2 by less than ε. The sequence $\{x_i\}_{i=1}^{\infty}$ is therefore convergent to 2, with respect to the Euclidean metric on $\Re$; $\lim x_i = 2$.

(ii) For any $i = 1, 2, 3, \ldots$, the least upper bound for the sequence $\{1 + \frac{i-1}{i}, 1 + \frac{i}{i+1}, 1 + \frac{i+1}{i+2}, \ldots\}$ is the number 2. Thus $\bar{s}_i = 2$ for $i = 1, 2, 3, \ldots$. Clearly this constant-valued sequence converges to its limit of 2. Thus $\limsup x_i = 2$.

(iii) The sequence $\{1, 1 + \frac{1}{2}, 1 + \frac{2}{3}, \ldots, 1 + \frac{i-1}{i}, \ldots\}$ is strictly monotonically increasing, so for each $i = 1, 2, 3, \ldots$, the greatest lower bound of the subsequence $\{1 + \frac{i-1}{i}, 1 + $

$\frac{i}{i+1}, 1 + \frac{i+1}{i+2}, \dots\}$ is the first, smallest element; *i.e.* $\underline{s}_i = 1 + \frac{i-1}{i}$ for $i = 1, 2, 3, \dots$. The sequence of infima $\{\underline{s}_i\}_{i=1}^{\infty} = \{1 + \frac{i-1}{i}\}_{i=1}^{\infty}$ is identical to the original sequence $\{x_i\}_{i=1}^{\infty}$. We can therefore repeat the proof for part (i) to establish that the sequence $\{\underline{s}_i\}_{i=1}^{\infty}$ converges to 2. Thus $\liminf x_i = 2$.

(iv) The sequence $\{x_i\}_{i=1}^{\infty}$ is convergent if and only if $\liminf x_i = \limsup x_i$. This is so, since $\liminf x_i = \limsup x_i = 2$. This confirms that $\lim x_i = 2$.

(v) The Euclidean distance between any pair of elements x_i and x_j in the sequence is

$$d_E(x_i, x_j) = |x_i - x_j| = \left| \frac{i-1}{i} - \frac{j-1}{j} \right| = \left| \frac{1}{j} - \frac{1}{i} \right|.$$

Choose any $\varepsilon > 0$, no matter how small. Then, for $i, j > 2/\varepsilon$,

$$\left| \frac{1}{j} - \frac{1}{i} \right| < \frac{1}{j} + \frac{1}{i} < \frac{\varepsilon}{2} + \frac{\varepsilon}{2} = \varepsilon,$$

so $d(x_i, x_j) < \varepsilon$ for all $i, j > M(\varepsilon) = 2/\varepsilon$. $\{x_i\}_{i=1}^{\infty}$ is therefore a Cauchy sequence. $\square$

Answer to Problem 4.2.

(i) Suppose that the sequence $\{x_i\}_{i=1}^{\infty}$ does have a limit; call it x_0. The Euclidean distance between the fixed number x_0 and the ith element in the sequence is

$$d_E(x_i, x_0) = |x_i - x_0| = \left| \sum_{j=1}^{i} \frac{1}{j} - x_0 \right| \to \infty \text{ as } i \to \infty$$

because $\sum_{j=1}^{i} \frac{1}{j} \to \infty$ as $i \to \infty$. Therefore, for any $\varepsilon > 0$ there does not exist any integer $M(\varepsilon)$ such that $d_E(x_i, x_0) < \varepsilon$ for all $i > M(\varepsilon)$. That is, $\{x_i\}_{i=1}^{\infty}$ is not convergent.

(ii) Without loss of generality, suppose that $i > k$. The Euclidean distance between the ith and k^{th} elements in the sequence is

$$d_E(x_i, x_k) = |x_i - x_k| = \left| \sum_{j=1}^{i} \frac{1}{j} - \sum_{j=1}^{k} \frac{1}{j} \right| = \sum_{j=k+1}^{i} \frac{1}{j} \to \infty \text{ as } i \to \infty.$$

Therefore, for any $\varepsilon > 0$, there does not exist any integer $M(\varepsilon)$ such that $d_E(x_i, x_k) < \varepsilon$ for all $i, k > M(\varepsilon)$. That is, $\{x_i\}_{i=1}^{\infty}$ is not a Cauchy sequence. $\square$

Answer to Problem 4.3.

(i) Choose any initial element $x_1 \in \Re$ and then generate the sequence $\{x_i\}_{i=1}^{\infty}$ using the algorithm that $x_{i+1} = f(x_i)$ for $i \geq 1$. The sequence $\{x_i\}_{i=1}^{\infty}$ is a Cauchy sequence if and only if, for any $\varepsilon > 0$, there exists an integer $M(\varepsilon)$ such that $d(x_i, x_j) < \varepsilon$ for every $i, j \geq M(\varepsilon)$.

Choose any $i \geq 2$. Then, since f is a contraction with modulus θ,

$$d_E(x_i, x_{i+1}) = d_E(f(x_{i-1}), f(x_i)) \leq \theta d_E(x_{i-1}, x_i)$$

and, similarly,

$$d_E(x_{i-1}, x_i) = d_E(f(x_{i-2}), f(x_{i-1})) \leq \theta d_E(x_{i-2}, x_{i-1}),$$

and so on. Thus

$$d_E(x_i, x_{i+1}) \leq \theta d_E(x_{i-1}, x_i) \leq \theta^2 d_E(x_{i-2}, x_{i-1}) \leq \cdots \leq \theta^{i-1} d_E(x_1, x_2). \qquad (4.3)$$

Choose any i and k with $i \neq k$. Without loss of generality, suppose that $i < k$, so that we may write $k = i + \Delta$ with $\Delta \geq 1$. By repeated applications of the triangular property of the metric function d_E,

$$d_E(x_i, x_{i+\Delta}) \leq d_E(x_i, x_{i+1}) + d_E(x_{i+1}, x_{i+2}) + \cdots + d_E(x_{i+\Delta-1}, x_{i+\Delta}). \qquad (4.4)$$

Using (4.3) term by term in (4.4) gives

$$d_E(x_i, x_{i+\Delta}) \leq d_E(x_1, x_2) \left(\theta^{i-1} + \theta^i + \cdots + \theta^{i+\Delta-2} \right) = \frac{\theta^{i-1}}{1 - \theta}(1 - \theta^\Delta) d_E(x_1, x_2).$$

$0 \leq \theta < 1$, so $\theta^{i-1} \to 0$ as $i \to \infty$. Hence, for any $\varepsilon > 0$, there is a value $\Delta(\varepsilon)$ for Δ, and thus a value $M(\varepsilon) = i + \Delta(\varepsilon)$, such that $d(x_i, x_k) < \varepsilon$ for all $i, k > M(\varepsilon)$. $\{x_i\}_{i=1}^\infty$ is therefore a Cauchy sequence.

(ii) First, note from part (iii) of Theorem 4.7 that any Cauchy sequence of real numbers is a bounded sequence. Then, from part (i) of this answer, we know that $\{x_i\}_{i=1}^\infty$ is a bounded sequence. The Bolzano-Weierstrass Theorem (Theorem 4.5) then tells us that our bounded sequence $\{x_i\}_{i=1}^\infty$ possesses a convergent subsequence. Finally, part (iv) of Theorem 4.7 tells us that our Cauchy sequence $\{x_i\}_{i=1}^\infty$ is convergent because it possesses a convergent subsequence.

(iii) The sequence is constructed using the algorithm that $x_{i+1} = f(x_i)$ for all $i \geq 1$. (4.3) shows that $d_E(x_i, x_{i+1}) = d_E(x_i, f(x_i)) \to 0$ as $i \to \infty$. Therefore the limit x_0 has the property that $d_E(x_0, f(x_0)) = 0$, which implies that $x_0 = f(x_0)$. $\qquad \square$

Problem 4.3 is a special case of *Banach's Fixed-Point Theorem*, a result of huge practical importance that was given to us in 1922 by the famous Polish mathematician

Stefan Banach. It is worth spending a few moments to understand why this result matters. Then, if you want more information about the theorem and its many uses, you can look elsewhere. One of my favorite references is Chapter 3 of Franklin 2002. The solution to an equation $x = f(x)$ is called a *fixed-point for f*. This might seem like a rather special equation, but it is not. In fact, the solution to any equation $g(x) = 0$ can be converted easily into a fixed-point equation. All we do is define $f(x) \equiv g(x) + x$. Then the generic equation $g(x) = 0$ has the same solution as the fixed-point equation $f(x) = g(x) + x = x$. So one way to think of solving any equation at all is to convert the equation into a fixed-point equation, and then use some fixed-point solution algorithm, like Banach's theorem, to compute numerically the value of the solution. Banach's Theorem applies only to contraction mappings, but there are simple ways to convert almost any mapping into a local contraction, so the theorem is more widely applicable than might at first be thought. Also, the theorem applies not just to mappings from and to the real line but to mappings in any *Banach space*; *i.e.* a complete and normed space. The Euclidean metric spaces are all Banach spaces, but there are all sorts of other Banach spaces, including some very important function spaces, so there is an enormous set of applications for Banach's wonderful theorem.

Chapter 5

Continuity

This chapter presents and explains four notions of continuity: *continuity, joint continuity, hemi-continuity,* and *semi-continuity.* By necessity it is a chapter that extensively uses the ideas of open sets, sequences and limits. Therefore, if you need to review these ideas, you should do so before proceeding into this chapter.

Most economists like to think that a small change to some economic policy variable, such as an interest rate or a tax rate, will result in only a small change to things that matter in the economy, such as incomes, quantities traded, total production, exchange rates, and so on. If this is true, then the relationships (mappings) between policy variables such as interest rates and tax rates, and outcome variables such as incomes and consumption levels, are continuous. But must this be so? Is it not possible, perhaps, that a small change to an interest rate could cause a sudden large change to incomes? Certainly an economist wants to know if this is so. In other words, every economist wants to know if important economic relationships are continuous mappings. It's a big idea.

How much of this chapter should you read? You can read the chapters dealing with constrained optimization without knowing anything about joint continuity, hemi-continuity, and semi-continuity. The only idea of continuity you need for those chapters is the continuity of a real-valued function. If you also want to understand the chapter on the properties of optimal solution correspondences, then you need to understand the ideas of joint continuity and hemi-continuity. That means reading just about everything in this chapter. So, you choose. Read what you want or need. You can always come back to this chapter if later on you find it necessary to do so.

Let us begin by defining some basic ideas. The first is the idea of a *map* or *mapping.* These terms mean the same thing, so we will use only "mapping." A mapping is a

145

"rule of association," meaning that a mapping associates an element from one set X with an element, or a subset of elements, in another set Y. X, the set that is mapped from, is called the *domain* of the mapping. Y, the set that is mapped to, is called the *codomain* of the mapping. You have met these ideas many times before now. We need be careful with some terminology that we will use in this and later chapters. Mathematicians have a variety of names for different types of mappings. Unfortunately the usage of some of these names seems to have changed over time, with some names replacing others and meanings changing. It gets confusing, so let's take a little time to define what *in this book* is meant by the terms that will matter to us.

5.1   Basic Ideas about Mappings

We will talk of two types of mappings: *functions* and *correspondences*. Let's start with the simpler of the two.

Definition 5.1 (Function). *A mapping from X to Y is a* function *if each element $x \in X$ is associated with (mapped to) a unique element $y \in Y$.*

A function is thus a "single-valued" mapping from an element of X to an element of Y. An example is the rule of association that maps x to $y = 2x$; a given value for x is mapped to only a single value for y. We will typically use lower-case letters such as f and g to denote functions. The mathematical way of writing the statement that a function f maps from a set X to a set Y is $f : X \mapsto Y$.

The rule of association that maps $x \geq 0$ to $\sqrt{x}$ is not a function since, for example, $x = 4$ is mapped to more than one value; $\sqrt{4} = \pm 2$. It would be more accurate, then, to say that the element $x = 4$ is mapped to the *set* $\{-2, +2\}$. This is an example of a mapping from an element in one set X to a subset of another set Y. We will call such a mapping a correspondence.

Definition 5.2 (Correspondence). *A mapping from X to Y is a* correspondence *if each element $x \in X$ is associated with (mapped to) a unique subset of Y.*

A correspondence is also a "single-valued" mapping in the sense that an element $x \in X$ is mapped to just *one subset* of Y. But this one subset of Y can contain many elements of Y, so you can think of a correspondence as allowing a single element in X to be mapped to *one or more elements* in Y. There are correspondences for which any element $x \in X$ is mapped to just a singleton subset of Y. There is no significant difference between such a correspondence and a function. Mappings that are correspondences typically will be denoted by capital letters such as F and G. The statement that a correspondence F maps from a set X to a set Y is just as for a function: $F : X \mapsto Y$. An example of a correspondence $F : \Re \mapsto \Re$ is $F(x) = [x, x+1]$. A domain element x is mapped to (associated with) the interval from x to $x + 1$ in the codomain. The set $[x, x + 1]$ is unique for given x, but contains many codomain elements.

To define a mapping completely we must specify both which elements in X are mapped from and which elements in Y are mapped to. These are called the *domain* and the *range* of the mapping.

The domain of a function f is the collection of all of the elements x that are actually mapped from by f.

Definition 5.3 (Domain of a Function). *The* domain of a function f *is*

$$\{x \in X \mid \text{there exists } y \in Y \text{ with } y = f(x)\}.$$

For example, if $Y = \Re$, then the domain of the function $f(x) = +\sqrt{x}$ (the "+" means take only the nonnegative square root) is the set of all of the nonnegative real numbers, $\Re_+$, and is not the entire real line (complex numbers are not allowed because $Y = \Re$ contains only real numbers).

Before we can talk of the domain of a correspondence, we must consider what subsets can be created from the set Y. The collection of all of the subsets that can be created from the elements of Y is the discrete topology on Y (also called the *power set* of Y), which we will denote by $\mathcal{P}(Y)$. The domain of a correspondence mapping from X to Y is the collection of all of the elements in X that are mapped to some nonempty subset of Y; *i.e.* to some member of $\mathcal{P}(Y)$ other than the empty set.

Definition 5.4 (Domain of a Correspondence). *The* domain of a correspondence F *is*

$$\{x \in X \mid F(x) \in \mathcal{P}(Y) \setminus \emptyset\}.$$

For example, if $Y = \Re$ the domain of the correspondence $F(x) = \{-\sqrt{x}, +\sqrt{x}\}$ is the set $\Re_+$ of the nonnegative real numbers. The $\setminus \emptyset$ bit of the above statement means "excluding the empty set."

The image or range of a function is the collection of all of the elements of Y that are mapped to by the function for at least one element in its domain.

Definition 5.5 (Image/Range of a Function). *The* image *or* range *of a function* $f : X \mapsto Y$ *is*

$$f(X) = \{y \in Y \mid y = f(x) \text{ for at least one } x \in X\} = \bigcup_{x \in X} \{f(x)\}.$$

Similarly, the range of a correspondence F is the collection of all of the elements in all of the subsets in $\mathcal{P}(Y)$ that are actually mapped to by F.

Definition 5.6 (Image/Range of a Correspondence). *The* image *or* range *of a correspondence* $F : X \mapsto Y$ *is*

$$F(X) = \bigcup_{x \in X} \{y \in Y \mid y \in F(x)\}.$$

For example, the image or range of the correspondence $F(x) = \pm\sqrt{x}$, where the square roots must be real numbers, is the union of the entire collection of pairs $\{(-\sqrt{x}, +\sqrt{x}) \mid x \geq 0\}$; *i.e.* the image or range is the entire real line $\Re$. We will use the terms image and range of a mapping interchangeably throughout the rest of this book.

It is possible that the range of a mapping is a strict subset of the mapping's codomain, but it is also possible that the range and the codomain are the same set. Special language distinguishes these two cases.

Definition 5.7 (Onto/Surjective Mapping). *A function* $f : X \mapsto Y$ *is called* onto *or* surjective *if* $Y = f(X)$. *A correspondence* $F : X \mapsto Y$ *is called* onto *or* surjective *if* $Y = F(X)$.

When a mapping is onto/surjective, every element in the codomain is mapped to by at least one element in the domain. Stated loosely, there are no "surplus" elements in the codomain. Consider, for example, the correspondence $F : [0, 1] \mapsto [0, 10]$ that is defined by

$$F(x) = [x + 1, x + 2] \text{ for } 0 \leq x \leq 1. \tag{5.1}$$

The image of F is $F([0, 1]) = [1, 3]$. There is no $x \in X = [0, 1]$ that maps to any of the codomain elements in $[0, 1) \cup (3, 10]$; these are "surplus" elements in the codomain $Y = [0, 10]$. F is not onto/surjective. If the correspondence (5.1) is instead defined as $F : [0, 1] \mapsto [1, 3]$, then it is onto/surjective.

It is also helpful to understand the meaning of terms such as *one-to-one* and *injective*.

Definition 5.8 (One-to-One or Injective Mapping). *A function $f : X \mapsto Y$ is called* one-to-one *or* injective *if*

$$\forall \, x', x'' \in X \text{ with } x' \neq x'', \quad f(x') \neq f(x'').$$

A correspondence $F : X \mapsto Y$ is called one-to-one *or* injective *if*

$$\forall \, x', x'' \in X \text{ with } x' \neq x'', \quad F(x') \cap F(x'') = \emptyset.$$

That is, when a mapping is one-to-one, each element in its domain is uniquely mapped to a distinct element, or a distinct set of elements, in its range. In other words, any element y in the image of the mapping is reached from only one element in the domain of the mapping. Is the correspondence (5.1) injective? For each $x \in [0, 1]$, the image $F(x)$ is uniquely the set $[x + 1, x + 2]$. But this does not make F injective. Why? Consider the range element $y = 2$. This is mapped to by every one of the elements in the domain $[0, 1]$; *i.e.* $2 \in [x + 1, x + 2]$ for every $x \in [0, 1]$. Thus F is not injective. In contrast, the correspondence $G : \Re_+ \mapsto \Re$ where $G(x) = \{-\sqrt{x}, +\sqrt{x}\}$ is injective because, for $x' \neq x''$, the images $G(x')$ and $G(x'')$ have no common element; $\{-\sqrt{x'}, +\sqrt{x'}\} \cap \{-\sqrt{x''}, +\sqrt{x''}\} = \emptyset$.

Definition 5.9 (Bijective Mapping). *A mapping is* bijective *if it is both surjective and injective.*

Clearly bijective mappings are special one-to-one mappings. Consider the function $f : \Re_+ \mapsto \Re$ that is defined by

$$f(x) = \frac{1}{1 + x} \, .$$

The image of f is the interval $(0, 1]$. The codomain of f is specified as $\Re$ and obviously $(0, 1]$ is a strict subset of $\Re$. Thus f is injective but it is not surjective, so f is not bijective. Now consider the function $g : \Re_+ \mapsto (0, 1]$ that is defined by the same equation as for f. The image and the codomain of g are the same, $(0, 1]$, so g is surjective. We already know that g is injective, so g is bijective.

The last idea that we need for now is that of the *graph* of a mapping.

Definition 5.10 (Graph of a Mapping). *The* graph *of a function $f : X \mapsto Y$ is*

$$G_f = \{(x, y) \mid x \in X \text{ and } y = f(x)\}.$$

The graph *of a correspondence $F : X \mapsto Y$ is*

$$G_F = \{(x, y) \mid x \in X \text{ and } y \in F(x)\}.$$

The graph of a mapping f or F is a subset of the direct product $X \times Y$ of the domain and the codomain of the mapping. Some examples will help to make the idea clear. Start with the function $f : [0, 2] \mapsto [1, 3]$ that is defined by $f(x) = x + 1$. The graph of f is the subset of $[0, 2] \times [1, 3] \subset \Re^2$ that is

$$G_f = \{(x, y) \mid 0 \leq x \leq 2 \text{ and } y = x + 1\}.$$

This set of pairs is the straight line in $\Re^2$ with endpoints at $(0, 1)$ and $(2, 3)$; see the left-side panel of Figure 5.1. Now consider the correspondence $F : [1, 3] \mapsto [1, 4]$ that is defined by $F(x) = [x, x + 1]$. The graph of F is the subset of $[1, 3] \times [1, 4] \subset \Re^2$ that is

$$G_F = \{(x, y) \mid 1 \leq x \leq 3 \text{ and } x \leq y \leq x + 1\}.$$

This is the set of points in the parallelogram with vertices at $(1, 1)$, $(1, 2)$, $(3, 3)$, and $(3, 4)$; see the right-side panel of Figure 5.1.

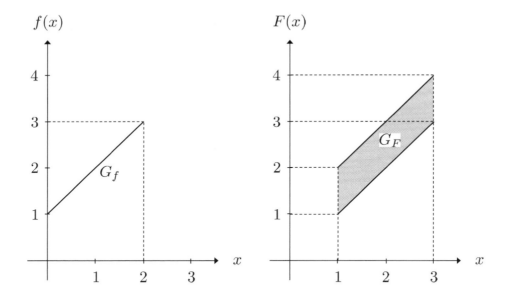

Figure 5.1: The graphs of f and F.

5.2   Continuity

Now let us turn to the idea of the continuity of a mapping. What does it mean to say that a mapping F is continuous at some point x_0 in its domain? We consider only slight movements from x_0 to close by values, say, x' and x''. Continuity of F means that the sets $F(x_0)$, $F(x')$ and $F(x'')$ must be almost the same or, if you prefer, because x' and x'' are close to x_0 the sets $F(x')$ and $F(x'')$ cannot be "suddenly different" from $F(x_0)$. This description is valid for mappings from real spaces to real spaces, and it is only these mappings that we will concentrate upon in this book. But before doing so, let's realize that continuity is an idea that is much more widely applicable.

We must start with a definition of continuity. As you will see in a moment, continuity of a mapping is an idea that depends upon specifications of topologies on the domain and the range of the mapping.

Definition 5.11 (Continuous Mapping). *Let $(X, \mathcal{T}_X)$ and $(Y, \mathcal{T}_Y)$ be topological spaces. Let the function $f : X \mapsto Y$. Let the correspondence $F : X \mapsto Y$.*

Relative to $(X, \mathcal{T}_X)$ and $(Y, \mathcal{T}_Y)$, f is continuous *on X if and only if, for every set $O \subset Y$ that is open with respect to $\mathcal{T}_Y$, the set $f^{-1}(O)$ is open with respect to $\mathcal{T}_X$.*

Relative to $(X, \mathcal{T}_X)$ and $(Y, \mathcal{T}_Y)$, F is continuous *on X if and only if, for every set $O \subset Y$ that is open with respect to $\mathcal{T}_Y$, the set $F^{-1}(O)$ is open with respect to $\mathcal{T}_X$.*

Let's build a weird example to get a better idea of the wide applicability of the idea of continuity. Let $X = \{$popcorn, blue, Rome$\}$. Let $Y = \{$shoes, radio, pansy$\}$.

$$\mathcal{T}(X) = \{\emptyset, \{\text{popcorn}\}, \{\text{blue}\}, \{\text{Rome }\}, \{\text{popcorn, blue}\}, \{\text{popcorn, Rome}\},$$
$$\{\text{blue, Rome}\}, \{\text{popcorn, blue, Rome}\}\}$$

is a topology on X, so all of the sets in the collection $\mathcal{T}(X)$ are open with respect to this topology. Similarly,

$$\mathcal{T}(Y) = \{\emptyset, \{\text{radio}\}, \{\text{shoes, radio}\}, \{\text{radio, pansy}\}, \{\text{shoes, radio, pansy}\}\}$$

is a topology on Y, so all of the sets in $\mathcal{T}(Y)$ are open with respect to $\mathcal{T}(Y)$. Now let's define the correspondence $F : X \mapsto Y$ as follows:

$$F(x) = \begin{cases} \{\text{radio}\} & , \ x = \text{blue} \\ \{\text{shoes, radio}\} & , \ x = \text{popcorn} \\ \{\text{radio, pansy}\} & , \ x = \text{Rome}. \end{cases}$$

Strange as it may seem at first glance, F is a correspondence that is continuous with respect to the topology $\mathcal{T}(X)$ on the domain X and the topology $\mathcal{T}(Y)$ on the codomain Y. Why? The set {radio} is open with respect to the codomain topology $\mathcal{T}(Y)$. The inverse image of this set is $F^{-1}(\{radio\}) = \{blue\}$, which is a set that is open with respect to the domain topology $\mathcal{T}(X)$. Next, the set {shoes, radio} is open with respect to the codomain topology $\mathcal{T}(Y)$. The inverse image of this set is $F^{-1}(\{shoes, radio\}) = \{popcorn\}$, which is a set that is open with respect to the domain topology $\mathcal{T}(X)$. Finally, the set {radio, pansy} is open with respect to the codomain topology $\mathcal{T}(Y)$. The inverse image of this set is $F^{-1}(\{radio, pansy\}) = \{Rome\}$, which is a set that is open with respect to the domain topology $\mathcal{T}(X)$. F satisfies Definition 5.11 and so is a continuous correspondence relative to the two given topologies. Fun though this example might be, we will spend most of our time thinking about continuity in cases where both the domain X and the codomain Y are *metrizable* (meaning that a metric function can be defined upon X and a, possibly different, metric function can be defined on Y).

Most of us are introduced to continuity in a case that is special for two reasons. First, the mappings are functions and, second, the mappings are from some real space to another real space, so think of a function $f : \Re^n \mapsto \Re^m$. The Euclidean metric d_E can be used to measure distances on both of these spaces. When we do so, we have constructed the Euclidean metric spaces $(\Re^n, d_E) \equiv E^n$ and $(\Re^m, d_E) \equiv E^m$. The typical basis element of the Euclidean metric topology for E^n is a ball (open, of course) $B(x, \varepsilon)$ of radius $\varepsilon > 0$ centered at a point $x \in X$. This ball is the set of all points that are distant (as measured by d_E) from x by strictly less than ε:

$$B(x, \varepsilon) = \{x' \in X \mid d_E(x, x') < \varepsilon\}.$$

The topology on X that is induced by the metric d_E is constructed by taking all possible unions of all of the balls $B(x, \varepsilon)$ for every $x \in X$ and for every $\varepsilon > 0$. Thus every point in a set that is open with respect to the Euclidean metric topology on X is surrounded by at least one such ball, and that ball is itself entirely within the open set. Similar statements apply to any set that is open with respect to the Euclidean metric topology on Y. This allows the following more familiar statement that is equivalent to Definition 5.11 when we restrict ourselves only to functions f mapping from one Euclidean metric space to another Euclidean metric space.

Definition 5.12 (Continuous Function in Euclidean Metric Spaces). *Let $X \subseteq \Re^n$ and $Y \subseteq \Re^m$. Let $f : X \mapsto Y$ be a function. With respect to the Euclidean metric topologies on $\Re^n$ and $\Re^m$, f is continuous at $x_0 \in X$ if and only if, for each $\varepsilon > 0$,* *there exists $\delta > 0$ such that*

$$d_E(x_0, x') < \delta \quad \Rightarrow \quad d_E(f(x_0), f(x')) < \varepsilon.$$

f is continuous on X if and only if f is continuous at every $x \in X$.

A lot of people find this statement hard to read, but really it is not. What it says is that, if x' is "close" to x_0 (distant from x_0 by less than δ), then the images $f(x')$ and $f(x_0)$ must also be close to each other (distant from each other by less than ε), and this "closeness" may be made as severe as one likes by making ε ever closer to zero. Put another way, the statement says that there cannot be a "break" or a "jump" in the graph of the function at the point $(x_0, f(x_0))$. Why? Because the statement says that a small distance between x' and x_0 cannot result in a big distance between $f(x')$ and $f(x_0)$. The idea is illustrated in Figure 5.2.

Any small distance between x_0 and any nearby x' causes only a small distance between the images $f(x_0)$ and $f(x')$; *i.e.* f is continuous at x_0.

For at least one x'' that is only a small distance from x_0 the distance between the images $f(x_0)$ and $f(x'')$ is not small; *i.e.* f is discontinuous at x_0.

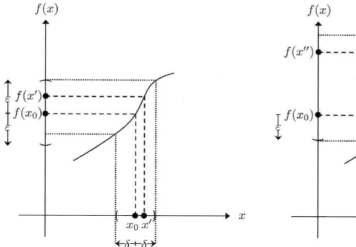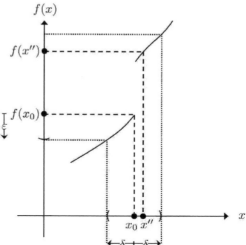

Figure 5.2: In the left-side panel, f is continuous at $x = x_0$. In the right-side panel, f is discontinuous at $x = x_0$.

We start by choosing *any* (possibly very small) strictly positive value for ε. We then look at all of the image values $f(x)$ that are in the codomain of f and are distant from $f(x_0)$ by less than ε. In the left-side panel of the figure, all of these image values are contained in the vertical axis interval $(f(x_0) - \varepsilon, f(x_0) + \varepsilon)$. In the right-side panel, all of these image values are contained in the vertical axis interval $(f(x_0) - \varepsilon, f(x_0)]$. Then we ask, "Is there a strictly positive number δ (not necessarily small) such that all of the x-values in the interval $(x_0 - \delta, x_0 + \delta)$ provide image values $f(x)$ that are not distant from $f(x_0)$ by ε or more?" For the function displayed in the left-side panel, the answer is "Yes." You see there displayed on the horizontal axis an interval $(x_0 - \delta, x_0 + \delta)$ with the property that, for any $x' \in (x_0 - \delta, x_0 + \delta)$, the distance between $f(x')$ and $f(x_0)$ is less than ε. No matter what value we choose for ε, the answer to the question will always be "Yes." In the right-side panel, there is at least one strictly positive value for ε such that the answer is "No." For the value chosen for ε in the right-side panel, there does not exist any strictly positive value for δ such that $f(x)$ is distant from $f(x_0)$ by less than ε for *every* value $x \in (x_0 - \varepsilon, x_0 + \varepsilon)$. There are values x'' larger than x_0 and distant from x_0 by less than δ with image values $f(x'')$ that are distant from $f(x_0)$ by more than ε. The source of the problem is the "jump" in the value of the function at $x = x_0$. Such a function is thus discontinuous at $x = x_0$.

It is important to understand that Definition 5.12 makes exactly the same statement as Definition 5.11 when the mapping being considered is a function that maps from one Euclidean metric space to another. Why is this so? Definition 5.12 says to choose a point x_0 and to choose a strictly positive distance ε. This allows us to define the ball (in the codomain $\Re^m$ of f),

$$B_Y(f(x_0), \varepsilon/2) = \{y \in Y \mid d_E(f(x_0), y) < \varepsilon/2\}.$$

This ball is a set that is open with respect to the Euclidean metric topology on $\Re^m$. The ball contains all points in Y that are distant from $f(x_0)$ by less than the given value $\varepsilon/2$. From Definition 5.11, f is continuous at x_0 if and only if the inverse image of the open set $B_Y(f(x_0), \varepsilon/2)$ is a subset of X that is open with respect to the Euclidean metric topology on the domain $\Re^n$. Necessarily, $x_0 \in f^{-1}(B_Y(f(x_0), \varepsilon/2))$, and so, because $f^{-1}(B_Y(f(x_0), \varepsilon/2))$ is an open set, there must exist a ball of some strictly positive radius $\delta/2$ containing all the points in X that are distant from x_0 by strictly less than $\delta/2$. This is the ball (in the domain of f),

$$B_X(x_0, \delta/2) = \{x \in X \mid d_E(x_0, x) < \delta/2\}.$$

Now note that, if we take any two points $x', x'' \in B_X(x_0, \delta/2)$, then, by the triangular inequality property of a metric function, the distance between x' and x'' is

$$d_E(x', x'') \leq d_E(x', x_0) + d_E(x_0, x'') < \frac{\delta}{2} + \frac{\delta}{2} = \delta.$$

$x', x'' \in B_X(x_0, \delta/2)$ if and only if $f(x')$ and $f(x'')$ both are elements of $B_Y(f(x_0), \varepsilon/2)$, so, again by the triangular inequality property of a metric function, the distance between $f(x')$ and $f(x'')$ is

$$d_E(f(x'), f(x'')) \le d_E(f(x'), f(x_0)) + d_E(f(x_0), f(x'')) < \frac{\varepsilon}{2} + \frac{\varepsilon}{2} = \varepsilon.$$

Hence,

$$d_E(x', x'') < \delta \quad \Rightarrow \quad d_E(f(x'), f(x'')) < \varepsilon.$$

This is the statement made in Definition 5.12. The two definitions coincide because sets that are open with respect to Euclidean topologies are always unions of (open) balls. In other topologies this need not be so; in any such case, Definition 5.12 is not equivalent to Definition 5.11.

5.3 Semi-Continuity and Continuity

Like full continuity, the ideas of lower-semi-continuity and upper-semi-continuity are defined with respect to topologies. However, they are much more restrictive than is continuity. Upper-semi-continuity and lower-semi-continuity are ideas that apply only to functions and, particularly, only to real-valued functions.

Definition 5.13 (Upper-Semi-Continuous Function). *Let $(X, \mathcal{T}_X)$ be a topological space. Let $Y \subset \Re$. Let $f : X \mapsto Y$ be a function. Relative to $\mathcal{T}_X$ and the Euclidean metric topology on the real line, f is* upper-semi-continuous *at $x_0 \in X$ if and only if the set $\{x \in X \mid f(x) < f(x_0)\}$ is open with respect to $\mathcal{T}_X$. f is* upper-semi-continuous *on X if and only if f is upper-semi-continuous at every $x \in X$.*

Definition 5.14 (Lower-Semi-Continuous Function). *Let $(X, \mathcal{T}_X)$ be a topological space. Let $Y \subset \Re$. Let $f : X \mapsto Y$ be a function. Relative to $\mathcal{T}_X$ and the Euclidean metric topology on the real line, f is* lower-semi-continuous *at $x_0 \in X$ if and only if the set $\{x \in X \mid f(x) > f(x_0)\}$ is open with respect to $\mathcal{T}_X$. f is* lower-semi-continuous *on X if and only if f is lower-semi-continuous at every $x \in X$.*

Figure 5.3 displays the graph of an upper-semi-continuous function. Notice that, at $x = x_0$, the image $f(x_0)$ is at the upper end of the jump discontinuity. This causes the set $\{x \in \Re \mid f(x) < f(x_0)\}$ not to include $x = x_0$, thereby making this set open with respect to E^1. Figure 5.4 displays the graph of a lower-semi-continuous function. Notice that the image $f(x_0)$ is at the lower end of the discontinuity at $x = x_0$. This

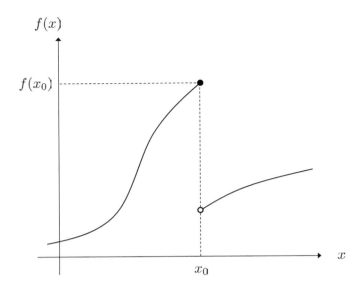

Figure 5.3: A graph of an upper-semi-continuous function.

causes the set $\{x \in \Re \mid f(x) > f(x_0)\}$ not to include $x = x_0$, so that the set is open with respect to E^1.

Here is a little teaser for you. Look again at Figure 5.3 and think of a horizontal line drawn at the height that is the right-side limit of $f(x)$ as $x \to x_0$ from above; *i.e.* $\lim_{x \to x_0^+} f(x)$. Is the set $\{x \mid f(x) < \lim_{x \to x_0^+} f(x)\}$ open with respect to E^1? Think about it. When you are ready, look at Problem 5.6 and its answer.

For a function to be continuous at a point $x = x_0$ there cannot be discontinuities of the type displayed in Figures 5.3 and 5.4, in which case the sets $\{x \in \Re \mid f(x) < f(x_0)\}$ and $\{x \in \Re \mid f(x) > f(x_0)\}$ will both be open with respect to E^1. This is the content of the following theorem, which we could, if we wished, use as an alternative way of defining continuity for a real-valued function.

Theorem 5.1. *Let $(X, \mathcal{T}_X)$ be a topological space. Let $Y \subset \Re$. Let $f : X \mapsto Y$ be a function. Relative to $\mathcal{T}_X$ and the Euclidean metric topology on the real line, f is continuous at $x_0 \in X$ if and only f is both lower-semi-continuous and upper-semi-continuous at x_0. f is continuous on X if and only if f is both lower-semi-continuous and upper-semi-continuous on X.*

The theorem offers an alternative way of defining continuity of a real-valued function (but not of more general mappings). How? Look again at Definition 5.11. Once

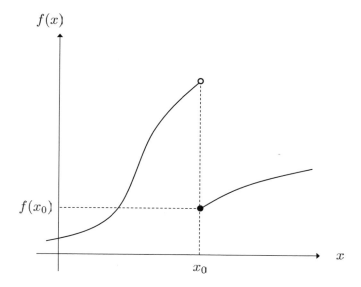

Figure 5.4: A graph of a lower-semi-continuous function.

we insist that the function f is real-valued, Definition 5.11 becomes the special case that we will call

Definition 5.15 (Continuous Real-Valued Function). *Let $(X, \mathcal{T}_X)$ be a topological space. Let $f : X \mapsto \Re$ be a function. Relative to $(X, \mathcal{T}_X)$ and the Euclidean metric topology on the real line, f is continuous at $x_0 \in X$ if and only if, for every open neighborhood $B_{d_E}(f(x_0), \varepsilon)$ about $f(x_0)$, the set $f^{-1}(B_{d_E}(f(x_0), \varepsilon))$ is open with respect to $\mathcal{T}_X$.*

Let's look closely at this statement and understand why it is equivalent to Definition 5.11 for the special case of real-valued functions. $B_{d_E}(f(x_0), \varepsilon)$ is a subset of the codomain $\Re$ that contains the point $f(x_0)$ and is open with respect to E^1. Because the topology on the codomain is the Euclidean metric topology, for every point $y \in B_{d_E}(f(x_0), \varepsilon)$, there must exist a ball with a strictly positive radius $\varepsilon(y) > 0$ that is centered on y and is entirely contained in $B_{d_E}(f(x_0), \varepsilon)$. In fact, the neighborhood $B_{d_E}(f(x_0), \varepsilon)$ is the union of all such balls:

$$B_{d_E}(f(x_0), \varepsilon) = \bigcup_{y \in B_{d_E}(f(x_0), \varepsilon)} B_{d_E}(y, \varepsilon(y)).$$

What is the inverse image of any one of these balls? It is $f^{-1}(B_{d_E}(y, \varepsilon(y)))$. Since f is continuous and since $B_{d_E}(y, \varepsilon(y))$ is open with respect to the topology on the codomain, $f^{-1}(B_{d_E}(y, \varepsilon(y)))$ must be open with respect to the topology on the domain. The inverse image of any union of sets in the codomain of a function is the union of the inverse images of these sets in the domain of the function, so,

$$f^{-1}(B_{d_E}(f(x_0), \varepsilon)) = \bigcup_{y \in B_{d_E}(f(x_0), \varepsilon)} f^{-1}(B_{d_E}(y, \varepsilon(y))).$$

Because any union of sets open with respect to a topology is a set that is open with respect to that topology, the set $f^{-1}(B_{d_E}(f(x_0), \varepsilon))$ must be open with respect to $\mathcal{T}_X$.

How does Definition 5.15 lead to Theorem 5.1? Think of any one of the balls $B_{d_E}(y, \varepsilon(y))$. Since the codomain of f is the real line, the ball is simply an open interval of the line:

$$\begin{aligned} B_{d_E}(y, \varepsilon(y)) &= \{y' \in Y \mid d_E(y, y') < \varepsilon(y)\} \\ &= (y - \varepsilon(y), y + \varepsilon(y)) \\ &= (-\infty, y + \varepsilon(y)) \cap (y - \varepsilon(y), \infty). \end{aligned}$$

Hence $B_{d_E}(y, \varepsilon(y))$ is open with respect to E^1 if and only if both of the sets $(y - \varepsilon(y), \infty)$ and $(-\infty, y + \varepsilon(y))$ are open with respect to E^1. This is true if and only if f is upper-semi-continuous at $f^{-1}(y + \varepsilon(y))$ and is lower-semi-continuous at $f^{-1}(y - \varepsilon(y))$.

Now think of any set $O \subset Y$ that is open with respect to E^1. This subset consists only of points that are interior to the set, which, in the Euclidean metric topology on $\Re$, means that each point $y \in O$ is contained in an open ball $B_{d_E}(y, \varepsilon(y))$ that is itself entirely within O. Moreover, O must be the union of all such balls. Thus,

$$\begin{aligned} O &= \bigcup_{y \in O} B_{d_E}(y, \varepsilon(y)) \\ &= \bigcup_{y \in O} \{(y - \varepsilon(y), \infty) \cap (-\infty, y + \varepsilon(y))\}. \end{aligned}$$

O is open with respect to E^1 if and only if every one of the intervals $(-\infty, y + \varepsilon(y))$ and $(y - \varepsilon(y), \infty)$ is open with respect to E^1, for every $y \in O$. For f to be continuous on X, we need *any* such subset O to be open with respect to E^1. This is true if and only if f is both upper-semi-continuous and lower-semi-continuous at *every* point $y \in Y$. This concludes the argument that establishes Theorem 5.1.

5.4   Hemi-Continuity and Continuity

The ideas of lower-hemi-continuity and upper-hemi-continuity have little to do with upper-semi-continuity and lower-semi-continuity. It is therefore important not to confuse the hemi-continuities with the semi-continuities. Be warned that in some older documents the term semi-continuity is used to mean what we here mean by hemi-continuity, so when you encounter the term semi-continuity, it is prudent to take a moment to check exactly what the author means by it.

Like continuity, upper-hemi-continuity and lower-hemi-continuity are ideas that are defined with respect to topologies. They are rather general notions, but, as we shall see, they do not apply to all types of correspondences. Each hemi-continuity, by itself, is a more general idea than is full continuity since, for a correspondence to be fully continuous, it must be both upper-hemi-continuous and lower-hemi-continuous. Neither an upper-hemi-continuous correspondence nor a lower-hemi-continuous correspondence need be (fully) continuous.

Why do we need to think about these hemi-continuity ideas at all? Do they have any practical merit? When we think of only functions, the idea of continuity is quite simple. We say that a function (remember, a function is a *single-valued* mapping) is continuous at some point $x_0 \in X$ if and only if, for every set $O \subset Y$ that is open in the topology on the codomain with $f(x_0) \in O$, the inverse image set $f^{-1}(O)$ is open in the topology on the domain and $x_0 \in f^{-1}(O)$. When f is a function, the set $f^{-1}(O)$ has just *one* meaning: it is the set of all of the domain elements that map to the elements in O. Unfortunately, when the mapping is a correspondence F that is not a function, there are *two* natural ways to think of the inverse image set $F^{-1}(O)$. A couple of examples will help you to understand the choice that is now before us.

Start by thinking of the function $f : [0, 4] \mapsto [1, 5]$ that is defined by $f(x) = x + 1$. Let $O = (2, 4)$. O is open in the codomain with respect to the Euclidean metric topology. The set $f^{-1}(O) = (1, 3)$, a set that is open in the domain with respect to the Euclidean metric topology. There is no question as to what is the set $f^{-1}(O)$, but there are two ways to interpret its meaning. Have a look at Figure 5.5. One interpretation is that $f^{-1}(O)$ is the collection of all values of $x \in [0, 4]$ for which the image set $f(x)$ is contained in $(2, 4)$; *i.e.* $x \in f^{-1}(O)$ if and only if $\{f(x)\} \subset O$. An alternative interpretation is that $f^{-1}(O)$ is the collection of all values of $x \in [0, 4]$ for which the image set $f(x)$ intersects $(2, 4)$; *i.e.* $x \in f^{-1}(O)$ if and only if $\{f(x)\} \cap O \neq \emptyset$. Because f is single-valued, these two different interpretations of the inverse image of the set $O = (2, 4)$ give us the same value, the interval $(1, 3)$, so we do not have to trouble ourselves over which of these two interpretations is "correct." Make sure you understand the statements of this paragraph before you proceed further.

Now think of the correspondence $F : [0, 4] \mapsto [1, 6]$ that is defined by $F(x) = [x + 1, x + 2]$. Again let $O = (2, 4)$. Look at Figure 5.6. What is now meant by $F^{-1}(O)$? Suppose we use the interpretation that $F^{-1}(O)$ is the collection of all values

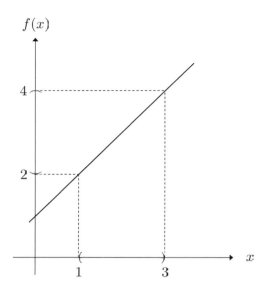

Figure 5.5: $f^{-1}(2,4) = (1,3) = \{x \in [0,4] \mid \{x+1\} \subset (2,4)\} = \{x \in [0,4] \mid \{x+1\} \cap (2,4) \neq \emptyset\}$.

of $x \in [0,4]$ for which the image set $F(x)$ is contained in $(2,4)$; *i.e.* $x \in F^{-1}(O)$ if and only if $F(x) \subset O$. Then $F^{-1}((2,4)) = (1,2)$. The alternative interpretation is that $F^{-1}(O)$ is the collection of all values of $x \in [0,4]$ for which $F(x)$ intersects $(2,4)$; *i.e.* $x \in F^{-1}(O)$ if and only if $F(x) \cap O \neq \emptyset$. Then $F^{-1}((2,4)) = (0,3)$. Obviously, $(1,2)$ and $(0,3)$ are different sets. Now it really does matter which way we interpret inverse images. As you will see shortly, one interpretation leads to upper-hemi-continuity while the other leads to lower-hemi-continuity.

When the inverse image $F^{-1}(O)$ is taken to mean the set of all elements x in the domain X such that the image of each x is completely contained in the set O, we obtain the set called the *upper inverse* of F at the set O. This we will denote by $F^{-1}(O)^+$:

$$F^{-1}(O)^+ = \{x \in X \mid F(x) \subset O\}. \tag{5.2}$$

It is the set of all domain elements that are mapped to sets in the codomain that contain *only* elements in the set O. We could, therefore, choose to define a correspondence F to be "continuous" at a point $x_0 \in X$ if and only if, for every set O that is open in the topology on the codomain of F and contains $F(x_0)$, the upper inverse $F^{-1}(O)^+$ is a set that is open in the topology on the domain of F. This idea of "continuity" that arises from using the upper inverse of F is called *upper-hemi-continuity*.

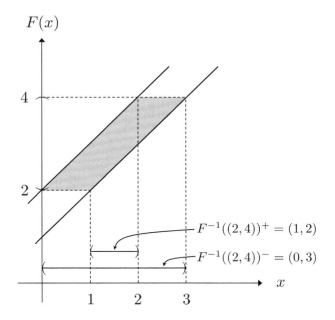

Figure 5.6: $F^{-1}((2,4))^+ = \{x \in [0,4] \mid [x+1, x+2] \subset (2,4)\} = (1,2)$, but $F^{-1}((2,4))^- = \{x \in [0,4] \mid [x+1, x+2] \cap (2,4) \neq \emptyset\} = (0,3)$.

When the inverse image $F^{-1}(O)$ is taken to mean the set of every element x in the domain X such that the image $F(x)$ intersects O, we obtain the set called the *lower inverse* of F at the set O. This will be denoted by $F^{-1}(O)^-$:

$$F^{-1}(O)^- = \{x \in X \mid F(x) \cap O \neq \emptyset\}. \tag{5.3}$$

It is the set of all domain elements that are mapped to sets in the codomain that contain *at least one* of the elements in the set O. Thus we could instead choose to define a correspondence F to be "continuous" at a point $x_0 \in X$ if and only if, for every set O that is open in the topology on the codomain of F and contains $F(x_0)$, the lower inverse $F^{-1}(O)^-$ is a set that is open in the topology on the domain of F. This idea of "continuity" that arises from using the lower inverse of F is called *lower-hemi-continuity.*

For any nonempty image set $F(x)$, $F(x) \subset O$ implies that $F(x) \cap O \neq \emptyset$. The converse is not true. Hence the upper-inverse of F at O is always a subset of the lower-inverse of F at O; $F^{-1}(O)^+ \subseteq F^{-1}(O)^-$.

The term "continuous correspondence" is reserved only for correspondences that are both upper-hemi-continuous and lower-hemi-continuous. Therefore, to understand clearly what is meant by the (full) continuity of a correspondence, it is necessary to understand both upper-hemi-continuity and lower-hemi-continuity. Let's start by thinking about upper-hemi-continuity.

Definition 5.16 (Upper-Hemi-Continuous Correspondence). *Let $(X, \mathcal{T}_X)$ and $(Y, \mathcal{T}_Y)$ be topological spaces. Let $F : X \mapsto Y$. Relative to $(X, \mathcal{T}_X)$ and $(Y, \mathcal{T}_Y)$, F is upper-hemi-continuous at $x_0 \in X$ if and only if, for every set O that is open in $\mathcal{T}_Y$ with $F(x_0) \subset O$, there exists a set $V \subset X$ that is open with respect to $\mathcal{T}_X$ and $x \in V$ implies that $F(x) \subset O$. F is upper-hemi-continuous on X if and only if F is upper-hemi-continuous at every $x \in X$.*

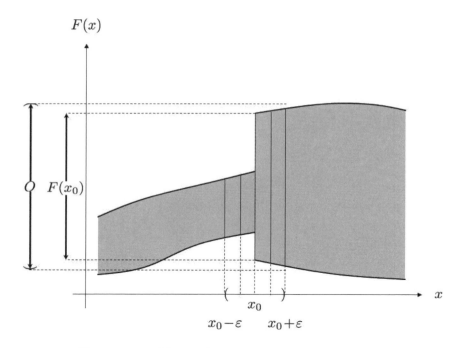

Figure 5.7: Upper-hemi-continuity at $x = x_0$.

This definition uses (5.2) as its interpretation of the inverse image $F^{-1}(O)$. The idea is quite simple. Take a point x_0 in the domain of F. Then look at its image $F(x_0)$. This is a set in the range Y; see Figure 5.7. Now take *any* open set O that contains the set $F(x_0)$. Think of O as setting boundaries on $F(x_0)$. Loosely stated, F is upper-hemi-continuous at x_0 if and only if, for *every* x that is "close" to x_0, the set $F(x)$

is "bounded on the outside" (in the sense of complete containment) by that *same* open set O. Now recollect that O is *any* open set in Y that contains $F(x_0)$, so, in particular, think of the open sets containing $F(x_0)$ that are almost the same as $F(x_0)$ (think of "shrink-wrapping" $F(x_0)$, as is displayed in Figure 5.7, where $F(x) \subset O$ for every x in the (open) ball of radius ε centered at x_0. O encloses $F(x_0)$ more tightly as $\varepsilon \to 0$). That means that the set $F(x_0)$ sets the outer boundaries mentioned above, so F is upper-hemi-continuous at x_0 if and only if, for all $x \in X$ that are really close to x_0, any set $F(x)$ that extends in any direction by more than does $F(x_0)$ does so by only very slightly more – see the sets $F(x)$ in Figure 5.7 for x just above x_0. But for x close to x_0, the sets $F(x)$ can suddenly be much smaller than the set $F(x_0)$ – see the sets $F(x)$ in Figure 5.7 for x just below x_0.

Lower-hemi-continuity has the opposite meaning to upper-hemi-continuity. As we shall see, when F is lower-hemi-continuous at x_0, the set $F(x_0)$ sets inner boundaries for all of the sets $F(x)$ for x "close" to x_0. Particularly, for every x close to x_0, any set $F(x)$ that extends in some direction less than does $F(x_0)$ must do so only very slightly – see the sets $F(x)$ in Figure 5.8 for x just above x_0. But for x close to x_0, the sets $F(x)$ can suddenly be much larger than the set $F(x_0)$ – see the sets $F(x)$ in Figure 5.8 for x just below x_0.

Definition 5.17 (Lower-Hemi-Continuous Correspondence). *Let $(X, \mathcal{T}_X)$ and $(Y, \mathcal{T}_Y)$ be topological spaces. Let $F : X \mapsto Y$. Relative to $(X, \mathcal{T}_X)$ and $(Y, \mathcal{T}_Y)$, F is lower-hemi-continuous at $x_0 \in X$ if and only if, for every set O that is open in $\mathcal{T}_Y$ with $F(x_0) \cap O \neq \emptyset$, there exists a set $V \subset X$ that is open with respect to $\mathcal{T}_X$ and $x \in V$ implies that $F(x) \cap O \neq \emptyset$. F is lower-hemi-continuous on X if and only if F is lower-hemi-continuous at every $x \in X$.*

This definition uses (5.3) as its interpretation of the inverse image $F^{-1}(O)$. As an example to help to visualize the meaning of lower-hemi-continuity, think of $F(x_0)$ as being an interval in Y, as displayed in Figure 5.8. Then think of a long but finite sequence of very small open sets $\{O_j\}_{j=1}^n$ such that every one of these sets intersects $F(x_0)$ and their union includes (*i.e.* covers) $F(x_0)$:

$$F(x_0) \cap O_j \neq \emptyset \ \forall \ j = 1, \ldots, n \quad \text{and} \quad F(x_0) \subset \bigcup_{j=1}^n O_j.$$

Lower-hemi-continuity insists that, for each one of the open sets O_j that intersect $F(x_0)$, for *every* x that is really close to x_0 the set $F(x)$ must also intersect each one of the open sets O_j. Picture in your mind that $F(x_0)$ is an interval of finite length in the vertical axis, that each open set O_j is a really small ball in the vertical axis that is centered somewhere in $F(x_0)$, that each of these tiny open balls overlaps its two neighbors, and that their union covers (*i.e.* contains) all of the set $F(x_0)$ like a string of overlapping links in a chain. In Figure 5.8 the union of the overlapping intervals (balls) O_1, O_2, and O_3 contains $F(x_0)$. The set of x-values for which $F(x) \cap O_1 \neq \emptyset$ is the open interval V_1. Similarly, the sets of x-values for which $F(x) \cap O_2 \neq \emptyset$ and $F(x) \cap O_3 \neq \emptyset$ are the open intervals V_2 and V_3. If $O = O_1 \cup O_2 \cup O_3$, then $V = V_1 \cup V_2 \cup V_3$.

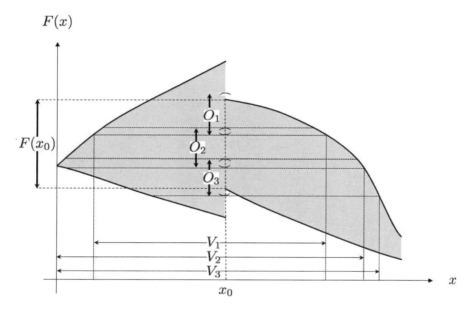

Figure 5.8: Lower-hemi-continuity at $x = x_0$.

Lower-hemi-continuity insists that, for *every* open set O_j that intersects $F(x_0)$, *all* of the sets $F(x)$ must also intersect the same open set O_j for *every* x that is really close to x_0. Thus $F(x)$ must intersect every single O_j and so must either be almost the same as $F(x_0)$ or else entirely enclose $F(x_0)$. In this sense, $F(x_0)$ is like an "inner bound" for each one of the sets $F(x)$. Look again at Figure 5.8. Notice that every value of x in V_1 that is "close" to x_0 creates an image $F(x)$ that intersects each of O_1, O_2, and O_3. Similarly, for $j = 2, 3$, every value of x in V_j that is "close" to x_0 creates an image $F(x)$ that intersects each of O_1, O_2, and O_3. We are allowed to choose the intervals O_1, O_2, and O_3 so this is only just true, in which case the union of O_1, O_2, and O_3 is an open set that essentially limits how small $F(x)$ can be for values of x that are really close to x_0.

What is the meaning of continuity of a correspondence? The basic idea of continuity is that a small change to x from an initial value x' to a new value x'' will result in a new image set $F(x'')$ that is only slightly different from the initial image set $F(x')$. In other words, a small change to x must cause only a small change to $F(x)$. We have seen that upper-hemi-continuity allows the change from x' to x'' to cause the image set of F to explode suddenly, but not by too much, since any sudden jump in the size or position of $F(x)$ will be bounded on the outside by an open set that just contains the set $F(x_0)$. We have also seen that lower-hemi-continuity allows the small change from x' to x'' to cause the image set of F to implode suddenly, but not by too much, since any sudden jump in the size or position of $F(x)$ will be bounded on the inside by $F(x_0)$. It seems reasonable to say that a correspondence F is fully continuous if and only if neither such explosions nor implosions occur when a small change is made to x. In other words, we define a correspondence to be continuous at a point x_0 if and only if it is both upper-hemi-continuous and lower-hemi-continuous at x_0.

Definition 5.18 (Continuous Correspondence). *Let $(X, \mathcal{T}_X)$ and $(Y, \mathcal{T}_Y)$ be topological spaces. Let $F : X \mapsto Y$. Relative to $(X, \mathcal{T}_X)$ and $(Y, \mathcal{T}_Y)$, F is continuous at $x_0 \in X$ if and only if F is both upper-hemi-continuous and lower-hemi-continuous at x_0. F is continuous on X if and only if F is continuous for every $x \in X$.*

Definition 5.18 might seem to have little to do with Definition 5.11, the correspondence part of which is restated below for your convenience. Yet both are definitions of the same thing – namely, the continuity of a correspondence at a point in its domain. Therefore the two statements must be equivalent.

Definition 5.11′ (Continuous Correspondence). *Let $(X, \mathcal{T}_X)$ and $(Y, \mathcal{T}_Y)$ be topological spaces. Let the correspondence $F : X \mapsto Y$. Relative to $(X, \mathcal{T}_X)$ and $(Y, \mathcal{T}_Y)$, F is continuous if and only if, for every set $O \subset Y$ that is open with respect to $\mathcal{T}_Y$ the set $F^{-1}(O)$ is open with respect to $\mathcal{T}_X$.*

According to Definition 5.18, a correspondence is continuous at a domain point x_0 if and only if both Definitions 5.16 and 5.17 are satisfied. That means that, for any set $O \subset Y$ that is open in the codomain of F and contains $F(x_0)$, there must exist a set $V \subset X$ that is open in the domain of F and $x \in V$ implies $F(x) \subset O$ and *also* that, for any set $O' \subset Y$ that is open in the codomain of F and intersects $F(x_0)$, there must exist a set $V' \subset X$ that is open in the domain of F and $x \in V'$ implies $F(x) \cap O' \neq \emptyset$. These two requirements reduce to the statement made for correspondences in Definition 5.11. Why?

The requirement that $F(x) \cap O \neq \emptyset$ ensures that $F(x) \neq \emptyset$; *i.e.* x must be in the *domain* of F. But why does it also imply that the image set $F(x_0)$ is not a sudden change in size or position compared to $F(x)$ for x very close to x_0? Again think of a long but finite sequence $\{O_j\}_{j=1}^n$ of sets open in the codomain topology with the properties that

$$O_j \cap F(x_0) \neq \emptyset \; \forall \; j = 1, \ldots, n \text{ and } \bigcup_{j=1}^n O_j = O \text{ and } F(x_0) \subset O. \qquad (5.4)$$

The picture is again of a long line of finitely many small chain links O_j, with each link overlapping with $F(x_0)$ by a bit and with their union O completely covering $F(x_0)$, but only just. Think again of O as a "shrink-wrapping" of $F(x_0)$. Look again at (5.4) and convince yourself that $F(x_0)$ is such a "chain-link-covered" set – draw a picture of it to help you follow what comes next.

Suppose that, for some x very close to x_0, the image set $F(x)$ is significantly smaller than $F(x_0)$. Then some of the little chain links O_j do not intersect with $F(x)$. But if F is continuous at x_0, then, from (5.4), this cannot happen.

Now suppose that, for some x very close to x_0, the image set $F(x)$ is significantly larger than $F(x_0)$. Then $F(x) \not\subset O$. But if F is continuous at x_0, then, from (5.4), this cannot happen.

Once you put the conclusions of the above two paragraphs together, it becomes clear that continuity of F at x_0 means that, as neighboring values of x become very close to x_0, the image sets $F(x)$ must become very close to $F(x_0)$.

Some examples of correspondences will help to make these ideas clearer to you. Consider the correspondence

$$F_1 : \Re \mapsto \Re \text{ that is } F_1(x) = [1, 2] \; \forall \; x \in \Re. \qquad (5.5)$$

Draw the graph before reading any further. Is this correspondence upper-hemi-continuous at some point $x_0 \in \Re$? The image $F_1(x_0) = [1, 2]$. Take any set O that is open in the codomain with respect to E^1 and contains the closed interval $[1, 2]$. Since O is open and $[1, 2]$ is closed, O must strictly include $[1, 2]$; *i.e.* O must be a "bit vertically longer" than $[1, 2]$ at both ends of $[1, 2]$. What is the upper-inverse of O? It is

$$F_1^{-1}(O)^+ = \{x \in \Re \mid F_1(x) \subset O\} = \Re. \qquad (5.6)$$

$\Re$ is an open subset of the domain $\Re$ with respect to E^1, so F_1 is upper-hemi-continuous at x_0. Since x_0 is an arbitrary choice from the domain $\Re$, F_1 is upper-hemi-continuous on $\Re$. Is the correspondence lower-hemi-continuous at some point $x_0 \in \Re$? The image $F_1(x_0) = [1, 2]$. Take any set O' that is open in the codomain with respect to E^1 and intersects the closed interval $[1, 2]$; $O' \cap [1, 2] \neq \emptyset$. What is the lower-inverse of O'? It is

$$F_1^{-1}(O')^- = \{x \in \Re \mid F_1(x) \cap O' \neq \emptyset\} = \Re. \tag{5.7}$$

$\Re$ is an open subset of the domain $\Re$ with respect to E^1, so F_1 is lower-hemi-continuous at x_0. Since x_0 is an arbitrary choice from the domain $\Re$, F_1 is lower-hemi-continuous on $\Re$. The correspondence F_1 is therefore (fully) continuous on $\Re$. This is hardly a surprise, since you would expect, I hope, that any constant-valued correspondence would be continuous.

Now consider the correspondence

$$F_2 : \Re \mapsto \Re \text{ that is } F_2(x) = [x, x + k], \text{ where } k > 0, \ \forall \ x \in \Re. \tag{5.8}$$

Draw the graph before reading any further. Is this correspondence upper-hemi-continuous at some point $x_0 \in \Re$? The image $F_2(x_0) = [x_0, x_0 + k]$. Take any set O that is open in the range with respect to E^1 and contains the closed interval $[x_0, x_0 + k]$. Since O is open and $[x_0, x_0 + k]$ is closed, O must strictly include $[x_0, x_0 + k]$; *i.e.* O must be a bit vertically longer than $[x_0, x_0 + k]$ at both ends of $[x_0, x_0 + k]$, so take $O = (a, b)$, where $a < x_0$ and $x_0 + k < b$. What is the upper-inverse of O? It is

$$F_2^{-1}(O)^+ = \{x \in \Re \mid F_2(x) \subset (a, b)\} = (a, b - k). \tag{5.9}$$

$(a, b - k)$ is an open subset of the domain $\Re$ with respect to E^1. We can make a similar argument for any open subset O that contains $[x_0, x_0 + k]$, so F_2 is upper-hemi-continuous at x_0. Since x_0 is an arbitrary choice from the domain $\Re$, F_2 is upper-hemi-continuous on $\Re$. Is the correspondence lower-hemi-continuous at some point $x_0 \in \Re$? The image $F_2(x_0) = [x_0, x_0 + k]$. Take any set O' that is open in the codomain with respect to E^1 and intersects the closed interval $[x_0, x_0 + k]$; $O' \cap [x_0, x_0 + k] \neq \emptyset$. Take $O' = (c, d)$, where $c < x_0 < d < x_0 + k$. What is the lower-inverse of O'? It is

$$F_2^{-1}(O')^- = \{x \in \Re \mid [x, x + k] \cap (c, d) \neq \emptyset\} = (c - k, d). \tag{5.10}$$

$(c - k, d)$ is an open subset of the domain $\Re$ with respect to E^1. We can make a similar argument for any open subset O' that intersects $[x_0, x_0 + k]$, so F_2 is lower-hemi-continuous at x_0. Since x_0 is an arbitrary choice from the domain $\Re$, F_2 is lower-hemi-continuous on $\Re$. The correspondence F_2 is therefore (fully) continuous on $\Re$.

Notice that the two correspondences that we have considered so far are both closed-valued; *i.e.* $F_1(x)$ and $F_2(x)$ are both closed sets in their codomains for every x in their domains. Does this matter? Consider

$$F_3 : \Re \mapsto \Re \text{ that is } F_3(x) = (1,2) \; \forall \; x \in \Re. \tag{5.11}$$

Draw the graph before reading any further. Is this correspondence upper-hemi-continuous at some point $x_0 \in \Re$? The image $F_3(x_0) = (1,2)$. Take any set O that is open in the codomain with respect to E^1 and contains the open interval $(1,2)$. Since O is open and $(1,2)$ is open, the smallest such set O is $(1,2)$ itself, so take $O = (a,b)$, where $a \leq 1$ and $2 \leq b$. What is the upper-inverse of O? It is

$$F_3^{-1}(O)^+ = \{x \in \Re \mid F_3(x) = (1,2) \subset (a,b)\} = \Re. \tag{5.12}$$

$\Re$ is an open subset of the domain $\Re$ with respect to E^1, so F_3 is upper-hemi-continuous at x_0. Since x_0 is an arbitrary choice from the domain $\Re$, F_3 is upper-hemi-continuous on $\Re$. Is the correspondence lower-hemi-continuous at some point $x_0 \in \Re$? The image $F_3(x_0) = (1,2)$. Take any set O' that is open in the codomain with respect to E^1 and intersects the open interval $(1,2)$; $O' \cap (1,2) \neq \emptyset$. What is the lower-inverse of O'? It is

$$F_3^{-1}(O')^- = \{x \in \Re \mid F_3(x) \cap O' = (1,2) \cap O' \neq \emptyset\} = \Re. \tag{5.13}$$

$\Re$ is an open subset of the domain $\Re$ with respect to E^1, so F_3 is lower-hemi-continuous at x_0. Since x_0 is an arbitrary choice from the domain $\Re$, F_3 is lower-hemi-continuous on $\Re$. The correspondence F_3 is therefore (fully) continuous on $\Re$. This example establishes that neither an upper-hemi-continuous correspondence, nor a lower-hemi-continuous correspondence, nor a continuous correspondence has to be closed-valued.

Another instructive example is the correspondence

$$F_4 : \Re \mapsto \Re \text{ that is } F_4(x) = (x, x+k) \text{ where } k > 0, \; \forall \; x \in \Re. \tag{5.14}$$

Draw the graph before reading any further. Is this correspondence upper-hemi-continuous at some point $x_0 \in \Re$? The image $F_4(x_0) = (x_0, x_0 + k)$. Take any set O that is open in the codomain with respect to E^1 and contains the open interval $(x_0, x_0 + k)$. Particularly, choose $O = (x_0, x_0 + k)$. What is the upper-inverse of O? It is

$$F_4^{-1}(O)^+ = \{x \in \Re \mid F_4(x) \subset (x_0, x_0 + k))\} = \{x_0\}. \tag{5.15}$$

$\{x_0\}$ is a closed subset of the domain $\Re$ with respect to E^1, so F_4 is not upper-hemi-continuous at x_0 and therefore is not upper-hemi-continuous on $\Re$. The correspondence F_4 is therefore not continuous on $\Re$. Is the correspondence lower-hemi-continuous at some point $x_0 \in \Re$? The image $F_4(x_0) = (x_0, x_0 + k)$. Take any set O' that is open in the codomain with respect to E^1 and intersects the open interval $(x_0, x_0 + k)$; $O' \cap (x_0, x_0 + k) \neq \emptyset$. Suppose, for example, that $O' = (c, d)$, where $c < x_0 < d < x_0 + k$. What is the lower-inverse of O'? It is

$$F_4^{-1}(O')^- = \{x \in \Re \mid (x, x + k) \cap (c, d) \neq \emptyset\} = (c - k, d). \tag{5.16}$$

$(c - k, d)$ is an open subset of the domain $\Re$ with respect to E^1. We can make a similar argument for any open subset O' that intersects $(x_0, x_0 + k)$, so F_4 is lower-hemi-continuous at x_0. Since x_0 is an arbitrary choice from the domain $\Re$, F_4 is lower-hemi-continuous on $\Re$.

Lastly, do you remember an example earlier in this section (see Figure 5.5) in which we concluded that, for a function, the upper-inverse and the lower-inverse sets are always the same? This is true for any function. With this in mind, construct a proof for the following theorem. It's an easy task.

Theorem 5.2 (Hemi-Continuous Function is Continuous). *Let $(X, \mathcal{T}_X)$ and $(Y, \mathcal{T}_Y)$ be topological spaces. Let $f : X \mapsto Y$ be a function.*

(i) If f is upper-hemi-continuous on X with respect to $\mathcal{T}_X$ and $\mathcal{T}_Y$, then f is continuous on X with respect to $\mathcal{T}_X$ and $\mathcal{T}_Y$.

(ii) If f is lower-hemi-continuous on X with respect to $\mathcal{T}_X$ and $\mathcal{T}_Y$, then f is continuous on X with respect to $\mathcal{T}_X$ and $\mathcal{T}_Y$.

5.5 Upper-Hemi-Continuity by Itself

The properties possessed by any correspondence depend greatly upon the types of topologies defined upon the domain and the range of the correspondence. In many instances an economist will be interested in mappings from one metric space to another. It turns out that upper-hemi-continuous correspondences have some rather nice properties when a metric topology is defined on the domain and a metric topology is defined on the range. Several of these are listed below.

Let's start by understanding the statement that a correspondence $F : X \mapsto Y$ is *compact-valued*. It means that, for any domain element $x \in X$, the image $F(x)$ is a set that is compact with respect to the topology on the codomain Y. We will often make reference to such correspondences in this section. One important theorem that underlies many of the others that will be stated here is the following.

Theorem 5.3. *Let (X, d_X) and (Y, d_Y) be metric spaces. Let $F : X \mapsto Y$ be an upper-hemi-continuous correspondence. If $K \subset X$ is compact with respect to the metric topology on X, then $F(K)$ is compact with respect to the metric topology on Y.*

Now we can proceed to examine one of the most commonly used characterizations of upper-hemi-continuous correspondences that map from a metric space to a metric space.

Theorem 5.4. *Let (X, d_X) and (Y, d_Y) be metric spaces. Let $F : X \mapsto Y$ be a correspondence.*

*(a) F is upper-hemi-continuous at $x_0 \in X$ **if**, for any sequence $\{x_n\}_{n=1}^{\infty}$ with $x_n \in X$ for every $n \geq 1$ and $x_n \to x_0$, any sequence $\{y_n\}_{n=1}^{\infty}$ with $y_n \in F(x_n)$ for every $n \geq 1$ possesses a subsequence $\{y_{n_k}\}_{k=1}^{\infty}$ such that $y_{n_k} \to y_0 \in F(x_0)$.*

*(b) If F is compact-valued, then the converse of (a) is true; i.e. F is upper-hemi-continuous at $x_0 \in X$ **only if**, for any sequence $\{x_n\}_{n=1}^{\infty}$ with $x_n \in X$ for every $n \geq 1$ and $x_n \to x_0$, any sequence $\{y_n\}_{n=1}^{\infty}$ with $y_n \in F(x_n)$ for every $n \geq 1$ possesses a subsequence $\{y_{n_k}\}_{k=1}^{\infty}$ such that $y_{n_k} \to y_0 \in F(x_0)$.*

Part (a) is a statement of sufficiency. Part (b) is a statement of necessity. We will see why these two statements are true in a moment, but for now note that the above theorem does not state that every correspondence F mapping from one metric space to another is upper-hemi-continuous at $x_0 \in X$ if and only if, for any sequence $\{x_n\}_{n=1}^{\infty}$ with $x_n \in X$ for every $n \geq 1$ and $x_n \to x_0$, any sequence $\{y_n\}_{n=1}^{\infty}$ with $y_n \in F(x_n)$ for every $n \geq 1$ possesses a subsequence $\{y_{n_k}\}_{k=1}^{\infty}$ such that $y_{n_k} \to y_0 \in F(x_0)$. Believing this to be true is a common error.

Let's have a closer look at part (a) of Theorem 5.4. The idea is illustrated in Figure 5.9. Take as true that, for any sequence $\{x_n\}_{n=1}^{\infty}$ with $x_n \in X$ for every $n \geq 1$ and $x_n \to x_0$, any sequence $\{y_n\}_{n=1}^{\infty}$ with $y_n \in F(x_n)$ for every $n \geq 1$ possesses a subsequence $\{y_{n_k}\}_{k=1}^{\infty}$ such that $y_{n_k} \to y_0 \in F(x_0)$. Why is it that F must then be upper-hemi-continuous at x_0? The sequence $x_n \to x_0$. This generates a sequence of image sets $F(x_n)$. We are allowed to select any one y_n from each set $F(x_n)$, and are assured that when we do so the sequence that we have created of values $y_n \in F(x_n)$ has a convergent subsequence $y_{n_k} \in F(x_{n_k})$ that converges to a value $y_0 \in F(x_0)$. Therefore there is an integer K such that $y_{n_k} \in F(x_0)$ for every $k > K$. In Figure 5.9 the sequence $x_1, x_2, \ldots \to x_0$. The sequence $y_1, y_2, \ldots$ need not converge, but it contains a subsequence $y_1', y_2', \ldots$ that converges to some element $y_0' \in F(x_0)$.

Because this is true *for every* sequence x_n and any sequence $y_n \in F(x_n)$, it follows that *every* possible limit point $y_0 \in F(x_0)$. This is possible only if every image $F(x_{n_k})$ is either contained in $F(x_0)$ (see the sets $F(x_n)$ just to the left of $F(x_0)$ in Figure 5.9) or are almost the same as $F(x_0)$ (see the sets $F(x_n)$ just to the right of $F(x_0)$ in the figure) for values x_{n_k} that are very close to x_0. This is exactly what is meant by F being upper-hemi-continuous at x_0.

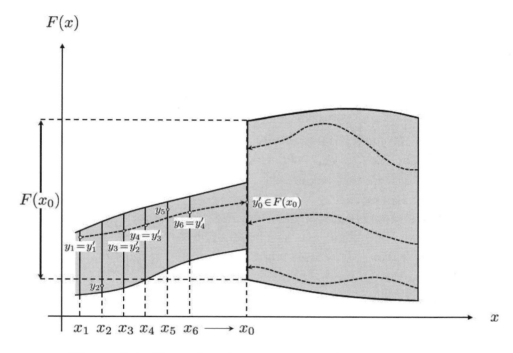

Figure 5.9: Upper-hemi-continuity at the point $x = x_0$.

Now let's examine part (b) of the theorem. Pick some point $x_0 \in X$ and a sequence $\{x_n\}_{n=1}^{\infty}$ in X with $x_n \to x_0$. This generates a sequence of image sets $F(x_n)$. For each n select as you please one element y_n from $F(x_n)$. Since F is compact-valued, the sequence $\{y_n\}_{n=1}^{\infty}$ must contain a subsequence $\{y_{n_k}\}_{k=1}^{\infty}$ that converges to a value we will call y_0. The question is, "Must y_0 belong to $F(x_0)$?" Suppose that $y_0 \notin F(x_0)$. Then is F upper-hemi-continuous at x_0? No. Why not? We are told that the subsequence of range values y_{n_k} converges to y_0. For each y_{n_k} there is an associated domain value x_{n_k}. Each x_{n_k} belongs to the x_n sequence that converges to x_0. *Every* subsequence of a convergent sequence is convergent, and to the same limit – see Corollary 4.1. Hence $x_{n_k} \to x_0$. Now $y_0 \notin F(x_0)$ and the sequence $y_{n_k} \to y_0$, so there is an integer K such that $y_{n_k} \notin F(x_0)$ for every $k > K$ (draw the picture).

Hence $F(x_{n_k}) \not\subset F(x_0)$ for *every* $k > K$. The picture you should have in your head at this moment is of a sequence of images $F(x_{n_k})$ that are not entirely contained in $F(x_0)$ for values x_{n_k} that are very close to x_0. Hence F cannot be upper-hemi-continuous at x_0.

Theorem 5.5. *Let (X, d_X) and (Y, d_Y) be metric spaces. If $F : X \mapsto Y$ is a compact-valued and upper-hemi-continuous correspondence, then F is closed-valued.*

The statement is that, if F is both compact-valued and upper-hemi-continuous, then, for any $x \in X$, the image $F(x)$ is a set that is closed in Y with respect to the metric topology defined on Y. Consider, for example, the constant-valued correspondence $F : \Re \mapsto \Re$ that is defined by

$$F(x) = (1, 2) \ \forall \ x \in \Re.$$

For any $x \in \Re$, the image set $(1, 2)$ is not closed with respect to E^1. Yet we have already seen that this correspondence is (fully) continuous, not just upper-hemi-continuous. Does this example contradict Theorem 5.5? No, because F is not a compact-valued correspondence.

More common misconceptions arise when the graph of an upper-hemi-continuous correspondence is considered, so let us now turn to thinking about the graph of a correspondence. Definition 5.10 states what is meant by the graph of a correspondence and is repeated here for your convenience.

Definition 5.10′ (Graph of a Correspondence) The *graph* G_F of a correspondence $F : X \mapsto Y$ is

$$G_F = \{(x, y) \mid x \in X \text{ and } y \in F(x)\}.$$

Definition 5.19 (Closed Graph). *Let $(X, \mathcal{T}_X)$ and $(Y, \mathcal{T}_Y)$ be topological spaces. Let the correspondence $F : X \mapsto Y$. F has a* closed graph *if and only if the set $G_F = \{(x, y) \mid x \in X \text{ and } y \in F(x)\}$ is closed with respect to the topology on the product space $X \times Y$.*

If we restrict ourselves to correspondences that map only from a metric space to a metric space, then the statement of Definition 5.19 is equivalent to the following statement.

Definition 5.20 (Closed Graph for Metric Spaces). *Let (X, d_X) and (Y, d_Y) be metric spaces. Let the correspondence $F : X \mapsto Y$. Let $x_0 \in X$. F is* closed-valued *at x_0 if and only if, for every sequence $\{x_n\}_{n=1}^{\infty}$ with $x_n \in X$ for all $n \geq 1$ and $x_n \to x_0$ and every sequence $\{y_n\}_{n=1}^{\infty}$ with $y_n \in F(x_n)$ for every $n \geq 1$ and $y_n \to y_0$, $y_0 \in F(x_0)$. F is closed-valued if and only if $F(x_0)$ is closed with respect to (X, d_X) at every $x_0 \in X$.*

Phrased in terms of the graph of a correspondence, the statement of Definition 5.20 is exactly the same as the following statement.

Definition 5.20' (Closed Graph for Metric Spaces). Let (X, d_X) and (Y, d_Y) be metric spaces. Let the correspondence $F : X \mapsto Y$. F has a closed graph G_F if and only if, for every sequence $\{(x_n, y_n)\}_{n=1}^{\infty}$ with $x_n \in X$ for all $n \geq 1$ and $x_n \to x_0$ and $y_n \in F(x_n)$ for every $n \geq 1$ and $y_n \to y_0$, $(x_0, y_0) \in G_F$.

For most people, accustomed to working and thinking in a Euclidean topological setting, a set is closed if and only if it contains all of its limit points, both interior limit points and boundary limit points. This is all that the two above definitions say. In each case there is a domain sequence of elements x_n that converges to some point x_0 in the domain. For each n there is another element y_n in the range. The sequence $\{y_n\}_{n=1}^{\infty}$ may or may not converge, but if it does, then it converges to a point y_0 that belongs to the image set $F(x_0)$. So any such convergent sequence y_n has its limit point in the set $F(x_0)$. This is what we see in figures such as 5.9 that display graphs of correspondences that are upper-hemi-continuous at a point x_0.

It is often asserted that a correspondence $F : X \mapsto Y$ is upper-hemi-continuous if and only if the graph of F is a set that is closed in the topology defined on the product space $X \times Y$. We have already seen that this cannot be true in general. Look again at the correspondence defined in (5.11). The graph of F_3 is the set

$$G_{F_3} = \{(x, y) \mid x \in \Re \text{ and } 1 < y < 2\}.$$

This is a set that is open with respect to the Euclidean topology on $\Re \times \Re = \Re^2$. Yet F_3 is upper-hemi-continuous. The truth of the matter is that the graph of an upper-hemi-continuous correspondence may be a closed set, but need not be, and that a correspondence with a closed graph may be, but need not be, upper-hemi-continuous. We have just had an example of the first of these two assertions. For an example of the second assertion, consider the correspondence $F_5 : \Re \mapsto \Re$, where

$$F_5(x) = \begin{cases} \{1, 4\} & ; x \neq 2 \\ \{2, 3\} & ; x = 2. \end{cases}$$

The graph of this correspondence is a set that is closed with respect to E^2, but the correspondence is not upper-hemi-continuous (F_5 is not lower-hemi-continuous either). The confusion typically arises from a misreading of the following theorem.

Theorem 5.6 (Closed Graph Theorem). *Let (X, d_X) and (Y, d_Y) be metric spaces. Let the correspondence $F : X \mapsto Y$.*

(a) If the graph of F is closed with respect to the topology on $X \times Y$ and if the range Y is compact with respect to the topology on Y, then F is upper-hemi-continuous on X.

(b) If F is upper-hemi-continuous on X and is closed-valued on X, then the graph of F is closed with respect to the topology on $X \times Y$.

An often-cited example of (a) that demonstrates the importance of requiring that the range Y be compact is as follows. Let $F_6 : [0,2] \mapsto \Re_+$, where

$$F_6(x) = \begin{cases} \{0\} & ; x = 0 \\ \left\{0, \dfrac{1}{x}\right\} & ; 0 < x \leq 2. \end{cases}$$

The graph of F_6 is a closed (but not a bounded) subset of $\Re_+^2$, and F_6 is not upper-hemi-continuous at $x = 0$. To the contrary, F_6 is lower-hemi-continuous at $x = 0$. Notice that the range of F_6 is $\Re_+$, which is a set that is closed but not bounded, and thus not compact, with respect to E^1.

What if we modified F_6 by insisting that its range Y be some bounded subset of $\Re_+$? Let's choose $Y = [0,10]$. Now we must ask "what are the images of the domain elements $x \in (0, 1/10)$." Suppose we set all these images equal to the doubleton $\{0, 10\}$. Then our modified correspondence is $F_7 : [0,2] \mapsto [0,10]$, where

$$F_7(x) = \begin{cases} \{0\} & ; x = 0 \\ \{0, 10\} & ; 0 < x < 1/10 \\ \left\{0, \dfrac{1}{x}\right\} & ; 1/10 \leq x \leq 2. \end{cases}$$

The graph of F_7 is a bounded but not closed (hence not compact) subset of $\Re_+^2$ (why?) and F_7 is not upper-hemi-continuous at $x = 0$.

Let's try again. Let's modify the image of F_7 at $x = 0$ from the singleton $\{0\}$ to the doubleton $\{0, 10\}$. This gives us the correspondence $F_8 : [0,2] \mapsto [0,10]$, where

$$F_8(x) = \begin{cases} \{0, 10\} & ; 0 \leq x < 1/10 \\ \left\{0, \dfrac{1}{x}\right\} & ; 1/10 \leq x \leq 2. \end{cases}$$

The graph of F_8 is a closed and bounded (hence compact) subset of $\Re_+^2$ and F_8 is upper-hemi-continuous at every $x \in [0,2]$.

5.6 Joint Continuity of a Function

What does it mean to say that a function is *jointly continuous*?

Definition 5.21 (Jointly Continuous Function). *Let $f : X \times \Gamma \mapsto Y$ be a function. f is* jointly continuous *with respect to (x, γ) at $(x_0, \gamma_0) \in X \times \Gamma$ if and only if, for every set $O \subset Y$ that is open with respect to the topology $\mathcal{T}_Y$ on Y, the set $f^{-1}(O) \subset X \times \Gamma$ is open with respect to the topology $\mathcal{T}_{X \times \Gamma}$ on $X \times \Gamma$.*

When we restrict ourselves to functions that map from a metric space to a metric space, Definition 5.21 becomes equivalent to the following statement.

Definition 5.22 (Jointly Continuous Function in Metric Spaces). *Let (X, d_X), (Γ, d_Γ) and (Y, d_Y) be metric spaces. Let $f : X \times \Gamma \mapsto Y$ be a function. f is* jointly continuous *in (x, γ) at $(x_0, \gamma_0) \in X \times \Gamma$ if and only if, for every sequence $\{(x_n, \gamma_n)\}_{n=1}^\infty$ with $(x_n, \gamma_n) \in X \times \Gamma$ for all $n \geq 1$ and $(x_n, \gamma_n) \to (x_0, \gamma_0)$, $\lim_{n \to \infty} f(x_n, \gamma_n) = f(x_0, \gamma_0)$.*

It should be clear that, if a function $f(x, \gamma)$ is jointly continuous with respect to (x, γ), then the function is continuous with respect to x for a fixed value of γ and the function is continuous with respect to γ for a fixed value of x. (What are the simple proofs of these two assertions?) It is tempting to infer that the reverse is true; *i.e.* that, if the function $f(x, \gamma)$ is continuous with respect to x for any fixed value of γ and the function is also continuous with respect to γ for any fixed value of x, then the function must be jointly continuous with respect to (x, γ). This is not true. The usual counterexample is the function $f : \Re_+^2 \mapsto \Re_+$ that is

$$f(x, \gamma) = \begin{cases} \dfrac{x\gamma}{x^2 + \gamma^2} & \text{, for } (x, \gamma) \neq (0, 0) \\ 0 & \text{, for } (x, \gamma) = (0, 0). \end{cases}$$

Fix γ at any value, and it is obvious that the function is continuous with respect to $x \in \Re_+$. Fix x at any value, and it is obvious that the function is continuous with respect to $\gamma \in \Re_+$. But is the function jointly continuous in (x, γ)? Consider a sequence $\{(x_n, \gamma_n)\}_{n=1}^\infty$ such that $(x_n, \gamma_n) \to (0, 0)$ with $x_n = \gamma_n$ for all $n \geq 1$. Then,

$$\lim_{n \to \infty} f(x_n, \gamma_n) = \frac{1}{2} \neq f(0, 0) = 0.$$

Therefore f is not jointly continuous at $(x, \gamma) = (0, 0)$ and so is not jointly continuous on $\Re_+^2$.

5.7   Using Continuity

This chapter was hard work, so there had better be a good reason for all that effort. In every chapter after this, continuity is used a lot. Almost every argument presented as a part of developing understanding of solving constrained optimization problems relies heavily upon continuity. Sometimes continuity is assumed to be there; sometimes it must be shown to be there. The next chapter considers when we can "separate" two sets from each other. Separation of sets is the idea at the core of constrained optimization. The tool that we use to attempt such separations is a continuous function called a "hyperplane." (You may not yet know it but for you this is an old idea if you have studied at least intermediate-level economics.) Continuity is a crucial feature of the methods we use to separate sets. In fact, if you don't understand continuity, then you cannot truly understand constrained optimization problems and their solutions. That is why this chapter matters and why all of the effort to understand its contents is worth it.

5.8 Problems

Definition 5.23. *Let X be a subset of $\Re^n$ and let $f : X \mapsto \Re$ be a function. Let $\alpha \in \Re$. The level-α contour set of f is the set $\{x \in X \mid f(x) = \alpha\}$.*

Definition 5.24. *Let X be a subset of $\Re^n$ and let $f : X \mapsto \Re$ be a function. Let $\alpha \in \Re$. The level-α upper contour set of f is the set $\{x \in X \mid f(x) \geq \alpha\}$.*

Definition 5.25. *Let X be a subset of $\Re^n$ and let $f : X \mapsto \Re$ be a function. Let $\alpha \in \Re$. The level-α lower contour set of f is the set $\{x \in X \mid f(x) \leq \alpha\}$.*

Definition 5.26. *Let X be a subset of $\Re^n$ and let $f : X \mapsto \Re$ be a function. f is* upper-semi-continuous *on X if and only if all of the upper-contour sets of f are closed in E^n.*

Definition 5.27. *Let X be a subset of $\Re^n$ and let $f : X \mapsto \Re$ be a function. f is* lower-semi-continuous *on X if and only if all of the lower-contour sets of f are closed in E^n.*

Problem 5.1. Give an example of a function that is upper-semi-continuous, but not continuous.

Problem 5.2. Give an example of a function that is lower-semi-continuous, but not continuous.

Problem 5.3. Let X be a subset of $\Re^n$ and let $f : X \mapsto \Re$ be a function. Prove that f is upper-semi-continuous on X if and only if $-f$ is lower-semi-continuous on X.

Problem 5.4. Let X be a subset of $\Re^n$ and let $f : X \mapsto \Re$ be a function. Prove that f is continuous on X if and only if f is both lower-semi-continuous on X and upper-semi-continuous on X.

Problem 5.5. Let X be a subset of $\Re^n$ and let $f : X \mapsto \Re$ be a function. Prove that f is continuous on X if and only if every upper-contour set and every lower-contour set of f is closed in E^n.

Problem 5.6. Figure 5.10 is Figure 5.3 to which has been added a horizontal line drawn at the height that is the right-side limit of $f(x)$ as $x \to x_0$ from above; *i.e.* $\lim_{x \to x_0^+} f(x)$. Claim: "The set $\{x \mid f(x) < \lim_{x \to x_0^+} f(x)\} = (-\infty, x') \cup \{x_0\}$. This set is not open with respect to E^1, so f is not upper-semi-continuous at $x = x_0$." Is this claim true or false? Explain.

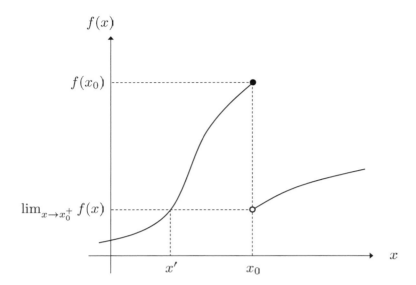

Figure 5.10: The graph for Problem 5.6.

Problem 5.7. (Weierstrass's Theorem for Upper-Semi-Continuous Functions) Let X be a nonempty and compact subset of $\Re^n$ and let $f : X \mapsto \Re$ be an upper-semi-continuous function. Prove that f attains a maximum on X.

Problem 5.8. Let X be a nonempty and compact subset of $\Re^n$ and let $f : X \mapsto \Re$ be a lower-semi-continuous function. Given an example that shows that f need not attain a maximum on X.

Problem 5.9. (Weierstrass's Theorem for Lower-Semi-Continuous Functions) Let X be a nonempty and compact subset of $\Re^n$ and let $f : X \mapsto \Re$ be a lower-semi-continuous function. Prove that f attains a minimum on X.

Problem 5.10. Let X be a nonempty and compact subset of $\Re^n$ and let $f : X \mapsto \Re$ be an upper-semi-continuous function. Given an example that shows that f need not attain a minimum on X.

Problem 5.11. (Weierstrass's Theorem for Continuous Functions) Let X be a nonempty and compact subset of $\Re^n$ and let $f : X \mapsto \Re$ be a continuous function. Prove that f attains both a maximum and a minimum on X.

Problem 5.12. The sets X and Y are

$$X = \{\text{hammer, saw, nail, drill, pencil, screw}\} \text{ and } Y = \{\text{bird, bee, snail}\}.$$

(i) Confirm that the collection of sets

$$\begin{aligned}
\mathcal{T}_X = \{&\emptyset, \{\text{saw}\}, \{\text{nail}\}, \{\text{hammer}\}, \{\text{nail, drill}\}, \{\text{nail, saw}\}, \{\text{nail, hammer}\}, \\
&\{\text{saw, hammer}\}, \{\text{saw, nail, drill}\}, \{\text{saw, nail, hammer}\}, \\
&\{\text{nail, drill, hammer}\}, \{\text{nail, drill, saw, hammer}\}, X\}
\end{aligned}$$

is a topology on X and that the collection of sets

$$\mathcal{T}_Y = \{\emptyset, \{\text{bird}\}, \{\text{bee}\}, \{\text{snail}\}, \{\text{bird, bee}\}, \{\text{bird, snail}\}, \{\text{bee, snail}\}, Y\}$$

is a topology on Y.

(ii) Define the mapping $f : X \mapsto Y$ by

$$\begin{aligned}
f(\text{saw}) &= \text{bird} \\
f(\text{drill}) &= \text{bee} \\
f(\text{nail}) &= \text{snail} \\
f(\text{hammer}) &= \text{bird}.
\end{aligned}$$

What is the domain of f? What is the range of f? What is the image of f? Is f a function? Is f surjective? Is f injective? Is f bijective? What is the graph of f? In what space is the graph of f contained?

(iii) Is f continuous relative to the topologies $\mathcal{T}_X$ and $\mathcal{T}_Y$?

Problem 5.13. Consider the correspondence $F : \Re_+ \mapsto \Re$ that is

$$F(x) = \pm\sqrt{x}; \; i.e. \; F(x) = \{-\sqrt{x}, \; +\sqrt{x}\} \text{ for } x \geq 0.$$

(i) What is the image of this correspondence? Is its image the same as its codomain? Is the correspondence surjective? Is it injective? Is it bijective? What is the graph of the correspondence? Is the graph a closed set and, if so, then closed with respect to which topology?

(ii) Is the correspondence F convex-valued? Is the graph of F a convex set?

(iii) Is the correspondence F closed-valued on $\Re_+$?

(iv) Is the correspondence F compact-valued on $\Re_+$? Is the range of F compact? Is the graph of F a compact set?

(v) Prove that F is upper-hemi-continuous on $\Re_+$ with respect to E^2.

(vi) Prove that F is lower-hemi-continuous on $\Re_+$ with respect to E^2.

(vii) Prove that F is continuous on $\Re_+$ with respect to E^2.

(viii) Can the Closed Graph Theorem be used to establish that F is upper-hemi-continuous on $\Re_+$ with respect to E^2? Why or why not?

Problem 5.14. Let $X \subset \Re^n$ and $Y \subset \Re^m$. Let $F : X \mapsto Y$ and $G : X \mapsto Y$ be correspondences. Define the correspondences $\Theta : X \mapsto Y$ and $\Psi : X \mapsto Y$ by

$$\Theta(x) = F(x) \cup G(x) \quad \text{and} \quad \Psi(x) = F(x) \cap G(x) \quad \forall\, x \in X.$$

(i) If F and G are convex-valued on X, then is Θ convex-valued on X?

(ii) If F and G are convex-valued on X, then is Ψ convex-valued on X?

(iii) If F and G are compact-valued on X, then is Θ compact-valued on X?

(iv) If F and G are compact-valued on X, then is Ψ compact-valued on X?

(v) If F and G are upper-hemi-continuous on X, then is Θ upper-hemi-continuous on X?

(vi) If F and G are lower-hemi-continuous on X, then is Θ lower-hemi-continuous on X?

(vii) If F and G are upper-hemi-continuous on X, then is Ψ upper-hemi-continuous on X?

(viii) If F and G are lower-hemi-continuous on X, then is Ψ lower-hemi-continuous on X?

(ix) If F and G are continuous on X, then is Θ continuous on X?

(x) If F and G are continuous on X, then is Ψ continuous on X?

(xi) If the graphs of F and G are closed with respect to E^{n+m}, then is the graph of Θ closed and, if so, then is Θ upper-hemi-continuous on X? If your answer is that Θ need not be upper-hemi-continuous, then state any additional condition(s) that will ensure that Θ is upper-hemi-continuous.

(xii) If the graphs of F and G are closed with respect to E^{n+m}, then is the graph of Ψ closed and, if so, then is Ψ upper-hemi-continuous on X? If your answer is that Ψ need not be upper-hemi-continuous, then state any additional condition(s) that will ensure that Ψ is upper-hemi-continuous.

5.9 Answers

Answer to Problem 5.1. Three examples are

$$g(x) = \begin{cases} x & , \text{ for } 0 \le x < 2 \\ x+1 & , \text{ for } 2 \le x \le 4 \end{cases},$$

$$h(x) = \begin{cases} x+2 & , \text{ for } 0 \le x \le 2 \\ 3-x & , \text{ for } 2 < x \le 4 \end{cases},$$

and

$$i(x) = \begin{cases} x & , \text{ for } 0 \le x < 2 \\ 5 & , \text{ for } x = 2 \\ x & , \text{ for } 2 < x \le 4. \end{cases} \qquad \square$$

Answer to Problem 5.2. Three examples are

$$u(x) = \begin{cases} x & , \text{ for } 0 \le x \le 2 \\ x+1 & , \text{ for } 2 < x \le 4 \end{cases},$$

$$v(x) = \begin{cases} x+2 & , \text{ for } 0 \le x < 2 \\ 3-x & , \text{ for } 2 \le x \le 4 \end{cases},$$

and

$$w(x) = \begin{cases} x & , \text{ for } 0 \le x < 2 \\ 1 & , \text{ for } x = 2 \\ x & , \text{ for } 2 < x \le 4. \end{cases} \qquad \square$$

Answer to Problem 5.3.

Proof. The statement that, for every $\alpha \in \Re$, the set $\{x \in X \mid f(x) \ge \alpha\}$ is closed in X is equivalent to the statement that, for every $-\alpha \in \Re$, the set $\{x \in X \mid -f(x) \le -\alpha\}$ is closed in X. $\qquad \square$

Answer to Problem 5.4.

Proof. Let's start by taking as given that f is both upper and lower-semi-continuous on X. Take any $x_0 \in X$. Then take any open ball in the codomain of f that contains $f(x_0)$. That is, take any $\delta > 0$ and consider the interval $O = (f(x_0) - \delta, f(x_0) + \delta)$ in the codomain of f. We need to show that the inverse image of O is a set that is open in the domain of f at x_0.

$$f^{-1}(O) = f^{-1}(f(x_0) - \delta, f(x_0) + \delta)$$
$$= \{x \in X \mid f(x) < f(x_0) + \delta\} \cap \{x \in X \mid f(x_0) - \delta < f(x)\}.$$

The set $\{x \in X \mid f(x) < f(x_0) + \delta\}$ is open in the domain of f because f is upper-semi-continuous on X. The set $\{x \in X \mid f(x_0) - \delta < f(x)\}$ is open in the domain of f because f is lower-semi-continuous on X. The intersection of two open sets is an open set, so $f^{-1}(O)$ is open at x_0. x_0 is an arbitrary choice from X, so f is continuous on X.

Now let's take as given that f is continuous on X. Take any $x_0 \in X$ and any $\delta > 0$ and consider the open ball in the range of f that is the interval $O = (f(x_0) - \delta, f(x_0) + \delta)$. The inverse image of O is open in the domain of f, since f is continuous at x_0. That is, the set

$$f^{-1}(O) = \{x \in X \mid f(x_0) - \delta < f(x) < f(x_0) + \delta\}$$
$$= \{x \in X \mid f(x) < f(x_0) + \delta\} \cap \{x \in X \mid f(x) > f(x_0) - \delta\}$$

is open in the domain of f, requiring that the sets $\{x \in X \mid f(x) < f(x_0) + \delta\}$ and $\{x \in X \mid f(x) > f(x_0) - \delta\}$ are open in the domain of f. This establishes that f is both upper and lower-semi-continuous at x_0. x_0 is an arbitrary choice from X, so f is both upper and lower-semi-continuous on X. $\qquad\square$

Answer to Problem 5.5.

Proof. f is continuous on X if and only f is both upper and lower semi-continuous on X. But f is upper semi-continuous on X if and only if all of the upper contour sets of f are closed in E^n, and f is lower-semi-continuous on X if and only if all of the lower contour sets of f are closed in E^n. $\qquad\square$

Answer to Problem 5.6: The claim is false. The set

$$\{x \mid f(x) < \lim_{x \to x_0^+} f(x)\} = (-\infty, x').$$

This set is open with respect to E^1. $\qquad\square$

Answer to Problem 5.7.

Proof. Let $\overline{f} = \sup_{x \in X} f(x)$. It must be shown that there is a value $x \in X$ for which the corresponding value of f is $\overline{f}$.

Since $\overline{f} = \sup_{x \in X} f(x)$, there exists in X a sequence $\{x_n\}_{n=1}^{\infty}$ such that

$$f(x_n) \to \overline{f}. \tag{5.17}$$

Since X is compact, this sequence must contain a convergent subsequence $\{x_{n_k}\}_{k=1}^{\infty}$. Let $\overline{x} = \lim_{k \to \infty} x_{n_k}$. $\overline{x} \in X$ because X is a closed set. Since f is upper-semi-continuous on X,

$$\lim_{k \to \infty} f(x_{n_k}) \leq f(\overline{x}). \tag{5.18}$$

Comparing (5.17) and (5.18) shows that $f(\overline{x}) = \overline{f}$. □

Answer to Problem 5.8. Let $X = [0, 4]$ and let the function be

$$v(x) = \begin{cases} x & , \text{ for } 0 \leq x \leq 2 \\ 5 - x & , \text{ for } 2 < x \leq 4. \end{cases}$$

This function is lower-semi-continuous on $[0, 4]$ and does not attain a maximum on $[0, 4]$. □

Answer to Problem 5.9.

Proof. Let $\underline{f} = \inf_{x \in X} f(x)$. It must be shown that there is a value $x \in X$ for which the corresponding value of f is $\underline{f}$.

Since $\underline{f} = \inf_{x \in X} f(x)$, there exists in X a sequence $\{x_n\}_{n=1}^{\infty}$ such that

$$f(x_n) \to \underline{f}. \tag{5.19}$$

Since X is compact, this sequence must contain a convergent subsequence $\{x_{n_k}\}_{k=1}^{\infty}$. Let $\underline{x} = \lim_{k \to \infty} x_{n_k}$. $\underline{x} \in X$ because X is a closed set. Since f is lower-semi-continuous on X,

$$\lim_{k \to \infty} f(x_{n_k}) \geq f(\underline{x}). \tag{5.20}$$

Comparing (5.19) and (5.20) shows that $f(\underline{x}) = \underline{f}$. □

Answer to Problem 5.10. Let $X = [0, 4]$ and let the function be

$$t(x) = \begin{cases} 5 - x & , \text{ for } 0 \leq x \leq 2 \\ x & , \text{ for } 2 < x \leq 4. \end{cases}$$

This function is upper-semi-continuous on $[0, 4]$ and does not attain a minimum on $[0, 4]$. □

Answer to Problem 5.11. A function is continuous if and only if it is both upper and lower-semi-continuous so the result follows from the answers to problems 5.7 and 5.9. □

Answer to Problem 5.12.
(i) Any union of sets in $\mathcal{T}_X$ is a set in $\mathcal{T}_X$ and any finite intersection of sets in $\mathcal{T}_X$ is a set in $\mathcal{T}_X$. Hence $\mathcal{T}_X$ is a topology on X. Any union of sets in $\mathcal{T}_Y$ is a set in $\mathcal{T}_Y$ and any finite intersection of sets in $\mathcal{T}_Y$ is a set in $\mathcal{T}_Y$. Hence $\mathcal{T}_Y$ is a topology on Y. In fact, $\mathcal{T}_Y$ is the discrete topology on Y since it is the collection of all possible subsets formed from the elements of Y.

(ii) The domain of f is

$$\{x \in X \mid f(x) \neq \emptyset\} = \{\text{saw, drill, nail, hammer}\}.$$

The range/image of f is $f(X) = \{\text{bird, bee, snail}\}$.

f is a function because $f(x)$ is a singleton for every x in the domain of f. The codomain and the image of f are the same set, so f is surjective. f is not injective since the element "bird" in the image of f is mapped to from more than one domain element; $f(\text{saw}) = f(\text{hammer}) = \text{bird}$. Thus f is not bijective.

The graph of f is the set

$$
\begin{aligned}
G_f &= \{(x, y) \mid x \in X \text{ and } y = f(x)\} \\
&= \{(\text{saw, bird}), (\text{drill, bee}), (\text{nail, snail}), (\text{hammer, bird})\}.
\end{aligned}
$$

This set is contained in the direct product of the domain and codomain,

$$
\begin{aligned}
X \times Y = \ &\{(\text{hammer, bird}), \ (\text{hammer, bee}), \ (\text{hammer, snail}), \\
&(\text{saw, bird}), \ (\text{saw, bee}), \ (\text{saw, snail}), \\
&(\text{nail, bird}), \ (\text{nail, bee}), \ (\text{nail, snail}), \\
&(\text{drill, bird}), \ (\text{drill, bee}), \ (\text{drill, snail}), \\
&(\text{pencil, bird}), \ (\text{pencil, bee}), \ (\text{pencil, snail}), \\
&(\text{screw, bird}), \ (\text{screw, bee}), \ (\text{screw, snail})\}.
\end{aligned}
$$

(iii) No. The sets $\{\text{bee}\}$ and $\{\text{bird, bee}\}$ are open with respect to $\mathcal{T}_Y$. The inverse images of these sets are

$$f^{-1}(\text{bee}) = \{\text{drill}\} \text{ and}$$
$$f^{-1}(\{\text{bird, bee}\}) = \{\text{saw, drill, hammer}\}.$$

But neither of the sets $\{\text{drill}\}$ and $\{\text{saw, drill, hammer}\}$ is open with respect to $\mathcal{T}_X$. Therefore f is not continuous relative to $\mathcal{T}_X$ and $\mathcal{T}_Y$. $\qquad\square$

Answer to Problem 5.13.
(i) The range/image is the real line, $\Re$. This is also the codomain of the correspondence. Hence the correspondence is surjective. The correspondence is injective because any image set $\{-\sqrt{x}, +\sqrt{x}\}$ is mapped to from exactly one x in the domain of the correspondence; *i.e.* for any $x', x'' \in \Re$ with $x' \neq x''$, $F(x') \cap F(x'') = \emptyset$. The

correspondence is both surjective and injective, so it is bijective. The graph of the correspondence is the set

$$G_F = \{(x, y) \mid x \in \Re_+, \ y \in \{-\sqrt{x}, +\sqrt{x}\}\}.$$

G_F is a subset of $\Re_+ \times \Re$ and is closed with respect to the Euclidean topology on $\Re_+ \times \Re$.

(ii) The correspondence is not convex-valued. For any $x \neq 0$, the image of f consists of the two distinct points $-\sqrt{x}$ and $+\sqrt{x}$ in $\Re$; this is not a convex set. Similarly, the graph is not a convex subset of $\Re_+ \times \Re$.

(iii) $F(0) = \{0\}$ is a singleton and so is closed in E^1. For any $x \neq 0$, $F(x)$ is a set consisting of two distinct points in $\Re$. Any such set is closed in E^1. Hence $F(x)$ is closed in E^1 for every element in the domain of F, meaning that the correspondence is closed-valued with respect to E^1.

(iv) $F(0) = \{0\}$ is obviously both closed and bounded, and hence compact, with respect to E^1. For any $x \neq 0$, $F(x)$ is closed with respect to E^1 and the number $M(x) = +2\sqrt{x}$ is a finite upper bound on the Euclidean distance between the points in the set. Hence $F(x)$ is bounded with respect to E^1 and is therefore compact with respect to E^1. Since $F(x)$ is compact with respect to E^1 for every x in the domain of F, F is compact-valued with respect to E^1. The range of F is $\Re$, which is not bounded, so the range is not compact with respect to E^1. The graph of F, G_F, is a subset of $\Re_+ \times \Re$ that is not bounded, so it is not compact with respect to the Euclidean topology on $\Re_+ \times \Re$.

(v) Proof 1. F is upper-hemi-continuous on $\Re_+$ if and only if the upper-inverse of any set O that is open in $\Re$ is a set V that is open in $\Re_+$, such that $x \in V$ implies that $F(x) \subset O$. So take a nonempty subset O in the range $\Re$ of F that is open with respect to E^1. Take any $y \in O$. Then there is a ball with a positive radius $\epsilon(y)$ that is centered on y and is entirely contained in O. This ball is the set $B_{d_E}(y, \epsilon(y)) = \{y' \in \Re \mid y - \epsilon(y) < y' < y + \epsilon(y)\}$.

$$y - \epsilon(y) < \sqrt{x} < y + \epsilon(y) \quad \Leftrightarrow \quad (y - \epsilon(y))^2 < x < (y + \epsilon(y))^2,$$

so the upper-inverse of F of $B_{d_E}(y, \epsilon(y))$ is

$$\begin{aligned}
F^{-1}(B_{d_E}(y, \epsilon(y)))^+ &= \{x \mid x \in \Re_+, \ F(x) \subset B_{d_E}(y, \epsilon(y))\} \\
&= \{x \mid x \in \Re_+, \ (y - \epsilon(y))^2 < x < (y + \epsilon(y))^2\}.
\end{aligned}$$

This is an interval in $\Re_+$ that is open with respect to the Euclidean topology on $\Re_+$. The upper-inverse of the entire set O is the union of the upper-inverses of all of the balls comprising O:

$$F^{-1}(O)^+ = \bigcup_{y \in O} F^{-1}(B_{d_E}(y, \epsilon(y)))^+.$$

Since it is the union of sets that are open with respect to the Euclidean topology on $\Re_+$, $F^{-1}(O)^+$ is open with respect to this topology. Therefore F is upper-hemi-continuous on $\Re_+$.   □

Proof 2. Since F is a *compact-valued* correspondence that maps from the Euclidean metric space $(\Re_+, d_E)$ to the Euclidean metric space $(\Re, d_E)$, F is upper-hemi-continuous at $x_0 \in \Re_+$ if and only if, for every sequence $\{x_n\}_{n=1}^\infty$ with $x_n \in \Re_+$ for all $n \geq 1$ and $x_n \to x_0$, every sequence $\{y_n\}_{n=1}^\infty$ with $y_n \in F(x_n)$ for all $n \geq 1$ contains a convergent subsequence $\{y_{n_k}\}_{k=1}^\infty$ with $y_{n_k} \to y_0 \in F(x_0)$.

Take any $x_0 \in \Re_+$ and any sequence $\{x_n\}_{n=1}^\infty$ with $x_n \in \Re_+$ for all $n \geq 1$ and $x_n \to x_0$. For each $n \geq 1$, $F(x_n) = \{-\sqrt{x_n}, +\sqrt{x_n}\}$. Select the sequence $y_n = +\sqrt{x_n}$ for all $n \geq 1$. As $x_n \to x_0$, $y_n \to y_0 = \sqrt{x_0} \in F(x_0)$. Similarly, select the sequence $y_n = -\sqrt{x_n}$ for all $n \geq 1$. As $x_n \to x_0$, $y_n \to y_0 = -\sqrt{x_0} \in F(x_0)$. Thus F is upper-hemi-continuous at x_0. But x_0 is an arbitrary choice from $\Re_+$, so F is upper-hemi-continuous on $\Re_+$ with respect to the Euclidean metric topologies on $\Re_+$ and $\Re$.   □

(vi) Proof 1. F is lower-hemi-continuous at $x_0 \in \Re_+$ if and only if the lower-inverse of any set O that is open with respect to E^1 with $F(x_0) \cap O \neq \emptyset$ is a set V that is open with respect to the Euclidean topology on $\Re_+$, such that $x \in V$ implies that $F(x) \cap O \neq \emptyset$. So take a nonempty subset O in the range $\Re$ of F that is open with respect to E^1, such that $\{-\sqrt{x_0}, +\sqrt{x_0}\} \cap O \neq \emptyset$. Then either $y_0^- = -\sqrt{x_0} \in O$, or $y_0^+ = +\sqrt{x_0} \in O$, or both. Suppose $y_0^+ \in O$. Then there is a ball with a positive radius $\epsilon(y_0^+)$ that is centered on y_0^+ and is entirely contained in O. This ball is the set $B_{d_E}(y_0^+, \epsilon(y_0^+)) = \{y' \in \Re \mid y_0^+ - \epsilon(y_0^+) < y' < y_0^+ + \epsilon(y_0^+)\}$.

$$y_0^+ - \epsilon(y_0^+) < +\sqrt{x} < y_0^+ + \epsilon(y_0^+) \quad \Leftrightarrow \quad (y_0^+ - \epsilon(y_0^+))^2 < x < (y_0^+ + \epsilon(y_0^+))^2,$$

so the lower-inverse of $B_{d_E}(y_0^+, \epsilon(y_0^+))$ is

$$F^{-1}(B_{d_E}(y_0^+, \epsilon(y_0^+)))^-$$
$$= \left\{x \mid x \in \Re_+, \ F(x) \cap B_{d_E}\left(y_0^+, \epsilon\left(y_0^+\right)\right) \neq \emptyset\right\}$$
$$= \left\{x \mid x \in \left(\left(y_0^+ - \epsilon\left(y_0^+\right)\right)^2, \left(y_0^+ + \epsilon\left(y_0^+\right)\right)^2\right), \ \{-\sqrt{x}, +\sqrt{x}\} \cap O \neq \emptyset\right\}.$$

The lower-inverse is not empty since it contains x_0. Moreover the lower-inverse is an interval in $\Re_+$ that is an open set. The lower-inverse of the entire set O is the union of the lower-inverses of all of the balls comprising O:

$$F^{-1}(O)^- = \bigcup_{y \in O} F^{-1}\left(B_{d_E}(y, \epsilon(y))\right)^-.$$

Since it is the union of sets that are open, it too is an open set. Therefore F is lower-hemi-continuous on $\Re_+$. $\qquad\square$

Proof 2. Since F is a *compact-valued* correspondence that maps from the Euclidean metric space $(\Re_+, d_E)$ to the Euclidean metric space $(\Re, d_E)$, F is lower-hemi-continuous at $x_0 \in \Re_+$ if and only if, for every sequence $\{x_n\}_{n=1}^\infty$ with $x_n \in \Re_+$ for all $n \geq 1$ and $x_n \to x_0$ and for every $y_0 \in F(x_0)$, there is a sequence $\{y_n\}_{n=1}^\infty$ with $y_n \in F(x_n)$ for every $n \geq 1$ and $y_n \to y_0$.

Take any $x_0 \in \Re_+$ and any sequence $\{x_n\}_{n=1}^\infty$ with $x_n \in \Re_+$ for all $n \geq 1$ and $x_n \to x_0$. $F(x_0) = \{-\sqrt{x_0}, +\sqrt{x_0}\}$. For each $n \geq 1$, $F(x_n) = \{-\sqrt{x_n}, +\sqrt{x_n}\}$. Select $y_0^+ = +\sqrt{x_0}$. The sequence $y_n = +\sqrt{x_n}$ for all $n \geq 1$ converges to y_0^+ as $n \to \infty$. Select $y_0^- = -\sqrt{x_0}$. The sequence $y_n = -\sqrt{x_n}$ converges to y_0^- as $n \to \infty$. Thus F is lower-hemi-continuous at x_0. x_0 is an arbitrary choice from $\Re_+$ so F is lower-hemi-continuous on $\Re_+$. $\qquad\square$

(vii) Proof. F is continuous on $\Re_+$ if and only if F is both upper and lower-hemi-continuous on $\Re_+$. Therefore, from parts (v) and (vi), F is continuous on $\Re_+$. $\qquad\square$

(viii) No. The Closed Graph Theorem requires the range of F to be a compact set. The range of F is $\Re$, which is not compact with respect to E^1. $\qquad\square$

Answer to Problem 5.14.
(i) F, G convex-valued on $X \not\Rightarrow \Theta$ is convex-valued on X.
Proof. For any $x \in X$, the sets $F(x)$ and $G(x)$ are convex subsets of $\Re^m$. The union of convex sets need not be a convex set, so $\Theta(x)$ need not be a convex subset of $\Re^m$. Thus Θ need not be a convex-valued correspondence. $\qquad\square$

(ii) F, G convex-valued on $X \Rightarrow \Psi$ is convex-valued on X.
Proof. For any $x \in X$, the sets $F(x)$ and $G(x)$ are convex subsets of $\Re^m$. The intersection of convex sets is a convex set, so $\Psi(x)$ is a convex subset of $\Re^m$. Thus Ψ is a convex-valued correspondence. $\qquad\square$

(iii) F, G compact-valued on $X \Rightarrow \Theta$ is compact-valued on X.
Proof. For any $x \in X$, the sets $F(x)$ and $G(x)$ are compact, with respect to E^m, subsets of $\Re^m$. The union of two compact sets is a compact set, so $\Theta(x)$ is a compact subset of $\Re^m$. Thus Θ is a compact-valued correspondence. $\qquad\square$

(iv) F, G compact-valued on $X \Rightarrow \Psi$ is compact-valued on X.

Proof. For any $x \in X$, the sets $F(x)$ and $G(x)$ are compact, with respect to E^m, subsets of $\Re^m$. The intersection of two compact sets is a compact set, so $\Psi(x)$ is a compact subset of $\Re^m$. Thus Ψ is a compact-valued correspondence. $\quad\square$

(v) F, G upper-hemi-continuous on $X \Rightarrow \Theta$ is upper-hemi-continuous on X.

Proof. Take any set O that is open with respect to E^m in the codomain of Θ with $\Theta(x) \subset O$ for some $x \in X$. The upper-inverse of O is

$$
\begin{aligned}
\Theta^{-1}(O)^+ &= \{x \in X \mid \Theta(x) \subset O\} \\
&= \{x \in X \mid (F(x) \cup G(x)) \subset O\} \\
&= \{x \in X \mid F(x) \subset O\} \cup \{x \in X \mid G(x) \subset O\} \\
&= F^{-1}(O)^+ \cup G^{-1}(O)^+.
\end{aligned}
$$

Since F is upper-hemi-continuous the upper-inverse image of F of O, $F^{-1}(O)^+$, is a set that is open in X. Similarly, $G^{-1}(O)^+$ is open in X. Therefore $\Theta^{-1}(O)^+$ is open in X, establishing that Θ is upper-hemi-continuous on X. $\quad\square$

(vi) F, G lower-hemi-continuous on $X \Rightarrow \Theta$ is lower-hemi-continuous on X.

Proof. Take any set O that is open with respect to E^m in the codomain of Θ with $\Theta(x) \cap O \neq \emptyset$ for some $x \in X$. The lower-inverse of O is

$$
\begin{aligned}
\Theta^{-1}(O)^- &= \{x \in X \mid \Theta(x) \cap O \neq \emptyset\} \\
&= \{x \in X \mid (F(x) \cup G(x)) \cap O \neq \emptyset\} \\
&= \{x \in X \mid F(x) \cap O \neq \emptyset\} \cup \{x \in X \mid G(x) \cap O \neq \emptyset\} \\
&= F^{-1}(O)^- \cup G^{-1}(O)^-.
\end{aligned}
$$

Since F is lower-hemi-continuous, the lower-inverse image of F of O, $F^{-1}(O)^-$, is a set that is open in X. Similarly, $G^{-1}(O)^-$ is open in X. Therefore $\Theta^{-1}(O)^-$ is open in X, establishing that Θ is lower-hemi-continuous on X. $\quad\square$

(vii) F, G upper-hemi-continuous on $X \Rightarrow \Psi$ is upper-hemi-continuous on X.

Proof. Take any set O that is open with respect to E^m in the codomain of Ψ. The upper-inverse of O is

$$
\begin{aligned}
\Psi^{-1}(O)^+ &= \{x \in X \mid \Psi(x) \subset O\} \\
&= \{x \in X \mid (F(x) \cap G(x)) \subset O\} \\
&= \{x \in X \mid F(x) \subset O\} \cap \{x \in X \mid G(x) \subset O\} \\
&= F^{-1}(O)^+ \cap G^{-1}(O)^+.
\end{aligned}
$$

Since F is upper-hemi-continuous, the upper-inverse image of O, $F^{-1}(O)^+$, is a set that is open in X. Similarly, $G^{-1}(O)^+$ is open in X. Therefore $\Psi^{-1}(O)^+$ is open in X, establishing that Ψ is upper-hemi-continuous on X. □

(viii) F, G lower-hemi-continuous on $X \Rightarrow \Psi$ is lower-hemi-continuous on X.

Proof. Take any set O that is open with respect to E^m in the codomain of Ψ with $\Psi(x) \cap O \neq \emptyset$ for some $x \in X$. The lower-inverse of O is

$$\begin{aligned}
\Psi^{-1}(O)^- &= \{x \in X \mid \Psi(x) \cap O \neq \emptyset\} \\
&= \{x \in X \mid (F(x) \cap G(x)) \cap O \neq \emptyset\} \\
&= \{x \in X \mid F(x) \cap O \neq \emptyset\} \cap \{x \in X \mid G(x) \cap O \neq \emptyset\} \\
&= F^{-1}(O)^- \cap G^{-1}(O)^-.
\end{aligned}$$

Since F is lower-hemi-continuous, the lower-inverse image of F of O, $F^{-1}(O)^-$, is a set that is open in X. Similarly, $G^{-1}(O)^-$ is open in X. Therefore $\Psi^{-1}(O)^-$ is open in X, establishing that Ψ is lower-hemi-continuous on X. □

(ix) F, G continuous on $X \Rightarrow \Theta$ is continuous on X.

Proof. Both F and G are continuous, and thus both upper-hemi-continuous and lower-hemi-continuous, on X. Therefore, from (v) and (vi), Θ is both upper-hemi-continuous and lower-hemi-continuous, and thus is continuous, on X. □

(x) F, G continuous on $X \Rightarrow \Psi$ is continuous on X.

Proof. Both F and G are continuous, and thus both upper-hemi-continuous and lower-hemi-continuous, on X. Therefore, from (vii) and (viii), Ψ is both upper-hemi-continuous and lower-hemi-continuous, and thus is continuous, on X. □

(xi) The graph of Θ is the set

$$\begin{aligned}
G_\Theta &= \{(x, y) \mid x \in X, \ y \in \Theta(x)\} \\
&= \{(x, y) \mid x \in X, \ y \in F(x) \cup G(x)\} \\
&= \{(x, y) \mid x \in X, \ y \in F(x)\} \cup \{(x, y) \mid x \in X, \ y \in G(x)\} \\
&= G_F \cup G_G.
\end{aligned}$$

G_Θ is the union of two closed sets and is therefore closed. By itself this does not ensure that Θ is upper-hemi-continuous on X. If, however, the range of Θ is a compact set, then Θ is upper-hemi-continuous on X if and only if the graph of Θ is a closed subset of $X \times Y$.

(xii) The graph of Ψ is the set

$$
\begin{aligned}
G_\Psi &= \{(x,y) \mid x \in X, \ y \in \Psi(x)\} \\
&= \{(x,y) \mid x \in X, \ y \in F(x) \cap G(x)\} \\
&= \{(x,y) \mid x \in X, \ y \in F(x)\} \cap \{(x,y) \mid x \in X, \ y \in G(x)\} \\
&= G_F \cap G_G.
\end{aligned}
$$

G_Ψ is the intersection of two closed sets and is therefore closed. By itself this does not ensure that Ψ is upper-hemi-continuous on X. If, however, the range of Ψ is a compact set, then Ψ is upper-hemi-continuous on X if and only if the graph of Ψ is a closed subset of $X \times Y$. $\qquad\square$

Chapter 6

Hyperplanes and Separating Sets

The whole idea of constrained optimization is to separate sets. If this seems odd to you, then consider the following familiar (to an economist) examples.

The main idea in demand theory is that a consumer chooses a consumption bundle that she most prefers from the bundles she can afford to purchase. The typical picture is displayed in Figure 6.1. The straight line that is the budget constraint separates two sets, S_1 and S_2. In this context $S_1 = \{x \in \Re_+^2 \mid x \succsim x^*\}$ is the set of consumption bundles that the consumer prefers at least as much as the bundle x^* and $S_2 = \{x \in \Re_+^2 \mid p_1 x_1 + p_2 x_2 \leq y\}$ is the consumer's budget set. The set $H = \{x \in \Re_+^2 \mid p_1 x_1 + p_2 x_2 = y\}$ that is the budget constraint is the hyperplane in $\Re_+^2$ that separates the sets S_1 and S_2.

One of the ideas central to the theory of the firm is that any firm seeks to produce a given quantity, y units, of its product at the smallest possible total production cost. Again the typical picture is displayed in Figure 6.1. This time $S_1 = \{x \in \Re_+^2 \mid f(x) \geq y\}$ is the set of input bundles that provide at least y units of output (f is the firm's production function) and $S_2 = \{x \in \Re_+^2 \mid w_1 x_1 + w_2 x_2 \leq w_1 x_1^* + w_2 x_2^*\}$ is the set of input bundles that cost no more than does the input bundle x^* that provides y output units. w_1 and w_2 are the per-unit prices of the inputs. The set $H = \{x \in \Re_+^2 \mid w_1 x_1 + w_2 x_2 = w_1 x_1^* + w_2 x_2^*\}$ is the isocost line that is the hyperplane in $\Re_+^2$ that separates the sets S_1 and S_2.

You are probably more familiar with these problems being posed to you as constrained optimization problems; *e.g.* a consumer wishing to maximize her utility subject to a budget constraint, or a firm wishing to minimize its cost of producing a specified quantity of its product. This should suggest to you the intimate relationship existing between constrained optimization problems and the separation of sets. It is

191

because of this relationship that in this chapter we study how and when a hyperplane may be used to separate sets. Let's start by seeing what is meant by the term *hyperplane*.

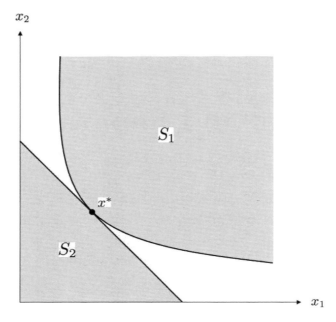

Figure 6.1: A hyperplane separating two sets.

6.1   Hyperplanes

Definition 6.1. *Given* $p \in \Re^n$ *with* $p \neq \underline{0}$ *and* $\|p\|_E < \infty$ *and given* $\alpha \in \Re$, *the set*

$$H(p, \alpha) = \{x \in \Re^n \mid p{\cdot}x = \alpha\} \qquad (6.1)$$

is the hyperplane in $\Re^n$ *with normal* p *and level* α.

This should be familiar to you. In $\Re^2$ a hyperplane is a (one-dimensional) straight line with the equation $p_1 x_1 + p_2 x_2 = \alpha$. In $\Re^3$ a hyperplane is a (two-dimensional) plane with the equation $p_1 x_1 + p_2 x_2 + p_3 x_3 = \alpha$. In $\Re^n$ a hyperplane is typically a plane of dimension $n - 1$.

The normal p of a hyperplane is the gradient vector with respect to x of the function $p{\cdot}x$; *i.e.*

$$\nabla_x \, p{\cdot}x = \left(\frac{\partial(p_1 x_1 + \cdots + p_n x_n)}{\partial x_1}, \ldots, \frac{\partial(p_1 x_1 + \cdots + p_n x_n)}{\partial x_n} \right) = (p_1, \ldots, p_n) = p^{\mathrm{T}}.$$

If we take any two points x' and $x' + \Delta x$ in the hyperplane then $p \cdot x' = \alpha$ and $p \cdot (x' + \Delta x) = \alpha$, so $p \cdot \Delta x = 0$. Thus p is orthogonal (*i.e.* "normal") to any vector Δx that is a "perturbation" from any one point in the hyperplane to any other point in the hyperplane.

Like any function mapping to the real line, the function $p \cdot x$ has contour sets, upper-contour sets and lower-contour sets. For a given α, the level-α contour set of $p \cdot x$ is the hyperplane itself. The upper and lower-contour sets of the hyperplane are called *half-spaces* because a hyperplane splits a space into two pieces. As you will see in the next section, the proper language is that a hyperplane *separates* a space into two half-spaces.

Definition 6.2 (Half-spaces). *Given $p \in \Re^n$ with $p \neq \underline{0}$ and $\|p\|_E < \infty$ and given $\alpha \in \Re$, the set*

$$UH(p, \alpha) = \{x \in \Re^n \mid p \cdot x \geq \alpha\}$$

is the upper half-space of the hyperplane $H(p, \alpha) = \{x \in \Re^n \mid p \cdot x = \alpha\}$ and the set

$$LH(p, \alpha) = \{x \in \Re^n \mid p \cdot x \leq \alpha\}$$

is the lower half-space of $H(p, \alpha)$.

A half-space in $\Re^n$ is a closed and weakly convex subset. By the way, in this chapter we consider only subsets of the real vector spaces $\Re^n$, so terms such as open, closed, bounded, and compact are all made with respect to the Euclidean metric topology on $\Re^n$.

6.2 Separations of Sets

What do we mean by "separating two sets by a hyperplane"? All it means is that one set lies entirely within one of the hyperplane's half-spaces and the other set lies entirely within the other half-space.

Definition 6.3 (Separation of Sets). *Let S_1 and S_2 be nonempty subsets of $\Re^n$. Let $H(p, \alpha)$ be a hyperplane in $\Re^n$. Then $H(p, \alpha)$ separates S_1 and S_2 if*

$$p \cdot x \geq \alpha \geq p \cdot y \ \forall \ x \in S_1, \ \forall \ y \in S_2. \tag{6.2}$$

Figure 6.2 displays some examples of separated sets. Notice that when two closed sets are separated they may still have one or more boundary points in common (see

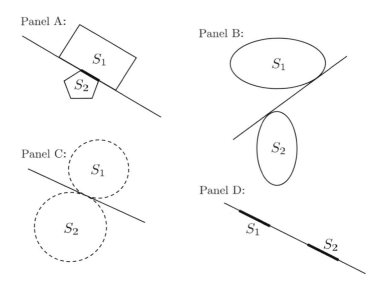

Figure 6.2: Separated sets.

panel A of the figure). If, however, one or both of two separated sets is an open set, then the two sets must be disjoint (see panel C of the figure).

Also notice from panel D of the figure that separation allows the possibility that the separated sets may both be contained in the separating hyperplane; *i.e.* $S_1 \cup S_2 \subseteq H$ is allowed by Definition 6.3. Since some may regard this as not real separation, we may insist that it not be allowed. Applying this restriction gives us the idea of *properly separating* the sets S_1 and S_2.

Definition 6.4 (Proper Separation of Sets). *Let S_1 and S_2 be nonempty subsets of $\Re^n$. Let $H(p, \alpha)$ be a hyperplane in $\Re^n$. Then $H(p, \alpha)$ properly separates S_1 and S_2 if*
(a) $H(p, \alpha)$ separates S_1 and S_2, and
(b) $S_1 \cup S_2$ is not a subset of $H(p, \alpha)$.

S_1 and S_2 are properly separated in panels A, B and C of Figure 6.2 but are only separated in panel D of the figure.

Then again you may wish to argue that two sets X and Y are not separated unless the value of $p \cdot x$ for any $x \in X$ is strictly larger than is the value of $p \cdot y$ for any $y \in Y$. For example, in panel A of Figure 6.2, the sets S_1 and S_2 have boundary points in common, so you might consider these sets to be not really separated. This is a reasonable view to take, and it is called *strict separation*.

Definition 6.5 (Strict Separation of Sets). *Let S_1 and S_2 be nonempty subsets of $\Re^n$. Let $H(p, \alpha)$ be a hyperplane in $\Re^n$. Then $H(p, \alpha)$ strictly separates S_1 and S_2 if*

$$p \cdot x > \alpha > p \cdot y \; \forall \; x \in S_1, \; \forall \; y \in S_2. \tag{6.3}$$

Figure 6.3 displays some examples of strict separations of sets. Notice that the sets S_1 and S_2 in panels B and D of Figures 6.2 and 6.3 are the same, but the hyperplanes are different. Thus the same pair of sets may be separated or strictly separated depending upon the position of the separating hyperplane. Notice also that the panels C of Figures 6.2 and 6.3 are the same. In the two panels C, the sets S_1 and S_2 are strictly separated because the sets are open. Therefore the sets are disjoint and neither set has a point in common with the separating hyperplane: $S_1 \cap S_2 = \emptyset$, $S_1 \cap H = \emptyset$ and $S_2 \cap H = \emptyset$.

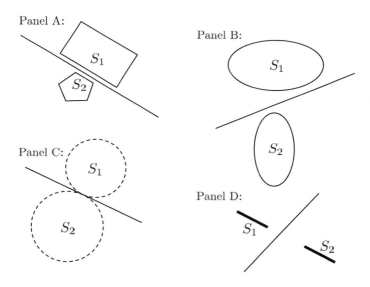

Figure 6.3: Strictly separated sets.

Even so, you could say that in your opinion the sets in panel C are "not really separated" because there are points in the two sets that are arbitrarily close to each other. You might argue that for two sets to really be separated there should be a strictly positive distance between their closest points. This is the idea of *strong separation*.

Definition 6.6 (Strong Separation of Sets)**.** *Let S_1 and S_2 be nonempty subsets of $\Re^n$. Let $H(p, \alpha)$ be a hyperplane in $\Re^n$. Then $H(p, \alpha)$ strongly separates S_1 and S_2 if, for some $\varepsilon > 0$,*

$$p{\cdot}x \geq \alpha + \varepsilon > \alpha - \varepsilon \geq p{\cdot}y \ \forall \ x \in S_1, \ \forall \ y \in S_2. \tag{6.4}$$

The sets in panels A, B, and D of Figure 6.3 are strongly separated. The sets in panel C of the figure are only strictly separated.

In the following definition, the *closure* of a set S is denoted by $\overline{S}$. $\overline{S}$ is the set S together with all of the boundary points of S. If S is a closed set, then $S = \overline{S}$. Otherwise, $S \subset \overline{S}$.

Definition 6.7 (Supporting Hyperplanes and Points of Support)**.** *Let $S \subseteq \Re^n$ be a nonempty set. Let $H(p, \alpha)$ be a hyperplane in $\Re^n$. If $x' \in \overline{S}$ is such that $p{\cdot}x' = \alpha$ and either $p{\cdot}x \geq \alpha$ for every $x \in S$ or $p{\cdot}x \leq \alpha$ for every $x \in S$, then x' is a* point of support *in H for S and H is a hyperplane* supporting *to S.*

Put into words, this definition says that a point x' in a hyperplane is a point of support for a set S if, first, S is contained entirely within one of the hyperplane's half-spaces (which half-space, upper or lower, does not matter) and, second, x' is a boundary point for S.

A point of support always belongs to the supporting hyperplane and may or may not also belong to the set being supported. In panel A of Figure 6.2, all of the points in the interval indicated by the thick line are points of support in the hyperplane for both of the closed sets $S_1 = \overline{S}_1$ and $S_2 = \overline{S}_2$. The points in the lower boundary of the rectangle S_1 that are not also members of the pentahedron S_2 are points of support in the hyperplane for S_1 only. The hyperplane supports both S_1 and S_2. In panel B there are two points of support in H, one for each of the closed sets $S_1 = \overline{S}_1$ and $S_2 = \overline{S}_2$, and the hyperplane supports both sets. In panel C the sets S_1 and S_2 are both open. There is a common point of support in the hyperplane for both sets. This point of support is not a member of either set, but it does belong to the closures $\overline{S}_1$ and $\overline{S}_2$ (it is a boundary point for both sets) of the sets. In panel D of Figure 6.3, the hyperplane strictly separates the sets S_1 and S_2, but there are no points of support because neither S_1 nor S_2 has a boundary point belonging to the hyperplane. This is an example of the fact that a hyperplane that strictly separates two sets may not support either set. Panel D is also an example of the fact that a hyperplane that strongly separates two sets contains no points of support.

6.3 Separating a Point from a Set

The place to begin our discussion is with the relatively simple problem of separating a set from a point that does not belong to the set. All of the more sophisticated results on separating sets with hyperplanes rely upon the answer to this initial problem.

Theorem 6.1 (Separating a Singleton Set from a Closed Set). *Let $S \subset \Re^n$ be a nonempty set that is closed with respect to E^n. Let $x_0 \in \Re^n$ with $x_0 \notin S$. Then*

(i) there exists $x' \in S$, such that $0 < d_E(x_0, x') \leq d_E(x_0, x) \ \forall \ x \in S$.

If, additionally, S is a convex set, then

(ii) x' is unique and there exists a hyperplane with normal $p \in \Re^n$, with $p \neq \underline{0}$ and $\|p\|_E < \infty$, such that

$$p{\cdot}x > p{\cdot}x_0 \ \forall \ x \in S.$$

For now let's concern ourselves with only part (i) of the theorem. The point x_0 is not a member of the set S. Since S is closed, x_0 is not a member of the boundary of S and so must lie some positive distance away from S; thus $0 < d_E(x_0, x)$ for every $x \in S$. Part (i) also says that the closed set S must contain at least one point x' that is closest to x_0. A picture makes clear why these statements are true, so look at Figure 6.4.

When we use the Euclidean metric to measure distances in $\Re^2$, a set of points equally distant from x_0 is a circle. The common distance of these points from x_0 is the radius of the circle. It is clear, then, that there will be a distance at which one of these circles just touches the boundary of S, possibly at more than one point, as is demonstrated in Figure 6.4. x' and x'' are thus both points in S that are as close as possible to the point x_0; *i.e.* $d_E(x_0, x') = d_E(x_0, x'') \leq d_E(x_0, x)$ for all $x \in S$. Since neither x' nor x'' is the same as x_0, we know that this minimal distance is strictly positive; *i.e.* $d_E(x_0, x') = d_E(x_0, x'') > 0$. Now that we know what part (i) says, let's prove it.

Proof of (i). Choose any value for a radius $\mu > 0$, such that the closed ball

$$\overline{B}_{d_E}(x_0, \mu) = \{x \in \Re^n \mid d_E(x_0, x) \leq \mu\} \cap S \neq \emptyset.$$

$\overline{B}_{d_E}(x_0, \mu)$ and S are both closed sets, so their intersection $\overline{B}_{d_E}(x_0, \mu) \cap S$ (the shaded region in Figure 6.4) is also a closed set. $\overline{B}_{d_E}(x_0, \mu) \cap S$ is also a bounded set because it is completely contained in the ball $\overline{B}_{d_E}(x_0, \mu)$. Hence $\overline{B}_{d_E}(x_0, \mu) \cap S$ is a nonempty and compact set.

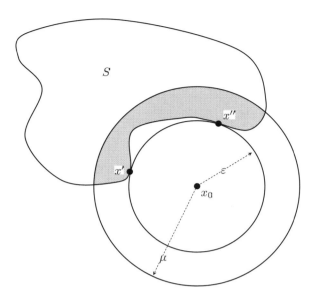

Figure 6.4: Part (i) of Theorem 6.1.

The Euclidean metric function $d_E(x_0, x)$ is a continuous function of x. Therefore, by Weierstrass's Theorem, the function attains a minimum at some point $x' \in \overline{B}_{d_E}(x_0, \mu) \cap S$. That is, there is a point x' in $\overline{B}_{d_E}(x_0, \mu) \cap S$ that is least distant from x_0:

$$\varepsilon = d_E(x_0, x') \leq d_E(x_0, x) \ \forall \ x \in \overline{B}_{d_E}(x_0, \mu) \cap S. \tag{6.5}$$

$\varepsilon > 0$ because $x' \in S$ and $x_0 \notin S$ imply that $x' \neq x_0$.

Now consider any point $x \in S$ that is not in the intersection $\overline{B}_{d_E}(x_0, \varepsilon) \cap S$. Then $x \notin \overline{B}_{d_E}(x_0, \varepsilon)$, and so $d_E(x_0, x) > d_E(x_0, x')$. $\square$

Now let's think about part (ii) of the theorem. The picture to have in mind now is Figure 6.5.

Now that S is a convex set, the closed ball centered at x_0 that only just touches S can touch in only one place, $x = x'$. It is easy to see that there will be lots of hyperplanes that separate the singleton closed set $\{x_0\}$ from the closed set S. In particular there will be a separating hyperplane passing through the point x' (see the figure). For now, don't worry about either the point x'' or the line joining it to the point x'. The proof is not complicated. We will construct a particular hyperplane and then show that it has the properties stated in part (ii). The normal of the hyperplane is the vector $p = x' - x_0$ shown in the figure. The level of the hyperplane

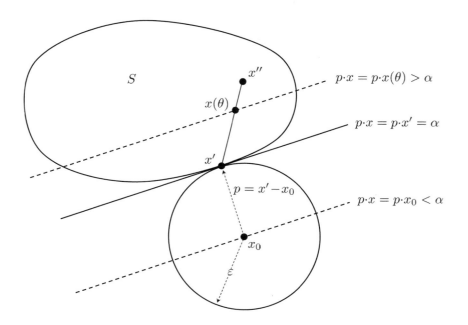

Figure 6.5: Part (ii) of Theorem 6.1.

is $\alpha = p{\cdot}x' = (x' - x_0){\cdot}x'$. The figure displays the hyperplane as the solid straight line labeled as $p{\cdot}x = \alpha$. It should be obvious from the figure that every point in S lies in the upper-half-space of the hyperplane, while x_0 lies strictly inside the hyperplane's lower-half-space, so $p{\cdot}x = (x' - x_0){\cdot}x \geq \alpha > p{\cdot}x_0 = (x' - x_0){\cdot}x_0$. Now let's prove part (ii).

Proof of Part (ii). Choose $p = x' - x_0$ and $\alpha = p{\cdot}x' = (x' - x_0){\cdot}x'$. $p \neq \underline{0}$ since, from part (i), $x' \neq x_0$. Also, $\|p\|_E = \|x' - x_0\|_E < \infty$ since there is only a finite distance between x' and x_0.

We will start by proving that $p{\cdot}x_0 < \alpha$.

$$p{\cdot}x_0 = (x' - x_0){\cdot}x_0 = (x' - x_0){\cdot}(x_0 - x' + x')$$
$$= -(x' - x_0){\cdot}(x' - x_0) + (x' - x_0){\cdot}x'.$$

$x' \neq x_0$ so $(x' - x_0){\cdot}(x' - x_0) > 0$. Therefore

$$p{\cdot}x_0 < (x' - x_0){\cdot}x' = p{\cdot}x' = \alpha.$$

Now we will show that $p{\cdot}x \geq \alpha$ for every $x \in S$. Choose any $x'' \in S$. We must show that $p{\cdot}x'' \geq \alpha = p{\cdot}x'$. Since S is a convex set and $x' \in S$, for any value of $\theta \in (0, 1]$

(notice that we choose not to allow $\theta = 0$) the point $x(\theta) = \theta x'' + (1 - \theta)x' \in S$; see Figure 6.5. In part (i) we established that x' is at least as close to x_0 as is other point $(x(\theta)$, for instance) in S, so

$$d_E(x_0, x') = \|x' - x_0\|_E$$
$$\leq d_E(x_0, x(\theta)) = \|\theta x'' + (1 - \theta)x' - x_0\|_E = \|\theta(x'' - x_0) + (1 - \theta)(x' - x_0)\|_E.$$

Squaring both sides of this equality gives us

$$(x' - x_0){\cdot}(x' - x_0)$$
$$\leq \theta^2(x'' - x_0){\cdot}(x'' - x_0) + 2\theta(1 - \theta)(x'' - x_0){\cdot}(x' - x_0) + (1 - \theta)^2(x' - x_0){\cdot}(x' - x_0).$$

That is,

$$0 \leq \theta^2(x'' - x_0){\cdot}(x'' - x_0) + 2\theta(1 - \theta)(x'' - x_0){\cdot}(x' - x_0) - \theta(2 - \theta)(x' - x_0){\cdot}(x' - x_0).$$

Because $\theta > 0$ (remember, $\theta = 0$ is not allowed), we may divide by θ and obtain

$$0 \leq \theta(x'' - x_0){\cdot}(x'' - x_0) + 2(1 - \theta)(x'' - x_0){\cdot}(x' - x_0) - (2 - \theta)(x' - x_0){\cdot}(x' - x_0). \quad (6.6)$$

The right-hand side of (6.6) is a continuous function of θ, so by allowing $\theta \to 0$, we learn that

$$0 \leq (x' - x_0){\cdot}(x'' - x_0) - (x' - x_0){\cdot}(x' - x_0) = (x' - x_0){\cdot}(x'' - x').$$

Since $p = x' - x_0$, this is the statement that $p{\cdot}x'' \geq p{\cdot}x' = \alpha$.

All that is left to do is to show that x' is unique. Suppose it is not unique; *i.e.* suppose that there is another point $\tilde{x} \neq x'$, such that $d_E(x_0, x') = d_E(x_0, \tilde{x})$. Notice that the closed ball $\overline{B}_{d_E}(x_0, \varepsilon)$ is a strictly convex set. Since $x', \tilde{x} \in \overline{B}_{d_E}(x_0, \varepsilon)$, for any $\theta \in (0, 1)$ the point $\hat{x} = \theta x' + (1 - \theta)\tilde{x}$ lies in the interior of $\overline{B}_{d_E}(x_0, \varepsilon)$, and so $d_E(x_0, \hat{x}) < \varepsilon$. Since S is a convex set, $\hat{x} \in S$ also. But then neither x' nor $\tilde{x}$ is a point in S that is closest to x_0. Contradiction. Hence x' is unique. $\square$

We now need to generalize part (ii) by removing the condition that S must be a closed set, so consider the more general problem of separating a point x_0 from any (closed, open, or neither) nonempty and convex subset S in $\Re^n$. Whenever we consider a theorem for a more general problem, we should anticipate that the result of the theorem will be less informative than for a special case of the problem, so what do you expect the more general theorem's statement to be? Think about it. (Hint: Draw a picture for the case when S is an open set.)

The change is that the strict inequality in part (ii) becomes only a weak inequality. Here is the theorem.

Theorem 6.2 (Separating a Point from Any Nonempty Convex Set). *Let $S \subset \Re^n$ be nonempty and convex. Let $x_0 \in \Re^n$ with $x_0 \notin S$. Then there exists a hyperplane with normal $p \in \Re^n$, with $p \neq \underline{0}$ and $\|p\|_E < \infty$, such that*

$$p{\cdot}x \geq p{\cdot}x_0 \ \forall \ x \in S.$$

Why is there no longer a part (i) as in Theorem 6.1? Remember that, in our proof of part (i) of Theorem 6.1, we used Weierstrass's Theorem to establish the existence of the point x' in S that is closest to x_0. To do so we needed to know that the intersection $\overline{B}_{d_E}(x, \mu) \cap S$ was a closed and bounded set. In the more general case, we know that the intersection is bounded, but it need not be a closed set. Because of this, a point such as x' may not exist (why not?).

Why does the strict inequality in part (ii) of Theorem 6.1 change to only a weak inequality in the more general case? Have a look at Figure 6.6. If the set S is open, then the point $x_0 \notin S$ could be a boundary point for S. In such a case, all we can say is that $p{\cdot}x \geq \alpha = p{\cdot}x_0$.

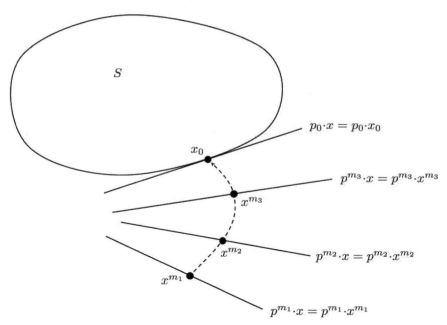

Figure 6.6: Case (ii), with x_0 a boundary point of the open set S.

The proof of the theorem has to consider two possible cases: (i) x_0 is not a boundary point of S, and (ii) x_0 is a boundary point of S (as is displayed in Figure 6.6). In the proof we will again use $\overline{S}$ to denote the closure of S.

Proof. Case (i): $x_0 \notin \overline{S}$. $\overline{S}$ is a closed set, so, by part (ii) of Theorem 6.1, there exists a hyperplane with normal $p \in \Re^n$, where $p \neq \underline{0}$ and $\|p\|_E < \infty$, such that $p \cdot x > p \cdot x_0$ for every $x \in \overline{S}$. Since $S \subseteq \overline{S}$, it follows that $p \cdot x > p \cdot x_0$ for every $x \in S$.

Case (ii): $x_0 \in \overline{S}$ and $x_0 \notin S$. Thus x_0 is a boundary point for S. Consider any open ball centered at x_0. This ball must contain points in $\overline{S}$ and points not in $\overline{S}$. From the points in the ball that are not in $\overline{S}$, we can form a sequence $\{x^m\}_{m=1}^{\infty}$ that converges to x_0. Each of these points x^m is exterior to the closed and convex set $\overline{S}$, so, for each point in turn, we can apply part (ii) of Theorem 6.1. This tells us that for each point x^m there is a hyperplane with normal $p^m \in \Re^m$, with $p^m \neq \underline{0}$ and $\|p^m\|_E < \infty$, such that $p^m \cdot x > p^m \cdot x^m$ for every $x \in \overline{S}$. So now we have two sequences, $\{x^m\}_{m=1}^{\infty}$ and its companion $\{p^m\}_{m=1}^{\infty}$. This gives us a sequence of hyperplanes, as displayed in Figure 6.6. We want to show that there is a subsequence of these hyperplanes that converges to a hyperplane that supports $\overline{S}$ at x_0. We cannot guarantee that the sequence $\{p^m\}_{m=1}^{\infty}$ converges, but, as you will see in a moment, it must possess a convergent subsequence.

Without any loss of generality, we will restrict ourselves to vectors p^m with "lengths" (actually norms: distances from the origin) that are not greater than unity: $\|p\|_E \leq 1$ (this amounts merely to rescaling units of measurement). Then the vectors p^m all belong to the compact ball centered at the origin $\underline{0} \in \Re^n$ with a radius of unity. Any sequence in a compact set possesses a convergent subsequence. Thus $\{p^m\}_{m=1}^{\infty}$ possesses a convergent subsequence that we will denote by $\{p^{m_k}\}_{k=1}^{\infty}$. Denote the limit of this subsequence by p_0; $p^{m_k} \to p_0$. Accompanying this subsequence is the subsequence $\{x^{m_k}\}_{k=1}^{\infty}$. The parent sequence $\{x^m\}_{m=1}^{\infty}$ converges to x_0, so any subsequence must also converge to x_0: $x^{m_k} \to x_0$.

The function $p \cdot x$ is jointly continuous with respect to p and x, so

$$\lim_{k \to \infty} (p^{m_k} \cdot x^{m_k}) = \left(\lim_{k \to \infty} p^{m_k} \right) \cdot \left(\lim_{k \to \infty} x^{m_k} \right) = p_0 \cdot x_0. \tag{6.7}$$

Also, for each $k = 1, 2, \ldots$, $p^{m_k} \cdot x > p^{m_k} \cdot x^{m_k}$ for every $x \in \overline{S}$, so

$$\lim_{k \to \infty} (p^{m_k} \cdot x) \geq \lim_{k \to \infty} (p^{m_k} \cdot x^{m_k}) \ \forall \ x \in \overline{S}. \tag{6.8}$$

Comparing (6.7) and (6.8) shows that

$$\lim_{k \to \infty} (p^{m_k} \cdot x) = \left(\lim_{k \to \infty} p^{m_k} \right) \cdot x = p_0 \cdot x \geq p_0 \cdot x_0 \ \forall \ x \in \overline{S}. \tag{6.9}$$

Since $S \subseteq \overline{S}$, it follows from (6.9) that

$$p_0 \cdot x \geq p_0 \cdot x_0 \ \forall \ x \in S. \qquad \square$$

6.4   Separating a Set from a Set

Theorems 6.1 and 6.2 describe the separation of two sets, but one of the sets is merely a singleton. We need to describe the separations of more general types of sets. For economists one of the most useful of the more general separation theorems is due to Hermann Minkowski. His theorem tells us that any pair of nonempty, disjoint, and convex sets can be separated by a hyperplane. The result is geometrically obvious (see all of the panels in Figures 6.2 and 6.3) and underlies much of constrained optimization theory and the theory of general equilibrium that primarily was developed by Kenneth Arrow, Gerard Debreu, and Lionel McKenzie.

Theorem 6.3 (Minkowski). *Let S_1 and S_2 be nonempty, convex and disjoint subsets of $\Re^n$. Then there exists a hyperplane with a normal $p \in \Re^n$, where $p \neq \underline{0}$ and $\|p\|_E < \infty$, and a level $\alpha \in \Re$, such that*

$$p \cdot x \geq \alpha \geq p \cdot y \; \forall \; x \in S_1 \; and \; \forall \; y \in S_2.$$

The proof is just a simple application of Theorem 6.2. Here is the idea. The sets S_1 and S_2 have no common element, so ask yourself "Does the set $S_1 + (-S_2)$ contain the origin, $\underline{0}$?" Think about it. If you have forgotten what is meant by the negative $-S$ of a set S, then have a look in Section 2.5.

If $\underline{0} \in S_1 + (-S_2)$, then there is an element $x \in S_1$ and an element $-x \in -S_2$. But then $x \in S_1$ and $x \in S_2$, in which case the sets S_1 and S_2 are not disjoint. Thus $\underline{0} \notin S_1 + (-S_2)$. Now set $x_0 = \underline{0}$ in Theorem 6.2 and we learn that there is a hyperplane with a normal p, such that $p \cdot (x + (-y)) \geq p \cdot \underline{0} = 0$ for all $x + (-y) \in S_1 + (-S_2)$. This is the same as saying that $p \cdot x \geq p \cdot y$ for all $x \in S_1$ and for all $y \in S_2$. It then follows that $\inf_{x \in S_1} p \cdot x \geq \sup_{y \in S_2} p \cdot y$, so to complete the result all we need to do is choose any value for α that is in the interval $[\sup_{y \in S_2} p \cdot y, \inf_{x \in S_1} p \cdot x]$. That's it!

6.5   How Do We Use What We Have Learned?

We can use what we have learned here in two distinct and valuable ways. The first is to use separating hyperplanes to implement computer algorithms for numerical computation of solutions to constrained optimization problems; this is a topic not discussed in this book. The second is to use hyperplanes to separate sets called *convex cones*. This is a method used to solve constrained optimization problems in which we may use the calculus. If you have already had some exposure to constrained optimization problems, then they probably were problems that you solved using some form of differentiation. When you solved such a problem, you were in fact using a hyperplane to separate two convex cones. This particular procedure is the one most often used when the solution sought to a constrained optimization problem is algebraic, rather than numeric. For example, if we attempt to solve a consumer demand problem not for numerical values of quantities demanded, but instead for demand functions, then typically we will use some form of differentiation to derive these functions. Or perhaps you want to solve a firm's profit maximization problem for an output supply function and input demand functions, rather than numerical values of quantity supplied and input quantities demanded. This is the approach most often taken by economists, so it is the approach that is emphasized in the chapters that follow. The next task, therefore, is look at the special sets that we call cones and convex cones. These are easy ideas, so don't worry.

6.6 Problems

Problem 6.1. Consider the choice problem of a consumer who has an endowment $\omega = (10, 5)$, faces prices $p = (3, 2)$, and has the direct utility function $U(x_1, x_2) = x_1^{1/3} x_2^{1/3}$.

(i) Compute the consumer's ordinary demands. Then compute the consumer's vector z of net trades. On a diagram, *accurately* draw the vectors p and z. Prove that p and z are orthogonal.

(ii) Now suppose that the consumer's utility function is $U(x_1, x_2, x_3) = x_1^{1/3} x_2^{1/3} x_3^{1/3}$. The consumer's endowment is now $\omega = (10, 5, 4)$ and prices are $p = (3, 2, 2)$. What is the consumer's vector z of net trades? Prove that z is orthogonal to p. Draw p and z on a three-dimensional diagram.

(iii) For each of the two above cases in turn, what hyperplane separates which sets, and what are the supports?

Problem 6.2. Why is it that, when we define a hyperplane in $\Re^n$, we insist that the hyperplane's normal vector p is not the n-dimensional zero vector? Answer this question by asking yourself what type of set would be a "hyperplane" with a zero vector for its normal.

Problem 6.3. Consider the closed and convex subset of $\Re^2$ that is $X = \{(x_1, x_2) \mid 2x_1^2 + x_2^2 \leq 9\}$. The boundary of this set is an ellipse centered at $(0, 0)$. Also consider the point $x_0 = (8, 2)$.

(i) Show that x_0 is exterior to the set X.

(ii) Using the Euclidean metric to measure distances, discover the point $x' \in X$ that is closest to x_0.

(iii) Discover the hyperplane that supports X at the point x'.

Problem 6.4. A separation theorem states that, if X is a closed, convex, and nonempty subset of $\Re^n$ and $x_0 \notin X$, then there exists a vector $p \in \Re^n$, $p \neq \underline{0}$ with $\|p\|_E < \infty$ and a scalar $\alpha \in \Re$, such that

$$p{\cdot}x_0 < \alpha \leq p{\cdot}x \ \forall \ x \in X. \tag{6.10}$$

Is the result valid if X is not a closed set?

Problem 6.5. Minkowski's separating hyperplane theorem states that, "If X and Y are nonempty, convex, and disjoint subsets of $\Re^n$, then there exists $p \in \Re^n$, $p \neq \underline{0}$, $\|p\|_E < \infty$, and $\alpha \in \Re$, such that $p{\cdot}x \leq \alpha$ for every $x \in X$ and $\alpha \leq p{\cdot}y$ for every

$y \in Y$." The sets X and Y are disjoint and at least weakly convex, so why is it that Minkowski did not strengthen his result to conclude that, for the given conditions, either

(a) $p \cdot x \leq \alpha < p \cdot y \ \forall \ x \in X, \ \forall \ y \in Y$, or

(b) $p \cdot x < \alpha \leq p \cdot y \ \forall \ x \in X, \ \forall \ y \in Y$?

Problem 6.6. Let X_1 and X_2 be two nonempty and convex subsets of $\Re^n$. The hyperplane with normal $p \in \Re^n$, $p \neq \underline{0}$, $\|p\|_E < \infty$ and level α supports X_1 at x_1^* and supports X_2 at x_2^*. Let $X = X_1 + X_2$. Does the hyperplane with normal p and level 2α support X at $x^* = x_1^* + x_2^*$? Prove your answer.

6.7 Answers

Answer to Problem 6.1. The consumer's utility function is $U(x_1, x_2) = x_1^{1/3} x_2^{1/3}$, her endowment is $\omega = (10, 5)$, and she faces prices $p = (3, 2)$.

(i) The consumer's ordinary demand functions are

$$x_1^*(p_1, p_2, \omega_1, \omega_2) = \frac{p_1\omega_1 + p_2\omega_2}{2p_1} \quad \text{and} \quad x_2^*(p_1, p_2, \omega_1, \omega_2) = \frac{p_1\omega_1 + p_2\omega_2}{2p_2},$$

so the consumer's net ordinary demand functions are

$$z_1(p_1, p_2, \omega_1, \omega_2) = x_1^*(p_1, p_2, \omega_1, \omega_2) - \omega_1 = \frac{p_1\omega_1 + p_2\omega_2}{2p_1} - \omega_1,$$

$$\text{and} \quad z_2(p_1, p_2, \omega_1, \omega_2) = x_2^*(p_1, p_2, \omega_1, \omega_2) - \omega_2 = \frac{p_1\omega_1 + p_1\omega_2}{2p_2} - \omega_2.$$

Evaluated for $(\omega_1, \omega_2) = (10, 5)$ and $(p_1, p_2) = (3, 2)$, the ordinary and net ordinary quantities demanded are

$$x_1^* = \frac{20}{3} \text{ and } x_2^* = 10, \quad \text{and} \quad z_1 = \frac{20}{3} - 10 = -\frac{10}{3} \text{ and } z_2 = 10 - 5 = 5.$$

Figure 6.7 displays the standard rational choice picture in which the highest available utility is achieved at the point $(x_1^*, x_2^*) = (20/3, 10)$ on the budget constraint (the separating hyperplane) that supports both the budget set S_1 and the set S_2 of bundles that are weakly preferred to (x_1^*, x_1^*). These are the two sets that are separated by the hyperplane. Figure 6.8 displays the vector of net trades $z = (z_1, z_2) = (-10/3, 5)$ and the price vector $p = (3, 2)$ that is the normal of the separating hyperplane. The Euclidean inner product of these vectors is zero, proving that p and z are orthogonal.

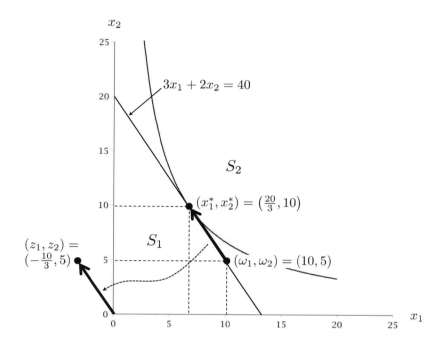

Figure 6.7: The budget constraint is a hyperplane that separates the budget set S_1 from the set S_2 of consumption bundles that are weakly preferred to the bundle $(20/3, 10)$.

(ii) The consumer's ordinary demand functions are

$$x_1^*(p_1, p_2, p_3, \omega_1, \omega_2, \omega_3) = \frac{p_1\omega_1 + p_2\omega_2 + p_3\omega_3}{3p_1},$$

$$x_2^*(p_1, p_2, p_3, \omega_1, \omega_2, \omega_3) = \frac{p_1\omega_1 + p_2\omega_2 + p_3\omega_3}{3p_2},$$

$$\text{and} \quad x_3^*(p_1, p_2, p_3, \omega_1, \omega_2, \omega_3) = \frac{p_1\omega_1 + p_2\omega_2 + p_3\omega_3}{3p_3},$$

so the consumer's net ordinary demand functions are

$$z_1(p_1, p_2, p_3, \omega_1, \omega_2, \omega_3) = x_1^*(p_1, p_2, p_3, \omega_1, \omega_2, \omega_3) - \omega_1 = \frac{p_1\omega_1 + p_2\omega_2 + p_3\omega_3}{3p_1} - \omega_1,$$

$$z_2(p_1, p_2, p_3, \omega_1, \omega_2, \omega_3) = x_2^*(p_1, p_2, p_3, \omega_1, \omega_2, \omega_3) - \omega_2 = \frac{p_1\omega_1 + p_2\omega_2 + p_3\omega_3}{3p_2} - \omega_2,$$

$$z_3(p_1, p_2, p_3, \omega_1, \omega_2, \omega_3) = x_3^*(p_1, p_2, p_3, \omega_1, \omega_2, \omega_3) - \omega_3 = \frac{p_1\omega_1 + p_2\omega_2 + p_3\omega_3}{3p_3} - \omega_3.$$

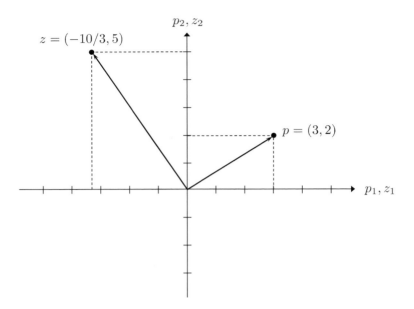

Figure 6.8: The hyperplane's normal p and the net trade vector z are orthogonal.

Evaluated for $(\omega_1, \omega_2, \omega_3) = (10, 5, 4)$ and $(p_1, p_2, p_3) = (3, 2, 2)$, the ordinary and the net ordinary quantities demanded are

$$x_1^* = \frac{16}{3}\ ,\ x_2^* = 8,\ x_3^* = 8 \quad \text{and} \quad z_1 = \frac{16}{3} - 10 = -\frac{14}{3},\ z_2 = 8 - 5 = 3,\ z_3 = 8 - 4 = 4.$$

Both panels of Figure 6.9 display the standard rational choice picture in which the highest achievable utility is achieved at the point $(x_1^*, x_2^*, x_3^*) = (16/3, 8, 8)$ on the budget constraint (the separating hyperplane) that supports both the budget set and the set of weakly preferred bundles. These are the two sets separated by the hyperplane. Figure 6.10 displays the net trade vector $z = (z_1, z_2, z_3) = (-14/3, 3, 4)$ and the price vector $p = (3, 2, 2)$ that is the normal of the separating hyperplane. The Euclidean inner product of these vectors is zero, so p and z are orthogonal.

(iii) For part (i), the budget hyperplane $\mathcal{H} = \{x \in \Re_+^2 \mid 3x_1 + 2x_2 = 40\}$ separates the budget set $\mathcal{B} = \{x \in \Re_+^2 \mid 3x_1 + 2x_2 \leq 40\}$ from the set $\mathcal{WP} = \{x \in \Re_+^2 \mid U(x_1, x_2) \geq (200/3)^{1/3}\}$. The point of support is $(x_1^*, x_2^*) = (20/3, 10)$; see Figure 6.7.

For part (ii), the budget hyperplane $\mathcal{H} = \{x \in \Re_+^3 \mid 3x_1 + 2x_2 + 2x_3 = 48\}$ separates the budget set $\mathcal{B} = \{x \in \Re_+^3 \mid 3x_1 + 2x_2 + 2x_3 \leq 48\}$ from the set $\mathcal{WP} = \{x \in \Re_+^3 \mid U(x_1, x_2, x_3) \geq (1024/3)^{1/3}\}$ of consumption bundles that are weakly preferred to the bundle $(x_1^*, x_2^*, x_3^*) = (16/3, 8, 8)$. The point of support is $(x_1^*, x_2^*, x_3^*) = (16/3, 8, 8)$;

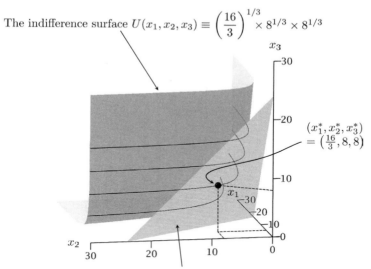

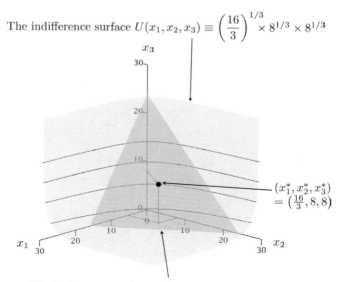

Figure 6.9: The budget constraint is a hyperplane that separates the budget set from the set of consumption bundles that are weakly preferred to the rationally chosen bundle $(16/3, 8, 8)$.

see both panels of Figure 6.9.   □

Answer to Problem 6.2. A hyperplane in $\Re^n$ with a normal $p = \underline{0}$ would be a set of the form

$$\mathcal{H} = \{(x_1, \ldots, x_n) \mid 0 \times x_1 + \cdots + 0 \times x_n = \alpha\},$$

where α is the level of the hyperplane. Necessarily, $\alpha = 0$. So what is the subset of $\Re^n$ that is the "hyperplane"

$$\mathcal{H} = \{(x_1, \ldots, x_n) \mid 0 \times x_1 + \cdots + 0 \times x_n = 0\}?$$

The answer is "All of $\Re^n$," which is not a set that we have in mind when we talk of a hyper*plane*.   □

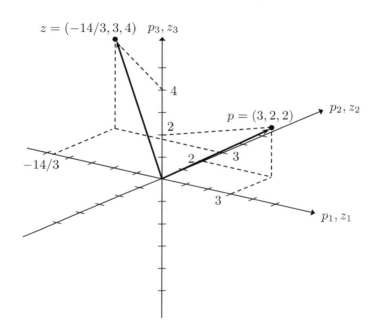

Figure 6.10: The net trade vector z and the normal p of the separating (budget constraint) hyperplane are orthogonal.

Answer to Problem 6.3.
(i) For $x_0 = (x_1, x_2) = (8, 2)$, the value of $2x_1^2 + x_2^2 = 132 > 9$, so $(8, 2)$ is exterior to the set X.

(ii) Clearly $x' = (x_1', x_2')$ is a boundary point for the set X, so $2(x_1')^2 + (x_2')^2 = 9$. The Euclidean distance between the point $x_0 = (8, 2)$ and the point (x_1', x_2') is

$$d_E((x_1', x_2'), (8, 2)) = +\sqrt{(x_1' - 8)^2 + (x_2' - 2)^2},$$

so the problem to be solved is the equality-constrained minimization problem

$$\min_{x_1, x_2} +\sqrt{(x_1 - 8)^2 + (x_2 - 2)^2} \quad \text{subject to} \quad g(x_1, x_2) = 2x_1^2 + x_2^2 = 9.$$

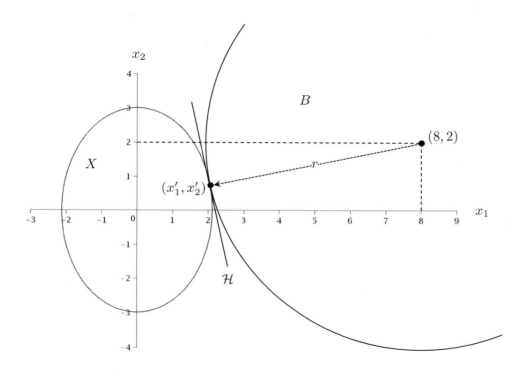

Figure 6.11: Finding the point (x_1', x_2') in X that is closest to the point $x_0 = (8, 2)$.

One way to solve this problem is to use the constraint $2x_1^2 + x_2^2 = 9$ to substitute for, say, x_2 as a function of x_1 in the problem's objective function and then to use differentiation to seek values for x_1 that may be the global minimizing solution to the problem. For an alternative approach, consider Figure 6.11. The figure shows that the point we seek, (x_1', x_2'), is not only on the elliptical boundary of X but is also a point at which the marginal rate of substitution (slope) along that boundary must be the same as the marginal rate of substitution (slope) along the boundary

$h(x_1, x_2) = (x_1 - 8)^2 + (x_2 - 2)^2 = r^2$ of the closed ball B with radius r centered at $(8, 2)$ with (x_1', x_2') contained in its circumference. These marginal rate of substitutions are

$$\mathrm{MRS}_g(x_1, x_2) = \frac{\mathrm{d}x_2}{\mathrm{d}x_1}\big|_{g\equiv 9} = -\frac{2x_1}{x_2} \quad \text{and} \quad \mathrm{MRS}_h(x_1, x_2) = \frac{\mathrm{d}x_2}{\mathrm{d}x_1}\big|_{h\equiv r^2} = -\frac{x_1 - 8}{x_2 - 2}.$$

Since these two marginal rates of substitution are equal at (x_1', x_2'),

$$\frac{2x_1'}{x_2'} = \frac{x_1' - 8}{x_2' - 2} \quad \Rightarrow \quad x_2' = \frac{4x_1'}{x_1' + 8}.$$

Since (x_1', x_2') is contained in the boundary of the ellipse,

$$9 = 2(x_1')^2 + \left(\frac{4x_1'}{x_1' + 8}\right)^2 \quad \Rightarrow \quad 2(x_1')^4 + 32(x_1')^3 + 135(x_1')^2 - 144x_1' - 576 = 0.$$

This quartic has four roots. Two of them are complex numbers, so they can be ignored. One of the other two roots is negative, so we can ignore that one too. The last root is $x_1' \approx 2{\cdot}04187$, implying that

$$x_2' \approx \frac{4 \times 2{\cdot}04187}{2{\cdot}04187 + 8} = 0{\cdot}81334.$$

The point in X that is closest to $x_0 = (8, 2)$ is thus $(x_1', x_2') \approx (2{\cdot}04187, 0{\cdot}81334)$.

(iii) The normal vector that we seek is the vector $p = x' - x_0 \approx (2{\cdot}04187, 0{\cdot}81334) - (8, 2) = (-5{\cdot}95813, -1{\cdot}18666)$. x' is contained in the hyperplane (denoted by $\mathcal{H}$ in Figure 6.11), so the level of this hyperplane is

$$\alpha = p{\cdot}x' \approx (-5{\cdot}95813, -1{\cdot}18666){\cdot}(2{\cdot}04187, 0{\cdot}81334) = -13{\cdot}13088.$$

It is clear from Figure 6.11 that there are many other hyperplanes that strictly separate x_0 from the set X. $\square$

Answer to Problem 6.4. The answer is "No"; *i.e.* the result cannot be extended to each and every not-closed subset of $\Re^n$. The result is true for some of these not-closed subsets, but it is not true for *all* such subsets.

Let's start by thinking of a case in which the result is true for a subset X that is not closed but not open with respect to E^n. For example, let x_0 be the point $(1, 1)$ and let $X = [2, 3] \times [2, 3]$ but with the point $(3, 3)$ removed from the set. Draw the picture. X is not closed, does not contain x_0, and the result is true in this case. And the result would be true even if we changed X to the open set $(2, 3) \times (2, 3)$.

The situation that is of most concern is when we have X as a not-closed set (not necessarily an open set) that has x_0 as a boundary point, so that the two sets X and $\{x_0\}$ are disjoint but "arbitrarily close" to each other. For example, $x_0 = (1,1)$ and $X = [1,2] \times [1,2]$ but with the point $(1,1)$ removed from X. We will show that in this case there does not exist even one pair (p, α), such that the hyperplane with normal $p \in \Re^2$ (with $p \neq \underline{0}$ and $\|p\|_E < \infty$) and level α satisfies $p \cdot x_0 < \alpha$ and $p \cdot x \geq \alpha$ for all $x \in X$; i.e. the result is false in this particular case.

Consider any p and any α for which x_0 and X are not in the same half-space of the hyperplane. Draw a picture (if it makes it easier for you, then use $p = (1,1)$ for your diagram). Your picture should indicate to you that the only way in which a hyperplane can separate $x_0 = (1,1)$ from X is if the hyperplane contains x_0. But then if we do as required and choose a level α, such that $p \cdot x_0 < \alpha$, the hyperplane passes through the interior of X, in which case there are some points in X close enough to the boundary point $(1,1)$ for which $p \cdot x < \alpha$. This violates the requirement that $\alpha \leq p \cdot x$ for every $x \in X$. In this example, then, the result is false.   □

Answer to Problem 6.5. The example provided in the answer to problem 6.4 is a counterexample to both assertions (a) and (b).   □

Answer to Problem 6.6. The answer is "No" in general. Here is a counterexample. Think of $\Re^2$. Let X_1 be the closed square with sides of length one starting at the origin and ending at (1,1); i.e. $X_1 = \{(x_1, x_2) \mid 0 \leq x_1 \leq 1, 0 \leq x_2 \leq 1\}$. Let X_2 be the closed square with sides of length one starting at (1,1) and ending at (2,2); i.e. $X_2 = \{(x_1, x_2) \mid 1 \leq x_1 \leq 2, 1 \leq x_2 \leq 2\}$. Draw these two squares. Their sum $X_1 + X_2$ is the square with sides of length two starting at (1,1) and ending at (3,3). Consider the hyperplane with normal $p = (1,1)$ and level $\alpha = 2$; i.e. $p_1 x_1 + p_2 x_2 = 2$. This hyperplane weakly separates X_1 from X_2. Notice that X_1 and X_2 are not in the same half-spaces defined by the hyperplane. The points of support are the same point: $x_1^* = x_2^* = (1,1)$. So $x_1^* + x_2^* = (1,1) + (1,1) = (2,2)$. But (2,2) is in the interior of $X_1 + X_2$ and so cannot be a point of support for $X_1 + X_2$. Use your diagram to check that this is true.

What follows is the case where the result is true.

To Be Proved. Let X_1 and X_2 be two nonempty and convex subsets of $\Re^n$. A hyperplane with normal $p \in \Re^n$, $p \neq \underline{0}$, $\|p\|_E < \infty$ and level α supports X_1 at x_1^* and supports X_2 at x_2^*. The hyperplane with normal p and level 2α supports $X_1 + X_2$ at $x^* = x_1^* + x_2^*$ if and only if X_1 and X_2 are in the same half-space of the hyperplane.

Proof. We will begin by showing that, if the sets X_1 and X_2 are in the same halfspace of the hyperplane with level α, then x^* is a point of support for $X_1 + X_2$

in the hyperplane with level 2α. Since the hyperplane supports X_1 and X_2 and since these sets are in the same half-space of the hyperplane, it must be, without loss of generality, that

$$p{\cdot}x_1 \le \alpha \ \forall \ x_1 \in X_1 \text{ and } p{\cdot}x_2 \le \alpha \ \forall \ x_2 \in X_2 \tag{6.11}$$

and

$$p{\cdot}x_1^* = \alpha = p{\cdot}x_2^*. \tag{6.12}$$

Therefore, from (6.11) and (6.12), for all $x_1 \in X_1$ and all $x_2 \in X_2$,

$$p{\cdot}(x_1 + x_2) \le 2\alpha \text{ and } p{\cdot}(x_1^* + x_2^*) = 2\alpha.$$

That is, the hyperplane with normal p and level 2α supports the set $X_1 + X_2$ at $x^* = x_1^* + x_2^*$.

Now suppose that the hyperplane supports X_1 at x_1^*, supports X_2 at x_2^*, and supports $X_1 + X_2$ at $x^* = x_1^* + x_2^*$. Without loss of generality, suppose that

$$p{\cdot}x \le 2\alpha \ \forall \ x \in X_1 + X_2. \tag{6.13}$$

Since x_1^* and x_2^* are members of the hyperplane,

$$p{\cdot}x_1^* = \alpha = p{\cdot}x_2^*. \tag{6.14}$$

Suppose that $p{\cdot}x_1' > \alpha$ for some $x_1' \in X_1$. Then, from (6.14), $x' = x_1' + x_2^* \in X_1 + X_2$ but $p{\cdot}x' > 2\alpha$. This contradicts (6.13). Similarly, if $p{\cdot}x_2'' > \alpha$ for some $x_2'' \in X_2$, then $x'' = x_1^* + x_2'' \in X_1 + X_2$ but $p{\cdot}x'' > 2\alpha$. This also contradicts (6.13). Therefore it must be that $p{\cdot}x_1 \le \alpha$ for every $x_1 \in X_1$ and that $p{\cdot}x_2 \le \alpha$ for every $x_2 \in X_2$. That is, X_1 and X_2 must lie in the same half-space of the hyperplane. $\square$

If $X_1, \dots, X_n$ were all nonempty and convex subsets of $\Re^n$, if a hyperplane with normal p and level α supported these sets at $x_1^*, \dots, x_n^*$, respectively, and if $X = \sum_{i=1}^n X_i$, would the hyperplane with normal p and level $n\alpha$ support X at $\sum_{i=1}^n x_i^*$? Prove your answer.

Answer. Again, and for the same reasons, the general answer is "No." The counterexample given above is a proof. Given below is the case for which the answer is true.

To Be Proved. Let $X_1, \dots, X_n$ be nonempty and convex subsets of $\Re^n$. A hyperplane with normal $p \in \Re^n$, $p \ne \underline{0}$, $\|p\|_E < \infty$ and level α supports X_i at x_i^* for $i = 1, \dots, n$. Let $X = \sum_{i=1}^n X_i$. Then the hyperplane with normal p and level $n\alpha$ supports X at $x^* = \sum_{i=1}^n x_i^*$ if and only if $X_1, \dots, X_n$ are in the same half-space of the hyperplane.

Proof. Since the hyperplane with level α supports $X_1, \ldots, X_n$ and since these sets are in the same half-space of the hyperplane, it must be, without loss of generality, that

$$p \cdot x_i \leq \alpha \ \forall \ x_i \in X_i, \ \forall \ i = 1, \ldots, n \tag{6.15}$$

and

$$p \cdot x_i^* = \alpha \ \forall \ i = 1, \ldots, n. \tag{6.16}$$

Therefore, from (6.15) and (6.16), for all $x_i \in X_i$ and for all $i = 1, \ldots, n$,

$$p \cdot (x_1 + \cdots + x_n) \leq n\alpha \text{ and } p \cdot (x_1^* + \cdots + x_n^*) = n\alpha. \tag{6.17}$$

That is, the hyperplane with normal p and level $n\alpha$ supports the set X at $x^* = x_1^* + \cdots + x_n^*$.

Now suppose that the hyperplane with level α supports $X_1, \ldots, X_n$ at $x_1^*, \ldots, x_n^*$, respectively, and that the hyperplane with level $n\alpha$ supports $X = X_1 + \cdots + X_n$ at $x^* = x_1^* + \cdots + x_n^*$. Without loss of generality, suppose that

$$p \cdot x \leq n\alpha \ \forall \ x \in X. \tag{6.18}$$

Since $x_1^*, \ldots, x_n^*$ are members of the hyperplane with level α,

$$p \cdot x_1^* = \cdots = p \cdot x_n^* = \alpha. \tag{6.19}$$

Suppose that $p \cdot x_1' > \alpha$ for some $x_1' \in X_1$. Then, from (6.19), $x' = x_1' + x_2^* + \cdots + x_n^* \in X$ but $p \cdot x' > n\alpha$. This contradicts (6.18). The same argument can be made in turn for each of $X_2, \ldots, X_n$. Therefore, for each $i = 1, \ldots, n$ it must be that $p \cdot x_i \leq \alpha$ for every $x_i \in X_i$; *i.e.* $X_1, \ldots, X_n$ must all lie in the same half-space of the hyperplane with level α. $\qquad \square$

Chapter 7

Cones

The most famous theorems to do with the solution of differentiable constrained optimization problems are the Karush-Kuhn-Tucker Theorem and Fritz John's Theorem. Both results describe whether or not certain gradient vectors are contained in sets called *convex cones*, so we need to understand what are these sets. This chapter explains cones and convex cones, and then provides explanations and proofs of Farkas's Lemma and Gordan's Lemma. These lemmas are really important results that are used in many applications of linear algebra. For us, their primary significance is that they can be used to prove the theorems by Karush, Kuhn, and Tucker, and by Fritz John. Descriptions of these two essential theorems, along with their proofs, are provided in Chapter 8. Let's get started by discovering the simple structure of the set we call a cone.

7.1 Cones

Definition 7.1 (Cone). *Let* $a^1, \ldots, a^m \in \Re^n$. *The* cone *with vertex at the origin* $\underline{0} \in \Re^n$ *that is generated by the vectors* $a^1, \ldots, a^m$ *is the set*

$$K(a^1, \ldots, a^m) = \{x \in \Re^n \mid x = \mu a^i, \ \mu \geq 0, \ i = 1, \ldots, m\}.$$

The definition says that to construct a cone we start with any one of the given vectors a^i and then collect all of the nonnegative multiples μa^i of a^i. What does this give us? Think about it – draw a picture for $n = 2$ and work it out before reading further.

Ready? OK then. Since μ can be zero, we know that the origin $\underline{0}$ is a member of the cone. And since μ can be any positive number at all, we collect every possible

216

positive multiple of a^i. Collect all these points together, and we have constructed the *ray* from the origin that passes through the point a^i. We do this in turn for each of the given vectors $a^1, \ldots, a^m$, so the cone is the set that is the union of the rays from the origin that pass through the points $a^1, \ldots, a^m$. Here is a simple example. Suppose we take the vectors $a^1 = (-1, 2)$ and $a^2 = (2, 3)$. What is the cone generated by these vectors? Have a look at Figure 7.1. Is it the set displayed in the left-hand panel or is it the set displayed in the right-hand panel? Think before you answer.

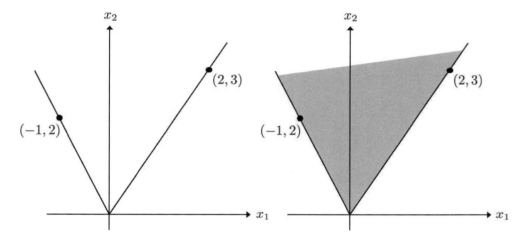

Figure 7.1: A cone and a convex cone.

The cone $K = \{x \in \Re^2 \mid x = \mu(-1, 2) \text{ or } x = \mu(2, 3), \ \mu \geq 0\}$ is the set displayed in the left-hand panel. It is the union of the two rays shown and, particularly, it does not contain any of the points in the shaded area shown on the right-hand panel. I hope it is clear that a cone is a set that is closed with respect to the Euclidean metric topology.

Why do we say the cone has a "vertex at the origin"? In other words, why is the "pointy end" of the cone located at the origin? Well, we can define a cone with a vertex at any vector v simply by taking a cone K with its vertex at the origin and then adding the vector v to every element of K. Such cones are called *affine cones*. For example, take the cone displayed in the left-hand panel of Figure 7.2, then "move it" by adding the vector $v = (1, 1)$ to every element of the cone. You now have the set that is displayed in the right-hand panel of Figure 7.2. This is an affine cone with its vertex at $v = (1, 1)$. The only cones that we will consider are those with vertices at the origin.

An Exercise. Is the singleton set $\{(0, 0)\}$ a cone with its vertex at $(0, 0)$ in $\Re^2$?

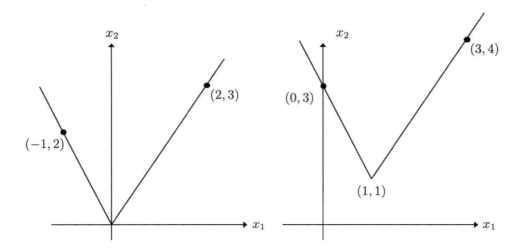

Figure 7.2: A cone and an affine cone.

Answer. Yes.

Another Exercise. Is any other singleton set other than $\{(0,0)\}$ a cone with its vertex at $(0,0)$ in $\Re^2$?

Answer. No.

7.2   Convex Cones

The set displayed in the right-hand panel of Figure 7.1 is not the cone generated by the two vectors displayed in that diagram. It is, instead, a *convex cone with its vertex at the origin*.

Definition 7.2 (Convex Cone). *Let K be a cone in $\Re^n$. The set*

$$CK = \{x \in \Re^n \mid x = y + z \text{ for all } y, z \in K\}$$

is the convex cone generated by the cone K.

So what do we have here? We start with a cone, just like the one in the left-hand panel of Figure 7.1. Then we take any two points in the cone. Adding them always gives us a point in the set called the convex cone. For example, the points $(-1,2)$ and $(2,3)$ belong to the cone. The sum of these points, $(1,5)$, does not belong to the cone. Instead it lies in the shaded interior of the set displayed in the right-hand panel of Figure 7.1. Try it for yourself. Pick any two points from the cone in the left-hand panel, add them together, and confirm that you have a member of the set in the right-hand panel. The convex cone generated from a cone is therefore the original cone in union with all of the points lying between the rays that constitute the original cone. Thus a convex cone is always a (weakly) convex set. The set displayed in the right-hand panel of Figure 7.1 is the convex cone generated by the cone displayed in the left-hand panel.

Equivalently, we can define the convex cone generated by a cone K to be the *convex hull* of K; *i.e.* the convex cone generated by a cone K is the smallest convex set that contains K.

Notice that a cone need not be a convex cone, but a convex cone is always a cone. It is obvious in Figure 7.1 that the cone displayed in the left-hand panel is not a convex set and so is not a convex cone. The convex cone in the right-hand panel is a cone. Why? Because for any point in the convex cone, the ray from the origin passing through that point is entirely in the convex cone. Thus the convex cone is a cone. Particularly, it is a cone that is generated by the infinitely many vectors a^i that are rays between the displayed (boundary) vectors. Although Figure 7.1 displays the typical case, it is nevertheless possible for a cone and the convex cone generated by it to be the same set. Can you see when this will be true? Think it over. Remember, a convex cone is always a weakly convex set.

Figured it out? If not, then here is another clue. Think of a cone that consists of just one ray – say, the ray from the origin passing through $(1, 1)$. What do you notice about this cone? Now try again to figure out the answer.

Let's see how you did. I hope you noticed that the cone consisting of just one ray is a convex set. The convex cone generated by a cone is the smallest convex set that contains the cone, so the cone and the convex cone generated by it are the same when the cone is its own convex hull. This happens if and only if the convex hull has an empty interior. There are just three possibilities – what are they?

One is that the cone consists of a single ray from the origin. The second is that the cone consists of two rays, each pointing in the exactly opposite direction to the other (so the cone is a hyperplane through the origin). The third possibility is that the cone is the singleton set $\{\underline{0}\}$.

Often the same convex cone can be generated by many cones. Think again of the cone displayed in the left-hand panel of Figure 7.1, and now add a third ray, one that lies between the original two rays; *e.g.* the ray that is the vertical axis. The convex cone generated by this new cone is still the set displayed in the right-hand panel. Add as many more rays as you want to the cone in the left-hand panel, but make sure each new ray lies between the original two. Each of these new cones generates the same convex cone, the one in the right-hand panel.

Sometimes adding a new ray to a cone can dramatically alter the convex cone it generates. Look again at the cone in the left-hand panel of Figure 7.1, then add to it the ray from the origin that passes through $(0, -1)$. What is the convex cone generated by this new cone? Think about it – what is the smallest convex set that contains the new cone?

The answer is $\Re^2$. Adding just one new vector can greatly increase the size of the convex cone.

Is it clear to you that, like a cone, a convex cone is a set that is closed with respect to the Euclidean topology?

What use are cones? You may be surprised to discover that most of the theory of differentiable constrained optimization makes heavy use of cones. Most of the major theorems to do with constrained optimization are statements describing something to do with cones. For example, the famous Karush-Kuhn-Tucker Theorem of constrained optimization theory is a description of conditions under which a particular vector lies inside a particular convex cone. So is its companion, the Fritz John Theorem. The two really useful theorems to do with cones that we need to understand are Farkas's Lemma and Gordan's Lemma. Both are examples of "theorems of the alternative." There are lots of such theorems and they all take the same form. Each is a statement that says here are two alternatives, A and B. One of them must be true, and when A is true, B is false and conversely. The alternatives A and B are thus mutually exclusive. Here is a rather silly, but valid, theorem of the alternative: "Alternative A is that the Earth is flat. Alternative B is that the Earth is not flat. The theorem is that A is true if and only if B is false, and that one of A and B must be true." It is time for us to have a close look at the two lemmas mentioned above. Let's start with the simpler of the two.

7.3   Farkas's Lemma

Gyuala Farkas (also known as Julius Farkas) was a Hungarian physicist and mathematician who in 1902 published the result named after him. Here it is.

Lemma 7.1 (Farkas's Lemma). *Given vectors $a^1, \ldots, a^m, b \in \Re^n$ with $b \neq \underline{0}$, one and only one of the following two statements is true.*

(i) There exist $\lambda_1, \ldots, \lambda_m \in \Re$, all nonnegative and not all zero, such that

$$b = \lambda_1 a^1 + \cdots + \lambda_m a^m. \tag{7.1}$$

(ii) There exists $x \in \Re^n$, such that

$$a^1 \cdot x \geq 0, \ldots, a^m \cdot x \geq 0 \text{ and } b \cdot x < 0. \tag{7.2}$$

When I first read this lemma, my reaction was something like, "What on earth is this talking about and why should I care?" Perhaps you are feeling the same way, so I suggest that we defer proving the result until we understand what it says. Good news – what it says is actually very simple. A picture will help. Look at Figure 7.3.

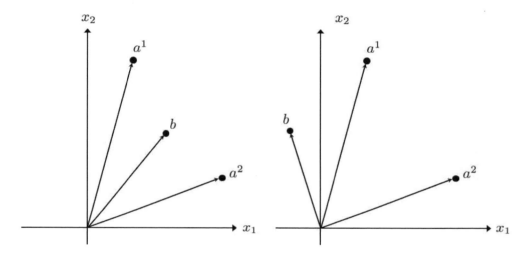

Figure 7.3: Farkas's two alternatives.

The left-hand panel shows the vector b as a member of the convex cone generated by a^1 and a^2. This is alternative (i), which says that b can be written as a *nonnegative* linear combination of a^1 and a^2. Any vector constructed as a nonnegative linear combination of two other vectors lies on a ray from the origin that is between the rays containing the two other vectors (see Figure 2.4 – use the parallelogram rule of vector addition). Since alternative (ii) is true when (i) is false, (ii) must describe the case when b is not a member of the convex cone generated by a^1 and a^2. This is displayed in the right-hand panel. I understand that it still might not be obvious to you that (7.2) describes this situation, so have a look at Figure 7.4, which is the same as Figure 7.3 except that I have added dashed lines that are orthogonal to each of b, a^1, and a^2.

The "closed" (solid dots at the ends) dotted half-circles show the regions of points x where $a^1 \cdot x \geq 0$ and $a^2 \cdot x \geq 0$. The "open" (hollow dots at the ends) dotted half-circle shows the regions of points x where $b \cdot x < 0$. In the left-hand panel, nowhere

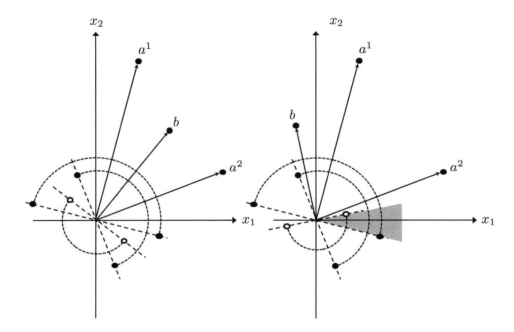

Figure 7.4: Farkas's second alternative.

do all of these three half-circles overlap each other, showing that, when (i) is true, there does not exist any x for which (7.2) is true. In the right-hand panel, there is a (shaded) region where all of the half-circles overlap; there are many points x satisfying (7.2), so (ii) is true. This is so because b is not a member of the convex cone generated by a^1 and a^2. Thus, (ii) is true if and only if (i) is false.

Before you proceed to the proof of Farkas's Lemma, try the following little exercise. Suppose that alternative (ii) is altered by changing $b \cdot x < 0$ to $b \cdot x \leq 0$. Is it now possible for both alternatives (i) and (ii) to be true? Draw yourself some diagrams like those in Figure 7.4 and discover why the answer is "Yes."

Now it is time to prove the lemma. Fear not. There is nothing hard in the proof. In fact, the heart of the proof is displayed in the right-hand panel of Figure 7.4. This panel is reproduced in Figure 7.5. Notice that, when (i) is false, the point b is outside the convex cone generated by a^1 and a^2. The singleton set $\{b\}$ is nonempty, convex, and closed. So is the convex cone. The convex cone and $\{b\}$ are disjoint. We know therefore (see Theorem 6.1) that there must be a hyperplane that separates the two sets. One of these hyperplanes is the hyperplane with normal x that passes through the origin – see the dotted line labelled $\mathcal{H}$ in Figure 7.5. This is the hyperplane $H = \{z \in \Re^2 \mid x \cdot z = 0\}$ and it should be clear that $x \cdot b < 0$ and $x \cdot z \geq 0$ for all points

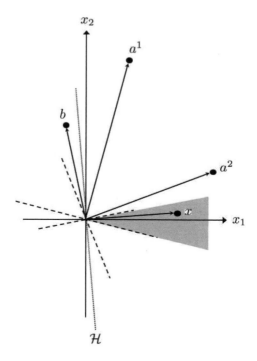

Figure 7.5: Farkas's second alternative is that a hyperplane through the origin separates the singleton set $\{b\}$ from the convex cone generated by a^1 and a^2.

on the right-hand side (*i.e.* the upper-half-space) of the hyperplane; this includes all points in the cone. Set z equal to a^1 and a^2 in particular and these inequalities are alternative (ii) of Farkas's Lemma.

Proof of Farkas's Lemma. We will show that (ii) is true if and only if (i) is false.

We will begin by showing that, if (i) is false, then (ii) is true, so take as a fact that there do not exist scalars $\lambda_1, \ldots, \lambda_m$ that are all nonnegative and not all zero that allow us to write the vector b as the linear combination (7.1). Use CK to denote the convex cone generated by $a^1, \ldots, a^m$. Since (7.1) is a statement that b is a vector contained in CK and since (7.1) is false, b must be a vector that lies outside CK. That is, the singleton set $\{b\}$ is disjoint from CK. Both $\{b\}$ and CK are nonempty, closed, and convex sets, so by Theorem 6.1 there exists a hyperplane with a normal $x \in \Re^n$, such that $x \neq \underline{0}$, $\|x\|_E < \infty$, $x \cdot b < 0$ and $x \cdot z \geq 0$ for every $z \in CK$. Since $a^1, \ldots, a^m \in CK$, we have proved that (i) is false implies that (ii) is true.

Now we will show that (ii) true implies that (i) is false, so take as a fact that there exists at least one $x \in \Re^n$, such that (7.2) is true. If (7.1) is also true, then

$$x{\cdot}b = \lambda_1 x{\cdot}a^1 + \cdots + \lambda_m x{\cdot}a^m. \tag{7.3}$$

$x{\cdot}a^1 \geq 0, \ldots, x{\cdot}a^m \geq 0$ because (ii) is true. If (i) is also true, then $\lambda_1 \geq 0, \ldots, \lambda_m \geq 0$ and so the right-hand side of (7.3) must be nonnegative; *i.e.* $x{\cdot}b \geq 0$, which contradicts that (ii) is true. Hence (i) cannot be true when (ii) is true.   □

Farkas's Lemma has a wide variety of valuable applications. It is, in fact, one of the fundamental results of linear algebra. The only application described in this book is to the proof of the famous Karush-Kuhn-Tucker Theorem on necessary optimality conditions for differentiable constrained optimization problems. This is found in Chapter 8, where you will find that the Karush-Kuhn-Tucker Theorem assumes something called a "constraint qualification." This is a bit of a nuisance when solving some types of constrained optimization problems. Fortunately another statement about necessary optimality conditions is available to us that does not require that any constraint qualification is satisfied. This is Fritz John's Theorem. It too is presented and proved in the constrained optimization chapter. The reason for mentioning it here is that its proof relies on a different theorem of the alternative, called Gordan's Lemma, that also describes things to do with convex cones. Because the Fritz John Theorem is so useful, we should understand Gordan's Lemma before we depart our inspection of cones and their uses.

7.4   Gordan's Lemma

We mentioned earlier that, like Farkas's Lemma, Gordan's Lemma is a theorem of the alternative. Also like Farkas's Lemma, Gordan's Lemma describes when a particular vector does and does not lie inside a particular convex cone.

Lemma 7.2 (Gordan's Lemma). *Given vectors $a^1, \ldots, a^m \in \Re^n$, one and only one of the following two statements is true.*
   (i) There exist $\lambda_1, \ldots, \lambda_m \in \Re$, all nonnegative and not all zero, such that

$$\lambda_1 a^1 + \cdots + \lambda_m a^m = \underline{0}. \tag{7.4}$$

(ii) There exists $x \in \Re^n$, such that

$$a^1{\cdot}x > 0, \ldots, a^m{\cdot}x > 0. \tag{7.5}$$

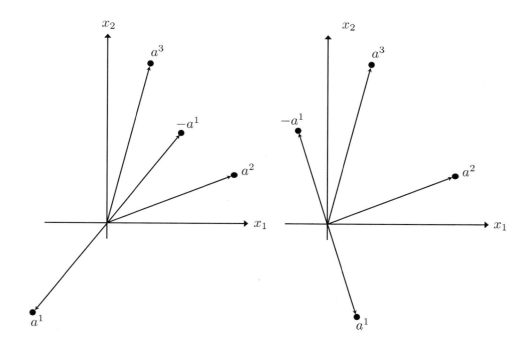

Figure 7.6: Gordan's two alternatives.

Figure 7.6 helps to make sense of what seems at first glance to mean not much. The figure is drawn for the case of $m = 3$ in $\Re^2$.

Suppose that (i) is true. Then we know, first, that there exist scalars $\lambda_1 \geq 0$, $\lambda_2 \geq 0$ and $\lambda_3 \geq 0$ that are not all zero. Therefore at least one of them is strictly positive. We will suppose that at least $\lambda_1 > 0$. Second, we know that

$$\lambda_1 a^1 + \lambda_2 a^2 + \lambda_3 a^3 = \underline{0}. \tag{7.6}$$

Since $\lambda_1 \neq 0$, we can rewrite (7.6) as

$$-a^1 = \frac{\lambda_2}{\lambda_1} a^2 + \frac{\lambda_3}{\lambda_1} a^3. \tag{7.7}$$

Now let's see – what does (7.7) say? We know that $\lambda_2/\lambda_1 \geq 0$ and $\lambda_3/\lambda_1 \geq 0$, so

$$\frac{\lambda_2}{\lambda_1} a^2 + \frac{\lambda_3}{\lambda_1} a^3$$

is a nonnegative linear combination of a^2 and a^3 and so is a vector contained in the convex cone generated by a^2 and a^3. (7.7) says that this vector is the negative of a^1.

The left-hand panel of Figure 7.6 displays this case. If alternative (i) is false, then $-a^1$ does not lie in the convex cone generated by a^2 and a^3. This is displayed in the right-hand panel of Figure 7.6. But I think I hear you muttering that you do not see why the dot products displayed in (7.5) tell you that we have the situation displayed in the right-hand panel. Things will look a bit clearer to you if I redraw Figure 7.6, so have a look at Figure 7.7. All I have done is add to Figure 7.6 the dotted lines that are orthogonal to a^1, a^2, and a^3.

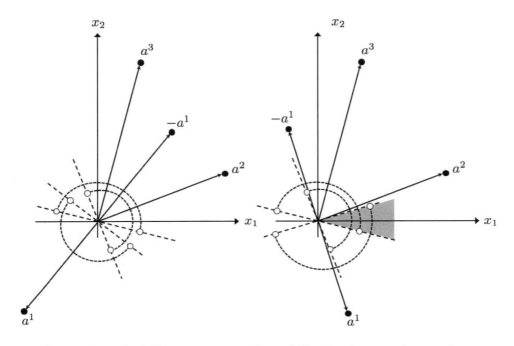

Figure 7.7: A different perspective of Gordan's two alternatives.

Start with the left-hand panel, where alternative (i) is true. Each semi-circle indicates the regions (open half-spaces, actually) in which there are points x that form a *strictly* positive inner product with a vector a^i (each semi-circle is "open" at its ends since at the ends the inner products are zero). You can see that nowhere do all three semi-circles overlap each other. In other words, there is no point x that forms a strictly positive inner product with all of a^1, a^2, and a^3. If alternative (i) is true, then alternative (ii) must be false.

Now look at the right-hand panel, where alternative (i) is false since $-a^1$ does not lie in the convex cone generated by a^2 and a^3. Observe that now the three semi-circles all overlap in the shaded region. The inner product of any point x in the shaded region with each of a^1, a^2, and a^3 is strictly positive. Hence alternative (ii) is true.

I hope you now have an idea of what Gordan's Lemma says. It probably still seems to you that the lemma is not of much use, but I promise you it really is and that it is worth the effort of proving. Let's do it.

Proof of Gordan's Lemma. We will begin by proving that, when (ii) is false, (i) must be true. The statement that (ii) is false is the statement that there does not exist even one $x \in \Re^n$, such that $a^1 {\cdot} x > 0, \ldots, a^m {\cdot} x > 0$. In other words,

$$\text{for every } x \in \Re^n, \; a^i {\cdot} x \leq 0 \text{ for at least one } i \in \{1, \ldots, m\}. \tag{7.8}$$

Define the set

$$V = \{(a^1 {\cdot} x, \ldots, a^m {\cdot} x) \mid x \in \Re^n\}. \tag{7.9}$$

Notice that any $v \in V$ has m, not n, elements $a^1 {\cdot} x$ up to $a^m {\cdot} x$ and so belongs to $\Re^m$, not $\Re^n$. The n-dimensional vectors $a^1, \ldots, a^m$ are fixed and given. V is the collection of all of the m-dimensional vectors formed by computing the inner products of the vectors $a^1, \ldots, a^m$ with every n-dimensional vector $x \in \Re^n$. Since (ii) is false, we know from (7.8) that there is no strictly positive vector in V; *i.e.* $v \not\gg \underline{0} \; \forall \; v \in V$. (Don't make the mistake of thinking that every vector in V consists only of negative or zero elements. A vector in V can have positive elements. But every vector in V must have at least one element that is either zero or negative.)

Now define the set

$$P = \{y \in \Re^m \mid y \gg \underline{0}\}. \tag{7.10}$$

You need to be clear that V and P are both subsets of $\Re^m$ (not of $\Re^n$). Notice that any vector $y \in P$ has only strictly positive elements. It follows that V and P are disjoint. Notice that $\underline{0}_m \notin P$ and that $\underline{0}_m \in V$ (because $(a^1 {\cdot} x, \ldots, a^m {\cdot} x) = \underline{0}_m$ when we choose $x = \underline{0}_n$).

Now is the time for you to try drawing the sets P and V in $\Re^2$. This is an important exercise, so take your time, think about it, and then create your picture. P is just $\Re^2_{++}$ – that's easy. Now try drawing V. I'll give you a warning – most people get it wrong, and that is why I am urging that you try your very best now so that I can later use your picture to help you out. Go on – give it a serious try before reading further. (Hint: Remember that $\underline{0}_m \in V$.)

It is obvious that P is nonempty, convex, and open with respect to E^m. It is similarly obvious that V is nonempty, and it is reasonably easy to see that V is closed in E^m, but perhaps it is not so obvious that V is a convex subset of R^m. Why is

V a convex subset of $\Re^m$? Take any two vectors $v', v'' \in V$. Then there are vectors $x', x'' \in \Re^n$, such that

$$v' = (a^1 \cdot x', \ldots, a^m \cdot x') \text{ and } v'' = (a^1 \cdot x'', \ldots, a^m \cdot x''). \tag{7.11}$$

For any $\theta \in [0, 1]$, write

$$\begin{aligned}
v(\theta) &= \theta v' + (1 - \theta) v'' \\
&= \theta(a^1 \cdot x', \ldots, a^m \cdot x') + (1 - \theta)(a^1 \cdot x'', \ldots, a^m \cdot x'') \\
&= (a^1 \cdot (\theta x' + (1 - \theta) x''), \ldots, a^m \cdot (\theta x' + (1 - \theta) x'')). \tag{7.12}
\end{aligned}$$

$\theta x' + (1 - \theta) x'' \in \Re^n$ since $\Re^n$ is a convex space and $x', x'' \in \Re^n$. Therefore $v(\theta) \in \Re^m$, establishing that V is a convex subset of $\Re^m$.

Now look at the picture you drew of P and V in $\Re^2$. You probably have drawn one of the diagrams displayed in Figure 7.8.

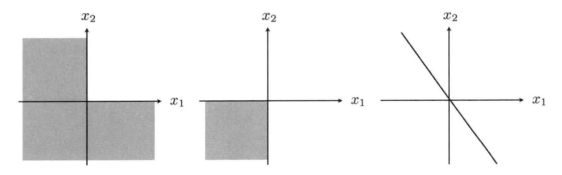

Figure 7.8: Where is the set V?

If you drew the diagram in the left-hand panel that says V is everything in $\Re^2$ except $\Re^2_{++}$, then you have made the mistake made by most first-timers (including me). Remember that V is a convex space, so it cannot be the nonconvex set displayed in the left-hand panel. What about the middle panel, which suggests that V is $\Re^2_-$, the negative orthant of $\Re^2$? No. Why not? Because vectors in V are allowed to have some positive elements. So we are looking for a convex space that contains the origin and does not intersect with $P = \Re^2_{++}$. There it is, in the right-hand panel. V is quite small. It is only a hyperplane passing through the origin and not intersecting with $\Re^2_{++}$. Take a minute and check out that there is no other possibility for V. Then try to draw both P and V in $\Re^3$. You will discover that $P = \Re^3_{++}$ and that V is a (two-dimensional) hyperplane passing through the origin of the three-dimensional space $\Re^3$ and not intersecting $\Re^3_{++}$. I hope it has become clear that in the general case V is an $(m-1)$-dimensional hyperplane in $\Re^m$ that passes through the origin $\underline{0}_m$ and does not intersect $\Re^m_{++}$. If this is clear to you, then the hard part is over and we are ready to complete our argument.

P and V are both nonempty and convex subsets of $\Re^m$. P and V are disjoint. Hence we can apply Minkowski's Separation Theorem and conclude that there exists at least one (normal) vector $\lambda \in \Re^m$ with $\lambda \neq \underline{0}_m$ and $\|\lambda\|_E < \infty$, and a level α, such that

$$\lambda \cdot v \leq \alpha \text{ for every } v \in V \text{ and } \lambda \cdot y \geq \alpha \text{ for every } y \in P. \qquad (7.13)$$

Recollect that $\underline{0}_m \in V$, so it is immediate from (7.13) that the separating hyperplane's level $\alpha \geq 0$. Look back at the right-hand panel of Figure 7.8. V is the hyperplane passing through the *origin*. What is the level of any such hyperplane? It must be zero. (Recall that a hyperplane is a set $\{x \in \Re^m \mid p \cdot x = \alpha\}$. p is the "normal" of the hyperplane and α is its "level.") This suggests that perhaps $\alpha = 0$ in (7.13). This is indeed the case, so we are now about to show that $\alpha > 0$ is impossible. The argument is by a simple contradiction. Suppose that $\alpha > 0$. Then we are asserting that there is a *strictly* positive upper bound, α, to the values of inner products $\lambda \cdot v$ for all of the elements $v \in V$, so there must be in V an element v' for which $\lambda \cdot v' > 0$. For any $\mu > 0$, $v' \in V$ implies that $\mu v' \in V$ (because $v' = (a^1 \cdot x', \ldots, a^m \cdot x')$ for some $x' \in \Re^n$ and $x' \in \Re^n$ implies that $\mu x' \in \Re^n$, so $\mu v' = (a^1 \cdot \mu x', \ldots, a^m \cdot \mu x') \in V$). By choosing μ to be as large as we want, we can cause $\lambda \cdot \mu v'$ to become as large as we like, so there cannot be a strictly positive upper bound on the values of these inner products. Contradiction. Hence $\alpha \not> 0$. Since $\alpha \geq 0$, we must conclude that $\alpha = 0$.

So now we know that $\lambda \cdot v \leq 0$ for all $v \in V$. The next step is to show that $\lambda \cdot v < 0$ is impossible. Suppose that there is a $v \in V$ for which $\lambda \cdot v < 0$. Then there is an $x \in \Re^n$ such that $v = (a^1 \cdot x, \ldots, a^m \cdot x)$. $x \in \Re^n$ implies that $-x \in \Re^n$ and, therefore, that $(a^1 \cdot (-x), \ldots, a^m \cdot (-x)) = -v \in V$. But then $\lambda \cdot (-v) > 0$, which contradicts that $\lambda \cdot v \leq 0$ for every $v \in V$. Thus there is no $v \in V$ for which $\lambda \cdot v < 0$. Consequently we have that $\lambda \cdot v = 0$ for every $v \in V$. This establishes that the set V is a hyperplane in $\Re^m$ passing through the origin.

Let's take a moment, collect our thoughts, and see what we still have to do. We have established that there exists a $\lambda \in \Re^m$, such that $\lambda \cdot v = 0$ for every $v \in V$. By construction, an element in V is a vector $v = (a^1 \cdot x, \ldots, a^m \cdot x)$ for some $x \in \Re^n$. We have yet to show that $\lambda_1 \geq 0, \ldots, \lambda_m \geq 0$, that at least one $\lambda_i > 0$, and that (7.4) is true. The good news is that none of these is difficult to do.

First, not every $\lambda_i = 0$ because Minkowski's Theorem tells us that $\lambda \neq \underline{0}_m$.

Second, suppose $\lambda_i < 0$ for at least one $i \in \{1, \ldots, m\}$. We know that P contains vectors y that have strictly positive values μ for their ith element and have all other elements equal to unity, where μ can be arbitrarily large. $\lambda \cdot y = \sum_{\substack{j=1 \\ j \neq i}}^{n} \lambda_j + \lambda_i \mu$, so $\lambda \cdot y < 0$ for a large enough value of μ, contradicting that $\lambda \cdot y \geq 0$ for every $y \in P$. Therefore $\lambda_i \geq 0$ for every $i = 1, \ldots, m$.

All that is left to show is that (7.4) is true. We are free to choose any $x \in \Re^n$ to construct an element of V, so let's choose $x'' = \lambda_1 a^1 + \cdots + \lambda_m a^m$. Then

$$
\begin{aligned}
0 &= \lambda \cdot (a^1 \cdot x'', \ldots, a^m \cdot x'') \\
&= (\lambda_1, \ldots, \lambda_m) \begin{pmatrix} a^1 \cdot x'' \\ \vdots \\ a^m \cdot x'' \end{pmatrix} \\
&= \lambda_1 a^1 \cdot x'' + \cdots + \lambda_m a^m \cdot x'' \\
&= (\lambda_1 a^1 + \cdots + \lambda_m a^m) \cdot x'' \\
&= (\lambda_1 a^1 + \cdots + \lambda_m a^m) \cdot (\lambda_1 a^1 + \cdots + \lambda_m a^m).
\end{aligned}
\tag{7.14}
$$

Hence

$$
\lambda_1 a^1 + \cdots + \lambda_m a^m = \underline{0}_n.
\tag{7.15}
$$

We are there; when (ii) is false, (i) is true.

That was quite a long argument, so you will be relieved to know that proving that (ii) is false when (i) is true is quick and simple. Suppose that (i) is true. Then there is at least one $\lambda_i > 0$. Without loss of generality, suppose that $\lambda_1 > 0$. Then we can rearrange (7.4) to

$$
a^1 = -\frac{\lambda_2}{\lambda_1} a^2 - \cdots - \frac{\lambda_m}{\lambda_1} a^m
\tag{7.16}
$$

and so obtain that

$$
a^1 \cdot x = -\frac{\lambda_2}{\lambda_1} a^2 \cdot x - \cdots - \frac{\lambda_m}{\lambda_1} a^m \cdot x.
\tag{7.17}
$$

Suppose that (ii) is true also. Then there is at least one $x \in \Re^n$ for which $a^1 \cdot x > 0$, $a^2 \cdot x > 0, \ldots, a^m \cdot x > 0$. Then the right-hand side of (7.17) is not positive, contradicting that $a^1 \cdot x > 0$. Hence when (i) is true, (ii) must be false. $\square$

I will make no effort here to convince you that all the hard work of proving the valuable lemmas of Farkas and Gordan is worth it. All I can do at this moment is ask you to trust me that it is so and to wait until we are working on constrained optimization problems to justify that trust.

7.5 Remarks

We have reached the end of what we might call preparatory materials. The next chapter introduces the type of constrained optimization problem mostly encountered by economists. Its solution uses all of the contents of the chapters on hyperplanes and cones. It will turn out, as a result of the work already done to understand hyperplanes and cones, that understanding the methods used to solve constrained optimization problems is not a big step from where we are now. In fact, mostly all we need to do is apply what we have already learned to the particular context of constrained optimization problems. In the next chapter we will understand and prove two of the major theorems that commonly are employed to solve constrained optimization problems. These are the first-order necessity results discovered by Karush, Kuhn, and Tucker, and by Fritz John. We will use both theorems to solve a variety of problems and draw lots of pictures to be sure that we see the quite simple geometry that explains the theorems and their applications. It is quite enjoyable, I think.

After that there remains a task that is very important to economists. Economists are particularly interested in the properties of solutions to constrained optimization problems. For example, an economist is interested in whether or not quantities demanded decrease as prices increase, and how quantities demanded change as consumers' disposable incomes change. Similarly, economists want to know the rates at which quantities supplied of products change as prices change. Answering such inquiries requires that the properties of a constrained optimization problem's optimal solution be discovered. Determining the properties of optimal solutions needs more information that is provided by either the Karush-Kuhn-Tucker or Fritz John Theorems. We also need information provided by a second-order necessary condition. Statements of this condition are usually made using something called a Lagrange function, so, after the next chapter, we will examine Lagrange functions and then carefully examine the second-order necessity condition. We are then ready to learn how to establish the properties of optimal solutions, a task that occupies the last three chapters of this book.

So, let's go. Let's, at last, get to grips with constrained optimization problems.

7.6 Problems

Problem 7.1.

$$a^1 = \begin{pmatrix} 2 \\ 1 \end{pmatrix}, \; a^2 = \begin{pmatrix} 0 \\ 1 \end{pmatrix}, \; a^3 = \begin{pmatrix} -1 \\ 2 \end{pmatrix}, \text{ and } b = \begin{pmatrix} 1 \\ 0 \end{pmatrix}. \tag{7.18}$$

(i) Draw the convex cone with vertex at the origin that is generated by the vectors a^1, a^2, and a^3.

(ii) Add the vector b to your diagram.

(iii) Which of Farkas's alternatives is true?

(iv) If the first of Farkas's alternatives is true, then solve $A\lambda = b$ for λ for at least two solutions and confirm for each that $\lambda \geq \underline{0}$. If the second alternative is true, then discover at least two $x \in \Re^2$ for which $Ax \geq \underline{0}$ and $b{\cdot}x < 0$.

(v) Now set $b = \begin{pmatrix} 1 \\ 1 \end{pmatrix}$ and repeat parts (i) to (iv) above.

Problem 7.2.

$$a^1 = \begin{pmatrix} 2 \\ 1 \end{pmatrix} \text{ and } a^2 = \begin{pmatrix} -6 \\ -3 \end{pmatrix}.$$

(i) What is the convex cone generated by the vectors a^1 and a^2?

(ii) Does there exist a vector $x \in \Re^2$ such that $a^1{\cdot}x \geq 0$ and $a^2{\cdot}x \geq 0$? If not, then why not? If so, then what is the complete collection of such vectors x?

Problem 7.3. Our statement of Farkas's Lemma is: Let $a^1, \ldots, a^m \in \Re^n$ and let $b \in \Re^n$, $b \neq \underline{0}$. Then exactly one of the following two alternatives is true:

(i) There exist $\lambda_1, \ldots, \lambda_m \in \Re$, all nonnegative and not all zero, such that

$$b = \sum_{j=1}^{m} \lambda_j a^j.$$

(ii) There exists $x \in \Re^n$ such that

$$b{\cdot}x < 0 \text{ and } a^j{\cdot}x \geq 0 \text{ for all } j = 1, \ldots, m.$$

Use Farkas's Lemma to show that, if A is an $(n \times m)$-matrix and $b \in \Re^n$, $b \neq \underline{0}$, then either there is at least one nonzero and nonnegative solution λ to the linear equation system $A\lambda = b$ or there exists an $x \in \Re^n$ for which $x^{\mathrm{T}}A \geq \underline{0}$ and $b{\cdot}x < 0$.

Problem 7.4. $a^2, a^3 \in \Re^2$ are nonzero and negatively collinear vectors. $a^1 \in \Re^2$ is a nonzero vector that is not collinear with a^2 or a^3. Explain why it is, in such a case, that

(i) there do not exist $\lambda_2 \geq 0$ and $\lambda_3 \geq 0$, not both zero, such that $a^1 = \lambda_2 a^2 + \lambda_3 a^3$, and why

(ii) there exist $\lambda_1 \geq 0$, $\lambda_2 \geq 0$ and $\lambda_3 \geq 0$, not all zero, such that $\lambda_1 a^1 + \lambda_2 a^2 + \lambda_3 a^3 = \underline{0}$.

Problem 7.5. Let $a^1, a^2, a^3 \in \Re^2$ be nonzero vectors. Suppose that there exists an $x \in \Re^2$ such that $a^1 \cdot x = 0$, $a^2 \cdot x > 0$ and $a^3 \cdot x > 0$. Explain why, for this circumstance,

(i) there do not exist scalars $\lambda_1 = 1$ and λ_2 and λ_3, both nonnegative and not both zero, such that $\lambda_1 a^1 = \lambda_2 a^2 + \lambda_3 a^3$, and

(ii) there do not exist scalars $\mu_1 = 1$ and μ_2 and μ_3, both nonnegative and not both zero, such that $\mu_1 a^1 + \mu_2 a^2 + \mu_3 a^3 = \underline{0}$.

Draw two accurate and well-labeled diagrams to illustrate your answers to parts (i) and (ii).

7.7 Answers

Answer to Problem 7.1.

(i) and (ii) See the upper panel of Figure 7.9.

(iii) and (iv) The vector $b = (1,0)^{\mathrm{T}}$ is not contained in the convex cone that is generated by the vectors a^1, a^2 and a^3. Therefore alternative 2 of Farkas's Lemma is true and alternative 1 is false. That is, there do not exist scalars λ_1, λ_2, and λ_3, all nonnegative and not all zero, such that

$$\lambda_1 \begin{pmatrix} 2 \\ 1 \end{pmatrix} + \lambda_2 \begin{pmatrix} 0 \\ 1 \end{pmatrix} + \lambda_3 \begin{pmatrix} -1 \\ 2 \end{pmatrix} = \begin{pmatrix} 1 \\ 0 \end{pmatrix}. \tag{7.19}$$

Equivalently, there exists at least one point (x_1, x_2) such that

$$a^1 \cdot x = (2,1) \begin{pmatrix} x_1 \\ x_2 \end{pmatrix} \geq 0, \quad a^2 \cdot x = (0,1) \begin{pmatrix} x_1 \\ x_2 \end{pmatrix} \geq 0, \quad a^3 \cdot x = (-1,2) \begin{pmatrix} x_1 \\ x_2 \end{pmatrix} \geq 0,$$

$$\text{and } b \cdot x = (1,0) \begin{pmatrix} x_1 \\ x_2 \end{pmatrix} < 0.$$

$$\tag{7.20}$$

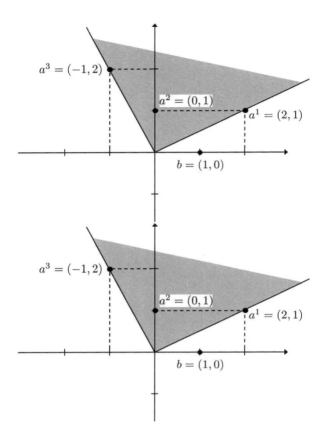

Figure 7.9: The graphs for problem 7.1.

The solutions to (7.19) are $\lambda_2 = 2 - 5\lambda_1$ and $\lambda_3 = 2\lambda_1 - 1$. $\lambda_2 \geq 0$ if $\lambda_1 \leq 2/5$, while $\lambda_3 \geq 0$ if $\lambda_1 \geq 1/2$. Thus there do not exist values for λ_1, λ_2, and λ_3 that are all nonnegative, not all zero, and satisfying (7.19). $x = (-1, 3)$ is one of many points satisfying (7.20).

(**v**) In the lower panel of Figure 7.9 the vector $b = (1, 1)^{\mathrm{T}}$ lies in the convex cone generated by the vectors a^1, a^2, and a^3, so alternative 1 of Farkas's Lemma is true and alternative 2 is false. There must exist nonnegative scalars λ_1, λ_2, and λ_3, not all zero, such that

$$\lambda_1 \begin{pmatrix} 2 \\ 1 \end{pmatrix} + \lambda_2 \begin{pmatrix} 0 \\ 1 \end{pmatrix} + \lambda_3 \begin{pmatrix} -1 \\ 2 \end{pmatrix} = \begin{pmatrix} 1 \\ 1 \end{pmatrix}. \tag{7.21}$$

Equivalently, there does not exist any point (x_1, x_2) such that

$$a^1 \cdot x = (2, 1) \begin{pmatrix} x_1 \\ x_2 \end{pmatrix} \geq 0, \ a^2 \cdot x = (0, 1) \begin{pmatrix} x_1 \\ x_2 \end{pmatrix} \geq 0, \ a^3 \cdot x = (-1, 2) \begin{pmatrix} x_1 \\ x_2 \end{pmatrix} \geq 0,$$

and $b \cdot x = (1, 1) \begin{pmatrix} x_1 \\ x_2 \end{pmatrix} < 0.$

$$(7.22)$$

The solutions to (7.21) are $\lambda_2 = 3 - 5\lambda_1$ and $\lambda_3 = 2\lambda_1 - 1$. $\lambda_2 \geq 0$ if $\lambda_1 \leq 3/5$, while $\lambda_3 \geq 0$ if $\lambda_1 \geq 1/2$. Thus (7.21) is satisfied by values of λ_1, λ_2, and λ_3 that are all nonnegative and not all zero for $1/2 \leq \lambda_1 \leq 3/5$. There is no point (x_1, x_2) that satisfies (7.22). □

Answer to Problem 7.2.
(i) The convex cone is the hyperplane with normal $p = (1, -2)$ and level $\alpha = 0$.
(ii) x is any vector that is orthogonal to the hyperplane; *e.g.* $x = p = (1, -2)$. The complete set of such vectors is the set $\{(x_1, x_2) \mid (x_1, x_2) = \mu(1, -2) \ \forall \ \mu \in \Re\}$. □

Answer to Problem 7.3. Expanded, the matrix equation

$$A\lambda = \begin{pmatrix} a_{11} & a_{12} & \cdots & a_{1m} \\ a_{21} & a_{22} & \cdots & a_{2m} \\ \vdots & \vdots & \ddots & \vdots \\ a_{n1} & a_{n2} & \cdots & a_{nm} \end{pmatrix} \begin{pmatrix} \lambda_1 \\ \lambda_2 \\ \vdots \\ \lambda_m \end{pmatrix} = b = \begin{pmatrix} b_1 \\ b_2 \\ \vdots \\ b_n \end{pmatrix}$$

is

$$a_{11}\lambda_1 + a_{12}\lambda_2 + \cdots + a_{1m}\lambda_m = b_1$$
$$a_{21}\lambda_1 + a_{22}\lambda_2 + \cdots + a_{2m}\lambda_m = b_2$$
$$\vdots \qquad\qquad \vdots$$
$$a_{n1}\lambda_1 + a_{n2}\lambda_2 + \cdots + a_{nm}\lambda_m = b_n.$$

This is the same as the vector equation

$$\lambda_1 \begin{pmatrix} a_{11} \\ a_{21} \\ \vdots \\ a_{n1} \end{pmatrix} + \lambda_2 \begin{pmatrix} a_{12} \\ a_{22} \\ \vdots \\ a_{n2} \end{pmatrix} + \cdots + \lambda_m \begin{pmatrix} a_{1m} \\ a_{2m} \\ \vdots \\ a_{nm} \end{pmatrix} = \lambda_1 a^1 + \lambda_2 a^2 + \cdots + \lambda_m a^m = \begin{pmatrix} b_1 \\ b_2 \\ \vdots \\ b_n \end{pmatrix}. \quad (7.23)$$

Farkas's Lemma states that there exist scalars $\lambda_1, \ldots, \lambda_m$, all nonnegative and not all zero, that solve (7.23) if and only if there does not exist any point $x = (x_1, \cdots, x_n)$ satisfying

$$b \cdot x < 0 \quad \text{and} \quad a^j \cdot x = x \cdot a^j \geq 0 \ \forall \ j = 1, \ldots, m.$$

That is, if and only if there does not exist an x satisfying

$$b \cdot x < 0 \quad \text{and} \quad (x_1, x_2, \cdots, x_n) \begin{pmatrix} a_{11} & a_{12} & \cdots & a_{1m} \\ a_{21} & a_{22} & \cdots & a_{2m} \\ \vdots & \vdots & \ddots & \vdots \\ a_{n1} & a_{n2} & \cdots & a_{nm} \end{pmatrix} \geq \begin{pmatrix} 0 \\ 0 \\ \vdots \\ 0 \end{pmatrix}. \qquad \square$$

Answer to Problem 7.4.

(i) Since a^2 and a^3 are nonzero and negatively collinear vectors, the convex cone that they generate is a hyperplane through the origin. The vector a^1 is not contained in this cone since a^1 is nonzero and is not collinear with a^2 or a^3. Therefore a^1 cannot be written as any linear combination $\lambda_2 a^2 + \lambda_3 a^3$, no matter what are the weights λ_2 and λ_3.

(ii) Since a^2 and a^3 are nonzero and negatively collinear, we may write $a^2 + \mu a^3 = \underline{0}$ for some $\mu > 0$. Now write $\lambda_3/\lambda_2 = \mu$ with $\lambda_2 > 0$ so that we have $\lambda_3 = \mu \lambda_2 > 0$. Then $\lambda_2 a^2 + \lambda_3 a^3 = \underline{0}$. Now set $\lambda_1 = 0$, and we have $\lambda_1 a^1 + \lambda_2 a^2 + \lambda_3 a^3 = \underline{0}$ with $\lambda_1 \geq 0$, $\lambda_2 \geq 0$, $\lambda_3 \geq 0$ and not all of λ_1, λ_2, and λ_3 zero. $\qquad \square$

Answer to Problem 7.5. In both panels of Figure 7.10, the set S of points x for which $a^2 \cdot x > 0$ and $a^3 \cdot x > 0$ is the shaded region bordered by the hyperplanes $a^2 \cdot x = 0$ and $a^3 \cdot x = 0$. The set contains no points belonging to either hyperplane.

(i) Examine the upper panel of Figure 7.10. The set of points a^1, such that $a^1 = \lambda_2 a^2 + \lambda_3 a^3$ with $\lambda_2 \geq 0$, $\lambda_3 \geq 0$ and λ_2, λ_3 not both zero, is the convex cone K, minus the origin, that is bordered by the rays containing a^2 and a^3. The question is, "Why is there not even one point x in the set S and one vector a^1 in the cone K that are orthogonal?" It should be clear from the figure that the vectors that are orthogonal to at least one of the vectors in the cone K are all contained in the subsets of $\Re^2$ labeled "Region I" and "Region II." These subsets contain vectors in the hyperplanes $a^2 \cdot x = 0$ and $a^3 \cdot x = 0$. But S does not, so there are no vectors common to the set S and either Region I or Region II.

(ii) Examine the lower panel of Figure 7.10. The set of points a^1, such that $a^1 + \lambda_2 a^2 + \lambda_3 a^3 = \underline{0}$ with $\lambda_2 \geq 0$, $\lambda_3 \geq 0$ and λ_2, λ_3 not both zero, is labeled $-K$ since this set of points is exactly the negative of the set K discussed in part (i). The question is, "Why is there not even one point x in the set S and one vector a^1 in the cone $-K$ that are orthogonal?" The vectors orthogonal to at least one of the vectors in the cone $-K$ are contained in the subsets of $\Re^2$ labeled "Region I" and "Region II." These subsets contain vectors in the hyperplanes $a^2 \cdot x = 0$ and $a^3 \cdot x = 0$. But S does not, so there are no vectors common to the set S and either Region I or Region II. $\quad\square$

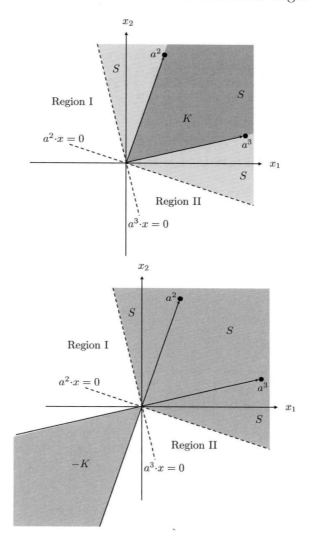

Figure 7.10: Diagrams for problem 7.5.

Chapter 8

Constrained Optimization, Part I

8.1   The Constrained Optimization Problem

Constrained optimization is the economist's primary means of modeling rational choice, the fundamental underpinning of modern economics. This chapter is therefore crucial to your understanding of most economic theories. The good news, and it is very good news, is that the core ideas of constrained optimization are rather obvious. Let's get started by setting out what is meant by the term *constrained optimization problem*.

Definition 8.1 (Constrained Optimization Problem). *Let $\mathcal{C}$ be a nonempty set. Let $f : \mathcal{C} \mapsto \Re$ be a function. Then the problem*

$$\max_{x \in \mathcal{C}} f(x) \equiv \max_{x} f(x) \; subject \; to \; x \in \mathcal{C} \tag{8.1}$$

is a constrained optimization problem.

objective function

feasible set

The set of all of the choices from which the decisionmaker may select is denoted by $\mathcal{C}$ and is called the "choice set," the "constraint set," or the "feasible set." Constraint set is not a good name for $\mathcal{C}$ because $\mathcal{C}$ is not a set of constraints. The other two names are perfectly reasonable, so let's follow the common convention of calling $\mathcal{C}$ the *feasible set*; *i.e.* a choice x is *feasible*, meaning available for selection, if and only if it satisfies all of the constraints imposed upon choices. A common economic example is the set of consumption bundle choices $x = (x_1, \ldots, x_n)$ that are feasible because they are affordable for a consumer who has \$$y$ to spend and faces prices $p = (p_1, \ldots, p_n)$;

$$\mathcal{C}(p_1, \ldots, p_n, y) = \{(x_1, \ldots, x_n) \mid x_1 \geq 0, \ldots, x_n \geq 0, p_1 x_1 + \cdots + p_n x_n \leq y\}.$$

Another example is the set of production plans $(x_1, \ldots, x_n, y)$ that are feasible from a production technology that is described by a production function g. This usually is called a technology set,

$$T(g) = \{(x_1, \ldots, x_n, y) \mid x_1 \geq 0, \ldots, x_n \geq 0, \ 0 \leq y \leq g(x_1, \ldots, x_n)\}.$$

The production function $g : \Re_+^n \mapsto \Re_+$ specifies the maximal output level y that the firm can obtain from an input vector $(x_1, \ldots, x_n)$, where x_i is the quantity used of input i. In this chapter it will always be presumed that $\mathcal{C}$ is a set of real numbers or vectors of real numbers, $\mathcal{C} \subseteq \Re^n$, but understand that this does not have to be so. In principle $\mathcal{C}$ can contain any elements that a decisionmaker may choose between; *e.g* cars, books, songs or jobs.

The function f ranks feasible choices by desirability. Since (8.1) is a maximization problem, a feasible choice $x' \in \mathcal{C}$ is *strictly preferred* to another feasible choice $x'' \in \mathcal{C}$ if and only if $f(x') > f(x'')$. Similarly, $f(x') = f(x'')$ if and only if x' and x'' are equally preferred, in which case we say that the decisionmaker is *indifferent* between x' and x''. If $f(x') \geq f(x'')$, then either x' and x'' are equally preferred or x' is strictly preferred to x''. We state this more briefly by saying that x' is *weakly preferred* to x''. The function f thus expresses the decisionmaker's objective, which is to select from the set $\mathcal{C}$ of available choices one that is as preferred as is possible, in the sense that the value of f is made as large as possible. For this reason f is typically called problem (8.1)'s *objective function*.

In case you are wondering if we have to consider minimization problems separately from maximization problems, the answer is "No." The reason is easy to see. Consider the minimization problem

$$\min_{x \in \mathcal{C}} h(x), \tag{8.2}$$

and now write $f(x) \equiv -h(x)$. Presto! You have the maximization problem (8.1) because any x that minimizes $h(x)$ must maximize $-h(x)$. Any minimization problem can be written as a maximization problem and *vice versa*.

Let's be clear that there are plenty of constrained optimization problems that do not have solutions. For example, can you achieve a maximum for $f(x) = x$ on the set $\mathcal{C} = \{x \mid x \geq 0\}$? Of course not. Yet there is a unique solution to the similar problem of achieving a maximum for $f(x) = x$ on the set $\mathcal{C} = \{x \mid x \leq 0\}$. Right?

Sometimes the feasible set $\mathcal{C}$ is finite; *i.e.* $\mathcal{C}$ contains only finitely many elements, such as $\{1, 2, 3\}$. Any constrained optimization problem with a finite feasible set always has a maximizing (and also a minimizing) solution because there must always be at least one member of that set that provides a highest (lowest) possible value for the objective function. For example, if $C = \{x_1, x_2, \ldots, x_n\}$, then there will be just n values $f(x_1), f(x_2), \ldots, f(x_n)$ for the objective function and one of these must be at least as big as the others. Whichever one, or more, of the x-values that provides the maximum achievable value for f is an *optimal solution* to the problem.

We talk of feasible solutions and of optimal solutions to a constrained optimization problem. The term "feasible solution" means the same as "feasible choice"; *i.e.* if $x \in C$, then x is a feasible solution or, equivalently, a feasible choice. The term "optimal solution" can be thought of in two ways, *global* and *local*.

A *globally optimal solution* is a feasible choice that provides the highest value for f that is achievable anywhere in the feasible set C.

Definition 8.2 (Globally Optimal Solution). $x^* \in C$ *is a globally optimal solution to problem* (8.1) *if and only if* $f(x^*) \geq f(x)$ *for every* $x \in C$.

Put simply, x^* is a most-preferred feasible choice among *all* of the feasible choices. Sometimes a constrained optimization problem has just one optimal solution, in which case we say that the problem's optimal solution is *unique*. For example, the problem $\max f(x) = x$, where $x \in C = \{1, 2, 3\}$, has the unique optimal solution $x^* = 3$. Other problems have nonunique, or *multiple*, optimal solutions. The problem $\max f(x) = x^2$, where $x \in C = \{-2, -1, 0, 1, 2\}$, has two globally optimal solutions, $x^* = -2$ and $x^{**} = 2$. The problem $\max f(x) = \cos x$, where $x \in C = \Re$, has infinitely many globally optimal solutions: $x^* = n\pi$ for $n = 0, \pm 2, \pm 4, \ldots$.

A *locally optimal solution* is a feasible choice that provides the highest value for f in at least a locality (*i.e.* a neighborhood) in the feasible set. A locally optimal solution could also be globally optimal (a globally optimal solution must also be a locally optimal solution), but need not be so. Consider the objective function

$$f(x) = \begin{cases} x & , \ x \leq 1 \\ 2 - x & , \ 1 < x \leq 2 \\ x - 2 & , \ 2 < x < 4 \\ 6 - x & , \ x \geq 4 \end{cases}$$

and take the feasible set to be $C = \Re$. Then this function has two local maxima, $x = 1$ and $x = 4$. One of these, $x = 4$, is also the global maximum.

Definition 8.3 (Locally Optimal Solution). $x' \in C$ *is a locally optimal solution to problem* (8.1) *in a nonempty neighborhood* $N \subseteq C$ *if and only if* $x' \in N$ *and* $f(x') \geq f(x)$ *for every* $x \in N$.

The earlier example of $f(x) = \cos x$ is interesting because, when the feasible set is the whole of the real line $\Re$, this function has infinitely many local maxima, each of which is also a global maximum.

8.2   The Typical Problem

There are lots of special cases we could consider, but economists mostly ponder only a few of them, so it is only to these cases that I suggest we turn our attention. The case of most interest has two crucial properties. We will call this case the "typical problem."

Definition 8.4 (The Typical Problem). *The* typical constrained optimization problem *is*

$$\max_{x \in \mathcal{C}} f(x), \tag{8.3}$$

where $f : \mathcal{C} \mapsto \Re$ is continuous on $\mathcal{C}$, $\mathcal{C} \neq \emptyset$, $\mathcal{C} \subset \Re^n$, and $\mathcal{C}$ is compact with respect to E^n.

What does all this mean? Let's start with $\mathcal{C}$. First of all, we are restricting ourselves to feasible choices that are real numbers or vectors of real numbers, so there will be no problems such as choosing between colors or pieces of furniture. Second, since we are considering only subsets of real numbers, a set is compact (with respect to the Euclidean topology on E^n) if and only if it is both closed and bounded. If you have already worked your way through Chapter 3, then this is old stuff. If you have not, then it will suffice for now to know that a set is bounded if it is completely contained in a sphere with only a finite radius, meaning that no part of the set continues on forever in some direction. And a nonempty set is closed (again, with respect to the Euclidean topology on E^n) if and only if it contains all of the points on its boundaries.

What does it mean to say that the objective function f is continuous? If you have worked through Chapter 5, then you already know this. If not, then for now understand that a function f that maps from some subset X of real numbers x to the real line is continuous on X if there is never an instance of an extremely small shift from one $x \in X$ to another causing a sudden jump in the value of f. Put in other words, any very small movement from one x to another must cause only a very small change to the value of f. (This is loose language, and I urge you to read Chapter 5 if you have not done so. Continuity of functions and other types of mappings is a really important idea.) Let's also note here that, while any differentiable function is continuous, there are lots of continuous functions that are not everywhere differentiable. An example is

$$f(x) = \begin{cases} 2 & ; \ x < 2 \\ x & ; \ 2 \leq x. \end{cases}$$

This function is continuous everywhere on $\Re$, but it is not differentiable at $x = 2$.

One of the nice features of the typical problem described above is that Weierstrass's Theorem for continuous functions assures us that the problem always possesses a globally optimal (not necessarily unique) solution.

8.3 First-Order Necessary Conditions

Now let's get to the main matter. What we seek is a complete description of the conditions that have to be true at an optimal solution to a constrained optimization problem. That is, we seek to discover statements that *necessarily* are true as a consequence of the information that some point x^* is an optimal solution to problem (8.3). The information provided by these necessarily true statements is what we will use to solve the problem.

Two types of conditions are necessarily true at a local maximum. These are first-order necessary conditions and second-order necessary conditions. In this chapter we will concern ourselves only with first-order necessary conditions. Second-order necessary conditions are described in Chapter 10.

We will consider only problems of the following form.

$$\begin{aligned} \max_{x_1,\ldots,x_n} \ & f(x_1,\ldots,x_n) \\ \text{subject to} \quad & g_1(x_1,\ldots,x_n) \ \leq \ b_1 \\ & \qquad \vdots \qquad\qquad \vdots \\ & g_m(x_1,\ldots,x_n) \ \leq \ b_m, \end{aligned} \qquad (8.4)$$

where all of the functions $f, g_1, \ldots, g_m$ are continuously differentiable. One immediate implication of this assumption is that the functions $g_1, \ldots, g_m$ are continuous. This, in turn, ensures that the feasible set

$$\mathcal{C} = \{x \in \Re^n \mid g_1(x) \leq b_1, \ldots, g_m(x) \leq b_m\} = \cap_{j=1}^m \{x \in \Re^n \mid g_j(x) \leq b_j\}$$

is a closed set. Why? Prove it.

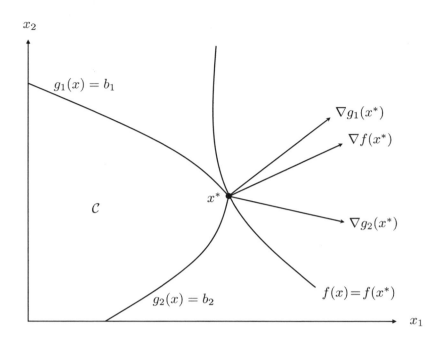

Figure 8.1: x^* is a local maximum for f on $\mathcal{C}$.

Have a look at Figure 8.1. The figure displays a compact feasible set $\mathcal{C}$ and a point $x^* \in \mathcal{C}$ that solves problem (8.4). At x^* there are two binding constraints, g_1 and g_2 (there might also be other slack constraints, but they can be ignored – only binding constraints matter), meaning that $g_1(x^*) = b_1$ and that $g_2(x^*) = b_2$. The figure displays three gradient vectors (which should really be displayed with respect to the origin, not with respect to x^* – see Section 2.14). $\nabla f(x^*)$ is the value at x^* of the objective function's gradient vector. This vector is orthogonal to small perturbation vectors Δx between x^* and nearby points $x^* + \Delta x$ in the contour set $\{x \in \Re^n \mid f(x) = f(x^*)\}$. The curve $\{x \in \Re^n \mid g_1(x) = b_1\}$ is the level-b_1 contour set for the first binding constraint function g_1, so the value at $x = x^*$ of its gradient vector, $\nabla g_1(x^*)$, is orthogonal to small perturbations Δx between x^* and nearby points $x^* + \Delta x$ in the contour set $\{x \in \Re^n \mid g_1(x) = b_1\}$. Similarly, the value $\nabla g_2(x^*)$ of the gradient vector of the second constraint g_2 that binds at $x = x^*$ is a vector that is orthogonal to small perturbations Δx between x^* and nearby points $x^* + \Delta x$ in the contour set $\{x \in \Re^n \mid g_2(x) = b_2\}$. The important feature of the figure is that the vector $\nabla f(x^*)$ lies in the convex cone that is generated by the vectors $\nabla g_1(x^*)$ and $\nabla g_2(x^*)$. Remember, from alternative (i) of Farkas's Lemma, that this means that there must exist nonnegative numbers, call them λ_1 and λ_2, that are not both zero such that $\nabla f(x^*) = \lambda_1 \nabla g_1(x^*) + \lambda_2 \nabla g_2(x^*)$. As you will soon see, this statement is the famous Karush-Kuhn-Tucker necessary condition for x^* to be a local maximum for f on $\mathcal{C}$.

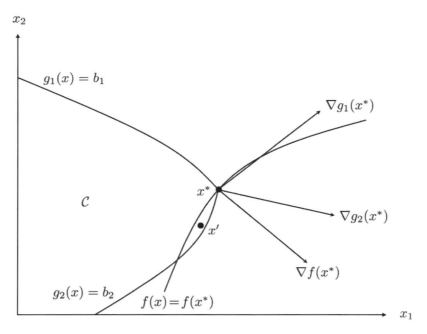

Figure 8.2: x^* is not a local maximum for f on $\mathcal{C}$.

Why is the condition necessary? Well, suppose the condition is not true, meaning that the objective function's gradient vector $\nabla f(x^*)$ does not lie in the convex cone generated by $\nabla g_1(x^*)$ and $\nabla g_2(x^*)$. This case is displayed in Figure 8.2. Because $\nabla f(x^*)$ is orthogonal to small perturbation vectors Δx between x^* and nearby points $x^* + \Delta x$ in the contour set $\{x \in \Re^n \mid f(x) = f(x^*)\}$, the consequence of $\nabla f(x^*)$ lying outside the convex cone is that the $f(x) = f(x^*)$ contour set "cuts inside" the feasible set $\mathcal{C}$. Consequently there are feasible points such as $x = x'$ for which $f(x') > f(x^*)$, contradicting that x^* is a local maximum for f on $\mathcal{C}$. This is really all there is to the Karush-Kuhn-Tucker Theorem, except for a detail called a "constraint qualification" that for now we will put aside. Albert Tucker and Harold Kuhn published their theorem in 1951 (see Kuhn and Tucker 1951) and for some time were regarded as the originators of the result. Only later did it become widely known that William Karush had already established the result in a Master of Science thesis written in 1939 at the University of Chicago (see Karush 1939) and, also, that a similar result, the Fritz

John Theorem, had been published in 1948.

Theorem 8.1 (Karush-Kuhn-Tucker Necessity Theorem). *Consider the problem*

$$\max_{x \in \Re^n} f(x) \text{ subject to } g_j(x) \leq b_j \text{ for } j = 1, \ldots, m,$$

where the objective function f and the constraint functions $g_1, \ldots, g_m$ are all continuously differentiable with respect to x, and the feasible set

$$\mathcal{C} = \{x \in \Re^n \mid g_j(x) \leq b_j \ \forall \ j = 1, \ldots, m\}$$

is not empty. Let x^* be a locally optimal solution to the problem. Let k denote the number of constraints that bind at $x = x^*$. Let $I(x^*)$ be the set of indices of the constraints that bind at $x = x^*$.

If $k = 0$, then $I(x^*) = \emptyset$ and $\nabla f(x^*) = \underline{0}$.

If $1 \leq k \leq m$ and if $\mathcal{C}$ satisfies a constraint qualification at x^* then there exist nonnegative scalars $\lambda_1^*, \ldots, \lambda_m^*$, not all zero, such that $\lambda_j^* \geq 0$ for all $j \in I(x^*)$, $\lambda_j^* = 0$ for all $j \notin I(x^*)$,

$$\nabla f(x^*) = \lambda_1^* \nabla g_1(x^*) + \cdots + \lambda_m^* \nabla g_m(x^*) \text{ and} \tag{8.5}$$

$$\lambda_j^* (b_j - g_j(x^*)) = 0 \ \forall \ j = 1, \ldots, m. \tag{8.6}$$

(8.5) is called the *Karush-Kuhn-Tucker necessary condition*. The m conditions (8.6) are the *complementary slackness* conditions. The proof of this famous theorem is but a simple application of Farkas's Lemma. Before we get to the proof, let me draw to your attention that the theorem assumes something called a "constraint qualification" that we have not yet examined. In most cases it is not good practice to state a theorem that contains an as-yet unexplained idea, but I'm going to do it this time and leave explaining what is meant by the term constraint qualification to the next section. I think that, overall, things will be clearer for you if I do this.

Proof. If $k = 0$, then none of the constraints bind at $x = x^*$, and so $I(x^*) = \emptyset$; *i.e.* $x = x^*$ is a point in the interior of $\mathcal{C}$. Obviously, then, necessarily $\nabla f(x^*) = \underline{0}$.

Suppose instead that $1 \leq k \leq m$. Thus $I(x^*) \neq \emptyset$. Without loss of generality, label the binding constraints by $j = 1, \ldots, k$, so $I(x^*) = \{1, \ldots, k\}$. Since x^* is a locally optimal solution to the problem, it must be true that $f(x^*)$ is at least as large as is the value of f at any nearby feasible choice $x^* + \Delta x$; *i.e.* for small enough Δx it must be true that

$$f(x^*) \geq f(x^* + \Delta x) \ \forall \ \Delta x \text{ such that } g_j(x^* + \Delta x) \leq g_j(x^*) = b_j \ \forall \ j = 1, \ldots, k. \tag{8.7}$$

Suppose that (8.5) is false; *i.e.* there do not exist scalars $\lambda_1, \ldots, \lambda_k$, all nonnegative and not all zero, such that

$$\nabla f(x^*) = \lambda_1^* \nabla g_1(x^*) + \cdots + \lambda_k^* \nabla g_k(x^*). \tag{8.8}$$

The feasible set $\mathcal{C}$ satisfies a constraint qualification, so Farkas's Lemma may be applied (an explanation of this mysterious assertion is provided in Section 8.6). (8.8) is alternative (i) in Farkas's Lemma, with $a^j = -\nabla g_j(x^*)$ and $b = -\nabla f(x^*)$. Since alternative (i) is false, it follows from alternative (ii) of the lemma that there exists a Δx such that

$$-\nabla g_1(x^*) \cdot \Delta x \geq 0, \ \ldots, \ -\nabla g_k(x^*) \cdot \Delta x \geq 0, \ -\nabla f(x^*) \cdot \Delta x < 0.$$

That is, there exists a Δx such that

$$\nabla g_1(x^*) \cdot \Delta x \leq 0, \ \ldots, \ \nabla g_k(x^*) \cdot \Delta x \leq 0, \ \nabla f(x^*) \cdot \Delta x > 0. \tag{8.9}$$

Since each of $f, g_1, \ldots, g_k$ is continuously differentiable, for small enough Δx,

$$\begin{aligned}
f(x^* + \Delta x) &= f(x^*) + \nabla f(x^*) \cdot \Delta x \quad \text{and} \\
g_j(x^* + \Delta x) &= g_j(x^*) + \nabla g_j(x^*) \cdot \Delta x \ \forall \ j = 1, \ldots, k.
\end{aligned}$$

Therefore, for small enough Δx, (8.9) is the statement that

$$f(x^* + \Delta x) > f(x^*), \ g_1(x^* + \Delta x) \leq g_1(x^*) = b_1, \ \ldots, \ g_k(x^* + \Delta x) \leq g_k(x^*) = b_k. \tag{8.10}$$

(8.10) is a statement that there is a feasible choice $x^* + \Delta x$ that is near to x^* and provides a higher objective function value than does x^*. But then x^* is not a local maximum; (8.10) contradicts (8.7). Thus (8.8) must be true if x^* is a locally optimal solution. Now choose $\lambda_{k+1}^* = \cdots = \lambda_m^* = 0$ for $j = k+1, \ldots, m$, and we have shown that (8.5) necessarily is true if x^* is a locally optimal solution.

(8.6) follows from the facts that $b_j - g_j(x^*) = 0$ for $j = 1, \ldots, k$ and $\lambda_j^* = 0$ for $j = k+1, \ldots, m$. $\qquad\qquad\square$

A few remarks need to be made before we go any further. First, notice that no mention has been made of a Lagrange function (this will be examined later), so if you are under the impression that you need a Lagrange function either to write down or to solve the Karush-Kuhn-Tucker conditions, then get rid of that impression – it is false.

Second, the theorem does not list all of the necessary optimization conditions. There is also a second-order necessary condition that will be described in Chapter 10.

Third, there may be more than one solution $(x_1^*, \ldots, x_n^*, \lambda_1^*, \ldots, \lambda_m^*)$ to the first-order optimality conditions (8.5) and (8.6). These conditions are only necessarily satisfied at any locally optimal solution. It is possible that other feasible choices, some perhaps locally optimal and some perhaps not, may also satisfy the first-order conditions.

Fourth, the theorem is subject to the requirement that the problem's feasible set $\mathcal{C}$ "satisfies a constraint qualification at x^*." It means that the Karush-Kuhn-Tucker Theorem cannot be applied to every constrained optimization problem of the type (8.4). We will examine the idea of a constraint qualification in the next section.

Last, the proof of the theorem uses the information that the problem satisfies a constraint qualification when applying Farkas's Lemma. Why this is so I cannot explain until we know what is a constraint qualification. So, for now, tuck this remark away, and I will explain it when we reach Section 8.6.

8.4   What Is a Constraint Qualification?

In the present context the word "qualification" means "restriction," so any constraint qualification is a restriction on the properties of the problem's constraint functions $g_1, \ldots, g_m$. Constraint qualifications have nothing to do with the problem's objective function f. Every one of the many constraint qualifications has the same purpose, which is to ensure that any locally optimal solution to problem (8.4) does not occur at a point in the feasible set $\mathcal{C}$ where the Karush-Kuhn-Tucker condition does not exist. Such points are called *irregularities*. More precisely, a feasible point $x \in \mathcal{C}$ is said to be *irregular* if and only if the Karush-Kuhn-Tucker condition does not exist at that point. Equivalently, a feasible point is *regular* if and only if the Karush-Kuhn-Tucker condition does exist at that point. The most commonly discussed example (there are others) of an irregularity is a *cusp*. What is a cusp and why does it matter? Have a look at Figure 8.3.

Once again there is displayed a compact feasible set $\mathcal{C}$, but, as you can see, the point x^* now lies at a "needle point" vertex on the boundary of $\mathcal{C}$ that is formed by the tangency at $x = x^*$ of two or more feasible set boundaries. Such a point is called a cusp. Suppose that x^* is a local maximum for f on $\mathcal{C}$. Why does it matter that x^* is a cusp? Look again at the figure and think about the values at $x = x^*$ of the gradient vectors $\nabla g_1(x)$ and $\nabla g_2(x)$ of the constraints that bind at $x = x^*$. Since the constraints' contour sets $\{x \in \Re^2 \mid g_1(x) = b_1\}$ and $\{x \in \Re^2 \mid g_2(x) = b_2\}$ are tangential at the cusp, what do you know about the gradient vectors $\nabla g_1(x^*)$ and

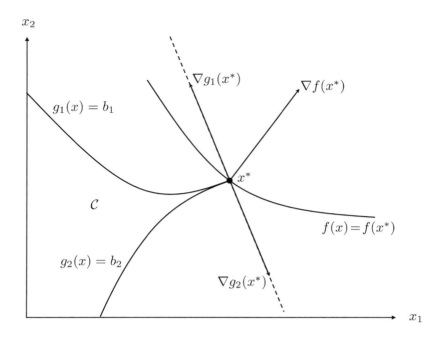

Figure 8.3: The feasible set $\mathcal{C}$ has a cusp at $x = x^*$.

$\nabla g_2(x^*)$? Think about it – this is the crucial point! Remember that the gradient vectors are orthogonal to small perturbation vectors Δx from x^* to nearby points $x^* + \Delta x$ in the contour sets.

The consequence of the tangency at x^* of the curves $g_1(x) = b_1$ and $g_2(x) = b_2$ is that $\nabla g_1(x^*)$ and $\nabla g_2(x^*)$ are *negatively collinear*; *i.e.* the vectors point in exactly opposite directions. Here is the next important question for you. What is the convex cone that is generated by the negatively collinear vectors $\nabla g_1(x^*)$ and $\nabla g_2(x^*)$? Don't proceed to the next paragraph until you have done your best to answer.

The convex cone is the hyperplane containing both vectors, shown as a dotted line in Figure 8.3 (remember that this hyperplane actually passes through the origin). The objective function's gradient vector $\nabla f(x)$ evaluated at x^* does not lie in the hyperplane. Consequently there do not exist any numbers λ_1 and λ_2 such that $\nabla f(x^*) = \lambda_1 \nabla g_1(x^*) + \lambda_2 \nabla g_2(x^*)$. *The Karush-Kuhn-Tucker first-order necessary condition (8.5) may not be true at a locally optimal solution that is a cusp (or any other type of irregular point) in the feasible set of the constrained optimization problem.*

This raises a troubling question: "For what particular types of constrained optimization problems can we be sure that the Karush-Kuhn-Tucker necessary condition will exist at the locally optimal solutions to the problems?" The conditions that identify these types of problems are the constraint qualifications – that is their sole purpose.

A cusp is not the only type of irregularity that can occur. Here is an example (due to Slater) of another. Consider the simple problem of maximizing $f(x) = x$ subject to the constraint $g(x) = x^2 \leq 0$ for only real values of x. Then the feasible set consists of just one point, $x = 0$, which must therefore be the optimal solution. Evaluated at $x = 0$, the gradients of f and g are $f'(0) = 1$ and $g'(0) = 0$. Clearly there is no value for λ such that $f'(0) = \lambda g'(0)$, so the Karush-Kuhn-Tucker condition fails. There is only one constraint in this problem, so there is no cusp in the feasible set. What's going on here? Why does the Karush-Kuhn-Tucker condition fail? Before we answer this question, suppose we alter the constraint to $g(x) = x^2 \leq \varepsilon$ for any $\varepsilon > 0$ that you wish. The feasible set becomes the interval $(-\sqrt{\varepsilon}, +\sqrt{\varepsilon})$, not just a single point, and the optimal solution becomes $x = +\sqrt{\varepsilon}$. Evaluated at $x = +\sqrt{\varepsilon}$, the gradients of f and g are $f'(+\sqrt{\varepsilon}) = 1$ and $g'(+\sqrt{\varepsilon}) = +2\sqrt{\varepsilon}$, so there is a positive value, $\lambda = 1/2\sqrt{\varepsilon}$, satisfying $f'(+\sqrt{\varepsilon}) = \lambda g'(+\sqrt{\varepsilon})$. Adding some extra elements to the feasible set seems to have made the irregularity go away. What do we make of all this? Look back at the proof of the Karush-Kuhn-Tucker Necessity Theorem. Particularly, note that in the proof we used as our notion of local optimality that the value of the objective function f at $x = x^*$ had to be at least as large as the value of f at any nearby feasible value $x = x^* + \Delta x$. Thus we assumed the existence of neighboring feasible values. The theorem does not apply to a case where there are no such neighbors, as in Slater's example.

8.5 Fritz John's Theorem

This raises a few practical problems. First, how would we discover if a problem's feasible set contains an irregular point? If the problem has only a few variables and only a few constraints, then it is probably not too hard to find out. But looking for a possible irregularity in the boundaries of the feasible set of a problem with many variables and many constraints requires a search that is neither simple nor rapid. Second, an irregular point does not present a difficulty unless it is also a locally optimal solution to the problem. Now we are in a nasty situation. If the optimal solution lies at an irregularity, then we cannot use the Karush-Kuhn-Tucker Necessity Theorem to solve for the value of the optimal solution, but without using the theorem locating the optimal solution will require an awful lot of hit-and-miss calculations. What are we to do? Perhaps we need a different tool than the Karush-Kuhn-Tucker Theorem? Indeed we do, and fortunately for us the tool exists. It is Fritz John's Theorem (see John 1948), a result that applies even if the problem's optimal solution is at an irregular point. It is one of the most important results available on solving differentiable constrained optimization problems. Let's have a look at it.

Theorem 8.2 (Fritz John's Necessity Theorem). *Consider the inequality constrained problem*

$$\max_{x \in \Re^n} f(x) \text{ subject to } g_j(x) \leq b_j \text{ for } j = 1, \ldots, m,$$

where the objective function f and the constraint functions $g_1, \ldots, g_m$ are all continuously differentiable with respect to x, and the feasible set

$$\mathcal{C} = \{x \in \Re^n \mid g_j(x) \leq b_j \ \forall \ j = 1, \ldots, m\}$$

is not empty. Let x^* be a locally optimal solution to the problem. Let k denote the number of constraints that bind at $x = x^*$. Let $I(x^*)$ be the set of indices of the constraints that bind at $x = x^*$.

If $k = 0$, then $I(x^*) = \emptyset$ and $\nabla f(x^*) = \underline{0}$.

If $1 \leq k \leq m$, then $I(x^*) \neq \emptyset$ and there exist nonnegative scalars $\lambda_0^*, \lambda_1^*, \ldots, \lambda_m^*$, not all zero, such that $\lambda_0^* \geq 0$, $\lambda_j^* \geq 0$ for all $j \in I(x^*)$, $\lambda_j^* = 0$ for all $j \notin I(x^*)$,

$$\lambda_0^* \nabla f(x^*) \quad = \quad \lambda_1^* \nabla g_1(x^*) + \cdots + \lambda_m^* \nabla g_m(x^*) \text{ and} \qquad (8.11)$$
$$\lambda_j^*(b_j - g_j(x^*)) \quad = \quad 0 \ \forall \ j = 1, \ldots, m. \qquad (8.12)$$

This is a really good moment for you to reread the Karush-Kuhn-Tucker Necessity Theorem and to compare it word-by-word to Fritz John's Theorem. Go ahead. I'll wait until you are done.

I'm sure that you have noticed that the m conditions (8.12) are the same complementary slackness conditions (8.6) described in the Karush-Kuhn-Tucker Theorem. (8.11) is the *Fritz John necessary condition* and it is the same as the Karush-Kuhn-Tucker necessary condition (8.5) except that there is an extra multiplier λ_0^* in front of the gradient of f at x^*. Indeed, if $\lambda_0^* = 1$, then Fritz John's necessary condition is exactly the Karush-Kuhn-Tucker necessary condition. Notice that none of the complementary slackness conditions involves λ_0^*. Also notice that Fritz John's Theorem does not require that the problem's feasible set $\mathcal{C}$ satisfies a constraint qualification. What this means is that Fritz John's Theorem can be applied to problems in which a local maximum x^* is an irregular point, while the Karush-Kuhn-Tucker Theorem cannot. It is hard to see what all this is about and why it matters without trying a couple of examples, so let's do that now.

We will start with a simple problem with a feasible set that does not contain a cusp or any other type of irregular point:

$$\max_{x_1, x_2} 5x_1 + x_2 \text{ subject to } g_1(x_1, x_2) = -x_1 \leq 0,$$

$$g_2(x_1, x_2) = -x_2 \leq 0 \text{ and } g_3(x_1, x_2) = x_1 + 2x_2 \leq 2.$$

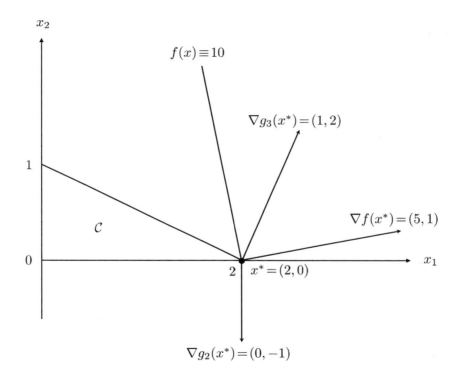

Figure 8.4: The optimal solution $x^* = (2, 0)$ is a regular point.

Figure 8.4 displays the problem. The optimal solution is $(x_1^*, x_2^*) = (2, 0)$. Constraint g_1 is slack at $(2, 0)$ and constraints g_2 and g_3 are binding at $(2, 0)$, so $I(x^*) = \{2, 3\}$. At $(2, 0)$ the values of the gradients of f, g_2 and g_3 are

$$\nabla f(2, 0) = (5, 1), \ \nabla g_2(2, 0) = (0, -1) \text{ and } \nabla g_3(2, 0) = (1, 2).$$

Fritz John's necessary condition (8.11) is thus

$$\lambda_0 \times 5 = \lambda_2 \times 0 + \lambda_3 \times 1$$
$$\text{and} \quad \lambda_0 \times 1 = \lambda_2 \times (-1) + \lambda_3 \times 2,$$

resulting in the infinite collection of solutions $\lambda_2 = 9\lambda_0$ and $\lambda_3 = 5\lambda_0$ in which λ_0 can take any positive value (positive, not zero, because we do not want *all* of λ_0, λ_1, λ_2, and λ_3 to be zero). The Karush-Kuhn-Tucker necessary condition (8.5) is

$$5 = \lambda_2 \times 0 + \lambda_3 \times 1$$
$$\text{and} \quad 1 = \lambda_2 \times (-1) + \lambda_3 \times 2,$$

resulting in the unique solution $\lambda_2 = 9$ and $\lambda_3 = 5$. This is the particular Fritz John solution that results from choosing $\lambda_0 = 1$. Indeed, so long as the problem's optimal solution is a regular point, then we might as well choose $\lambda_0 = 1$ and apply the Karush-Kuhn-Tucker Theorem. But now consider a similar problem in which the optimal solution is an irregular point, a cusp, in the feasible set:

$$\max_{x_1, x_2} 5x_1 + x_2 \text{ subject to } g_1(x_1, x_2) = -x_1 \le 0,$$
$$g_2(x_1, x_2) = -x_2 \le 0 \text{ and } g_3(x_1, x_2) = x_2 + (x_1 - 2)^3 \le 0.$$

Figure 8.5 displays the problem. The optimal solution is again $(x_1^*, x_2^*) = (2, 0)$. Confirm for yourself that this point is a cusp in the problem's feasible set. Constraint g_1 is slack and constraints g_2 and g_3 bind at $(2, 0)$, so $I(x^*) = \{2, 3\}$. At $(2, 0)$ the values of the gradients of f, g_2 and g_3 are

$$\nabla f(2, 0) = (5, 1), \quad \nabla g_2(2, 0) = (0, -1), \text{ and } \nabla g_3(2, 0) = (0, 1).$$

The Fritz John necessary condition (8.11) is

$$\lambda_0 \times 5 = \lambda_2 \times 0 + \lambda_3 \times 0$$
$$\text{and} \quad \lambda_0 \times 1 = \lambda_2 \times (-1) + \lambda_3 \times 1.$$

There is an infinity of solutions to these equations, all of the form $\lambda_0 = 0$ and $\lambda_2 = \lambda_3$. The two important things to notice here are that, first, there is at least one solution to the Fritz John conditions and, second, for *every* solution $\lambda_0 = 0$. The Karush-Kuhn-Tucker necessary condition (8.5) is

$$5 = \lambda_2 \times 0 + \lambda_3 \times 0$$
$$\text{and} \quad 1 = \lambda_2 \times (-1) + \lambda_3 \times 1.$$

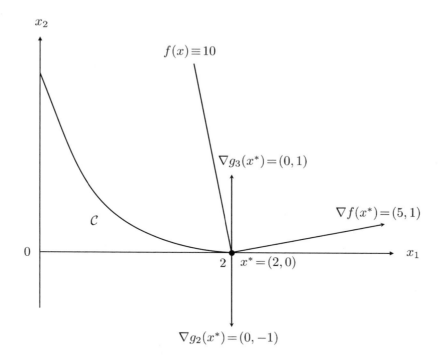

Figure 8.5: The feasible set has a cusp at the optimal solution $x^* = (2, 0)$.

These are equations with no solution. This demonstrates the extra generality of Fritz John's necessary optimality condition. It can be used whether the problem's feasible set has an irregular point or not. If the problem's optimal solution lies at an irregularity, then Fritz John's necessary condition reports this by showing that necessarily $\lambda_0 = 0$. But what does $\lambda_0 = 0$ mean? Well, what is the whole idea of the Karush-Kuhn-Tucker necessary condition? It is that, at any regular optimal solution to a problem, there must exist a non-zero and nonnegative vector $\lambda = (\lambda_1, \ldots, \lambda_m)$, such that $\nabla f(x^*) = \sum_{j=1}^{m} \lambda_j \nabla g(x^*)$. Only if this is so does the value of the objective function's gradient vector at x^*, $\nabla f(x^*)$, lie inside the convex cone defined by the values $\nabla g_j(x^*)$ of the gradient vectors of the constraints $j \in I(x^*)$ that bind at x^*. When there is a cusp at x^*, this convex cone typically does not contain $\nabla f(x^*)$, so the solutions to $\lambda_0 \nabla f(x^*) = \sum_{j=1}^{m} \lambda_j \nabla g(x^*)$ all require that $\lambda_0 = 0$. It is, in effect, a statement that $\nabla f(x^*)$ cannot be written as a nonnegative and nonzero linear combination of any of the $\nabla g_j(x^*)$ for $j \in I(x^*)$. Or, if you prefer, only by multiplying $\nabla f(x^*)$ by zero to create the zero vector can we create a vector $\lambda_0 \nabla f(x^*)$ that is contained in the hyperplane through the origin that is the convex cone generated by the negatively collinear gradient vectors of the constraints that bind at a cusp.

But why does $\lambda_0^* = 0$ tell us that there is an irregularity at $x = \hat{x}$? Let's think of the case in which two constraints, say g_1 and g_2, are binding and form a cusp at $\hat{x}$. If $\lambda_0^* = 0$, then Fritz John's necessary condition is

$$\lambda_0^* \nabla f(x^*) = \underline{0} = \lambda_1^* \nabla g_1(x^*) + \lambda_2^* \nabla g_2(x^*),$$

which tells us that

$$\nabla g_1(x^*) = -\frac{\lambda_2^*}{\lambda_1^*} \nabla g_2(x^*).$$

So $\lambda_0^* = 0$ only if the vectors $\nabla g_1(x^*)$ and $\nabla g_2(x^*)$ are collinear and point in opposite (because $-\lambda_2^*/\lambda_1^* \leq 0$) directions. Consequently the two vectors $\nabla g_1(x^*)$ and $\nabla g_2(x^*)$ generate a hyperplane when $x = \hat{x}$ is a cusp.

Now let's think of Slater's example. Why is it that necessarily $\lambda_0^* = 0$ in that case? In Slater's example the feasible set contains only the point $x^* = 0$ and, at that point, $\nabla f(0) = 1$ and $\nabla g(0) = 0$. The only way to satisfy Fritz John's necessary condition that there exist scalars λ_0^* and λ_1^*, both nonnegative and not both zero, satisfying $\lambda_0^* \nabla f(0) = \lambda_1^* \nabla g(0)$ is with $\lambda_0^* = 0$. $\lambda_0^* = 0$ says that $\nabla f(0)$ is not a positive multiple of $\nabla g(0)$, which is, for Slater's example, what the Karush-Kuhn-Tucker condition (impossibly) attempts to demand.

The Karush-Kuhn-Tucker necessary condition is the special case of the Fritz John necessary condition in which $\lambda_0 = 1$, so it would be entirely reasonable for you to conjecture that, since we used Farkas's Lemma to prove the Karush-Kuhn-Tucker Theorem, we will again use Farkas's Lemma to prove Fritz John's Theorem. This is not so. To prove Fritz John's Theorem we will instead use Gordan's Lemma. It is probably a good idea to take a few minutes to review Gordan's Lemma before examining the following proof.

Proof of Fritz John's Necessity Theorem. If $k = 0$, then none of the constraints bind at $x = x^*$; *i.e.* $I(x^*) = \emptyset$ and $x = x^*$ is interior to $\mathcal{C}$. Obviously, then, necessarily $\nabla f(x^*) = \underline{0}$.

Suppose instead that $1 \leq k \leq m$. Without loss of generality, label the binding constraints by $j = 1, \ldots, k$. Then $I(x^*) = \{1, \ldots, k\}$. Suppose that there do not exist $\lambda_0^*, \lambda_1^*, \ldots, \lambda_k^*$, all nonnegative and not all zero, such that

$$\lambda_0^* \nabla f(x^*) + \lambda_1^* (-\nabla g_1(x^*)) + \cdots + \lambda_k^* (-\nabla g_k(x^*)) = \underline{0}. \tag{8.13}$$

Then alternative (i) of Gordan's Lemma is false and so, from alternative (ii) of the lemma, there exists Δx such that

$$\nabla f(x^*) \cdot \Delta x > 0, \quad -\nabla g_1(x^*) \cdot \Delta x > 0, \ldots, \quad -\nabla g_k(x^*) \cdot \Delta x > 0. \tag{8.14}$$

That is,

$$\nabla f(x^*)\cdot\Delta x > 0, \ \nabla g_1(x^*)\cdot\Delta x < 0, \ldots, \ \nabla g_k(x^*)\cdot\Delta x < 0. \tag{8.15}$$

This is a statement that, for small enough Δx, there exists a *feasible* point $x^* + \Delta x$ near to x^* and *in the interior* of the feasible set for which $f(x^* + \Delta x) > f(x^*)$. This contradicts that x^* is a locally optimal solution. Therefore, because x^* is a locally optimal solution, necessarily there exist $\lambda_0^*, \lambda_1^*, \ldots, \lambda_k^*$, all nonnegative and not all zero, such that

$$\lambda_0^*\nabla f(x^*) = \lambda_1^*\nabla g_1(x^*) + \cdots + \lambda_k^*\nabla g_k(x^*). \tag{8.16}$$

Now choose $\lambda_{k+1}^* = \cdots = \lambda_m^* = 0$, and both (8.11) and (8.12) are established. □

Let's notice a detail in the proof that is easily overlooked. Notice that the inequalities $\nabla g_j(x^*)\cdot\Delta x < 0$ in (8.15) are *strict*, not weak. So the proof relies upon the existence of feasible points $x^* + \Delta x$ near to x^* that are in the *interior* of the feasible set; *i.e.* nearby points $x^* + \Delta x$ for which $g_j(x^* + \Delta x) = g_j(x^*) + \nabla g_j(x^*)\cdot\Delta x = b_j + \nabla g_j(x^*)\cdot\Delta x < b_j$ (note: $< b_j$, not $\leq b_j$) because $\nabla g_j(x^*)\cdot\Delta x < 0$. For this to be possible, the feasible set must locally have a nonempty interior, requiring that none of the constraints that bind at x^* is an equality constraint. That is why the title of John's paper is *Extremum Problems with **Inequalities** as Subsidiary Conditions* (emphasis added). The Fritz John necessary condition does not apply to constrained optimization problems with even one equality constraint that binds at a locally optimal solution.

The Karush-Kuhn-Tucker Theorem is more general than Fritz John's Theorem in that the Karush-Kuhn-Tucker Theorem applies to problems with any mixture of equality and inequality constraints, but is less general than Fritz John's Theorem in that it applies only to problems with feasible sets satisfying a constraint qualification. This is because the proof of the Karush-Kuhn-Tucker Theorem uses Farkas's Lemma, which does not imply the Karush-Kuhn-Tucker first-order necessary condition at a feasible solution unless a constraint qualification is satisfied at that point. Why this is so is explained in the next section.

8.6 Constraint Qualifications and Farkas's Lemma

Now it is time to clear up a point that I deferred when explaining the proof of the Karush-Kuhn-Tucker Necessity Theorem. Do you recollect that, in the proof, I said, "The feasible set $\mathcal{C}$ satisfies a constraint qualification so Farkas's Lemma may be applied."? Look again at the statement of Farkas's Lemma so that you are sure of what it says. In that statement do you see any caveat that the lemma can be used only if a constraint qualification is satisfied? No, you do not. So why insist upon there being a constraint qualification satisfied before making use of the lemma?

The difficulty is not with Farkas's Lemma. It is with the constrained optimization problem. The proof of the Karush-Kuhn-Tucker Theorem aims to show that, if $x = x^*$ is a maximum for f in a neighborhood of feasible points around x^*, then necessarily the Karush-Kuhn-Tucker condition (8.5) is satisfied. But, as we have seen, this is not always true. Particularly, if $x = x^*$ is some sort of irregular point in the feasible set $\mathcal{C}$ then the condition will not be satisfied. What does this have to do with Farkas's Lemma?

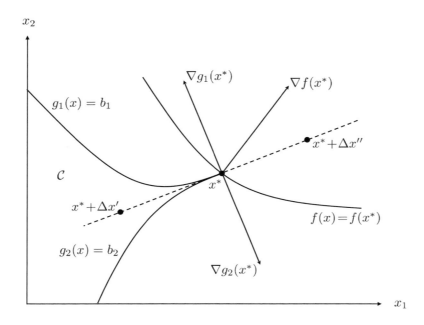

Figure 8.6: The feasible set has a cusp at the optimal solution. Farkas's second alternative is true.

Let's suppose that the optimal solution x^* is a cusp. Look at Figure 8.6. Because the gradients of the binding constraints are negatively collinear, the set of perturbations Δx from x^*, such that $\nabla g_1(x^*) \cdot \Delta x \leq 0$ and $\nabla g_2(x^*) \cdot \Delta x \leq 0$, is

$H = \{\Delta x \mid \nabla g_1(x^*) \cdot \Delta x = 0 \text{ and } \nabla g_1(x^*) \cdot \Delta x = 0\}$. This set is a hyperplane through the origin. The perturbations Δx in the hyperplane create a straight line locus of points $x^* + \Delta x$ that is displayed as a dashed line in the figure. There are points such as $x^* + \Delta x'$ in the locus that are in the feasible set, as well as points such as $x^* + \Delta x''$ that are outside the feasible set. Notice that

$$\nabla g_1(x^*) \cdot \Delta x'' = 0, \ \nabla g_2(x^*) \cdot \Delta x'' = 0 \text{ and } \nabla f(x^*) \cdot \Delta x'' > 0,$$

so we have found at least one value for Δx that satisfies alternative (ii) of Farkas's Lemma (with $a^1 = -\nabla g_1(x^*)$, $a^2 = -\nabla g_2(x^*)$ and $b = -\nabla f(x^*)$). Hence alternative (i) is false, and it is alternative (i) upon which we rely to establish the Karush-Kuhn-Tucker necessary optimality condition. Thus, to establish the Karush-Kuhn-Tucker result, we must confine ourselves to constrained optimization problems in which alternative (ii) is false. These are exactly the problems wherein the optimal solution is a regular point. One way to do this is to consider only problems in which the feasible set of the problem never has a locally maximal solution at an irregular point. The constraint qualifications tell us which are some of these problems.

8.7   Particular Constraint Qualifications

There are many constraint qualifications. This section presents just a representative few of them. So long as you understand what a constraint qualification does, you can safely skip this section. But there is some merit in reading at least the first few of the qualifications explained below since they are in common use by economists.

Slater's Constraint Qualification. The feasible set $\mathcal{C}$ of the constrained optimization problem is compact with respect to E^n, is convex, and has a nonempty interior.

The feasible set is thus required to be as is displayed, for example, in Figures 8.1 and 8.4, and not as is displayed in Figure 8.6. The nonempty interior requirement means that the feasible set can be neither empty nor a singleton (thus avoiding the difficulty demonstrated in Slater's example). The convexity of the set together with its nonempty interior means that there cannot be a cusp at any point in the set. Karlin's Constraint Qualification, stated below, is equivalent to Slater's, even though it might not seem so at a first glance.

Karlin's Constraint Qualification.   For any $p \in \Re_+^m$ with $p \neq \underline{0}$ and $\|p\|_E < \infty$ there exists an $x' \in \mathcal{C}$, such that $p \cdot (b - g(x')) = \sum_{j=1}^m p_j (b_j - g_j(x')) > 0$.

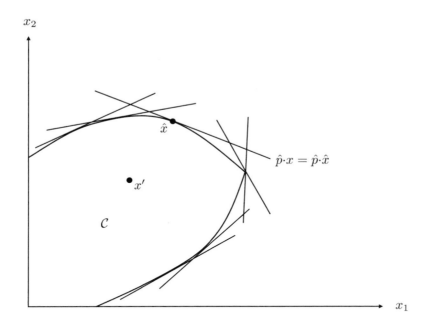

Figure 8.7: The Slater/Karlin Constraint Qualification.

It is not hard to see why Slater's and Karlin's statements are equivalent. The idea is illustrated in Figure 8.7 and is as follows. Take any point $\hat{x}$ on the boundary of the feasible set $\mathcal{C}$. Then $g_j(\hat{x}) = b_j$ for at least one $j \in \{1, \ldots, n\}$ and $g_k(\hat{x}) \le b_k$ for all $k \in \{1, \ldots, n\}$, $k \neq j$. There will be a normal $\hat{p}$ for which the hyperplane $\hat{p}{\cdot}x = \hat{p}{\cdot}\hat{x}$ is tangential to $\mathcal{C}$ at $\hat{x}$. Since $p \in \Re_+^m$ and $p \neq \underline{0}_m$, every one of $p_1, \ldots, p_m \ge 0$ with at least one strictly positive. Hence $p{\cdot}(b - g(x')) \ge 0$. Karlin's requirement is that there must be another point x' that is in the interior of $\mathcal{C}$, for then $g_j(x') < b_j$ for every $j = 1, \ldots, m$, causing $p{\cdot}(b - g(x')) > 0$; *i.e.* the interior of $\mathcal{C}$ is not empty, as is required by Slater's Qualification. Why does Karlin's Qualification ensure that $\mathcal{C}$ is a convex set? It says that all of the interior points of $\mathcal{C}$ lie in the lower half-spaces of hyperplanes that are tangential to (supporting to) the feasible set $\mathcal{C}$. In other words, the interior of $\mathcal{C}$ must be the intersection of all such possible lower half-spaces. Half-spaces are convex sets, so their intersection is a convex set, Slater's other requirement, as you can see from Figure 8.7.

Since it seems that all we really need to do is insist that the gradients of the constraints that bind at $x = \hat{x}$ are linearly independent, we can construct a constraint qualification by demanding exactly that. This is the Rank Constraint Qualification.

Rank Constraint Qualification.   If the number of constraints that bind at $\hat{x}$

is $k \geq 1$, then the rank of the Jacobian matrix consisting of the values at $\hat{x}$ of the gradients of the constraints that bind at $\hat{x}$ is k.

The usual shorthand notation for this Jacobian is

$$J(\hat{x}) = \left(\nabla g_j(\hat{x})\right)_{j \in I(\hat{x})}.$$

Think of a problem with, say, five variables $x_1, \ldots, x_5$ and four constraints labeled by $j = 1, 2, 3, 4$. Suppose that the fourth constraint is slack at $x = \hat{x}$. Then the index set for the binding constraints is $I(\hat{x}) = \{1, 2, 3\}$ and the Jacobian matrix is

$$J(\hat{x}) = \begin{pmatrix} \nabla g_1(x) \\ \nabla g_2(x) \\ \nabla g_3(x) \end{pmatrix} \Bigg|_{x=\hat{x}} = \begin{pmatrix} \dfrac{\partial g_1(x)}{\partial x_1} & \dfrac{\partial g_1(x)}{\partial x_2} & \dfrac{\partial g_1(x)}{\partial x_3} & \dfrac{\partial g_1(x)}{\partial x_4} & \dfrac{\partial g_1(x)}{\partial x_5} \\ \dfrac{\partial g_2(x)}{\partial x_1} & \dfrac{\partial g_2(x)}{\partial x_2} & \dfrac{\partial g_2(x)}{\partial x_3} & \dfrac{\partial g_2(x)}{\partial x_4} & \dfrac{\partial g_2(x)}{\partial x_5} \\ \dfrac{\partial g_3(x)}{\partial x_1} & \dfrac{\partial g_3(x)}{\partial x_2} & \dfrac{\partial g_3(x)}{\partial x_3} & \dfrac{\partial g_3(x)}{\partial x_4} & \dfrac{\partial g_3(x)}{\partial x_5} \end{pmatrix} \Bigg|_{x=\hat{x}},$$

where every derivative is evaluated at $x = \hat{x}$. The rank of this matrix is at most 3. Suppose that $\hat{x}$ is a cusp. Then at least two of the gradient vectors $\nabla g_j(\hat{x})$ for $j = 1, 2, 3$ are collinear, and so are linearly dependent, so the rank of $J(\hat{x})$ is at most 2, not 3. Conversely, suppose the rank of $J(\hat{x}) = 3$. Then all of the gradient vectors are linearly independent. Hence $\hat{x}$ cannot be a cusp. Look back at Figure 8.6, where $x = x^*$ is a cusp, and observe that

$$I(x^*) = \{1, 2\}, \quad J(x^*) = \begin{pmatrix} \dfrac{\partial g_1(x)}{\partial x_1} & \dfrac{\partial g_1(x)}{\partial x_2} \\ \dfrac{\partial g_2(x)}{\partial x_1} & \dfrac{\partial g_2(x)}{\partial x_2} \end{pmatrix} \Bigg|_{x=x^*} \quad \text{and Rank } J(x^*) = 1 < 2.$$

I wish I could tell you that every constraint qualification is as easy to comprehend as are the above three, but, sad to say, some of them take quite a bit of puzzling over. Even more unfortunately, there is such a constraint qualification that is too important to be ignored. This is the Kuhn-Tucker Constraint Qualification, usually abbreviated to KTCQ. To make sense of it, we need to understand the terms *constrained direction* and *constrained path*. Then I will state the KTCQ and, with the help of a picture or two, we will figure out what it says and how it ensures that any feasible solution that satisfies it is a regular point.

Definition 8.5 (Constrained Direction). *Let $x' \in \mathcal{C}$. Let $I(x')$ denote the set of indices of the constraints $g_1(x) \leq b_1, \ldots, g_m(x) \leq b_m$ that bind at $x = x'$. A vector $\Delta x \in \Re^n$ is a* constrained direction *from x' if $\nabla g_j(x') \cdot \Delta x \leq 0 \ \forall \ j \in I(x')$.*

The set of constrained directions Δx from x' is a closed convex cone that we will denote by

$$\mathrm{CD}(x') = \{\Delta x \in \Re^n \mid \nabla g_j(x') \cdot \Delta x \leq 0 \ \forall \ j \in I(x')\}.$$

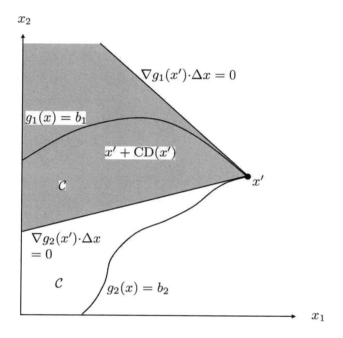

Figure 8.8: The affine closed convex cone $x' + \mathrm{CD}(x')$ for the regular point $x = x'$.

The shaded region of Figure 8.8 displays the points $x' + \Delta x$ created by such a cone. A convex cone of constrained directions does not have to create points $x' + \Delta x$ only in the problem's feasible set $\mathcal{C}$, as is illustrated in Figure 8.8. Note that the set of points $x' + \Delta x$ "points inwards into $\mathcal{C}$ from x'" when x' is a regular feasible point. However, if x' is an irregular point, a cusp perhaps, then the set of constrained directions is still a closed cone but it is rather different in shape. Figure 8.9 displays the cone when x' is a cusp. Notice, because this is important, that in this case the cone is a hyperplane containing points near to x' that are in $\mathcal{C}$ and points near to x' that are outside $\mathcal{C}$.

Do you remember Slater's example, in which the feasible set is only a singleton? What is the closed convex cone of constrained directions in such a case? Look again at Figure 8.8 and suppose this time that the two constraints are equalities instead of weak inequalities; *i.e.* the constraints are $g_1(x_1, x_2) = b_1$ and $g_2(x_1, x_2) = b_2$. Then the feasible set is only the singleton set $\{x'\}$. What now is the set $x' + \mathrm{CD}(x')$? I'll

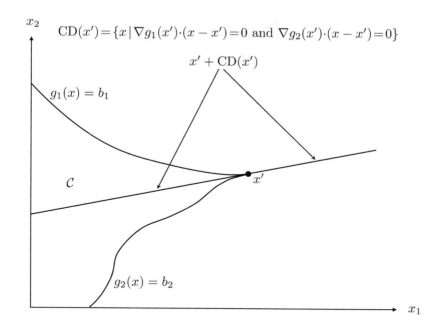

Figure 8.9: The affine closed convex cone $x' + \mathrm{CD}(x')$ for the cusp $x = x'$.

give you a clue. Look again at Definition 8.5. Notice that the movements Δx do not have to result in *feasible* points $x' + \Delta x$. So, where in Figure 8.8 is the set $x' + \mathrm{CD}(x')$?

The answer is that $x' + \mathrm{CD}(x')$ is exactly where the figure shows it to be. Turning the feasible set into a singleton does not alter the position of the cone because the points $x' + \Delta x$ do not have to be feasible.

Now it is time to turn to the second idea we need, the idea of a *constrained path*.

Definition 8.6 (Constrained Path). *Let $x' \in \mathcal{C}$. Let $\Delta x \in \Re^n$, $\Delta x \neq \underline{0}$. A constrained path from x' in the direction Δx is a function $h : [0,1) \mapsto \Re^n$ that is first-order continuously differentiable and has the properties that*

(i) $h(0) = x'$,

(ii) $h'(0) = \alpha \Delta x$ where $\alpha > 0$ is a scalar, and

(iii) $h(t) \in \mathcal{C}$ for all $t \in [0,1)$.

A constrained path from x' in the direction Δx is a smooth (because it is differentiable) curve that starts at $x = x'$, is entirely contained in $\mathcal{C}$, and is tangential at x' to the vector Δx. For a given x' and Δx, there can be many such paths. Figure 8.10 displays two constrained paths, $h^1(t)$ and $h^2(t)$.

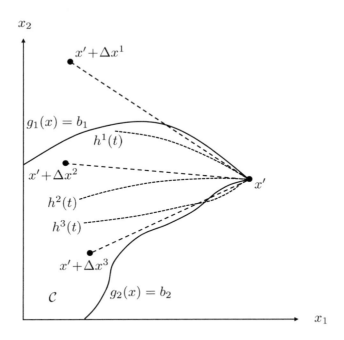

Figure 8.10: h^1 and h^2 are constrained paths from $x = x'$. h^3 is not.

Notice that, while $x' \in \mathcal{C}$, it is possible that some of the points $x = x' + \alpha\Delta x$ are not in $\mathcal{C}$. You see an example of this in Figure 8.10, where $x = x' + \Delta x^1 \notin \mathcal{C}$. However, the path $h^1(t)$ is entirely within $\mathcal{C}$, converges to $x = x'$, and becomes tangential to the line from x' to $x' + \Delta x^1$ as it converges to x'. Thus the curve $h^1(t)$ is a constrained path from x' in the direction Δx^1. Similarly, the path $h^2(t)$ is entirely within $\mathcal{C}$, converges to $x = x'$, and becomes tangential to the line from x' to $x' + \Delta x^2$ as it converges to x'. Thus the curve $h^2(t)$ is a constrained path from x' in the direction Δx^2. The curve $h^3(t)$ is not a constrained path because, as the curve approaches x' in the direction of Δx^3, the curve is forced outside of $\mathcal{C}$ in order to be tangential to the line from x' to $x' + \Delta x^3$. Be clear that the value of a constrained path h at a given value of t is a vector in $\Re^n$; *i.e.* $h(t) = (h_1(t), \ldots, h_n(t))$ where each of $h_1(t), \ldots, h_n(t)$ is a real number. In Figure 8.10, for example, $n = 2$, $h^1(0) = x' = (x_1', x_2')$ and for $0 < t < 1$,

$h^1(t) = (h_1^1(t), h_2^1(t))$ is a point (x_1, x_2) on the line $h^1(t)$. At last we are ready to understand the Kuhn-Tucker Constraint Qualification. Here it is.

The Kuhn-Tucker Constraint Qualification (KTCQ). Let $x' \in \mathcal{C}$ be a point for which at least one of the constraints $g_1(x) \leq b_1, \dots, g_m(x) \leq b_m$ binds. Let $I(x')$ denote the set of indices of the constraints that bind at $x = x'$. Let $\Delta x \in \Re^n$ be a constrained direction from x'. There exists a constrained path from x' in the direction Δx.

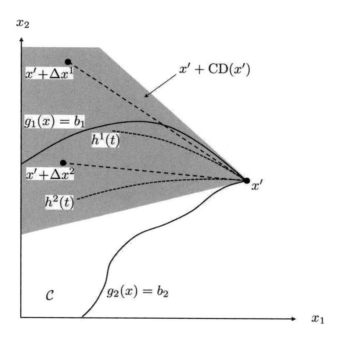

Figure 8.11: The Kuhn-Tucker Constraint Qualification is satisfied at $x = x'$.

Most people find this statement about as clear as mud when reading it for the first time. What it says, however, is not too hard to figure out by looking at two pictures. Start with Figure 8.11. As you can see there, $x = x'$ is a regular point. The set of indices of the constraints that bind at x' is $I(x') = \{1, 2\}$. The closed convex cone $\mathrm{CD}(x')$ containing all of the constrained directions from x' added to x' is the shaded area $x' + \mathrm{CD}(x')$. Take any point $x' + \Delta x$ you like in $x' + \mathrm{CD}(x')$, such as $x' + \Delta x^1$ or $x' + \Delta x^2$, and there is always at least one constrained path from x' in the direction of Δx. Thus, whenever x' is a regular feasible point the KTCQ is satisfied.

Now have a look at Figure 8.12, where the point x' is a cusp. The closed convex cone of constrained directions is the hyperplane $\mathrm{CD}(x') = \{\Delta x \mid \nabla g_1(x') \cdot \Delta x =$

0 and $\nabla g_2(x') \cdot \Delta x = 0$} through the origin. The set $x' + \mathrm{CD}(x')$ is the straight line passing through x' and containing points such as $x' + \Delta \hat{x}$ and $x' + \Delta \tilde{x}$.

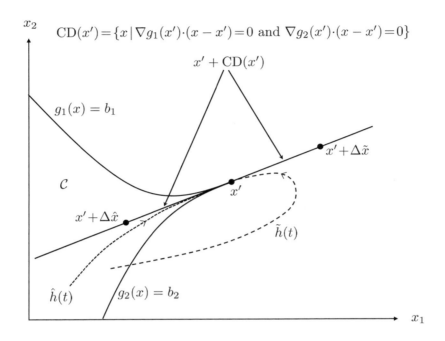

Figure 8.12: The Kuhn-Tucker Constraint Qualification is not satisfied at $x = x'$.

If we select a constrained direction such as $\Delta \hat{x}$ for which $x' + \Delta \hat{x}$ is in the "inside $\mathcal{C}$" part of the line $x' + \mathrm{CD}(x')$, then we can always find at least one constrained path, such as $\hat{h}(t)$, from x' in the direction $\Delta \hat{x}$ – see the figure. But if we select a constrained direction such as $\Delta \tilde{x}$ for which $x' + \Delta \tilde{x}$ is in the "outside $\mathcal{C}$" part of the line $x' + \mathrm{CD}(x')$, then we cannot find even one constrained path from x' in the direction $\Delta \tilde{x}$ – see the curve $\tilde{h}(t)$ in the figure. Even though this smooth (remember, it is differentiable) curve starts inside $\mathcal{C}$, it must eventually pass outside of $\mathcal{C}$ in order to approach x' from the direction $\Delta \tilde{x}$. Therefore the curve $\tilde{h}(t)$ is not a constrained path. By insisting that there must be at least one constrained path from x' for every constrained direction from x', the KTCQ insists that x' is not a cusp.

Let's again consider Slater's example, in which the feasible set is a singleton. How exactly is this prohibited by the KTCQ? Look again at Definition 8.6 and notice that any constrained path must be entirely within the feasible set $\mathcal{C} = \{x'\}$. Therefore $h(t) \equiv x'$ (*i.e.* h is constant-valued) for all $t \in [0, 1)$. Hence its derivative is the zero vector for all t, including at $t = 0$. Thus $h'(0) = \underline{0}$. Part (ii) of Definition 8.6 insists that, for a constrained direction $\Delta x \neq \underline{0}$ from x' and for $\alpha > 0$, we can write $h'(0) = \alpha \Delta x$. This is impossible when $h'(0) = \underline{0}$, so the KTCQ demands also that the feasible set not be a singleton.

As I said earlier, the constraint qualifications explained in this section are but a few of many. I selected the ones described above because of their usefulness to economists, but it may happen that none of the qualifications described here meets your needs. Do not despair – there are many other qualifications and one of them may be what you require.

8.8 Remarks

We have reached the end of our discussion of the first-order optimality conditions for constrained optimization problems. A lot has been covered, and it is easy to lose sight of the essential points when trying to deal with all of the details. So let's take a moment to review what we have learned and to set the stage for what still awaits us.

The crucial idea is that, for most of the constrained optimization problems that are of interest to economists, a feasible point x^* is locally optimal only if the value at x^* of the gradient of the objective function is a vector that is contained in the convex cone generated by the values at x^* of the gradient vectors of the constraint functions that bind at x^*. This is the meaning of the Karush-Kuhn-Tucker and Fritz John necessary first-order optimality conditions. For each constraint, binding or not, another set of conditions has to be true at a local optimum. These are the complementary slackness conditions. Each necessary condition must individually be true at a local optimum; if any one of them is not true at x^*, then x^* cannot be a local optimum.

We also learned that the Karush-Kuhn-Tucker Theorem and the Fritz John Theorem each applies to different classes of constrained optimization problems. The good news about the Karush-Kuhn-Tucker Theorem is that it applies to constrained optimization problems with any mixture of equality and/or inequality constraints. The bad news is that there may exist feasible, possibly optimal, points at which the Karush-Kuhn-Tucker necessary condition does not exist. We attempt to identify problems that do not contain such irregular points by insisting that the problems satisfy at least one of the many constraint qualifications. The Karush-Kuhn-Tucker Theorem can be applied only to such problems. There is good and bad news about Fritz John's Theorem also. The bad news is that the theorem applies only to constrained optimization problems with only inequality constraints – no equality constraints are allowed. The good news is that, for such problems, the Fritz John necessary condition is well defined at any feasible point, irregular or not. The two theorems thus complement each other. Neither is a special case of the other.

All that we have done in this chapter is subject to one obvious weakness. The first-order local optimality conditions that we have discovered may be satisfied also for points that are not local maxima (local minima, for example), so we now need to discover a method for distinguishing between local maxima and points that are not local maxima even though they too solve the necessary first-order optimality conditions. This is the central matter of Chapter 10. The ideas explained in Chapter 10 make extensive use of *Lagrange functions*, so Chapter 9 explains these functions and some of their valuable uses.

8.9 Problems

Problem 8.1. Here is a constrained optimization problem:

$$\max_{x_1, x_2} f(x_1, x_2) = 4x_1 + x_2 \text{ subject to } g_1(x_1, x_2) = -2 - 2x_1 + \frac{(x_1 - 20)^3}{500} + x_2 \leq 0,$$

$$g_2(x_1, x_2) = 2x_1 - x_2 \leq 0, \ g_3(x_1, x_2) = -x_1 \leq 0, \text{ and } g_4(x_1, x_2) = -x_2 \leq 0.$$

(i) Try using the Karush-Kuhn-Tucker necessary condition to solve the problem. Hint: The globally optimal solution is $x^* = (x_1^*, x_2^*) = (30, 60)$.

(ii) Try using the Fritz John necessary condition to solve the problem.

(iii) What difference, if any, is there in the outcomes of the approaches used in parts (i) and (ii)?

(iv) Draw the feasible set. See for yourself that the point $x^* = (30, 60)$ is regular and that the gradient $\nabla f(x^*) = (4, 1)$ of the objective function at $x^* = (30, 60)$ is contained in the convex cone that is generated by the gradients $\nabla g_1(x^*) = (-7/5, 1)$ and $\nabla g_2(x^*) = (2, -1)$ of the constraints that bind at $x^* = (30, 60)$.

(v) Is the Slater/Karlin constraint qualification satisfied for the constrained optimization problem's feasible set? Is the rank constraint qualification satisfied at the feasible solution $(x_1, x_2) = (30, 60)$?

Problem 8.2. The problem presented below is the same as problem 8.1 except that the constraint function g_1 has been slightly changed:

$$\max_{x_1, x_2} f(x_1, x_2) = 4x_1 + x_2 \text{ subject to } g_1(x_1, x_2) = -2x_1 + \frac{(x_1 - 20)^3}{500} + x_2 \leq 0,$$

$$g_2(x_1, x_2) = 2x_1 - x_2 \leq 0, \ g_3(x_1, x_2) = -x_1 \leq 0, \text{ and } g_4(x_1, x_2) = -x_2 \leq 0.$$

(i) Try using the Karush-Kuhn-Tucker necessary condition to solve the problem. Hint: The globally optimal solution is $x^* = (x_1^*, x_2^*) = (20, 40)$.

(ii) Try using the Fritz John necessary condition to solve the problem.

(iii) What difference, if any, is there in the outcomes of the approaches used in parts (i) and (ii)?

(iv) Draw the feasible set. See for yourself that the point $x^* = (20, 40)$ is irregular and that the gradient $\nabla f(x^*) = (4, 1)$ of the objective function at $x^* = (20, 40)$ is not contained in the convex cone that is generated by the gradients $\nabla g_1(x^*) = (-2, 1)$ and $\nabla g_2(x^*) = (2, -1)$ of the constraints that bind at $x^* = (20, 40)$.

(v) Is the Slater/Karlin constraint qualification satisfied for the constrained optimization problem's feasible set? Is the rank constraint qualification satisfied at the feasible solution $(x_1, x_2) = (20, 40)$?

Problem 8.3. Here is another constrained optimization problem:

$$\max_{x_1, x_2} f(x_1, x_2) = -4(x_1 - 2)^2 + x_2 \text{ subject to } g_1(x_1, x_2) = (x_1 - 2)^3 + x_2 \le 8,$$

$$g_2(x_1, x_2) = (x_1 - 2)^3 - x_2 \le -8, \ g_3(x_1, x_2) = -x_1 \le 0, \text{ and } g_4(x_1, x_2) = -x_2 \le 0.$$

(i) Try using the Karush-Kuhn-Tucker necessary condition to solve the problem. Hint: The globally optimal solution is $x^* = (x_1^*, x_2^*) = (2, 8)$. Draw the feasible set and the contour set for the objective function that contains the point $(2, 8)$.

(ii) Why is it, in this problem, that the Karush-Kuhn-Tucker necessary condition is well-defined at the global optimum even though the global optimum is a cusp? Add to your diagram of the feasible set the gradients, evaluated at $(2, 8)$, of the objective function and the two binding constraints. What do you see?

(iii) Try using the Fritz John necessary condition to solve the problem.

Problem 8.4. Consider the constrained optimization problem:

$$\max_{x \in \mathcal{C}} f(x), \text{ where } \mathcal{C} = \{x \in \Re^n \mid g_j(x) \le b_j \text{ for } j = 1, \dots, m\}.$$

$f, g_1, \dots, g_m$ are all C^1 functions defined on $\Re^n$. x^* denotes a locally optimal solution to this problem.

(i) Is satisfaction of a constraint qualification at x^* a condition that is necessary for this problem to have a locally optimal solution x^*? Explain.

(ii) Is satisfaction of a constraint qualification at x^* a condition that is sufficient for this problem to have a locally optimal solution x^*? Explain.

(iii) Is satisfaction of a constraint qualification at x^* a condition that is necessary for the Karush-Kuhn-Tucker necessary condition to be well-defined at x^*? Explain.

(iv) Is satisfaction of a constraint qualification at x^* a condition that is sufficient for the Karush-Kuhn-Tucker necessary condition to be well-defined at x^*? Explain.

Problem 8.5. Consider the following constrained optimization problem:

$$\max_{x_1, x_2} f(x_1, x_2) = +\sqrt{x_1} + x_2 \text{ subject to } g_1(x_1, x_2) = x_1^2 + x_2^2 \le 16,$$

$$g_2(x_1, x_2) = x_1 + x_2 \le 5, \ g_3(x_1, x_2) = -x_1 \le 0, \text{ and } g_4(x_1, x_2) = -x_2 \le 0.$$

Note: When evaluating f, use only the positive value of the square root of x_1.
(i) Draw a diagram that displays the feasible set

$$\mathcal{C} = \{(x_1, x_2) \mid x_1 \ge 0, \ x_2 \ge 0, \ x_1^2 + x_2^2 \le 16, \ x_1 + x_2 \le 5\}.$$

(ii) What properties does $\mathcal{C}$ possess?
(iii) Must this constrained optimization problem have an optimal solution?
(iv) Add a typical contour set for the objective function to your diagram.
(v) Use the Karush-Kuhn-Tucker necessary local maximization conditions to locate possible local maxima for f on $\mathcal{C}$.

Problem 8.6. Consider the following constrained optimization problem:

$$\max_{x_1, x_2} f(x_1, x_2) = x_1^2 - \frac{33}{4}x_1 + 21 + x_2 \text{ subject to } g_1(x_1, x_2) = -\sqrt{x_1} - x_2 \leq -6,$$

$$g_2(x_1, x_2) = x_1 + 4x_2 \leq 20, \ g_3(x_1, x_2) = -x_1 \leq 0, \text{ and } g_4(x_1, x_2) = -x_2 \leq 0.$$

(i) Draw a diagram that displays the problem's feasible set.
(ii) The optimal solution to this problem is $(x_1^*, x_2^*) = (4, 4)$. Can you write down the Karush-Kuhn-Tucker necessary optimality condition at this point? Explain.

Problem 8.7. Consider the following constrained optimization problem:

$$\max_{x_1, x_2} f(x_1, x_2) = x_1 + x_2 \text{ subject to } g_1(x_1, x_2) = (x_1 - 4)^2 + x_2 \leq 7,$$

$$\text{and } g_2(x_1, x_2) = (x_1 - 5)^3 - 12x_2 \leq -60.$$

(i) Draw a diagram that displays the feasible set.
(ii) Write down the Karush-Kuhn-Tucker necessary optimality condition together with the complementary slackness conditions.
(iii) Solve the problem.

8.10   Answers

Answer to Problem 8.1.
(i) See Figure 8.13. At $x^* = (30, 60)$, constraints g_3 and g_4 are slack. Constraints g_1 and g_2 bind at $x^* = (30, 60)$. The gradients of the objective function and the constraint functions g_1 and g_2 are

$$\nabla f(x) = (4, 1), \ \nabla g_1(x) = \left(-2 + \frac{3(x_1 - 20)^2}{500}, 1\right), \text{ and } \nabla g_2(x) = (2, -1).$$

Evaluated at $x^* = (30, 60)$, these gradients are

$$\nabla f(x^*) = (4, 1), \ \nabla g_1(x^*) = \left(-\frac{7}{5}, 1\right), \text{ and } \nabla g_3(x^*) = (2, -1).$$

The gradients $\nabla g_1(x^*)$ and $\nabla g_2(x^*)$ of the binding constraints are not collinear, so the feasible point $x^* = (30, 60)$ is regular. Hence we may use the Karush-Kuhn-Tucker first-order necessary condition and write that

$$(4, 1) = \lambda_1 \left(-\frac{7}{5}, 1 \right) + \lambda_2(2, -1) \quad \Rightarrow \quad \lambda_1^* = 10, \ \lambda_2^* = 9.$$

The values λ_1^* and λ_2^* are both nonnegative and at least one is strictly positive.

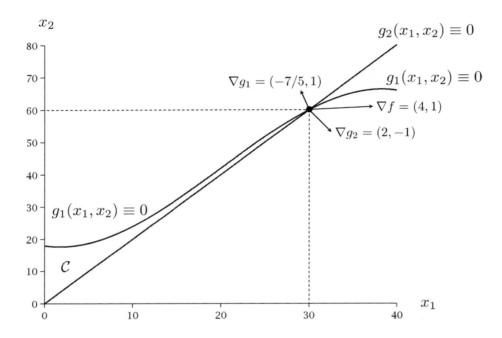

Figure 8.13: The feasible set, the optimal solution, and the gradient vectors for problem 8.1.

(ii) Fritz John's first-order necessary condition is that

$$\lambda_0(4, 1) = \lambda_1 \left(-\frac{7}{5}, 1 \right) + \lambda_2(2, -1) \quad \Rightarrow \quad \lambda_1^* = 10\lambda_0, \ \lambda_2^* = 9\lambda_0.$$

Clearly there is an infinity of positive values for λ_0 that cause both λ_1^* and λ_2^* also to have positive values.

(iii) The Karush-Kuhn-Tucker approach insists that the objective function multiplier $\lambda_0 = 1$. In the Fritz John approach, λ_0 can be assigned any positive value, and the other multiplier values are then determined conditional upon the value assigned to λ_0.

(iv) See Figure 8.13.

(v) The feasible set C has a nonempty interior but is not a convex set, so the Slater/Karlin constraint qualification is not satisfied by this problem's feasible set. The Jacobian matrix formed by the values at $(x_1, x_2) = (30, 60)$ of the gradient vectors of the binding constraints is

$$J_g(30, 60) = \begin{pmatrix} \nabla g_1(x_1, x_2) \\ \nabla g_2(x_1, x_2) \end{pmatrix} \Bigg|_{\substack{(x_1, x_2) = \\ (30, 60)}} = \begin{pmatrix} -7/5 & 1 \\ 2 & -1 \end{pmatrix}.$$

The row vectors of this matrix are linearly independent of each other. Equivalently, the rank of this matrix is 2, equal to the number of constraints that bind at $(30, 60)$. So the rank constraint qualification is satisfied at $(30, 60)$, establishing that $(x_1, x_2) = (30, 60)$ is a regular feasible solution. $\qquad\square$

Answer to Problem 8.2.

(i) See Figure 8.14. At $x^* = (20, 40)$ constraints g_3 and g_4 are slack. Constraints g_1 and g_2 bind at $x^* = (20, 40)$. The gradients of the objective function and the constraint functions g_1 and g_2 are

$$\nabla f(x) = (4, 1), \ \nabla g_1(x) = \left(-2 + \frac{3(x_1 - 20)^2}{500}, 1 \right), \ \text{and} \ \nabla g_2(x) = (2, -1).$$

Evaluated at $x^* = (20, 40)$, these gradients are

$$\nabla f(x^*) = (4, 1), \ \nabla g_1(x^*) = (-2, 1), \ \text{and} \ \nabla g_3(x^*) = (2, -1).$$

The gradients $\nabla g_1(x^*)$ and $\nabla g_2(x^*)$ of the binding constraints are negatively collinear, so the feasible point $x^* = (20, 40)$ is irregular (a cusp, actually). Hence it may not be possible to use the Karush-Kuhn-Tucker first-order necessary condition. If we try to do so, we get

$$(4, 1) = \lambda_1 (-2, 1) + \lambda_2 (2, -1).$$

That is,

$$4 = -2\lambda_1 + 2\lambda_2 \quad \text{and} \quad 1 = \lambda_1 - \lambda_2.$$

These are inconsistent equations, so there no values for λ_1^* and λ_2^* satisfying the Karush-Kuhn-Tucker necessary condition.

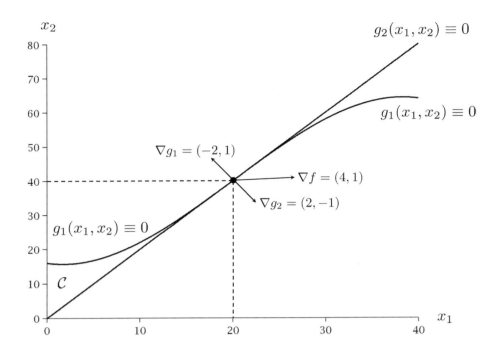

Figure 8.14: The feasible set, the optimal solution, and the gradient vectors for problem 8.2.

(ii) Fritz John's first-order necessary condition is that there are nonnegative scalars λ_0, λ_1 and λ_2, not all zero, such that

$$\lambda_0(4,1) = \lambda_1(-2,1) + \lambda_2(2,-1) \quad \Rightarrow \quad \lambda_1^* = 10\lambda_0, \ \lambda_2^* = 9\lambda_0.$$

That is,

$$4\lambda_0 = -2\lambda_1 + 2\lambda_2 \quad \text{and} \quad \lambda_0 = \lambda_1 - \lambda_2.$$

The family of solutions is $\lambda_0 = 0$ and $\lambda_1 = \lambda_2 > 0$ (because not all of λ_0, λ_1 and λ_2 are zero). That is, there is an infinity of solutions satisfying the Fritz John necessary condition. In each of these solutions $\lambda_0 = 0$.

(iii) The Karush-Kuhn-Tucker necessary condition does not exist at $x^* = (20, 40)$. The condition assumes (a constraint qualification) that the gradient of the objective function lies within the convex cone generated by the gradients of the constraints that bind at $x^* = (20, 40)$. But this is not so. The Fritz John necessary condition points this out by reporting that necessarily $\lambda_0 = 0$.

(iv) See Figure 8.14.

(v) The feasible set $\mathcal{C}$ has a nonempty interior but is not a convex set, so the Salter/Karlin constraint qualification is not satisfied by this problem's feasible set. The Jacobian matrix formed by the values at $(x_1, x_2) = (240, 0)$ of the gradient vectors of the binding constraints is

$$J_g(30, 60) = \begin{pmatrix} \nabla g_1(x_1, x_2) \\ \nabla g_2(x_1, x_2) \end{pmatrix} \bigg|_{\substack{(x_1, x_2)= \\ (20, 40)}} = \begin{pmatrix} -2 & 1 \\ 2 & -1 \end{pmatrix}.$$

The row vectors of this matrix are linearly dependent; each is the negative of the other. Thus the rank of this matrix is $1 < 2$, the number of constraints that bind at $(20, 40)$; the rank constraint qualification is not satisfied at $(x_1, x_2) = (20, 40)$.   □

Answer to Problem 8.3.
(i) See Figure 8.15. At $x^* = (2, 8)$, constraints g_3 and g_4 are slack. Constraints g_1 and g_2 bind at $x^* = (2, 8)$. The feasible set is displayed in Figure 8.15.

The gradients of the objective function and the constraint functions g_1 and g_2 are

$$\nabla f(x) = (-8(x_1 - 2), 1), \quad \nabla g_1(x) = (3(x_1 - 2)^2, 1), \quad \text{and} \quad \nabla g_2(x) = (3(x_1 - 2)^2, -1).$$

Evaluated at $x^* = (2, 8)$, these gradients are

$$\nabla f(x^*) = (0, 1), \quad \nabla g_1(x^*) = (0, 1), \quad \text{and} \quad \nabla g_2(x^*) = (0, -1).$$

Notice that the gradients $\nabla g_1(x^*)$ and $\nabla g_2(x^*)$ of the binding constraints are negatively collinear. The Karush-Kuhn-Tucker first-order necessary condition is that there are nonnegative values λ_1 and λ_2, not both zero, such that

$$(0, 1) = \lambda_1(0, 1) + \lambda_2(0, -1).$$

There are many solutions, all of the form $(\lambda_1, \lambda_2) = (\lambda_1, \lambda_1 - 1)$. One such solution, for example, is $\lambda_1 = 2$ and $\lambda_2 = 1$. These values for λ_1^* and λ_2^* are both nonnegative and at least one is strictly positive. Thus, even though the feasible (and globally optimal) point $(2, 8)$ is a cusp, the Karush-Kuhn-Tucker necessary condition is satisfied. For this problem, then, the point $(2, 8)$ is a regular point, even though it is a cusp. If this seems contradictory, then remember that any constraint qualification is a condition *sufficient*, but *not necessary*, for the Karush-Kuhn-Tucker necessary condition to be satisfied at a local optimum.
(ii) The gradients $(0, 1)$ and $(0, -1)$ of the two constraints that bind at $(2, 8)$ are negatively collinear, so the convex cone they generate is the hyperplane that is the

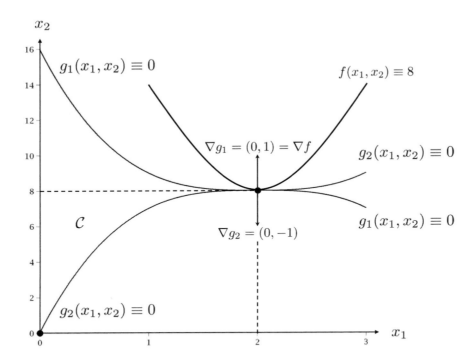

Figure 8.15: The feasible set, the optimal solution, and the gradient vectors for problem 8.3.

set $\{(x_1, x_2) \mid x_1 = 0\}$. In this particular problem, the value $(0, 1)$ of the gradient vector of the objective function at $(2, 8)$ happens to lie in this hyperplane. This is why the Karush-Kuhn-Tucker condition is true. The Karush-Kuhn-Tucker condition makes no sense only when the gradient of the objective function is not contained in the convex cone that is generated by the gradient vectors of the binding constraints. **(iii)** The Fritz John first-order necessary condition is that there exist nonnegative scalars λ_0, λ_1 and λ_2, not all zero, such that

$$\lambda_0(0, 1) = \lambda_1(0, 1) + \lambda_2(0, -1).$$

There is an infinity of nonnegative values for λ_0, λ_1, and λ_2, not all zero, that satisfy the Fritz John condition. Each solution is of the form $(\lambda_0, \lambda_1, \lambda_2) = (\lambda_0, \lambda_1, \lambda_1 - \lambda_0)$, with $\lambda_0 \geq 0$ and $\lambda_1 \geq \lambda_0$. An example is $(\lambda_0, \lambda_1, \lambda_2) = (1, 2, 1)$. Another is

$(\lambda_0, \lambda_1, \lambda_2) = (0, 1, 0)$. Notice that, even though $(2, 8)$ is a cusp, it is *not necessary* that $\lambda_0 = 0$. Why? $\lambda_0 = 0$ necessarily occurs when the gradient of the objective function is not contained in the hyperplane generated by the convex cone of the gradients of the constraints that bind. In this problem, however, the gradient vector $(0, 1)$ of the objective function at $(2, 8)$ happens to be contained in the convex cone generated by the gradient vectors of the constraints that bind. Consequently it is not necessary that $\lambda_0 = 0$. □

Answer to Problem 8.4.

(i) No. A constraint qualification makes no statement about the existence of an optimal solution to the constrained optimization problem. The only thing that a constraint qualification makes a statement about is the shape of the boundary of the feasible set. Existence of an optimal solution to the constrained optimization problem is not an issue dealt with by any constraint qualification. The only difficulty is that, at an irregular feasible point, there is no guarantee that the Karush-Kuhn-Tucker first-order necessary condition is defined.

Some constraint qualifications impose restrictions upon the entirety of the feasible set. An example is the Slater/Karlin constraint qualification. Other constraint qualifications impose a restriction only upon a particular point in the feasible set. An example is the rank constraint qualification. So suppose that $\mathcal{C}$ contains an irregular point, but not at the maximizing solution to the constrained optimization problem. Then a constraint qualification such as Slater/Karlin will fail, while the rank qualification will be satisfied at the optimal solution to the constrained optimization problem, so the Karush-Kuhn-Tucker first-order necessary condition will be well-defined at this optimal solution and can be used to locate the solution.

(ii) No. Consider the constrained optimization problem:

$$\max_{x_1, x_2} x_1 + x_2 \text{ subject to } x_1 \geq 0 \text{ and } x_2 \geq 0.$$

The feasible set is $\mathcal{C} = \{(x_1, x_2) \mid x_1 \geq 0, x_2 \geq 0\}$. This set contains only regular points, and so satisfies each and every constraint qualification. Even so, there is no optimal solution to this constrained optimization problem because the objective function is strictly increasing and the feasible set is unbounded above.

(iii) No. Again consider problem 8.3. The constrained optimization problem therein has an optimal solution at a cusp. No constraint qualification applies at such a point. Yet, at this optimal solution, the Karush-Kuhn-Tucker necessary first-order condition is well-defined. Again, the crucial point is that satisfaction at any locally optimal solution of any one of the constraint qualifications is a condition *sufficient,* but not necessary, for that locally optimal solution to be a regular point, a point at which the Karush-Kuhn-Tucker condition is well-defined.

(iv) Yes. By definition, if a constraint qualification applies at a locally optimal solution, then that point is regular and the Karush-Kuhn-Tucker first-order condition is well-defined at that locally optimal solution.   □

Answers to Problem 8.5.

(i) $S_1 = \{(x_2, x_2) \mid x_1^2 + x_2^2 \leq 16\}$ is the disc centered at the origin with a radius of 4. $S_2 = \{(x_1, x_2) \mid x_1 + x_2 \leq 5\}$ is the lower half-space in $\Re^2$ of the hyperplane with normal $(1, 1)$ that contains the points $(0, 5)$ and $(5, 0)$. $S_3 = \{(x_1, x_2) \mid x_1 \geq 0\}$ is the upper half-space in $\Re^2$ of the hyperplane with normal $(1, 0)$ that includes the origin $(0, 0)$. $S_4 = \{(x_1, x_2) \mid x_2 \geq 0\}$ is the upper half-space in $\Re^2$ of the hyperplane with normal $(0, 1)$ that includes the origin $(0, 0)$. The feasible set $\mathcal{C} = S_1 \cap S_2 \cap S_3 \cap S_4$ is the shaded region displayed in the upper panel of Figure 8.16.

(ii) Because $g_1(x_1, x_2) = x_1^2 + x_2^2$ is continuous on $\Re^2$, the set S_1 is closed in E^2. Similarly, S_2, S_3, and S_4 are also closed in E^2. Therefore $\mathcal{C} = S_1 \cap S_2 \cap S_3 \cap S_4$ is closed in E^2.

S_1 is a strictly convex set. S_2, S_3, and S_4 are weakly convex sets. Therefore $S_1 \cap S_2 \cap S_3 \cap S_4$ is a (weakly) convex set.

S_2, S_3, and S_4 are not bounded sets, but S_1 is bounded in E^2. Therefore $\mathcal{C} = S_1 \cap S_2 \cap S_3 \cap S_4$ is bounded in E^2.

Since $\mathcal{C}$ is both closed and bounded in E^2, $\mathcal{C}$ is compact in E^2.

Finally, it is easy to see that $\mathcal{C}$ is not empty and has a nonempty interior.

(iii) Yes. The objective function is continuous over the feasible set, and the feasible set is nonempty and is compact in E^2. Weierstrass's Theorem confirms that there must exist at least one element in $\mathcal{C}$ that achieves a maximum for f on $\mathcal{C}$.

(iv) For level $k = 0$, the objective function's contour set is the singleton containing only the origin. For any level $k > 0$, the objective function's level-k contour set is

$$S(k) = \{(x_1, x_2) \mid +\sqrt{x_1} + x_2 = k,\ x_1 \geq 0,\ x_2 \geq 0\}.$$

This is the set described by the curve $x_2 = k - \sqrt{x_1}$ in $\Re_+^2$. It is easy to see that the upper-contour set is always a weakly convex subset of $\Re_+^2$. Therefore f is a quasi-concave function on $\Re_+^2$. The lower panel of Figure 8.16 displays two of the objective function's contour sets.

(v) The gradient vectors of the objective function f and of the constraint functions g_1 and g_2 are

$$\nabla f(x_1, x_2) = \left(\frac{1}{2\sqrt{x_1}},\ 1\right),\quad \nabla g_1(x_1, x_2) = (2x_1,\ 2x_2),\quad \text{and}\quad \nabla g_2(x_1, x_2) = (1, 1).$$

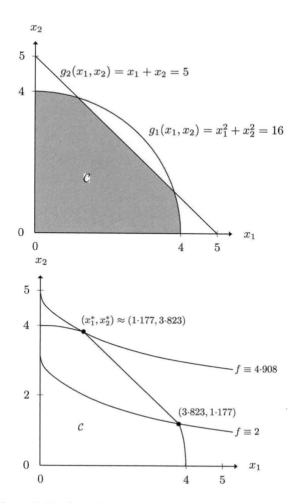

Figure 8.16: Problem 8.5's feasible set and two objective function contour sets.

Because the objective function is strictly increasing in both x_1 and x_2 the obvious places to first check for a local maximum are the two intersections of the boundaries of the constraints g_1 and g_2. The solutions to $x_1 + x_2 = 5$ and $x_1^2 + x_2^2 = 16$ are the points $(x_1, x_2) = \big((5 - \sqrt{7})/2, (5 + \sqrt{7})/2\big) \approx (1{\cdot}177, 3{\cdot}823)$ and $(x_1, x_2) = \big((5 + \sqrt{7})/2, (5 - \sqrt{7})/2\big) \approx (3{\cdot}823, 1{\cdot}177)$. The values at $(1{\cdot}177, 3{\cdot}823)$ of the above gradient vectors are

$$\nabla f(1{\cdot}177, 3{\cdot}823) = (0{\cdot}461, 1), \ \ \nabla g_1(1{\cdot}177, 3{\cdot}823) = (2{\cdot}354, 7{\cdot}646),$$
$$\text{and } \nabla g_2(1{\cdot}177, 3{\cdot}823) = (1, 1).$$

These gradient vectors are displayed in Figure 8.17. The gradient vector of the objective function is contained in the interior of the convex cone generated by the gradient vectors of the two binding constraint functions, so there must exist two strictly positive numbers λ_1 and λ_2, such that

$$(0 \cdot 461, 1) = \lambda_1(2 \cdot 354, 7 \cdot 646) + \lambda_2(1, 1).$$

These numbers are $\lambda_1 = 0 \cdot 102$ and $\lambda_2 = 0 \cdot 221$. Thus the Karush-Kuhn-Tucker necessary condition is satisfied at $(x_1, x_2) = (1 \cdot 177, 3 \cdot 823)$, which might, therefore, be a local maximum for f on $\mathcal{C}$.

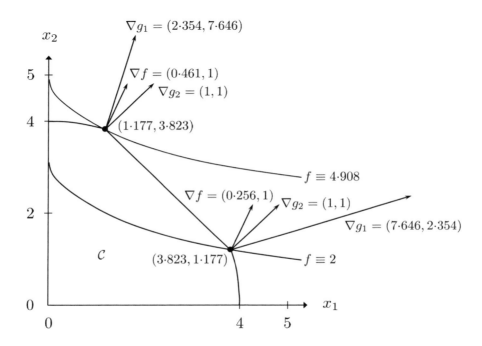

Figure 8.17: The gradients of f, g_1 and g_2 at $(x_1, x_2) = (1 \cdot 177, 3 \cdot 823)$ and at $(x_1, x_2) = (3 \cdot 823, 1 \cdot 177)$.

Evaluated at $(3 \cdot 823, 1 \cdot 177)$, the above gradient vectors are

$$\nabla f(3 \cdot 823, 1 \cdot 177) = (0 \cdot 256, 1), \quad \nabla g_1(3 \cdot 823, 1 \cdot 177) = (7 \cdot 646, 2 \cdot 354),$$
$$\text{and} \quad \nabla g_2(3 \cdot 823, 1 \cdot 177) = (1, 1).$$

These gradient vectors are also displayed in Figure 8.17. The gradient vector of the objective function is not contained in the convex cone generated by the gradient vectors of the two constraint functions. That is, the Karush-Kuhn-Tucker necessity condition is not satisfied at $(x_1, x_2) = (3 \cdot 823, 1 \cdot 177)$. Necessarily, therefore, this point is not a local maximum for f on $\mathcal{C}$.

How do we know that $(x_1, x_2) = (1 \cdot 177, 3 \cdot 823)$ is indeed a local maximum? Why is it not a local minimum, for example? The objective function's upper-contour sets are convex. The feasible set $\mathcal{C}$ is convex. Add to this that the objective function f is strictly increasing and that its upper-contour set is locally *strictly* convex at $(1 \cdot 177, 3 \cdot 823)$, and it follows immediately that $(1 \cdot 177, 3 \cdot 823)$ is a local maximum and is the only local maximum for f on $\mathcal{C}$. Thus $(x_1, x_2) = (1 \cdot 177, 3 \cdot 823)$ is the global maximum for f on $\mathcal{C}$. $\qquad\square$

Answer to Problem 8.6.

(i) See Figure 8.18. The feasible set is the singleton $\mathcal{C} = \{(4, 4)\}$.

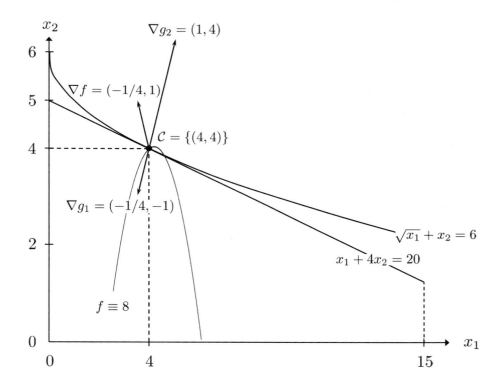

Figure 8.18: The singleton feasible set $\mathcal{C}$ and the gradient vectors for problem 8.6.

(ii) At $(x_1, x_2) = (4, 4)$, constraints g_1 and g_2 bind, and constraints g_3 and g_4 are slack. The gradient vectors of the objective function and the binding constraints are

$$\nabla f(x_1, x_2) = \left(2x_1 - \frac{33}{4}, 1\right), \quad \nabla g_1(x_1, x_2) = \left(-\frac{1}{2\sqrt{x_1}}, -1\right), \quad \nabla g_2(x_1, x_2) = (1, \ 4).$$

The values at $(x_1, x_2) = (4, 4)$ of these gradient vectors are

$$\nabla f(4, 4) = \left(-\frac{1}{4}, 1\right), \quad \nabla g_1(4, 4) = \left(-\frac{1}{4}, -1\right), \quad \text{and} \quad \nabla g_2(4, 4) = (1, \ 4).$$

The gradient vectors of the binding constraints are negatively collinear, so the convex cone that they generate is the hyperplane with normal $(-4, 1)$ that includes the origin. The objective function's gradient vector $(-1/4, 1)$ is not contained in this cone, so the Karush-Kuhn-Tucker necessary condition is not defined at the point $(x_1, x_2) = (4, 4)$. If we nevertheless attempt to solve the Karush-Kuhn-Tucker necessary condition, then we are attempting to find nonnegative scalars λ_1 and λ_2, not both zero, such that

$$\nabla f(4, 4) = \left(-\frac{1}{4}, \ 1\right) = \lambda_1 \nabla g_1(4, 4) + \lambda_2 \nabla g_2(4, 4) = \lambda_1 \left(-\frac{1}{4}, \ -1\right) + \lambda_2(1, \ 4).$$

That is, we are attempting to solve

$$-\frac{1}{4} = -\frac{1}{4}\lambda_1 + \lambda_2 \quad \text{and} \quad 1 = -\lambda_1 + 4\lambda_2.$$

These are inconsistent equations. This is a statement that the Karush-Kuhn-Tucker condition does not exist at the optimal solution to the problem. The problem is an example of the difficulty pointed out by Slater, which is why the proof of the Karush-Kuhn-Tucker Theorem assumes that there are points in the problem's feasible set that are *neighboring* to the locally maximal point. That assumption is not met in the present problem, so the Karush-Kuhn-Tucker necessary condition fails.   □

Answer to Problem 8.7.
(i) The problem's feasible set is displayed in Figure 8.19. The optimal solution is $(x_1^*, x_2^*) = (9/2, 27/4)$. The only constraint that binds at the optimal solution is g_1.
(ii) The complete collection of first-order necessary maximization conditions consists of the Karush-Kuhn-Tucker condition and the two complementary slackness conditions. The Karush-Kuhn-Tucker condition is that there exist nonnegative scalars λ_1 and λ_2, not both zero, that at a local maximum (x_1, x_2) satisfy

$$\nabla f(x_1, x_2) = \lambda_1 \nabla g_1(x_1, x_2) + \lambda_2 \nabla g_2(x_1, x_2).$$

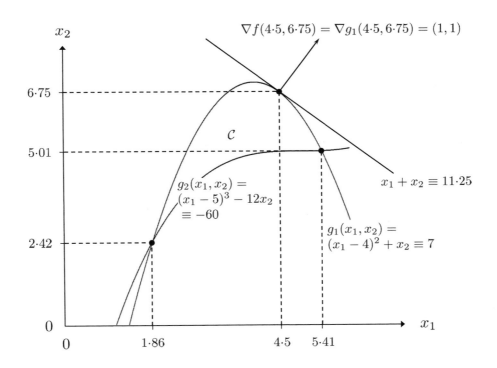

Figure 8.19: The feasible set, the optimal solution, and the gradient vectors for problem 8.7.

That is,

$$(1,1) = \lambda_1(2(x_1 - 4), 1) + \lambda_2(3(x_1 - 5)^2, -12). \qquad (8.17)$$

The complementary slackness conditions are

$$\lambda_1(7 - (x_1 - 4)^2 - x_2) = 0 \quad \text{and} \quad \lambda_2(-60 - (x_1 - 5)^3 + 12x_2) = 0. \qquad (8.18)$$

Suppose that we cannot draw Figure 8.19 and so have to rely upon the necessary optimality conditions (8.17) and (8.18) to locate possible local maxima. How do we use these equations? There are four possibilities. One possibility is that both of the constraints are slack. But this makes no sense since the objective function is strictly increasing.

Another possibility is that both constraints bind. To locate such a point we must simultaneously solve

$$(x_1 - 4)^2 + x_2 = 7 \quad \text{and} \quad (x_1 - 5)^3 - 12x_2 = -60.$$

There are two solutions; $(x_1, x_2) \approx (1 \cdot 860, 2 \cdot 420)$ and $(x_1, x_2) \approx (5 \cdot 412, 5 \cdot 006)$. We must check if the Karush-Kuhn-Tucker condition (8.17) is satisfied at either one, or both, of these solutions.

At $(x_1, x_2) = (1 \cdot 860, 2 \cdot 420)$, the Karush-Kuhn-Tucker condition (8.17) is

$$(1, 1) = \lambda_1(-4 \cdot 28, 1) + \lambda_2(29 \cdot 6, -12) \quad \Rightarrow \quad \lambda_1 = -1 \cdot 91 \text{ and } \lambda_2 = -0 \cdot 243.$$

$\lambda_1 < 0$ and $\lambda_2 < 0$ inform us that, at $(x_1, x_2) = (1 \cdot 860, 2 \cdot 420)$, the gradient vector of the objective function is not contained in the convex cone that is generated by the gradient vectors at $(x_1, x_2) = (1 \cdot 860, 2 \cdot 420)$ of constraints 1 and 2. Thus $(x_1, x_2) = (1 \cdot 860, 2 \cdot 420)$ cannot be a local maximum for the constrained optimization problem.

At $(x_1, x_2) = (5 \cdot 412, 5 \cdot 006)$, the Karush-Kuhn-Tucker condition is

$$(1, 1) = \lambda_1(2 \cdot 824, 1) + \lambda_2(0 \cdot 509, -12) \quad \Rightarrow \quad \lambda_1 = 0 \cdot 364 \text{ and } \lambda_2 = -0 \cdot 053.$$

$\lambda_2 < 0$ informs us that, at $(x_1, x_2) = (5 \cdot 412, 5 \cdot 006)$, the gradient vector of the objective function is not contained in the convex cone that is generated by the gradient vectors at $(x_1, x_2) = (5 \cdot 412, 5 \cdot 006)$ of constraints 1 and 2. Thus $(x_1, x_2) = (5 \cdot 412, 5 \cdot 006)$ cannot be a local maximum for the constrained optimization problem.

The next possibility is that only constraint g_2 binds at the problem's optimal solution. If so, then g_1 is slack and so, necessarily, $\lambda_1 = 0$. But then, from (8.17), we observe that necessarily $1 = -12\lambda_2$, implying that $\lambda_2 < 0$, which violates the Karush-Kuhn-Tucker necessary condition.

The only remaining possibility is that only constraint g_1 binds at the problem's optimal solution. If so, then g_2 is slack and so, necessarily, $\lambda_2 = 0$. Then, from (8.17) we observe that necessarily $\lambda_1 = 1$. OK so far. Using $\lambda_1 = 1$ in (8.17) shows that necessarily $1 = 2(x_1 - 4)$, requiring that $x_1 = 9/2$. Since constraint g_1 is presumed to be binding, it then follows that

$$7 = \left(\frac{9}{2} - 4\right)^2 + x_2 \quad \Rightarrow \quad x_2 = \frac{27}{4}.$$

We have determined that there is exactly one point, $(x_1, x_2) = (9/2, 27/4)$, that satisfies the necessary first-order optimality conditions. This point must, therefore, be the problem's optimal solution. □

Chapter 9

Lagrange Functions

9.1 What Is a Lagrange Function?

At no point in our Chapter 8 discussion of first-order necessary optimality conditions for differentiable constrained optimization problems did we refer to or use a *Lagrange function*. Yet many discussions of solving constrained optimization problems introduce a Lagrange function at an early stage and use it intensively. Is a Lagrange function necessary for such a discussion? Obviously not, since we did not use it. But there must be something useful about such a function since, otherwise, few would mention it when describing how to solve constrained optimization problems. So let us now discover some of the valuable properties and uses of Lagrange functions. In Chapter 10 we will see that Lagrange functions are very helpful when deriving and using second-order optimality conditions. Chapters 12 and 13 explain the usefulness of Lagrange functions in comparative statics analysis.

It may interest you to know that the spectacular mathematician whom we know as Joseph-Louis Lagrange was born in Turin, Italy, in 1736 as Giuseppe Luigi Lagrangia. Lagrange changed his name when he left Italy as a young man to live and work in Prussia. Eventually he moved to France, where he narrowly avoided serious trouble with the French revolutionaries. He died in 1810, shortly after receiving one of France's greatest honors.

Throughout the book I have used lower-case letters like f and g to denote functions and upper-case letters like F and G to denote correspondences. I'm going to make an exception to this convention by using capital L to denote Lagrange functions. I promise I will not use L to denote anything other than a Lagrange function. Why do this? Because Lagrange is a proper noun (it's a person's name) and, to my knowledge, in the English language every proper noun starts with a capital letter.

Definition 9.1 (Lagrange Functions). *The* Karush-Kuhn-Tucker Lagrange function *for the inequality constrained optimization problem*

$$\max_{x_1,\dots,x_n} f(x_1,\dots,x_n) \text{ subject to } g_j(x_1,\dots,x_n) \le b_j \text{ for } j=1,\dots,m \tag{9.1}$$

is the function $L : \Re^n \times \Re_+^m \mapsto \Re$ *that is*

$$L(x_1,\dots,x_n,\lambda_1,\dots,\lambda_m) = f(x_1,\dots,x_n) + \sum_{j=1}^{m} \lambda_j(b_j - g_j(x_1,\dots,x_n)), \tag{9.2}$$

where $\lambda_1,\dots,\lambda_m \ge 0$.

The Fritz-John Lagrange function *for the inequality constrained problem* (9.1) *is the function* $L : \Re^n \times \Re_+^{m+1} \mapsto \Re$ *that is*

$$L(x_1,\dots,x_n,\lambda_0,\lambda_1,\dots,\lambda_m) = \lambda_0 f(x_1,\dots,x_n) + \sum_{j=1}^{m} \lambda_j(b_j - g_j(x_1,\dots,x_n)), \tag{9.3}$$

where $\lambda_0,\lambda_1,\dots,\lambda_m \ge 0$.

The nonnegative scalar variables $\lambda_0,\lambda_1,\dots,\lambda_m$ are called the *Lagrange multipliers*. Notice that, for the Lagrange functions, the values of $x_1,\dots,x_n$ are *unconstrained*; the "x-part" of the domain of the Lagrange functions is all of $\Re^n$. In contrast the values of the multipliers $\lambda_0,\lambda_1,\dots,\lambda_m$ are restricted to being nonnegative (note: multipliers can take negative values in problems with equality constraints). Some of the properties of the Lagrange function L are inherited from the properties of its component functions $f,g_1,\dots,g_m$. For example, if each of these component functions is differentiable with respect to $x_1,\dots,x_n$, then so too will be L.

To avoid a lot of duplication, from here onwards the discussion will assume that a constraint qualification applies so that we can set $\lambda_0 = 1$ and talk only of the Karush-Kuhn-Tucker Lagrange function.

The immediate appeal of a Lagrange function is that it offers a convenient way to write down the Karush-Kuhn-Tucker necessary condition. Unfortunately, sometimes false assertions are made about the uses and properties of Lagrange functions. Because these functions are so useful, it is important to be clear about what is true and what is falsely claimed about them. Probably the best way to begin this discussion is to start with what Lagrange told us, in 1788, about the functions named after him.

The particular problem in which Lagrange was interested is an *equality* constrained optimization problem; *i.e.* a problem of the form

$$\max_{x_1,\ldots,x_n} f(x_1,\ldots,x_n) \text{ subject to } g_j(x_1,\ldots,x_n) = b_j \text{ for } j = 1,\ldots,k, \qquad (9.4)$$

in which $n > k$ and a constraint qualification holds. The Lagrange function for such a problem is

$$\begin{aligned} L(x_1,&\ldots,x_n,\lambda_1,\ldots,\lambda_k) \\ &= f(x_1,\ldots,x_n) + \lambda_1(b_1 - g_1(x_1,\ldots,x_n)) + \cdots + \lambda_k(b_k - g_k(x_1,\ldots,x_n)). \end{aligned} \qquad (9.5)$$

The first-order derivatives of this function are

$$\frac{\partial L}{\partial x_1} = \frac{\partial f}{\partial x_1} - \lambda_1 \frac{\partial g_1}{\partial x_1} - \cdots - \lambda_k \frac{\partial g_k}{\partial x_1}$$

$$\vdots \qquad\qquad \vdots \qquad\qquad (9.6)$$

$$\frac{\partial L}{\partial x_n} = \frac{\partial f}{\partial x_n} - \lambda_1 \frac{\partial g_1}{\partial x_n} - \cdots - \lambda_k \frac{\partial g_k}{\partial x_n}$$

$$\text{and} \quad \frac{\partial L}{\partial \lambda_1} = b_1 - g_1(x_1,\ldots,x_n)$$

$$\vdots \qquad\qquad \vdots \qquad\qquad (9.7)$$

$$\frac{\partial L}{\partial \lambda_k} = b_k - g_k(x_1,\ldots,x_n).$$

Notice that the value of each of the k partial derivatives in (9.7) is zero for any feasible (not necessarily optimal) point $(x_1,\ldots,x_n)$ because the constraints in problem (9.4) are equalities. Now suppose that $(x_1^*,\ldots,x_n^*)$ is a local optimum for problem (9.4). Then each of the n partial derivatives in (9.6) is zero, too, because the Karush-Kuhn-Tucker condition is that this necessarily is so. What have we discovered? We have discovered that any locally optimal solution to problem (9.4) necessarily is a *critical point* for the problem's Lagrange function.

Theorem 9.1 (Lagrange). *If $(x^*, \lambda^*) = (x_1^*,\ldots,x_n^*,\lambda_1^*,\ldots,\lambda_k^*)$ is a locally optimal solution to problem (9.4), then (x^*, λ^*) is a critical point of the Lagrange function for problem (9.4).*

The theorem does not assert that the Lagrange function is maximized or minimized at (x^*, λ^*). Such claims are false, in fact. All the theorem asserts is that the $n + k$ directional slopes of the Lagrange function must all be zero at (x^*, λ^*).

Can we apply Lagrange's Theorem to the inequality constrained problem (9.1)? Yes, but with one caution. We must allow for the possibility that some of the problem's constraints are slack at a locally optimal solution. So suppose that (x^*, λ^*) is a locally optimal solution for problem (9.1) and that at this point k of the m constraints bind, where $k \in \{1, \ldots, m\}$. Without loss of generality, suppose that the indices of the constraints that bind at x^* are $j = 1, \ldots, k$. Then the locally optimal solution $(x_1^*, \ldots, x_n^*)$ to the inequality constrained problem (9.1) with its accompanying multipliers $(\lambda_1^*, \ldots, \lambda_k^*, \underbrace{0, \ldots, 0}_{m-k \text{ zeros}})$ is a locally optimal solution, with accompanying multipliers $(\lambda_1^*, \ldots, \lambda_k^*)$, to the equality constrained problem (9.4). It is to this equality constrained problem that Lagrange's Theorem is applied.

9.2   Revisiting the Karush-Kuhn-Tucker Condition

The Karush-Kuhn-Tucker condition is the statement that the Lagrange function's gradient vector in the x-space is the n-dimensional zero vector; *i.e.*

$$\nabla_x L(x, \lambda) = \left(\frac{\partial L}{\partial x_1}, \ldots, \frac{\partial L}{\partial x_n} \right) = \left(\frac{\partial f}{\partial x_1} - \sum_{j=1}^{m} \lambda_j \frac{\partial g_j(x)}{\partial x_1}, \ldots, \frac{\partial f}{\partial x_n} - \sum_{j=1}^{m} \lambda_j \frac{\partial g_j}{\partial x_n} \right)$$
$$= \underline{0}_n. \tag{9.8}$$

This allows a restatement of the Karush-Kuhn-Tucker Necessity Theorem.

Theorem 9.2 (Restatement of the Karush-Kuhn-Tucker Necessity Theorem). *Consider the problem*

$$\max_{x \in \Re^n} f(x) \text{ subject to } g_j(x) \le b_j \text{ for } j = 1, \ldots, m, \tag{9.9}$$

where the objective function f and the constraint functions $g_1, \ldots, g_m$ are all continuously differentiable with respect to x, and the feasible set

$$\mathcal{C} = \{ x \in \Re^n \mid g_j(x) \le b_j \ \forall \ j = 1, \ldots, m \}$$

is not empty. The problem's Lagrange function is

$$L(x, \lambda) = f(x) + \lambda_1(b_1 - g_1(x)) + \cdots + \lambda_m(b_m - g_m(x)).$$

Let x^* be a locally optimal solution to the problem. If a constraint qualification is satisfied at x^*, then there exist nonnegative values $\lambda_1^*, \ldots, \lambda_m^*$, not all zero, such that

$$\frac{\partial L(x; \lambda^*)}{\partial x_i}\Big|_{x=x^*} = 0 \text{ for all } i = 1, \ldots, n \tag{9.10}$$

$$\text{and} \quad \lambda_j^*(b_j - g_j(x^*)) = 0 \text{ for all } j = 1, \ldots, m. \tag{9.11}$$

Any critical point for the Lagrange function with respect to x is a point at which the slopes of L in the $x_1, \ldots, x_n$ directions are all zero. This is what (9.10) states. But how do we know that such a value of x is feasible? The complementary slackness conditions eliminate infeasible values of x; *i.e.* x^* is feasible only if x^* satisfies (9.11). Why?

Suppose that, at some locally optimal solution x^*, at least one (let's say the first) of the complementary slackness conditions is not satisfied. That is, $\lambda_1^*(b_1 - g_1(x^*)) \neq 0$. Let's suppose, then, that $\lambda_1^*(b_1 - g_1(x^*)) < 0$. Since $\lambda_1^* \geq 0$, this implies that $g_1(x^*) > b_1$. But then x^* is not a feasible solution. So now let's suppose that $\lambda_1^*(b_1 - g_1(x^*)) > 0$. Then $\lambda_1^* > 0$ and $g_1(x^*) < b_1$. But $\lambda_1^* > 0$ only if constraint g_1 is binding at x^*, so we have a contradiction.

There is nothing to be gained by writing down a Lagrange function and then differentiating it to derive the Karush-Kuhn-Tucker and complementary slackness conditions. We might as well directly write down these first-order necessary optimality conditions, just as we did throughout Chapter 8. Nevertheless, there are at least four important reasons to consider the Lagrange function. First, if the Lagrange function possesses a particular type of saddle-point, then the "x-part" of the saddle-point is the *global* solution to the constrained optimization problem. Second, the Lagrange function is very useful when considering the *primal-dual* version of the constrained optimization problem. What this means is explained in Chapter 12. Third, as we will see in Chapter 10, the Lagrange function simplifies the task of considering second-order optimality conditions. Fourth, the Lagrange function simplifies deriving some types of comparative statics results about the properties of optimal solutions to constrained optimization problems. This is explained in Chapters 12 and 13.

9.3 Saddle-Points for Lagrange Functions

Saddle-points were discussed in Section 2.19. If you have not read this discussion, or have forgotten what you read, then you should review this material before proceeding further in this section.

Because the Lagrange function for problem (9.4) is a function of $n + k$ variables, it can possess many types of saddle-points $(\hat{x}, \hat{\lambda}) = (\hat{x}_1, \ldots, \hat{x}_n, \hat{\lambda}_1, \ldots, \hat{\lambda}_k)$. One particular type is especially interesting. This is the saddle-point in which the Lagrange function is maximized with respect to the choice variables $x_1, \ldots, x_n$ at the point $(\hat{x}_1, \ldots, \hat{x}_n)$, when the values of the multipliers are fixed at $\hat{\lambda}_1, \ldots, \hat{\lambda}_k$, and, also, is minimized with respect to $\lambda_1, \ldots, \lambda_k$ at the point $(\hat{\lambda}_1, \ldots, \hat{\lambda}_k)$, when the values of the choice variables are fixed at $\hat{x}_1, \ldots, \hat{x}_n$. We will call this an "$x$-max, λ-min saddle-point."

Definition 9.2 (x-max, λ-min Saddle-Point). $(\hat{x}, \hat{\lambda}) = (\hat{x}_1, \ldots, \hat{x}_n, \hat{\lambda}_1, \ldots, \hat{\lambda}_k)$ *is a local x-max, λ-min saddle-point for the Lagrange function* (9.5) *in a neighborhood* $N(\hat{x}, \hat{\lambda}) \subset \Re^n \times \Re_+^k$ *if and only if, for all* $(x, \lambda) \in N(\hat{x}, \hat{\lambda})$,

$$L^r(x_1, \ldots, x_n; \hat{\lambda}_1, \ldots, \hat{\lambda}_k) \leq L(\hat{x}_1, \ldots, \hat{x}_n, \hat{\lambda}_1, \ldots, \hat{\lambda}_k) \leq L^r(\lambda_1, \ldots, \lambda_k; \hat{x}_1, \ldots, \hat{x}_n).$$
(9.12)

The function $L^r(x; \hat{\lambda})$ denotes the Lagrange function restricted by having the values of the multipliers fixed at $\hat{\lambda}_1, \ldots, \hat{\lambda}_k$. The function $L^r(\lambda; \hat{x})$ denotes the Lagrange function restricted by having the values of the choice variables fixed at $\hat{x}_1, \ldots, \hat{x}_n$. The superscripts r denote *restricted*.

For an example of another type of saddle-point we might consider one in which the Lagrange function is minimized with respect to the choice variables $x_1, \ldots, x_n$ at the point $(\hat{x}_1, \ldots, \hat{x}_n)$ when the values of the multipliers are fixed at $\hat{\lambda}_1, \ldots, \hat{\lambda}_k$ and, also, is maximized with respect to $\lambda_1, \ldots, \lambda_k$ at the point $(\hat{\lambda}_1, \ldots, \hat{\lambda}_k)$ when the values of the choice variables are fixed at $\hat{x}_1, \ldots, \hat{x}_n$. We will call this an "$x$-min, λ-max saddle-point".

Definition 9.3 (x-min, λ-max Saddle-Point). $(\hat{x}, \hat{\lambda}) = (\hat{x}_1, \ldots, \hat{x}_n, \hat{\lambda}_1, \ldots, \hat{\lambda}_k)$ *is a local x-min, λ-max saddle-point for the Lagrange function* (9.5) *in a neighborhood* $N(\hat{x}, \hat{\lambda}) \subset \Re^n \times \Re_+^k$ *if and only if, for all* $(x, \lambda) \in N(\hat{x}, \hat{\lambda})$,

$$L^r(x_1, \ldots, x_n; \hat{\lambda}_1, \ldots, \hat{\lambda}_k) \geq L(\hat{x}_1, \ldots, \hat{x}_n, \hat{\lambda}_1, \ldots, \hat{\lambda}_k) \geq L^r(\lambda_1, \ldots, \lambda_k; \hat{x}_1, \ldots, \hat{x}_n).$$
(9.13)

In both of the above definitions, if the neighborhood $N(\hat{x}, \hat{\lambda}) = \Re^n \times \Re_+^k$ (*i.e.* if (9.12) or (9.13) is true for all $x \in \Re^n$ and for all $\lambda \in \Re_+^k$) then the saddle-point is *global*.

Let's have a look at an example of each of these two types of saddle-points. Consider the constrained optimization problem that is to maximize $f(x) = +4\sqrt{x}$ for $x \in [0, 2]$. Write the problem as

$$\max_x f(x) = +4\sqrt{x} \text{ subject to } g_1(x) = -x \leq 0 \text{ and } g_2(x) = x \leq 2. \qquad (9.14)$$

The globally optimal solution is $x^* = 2$. Constraint g_1 is slack at the optimal solution, so we can ignore it. Constraint g_2 binds at the optimal solution with a multiplier value $\lambda_2^* = +\sqrt{2}$, so (9.14) has the same optimal solution as the equality constrained problem

$$\max_x f(x) = +4\sqrt{x} \text{ subject to } g_2(x) = x = 2. \qquad (9.15)$$

The Lagrange function for this equality constrained problem is

$$L(x, \lambda_2) = +4\sqrt{x} + \lambda_2(2 - x). \qquad (9.16)$$

Figure 9.1 displays the graph of the Lagrange function (9.16). The point $(x^*, \lambda_2^*) = (2, \sqrt{2}\,)$ is a global x-max, λ-min saddle-point for this Lagrange function.

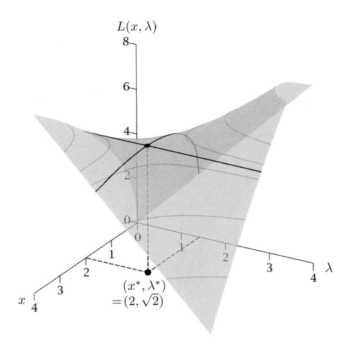

Figure 9.1: The Lagrange function $L(x, \lambda_2) = 4\sqrt{x} + \lambda_2(2 - x)$ has a global x-max, λ-min saddle-point at $(x, \lambda_2) = (2, \sqrt{2}\,)$.

Now consider the similar problem that is to maximize $f(x) = x^2$ for $x \in [0, 2]$. Write the problem as

$$\max_x f(x) = x^2 \text{ subject to } g_1(x) = -x \le 0 \text{ and } g_2(x) = x \le 2. \qquad (9.17)$$

The globally optimal solution is again $x^* = 2$. Constraint g_1 is slack at the optimal solution. Constraint g_2 binds at the optimal solution with a multiplier value $\lambda_2^* = 4$, so problem (9.17) has the same optimal solution as the equality constrained problem

$$\max_x f(x) = x^2 \text{ subject to } g_2(x) = x = 2. \tag{9.18}$$

The Lagrange function for this problem is

$$L(x, \lambda_2) = x^2 + \lambda_2(2 - x). \tag{9.19}$$

Figure 9.2 displays the graph of the Lagrange function (9.19). The point $(x^*, \lambda_2^*) = (2, 4)$ is a global x-min, λ-max saddle-point for this Lagrange function.

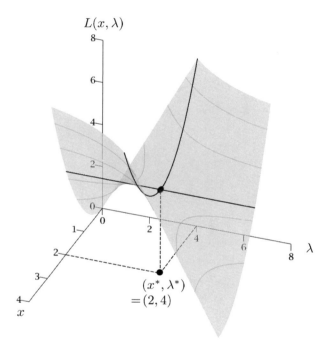

Figure 9.2: The Lagrange function $L(x, \lambda_2) = x^2 + \lambda_2(2 - x)$ has a global x-min, λ-max saddle-point at $(x, \lambda_2) = (2, 4)$.

At this point you should be asking, "Is this stuff about saddle-points for Lagrange functions important?" The answer is "Yes" because any point that satisfies a constraint qualification and is a solution to the Karush-Kuhn-Tucker condition and the complementary slackness conditions for a constrained optimization problem is a saddle-point of some sort for the Lagrange function.

Let's turn to contradicting two erroneous statements that seem to have developed some standing among economists. It is sometimes asserted that, to locate a local maximum for a constrained optimization problem, we must locally "maximize the Lagrange function." This is *never* true. Any local maximum $(\hat{x}, \hat{\lambda})$ for the constrained optimization problem is a critical point for the Lagrange function, but this critical point is always a saddle-point of some sort for the Lagrange function and so is never a local maximum for the Lagrange function.

Another assertion is that a local maximum $(\hat{x}, \hat{\lambda})$ for a constrained optimization problem "maximizes the *restricted* Lagrange function" $L^r(x; \hat{\lambda})$, in which the values of the multipliers of the Lagrange function are fixed at $\hat{\lambda} = (\hat{\lambda}_1, \ldots, \hat{\lambda}_k)$. Although this assertion can be true for particular problems, it is not true in general. Again consider problem (9.15). The optimal solution to the problem is $(\hat{x}, \hat{\lambda}) = (2, \sqrt{2})$. From (9.16), the restricted Lagrange function $L(^r x; \hat{\lambda})$ for this problem is

$$L^r\left(x; \lambda = \sqrt{2}\right) = 4\sqrt{x} + \sqrt{2}\,(2 - x).$$

This function achieves a global maximum at $x = 2$, so, in this instance, the restricted Lagrange function is indeed maximized at $\hat{x} = 2$. However, now consider again problem (9.18). The optimal solution to the problem is $(\hat{x}, \hat{\lambda}) = (2, 4)$, so, from (9.19), the restricted Lagrange function $L^r(x; \hat{\lambda})$ is

$$L^r(x; \lambda = 4) = x^2 + 4(2 - x).$$

This function achieves a global *minimum* at $x = 2$, contradicting the assertion that the restricted Lagrange function is always locally maximized at a locally optimal solution to the constrained optimization problem.

9.4   Saddle-Points and Optimality

We have established that a local optimum for a constrained optimization problem is a saddle-point of some sort for the problem's Lagrange function. Must a saddle-point for a problem's Lagrange function be a local optimum for that problem? The answer is "No." However, there does exist one rather remarkable result of this type: if the saddle-point is a global x-max, λ-min saddle-point, then the "x-part" of the saddle-point is a global optimum for the constrained optimization problem. Here is the theorem.

Theorem 9.3 (Kuhn-Tucker Saddle-Point Theorem). *If the Lagrange function for the constrained optimization problem* (9.1) *possesses a global x-max, λ-min saddle-point* (x^*, λ^*), *then* x^* *is a globally optimal solution to problem* (9.1).

Proof. The proof proceeds in two steps. The first step is to show that the global x-max, λ-min saddle-point property implies that x^* is a feasible solution. The second step is then to show that x^* is a globally optimal solution.

(x^*, λ^*) is a global x-max, λ-min saddle-point for L, so $L(x^*, \lambda^*) \leq L^r(\lambda; x^*)$ for all $\lambda \in \Re_+^m$. That is,

$$f(x^*) + \sum_{j=1}^{m} \lambda_j^*(b_j - g_j(x^*)) \leq f(x^*) + \sum_{j=1}^{m} \lambda_j(b_j - g_j(x^*))$$

for all $\lambda_j \geq 0$ and for all $j = 1, \ldots, m$. Hence

$$\sum_{j=1}^{m} \lambda_j^*(b_j - g_j(x^*)) \leq \sum_{j=1}^{m} \lambda_j(b_j - g_j(x^*)) \; \forall \; \lambda_j \geq 0, \; \forall \; j = 1, \ldots, m. \qquad (9.20)$$

Let's be clear that the left-hand side of (9.20) is a constant since x^* and λ^* are given vectors. The right-hand side of (9.20) is a linear function only of $\lambda_1, \ldots, \lambda_m$ and each is nonnegative (see Definition 9.1).

(9.20) cannot be true if, for even one j, we have $g_j(x^*) > b_j$ since then $b_j - g_j(x^*) < 0$, and by choosing λ_j to be as large as we like, we can make the right-hand side of (9.20) as negative as we wish. This contradicts that the right-hand side of (9.20) has a finite lower bound, which is the (constant) value of the left-hand side of (9.20). Therefore $g_j(x^*) \leq b_j$ for all $j = 1, \ldots, m$. Thus x^* is a feasible solution.

Now we need to show that x^* is a globally optimal solution. Since $\lambda_j^* \geq 0$ and $b_j - g_j(x^*) \geq 0$ for all $j = 1, \ldots, m$, it follows that

$$\sum_{j=1}^{m} \lambda_j^*(b_j - g_j(x^*)) \geq 0. \qquad (9.21)$$

We are now going to show that the sum in (9.21) cannot be strictly positive and thus must be exactly zero. The argument is by contradiction, so suppose that

$$\sum_{j=1}^{m} \lambda_j^*(b_j - g_j(x^*)) = k > 0. \qquad (9.22)$$

Now choose $\lambda_j = \lambda_j^*/2$ for each $j = 1, \ldots, m$. $\lambda_j^* \geq 0$ shows that $\lambda_j \geq 0$ also. But then

$$\sum_{j=1}^{m} \lambda_j (b_j - g_j(x^*)) = \frac{k}{2} < k = \sum_{j=1}^{m} \lambda_j^* (b_j - g_j(x^*)).$$

This contradicts that $\lambda_1^*, \ldots, \lambda_m^*$ are values of $\lambda_1, \ldots, \lambda_m$ that minimize $L^r(\lambda; x^*)$. Therefore

$$\sum_{j=1}^{m} \lambda_j^* (b_j - g_j(x^*)) = 0. \tag{9.23}$$

Since (x^*, λ^*) is a global x-max, λ-min saddle-point for L, $L^r(x; \lambda^*) \leq L(x^*, \lambda^*)$ for all $x \in \Re^n$; *i.e.*

$$f(x) + \sum_{j=1}^{m} \lambda_j^* (b_j - g_j(x)) \leq f(x^*) + \sum_{j=1}^{m} \lambda_j^* (b_j - g_j(x^*)) = f(x^*) \tag{9.24}$$

by (9.23). But $b_j - g_j(x) \geq 0$ for *any feasible* x, so, $f(x) \leq f(x^*)$ everywhere on $\mathcal{C}$. □

There is much that is attractive about this result. First, it does not require that any of the functions $f, g, \ldots, g_m$ be differentiable. Second, it is not required that the feasible set of the constrained optimization problem satisfy a constraint qualification. Third, no particular curvatures are demanded of f or any of $g_1, \ldots, g_m$. Against all of these attributes is the demanding requirement that the problem's Lagrange function have a global x-max, λ-min saddle-point.

Notice that the proof of the theorem comes very close to establishing (see (9.23)) a useful but less important result that merits emphasis by stating it separately.

Theorem 9.4 (x-max, λ-min Saddle-Point Implies Complementary Slackness). *If the Lagrange function for the constrained optimization problem* (9.1) *possesses a global x-max, λ-min saddle-point* (x^*, λ^*), *then* $\lambda_j^* (b_j - g_j(x^*)) = 0$ *for each* $j = 1, \ldots, m$.

Proof. By Theorem 9.3, x^* is optimal and therefore feasible, so $\lambda_j^* \geq 0$ and $b_j - g_j(x^*) \geq 0$ for all $j = 1, \ldots, m$. Hence $\lambda_j^* (b_j - g_j(x^*)) \geq 0$ for all $j = 1, \ldots, m$. If, for any j, the product $\lambda_j (b_j - g_j(x^*)) > 0$, then it follows from (9.23) that $\lambda_k (b_k - g_k(x^*)) < 0$ for some $k \neq j$. Contradiction. Hence $\lambda_j^* (b_j - g_j(x^*)) = 0$ for each $j = 1, \ldots, m$. □

9.5 Concave Programming Problems

The usual method for solving a differentiable constrained optimization problem starts by solving the first-order local optimality conditions. Examining the second-order conditions then eliminates solutions that are not local optima. Each local optimum is then evaluated to determine the global optimum. Examining second-order conditions is typically a lot of work, so it would be nice if the first-order conditions were both necessary and sufficient for a local optimum. This is not so in general, but, there is one important type of constrained optimization problem for which it is so. This is the *concave programming problem.*

Definition 9.4 (Concave Programming Problem). *A constrained optimization problem*

$$\max_{x \in \Re^n} f(x) \ subject \ to \ g_j(x) \le b_j \ for \ j = 1, \ldots, m \tag{9.25}$$

is a concave programming problem *if f is concave with respect to x and each of $g_1, \ldots, g_m$ is convex with respect to x.*

Theorem 9.5 (Solution to a Concave Programming Problem). *Consider a concave programming problem (9.25) in which the functions $f, g_1, \ldots, g_m$ are all differentiable with respect to $x_1, \ldots, x_n$ and the interior of the feasible set is not empty. Let (x^*, λ^*) be a solution to the problem's first-order optimality conditions. Then (x^*, λ^*) is a global x-max, λ-min saddle-point for the problem's Lagrange function and x^* is a globally optimal solution to the problem. If f is strictly concave with respect to x, then x^* is the unique global solution to the problem.*

   This result should not surprise you. Let's think about it. Suppose, for a moment, that the problem is unconstrained. Then the problem's Lagrange function is just $L(x_1, \ldots, x_n) = f(x_1, \ldots, x_n)$ and, at a local maximum $x = x^*$ for f, the Karush-Kuhn-Tucker condition, $\nabla f(x^*) = \underline{0}$, necessarily is satisfied. This same condition is also sufficient for $x = x^*$ to be a global maximum for f because f is a concave function of x. Now let's put the constraints back. The problem's Lagrange function is

$$L(x_1, \ldots, x_n, \lambda_1, \ldots, \lambda_m) = f(x_1, \ldots, x_n) + \sum_{j=1}^m \lambda_j(b_j - g_j(x_1, \ldots, x_n)).$$

f is concave with respect to x. Each of $-g_1, \ldots, -g_m$ is concave with respect to x (the negative of a convex function is a concave function) and $\lambda_1 \ge 0, \ldots, \lambda_m \ge 0$. So L is a nonnegative linear combination of functions that are concave with respect to x. L is therefore concave with respect to x. A local optimum to any differentiable constrained optimization problem necessarily is a critical point for the problem's Lagrange function. Hence the gradient of the Lagrange function with respect to x is a zero vector. But L is concave with respect to x, so the first-order zero gradient condition is sufficient for the restricted Lagrange function $L^r(x; \lambda^*)$ to be globally maximized at $x = x^*$ (*i.e.* the left-hand inequality in (9.12) is satisfied). Last, the other restricted Lagrange function,

$$L^r(\lambda; x^*) = f(x^*) + \lambda_1(b_1 - g_1(x^*)) + \cdots + \lambda_m(b_m - g(x^*)),$$

is just an affine function of $\lambda_1, \ldots, \lambda_m$. Each $\lambda_j \geq 0$ and each $b_j - g_j(x^*) \geq 0$, since x^* is a feasible solution. Thus the smallest possible value of $L^r(\lambda; x^*)$ is achieved when $\lambda_1(b_1 - g_1(x^*)) + \cdots + \lambda_m(b_m - g(x^*)) = 0$. The complementary slackness conditions state that this necessarily is so and thus the right-hand inequality in (9.12) is also established.

Proof of Theorem 9.5. We are given that the first-order optimality conditions are true at the point (x^*, λ^*). Our task is to show that this information implies that x^* is the globally optimal solution to problem (9.25).

We will start by establishing that the problem's feasible set satisfies Slater's constraint qualification. Each of the constraint functions g_j is convex with respect to x and so is continuous and quasi-convex with respect to x. Therefore each of the lower-contour sets $\{x \in \Re^n \mid g_j(x) \leq b_j\}$ is a closed and convex set. The problem's feasible set,

$$\mathcal{C} = \{x \in \Re^n \mid g_1(x) \leq b_1, \ldots, g_m(x) \leq b_m\} = \cap_{j=1}^m \{x \in \Re^n \mid g_j(x) \leq b_j\},$$

is therefore an intersection of finitely many closed and convex sets and thus is a closed and convex set. Its interior is not empty by hypothesis, so Slater's constraint qualification is satisfied and the Karush-Kuhn-Tucker condition is well-defined at any $x \in \mathcal{C}$.

For each $j = 1, \ldots, m$ the function $-g_j(x)$ is concave with respect to x and $\lambda_j \geq 0$. The Lagrange function

$$L(x, \lambda) = f(x) + \sum_{j=1}^m \lambda_j(b_j - g_j(x))$$

is therefore a nonnegative linear combination of functions that are concave with respect to x and so is a function that is concave with respect to x.

(x^*, λ^*) is a solution to the Karush-Kuhn-Tucker condition, so

$$\frac{\partial L^r(x; \lambda^*)}{\partial x_i}\Big|_{x=x^*} = 0 \ \forall \ i = 1, \ldots, n.$$

Because $L^r(x; \lambda^*)$ is concave with respect to x, it follows that $L^r(x; \lambda^*) \leq L(x^*, \lambda^*)$ for all $x \in \Re^n$ and for all $x \in \mathcal{C}$ in particular.

Also, since $\lambda_j^*(b_j - g_j(x^*)) = 0$ and $\lambda_j(b_j - g_j(x^*)) \geq 0$ for all $j = 1, \ldots, m$,

$$L(x^*, \lambda^*) = f(x^*) = f(x^*) + \sum_{j=1}^{m} \lambda_j^*(b_j - g_j(x^*))$$

$$\leq f(x^*) + \sum_{j=1}^{m} \lambda_j(b_j - g_j(x^*)) = L^r(\lambda; x^*) \; \forall \; \lambda \in \Re_+^m.$$

We have now established that (x^*, λ^*) is an x-max, λ-min saddle-point for the problem's Lagrange function, so Theorem 9.3 informs us that x^* is a globally optimal solution to the problem.

Suppose that f is strictly concave with respect to x. The argument establishing that x^* is then unique is by contradiction. Suppose that (x', λ') and (x'', λ''), with $x' \neq x''$, are both solutions to the problem's first-order optimality conditions. Then both x' and x'' are globally optimal solutions, and thus feasible solutions, to the problem. $\mathcal{C}$ is a convex set with a nonempty interior, so, for any $\theta \in (0, 1)$, $x(\theta) = \theta x' + (1 - \theta)x'' \in \mathcal{C}$ and $f(x(\theta)) > f(x') = f(x'')$ because f is strictly concave with respect to x. This contradicts the global optimality of x' and x'', so there is just one solution to the problem's first-order optimality conditions and thus a unique global optimal solution to the problem. □

Theorem 9.5 is easily generalized. Let's think using simple geometry. What is the idea at the heart of the above result? It is that the feasible set $\mathcal{C}$ is a convex set with a nonempty interior, and that the objective function f is concave with respect to x. Then any value for $x \in \mathcal{C}$ that locally maximizes f, must be a global maximum for f on $\mathcal{C}$. Right? A less restrictive way to ensure that $\mathcal{C}$ is convex is to insist that each of the constraint functions $g_1, \ldots, g_m$ is quasi-convex with respect to x (a function defined on $\Re^n$ is quasi-(strictly)-convex if and only if all of its lower-contour sets are (strictly) convex sets). Then, once again, $\mathcal{C}$ is the intersection of convex sets and so is a convex set. There is no need to insist upon the stronger condition that the constraint functions be convex with respect to x (a quasi-convex function does not have to be a convex function). The result we obtain by this reasoning is as follows.

Theorem 9.6. *Consider a problem (9.1) in which the objective function f is differentiable and concave with respect to $x_1, \ldots, x_n$, the constraint functions $g_1, \ldots, g_m$ are all differentiable and quasi-convex with respect to $x_1, \ldots, x_n$, and the interior of the feasible set $\mathcal{C}$ is not empty. Let $\mathcal{C} \subset \Re_+^n$. Let (x^*, λ^*) be a solution to the problem's* *first-order optimality conditions. Then x^* is a globally optimal solution to the problem. If f is strictly concave with respect to x, then x^* is the unique globally optimal solution to the problem.*

If you want to read a proof, then try the original in Arrow and A. Enthoven. 1961. Notice that, although the conditions of this theorem are less restrictive than those of Theorem 9.5 in that the constraint functions now need to be only quasi-convex, the conditions are more restrictive in that only nonnegative vectors x are allowed; *i.e.* $\mathcal{C} \subset \Re_+^n$. Also notice that there is no mention of an x-max, λ-min saddle-point. This is for a very good reason: once we generalize from convex to quasi-convex constraint functions, the problem's Lagrange function may not have an x-max, λ-min saddle-point.

9.6   Remarks

We have explored just a few uses of Lagrange functions. Least important is that Lagrange functions let us use almost mindless differentiation to write down the Karush-Kuhn-Tucker necessary condition for a local constrained optimum. Lagrange functions have more valuable uses that will be explored in the following chapters. The first of these, and arguably the most important, is explained in the next chapter, where we will discover that the information that a point (x^*, λ^*) is a locally optimal solution implies a valuable necessary second-order condition that so far we have neither explored nor exploited. This second-order condition allows us to establish a variety of properties possessed by optimal solutions. These are the properties that most economists rely upon when applying economic theory. They allow us, for example, to predict the effects of a change to a tax rate or an interest rate. Chapters 11, 12, and 13 explain how to obtain such results.

9.7   Problems

Problem 9.1. Consider a rational consumer with a Cobb-Douglas direct utility function who chooses an affordable consumption bundle. The problem is

$$\max_{x_1, x_2} U(x_1, x_2; \alpha) = x_1^\alpha x_2^\alpha \text{ subject to } g_1(x_1, x_2) = -x_1 \leq 0,$$
$$g_2(x_1, x_2) = -x_2 \leq 0 \text{ and } g_3(x_1, x_2) = p_1 x_1 + p_2 x_2 \leq y. \tag{9.26}$$

For $\alpha_1 > 0$, $p_1 > 0$, $p_2 > 0$, and $y > 0$, the optimal solution $(x_1^*(p_1, p_2, y), x_2^*(p_1, p_2, y))$ is interior to $\Re_+^2$; *i.e.* $x_1^*(p_1, p_2, y) > 0$ and $x_2^*(p_1, p_2, y) > 0$. Moreover, this optimal solution is unique. Consequently the optimal solution to the inequality constrained problem (9.26) is the same as the unique optimal solution to the equality constrained problem

$$\max_{x_1, x_2} U(x_1, x_2; \alpha) = (x_1 x_2)^\alpha \text{ subject to } g_3(x_1, x_2) = p_1 x_1 + p_2 x_2 = y. \tag{9.27}$$

The first-order necessary optimality conditions for (9.27) are

$$\left(\alpha \left(x_1^*\right)^{\alpha-1} \left(x_2^*\right)^\alpha, \ \alpha \left(x_1^*\right)^\alpha \left(x_2^*\right)^{\alpha-1}\right) = \lambda_3^*(p_1, p_2) \text{ and } p_1 x_1^* + p_2 x_2^* = y, \tag{9.28}$$

resulting in the Cobb-Douglas ordinary demand functions

$$x_1^*(p_1, p_2, y) = \frac{y}{2p_1} \quad \text{and} \quad x_2^*(p_1, p_2, y) = \frac{y}{2p_2}. \tag{9.29}$$

The associated value for the multiplier λ_3 is

$$\lambda_3^*(p_1, p_2, y, \alpha) = \left(\frac{\alpha}{p_1}\right)^\alpha \left(\frac{\alpha}{p_2}\right)^\alpha \left(\frac{2\alpha}{y}\right)^{1-2\alpha}. \tag{9.30}$$

The Lagrange function for the equality constrained problem (9.27) is

$$L(x_1, x_2, \lambda_3; \alpha) = (x_1 x_2)^\alpha + \lambda_3(y - p_1 x_1 - p_2 x_2). \tag{9.31}$$

Lagrange's Theorem is that the point $(x_1^*(p_1, p_2, y), x_2^*(p_1, p_2, y), \lambda_3^*(p_1, p_2, y, \alpha))$ necessarily is a critical point for the Lagrange function (9.31). We now know that this critical point is some type of saddle-point for this Lagrange function. Let us explore just what type of saddle-point it might be. Is it, for example, an x-max, λ-min saddle-point?

(i) If $0 < \alpha < \frac{1}{2}$, then is $(x_1^*(p_1, p_2, y), x_2^*(p_1, p_2, y), \lambda_3^*(p_1, p_2, y))$ an x-max, λ-min saddle-point for the Lagrange function (9.31)?

(ii) If $1 < \alpha$, then is $(x_1^*(p_1, p_2, y), x_2^*(p_1, p_2, y), \lambda_3^*(p_1, p_2, y))$ an x-max, λ-min saddle-point for the Lagrange function (9.31)?

(iii) If $\frac{1}{2} < \alpha < 1$, then is $(x_1^*(p_1, p_2, y), x_2^*(p_1, p_2, y), \lambda_3^*(p_1, p_2, y))$ an x-max, λ-min saddle-point for the Lagrange function (9.31)?

Problem 9.2. Theorem 9.3 takes as given only an x-max, λ-min type of saddle-point. Suppose instead that you know that a point (x^*, λ^*) for some constrained optimization problem is an x-min, λ-max saddle-point for the problem's Lagrange function. Is there a theorem, analogous to Theorem 9.3, that applies to such a case? If so, then what is the theorem? If not, then why not?

Problem 9.3. We are given that a point $(x^*, \lambda^*) = (x_1^*, \ldots, x_n^*, \lambda_1^*, \ldots, \lambda_m^*)$ is a saddle-point for the Lagrange function for the constrained optimization problem (9.1).

(i) If the saddle-point is not an x-max, λ-min saddle-point, then can x^* be the globally optimal solution to problem (9.1)? Explain.

(ii) Suppose that x^* is the globally optimal solution to problem (9.1)? Must (x^*, λ^*) be an x-max, λ-min saddle-point? Explain.

9.8 Answers

Answer to Problem 9.1. We must consider in turn each one of the restricted Lagrange functions $L^r(x_1, x_2; \lambda_3^*)$ and $L^r(\lambda_3; x_1^*, x_2^*)$. We need to determine if these functions are minimized or maximized at the saddle-point.

(i) The answer is "Yes." The Hessian matrix for the restricted Lagrange function $L^r(x_1, x_2; \lambda_3^*)$ is

$$H_{L^r(x_1, x_2; \lambda_3^*)}(x_1, x_2) = \begin{pmatrix} -\alpha(1-\alpha)x_1^{\alpha-2}x_2^\alpha & \alpha^2(x_1 x_2)^{\alpha-1} \\ \alpha^2(x_1 x_2)^{\alpha-1} & -\alpha(1-\alpha)x_1^\alpha x_2^{\alpha-2} \end{pmatrix}. \qquad (9.32)$$

This is a symmetric matrix, so to determine if the matrix's quadratic form has a definiteness property all we need do is check the signs of the first and second principal minors of the matrix. These minors are

$$M_1 = -\alpha(1-\alpha)x_1^{\alpha-2}x_2^\alpha \quad \text{and} \quad M_2 = \alpha^2(1-2\alpha)(x_1 x_2)^{2(\alpha-1)}.$$

If $0 < \alpha < \frac{1}{2}$, then $M_1 < 0$ and $M_2 > 0$, establishing that $L^r(x_1, x_2; \lambda_3^*)$ is a strictly concave function of x_1 and x_2 (or, equivalently, that the Hessian matrix is negative-definite for any $x_1 > 0$ and for any $x_2 > 0$). Any critical point for such a function must be a global (note: global, not just local) maximum with respect to x_1 and x_2. Thus we have that, if $0 < \alpha < \frac{1}{2}$,

$$L^r(x_1, x_2; \lambda_3^*) < L^r(x_1^*, x_2^*; \lambda_3^*) = L(x_1^*, x_2^*, \lambda_3^*) \ \forall \ x_1, x_2 \in \Re, \ (x_1, x_2) \neq (x_1^*, x_2^*).$$
(9.33)

The restricted Lagrange function $L^r(\lambda_3; x_1^*, x_2^*) = (x_1^* x_2^*)^\alpha + \lambda_3(y - p_1 x_1^* - p_2 x_2^*) \equiv (x_1^* x_2^*)^\alpha$ is constant-valued with respect to λ_3, so

$$L^r(\lambda_3; x_1^*, x_2^*) = L^r(\lambda_3^*; x_1^*, x_2^*) = L(x_1^*, x_2^*, \lambda_3^*) \ \forall \ \lambda_3 \geq 0.$$
(9.34)

(9.33) and (9.34) establish that the point $(x_1^*(p_1, p_2, y), x_2^*(p_1, p_2, y), \lambda_3^*(p_1, p_2, y, \alpha))$ is an x-max, λ-min saddle-point for the Lagrange function (9.31) when $0 < \alpha < \frac{1}{2}$.

(ii) The answer is "No." If $1 < \alpha$, then $M_1 > 0$ and $M_2 < 0$, establishing (see Theorem 2.11) that the Hessian matrix of the restricted Lagrange function $L^r(x_1, x_2; \lambda_3^*)$ is indefinite and that the restricted Lagrange function $L^r(x_1, x_2; \lambda_3^*)$ is neither maximized nor minimized with respect to *both* x_1 and x_2 at $(x_1, x_2) = (x_1^*, x_2^*)$ (indeed, the function does not possess a maximum in $\Re_+^2$ with respect to both x_1 and x_2). In fact, if $1 < \alpha$, then the point (x_1^*, x_2^*) is a saddle-point (not a maximum and not a minimum) with respect to x_1 and x_2 for the restricted Lagrange function $L^r(x_1, x_2; \lambda_3^*)$. Thus the point $(x_1^*(p_1, p_2, y), x_2^*(p_1, p_2, y), \lambda_3^*(p_1, p_2, y, \alpha))$ is not an x-max, λ-min saddle-point for the (unrestricted) Lagrange function when $1 < \alpha$.

(iii) The answer is "No." If $\frac{1}{2} < \alpha < 1$, then $M_1 < 0$ and $M_2 < 0$, establishing (see Theorem 2.11) that the Hessian matrix of the restricted Lagrange function $L^r(x_1, x_2; \lambda_3^*)$ is indefinite and that the restricted Lagrange function $L^r(x_1, x_2; \lambda_3^*)$ is neither maximized nor minimized with respect to x_1 and x_2 at $(x_1, x_2) = (x_1^*, x_2^*)$. Instead the point (x_1^*, x_2^*) is again a saddle-point (not a maximum and not a minimum) with respect to x_1 and x_2 for the restricted Lagrange function $L^r(x_1, x_2; \lambda_3^*)$ and so, again, the point $(x_1^*(p_1, p_2, y), x_2^*(p_1, p_2, y), \lambda_3^*(p_1, p_2, y, \alpha))$ is not an x-max, λ-min saddle-point for the (unrestricted) Lagrange function when $\frac{1}{2} < \alpha < 1$. $\qquad\square$

Answer to Problem 9.2. We are given a Lagrange function

$$L(x_1, \ldots, x_n, \lambda_1, \ldots, \lambda_k) = f(x_1, \ldots, x_n) + \sum_{j=1}^{k} \lambda_j(b - g_j(x_1, \ldots, x_n))$$
(9.35)

and that (x^*, λ^*) is a global x-min, λ-max saddle-point for this function. That is, for all $x \in \Re^n$ and for all $\lambda \in \Re_+^k$,

$$L^r(x_1, \ldots, x_n; \lambda_1^*, \ldots, \lambda_k^*) \geq L(x_1^*, \ldots, x_n^*, \lambda_1^*, \ldots, \lambda_k^*) \geq L^r(\lambda_1, \ldots, \lambda_k; x_1^*, \ldots, x_n^*).$$
(9.36)

The proof of Theorem 9.3 is in two parts, the first of which is a demonstration that the λ-min part of the x-max, λ-min saddle-point property implies that x^* is a feasible solution. Let's see if the λ-max part of the x-min, λ-max saddle-point property implies the same thing. The right-side inequality in (9.36) is

$$f(x^*) + \sum_{j=1}^{k} \lambda_j^*(b_j - g_j(x^*)) \geq f(x^*) + \sum_{j=1}^{k} \lambda_j(b_j - g_j(x^*)) \ \forall \ \lambda_j \geq 0, \ j = 1, \ldots, k,$$

so $$\sum_{j=1}^{k} \lambda_j^*(b_j - g_j(x^*)) \geq \sum_{j=1}^{k} \lambda_j(b_j - g_j(x^*)) \text{ for all } \lambda_1 \geq 0, \ldots, \lambda_k \geq 0. \quad (9.37)$$

The left side of (9.37) is a fixed number. Just as in the proof of Theorem 9.3, we now attempt to show that this fixed number is zero. Suppose it is not. Particularly, suppose that $\sum_{j=1}^{k} \lambda_j^*(b_j - g_j(x^*)) > 0$. Then, since $\lambda_1^* \geq 0, \ldots, \lambda_k^* \geq 0$, each of $\tilde{\lambda}_j = \mu \lambda_j^* \geq 0$ for $j = 1, \ldots, k$, where $\mu > 0$. By making μ large enough, we make the right side of (9.37) larger than the fixed value of the left side of (9.37). Hence $\sum_{j=1}^{k} \lambda_j^*(b_j - g_j(x^*)) \leq 0$. Now suppose that $\sum_{j=1}^{k} \lambda_j^*(b_j - g_j(x^*)) < 0$. Since $\lambda_j \geq 0$ for all $j = 1, \ldots, k$, there must be at least one value of j for which $g_j(x^*) > b_j$. But then x^* is not feasible. So, if x^* is a feasible solution to the constrained optimization problem, then necessarily $\sum_{j=1}^{k} \lambda_j^*(b_j - g_j(x^*)) \geq 0$. Necessarily, then, $\sum_{j=1}^{k} \lambda_j^*(b_j - g_j(x^*)) = 0$.

This information together with the left side inequality in (9.36) tells us that

$$f(x) + \sum_{j=1}^{k} \lambda_j^*(b_j - g_j(x)) \geq f(x^*) + \sum_{j=1}^{k} \lambda_j^*(b_j - g_j(x^*)) = f(x^*). \quad (9.38)$$

For feasible choices x, $\sum_{j=1}^{k} \lambda_j^*(b_j - g_j(x)) \geq 0$, so we cannot deduce from (9.38) that $f(x^*) \geq f(x)$. There is no analogue to Theorem 9.3 for an x-min, λ-max saddle-point for the Lagrange function (9.35). $\qquad\square$

Answer to Problem 9.3.

(i) Yes. Examples are problem (9.17) and problem (9.26) with $1 < \alpha$.

(ii) No. Theorem 9.3 is a *sufficiency* statement. It says that, if (x^*, λ^*) is a global x-max, λ-min type of saddle-point for the constrained optimization problem's Lagrange function, then x^* is a globally optimal solution to the problem. The theorem does not say the reverse. That is, the theorem does not say that, if x^* is a globally optimal solution to the constrained optimization problem, then the saddle-point at (x^*, λ^*) for the problem's Lagrange function must be an x-max, λ-min type of saddle-point. Problem (9.17) is a counterexample to this false assertion. $\qquad\square$

Chapter 10

Constrained Optimization, Part II

Chapter 8 described the first-order conditions that necessarily are true at a local maximum to the constrained optimization problem

$$\max_{x_1, \ldots, x_n} f(x_1, \ldots, x_n) \text{ subject to } g_1(x_1, \ldots, x_n) \leq b_1, \ldots, g_m(x_1, \ldots, x_n) \leq b_m, \quad (10.1)$$

in which the objective function f and the constraint functions $g_1, \ldots, g_m$ are all continuously differentiable with respect to each of $x_1, \ldots, x_n$. In this chapter we will require these functions to all be twice-continuously differentiable. Reminder: A function is twice-continuously differentiable with respect to $x_1, \ldots, x_n$ if and only if all of the function's second-order derivatives are continuous functions of $x_1, \ldots, x_n$. The $m + 1$ first-order conditions consist of the Karush-Kuhn-Tucker condition

$$\nabla f(x^*) = \lambda_1^* \nabla g_1(x^*) + \cdots + \lambda_m^* \nabla g_m(x^*), \quad (10.2)$$

where the nonnegative scalars $\lambda_1^*, \ldots, \lambda_m^*$ are not all zero, and the complementary slackness conditions

$$\lambda_j^*(b_j - g_j(x^*)) = 0 \ \forall \ j = 1, \ldots, m. \quad (10.3)$$

There is an additional condition that necessarily is true at a local optimum, a second-order condition that will shortly be described. Following that, this chapter discusses sets of conditions that are sufficient for a feasible point to be a local optimum.

10.1 Necessary *vs.* Sufficient Conditions

Let's take a minute to review the fundamental differences between necessary and sufficient optimality conditions. The basic difference is as follows. Necessary optimality conditions are conditions that *individually* have to be true at an optimum, so the flow of the logic is, because $\tilde{x}$ is a local optimum, we know that each one of the conditions A, B, and so on must be (is necessarily) true at $\tilde{x}$. Equivalently, if *any one* of the conditions A, B, and so on is not true at $x = \tilde{x}$, then $\tilde{x}$ is not a local optimum. Necessary local optimality conditions are individually true when $\tilde{x}$ is a local optimum. In contrast, a *set* of conditions all true at $x = \tilde{x}$ is sufficient for $x = \tilde{x}$ to be a local optimum if, *collectively*, these conditions ensure that $x = \tilde{x}$ is a local optimum. Equivalently, if $x = \tilde{x}$ is not a local optimum then at least one of the sufficiency conditions must not be true at $\tilde{x}$. It is easy to get all of this confused, so take some time to think it through and understand it before proceeding further.

We are going to start by making a very general statement about what necessarily is true at some local optimum $x = \tilde{x}$. This will be our general "statement of necessity."

Statement of Necessity. If f is locally maximized on $\mathcal{C}$ at $x = \hat{x}$, then the value of f at $\hat{x}$ is at least as large as the value of f at every point $\hat{x} + \Delta x$ in $\mathcal{C}$ that is close to $\hat{x}$. Put more formally, if $\tilde{x}$ is a local maximizer for f on $\mathcal{C}$, then necessarily there is an $\varepsilon > 0$ for which

$$f(\tilde{x} + \Delta x) \leq f(\tilde{x}) \ \forall \ \tilde{x} + \Delta x \in B_{d_E}(\tilde{x}, \varepsilon) \cap \mathcal{C}. \tag{10.4}$$

If (10.4) is false, then $\tilde{x}$ is not a local maximizer.

$f, g_1, \ldots, g_m$ are continuously differentiable with respect to $x_1, \ldots, x_n$, so, for small enough ε (and thus for small enough perturbations Δx), we can use the first-order version of Taylor's Theorem to write

$$f(\tilde{x} + \Delta x) \approx f(\tilde{x}) + \nabla f(\tilde{x}) \cdot \Delta x \tag{10.5}$$

and, for each $j = 1, \ldots, m$, to write

$$g_j(\tilde{x} + \Delta x) \approx g_j(\tilde{x}) + \nabla g_j(\tilde{x}) \cdot \Delta x. \tag{10.6}$$

(10.5) and (10.6) let us rewrite (10.4) as: If $\tilde{x}$ is a local maximizer for f on $\mathcal{C}$, then

$$\nabla f(\tilde{x}) \cdot \Delta x \leq 0 \text{ for all } \Delta x \text{ for which } \nabla g_j(\tilde{x}) \cdot \Delta x \leq 0 \ \forall \ j \in I(\tilde{x}), \tag{10.7}$$

where $I(\tilde{x})$ is the set of the indices of the constraints that bind at $x = \tilde{x}$ and the size (*i.e.* norm) of any perturbation Δx is less than ε. Statement (10.7) was used to derive the first-order necessary optimization conditions explained in Chapter 8. A single statement of necessity results in a single *complete* list of conditions that *individually* are necessarily true when $\tilde{x}$ is a local optimum.

Statements of Sufficiency. Notice the use of the plural; *i.e.* "statement<u>s</u>," not "statement." Typically we can find more than one set of conditions that ensure some point is a local optimum. For example, I could make the statement, "if x^* is a global optimum, then x^* is a local optimum." I could also say that, "if the value at $x^* \in \mathcal{C}$ of the function f is larger than the values of f at every other feasible point x in a neighborhood about x^*, then x^* is a local optimum for f on $\mathcal{C}$." I'm sure that you can dream up a few more such sufficiency statements for yourself. My points are, first, that there can be more than one statement that is sufficient for x^* to be a local optimum and, second, that each such statement will typically consist of a different collection of conditions that together are sufficient for x^* to be a local optimum. Well then, which one of the sufficiency statements shall we choose? The statement that usually is employed is the following:

Particular Statement of Sufficiency. If the value of f at $\hat{x}$ is strictly larger than the value of f at every point $\hat{x} + \Delta x$ in $\mathcal{C}$ with $\Delta \neq \underline{0}$ that is close to $\hat{x}$, then $\hat{x}$ locally maximizes f on $\mathcal{C}$. Put more formally, if for some $\varepsilon > 0$, $f(x^* + \Delta x) < f(x^*)$ for every perturbation $\Delta x \neq \underline{0}$, such that $x^* + \Delta x \in B_{d_E}(x^*, \varepsilon) \cap \mathcal{C}$, then x^* is locally maximal for f on $\mathcal{C}$.

From this statement we will later in this chapter derive a particular set of conditions that *jointly* ensure that x^* is a local optimum. I emphasize "jointly" because the conditions that are sufficient for local maximality are collectively but not individually sufficient. Think of the simple problem of maximizing $f(x) = -x^2$ on $\Re$. To solve this problem most of us would compute the first-derivative, $f'(x) = -2x$, and then solve $f'(x) = 0$ to obtain $x^* = 0$. Next we would check that the value at $x^* = 0$ of the second-order derivative, $f''(0) \equiv -2$, is negative. Would you assert that $f''(\hat{x}) < 0$ is sufficient for $x = \hat{x}$ to be a local optimum for $f(x) = -x^2$? I hope not, since your assertion would be wrong (after all, $f''(x) = -2$ at, for example, $x = 1$ also, but $x = 1$ is not a local optimum). A correct statement is, "$f'(x^*) = 0$ and $f''(x^*) < 0$ are together sufficient for $x^* = 0$ to be a local maximum for $f(x) = -x^2$." Thus we do not usually talk of an individual condition as being enough to ensure that a point x^* is a local optimum. Instead we talk of a *set* of conditions that together are sufficient for local optimality.

10.2   Second-Order Necessary Conditions

Let's briefly review some basic calculus. Suppose you have a twice-differentiable function $f : \Re \mapsto \Re$ with a local maximum at $x = x^*$. You are asked to locate x^*.

There are no constraints. How would you do it? I imagine that you would obtain the function's first-order derivative $f'(x)$ and solve $f'(x) = 0$. The solutions to this equation are the critical points of the function. Let's suppose there is only one critical point, $x = \tilde{x}$. I imagine further that you would then obtain the function's second-order derivative $f''(x)$ and evaluate it at $x = \tilde{x}$. If $f''(\tilde{x}) < 0$, then you would conclude that $\tilde{x}$ is x^*, the value of x that locally maximizes the value of f. If that is a reasonable description of what you would do, then I ask you now to consider carefully what is the *complete* list of conditions that necessarily, individually are true when $x = \tilde{x}$ is a local maximum for f. What is this list?

We know that $f'(\tilde{x}) = 0$ is a necessary condition. So is $f''(\tilde{x}) \leq 0$. Why? Suppose instead that $f''(\tilde{x}) > 0$. Then $\tilde{x}$ is not a local maximum for f, is it? Hence, if $\tilde{x}$ is a local maximizer for f, then necessarily $f''(\tilde{x}) \ngtr 0$. The reason becomes clear when we use a second-order Taylor's series (this is why we require order-2 continuous differentiability for f) to approximate $f(\tilde{x} + \Delta x)$ in our necessity statement; *i.e.* we write $f(\tilde{x} + \Delta x) \leq f(\tilde{x})$ as

$$f(\tilde{x}) + f'(\tilde{x})\Delta x + \frac{1}{2}f''(\tilde{x})\left(\Delta x\right)^2 \leq f(\tilde{x}).$$

Since necessarily $f'(\tilde{x}) = 0$, the local maximality of $\tilde{x}$ tells us that necessarily

$$f''(\tilde{x}) \leq 0. \tag{10.8}$$

What if $f : \Re^n \mapsto \Re$? Again, using a second-order Taylor's series lets us write $f(\tilde{x} + \Delta x) \leq f(\tilde{x})$, for all $\tilde{x} + \Delta x \in B_{d_E}(\tilde{x}, \varepsilon)$ and small $\varepsilon > 0$, as

$$f(\tilde{x}) + \nabla f(\tilde{x}) \cdot \Delta x + \frac{1}{2}\Delta x^T H_f(\tilde{x})\Delta x \leq f(\tilde{x}).$$

Necessarily $\nabla f(\tilde{x}) = \underline{0}$, so it is also necessary that

$$\Delta x^T H_f(\tilde{x})\Delta x \leq 0 \ \forall \ \Delta x \text{ such that } \tilde{x} + \Delta x \in B_{d_E}(\tilde{x}, \varepsilon). \tag{10.9}$$

H_f is the Hessian matrix of f. $\Delta x^T H_f(x)\Delta x$ is the quadratic function of $\Delta x_1, \ldots, \Delta x_n$ that is called the "quadratic form of the matrix H_f." The matrix is the ordered collection of all of the second-order derivatives of f; *i.e.*

$$H_f(x) = \begin{pmatrix} \dfrac{\partial^2 f(x)}{\partial x_1^2} & \cdots & \dfrac{\partial^2 f(x)}{\partial x_1 \partial x_n} \\ \vdots & \ddots & \vdots \\ \dfrac{\partial^2 f(x)}{\partial x_n \partial x_1} & \cdots & \dfrac{\partial^2 f(x)}{\partial x_n^2} \end{pmatrix}. \tag{10.10}$$

A matrix with a quadratic form that never takes a positive value is called a negative-semi-definite matrix, so (10.9) says that, if $\tilde{x}$ is a local maximizer for f, then necessarily the Hessian matrix of f evaluated at $x = \tilde{x}$ is negative-semi-definite. (10.8) is exactly this statement for $n = 1$.

(10.9) has a simple meaning. The necessary condition $\nabla f(\tilde{x}) = \underline{0}$ says that *at $\tilde{x}$* the graph of f is flat in every direction. (10.9) says that, if $\tilde{x}$ is a local maximum, then necessarily in a small neighborhood *around $\tilde{x}$* the graph of f must not in any direction "curl upwards." Look at Figure 10.1. There, $\tilde{x} = (1,1)$ is a local maximizer for f. The slope of the graph of f in any direction is zero at $\tilde{x}$ and for any small movement in any direction away from the point $\tilde{x}$ the graph of f does not curl upwards.

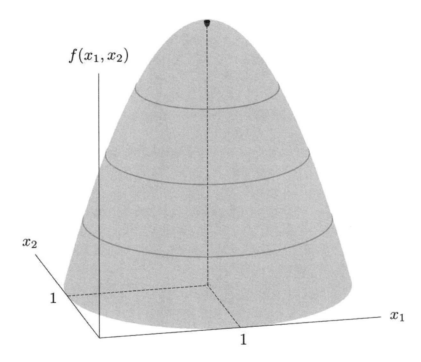

Figure 10.1: The first-order and second-order necessary conditions that are implied by f being maximized at $\tilde{x} = (1,1)$.

Now look at Figure 10.2. Again the slope of the graph of f at $\tilde{x} = (1,1)$ is zero in any direction, but this time in every small neighborhood *around $\tilde{x}$* the graph curls upwards in at least one direction. Thus $\tilde{x}$ cannot be a maximizer for f.

All of our discussion so far has been of unconstrained optimization problems. Let's now examine constrained optimization problems. Our problem is again (10.1).

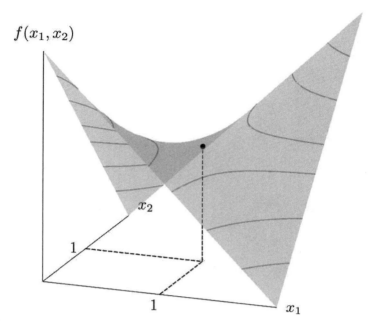

Figure 10.2: f satisfies the first-order necessary condition but not the second-order necessary condition at $\tilde{x} = (1,1)$, which is therefore not a local maximum for f.

Imagine that we have solved the first-order optimality conditions and that $\tilde{x}$ is one of the solutions. Again use $I(\tilde{x})$ to denote the set of the indices of the constraints that bind at $\tilde{x}$. If $I(\tilde{x}) = \emptyset$ and $\tilde{x}$ is a local maximizer for f, then we are dealing with an unconstrained solution, and the necessary local optimality conditions are just $\nabla f(\tilde{x}) = \underline{0}$ and (10.9), so consider the case in which at least one constraint binds at $\tilde{x}$; *i.e.* $I(\tilde{x}) \neq \emptyset$. Without loss of generality, suppose that the first k constraints bind at $\tilde{x}$; *i.e.* $I(\tilde{x}) = \{1, \ldots, k\}$ with $1 \leq k \leq m$.

For a constrained optimization problem such as (10.1), our necessity statement (10.4) becomes, "If $\tilde{x}$ is a local maximizer for f subject to $g_1(x) \leq b_1, \ldots, g_m(x) \leq b_m$, then necessarily there is an $\varepsilon > 0$ for which

$$f(\tilde{x} + \Delta x) \leq f(\tilde{x}) \ \forall \ \Delta x \text{ such that } \tilde{x} + \Delta x \in B_{d_E}(\tilde{x}, \varepsilon)$$
$$\text{and } g_j(\tilde{x} + \Delta x) \leq b_j \ \forall \ j = 1, \ldots, m." \tag{10.11}$$

The last $m - k$ constraints are slack at $\tilde{x}$; *i.e.* $g_j(\tilde{x}) < b_j$ for $j = k+1, \ldots, m$. We are considering only problems in which each constraint function is continuous with respect to x, so there are values for ε that are so close to zero that the neighborhood $B_{d_E}(\tilde{x}, \varepsilon)$ is so small that every constraint that is slack at $\tilde{x}$ is also slack for every feasible point

$\tilde{x} + \Delta x \in B_{d_E}(\tilde{x}, \varepsilon)$. Within this small neighborhood, then, we can ignore the slack constraints. Hence (10.11) informs us that the following, more special, statement is also true: "If $\tilde{x}$ is a local maximizer for f subject to $g_1(x) \le b_1, \ldots, g_m(x) \le b_m$, then necessarily there is an $\varepsilon > 0$ for which

$$f(\tilde{x} + \Delta x) \le f(\tilde{x}) \; \forall \; \Delta x \text{ such that } \tilde{x} + \Delta x \in B_{d_E}(\tilde{x}, \varepsilon)$$
$$\text{and } g_j(\tilde{x} + \Delta x) \le b_j \; \forall \; j = 1, \ldots, k."$$

(10.12)

For small ε, a second-order Taylor's series for f lets us write (10.12) as

$$\nabla f(\tilde{x}) \cdot \Delta x + \frac{1}{2} \Delta x^T H_f(\tilde{x}) \Delta x \le 0 \; \forall \; \Delta x \text{ such that } \tilde{x} + \Delta x \in B_{d_E}(\tilde{x}, \varepsilon)$$
$$\text{and } g_j(\tilde{x} + \Delta x) \le b_j \; \forall \; j = 1, \ldots, k.$$

(10.13)

In this constrained case, the Karush-Kuhn-Tucker condition is not $\nabla f(\tilde{x}) = \underline{0}$. It is

$$\nabla f(\tilde{x}) = \sum_{j=1}^{m} \tilde{\lambda}_j \nabla g_j(\tilde{x}) = \sum_{j=1}^{k} \tilde{\lambda}_j \nabla g_j(\tilde{x}) \quad (\text{because } \tilde{\lambda}_{k+1} = \cdots = \tilde{\lambda}_m = 0), \quad (10.14)$$

where $\tilde{\lambda}_1, \ldots, \tilde{\lambda}_k$ are the values of the multipliers for the binding constraints obtained from the Karush-Kuhn-Tucker and complementary slackness conditions evaluated at $\tilde{x}$. Using (10.14) in (10.13) gives us, "If $\tilde{x}$ is a local maximizer for f subject to $g_1(x) \le b_1, \ldots, g_m(x) \le b_m$, then necessarily there is an $\varepsilon > 0$ for which

$$\tilde{\lambda}_1 \nabla g_1(\tilde{x}) \cdot \Delta x + \cdots + \tilde{\lambda}_k \nabla g_k(\tilde{x}) \cdot \Delta x + \frac{1}{2} \Delta x^T H_f(\tilde{x}) \Delta x \le 0 \qquad (10.15)$$

$$\forall \; \Delta x \text{ such that } \tilde{x} + \Delta x \in B_{d_E}(\tilde{x}, \varepsilon) \text{ and } g_j(\tilde{x} + \Delta x) \le b_j \; \forall \; j = 1, \ldots, k." \quad (10.16)$$

(10.15) necessarily is true for two types of perturbations Δx: those that satisfy (10.16) with $<$ and those that satisfy (10.16) with $=$. From here onwards we will consider only the perturbations that satisfy (10.16) with equality.

Second-order Taylor's series approximations let us write the feasibility-preserving requirements $g_j(\tilde{x} + \Delta x) = g_j(\tilde{x}) = b_j$ for $j = 1, \ldots, k$ as

$$g_j(\tilde{x} + \Delta x) = g_j(\tilde{x}) + \nabla g_j(\tilde{x}) \cdot \Delta x + \frac{1}{2} \Delta x^T H_{g_j}(\tilde{x}) \Delta x = g_j(\tilde{x}) = b_j \text{ for } j = 1, \ldots, k.$$

That is,

$$\nabla g_j(\tilde{x}) \cdot \Delta x = -\frac{1}{2} \Delta x^T H_{g_j}(\tilde{x}) \Delta x \text{ for each } j = 1, \ldots, k. \qquad (10.17)$$

So (10.15) and (10.17) give us the still more special necessity statement, "If $\tilde{x}$ is a local maximizer for f subject to $g_1(x) \leq b_1, \ldots, g_m(x) \leq b_m$, then necessarily there is an $\varepsilon > 0$ for which

$$\Delta x^T \left[H_f(\tilde{x}) - \tilde{\lambda}_1 H_{g_1}(\tilde{x}) - \cdots - \tilde{\lambda}_k H_{g_k}(\tilde{x}) \right] \Delta x \leq 0 \; \forall \; \Delta x \text{ such that} \qquad (10.18)$$

$$\tilde{x} + \Delta x \in B_{d_E}(\tilde{x}, \varepsilon) \text{ and } g_j(\tilde{x} + \Delta x) = b_j \text{ for } j = 1, \ldots, k." \qquad (10.19)$$

The matrix inside the square brackets in (10.18) is the Hessian matrix (with respect to $x_1, \ldots, x_n$ only) of the restricted Lagrange function

$$L^r(x_1, \ldots, x_n; \tilde{\lambda}_1, \ldots, \tilde{\lambda}_k) = f(x_1, \ldots, x_n) + \sum_{j=1}^k \tilde{\lambda}_j(b_j - g_j(x_1, \ldots, x_n)) \qquad (10.20)$$

for problem (10.1) with the *multipliers fixed* at the values that satisfy the Karush-Kuhn-Tucker condition at $\tilde{x}$; *i.e.* $\lambda_j = \tilde{\lambda}_j$ for $j = 1, \ldots, k$ and $\lambda_j = 0$ for $j = k+1, \ldots, m$.

Why is (10.18) a statement that the function $L^r(\tilde{x} + \Delta x; \tilde{\lambda})$ does not locally increase its value above its value $L^r(\tilde{x}; \tilde{\lambda})$ at $\tilde{x}$ for perturbations satisfying (10.19)? To a second-order approximation (remember, the multiplier values are fixed),

$$L^r(\tilde{x} + \Delta x; \tilde{\lambda}) = L^r(\tilde{x}; \tilde{\lambda}) + \nabla_x L^r(x; \tilde{\lambda})|_{x=\tilde{x}} \cdot \Delta x + \frac{1}{2} \Delta x^T H_{L^r}(x; \tilde{\lambda})|_{x=\tilde{x}} \Delta x. \qquad (10.21)$$

The Karush-Kuhn-Tucker condition is necessarily satisfied at $\tilde{x}$; *i.e.*

$$\nabla f(\tilde{x}) = \sum_{j=1}^k \tilde{\lambda}_j \nabla g_j(\tilde{x}) \quad \Leftrightarrow \quad \nabla_x L^r(x; \tilde{\lambda})|_{x=\tilde{x}} = \underline{0}_n. \qquad (10.22)$$

Thus the statement that $L^r(\tilde{x} + \Delta x; \tilde{\lambda}) \leq L^r(\tilde{x}; \tilde{\lambda})$ implies both of the statements

$$\nabla_x L^r(x; \tilde{\lambda})|_{x=\tilde{x}} = \underline{0} \quad \text{and} \quad \Delta x^T H_{L^r}(x; \tilde{\lambda})|_{x=\tilde{x}} \Delta x \leq 0. \qquad (10.23)$$

The second of these two statements is exactly (10.18), since

$$H_f(x) - \tilde{\lambda}_1 H_{g_1}(x) - \cdots - \tilde{\lambda}_k H_{g_k}(x) = H_{L^r}(x; \tilde{\lambda}). \qquad (10.24)$$

Written out in full, this square order-n matrix is

$$H_{L^r}(x_1,\ldots,x_n;\tilde{\lambda}_1,\ldots,\tilde{\lambda}_k) = \begin{pmatrix} \dfrac{\partial^2 L^r(x;\tilde{\lambda})}{\partial x_1^2} & \cdots & \dfrac{\partial^2 L^r(x;\tilde{\lambda})}{\partial x_n \partial x_1} \\ \vdots & \ddots & \vdots \\ \dfrac{\partial^2 L^r(x;\tilde{\lambda})}{\partial x_1 \partial x_n} & \cdots & \dfrac{\partial^2 L^r(x;\tilde{\lambda})}{\partial x_n^2} \end{pmatrix}$$

$$= \begin{pmatrix} \dfrac{\partial^2 f(x)}{\partial x_1^2} - \displaystyle\sum_{j=1}^{k} \tilde{\lambda}_j \dfrac{\partial^2 g_j(x)}{\partial x_1^2} & \cdots & \dfrac{\partial^2 f(x)}{\partial x_n \partial x_1} - \displaystyle\sum_{j=1}^{k} \tilde{\lambda}_j \dfrac{\partial^2 g_j(x)}{\partial x_n \partial x_1} \\ \vdots & \ddots & \vdots \\ \dfrac{\partial^2 f(x)}{\partial x_1 \partial x_n} - \displaystyle\sum_{j=1}^{k} \tilde{\lambda}_j \dfrac{\partial^2 g_j(x)}{\partial x_1 \partial x_n} & \cdots & \dfrac{\partial^2 f(x)}{\partial x_n^2} - \displaystyle\sum_{j=1}^{k} \tilde{\lambda}_j \dfrac{\partial^2 g_j(x)}{\partial x_n^2} \end{pmatrix}. \tag{10.25}$$

Let's be clear what we have discovered so far. It is that the original necessity statement (10.11) implies the more specialized statement that, "If $\tilde{x}$ is a local maximizer for f subject to $g_1(x) \leq b_1, \ldots, g_m(x) \leq b_m$, then necessarily there is an $\varepsilon > 0$ for which

$$\Delta x^T H_{L^r}(x;\tilde{\lambda})|_{x=\tilde{x}}\Delta x \leq 0 \; \forall \; \Delta x \text{ such that} \tag{10.26}$$
$$\tilde{x} + \Delta x \in B_{d_E}(\tilde{x},\varepsilon) \text{ and } g_j(\tilde{x} + \Delta x) = b_j \text{ for all } j = 1,\ldots,k, \tag{10.27}$$

where $L^r(x;\tilde{\lambda})$ is given by (10.20)."

Be careful not to interpret (10.26) and (10.27) as stating that the Hessian matrix of the optimization problem's Lagrange function necessarily is negative-semi-definite at a local constrained optimum $\tilde{x}$. Such a statement is wrong for two reasons. First, the problem's Lagrange function $L(x_1,\ldots,x_n,\lambda_1,\ldots,\lambda_m)$ is a function in which all of $x_1,\ldots,x_n$ and $\lambda_1,\ldots,\lambda_m$ are variable. The restricted Lagrange function mentioned in (10.26) is a function only of $x_1,\ldots,x_n$, since the values of $\lambda_1,\ldots,\lambda_k,\lambda_{k+1},\ldots,\lambda_m$ are fixed at $\tilde{\lambda}_1,\ldots,\tilde{\lambda}_k,0,\ldots,0$. Second, (10.26) is necessarily true only for the small enough perturbations Δx that satisfy (10.27). A statement that the Hessian of $L^r(x;\tilde{\lambda})$ is a negative-semi-definite matrix requires that (10.26) be true for every possible Δx, whether it satisfies (10.27) or not.

Keep in mind that the necessary second-order condition (10.26) depends upon the necessary first-order Karush-Kuhn-Tucker condition and also upon the complementary slackness conditions. (10.26) depends upon the Karush-Kuhn-Tucker condition because it was used to rewrite the necessity statement from (10.13) to (10.15). (10.26) depends upon the complementary slackness conditions because they, along with the Karush-Kuhn-Tucker condition, were used to compute the values $\tilde{\lambda}_1, \ldots, \tilde{\lambda}_k$.

What we have learned in this section provides the following theorem.

Theorem 10.1 (Necessary Second-Order Local Optimality Condition). *Let $\tilde{x}$ be a locally optimal solution to problem (10.1). Let $I(\tilde{x}) \neq \emptyset$ be the set of indices of the constraints that strictly bind at $\tilde{x}$. Let $\tilde{\lambda}_j$ for $j \in I(\tilde{x})$ be the solution at $\tilde{x}$ to the Karush-Kuhn-Tucker condition*

$$\nabla f(\tilde{x}) = \sum_{j \in I(\tilde{x})} \lambda_j \nabla g_j(\tilde{x})$$

and the complementary slackness conditions

$$\lambda_j(b_j - g_j(\tilde{x})) = 0 \text{ for } j \in I(\tilde{x}).$$

Let

$$L^r(x_1, \ldots, x_n; \tilde{\lambda}_1, \ldots, \tilde{\lambda}_k) = f(x_1, \ldots, x_n) + \sum_{j \in I(\tilde{x})} \tilde{\lambda}_j(b_j - g_j(x_1, \ldots, x_n)).$$

Then necessarily there is an $\varepsilon > 0$, such that $\Delta x^T H_{L^r}(x; \tilde{\lambda})|_{x=\tilde{x}} \Delta x \leq 0$ for all Δx such that $\tilde{x} + \Delta x \in B_{d_E}(\tilde{x}, \varepsilon)$ and $g_j(\tilde{x} + \Delta x) = b_j \ \forall \ j \in I(\tilde{x})$.

This second-order necessary local optimality condition has many valuable uses, as we will later see.

10.3 The Geometry of the Second-Order Necessary Condition

What is the geometric interpretation of the second-order necessary condition (10.26) and (10.27)? Until now we have said that a point $\tilde{x}$ is a local maximum for a function f only if the slopes of f at $\tilde{x}$ in every direction are all zero and only if the graph of f does not "curl upwards" in any direction for a small neighborhood around $\tilde{x}$. But this statement was made for an unconstrained optimization problem. It does not apply to a constrained optimization problem.

Some examples will be instructive. Consider, first, a problem we have met before:

$$\max_{x_1, x_2} f(x_1, x_2) = x_1^2 x_2^2 \text{ subject to } g_1(x_1) = -x_1 \leq 0,$$

$$g_2(x_2) = -x_2 \leq 0 \text{ and } g_3(x_1, x_2) = x_1 + x_2 \leq 2. \tag{10.28}$$

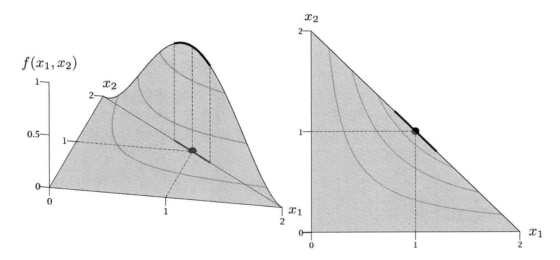

Figure 10.3: The second-order necessary condition for problem (10.28).

The panels in Figure 10.3 display the problem. $\tilde{x} = (1, 1)$ is a locally optimal solution. Only the third constraint binds at $\tilde{x} = (1, 1)$, so the Karush-Kuhn-Tucker condition is

$$\nabla f(\tilde{x}) = (2\tilde{x}_1\tilde{x}_2^2, 2\tilde{x}_1^2\tilde{x}_2) = (2, 2) = \tilde{\lambda}_3 \nabla g_3(\tilde{x}) = \tilde{\lambda}_3(1, 1) \ \Rightarrow \ \tilde{\lambda}_3 = 2 > 0. \quad (10.29)$$

The perturbations $\Delta x = (\Delta x_1, \Delta x_2)$ that preserve feasibility and keep the binding constraint binding in a small neighborhood about $(1, 1)$ must satisfy

$$b_3 = 2 = g_3((1, 1) + \Delta x) = g_3(1, 1) + \nabla g_3(1, 1) \cdot \Delta x + \frac{1}{2} \Delta x^T H_{g_3}(x)|_{x=(1,1)} \Delta x,$$

which, since $g_3(1, 1) = 2$, $\nabla g_3(1, 1) = (1, 1)$ and $H_{g_3}(1, 1) = \left(\begin{smallmatrix} 0 & 0 \\ 0 & 0 \end{smallmatrix}\right)$, is the requirement that each Δx satisfies

$$0 = \Delta x_1 + \Delta x_2 \quad \Rightarrow \quad \Delta x_1 = -\Delta x_2. \quad (10.30)$$

The second-order necessary local maximality condition (10.18) is therefore

$$(\Delta x_1, \Delta x_2) \left(\left(\begin{matrix} 2\tilde{x}_2^2 & 4\tilde{x}_1\tilde{x}_2 \\ 4\tilde{x}_1\tilde{x}_2 & 2\tilde{x}_1^2 \end{matrix} \right) \Bigg|_{\tilde{x}=(1,1)} - \tilde{\lambda}_3 \left(\begin{matrix} 0 & 0 \\ 0 & 0 \end{matrix} \right) \Bigg|_{\tilde{\lambda}_3=2} \right) \left(\begin{matrix} \Delta x_1 \\ \Delta x_2 \end{matrix} \right)$$

$$= (\Delta x_1, \Delta x_2) \left(\begin{matrix} 2 & 4 \\ 4 & 2 \end{matrix} \right) \left(\begin{matrix} \Delta x_1 \\ \Delta x_2 \end{matrix} \right)$$

$$= 2 \left(\Delta x_1^2 + 4\Delta x_1 \Delta x_2 + \Delta x_2^2 \right) \quad (10.31)$$

$$= -4 \left(\Delta x_1 \right)^2 \leq 0 \text{ for } \Delta x_1 = -\Delta x_2 \text{ (see (10.30))}. \quad (10.32)$$

What does it mean? Around $(1,1)$, the feasibility-preserving perturbations that keep the constraint $x_1 + x_2 = 2$ binding are perturbations from $(1,1)$ only along the line $x_1 + x_2 = 2$; thus $\Delta x_1 = -\Delta x_2$. Think, then, of a small interval on that line around $(1,1)$, as is indicated in both panels of Figure 10.3 by the short thicker lines. For the points (x_1, x_2) in this interval, the equation of the objective function is

$$\psi(x_1) \equiv f(x_1, x_2 = 2 - x_1) = x_1^2(2 - x_1)^2 = x_1^4 - 4x_1^3 + 4x_1^2. \tag{10.33}$$

The values at $(x_1, x_2) = (1,1)$ of the first-order and second-order derivatives of this function are $\psi'(x_1) = 4x_1^3 - 12x_1^2 + 8x_1 = 0$ for $x_1 = 1$ and $\psi''(x_1) = 12x_1^2 - 24x_1 + 8 = -4 < 0$ for $x_1 = 1$. Thus, over this small interval, the first-order necessary and the second-order necessary local optimality conditions are true. Notice that the Lagrange function

$$L(x_1, x_2, \lambda_1, \lambda_2, \lambda_3) = x_1^2 x_2^2 + \lambda_1 x_1 + \lambda_2 x_2 + \lambda_3(2 - x_1 - x_2)$$

becomes

$$L^r(x_1, x_2; 0, 0, 2) = x_1^2 x_2^2 + 2(2 - x_1 - x_2)$$

once the function is restricted by setting $\lambda_1 = \tilde{\lambda}_1 = 0$, $\lambda_2 = \tilde{\lambda}_2 = 0$, and $\lambda_3 = \tilde{\lambda}_3 = 2$. Thus the restricted Lagrange function

$$L^r(x_1, x_2; 0, 0, 2) \equiv \psi(x_1)$$

on the set $\{(x_1, x_2) \mid x_1 + x_2 = 2\}$.

Now consider a new problem that is similar to the first, differing only in that the third constraint has been changed:

$$\max_{x_1, x_2} f(x_1, x_2) = x_1^2 x_2^2 \text{ subject to } g_1(x_1) = -x_1 \leq 0,$$

$$g_2(x_2) = -x_2 \leq 0, \text{ and } g_3(x_1, x_2) = x_1^2 + x_2^2 \leq 2. \tag{10.34}$$

The panels in Figure 10.4 display the problem. $\tilde{x} = (1,1)$ is again a locally optimal solution. Only the third constraint binds at $\tilde{x}$, so the Karush-Kuhn-Tucker condition is

$$\nabla f(\tilde{x}) = (2\tilde{x}_1 \tilde{x}_2^2, 2\tilde{x}_1^2 \tilde{x}_2) = (2, 2) = \tilde{\lambda}_3 \nabla g_3(\tilde{x}) = \tilde{\lambda}_3(2\tilde{x}_1, 2\tilde{x}_2) = \tilde{\lambda}_3(2, 2)$$

$$\Rightarrow \tilde{\lambda}_3 = 1 > 0. \tag{10.35}$$

The feasibility-preserving perturbations $\Delta x = (\Delta x_1, \Delta x_2)$ that keep the third constraint binding in a small neighborhood about $(1,1)$ must again satisfy

$$b_3 = 2 = g_3((1,1) + \Delta x) = g_3(1,1) + \nabla g_3(1,1) \cdot \Delta x + \frac{1}{2} \Delta x^T H_{g_3}(x)|_{x=(1,1)} \Delta x,$$

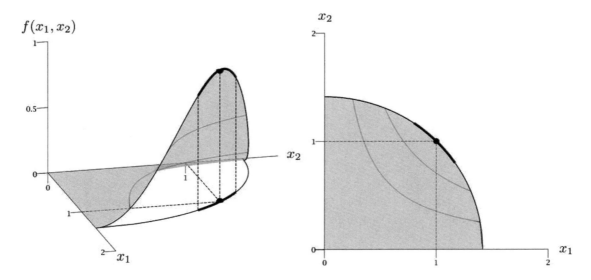

Figure 10.4: The second-order necessary condition for problem (10.34).

which, since $g_3(1,1) = 2$, $\nabla g_3(1,1) = (2,2)$, and $H_{g_3}(1,1) \equiv \left(\begin{smallmatrix} 2 & 0 \\ 0 & 2 \end{smallmatrix}\right)$, is now the requirement that each Δx satisfies

$$0 = 2\Delta x_1 + 2\Delta x_2 + (\Delta x_1)^2 + (\Delta x_2)^2. \tag{10.36}$$

The second-order necessary local maximality condition (10.18) is that

$$\begin{aligned} Q &= (\Delta x_1, \Delta x_2) \left(\left(\begin{matrix} 2\tilde{x}_2^2 & 4\tilde{x}_1\tilde{x}_2 \\ 4\tilde{x}_1\tilde{x}_2 & 2\tilde{x}_1^2 \end{matrix}\right)\Bigg|_{\tilde{x}=(1,1)} - \tilde{\lambda}_3 \left(\begin{matrix} 2 & 0 \\ 0 & 2 \end{matrix}\right)\Bigg|_{\tilde{\lambda}_3=1} \right) \left(\begin{matrix} \Delta x_1 \\ \Delta x_2 \end{matrix}\right) \\ &= (\Delta x_1, \Delta x_2) \left(\begin{matrix} 0 & 4 \\ 4 & 0 \end{matrix}\right) \left(\begin{matrix} \Delta x_1 \\ \Delta x_2 \end{matrix}\right) \\ &= 8\Delta x_1 \Delta x_2 \leq 0 \end{aligned} \tag{10.37}$$

for every small enough perturbation $(\Delta x_1, \Delta x_2)$ that satisfies (10.36). Is this so? Rearranging (10.36) gives

$$\Delta x_2 = -1 + \sqrt{2 - (\Delta x_1 + 1)^2}. \tag{10.38}$$

Using this for Δx_2 in (10.37) gives

$$Q = 8\Delta x_1 \left(-1 + \sqrt{2 - (\Delta x_1 + 1)^2} \right).$$

It is easy to see that $Q = 0$ for $\Delta x_1 = 0$ and that $Q < 0$ for $\Delta x_1 \in [-1, 0) \cup (0, \sqrt{2}-1]$, so there do exist small enough, strictly positive values for ε for which the second-order necessary condition is satisfied. Another way to verify this is to recognize that the objective function defined only on the set $\{(x_1, x_2) \mid x_1^2 + x_2^2 = 2\}$ is the function

$$\theta(x_1) \equiv f\left(x_1, x_2 = \sqrt{2 - x_1^2}\right) = x_1^2(2 - x_1^2).$$

$\theta'(x_1) = 4x_1(1 - x_1^2) = 0$ for $x_1 = 0$ and $x_1 = 1$ ($x_1 = -1$ violates the first constraint). But $\theta''(x_1) = 4(1 - 3x_1^2) > 0$ for $x_1 = 0$, while $\theta''(1) < 0$. Thus $\theta(x_1)$ achieves a local maximum at $x_1 = 1$ (thus $x_2 = 1$) on the set $\{(x_1, x_2) \in \Re_+^2 \mid x_1^2 + x_2^2 = 2\}$. Because at $\tilde{x} = (1, 1)$ the Lagrange multiplier values are $\tilde{\lambda}_1 = 0$, $\tilde{\lambda}_2 = 0$, and $\tilde{\lambda}_3 = 1$, the restricted Lagrange function is

$$L^r(x_1, x_2; \tilde{\lambda}_1, \tilde{\lambda}_2, \tilde{\lambda}_3) = x_1^2 x_2^2 + 2 - x_1^2 - x_2^2 \equiv \theta(x_1)$$

on the set $\{(x_1, x_2) \in \Re_+^2 \mid x_1^2 + x_2^2 = 2\}$.

The necessary conditions (10.32) and (10.37) are not the same. Why not? After all, the two problems have the same objective function $f(x_1, x_2) = x_1^2 x_2^2$, the same locally optimal solution $\tilde{x} = (1, 1)$, only one constraint binds, and the gradients of the binding constraint in each example point in exactly the same direction at $\tilde{x} = (1, 1)$. The second-order necessary condition for the first problem tells us that the objective function $f(x_1, x_2) = x_1^2 x_2^2$ *restricted to points* $(x_1, x_2) = (1 + \Delta x_1, 1 + \Delta x_2)$ *on the path* $x_1 + x_2 = 2$ necessarily is weakly concave in a small enough neighborhood on this path about the point $(1, 1)$. The second-order necessary condition for the second problem tells us that the objective function $f(x_1, x_2) = x_1^2 x_2^2$ *restricted to points* $(x_1, x_2) = (1 + \Delta x_1, 1 + \Delta x_2)$ *on the path* $x_1^2 + x_2^2 = 2$ necessarily is weakly concave in a small enough neighborhood on this *different* path about the point $(1, 1)$. The left-hand panel of Figure 10.3 displays the objective function's graph over the path $x_1 + x_2 = 2$. The left-hand panel of Figure 10.4 displays the objective function's graph over the path $x_1^2 + x_2^2 = 2$. Clearly the two graphs are different, even though they both achieve the same maximum value $f(1, 1) = 1$ at the same point $(1, 1)$.

It is sometimes asserted that the necessary second-order condition says that the objective function of the constrained optimization problem is locally (at least weakly) concave at a local optimum. This is false, as the two above examples demonstrate. For either problem, look at the graph of the objective function above the line from the origin to the point $(1, 1)$. This is the line along which $x_1 = x_2$, so the objective function has the equation $f(x_1) = x_1^4$ along this path. This is a strictly convex function, including at and near to the point $(1, 1)$. What *is* true is that, "at a local optimum $\tilde{x}$, the objective function necessarily is locally (at least weakly) concave along any path from $\tilde{x}$ that keeps binding all of the constraints that bind at $\tilde{x}$."

Another false assertion is that the necessary second-order condition says that the restricted Lagrange function of the constrained optimization problem is locally (at least weakly) concave at a local optimum. Both of the above examples demonstrate that this is not true. Once again, for either problem, look at the graph of the objective function above the line $x_1 = x_2$ from the origin to the point $(1, 1)$. In the first example, the restricted Lagrange function $L^r(x_1, x_2; \tilde{\lambda})$ with $x_1 = x_2$ is

$$L^r(x_1, x_1; 0, 0, 2) = x_1^4 + 2(2 - 2x_1) = x_1^4 - 4x_1 + 4.$$

This is a strictly convex function for any $x_1 > 0$, including at and near to $x_1 = 1$. Similarly, in the second example, the restricted Lagrange function $L^r(x_1, x_2; \tilde{\lambda})$ with $x_1 = x_2$ is

$$L^r(x_1, x_1; 0, 0, 1) = x_1^4 + 2 - 2x_1^2.$$

This too is a strictly convex function at and near to $x_1 = 1$. Again, what is true is that, "at a local optimum $\tilde{x}$, the problem's restricted Lagrange function $L^r(x_1, x_2; \tilde{\lambda})$ necessarily is locally (at least weakly) concave along any path from $\tilde{x}$ that keeps binding all of the constraints that bind at $\tilde{x}$."

Why are the above two statements in quotation marks so similar even though the first refers to the problem's objective function and the second refers to the problem's restricted Lagrange function? It is because the two statements are the same statement. Along any path from $\tilde{x}$ that keeps binding all of the constraints that bind at $\tilde{x}$, the problem's objective function $f(x_1, x_2)$ and the problem's restricted Lagrange function $L^r(x_1, x_2; \tilde{\lambda})$ are the same. Why?

A third example will further improve your understanding of the necessary second-order condition. The problem is:

$$\max_{x_1, x_2} f(x_1, x_2) = (x_1 + 1)^2 + (x_2 + 1)^2 \quad \text{subject to}$$
$$g_1(x_1) = -x_1 \leq 0, \ g_2(x_2) = -x_2 \leq 0, \ \text{and} \ g_3(x_1, x_2) = x_1^2 + x_2^2 \leq 2. \tag{10.39}$$

Figure 10.5 displays the problem. $\tilde{x} = (1, 1)$ is a locally optimal solution. Clearly $\tilde{\lambda}_1 = \tilde{\lambda}_2 = 0$. The Karush-Kuhn-Tucker condition is

$$\nabla f(1, 1) = (2(x_1 + 1), 2(x_2 + 1))|_{x=(1,1)} = (4, 4) = \tilde{\lambda}_3 \nabla g_3(1, 1)$$
$$= \tilde{\lambda}_3 (2x_1, 2x_2)|_{x=(1,1)} = \tilde{\lambda}_3 (2, 2).$$

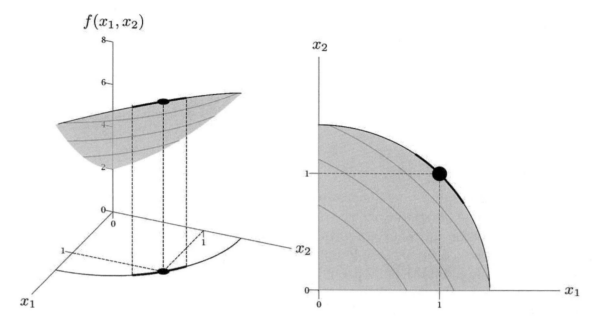

Figure 10.5: The second-order necessary condition for problem (10.39).

Thus $\tilde{\lambda}_3 = 2 > 0$. The restricted Lagrange function is

$$L^r(x; \tilde{\lambda}) = L^r(x_1, x_2; 0, 0, 2) = (x_1 + 1)^2 + (x_2 + 1)^2 + 2(2 - x_1^2 - x_2^2).$$

The Hessian matrix of this function is constant-valued on $\Re_+^2$, and is

$$H_{L^r}(x; \tilde{\lambda}) \equiv \begin{pmatrix} -2 & 0 \\ 0 & -2 \end{pmatrix}.$$

The matrix is negative-definite (thus negative-semi-definite), so the necessary second-order condition is satisfied. The objective function $f(x_1, x_2) = (x_1 + 1)^2 + (x_2 + 1)^2$ is strictly convex everywhere on $\Re_+^2$, so this example makes the point that the necessary second-order condition does not imply that the constrained optimization problem's objective function must be even weakly concave. However, the problem's objective function constrained to the set $\{(\Delta x_1, \Delta x_2) \mid (1 + \Delta x_1)^2 + (1 + \Delta x_2)^2 = 2\}$ is concave. Let's see why. From (10.38),

$$\Gamma(\Delta x_1) \equiv f(1 + \Delta x_1, 1 + \Delta x_2) = (2 + \Delta x_1)^2 + (2 + \Delta x_2)^2$$
$$= 6 + 2\Delta x_1 + 2\sqrt{2 - (1 + \Delta x_1)^2}.$$

The first-order derivative of this function is

$$\Gamma'(\Delta x_1) = 2 - \frac{2(1 + \Delta x_1)}{\sqrt{2 - (1 + \Delta x_1)^2}} \, .$$

$\Gamma'(\Delta x_1) = 0$ for $\Delta x_1 = 0$. The second-order derivative of Γ is

$$\Gamma''(\Delta x_1) = - \frac{4}{(2 - (1 + \Delta x_1)^2)^{3/2}} < 0$$

for $-1 - \sqrt{2} < \Delta x_1 < \sqrt{2} - 1$. Thus, as we saw in the first two examples, the problem's restricted Lagrange function, with the multipliers fixed at the values $\tilde{\lambda}$ that satisfy the problem's first-order optimality conditions at $\tilde{x}$, necessarily is at least weakly concave in a neighborhood about the locally optimal point $\tilde{x}$ when the function is confined to the set of feasible points that keep binding all of the constraints that bind at $\tilde{x}$.

All of the examples so far have in common that only one constraint binds at the local optimum. The next, and last, example changes that. Figure 10.6 displays the solution to the problem:

$$\max_{x_1, x_2} f(x_1, x_2) = x_1 x_2 \text{ subject to } g_1(x_1) = -x_1 \le 0, \ g_2(x_2) = -x_2 \le 0,$$
$$g_3(x_1, x_2) = x_1 + 2x_2 \le 3, \text{ and } g_4(x_1, x_2) = 2x_1 + x_2 \le 3. \tag{10.40}$$

Once again $\tilde{x} = (1, 1)$ is a locally optimal solution. At this point both the constraints g_3 and g_4 bind. Evaluated at $(1, 1)$, the gradients of f, g_3 and g_4 are $\nabla f(1, 1) = (1, 1)$, $\nabla g_3(1, 1) = (1, 2)$, and $\nabla g_4(1, 1) = (2, 1)$. The Karush-Kuhn-Tucker condition is thus

$$(1, 1) = (\tilde{\lambda}_3, \tilde{\lambda}_4) \begin{pmatrix} 1 & 2 \\ 2 & 1 \end{pmatrix} \quad \Rightarrow \quad \tilde{\lambda}_3 = \tilde{\lambda}_4 = \frac{1}{3} \, .$$

The problem's restricted Lagrange function $L^r(x; \tilde{\lambda})$ for this local optimum is therefore

$$L^r(x_1, x_2; 0, 0, 1/3, 1/3) = x_1 x_2 + \frac{1}{3}(3 - x_1 - 2x_2) + \frac{1}{3}(3 - 2x_1 - x_2)$$
$$= x_1 x_2 - x_1 - x_2 + 2.$$

Evaluated at $\tilde{x} = (1, 1)$, the Hessian matrix of this restricted Lagrange function is

$$H_{L^r}(x; \tilde{\lambda})|_{x=(1,1)} = \begin{pmatrix} 0 & 1 \\ 1 & 0 \end{pmatrix} .$$

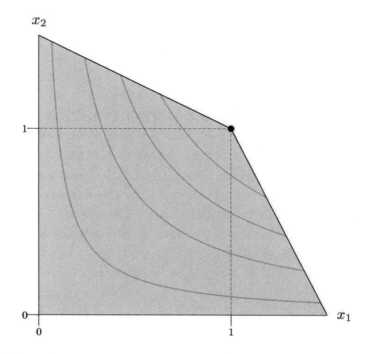

Figure 10.6: The only perturbation that keeps both constraints binding is $(0,0)$.

The second-order necessary condition is that there is an $\varepsilon > 0$ such that

$$(\Delta x_1, \Delta x_2) \begin{pmatrix} 0 & 1 \\ 1 & 0 \end{pmatrix} \begin{pmatrix} \Delta x_1 \\ \Delta x_2 \end{pmatrix} = 2\Delta x_1 \Delta x_2 \leq 0 \tag{10.41}$$

$\forall \, (\Delta x_1, \Delta x_2)$ satisfying $(1 + \Delta x_1, 1 + \Delta x_2) \in B_{d_E}((1,1), \varepsilon)$,

$$1 + \Delta x_1 + 2(1 + \Delta x_2) = 3 \;\Rightarrow\; \Delta x_1 = -2\Delta x_2, \tag{10.42}$$

$$\text{and } 2(1 + \Delta x_1) + 1 + \Delta x_2 = 3 \;\Rightarrow\; 2\Delta x_1 = -\Delta x_2. \tag{10.43}$$

The *only* values for Δx_1 and Δx_2 that satisfy (10.42) and (10.43) are $\Delta x_1 = \Delta x_2 = 0$. Thus there are no feasibility-preserving perturbations Δx to consider in this case – the necessary second-order condition is true, but only trivially. How would we know when we are dealing with such a case? The answer is not complex. In our present example we have two linearly independent affine constraints g_3 and g_4 that bind at $(1,1)$. Since we have only two choice variables, x_1 and x_2, there is just one point at which these two constraints bind, so the only feasibility-preserving perturbations are the "non-perturbations" $\Delta x_1 = \Delta x_2 = 0$. In each of our three earlier examples, there are nontrivial perturbations that keep the binding constraint binding. If, as in our last example, the constraints that bind at a local optimum $\tilde{x}$ do so only at a single point, then the only allowed feasibility-preserving perturbations are $\Delta x_1 = \cdots = \Delta x_n = 0$, and the second-order necessary condition is true, but only trivially and uninformatively.

10.4   Second-Order Necessary Condition Testing

Suppose we have solved the first-order optimality conditions for a constrained optimization problem and that $\tilde{x}$ is one of the solutions. How can we check if the value at $x = \tilde{x}$ of the Hessian matrix of the function $L^r(x; \tilde{\lambda})$ is negative-semi-definite for all small enough perturbations Δx from $\tilde{x}$ that keep binding all of the constraints that bind at $\tilde{x}$? You have already seen some simple examples of how to do it. In general you need, first, to find for a small enough $\varepsilon > 0$ the set of perturbations that keep binding all of the constraints that bind at $\tilde{x}$. This set is

$$\Delta(\tilde{x}, \varepsilon) \equiv \{\Delta x \in \Re^n \mid g_j(\tilde{x} + \Delta x) = b_j \ \forall \ j \in I(\tilde{x}) \text{ and } \tilde{x} + \Delta x \in B_{d_E}(\tilde{x}, \varepsilon)\}.$$

Then you must determine if the function $L^r(\tilde{x} + \Delta x; \tilde{\lambda})$ is at least weakly concave on the set $\Delta(\tilde{x}, \varepsilon)$. With complicated problems, you may need to do this numerically. But there is a special case in which this computation is relatively easy. It is the case in which all of the constraints that bind at a local optimum are linear functions of $x_1, \ldots, x_n$; i.e. each binding constraint g_j is of the form $g_j(x) = a_{j1}x_1 + \cdots + a_{jn}x_n$, where $a_{j1}, \ldots, a_{jn}$ are constants. The requirement that a perturbation Δx keeps such a constraint binding is

$$b_j = g_j(\tilde{x} + \Delta x) = g_j(\tilde{x}) + \nabla g_j(\tilde{x}) \cdot \Delta x = b_j + \nabla g_j(\tilde{x}) \cdot \Delta x$$
$$\Rightarrow \nabla g_j(\tilde{x}) \cdot \Delta x = (a_{j1}, \ldots, a_{jn}) \cdot (\Delta x_1, \ldots, \Delta x_n) = 0. \tag{10.44}$$

Hence, whenever all of the constraints that bind at a local optimum $\tilde{x}$ are linear functions of x, statement (10.26) and (10.27) becomes, "If $\tilde{x}$ is a local maximizer for f subject to $g_1(x) \leq b_1, \ldots, g_m(x) \leq b_m$, then necessarily there is an $\varepsilon > 0$ for which

$$\Delta x^T H_{L^r}(x; \tilde{\lambda})|_{x=\tilde{x}} \Delta x \leq 0 \tag{10.45}$$

$\forall \ \Delta x$ such that $\tilde{x} + \Delta x \in B_{d_E}(\tilde{x}, \varepsilon)$, and $\nabla g_j(\tilde{x}) \cdot \Delta x = 0$ for all $j = 1, \ldots, k$."

$$\tag{10.46}$$

The condition that $\nabla g_j(\tilde{x}) \cdot \Delta x = 0$ for all $j = 1, \ldots, k$ is the same as $J_g(\tilde{x}) \Delta x = \underline{0}_k$, where $J_g(\tilde{x})$ is the value at $x = \tilde{x}$ of the Jacobian matrix formed from the gradients of the constraints that bind at $x = \tilde{x}$. Checking if (10.45) is true subject to the conditions (10.46) is relatively easy thanks to a theorem we will see shortly. The theorem relies upon determinants formed from a matrix called a *bordered Hessian* that we will denote by $\overline{H}$. $\overline{H}$ is the Hessian with respect to $x_1, \ldots, x_n$ of the restricted Lagrange function $L^r(x; \hat{\lambda})$, augmented, on the left and top sides, by a border consisting of the gradient vectors of the constraints that bind at $x = \tilde{x}$. The border is thus the Jacobian matrix consisting of the gradient vectors of the constraints that bind at $\tilde{x}$. If no constraint binds at $x = \tilde{x}$, then there is no border, and the "bordered" Hessian is the unbordered Hessian of the restricted Lagrange function.

Definition 10.1 (Bordered Hessian Matrix). *Let $\tilde{x} \in \mathcal{C}$. Let $I(\tilde{x})$ denote the set of indices of the constraints $g_1, \ldots, g_m$ that bind at $\tilde{x}$. Let $\overline{H}_{L^r}(\tilde{x}; \tilde{\lambda})$ denote the value at $x = \tilde{x}$ of the bordered Hessian of $L^r(x; \tilde{\lambda})$.*

If $I(\tilde{x}) = \emptyset$, then $\overline{H}_{L^r}(\tilde{x}; \tilde{\lambda}) = H_f(\tilde{x})$. If $I(\tilde{x}) \neq \emptyset$, then let $I(\tilde{x}) = \{1, \ldots, k\}$ for $1 \leq k \leq m$. Then

$$\overline{H}_{L^r}(\tilde{x}; \tilde{\lambda}) = \begin{pmatrix} 0 & \cdots & 0 & \frac{\partial g_1(x)}{\partial x_1} & \cdots & \frac{\partial g_1(x)}{\partial x_n} \\ \vdots & \ddots & \vdots & \vdots & & \vdots \\ 0 & \cdots & 0 & \frac{\partial g_k(x)}{\partial x_1} & \cdots & \frac{\partial g_k(x)}{\partial x_n} \\ \frac{\partial g_1(x)}{\partial x_1} & \cdots & \frac{\partial g_k(x)}{\partial x_1} & \frac{\partial^2 L^r(x; \tilde{\lambda})}{\partial x_1^2} & \cdots & \frac{\partial^2 L^r(x; \tilde{\lambda})}{\partial x_1 \partial x_n} \\ \vdots & & \vdots & \vdots & \ddots & \vdots \\ \frac{\partial g_1(x)}{\partial x_n} & \cdots & \frac{\partial g_k(x)}{\partial x_n} & \frac{\partial^2 L^r(x; \tilde{\lambda})}{\partial x_n \partial x_1} & \cdots & \frac{\partial^2 L^r(x; \tilde{\lambda})}{\partial x_n^2} \end{pmatrix} =$$

$$\begin{pmatrix} 0 & \cdots & 0 & \frac{\partial g_1(x)}{\partial x_1} & \cdots & \frac{\partial g_1(x)}{\partial x_n} \\ \vdots & \ddots & \vdots & \vdots & & \vdots \\ 0 & \cdots & 0 & \frac{\partial g_k(x)}{\partial x_1} & \cdots & \frac{\partial g_k(x)}{\partial x_n} \\ \frac{\partial g_1(x)}{\partial x_1} & \cdots & \frac{\partial g_k(x)}{\partial x_1} & \frac{\partial^2 f(x)}{\partial x_1^2} - \sum_{j=1}^{k} \tilde{\lambda}_j \frac{\partial^2 g_j(x)}{\partial x_1^2} & \cdots & \frac{\partial^2 f(x)}{\partial x_n \partial x_1} - \sum_{j=1}^{k} \tilde{\lambda}_j \frac{\partial^2 g_j(x)}{\partial x_n \partial x_1} \\ \vdots & & \vdots & \vdots & \ddots & \vdots \\ \frac{\partial g_1(x)}{\partial x_n} & \cdots & \frac{\partial g_k(x)}{\partial x_n} & \frac{\partial^2 f(x)}{\partial x_1 \partial x_n} - \sum_{j=1}^{k} \tilde{\lambda}_j \frac{\partial^2 g_j(x)}{\partial x_1 \partial x_n} & \cdots & \frac{\partial^2 f(x)}{\partial x_n^2} - \sum_{j=1}^{k} \tilde{\lambda}_j \frac{\partial^2 g_j(x)}{\partial x_n^2} \end{pmatrix},$$

$$(10.47)$$

where all of the derivatives are evaluated at $x = \tilde{x}$.

The bordered Hessian is a square order-$(k + n)$ matrix that is made up of four blocks. The upper-left $k \times k$ block is the order-k zero matrix, 0_k. The upper-right $k \times n$ block is the Jacobian matrix $J_g(x)$, evaluated at $x = \tilde{x}$, that is formed by the gradient vectors of the constraints that bind at $x = \tilde{x}$. The lower-left $n \times k$ block is the transpose of this Jacobian, $J_g(\tilde{x})^T$. The lower-right $n \times n$ block is $H_{L^r}(\tilde{x}; \tilde{\lambda})$, the value at $x = \tilde{x}$ of the Hessian matrix of $L^r(x; \tilde{\lambda})$. It is often notationally convenient to write the bordered Hessian in its "block form," which is

$$\overline{H}_{L^r}(\tilde{x}; \tilde{\lambda}) = \begin{pmatrix} 0_k & J_g(x) \\ J_g(x)^T & H_{L^r}(x; \tilde{\lambda}) \end{pmatrix} \Bigg|_{x=\tilde{x}}. \tag{10.48}$$

Sometimes the bordered Hessian is written with the borders at the right side and the bottom of the matrix; *i.e.*

$$\overline{H}_{L^r}(\tilde{x}; \tilde{\lambda}) = \begin{pmatrix} H_{L^r}(x; \tilde{\lambda} & J_g(x)^T \\ J_g(x) & 0_k \end{pmatrix} \Bigg|_{x=\tilde{x}}.$$

This form of the matrix is just as useful as (10.48), so choose whichever you wish. If you choose this second form, then you will need to rewrite for yourself the determinants that I will introduce to you in a moment (doing so is a simple exercise that will help to develop your understanding).

It will help if we work with an example. Let's use the problem:

$$\max_{x \in \Re^3} f(x_1, x_2, x_3) = x_1 x_2 x_3 \text{ subject to } g_1(x_1) = -x_1 \leq 0, \ g_2(x_2) = -x_2 \leq 0,$$

$$g_3(x_3) = -x_3 \leq 0, \text{ and } g_4(x_1, x_2, x_3) = 3x_1 + x_2 + x_3 \leq 9. \tag{10.49}$$

Verify for yourself that $(\tilde{x}_1, \tilde{x}_2, \tilde{x}_3) = (1, 3, 3)$ is a locally optimal solution to this problem, that only the fourth constraint binds at $\tilde{x} = (1, 3, 3)$, and that the associated values of the multipliers are $\tilde{\lambda}_1 = \tilde{\lambda}_2 = \tilde{\lambda}_3 = 0$, and $\tilde{\lambda}_4 = 3$. The value at $\tilde{x} = (1, 3, 3)$ of the bordered Hessian matrix for this problem is therefore

$$\overline{H}_{L^r}(\tilde{x}; \tilde{\lambda}) = \begin{pmatrix} 0 & 3 & 1 & 1 \\ 3 & 0 & \tilde{x}_3 & \tilde{x}_2 \\ 1 & \tilde{x}_3 & 0 & \tilde{x}_1 \\ 1 & \tilde{x}_2 & \tilde{x}_1 & 0 \end{pmatrix} = \begin{pmatrix} 0 & 3 & 1 & 1 \\ 3 & 0 & 3 & 3 \\ 1 & 3 & 0 & 1 \\ 1 & 3 & 1 & 0 \end{pmatrix}. \tag{10.50}$$

Strange as it may seem, the properties of the bordered Hessian matrix describe completely the necessary second-order local optimality condition (10.45) and (10.46). The information that we require to test the condition is provided by the signs of particular determinants formed from the elements of the bordered Hessian. These determinants are called the *bordered principal minors* of the bordered Hessian.

Definition 10.2 (Bordered Principal Minor). *For $i = 1, \ldots, n$, let $\pi_i = \{l_1, \ldots, l_i\}$ be any permutation of i integers from the set $\{1, \ldots, n\}$. Let*

$$A(\pi_i) = \begin{pmatrix} \dfrac{\partial g_1}{\partial x_{l_1}} & \dfrac{\partial g_1}{\partial x_{l_2}} & \cdots & \dfrac{\partial g_1}{\partial x_{l_i}} \\[2mm] \dfrac{\partial g_2}{\partial x_{l_1}} & \dfrac{\partial g_2}{\partial x_{l_2}} & \cdots & \dfrac{\partial g_2}{\partial x_{l_i}} \\[2mm] \vdots & \vdots & & \vdots \\[2mm] \dfrac{\partial g_k}{\partial x_{l_1}} & \dfrac{\partial g_k}{\partial x_{l_2}} & \cdots & \dfrac{\partial g_k}{\partial x_{l_i}} \end{pmatrix}.$$

Let

$$B(\pi_i) = \begin{pmatrix} \dfrac{\partial^2 L^r(x;\tilde{\lambda})}{\partial x_{l_1}^2} & \dfrac{\partial^2 L^r(x;\tilde{\lambda})}{\partial x_{l_2}\partial x_{l_1}} & \cdots & \dfrac{\partial^2 L^r(x;\tilde{\lambda})}{\partial x_{l_i}\partial x_{l_1}} \\[3mm] \dfrac{\partial^2 L^r(x;\tilde{\lambda})}{\partial x_{l_1}\partial x_{l_2}} & \dfrac{\partial^2 L^r(x;\tilde{\lambda})}{\partial x_{l_2}^2} & \cdots & \dfrac{\partial^2 L^r(x;\tilde{\lambda})}{\partial x_{l_i}\partial x_{l_2}} \\[3mm] \vdots & \vdots & \ddots & \vdots \\[3mm] \dfrac{\partial^2 L^r(x;\tilde{\lambda})}{\partial x_{l_1}\partial x_{l_i}} & \dfrac{\partial^2 L^r(x;\tilde{\lambda})}{\partial x_{l_2}\partial x_{l_i}} & \cdots & \dfrac{\partial^2 L^r(x;\tilde{\lambda})}{\partial x_{l_i}^2} \end{pmatrix}.$$

The order-$(k + i)$ determinant

$$\overline{M}(\pi_i) = \det \begin{pmatrix} 0_k & A(\pi_i) \\ A(\pi_i)^T & B(\pi_i) \end{pmatrix} \tag{10.51}$$

is an order-$(k + i)$ bordered principal minor of $\overline{H}_{L^r}(x;\tilde{\lambda})$.

Consider again the bordered Hessian matrix (10.50). For this matrix, $k = 1$ and $n = 3$, so $i \in \{1, 2, 3\}$. Let's start with $i = 1$. The $^3P_1 = 3$ ordered ways of selecting one value from the set $\{1, 2, 3\}$ are the permutations $\pi_1 = \{1\}$, $\pi_1 = \{2\}$, and $\pi_1 = \{3\}$. Thus there are three bordered principal minors of order-2:

$$
\overline{M}(\{1\}) = \det \left. \begin{pmatrix} 0 & \dfrac{\partial g_4}{\partial x_1} \\[2mm] \dfrac{\partial g_4}{\partial x_1} & \dfrac{\partial^2 L^r(x; \tilde{\lambda})}{\partial x_1^2} \end{pmatrix} \right|_{\substack{x_1=1 \\ x_2=3 \\ x_3=3}} = \det \begin{pmatrix} 0 & 3 \\ 3 & 0 \end{pmatrix} = -9,
$$

$$
\overline{M}(\{2\}) = \det \left. \begin{pmatrix} 0 & \dfrac{\partial g_4}{\partial x_2} \\[2mm] \dfrac{\partial g_4}{\partial x_2} & \dfrac{\partial^2 L^r(x; \tilde{\lambda})}{\partial x_2^2} \end{pmatrix} \right|_{\substack{x_1=1 \\ x_2=3 \\ x_3=3}} = \det \begin{pmatrix} 0 & 1 \\ 1 & 0 \end{pmatrix} = -1, \qquad (10.52)
$$

$$
\text{and} \quad \overline{M}(\{3\}) = \det \left. \begin{pmatrix} 0 & \dfrac{\partial g_4}{\partial x_3} \\[2mm] \dfrac{\partial g_4}{\partial x_3} & \dfrac{\partial^2 L^r(x; \tilde{\lambda})}{\partial x_3^2} \end{pmatrix} \right|_{\substack{x_1=1 \\ x_2=3 \\ x_3=3}} = \det \begin{pmatrix} 0 & 1 \\ 1 & 0 \end{pmatrix} = -1.
$$

For $i = 2$, there are $^3P_2 = 6$ ordered ways of selecting two values from the set $\{1, 2, 3\}$. These are $\pi_2 = \{1, 2\}$, $\pi_2 = \{2, 1\}$, $\pi_2 = \{1, 3\}$, $\pi_2 = \{3, 1\}$, $\pi_2 = \{2, 3\}$, and $\pi_2 = \{3, 2\}$. The bordered principal minor created from the permutation $\pi_2 = \{3, 2\}$ is

$$
\overline{M}(\{3, 2\}) = \det \left. \begin{pmatrix} 0 & \dfrac{\partial g_4}{\partial x_3} & \dfrac{\partial g_4}{\partial x_2} \\[2mm] \dfrac{\partial g_4}{\partial x_3} & \dfrac{\partial^2 L^r(x; \tilde{\lambda})}{\partial x_3^2} & \dfrac{\partial^2 L^r(x; \tilde{\lambda})}{\partial x_3 \partial x_2} \\[2mm] \dfrac{\partial g_4}{\partial x_2} & \dfrac{\partial^2 L^r(x; \tilde{\lambda})}{\partial x_2 \partial x_3} & \dfrac{\partial^2 L^r(x; \tilde{\lambda})}{\partial x_2^2} \end{pmatrix} \right|_{\substack{x_1=1 \\ x_2=3 \\ x_3=3}} = \det \begin{pmatrix} 0 & 1 & 1 \\ 1 & 0 & 1 \\ 1 & 1 & 0 \end{pmatrix} = 2.
$$

$$
(10.53)
$$

The other five bordered principal minors of order-3 are:

$$\overline{M}(\{1,2\}) = \det \begin{pmatrix} 0 & 3 & 1 \\ 3 & 0 & 3 \\ 1 & 3 & 0 \end{pmatrix} = 18, \quad \overline{M}(\{2,1\}) = \det \begin{pmatrix} 0 & 1 & 3 \\ 1 & 0 & 3 \\ 3 & 3 & 0 \end{pmatrix} = 18,$$

$$\overline{M}(\{1,3\}) = \det \begin{pmatrix} 0 & 3 & 1 \\ 3 & 0 & 3 \\ 1 & 3 & 0 \end{pmatrix} = 18, \quad \overline{M}(\{3,1\}) = \det \begin{pmatrix} 0 & 1 & 3 \\ 1 & 0 & 3 \\ 3 & 3 & 0 \end{pmatrix} = 18, \quad (10.54)$$

$$\text{and } \overline{M}(\{2,3\}) = \det \begin{pmatrix} 0 & 1 & 1 \\ 1 & 0 & 1 \\ 1 & 1 & 0 \end{pmatrix} = 2.$$

For $i = 3$, there are $^3P_3 = 6$ ordered ways to select three numbers from the set $\{1, 2, 3\}$, so there are six bordered principal minors of order-4, but each has the same value. Why? When $i = n$, any permutation is a sequence of exchanges of the positions of full rows of the bordered Hessian accompanied by the same sequence of exchanges of the positions of full columns of the matrix. Each time you exchange the position of any two rows, you change the sign, but not the size, of the determinant of the Hessian. The same is true whenever you exchange the position of any two columns of the matrix. Thus any such sequences of pairs of exchanges (one row exchange accompanied by one column exchange) leaves the value of the determinant of the bordered Hessian unchanged, so we need compute only the value of any one of the Hessian's order-4 bordered principal minors, such as

$$\det \begin{pmatrix} 0 & 3 & 1 & 1 \\ 3 & 0 & 3 & 3 \\ 1 & 3 & 0 & 1 \\ 1 & 3 & 1 & 0 \end{pmatrix} = -27. \qquad (10.55)$$

How do we use the bordered principal minors to see if the necessary second-order local optimality condition (10.45) and (10.46) is true when all of the binding constraints are linear? The answer is supplied in the following theorem (see Debreu 1952).

Theorem 10.2 (Second-Order Necessary Condition Test). *Let $\tilde{x}$ be locally optimal for the constrained optimization problem (10.1). If the bordered Hessian matrix $\overline{H}_{L^r}(\tilde{x}; \tilde{\lambda})$ is symmetric, then there exists $\varepsilon > 0$ such that the quadratic form $\Delta x^T H_{L^r}(\tilde{x}; \tilde{\lambda}) \Delta x \leq 0$ for all perturbations Δx satisfying $\tilde{x} + \Delta x \in B_{d_E}(\tilde{x}, \varepsilon)$ and $\nabla g_j(\tilde{x}) \cdot \Delta x = 0$ for every $j \in I(\tilde{x})$, if and only if, for all $i = k+1, \ldots, n$, every bordered principal minor (10.51) of order-$(k + i)$ is either zero or has the same sign as $(-1)^i$.*

The theorem says that we do not need to check all of the bordered principal minors. Instead we must check the signs of only the minors with orders from $2k + 1$ to $k + n$. Recall that, in our example, $k = 1$ and $n = 3$. Thus we must check the signs of only the minors of order-3 and order-4. The six bordered principal minors of order-3 are all positive (see (10.53) and (10.54)) and so meet the condition of all being either zero or having the same sign as $(-1)^2$. Also, all six bordered principal minors of order-4 are negative and so meet the condition of being either zero or having the same sign as $(-1)^3$ (see (10.55)). Thus the second-order necessary local maximization condition is satisfied for $(\tilde{x}_1, \tilde{x}_2, \tilde{x}_3) = (1, 3, 3)$ (as it must be, since this is the globally optimal solution to problem (10.49)).

Note that Theorem 10.2 applies only to symmetric Hessian matrices. Recall that we have assumed that all of the functions $f, g_1, \ldots, g_m$ are twice-continuously differentiable with respect to x. This ensures that both the Hessian matrix H and the bordered Hessian matrix $\overline{H}$ are symmetric.

When all of the constraints that bind at $x = \tilde{x}$ are linear with respect to x, you may see the bordered Hessian matrix written as

$$\overline{H}(\tilde{x}; \tilde{\lambda}) = \begin{pmatrix} 0_k & J_g(x) \\ J_g^T(x) & H_f(x) \end{pmatrix} \bigg|_{x=\tilde{x}}, \qquad (10.56)$$

with the lower-right block being the Hessian matrix of the objective function f. When all of the binding constraints are linear in x, the restricted Lagrange function's Hessian matrix is the same as the Hessian matrix of the objective function, making (10.56) and (10.48) the same matrix.

10.5   Sufficient Conditions

The usual particular statement of conditions that together are sufficient for $\tilde{x}$ to be a local maximizer for f on $\mathcal{C}$ is that *every* point $\tilde{x} + \Delta x$ that is close to $\tilde{x}$, but not $\tilde{x}$, gives an objective function value $f(\tilde{x} + \Delta x)$ that is *strictly* less than $f(\tilde{x})$. That is, "If for some $\varepsilon > 0$

$$f(\tilde{x} + \Delta x) < f(\tilde{x}) \; \forall \; \Delta x \neq \underline{0} \text{ such that } \tilde{x} + \Delta x \in B_{d_E}(\tilde{x}, \varepsilon) \qquad (10.57)$$
$$\text{and } g_j(\tilde{x} + \Delta x) \leq b_j \; \forall \; j = 1, \ldots, m, \qquad (10.58)$$

then $\tilde{x}$ is a local maximizer for f on $\mathcal{C}$."

Again let $I(\tilde{x})$ be the set of the indices of the constraints that bind at $x = \tilde{x}$. If $I(\tilde{x}) = \emptyset$, then, as you already know, the conditions

$$\nabla f(\tilde{x}) = \underline{0} \text{ and } \Delta x^T H_f(\tilde{x}) \Delta x < 0 \text{ for all } \Delta x \neq \underline{0} \text{ satisfying } \tilde{x} + \Delta x \in B_{d_E}(\tilde{x}, \varepsilon)$$

for some $\varepsilon > 0$ are jointly sufficient for $\tilde{x}$ to be either an unconstrained local optimum for f or for $\tilde{x}$ to be an interior locally optimal solution to the constrained optimization problem (10.1).

If $I(\tilde{x}) \neq \emptyset$, then we can replicate the reasoning used in Section 10.2 to discover a sufficiency statement that uses a local strict concavity requirement for the problem's restricted Lagrange function. Again suppose that $I(\tilde{x}) = \{1, \ldots, k\}$, where $1 \leq k \leq m$. As before we use second-order Taylor's series approximations for each of $f, g_1, \ldots, g_k$ to write (10.57) and (10.58) as, "If, for some $\varepsilon > 0$,

$$\nabla f(\tilde{x}) \cdot \Delta x + \frac{1}{2} \Delta x^T H_f(\tilde{x}) \Delta x < 0 \ \forall \ \Delta x \neq \underline{0} \text{ such that} \qquad (10.59)$$

$$\tilde{x} + \Delta x \in B_{d_E}(\tilde{x}, \varepsilon) \text{ and } \nabla g_j(\tilde{x}) \cdot \Delta x + \frac{1}{2} \Delta x^T H_{g_j}(\tilde{x}) \Delta x \leq 0 \ \forall \ j = 1, \ldots, k, \quad (10.60)$$

then $\tilde{x}$ is a local maximizer for f on $\mathcal{C}$."

Suppose that $\tilde{x}$ is a regular point in the feasible set. Then $\tilde{x}$ cannot be a local optimum unless the first-order conditions are satisfied at $\tilde{x}$, so any set of conditions that together are sufficient for $\tilde{x}$ to be a local optimum must include that there exist nonnegative values $\tilde{\lambda}_1, \ldots, \tilde{\lambda}_m \geq 0$, not all zero, satisfying

$$\nabla f(\tilde{x}) = \sum_{j=1}^{m} \lambda_j \nabla g_j(\tilde{x}) \text{ and } \lambda_j(b_j - g_j(\tilde{x})) = 0 \text{ for all } j = 1, \ldots, m. \qquad (10.61)$$

We already know that the complementary slackness conditions require $\tilde{\lambda}_j = 0$ for every $j \notin I(\tilde{x})$. Thus we obtain from (10.59), (10.60), and (10.61) the statement that, "If there exist values $\tilde{\lambda}_1, \ldots, \tilde{\lambda}_k \geq 0$, not all zero, satisfying (10.61) and if, for some $\varepsilon > 0$,

$$\sum_{j=1}^{k} \tilde{\lambda}_j \nabla g_j(\tilde{x}) \cdot \Delta x + \frac{1}{2} \Delta x^T H_f(\tilde{x}) \Delta x < 0 \ \forall \ \Delta x \neq \underline{0} \text{ such that} \qquad (10.62)$$

$$\tilde{x} + \Delta x \in B_{d_E}(\tilde{x}, \varepsilon) \text{ and } \nabla g_j(\tilde{x}) \cdot \Delta x + \frac{1}{2} \Delta x^T H_{g_j}(\tilde{x}) \Delta x \leq 0 \ \forall \ j = 1, \ldots, k, \quad (10.63)$$

then $\tilde{x}$ is a local maximizer for f on $\mathcal{C}$."

Once we specialize by considering only perturbations Δx that keep binding the constraints that bind at $\tilde{x}$, the sufficiency statement becomes, "If there exist values $\tilde{\lambda}_1, \ldots, \tilde{\lambda}_k \geq 0$ satisfying (10.61) and if, for some $\varepsilon > 0$,

$$\sum_{j=1}^{k} \tilde{\lambda}_j \nabla g_j(\tilde{x}) \cdot \Delta x + \frac{1}{2} \Delta x^T H_f(\tilde{x}) \Delta x < 0 \ \forall \ \Delta x \neq \underline{0} \text{ such that} \tag{10.64}$$

$$\tilde{x} + \Delta x \in B_{d_E}(\tilde{x}, \varepsilon) \text{ and } \nabla g_j(\tilde{x}) \cdot \Delta x = -\frac{1}{2} \Delta x^T H_{g_j}(\tilde{x}) \Delta x \ \forall \ j = 1, \ldots, k, \tag{10.65}$$

then $\tilde{x}$ is a local maximizer for f on $\mathcal{C}$." This is the same as the statement, "If there exist values $\tilde{\lambda}_1, \ldots, \tilde{\lambda}_k \geq 0$ satisfying (10.61), and if, for some $\varepsilon > 0$,

$$\Delta x^T \left[H_f(\tilde{x}) - \tilde{\lambda}_1 \nabla g_1(\tilde{x}) - \cdots - \tilde{\lambda}_k \nabla g_k(\tilde{x}) \right] \Delta x < 0 \ \forall \ \Delta x \neq \underline{0} \text{ such that} \tag{10.66}$$

$$\tilde{x} + \Delta x \in B_{d_E}(\tilde{x}, \varepsilon) \text{ and } g_j(\tilde{x} + \Delta x) = b_j \ \forall \ j = 1, \ldots, k, \tag{10.67}$$

then $\tilde{x}$ is a local maximizer for f on $\mathcal{C}$."

The effort put into understanding the necessary second-order local optimality condition should make it not difficult for you to understand what this sufficiency statement asserts. First, the statement is a collection of conditions. Remove any one from the collection and you may not have a set of conditions sufficient for $\tilde{x}$ to be locally optimal. Second, all of the necessary conditions are an essential part of any set of collectively sufficient conditions. If it is not clear to you that this must be so, then think about it. Third, condition (10.67) is not quite the same as condition (10.27). Why not? The collectively sufficient conditions include that $\Delta x \neq \underline{0}$, whereas $\Delta x = \underline{0}$ is allowed in the necessary second-order condition. Fourth, condition (10.66) is a demand that, in small enough neighborhoods about $\tilde{x}$, the restricted Lagrange function $L^r(x; \tilde{\lambda})$ is *strictly* concave at every point $\tilde{x} + \Delta x$ for which the constraints that bind at $\tilde{x}$ also all bind at $\tilde{x} + \Delta x$. Note carefully that the demand is not that $L^r(x; \tilde{\lambda})$ is strictly concave at *every* neighboring point $\tilde{x} + \Delta x$. It is only that $L^r(x; \tilde{\lambda})$ is strictly concave at all neighboring point $\tilde{x} + \Delta x$ with Δx satisfying (10.67).

You will find it helpful to reconsider the examples (10.28), (10.34), and (10.39). Verify for each example that the entire collection (10.61), (10.66), and (10.67) of sufficiency conditions is satisfied, and therefore that each of the points $\tilde{x}$ mentioned in those examples truly is a local optimum. The set of sufficiency conditions does not apply to example (10.40) because, for that example, the only allowed perturbation is $\Delta x = (0, 0)$, which does not satisfy condition (10.67), which uses only nonzero perturbations. This does not imply that the point $x = (1, 1)$ is not a local optimum (it is), since it is only a set of *sufficiency* conditions that does not apply in this case.

10.6 Second-Order Sufficient Condition Testing

What is the procedure for applying the conditions (10.61), (10.66), and (10.67) in an effort to verify that a point $\tilde{x}$ is a local optimum? It is almost the same as the procedure for testing the necessary second-order local optimality condition. Once again the first step is to verify that there are small enough values of $\varepsilon > 0$ for which there are nonempty sets of *nonzero* perturbations that keep binding all of the constraints that bind at $\tilde{x}$. That is, you must verify that, for small enough values of $\varepsilon > 0$, the set

$$\overline{\Delta}(\tilde{x}, \varepsilon) \equiv \{\Delta x \in \Re^n \mid \Delta x \neq \underline{0},\ g_j(\tilde{x} + \Delta x) = b_j\ \forall\ j \in I(\tilde{x}),\ \tilde{x} + \Delta x \in B_{d_E}(\tilde{x}, \varepsilon)\} \neq \emptyset.$$

Then you must determine if the function $L(\tilde{x} + \Delta x; \tilde{\lambda})$ is strictly concave with respect to Δx on the set $\overline{\Delta}(\tilde{x}, \varepsilon)$. With more complicated problems, it may be necessary to do this numerically.

As before, in the special case in which the only constraints that bind at $\tilde{x}$ are linear with respect to x, the testing of (10.66) and (10.67) can be done relatively easily by computing the values of bordered principal minors of the bordered Hessian of the function $L^r(x; \tilde{\lambda})$. In fact, only a few of the bordered principal minors need to be evaluated. These are the ***successive*** bordered principal minors of the bordered Hessian matrix.

Definition 10.3 (Successive Principal Bordered Minor). *For $i = 1, \ldots, n$, the ith successive bordered principal minor of the bordered Hessian matrix (10.47) is the determinant consisting of the first $k + i$ row and column elements of the matrix; i.e.*

$$\overline{\overline{M}}_i = \det \begin{pmatrix} 0 & \cdots & 0 & \dfrac{\partial g_1}{\partial x_1} & \cdots & \dfrac{\partial g_1}{\partial x_i} \\ \vdots & \ddots & \vdots & \vdots & & \vdots \\ 0 & \cdots & 0 & \dfrac{\partial g_k}{\partial x_1} & \cdots & \dfrac{\partial g_k}{\partial x_i} \\ \dfrac{\partial g_1}{\partial x_1} & \cdots & \dfrac{\partial g_k}{\partial x_1} & \dfrac{\partial^2 L^r(x; \tilde{\lambda})}{\partial x_1^2} & \cdots & \dfrac{\partial^2 L^r(x; \tilde{\lambda})}{\partial x_1 \partial x_i} \\ \vdots & & \vdots & \vdots & \ddots & \vdots \\ \dfrac{\partial g_1}{\partial x_i} & \cdots & \dfrac{\partial g_k}{\partial x_i} & \dfrac{\partial^2 L^r(x; \tilde{\lambda})}{\partial x_i \partial x_1} & \cdots & \dfrac{\partial^2 L^r(x; \tilde{\lambda})}{\partial x_i^2} \end{pmatrix}. \qquad (10.68)$$

In example (10.49), the $n = 3$ successive bordered principal minors are, from (10.50),

$$\overline{\overline{M}}_1 = \det \begin{pmatrix} 0 & 3 \\ 3 & 0 \end{pmatrix} = -9, \quad \overline{\overline{M}}_2 = \det \begin{pmatrix} 0 & 3 & 1 \\ 3 & 0 & 3 \\ 1 & 3 & 0 \end{pmatrix} = 18,$$

$$\text{and} \quad \overline{\overline{M}}_3 = \det \begin{pmatrix} 0 & 3 & 1 & 1 \\ 3 & 0 & 3 & 3 \\ 1 & 3 & 0 & 1 \\ 1 & 3 & 1 & 0 \end{pmatrix} = -27. \tag{10.69}$$

Theorem 10.3 (Second-Order Sufficient Optimality Condition Test). *Let $\tilde{x}$ be a feasible solution for problem (10.1). Let $I(\tilde{x}) \neq \emptyset$ be the set of the indices of the constraints that bind at $\tilde{x}$. If*

(i) for each $j \in I(\tilde{x})$, $\tilde{\lambda}_j$ solves the first-order necessary conditions at $\tilde{x}$ with each $\tilde{\lambda}_j \geq 0$ and not all zero, and if

(ii) the bordered Hessian matrix $\overline{H}_{L^r}(\tilde{x}; \tilde{\lambda})$ is symmetric, then there exists $\varepsilon > 0$, such that $\Delta x^T H_{L^r}(\tilde{x}; \tilde{\lambda}) \Delta x < 0$ for all perturbations $\Delta x \neq \underline{0}$ satisfying $\tilde{x} + \Delta x \in B_{d_E}(\tilde{x}, \varepsilon)$ and $\nabla g_j(\tilde{x}) \cdot \Delta x = 0$ for every $j \in I(\tilde{x})$, if and only if, for each $i = k + 1, \ldots, n$, the successive bordered principal minor (10.68) of order-$(k + i)$ is not zero and has the same sign as $(-1)^i$.

That is, the last $n - k$ successive bordered principal minors are all nonzero and alternate in sign, with the sign of the last minor being the sign of $(-1)^n$. In our example, $k = 1$ and $n = 3$, so the only successive bordered principal minors that need to be examined are for $i = 2, 3$. $\overline{\overline{M}}_2 = 18$ is nonzero and has the same sign as $(-1)^2$. $\overline{\overline{M}}_3 = -27$ is nonzero and has the same sign as $(-1)^3$. Therefore the second-order sufficiency condition for a local maximum is satisfied.

Recollect that this second-order condition is, by itself, not sufficient for a point to be locally maximal. It is the set consisting of this second-order condition along with the Karush-Kuhn-Tucker and the complementary slackness conditions that collectively is sufficient for a point to be locally maximal.

This concludes our examination of the essentials of constrained optimization problems in which the objective and constraint functions are differentiable. It is worth mentioning that the essential ideas developed here can be extended without too much additional effort to problems with objective and constraint functions that are not all differentiable. The basic tool is Minkowski's Separating Hyperplane Theorem. The geometries of the solutions of these problems are similar to those we have explored for our differentiable problems.

10.7   Remarks

Well, now what? What do we do with the knowledge we have gained so far into solving constrained optimization problems? What we have focused upon so far are the questions of when does a problem have a solution and, if so, then how do we locate it? Next on the to-be-answered list is the question, "Given that a constrained optimization problem has an optimal solution, what are the properties of the optimal solution?" This is the theme of Chapters 11, 12, and 13. Chapter 11 examines in a reasonably general way the properties of optimal solution mappings and maximum-value functions. This chapter relies upon continuity a lot, so you will need to be familiar with the contents of Chapter 5 to understand all that is presented. Chapters 12 and 13 use calculus to explain how to derive differential descriptions of the properties of optimal solution functions and maximum-value functions. These chapters rely heavily upon the second-order necessary maximization condition explained in the current chapter.

10.8   Problems

Problem 10.1. A firm wishes to minimize its cost of producing a specified quantity $y \geq 0$ of its product. The firm's production function is $y = x_1^{1/2} x_2^{1/2}$, where x_1 and x_2 denote the quantities used by the firm of inputs 1 and 2. The per-unit input prices are $w_1 > 0$ and $w_2 > 0$. Thus the firm's problem is:

$$\min_{x_1, x_2} w_1 x_1 + w_2 x_2 \text{ subject to } x_1 \geq 0, \ x_2 \geq 0 \text{ and } y \leq x_1^{1/2} x_2^{1/2}.$$

Rewritten as a maximization problem, this is

$$\max_{x_1, x_2} -w_1 x_1 - w_2 x_2 \text{ subject to } g_1(x_1) = -x_1 \leq 0, \ g_2(x_2) = -x_2 \leq 0,$$

$$\text{and } g_3(x_1, x_2) = -x_1^{1/2} x_2^{1/2} \leq -y.$$

The cost-minimizing input bundle, the optimal solution to this problem, is the conditional input demand pair consisting of

$$x_1^*(w_1, w_2, y) = \left(\frac{w_2}{w_1}\right)^{1/2} y \quad \text{and} \quad x_2^*(w_1, w_2, y) = \left(\frac{w_1}{w_2}\right)^{1/2} y. \tag{10.70}$$

The first and second constraints are slack at the optimal solution. The third constraint strictly binds. The multipliers are $\lambda_1^*(w_1, w_2, y) = 0$, $\lambda_2^*(w_1, w_2, y) = 0$ and $\lambda_3^*(w_1, w_2, y) = 2(w_1 w_2)^{1/2} > 0$.

(i) Let Δx_1 and Δx_2 denote small perturbations of the variables x_1 and x_2 from the values x_1^* and x_2^*. In order to keep the third constraint binding, what relationship must exist between Δx_1 and Δx_2?

(ii) What is the problem's objective function when its domain is confined to the small perturbations discovered in part (i)? Rewrite this mapping as a function of only Δx_1 and denote it by $\tilde{f}$.

(iii) Show that $\tilde{f}$ is an at least weakly concave function of Δx_1, for small values of Δx_1.

(iv) Write down the problem's Lagrange function. Then write down the restricted Lagrange function $L^r(x_1, x_2; \lambda_1^*, \lambda_2^*, \lambda_3^*)$.

(v) Write down the Hessian matrix $H_{L^r}(x_1, x_2; \lambda_1^*, \lambda_2^*, \lambda_3^*)$ of the restricted Lagrange function.

(vi) Let $\Delta x = (\Delta x_1, \Delta x_2)^T$. Write down the value at (x_1^*, x_2^*) of the quadratic form $\Delta x^T H_{L^r}(x_1^*, x_2^*; \lambda_1^*, \lambda_2^*, \lambda_3^*) \Delta x$ of the Hessian matrix. Use your answer to part (i) to write this quadratic as a function of only Δx_1. Then show that this function is never positive for small values of Δx_1 that satisfy the relationship discovered in part (i), thereby confirming the necessary second-order local maximality condition.

(vii) Is the binding constraint function linear with respect to x_1 and x_2? Is it valid to evaluate the bordered principal permutation minors of the bordered Hessian matrix for this problem in order to deduce whether or not the second-order necessary condition is true at (x_1^*, x_2^*)?

Problem 10.2. Consider the problem:

$$\max_{x_1, x_2, x_3} f(x_1, x_2, x_3) = x_1 x_2 x_3 \text{ subject to } g_1(x_1) = -x_1 \leq 0, \ g_2(x_2) = -x_2 \leq 0,$$

$$g_3(x_3) = -x_3 \leq 0, \ g_4(x_1, x_2, x_3) = 2x_1 + x_2 + x_3 \leq 18, \text{ and}$$

$$g_5(x_1, x_2, x_3) = x_1 + 2x_2 + x_3 \leq 18.$$

The optimal solution is $(x_1^*, x_2^*, x_3^*) = (4, 4, 6)$. The associated multiplier values are $\lambda_1^* = \lambda_2^* = \lambda_3^* = 0$, $\lambda_4^* = 8$, and $\lambda_5^* = 8$.

(i) Let Δx_1, Δx_2, and Δx_3 denote small perturbations of the variables x_1, x_2, and x_3 from the values $x_1^* = 4$, $x_2^* = 4$, and $x_3^* = 6$. In order to keep the fourth and fifth constraints binding, what relationships must exist between Δx_1, Δx_2, and Δx_3?

(ii) What is the problem's objective function when its domain is confined to the small perturbations discovered in part (i)? Rewrite this mapping as a function of only Δx_1 and denote it by $\tilde{f}$.

(iii) Show that $\tilde{f}$ is an at least weakly concave function of Δx_1, for small values of Δx_1.

(iv) Write down the problem's Lagrange function. Then write down the restricted Lagrange function $L^r(x_1, x_2, x_3; \lambda_1^*, \lambda_2^*, \lambda_3^*, \lambda_4^*, \lambda_5^*)$.

(v) Write down the Hessian matrix $H_{L^r}(x_1, x_2, x_3; \lambda_1^*, \lambda_2^*, \lambda_3^*, \lambda_4^*, \lambda_5^*)$ of the restricted Lagrange function.

(vi) Let $\Delta x = (\Delta x_1, \Delta x_2, \Delta x_3)^T$. Write down the value at (x_1^*, x_2^*, x_3^*) of the quadratic form $\Delta x^T H_{L^r}(x_1, x_2, x_3; \lambda_1^*, \lambda_2^*, \lambda_3^*, \lambda_4^*, \lambda_5^*)\Delta x$ of the Hessian matrix. Use your answer to part (i) to write this quadratic as a function of only Δx_1. Then show that this function is never positive for small values of Δx_1, thereby confirming the necessary second-order local maximality condition.

(vii) Explain why, for the present problem, it is valid to use Theorem 10.2 to evaluate the necessary second-order local maximality condition.

(viii) What is the value at $(x_1^*, x_2^*, x_3^*) = (4, 4, 6)$ of the problem's bordered Hessian matrix?

(ix) Apply Theorem 10.2 to the bordered Hessian matrix to confirm the necessary second-order local maximality condition.

Problem 10.3. Consider again problem 10.2. Use the Karush-Kuhn-Tucker condition, the five complementary slackness conditions, and the second-order sufficiency condition to verify that $(x_1, x_2, x_3) = (4, 4, 6)$ is a local maximum for the problem.

Problem 10.4. Consider again problem 8.6. Another quick look at Figure 8.18 will be helpful. The optimal solution is the point $(x_1^*, x_2^*) = (4, 4)$. Confirm the second-order necessary local maximality condition at this point. Can the second-order local maximality sufficiency condition be verified?

Problem 10.5. Consider again problem 8.7. Take another peek at Figure 8.19. We earlier established that the optimal solution is the point $(x_1^*, x_2^*) = (4\cdot5, 6\cdot75)$. At this point, the constraint $g_1(x_1, x_2) = (x_1 - 4)^2 + x_2 \leq 7$ binds and the constraint $g_2(x_1, x_2) = (x_1 - 5)^3 - 12x_2 \leq -60$ is slack. Another feasible, not optimal, solution is the point $(x_1, x_2) \approx (5\cdot412, 5\cdot006)$, at which both of the constraints bind.
(i) Confirm that the necessary second-order condition is true at the optimal solution $(x_1^*, x_2^*) = (4\cdot5, 6\cdot75)$. I know – it must be true, but check it anyway, just for the practice.
(ii) Is the necessary second-order condition true at the feasible solution $(x_1, x_2) \approx (5\cdot412, 5\cdot006)$? What do you learn from this?

10.9 Answers

Answer to Problem 10.1.
(i) At the optimal solution only the third constraint binds, so the second-order necessary condition considers only small perturbations Δx_1 and Δx_2 from (x_1^*, x_2^*) to nearby input bundles $(x_1^* + \Delta x_1, x_2^* + \Delta x_2)$ for which the third constraint continues to bind; that is, Δx_1 and Δx_2 satisfy

$$g_3(x_1^* + \Delta x_1, x_2^* + \Delta x_2) = g_3(x_1^*, x_2^*) = y;$$
$$i.e. \quad (x_1^* + \Delta x_1)^{1/2} (x_2^* + \Delta x_2)^{1/2} = (x_1^*)^{1/2} (x_2^*)^{1/2} = y.$$

Squaring followed by a little rearranging gives

$$\Delta x_2 = -\frac{x_2^* \Delta x_1}{x_1^* + \Delta x_1} . \tag{10.71}$$

(ii) Evaluated for input bundles $(x_1^* + \Delta x_1, x_2^* + \Delta x_2)$, the problem's objective function is

$$f(x_1^* + \Delta x_1, x_2^* + \Delta x_2; w_1, w_2) = -w_1(x_1^* + \Delta x_1) - w_2(x_2^* + \Delta x_2).$$

Substitution from (10.71) then shows the value of the objective function at input bundles where Δx_1 and Δx_2 satisfy (10.71) to be

$$\tilde{f}(\Delta x_1; x_1^*, x_2^*, w_1, w_2) = -w_1 x_1^* - w_2 x_2^* - w_1 \Delta x_1 + w_2 x_2^* \times \frac{\Delta x_1}{x_1^* + \Delta x_1} . \qquad (10.72)$$

(iii) The second-order derivative of $\tilde{f}$ with respect to Δx_1 is

$$\frac{\mathrm{d}^2 \tilde{f}(\Delta x_1; x_1^*, x_2^*, w_1, w_2)}{\mathrm{d}\Delta x_1^2} = -\frac{2 w_2 x_1^* x_2^*}{(x_1^* + \Delta x_1)^3} = -\frac{2 w_2 y^2}{\left(\left(\frac{w_2}{w_1} \right)^{1/2} y + \Delta x_1 \right)^3} , \qquad (10.73)$$

after substitution from (10.70). If Δx_1 is small, then this second-derivative is not positive, confirming the second-order local maximality condition that we already knew had to be true as a consequence of the local optimality of the input bundle (10.70).

(iv) The problem's Lagrange function is

$$L(x_1, x_2, \lambda_1, \lambda_2, \lambda_3; w_1, w_2, y) = -w_1 x_1 - w_2 x_2 + \lambda_1 x_1 + \lambda_2 x_2 + \lambda_3 \left(-y + x_1^{1/2} x_2^{1/2} \right) .$$

The Lagrange function restricted by $\lambda_1 = \lambda_1^* = 0$, $\lambda_2 = \lambda_2^* = 0$, and $\lambda_3 = \lambda_3^* = 2(w_1 w_2)^{1/2} y$ is

$$L^r(x_1, x_2; \lambda_1^*, \lambda_2^*, \lambda_3^*, w_1, w_2, y) = -w_1 x_1 - w_2 x_2 + 2(w_1 w_2)^{1/2} y \left(-y + x_1^{1/2} x_2^{1/2} \right) .$$

(v) The Hessian matrix of the restricted Lagrange function is

$$H_{L^r}(x_1, x_2; \lambda_1^*, \lambda_2^*, \lambda_3^*) = \frac{(w_1 w_2)^{1/2} y}{2} \begin{pmatrix} -x_1^{-3/2} x_2^{1/2} & x_1^{-1/2} x_2^{-1/2} \\ x_1^{-1/2} x_2^{-1/2} & -x_1^{1/2} x_2^{-3/2} \end{pmatrix} .$$

(vi) For perturbations Δx_1 and Δx_2, the quadratic form of the Hessian matrix of the restricted Lagrange function is

$$Q(\Delta x_1, \Delta x_2) = \frac{(w_1 w_2)^{1/2} y}{2} (\Delta x_1, \Delta x_2) \begin{pmatrix} -x_1^{-3/2} x_2^{1/2} & x_1^{-1/2} x_2^{-1/2} \\ x_1^{-1/2} x_2^{-1/2} & -x_1^{1/2} x_2^{-3/2} \end{pmatrix} \begin{pmatrix} \Delta x_1 \\ \Delta x_2 \end{pmatrix}$$

$$= \frac{(w_1 w_2)^{1/2} y}{2} \left(-x_1^{-3/2} x_2^{1/2} (\Delta x_1)^2 + 2 x_1^{-1/2} x_2^{-1/2} \Delta x_1 \Delta x_2 - x_1^{1/2} x_2^{-3/2} (\Delta x_2)^2 \right) .$$

Evaluating the Hessian matrix at (x_1^*, x_2^*) and considering only the perturbations that satisfy (10.71) gives us the function of Δx_1 that is

$$\tilde{Q}(\Delta x_1) = \frac{(w_1 w_2)^{1/2} y}{2} \Big(-(x_1^*)^{-3/2}(x_2^*)^{1/2}(\Delta x_1)^2 +$$

$$2(x_1^*)^{-1/2}(x_2^*)^{-1/2}\Delta x_1 \left(-\frac{x_2^* \Delta x_1}{x_1^* + \Delta x_1} \right) - (x_1^*)^{1/2}(x_2^*)^{-3/2} \left(-\frac{x_2^* \Delta x_1}{x_1^* + \Delta x_1} \right)^2 \Big)$$

$$= -\frac{(w_1 w_2)^{1/2} y}{2} \left(1 + \frac{2x_1^*}{x_1^* + \Delta x_1} + \frac{(x_1^*)^2}{(x_1^* + \Delta x_1)^2} \right) (x_1^*)^{-3/2}(x_2^*)^{1/2}(\Delta x_1)^2.$$

This function is nonpositive for small values of Δx_1, confirming the second-order local maximality condition that we already knew necessarily to be true as a consequence of the local optimality of the input bundle (10.70).

(vii) Theorem 10.2 is valid for small perturbations Δx_1 and Δx_2 from x_1^* and x_2^* that satisfy the *linear* relationship between Δx_1 and Δx_2 that is $\nabla g_3(x_1^*, x_2^*) \cdot (\Delta x_1, \Delta x_2) = 0$. This relationship is

$$-\frac{1}{2} \left(\left(\frac{x_2^*}{x_1^*} \right)^{1/2}, \left(\frac{x_1^*}{x_2^*} \right)^{-1/2} \right) \cdot (\Delta x_1, \Delta x_2) = 0 \;\Rightarrow\; \Delta x_2 = \frac{x_2^*}{x_1^*} \Delta x_1. \qquad (10.74)$$

The correct relationship between Δx_1 and Δx_1 is the nonlinear relationship (10.71). Theorem 10.2 should not be used for the present problem. $\square$

Answer to Problem 10.2.

(i) At the optimal solution only the fourth and fifth constraints bind, so the second-order necessary condition considers only small perturbations Δx_1, Δx_2 and Δx_3 from (x_1^*, x_2^*, x_3^*) to nearby input bundles $(x_1^* + \Delta x_1, x_2^* + \Delta x_2, x_3^* + \Delta x_3)$ for which the fourth and fifth constraints continue to bind; *i.e.* Δx_1, Δx_2 and Δx_3 satisfy

$$2(x_1^* + \Delta x_1) + (x_2^* + \Delta x_2) + (x_3^* + \Delta x_3) = 2x_1^* + x_2^* + x_3^* = 18,$$

$$\text{and} \quad (x_1^* + \Delta x_1) + 2(x_2^* + \Delta x_2) + (x_3^* + \Delta x_3) = x_1^* + 2x_2^* + x_3^* = 18,$$

$$\Rightarrow \quad 2\Delta x_1 + \Delta x_2 + \Delta x_3 = 0 \quad \text{and} \quad \Delta x_1 + 2\Delta x_2 + \Delta x_3 = 0.$$

From these equations we obtain that the small perturbations to be considered satisfy

$$\Delta x_2 = \Delta x_1 \quad \text{and} \quad \Delta x_3 = -3\Delta x_1. \qquad (10.75)$$

(ii) Evaluated for points $(x_1^* + \Delta x_1, x_2^* + \Delta x_2, x_3^* + \Delta x_3)$, the problem's objective function is

$$f(x_1^* + \Delta x_1, x_2^* + \Delta x_2, x_3^* + \Delta x_3) = (x_1^* + \Delta x_1)(x_2^* + \Delta x_2)(x_3^* + \Delta x_3).$$

Substitution from (10.75) then shows the value of the objective function at points where Δx_1, Δx_2 and Δx_3 satisfy (10.75) to be

$$\tilde{f}(\Delta x_1; x_1^*, x_2^*, x_3^*) = (x_1^* + \Delta x_1)(x_2^* + \Delta x_1)(x_3^* - 3\Delta x_1) = (4 + \Delta x_1)^2(6 - 3\Delta x_1). \quad (10.76)$$

(iii) The second-order derivative of $\tilde{f}$ with respect to Δx_1 is

$$\frac{\mathrm{d}^2 \tilde{f}(\Delta x_1; x_1^*, x_2^*, x_3^*)}{\mathrm{d}\Delta x_1^2} = -18(2 + \Delta x_1).$$

If Δx_1 is small, then this second-derivative is not positive, thus confirming the second-order local maximality condition that must be true as a consequence of the local optimality of the point $(x_1^*, x_2^*, x_3^*) = (4, 4, 6)$.

(iv) The problem's Lagrange function is

$$L(x_1, x_2, \lambda_1, \lambda_2, \lambda_3, \lambda_4, \lambda_5) = x_1 x_2 x_3 + \lambda_1 x_1 + \lambda_2 x_2 + \lambda_3 x_3 + \lambda_4(18 - 2x_1 - x_2 - x_3)$$
$$+ \lambda_5(18 - x_1 - 2x_2 - x_3).$$

The Lagrange function restricted by $\lambda_1 = \lambda_1^* = 0$, $\lambda_2 = \lambda_2^* = 0$, $\lambda_3 = \lambda_3^* = 0$, $\lambda_4 = \lambda_4^* = 8$, and $\lambda_5 = \lambda_5^* = 8$ is

$$L^r(x_1, x_2; \lambda_1^*, \lambda_2^*, \lambda_3^*, \lambda_4^*, \lambda_5^*) = x_1 x_2 x_3 + 8(18 - 2x_1 - x_2 - x_3) + 8(18 - x_1 - 2x_2 - x_3)$$
$$= x_1 x_2 x_3 - 24x_1 - 24x_2 - 16x_3 + 288.$$

(v) The Hessian matrix of the restricted Lagrange function is

$$H_{L^r}(x_1, x_2, x_3; \lambda_1^*, \lambda_2^*, \lambda_3^*, \lambda_4^*, \lambda_5^*) = \begin{pmatrix} 0 & x_3 & x_2 \\ x_3 & 0 & x_1 \\ x_2 & x_1 & 0 \end{pmatrix}.$$

Evaluated at the optimal solution $(x_1^*, x_2^*, x_3^*) = (4, 4, 6)$, this is the matrix

$$H_{L^r}(4, 4, 6; 0, 0, 0, 8, 8) = \begin{pmatrix} 0 & 6 & 4 \\ 6 & 0 & 4 \\ 4 & 4 & 0 \end{pmatrix}.$$

(vi) For perturbations Δx_1, Δx_2, and Δx_3, the quadratic form of the Hessian matrix of the restricted Lagrange function is

$$Q(\Delta x_1, \Delta x_2, \Delta x_3) = (\Delta x_1, \Delta x_2, \Delta x_3) \begin{pmatrix} 0 & 6 & 4 \\ 6 & 0 & 4 \\ 4 & 4 & 0 \end{pmatrix} \begin{pmatrix} \Delta x_1 \\ \Delta x_2 \\ \Delta x_3 \end{pmatrix}$$
$$= 12\Delta x_1 \Delta x_2 + 8\Delta x_1 \Delta x_3 + 8\Delta x_2 \Delta x_3.$$

Considering only the perturbations that satisfy (10.75) gives us the function of Δx_1 that is

$$\tilde{Q}(\Delta x_1) = 12(\Delta x_1)^2 - 24(\Delta x_1)^2 - 24(\Delta x_1)^2 = -36(\Delta x_1)^2.$$

This function is nonpositive, confirming the second-order local maximality condition that must be true as a consequence of the local optimality of the point $(x_1, x_2, x_3) = (4, 4, 6)$.

(vii) The relationships between the perturbations Δx_1, Δx_2, and Δx_3 are all linear, so Theorem 10.2 may be used for the current problem.

(viii) The bordered Hessian is

$$\overline{H}_{L^r}(x_1, x_2, x_3; \lambda_1^*, \lambda_2^*, \lambda_3^*, \lambda_4^*, \lambda_5^*) = \begin{pmatrix} 0 & 0 & 2 & 1 & 1 \\ 0 & 0 & 1 & 2 & 1 \\ 2 & 1 & 0 & x_3 & x_2 \\ 1 & 2 & x_3 & 0 & x_1 \\ 1 & 1 & x_2 & x_1 & 0 \end{pmatrix}.$$

The value of the matrix at $(x_1^*, x_2^*, x_3^*) = (4, 4, 6)$ is

$$\overline{H}_{L^r}(4, 4, 6; 0, 0, 0, 8, 8) = \begin{pmatrix} 0 & 0 & 2 & 1 & 1 \\ 0 & 0 & 1 & 2 & 1 \\ 2 & 1 & 0 & 6 & 4 \\ 1 & 2 & 6 & 0 & 4 \\ 1 & 1 & 4 & 4 & 0 \end{pmatrix}. \tag{10.77}$$

(ix) The number of choice variables is $n = 3$, so the set of integers to be permuted when designing the bordered principal permutation minors is $\{1, 2, 3\}$. The number of binding constraints is $k = 2$. Theorem 10.2 informs us that we must check the values of each of the minors of orders $i = k+1, \ldots, n$, so, for the present problem, we need to check the values of only the order-3 minors. And, since each of the order-3 permutation minors has the same value, we need to compute the value of only one of them. So let's compute the determinant of (10.77). This is

$$\overline{M} = \det \begin{pmatrix} 0 & 0 & 2 & 1 & 1 \\ 0 & 0 & 1 & 2 & 1 \\ 2 & 1 & 0 & 6 & 4 \\ 1 & 2 & 6 & 0 & 4 \\ 1 & 1 & 4 & 4 & 0 \end{pmatrix} = -36.$$

Since this determinant has the same sign as $(-1)^i = (-1)^3$, the second-order necessary condition for a local maximum is true. $\square$

Answer to Problem 10.3. The problem's feasible set satisfies the Slater/Karlin constraint qualification, so we are assured that the Karush-Kuhn-Tucker condition is well-defined at any feasible solution. The Karush-Kuhn-Tucker condition evaluated at $(x_1, x_2, x_3) = (4, 4, 6)$ is

$$\nabla f = (x_2 x_3, x_1 x_3, x_1 x_2) = (24, 24, 16)$$
$$= \lambda_1(-1, 0, 0) + \lambda_2(0, -1, 0) + \lambda_3(0, 0, -1) + \lambda_4(2, 1, 1) + \lambda_5(1, 2, 1),$$

where $\lambda_1 \geq 0$, $\lambda_2 \geq 0$, $\lambda_3 \geq 0$, $\lambda_4 \geq 0$, $\lambda_5 \geq 0$, and not all zero. The complementary slackness conditions evaluated at $(x_1, x_2, x_3) = (4, 4, 6)$ are

$$\lambda_1 x_1 = 0 = \lambda_1 \times 4 \qquad\qquad \Rightarrow \quad \lambda_1^* = 0,$$
$$\lambda_2 x_2 = 0 = \lambda_2 \times 4 \qquad\qquad \Rightarrow \quad \lambda_2^* = 0,$$
$$\lambda_3 x_3 = 0 = \lambda_3 \times 6 \qquad\qquad \Rightarrow \quad \lambda_3^* = 0,$$
$$\lambda_4(18 - 2x_1 - x_2 - x_3) = 0 = \lambda_4 \times 0 \qquad \Rightarrow \quad \lambda_4^* \geq 0,$$
$$\text{and} \quad \lambda_5(18 - x_1 - 2x_2 - x_3) = 0 = \lambda_5 \times 0 \qquad \Rightarrow \quad \lambda_5^* \geq 0.$$

The Karush-Kuhn-Tucker condition thus requires

$$24 = 2\lambda_4^* + \lambda_5^*, \ 24 = \lambda_4^* + 2\lambda_5^* \quad \text{and} \quad 16 = \lambda_4^* + \lambda_5^* \quad \Rightarrow \quad \lambda_4^* = \lambda_5^* = 8.$$

The fourth and fifth constraints are strictly binding at $(x_1, x_2, x_3) = (4, 4, 6)$. Since these are constraints that are linear with respect to x_1, x_2, and x_3, we may apply Theorem 10.3. The number of choice variables is $n = 3$. The number of binding constraints is $k = 2$. Therefore Theorem 10.3 tells us to evaluate only the order-3 successive bordered principal minor of the bordered Hessian matrix evaluated at $(x_1, x_2, x_3) = (4, 4, 6)$. From (10.77), this is

$$\overline{\overline{M}} = \det \begin{pmatrix} 0 & 0 & 2 & 1 & 1 \\ 0 & 0 & 1 & 2 & 1 \\ 2 & 1 & 0 & 6 & 4 \\ 1 & 2 & 6 & 0 & 4 \\ 1 & 1 & 4 & 4 & 0 \end{pmatrix} = -36.$$

This minor is not zero and has the same sign as $(-1)^i = (-1)^3$, so the second-order sufficiency condition is satisfied at $(x_1, x_2, x_3) = (4, 4, 6)$. Collectively, the Karush-Kuhn-Tucker condition, the complementary slackness conditions, and the second-order sufficiency condition establish that $(x_1, x_2, x_3) = (4, 4, 6)$ is locally maximal for the constrained optimization problem. $\square$

Answer to Problem 10.4. The feasible set for problem 8.6 is a singleton, and two constraints are strictly binding at the optimal and only feasible solution $(x_1, x_2) = (4, 4)$. Consequently the only perturbations Δx_1 and Δx_2 that continue to keep the binding constraints binding are $\Delta x_1 = \Delta x_2 = 0$. Thus the second-order necessary local maximality condition is trivially true. The second-order local maximality sufficiency condition considers only nonzero perturbations that keep the binding constraints binding. There are no such perturbations, so the second-order local maximality sufficiency condition cannot be applied.   □

Answer to Problem 10.5. Consider first the point that is the optimal solution $(x_1^*, x_2^*) = \left(4\frac{1}{2}, 6\frac{3}{4}\right)$. The second-order condition considers small perturbations, Δx_1 and Δx_2, such that the binding constraint g_1 continues to bind. That is, Δx_1 and Δx_2 are required to satisfy

$$g_1(x_1^* + \Delta x_1, x_2^* + \Delta x_2) = (x_1^* + \Delta x_1 - 4)^2 + x_2^* + \Delta x_2 = g_1(x_1^*, x_2^*) = (x_1^* - 4)^2 + x_2^* = 7.$$

Rearranging gives

$$\Delta x_2 = -(2x_1^* - 8 + \Delta x_1)\Delta x_1 = -(1 + \Delta x_1)\Delta x_1, \tag{10.78}$$

since $x_1^* = 4\frac{1}{2}$. Evaluated only for points $(x_1^* + \Delta x_1, x_2^* + \Delta x_2)$ nearby to (x_1^*, x_2^*), the problem's objective function is

$$f(x_1^* + \Delta x_1, x_2^* + \Delta x_2) = x_1^* + \Delta x_1 + x_2^* + \Delta x_2 = 11\frac{1}{4} + \Delta x_1 + \Delta x_2.$$

When evaluated only for perturbations satisfying (10.78), the problem's objective function is

$$\tilde{f}(\Delta x_1) = 11\frac{1}{4} + \Delta x_1 - (1 + \Delta x_1)\Delta x_1 = 11\frac{1}{4} - (\Delta x_1)^2,$$

a function that obviously is concave with respect to Δx_1. The second-order necessary local maximality condition is thus true, as it must be, because $(x_1^*, x_2^*) = \left(4\frac{1}{2}, 6\frac{3}{4}\right)$ is locally maximal.

Now let's consider the feasible, not locally maximal, point $(x_1, x_2) \approx (5\cdot412, 5\cdot006)$. At this point both constraints g_1 and g_2 bind. It should be clear from Figure 8.19 that the only perturbations Δx_1 and Δx_2 that keep both constraints binding are the "nonperturbations" $\Delta x_1 = \Delta x_2 = 0$. For these perturbations is the necessary second-order local maximality condition true? Yes – only trivially, but it is true. What do we learn from this? We get a reminder that, while necessary optimality conditions *must* be true at a local optimum, these same necessary optimality conditions *may* be true at a point that is not a local optimum. Be careful.   □

Chapter 11

Optimal Solutions and Maximum Values

11.1   Questions to Be Answered

Now that we have understood how to obtain solutions to differentiable constrained optimization problems, together with their maximum values, it is time to turn to the question of what properties might be possessed by optimal solution mappings and maximum-value functions. This question can reasonably be divided into two parts.

The first part is the more technical question of whether or not the mappings that are the optimal solution and the maximum value to some problem are functions, are continuous in some way, or are differentiable, and so on. And when can we be sure that optimal solutions and maximum values exist? This chapter provides some answers to these types of questions.

The second part is to examine how the values of the optimal solution and the maximum value for a constrained optimization problem alter with the values of the problem's parameters. For example, does the quantity demanded by a firm of some input change when the price for the firm's product changes? Does the quantity of a product supplied by a firm change if the rate of tax on its profit increases? And at what rates do these changes occur? These types of questions are answered by a method called *comparative statics analysis*. Chapters 12 and 13 present three comparative statics analysis methodologies.

11.2   Solution Correspondences, Maximum Values

What do we mean when we talk of "the optimal solution to a constrained optimization problem"? Consider the problem $\max_x -ax^2 + bx + c$, where $a > 0$, b, and c are parameters. Take a moment and think carefully about what *you* mean by the optimal solution to this problem.

You probably have decided that the optimal solution is $x = -b/2a$. This is a statement that the optimal solution is a *mapping*. It is a mapping from the set of parameter vectors (a, b, c) that are admissible to the problem. The optimal solution is always a real number, so it maps to the set $\Re$. Consequently it is more informative to write the optimal solution using a notation such as

$$x^*(a, b, c) = -\frac{b}{2a} \tag{11.1}$$

that clearly asserts the dependence of the value of the problem's optimal solution upon the values of the problem's parameters. Thus we write the optimal solution mapping for this problem as $x^* : \Re_{++} \times \Re \times \Re \mapsto \Re$, with x^* defined by (11.1). We will find that much the same is true for the optimal solution mappings for constrained optimization problems; *i.e.* an optimal solution to a constrained optimization problem is a mapping from the parameters of the problem (the parameters of the objective function, the parameters of the constraint functions, and the levels of the constraints) to a real number space.

You may recall a notational convention that I used in Section 2.7 to distinguish between quantities that are variables for a mapping and quantities that are parameters for that mapping. The convention is that all of the quantities listed before (to the left of) a semicolon are variables, while all of the quantities listed after (to the right of) the semicolon are parameters. So, if I write $H(t, z)$, then, since there is no semicolon, I mean a mapping in which both t and z are variables. If I write instead $H(t; z)$, then, since t is to the left of the semicolon and z is to its right, I mean that t is a variable, while z is a parameter. Writing $H(z; t)$ means instead that z is a variable, while t is a parameter. For example, if $H(t, z) = t^2(z+2)$, then $H(t; z = 3) = 5t^2$ and $H(z; t = 2) = 4(z + 2)$. We will often call $H(t; z)$ and $H(z; t)$ *restricted* versions of $H(t, z)$, since $H(t; z')$ is $H(t, z)$ subject to the restriction that z is fixed at the value z', and $H(z; t')$ is $H(t, z)$ subject to the restriction that t is fixed at the value t'.

Let's take a moment to refresh our memories of the notation used in earlier chapters. The constrained optimization problem that we spent a lot of time thinking about in Chapters 8 and 10 is:

$$\max_{x_1,\dots,x_n} f(x_1,\dots,x_n) \text{ subject to } g_j(x_1,\dots,x_n) \le b_j \text{ for } j = 1,\dots,m. \qquad (11.2)$$

I would like to modify the notation used in (11.2) to make explicit the way that this problem and its solutions depend upon parameters, so let me rewrite (11.2) as

$$\max_{x \in \Re^n} f(x; \alpha) \text{ subject to } g_j(x; \beta_j) \le b_j \text{ for } j = 1,\dots,m. \qquad (11.3)$$

In (11.3), α is a vector list of the parameters of the objective function and β_j is a vector list of the parameters of the jth constraint function. It is convenient to concatenate (*i.e.* join together as a chain) these vectors, so let's define

$$\beta \equiv \begin{pmatrix} \beta_1 \\ \vdots \\ \beta_m \end{pmatrix}, \quad b \equiv \begin{pmatrix} b_1 \\ \vdots \\ b_m \end{pmatrix}, \quad \text{and} \quad \gamma \equiv \begin{pmatrix} \alpha \\ \beta \\ b \end{pmatrix}.$$

The *concatenation operator* is usually denoted by a colon, so we can also write $\beta = (\beta_1 : \cdots : \beta_m)$ and $\gamma \equiv (\alpha : \beta : b)$. The set of all allowed values for the parameter vector γ is called the problem's *parameter space*. We will use Γ to denote the problem's parameter space, so every allowed parameter vector $\gamma \in \Gamma$.

An example is the profit-maximization problem

$$\max_{y, x_1, x_2} py - w_1 x_1 - w_2 x_2 \text{ subject to } y \ge 0, \ x_1 \ge 0, \ x_2 \ge 0, \text{ and } y - x_1^{\beta_1} x_2^{\beta_2} \le 0 \quad (11.4)$$

that confronts a firm facing a given product price $p > 0$, given input prices $w_1 > 0$ and $w_2 > 0$, and using a technology parameterized by $\beta_1 > 0$, $\beta_2 > 0$, and $\beta_1 + \beta_2 < 1$. In terms of the notation used in (11.3), the functions in (11.4) are

$$f(y, x_1, x_2; p, w_1, w_2) = py - w_1 x_1 - w_2 x_2, \quad g_1(y) = -y,$$

$$g_2(x_1) = -x_1, \quad g_3(x_2) = -x_2, \text{ and } g_4(y, x_1, x_2; \beta_1, \beta_2) = y - x_1^{\beta_1} x_2^{\beta_2}.$$

Notice that some of the parameters of (11.4) are numerically specified ($b_1 = b_2 = b_3 = b_4 = 0$), while others (*i.e.* p, w_1, w_2, β_1, and β_2) are left as symbols without specified values. This indicates that the optimal solution correspondence is to be stated as a mapping of the parameters p, w_1, w_2, β_1, and β_2. With this in mind, then, the parameter vectors of interest for (11.4) are

$$\alpha = \begin{pmatrix} p \\ w_1 \\ w_2 \end{pmatrix} \quad \text{and} \quad \beta = \begin{pmatrix} \beta_1 \\ \beta_2 \end{pmatrix}, \quad \text{so} \quad \gamma = \begin{pmatrix} p \\ w_1 \\ w_2 \\ \beta_1 \\ \beta_2 \end{pmatrix},$$

and the parameter space $\Gamma = \Re_{++}^3 \times \{(\beta_1, \beta_2) \mid \beta_1 > 0, \ \beta_2 > 0, \ \beta_1 + \beta_2 < 1\}$.

The optimal solution to our example (11.4) is the vector of functions $(y^*(\gamma), x_1^*(\gamma),$ $x_2^*(\gamma), \lambda_1^*(\gamma), \lambda_2^*(\gamma), \lambda_3^*(\gamma), \lambda_4^*(\gamma))$ that state the values of the input and output levels that maximize the firm's profit and the values of the constraints' multipliers. These functions of p, w_1, w_2, β_1, and β_2 are

$$y^*(p, w_1, w_2, \beta_1, \beta_2) = \left(\frac{p^{\beta_1 + \beta_2} \beta_1^{\beta_1} \beta_2^{\beta_2}}{w_1^{\beta_1} w_2^{\beta_2}} \right)^{1/(1 - \beta_1 - \beta_2)}, \qquad (11.5\text{a})$$

$$x_1^*(p, w_1, w_2, \beta_1, \beta_2) = \left(\frac{p \beta_1^{1 - \beta_2} \beta_2^{\beta_2}}{w_1^{1 - \beta_2} w_2^{\beta_2}} \right)^{1/(1 - \beta_1 - \beta_2)}, \qquad (11.5\text{b})$$

$$x_2^*(p, w_1, w_2, \beta_1, \beta_2) = \left(\frac{p \beta_1^{\beta_1} \beta_2^{1 - \beta_1}}{w_1^{\beta_1} w_2^{1 - \beta_1}} \right)^{1/(1 - \beta_1 - \beta_2)}, \qquad (11.5\text{c})$$

$$\lambda_1^*(p, w_1, w_2, \beta_1, \beta_2) = 0, \qquad (11.5\text{d})$$

$$\lambda_2^*(p, w_1, w_2, \beta_1, \beta_2) = 0, \qquad (11.5\text{e})$$

$$\lambda_3^*(p, w_1, w_2, \beta_1, \beta_2) = 0, \qquad (11.5\text{f})$$

$$\text{and} \quad \lambda_4^*(p, w_1, w_2, \beta_1, \beta_2) = p. \qquad (11.5\text{g})$$

Each of y^*, x_1^*, x_2^*, λ_1^*, λ_2^*, λ_3^*, and λ_4^* is a mapping from the parameter space of the firm's problem to the nonnegative part of the real line.

Let us return to our more general statement (11.3) of our constrained optimization problem. A will be used to denote the set of values that can be taken by the parameter vector α. For each $j = 1, \ldots, m$, the set of all possible values for β_j will be denoted by B_j. $\boldsymbol{b}$ will denote the set of all possible values for the vector b. The problem's parameter space is thus

$$\Gamma \equiv A \times B_1 \times \cdots \times B_m \times \boldsymbol{b}.$$

The feasible set $\mathcal{C}(\beta, b) \subseteq X$ for a particular problem (11.3) is determined only by the problem's constraints (not by the problem's objective function), and so depends upon the parameter vectors β and b but is independent of the parameter vector α that determines only the objective function. The mapping from the problem's parameter space to the set of all possible feasible sets is called the problem's *feasible solution correspondence*.

Definition 11.1 (Feasible Set Correspondence). *The* feasible solution correspondence *for problem* (11.3) *is the mapping* $\mathcal{C} : \times_{j=1}^m B_j \times \boldsymbol{b} \mapsto X$ *that is*

$$C(\beta, b) = \{x \in X \mid g_1(x; \beta_1) \leq b_1, \ldots, g_m(x; \beta_m) \leq b_m\} \ \textit{for} \ (\beta, b) \in \times_{j=1}^m B_j \times \boldsymbol{b}.$$

An example is the set of consumption bundles that are feasible (affordable) for a consumer with a budget of y who faces prices $p_1, \ldots, p_n$ for commodities $1, \ldots, n$. For this problem, the feasible set correspondence is the budget set correspondence

$$\mathcal{C}(p_1, \ldots, p_n, y) = \{(x_1, \ldots, x_n) \mid x_1 \geq 0, \ldots, x_n \geq 0, \ p_1 x_1 + \cdots + p_n y_n \leq y\}$$

for $(p_1, \ldots, p_n, y) \in \Re^n_{++} \times \Re_+$.

The feasible set correspondence for problem (11.4) is the firm's technology set; *i.e.* it is the set of all technically feasible production plans,

$$\mathcal{C}(\beta_1, \beta_2) = \left\{(x_1, x_2, y) \mid x_1 \geq 0, \ x_2 \geq 0, \ 0 \leq y \leq x_1^{\beta_1} x_2^{\beta_2}\right\}$$

for all $(\beta_1, \beta_2) \in \{(\beta_1, \beta_2) \mid \beta_1 > 0, \ \beta_2 > 0, \ 0 < \beta_1 + \beta_2 < 1\}$.

The set of solutions that are optimal for problem (11.3) for a particular parameter vector typically depends upon all of the parameter vectors α, β, and b. Particular values for β and b determine a particular feasible set. A particular value for α then determines the particular objective function for the problem, and so determines which of the feasible solutions is/are optimal. For a particular $\gamma \in \Gamma$, the set of optimal solutions to the particular constrained optimization problem parameterized by γ is called the *optimal solution set*. The mapping from the problem's parameter space to the set of optimal solutions is called the problem's *optimal solution correspondence*.

Definition 11.2 (Optimal Solution Correspondence). *The* optimal solution correspondence *for problem (11.3) is the mapping* $X^* : \Gamma \mapsto X$ *that is*

$$X^*(\alpha, \beta, b) = \{x^* \in \mathcal{C}(\beta, b) \mid f(x^*; \alpha) \geq f(x; \alpha) \ \forall \ x \in \mathcal{C}(\beta, b)\} \ for \ (\alpha, \beta, b) \in \Gamma.$$

A familiar economics example is the consumer budget allocation problem in which a consumer with a Cobb-Douglas direct utility function chooses a most-preferred consumption bundle from those he can afford. For two commodities the problem is

$$\max_{x_1, x_2} U(x_1, x_2) = x_1^{\alpha_1} x_2^{\alpha_2} \text{ subject to } x_1 \geq 0, \ x_2 \geq 0, \text{ and } p_1 x_1 + p_2 x_2 \leq y,$$

where $\alpha_1 > 0$, $\alpha_2 > 0$, $p_1 > 0$, $p_2 > 0$, and $y \geq 0$. The optimal solution correspondence is the mapping

$$X^*(\alpha_1, \alpha_2, p_1, p_2, y) = \left(x_1^*(\alpha_1, \alpha_2, p_1, p_2, y), \ x_2^*(\alpha_1, \alpha_2, p_1, p_2, y)\right)$$

$$= \left(\frac{\alpha_1 y}{(\alpha_1 + \alpha_2)p_1}, \ \frac{\alpha_2 y}{(\alpha_1 + \alpha_2)p_2}\right)$$

from the parameter space $\Gamma = \{(\alpha_1, \alpha_2, p_1, p_2, y) \mid \alpha_1 > 0, \ \alpha_2 > 0, \ p_1 > 0, \ p_2 > 0, \ y \geq 0\} = \Re_{++}^4 \times \Re_+$ to the commodity space $\Re_+^2$.

For problem (11.4) the optimal solution correspondence is, from (11.5a), (11.5b), and (11.5c),

$$
\begin{aligned}
&X^*(p, w_1, w_2, \beta_1, \beta_2) \\
&= \left((y^*(p, w_1, w_2, \beta_1, \beta_2), \ x_1^*(p, w_1, w_2, \beta_1, \beta_2), \ x_2^*(p, w_1, w_2, \beta_1, \beta_2) \right) \\
&= \left(\left(\frac{p^{\beta_1+\beta_2} \beta_1^{\beta_1} \beta_2^{\beta_2}}{w_1^{\beta_1} w_2^{\beta_2}} \right)^{1/(1-\beta_1-\beta_2)}, \ \left(\frac{p\beta_1^{1-\beta_2} \beta_2^{\beta_2}}{w_1^{1-\beta_2} w_2^{\beta_2}} \right)^{1/(1-\beta_1-\beta_2)}, \ \left(\frac{p\beta_1^{\beta_1} \beta_2^{1-\beta_1}}{w_1^{\beta_1} w_2^{1-\beta_1}} \right)^{1/(1-\beta_1-\beta_2)} \right).
\end{aligned}
$$

This is a mapping from the problem's parameter space $\Gamma = \{(p, w_1, w_2, \beta_1, \beta_2) \mid p > 0, \ w_1 > 0, \ w_2 > 0, \ \beta_1 > 0, \ \beta_2 > 0, \ 0 < \beta_1 + \beta_2 < 1\}$ to the production plan space $\Re_+^3$.

What is the value provided by an optimal solution? It is the maximum value that is achievable given the constraints on choices; *i.e.* it is the largest value for the problem's objective function that is possible from all of the choices in the feasible set. So it is natural that we call this maximum value exactly that: the maximum value possible for the specified values (α, β, b) of the problem's parameters. The mapping so constructed is the problem's *maximum-value function.*

Definition 11.3 (Maximum-Value Function). *The* maximum-value function *for problem (11.3) is the mapping* $v : \Gamma \mapsto \Re$ *that is*

$$
v(\alpha, \beta, b) = f(x^*(\alpha, \beta, b); \alpha) \ \text{for} \ x^*(\alpha, \beta, b) \in X^*(\alpha, \beta, b), \ \forall \ (\alpha, \beta, b) \in \Gamma.
$$

The maximum-value mapping is a function; *i.e.* associated with each possible vector of parameters there is only a single maximum value for the objective function. Why is this? Figure it out for yourself by asking what if it is not unique? For example, suppose for some particular vector of parameters there were two maximum values, say, $v = 33$ and $v = 37$. This is a contradiction. Why?

For the above example of the consumer's budget allocation problem, the maximum-value function reveals how the consumer's maximum achievable utility level depends upon the problem's parameters. Economists call this function the consumer's *indirect utility function.* For our example it is the function $v : \Re_{++}^2 \times \Re_+ \mapsto \Re$ that is

$$
v(p_1, p_2, y) = U(x_1^*(p_1, p_2, y), x_2^*(p_1, p_2, y)) = \left(\frac{\alpha_1 y}{(\alpha_1 + \alpha_2)p_1} \right)^{\alpha_1} \left(\frac{\alpha_2 y}{(\alpha_1 + \alpha_2)p_2} \right)^{\alpha_2}.
$$

$$(11.6)$$

For problem (11.4) the maximum-value function reveals how the firm's maximum achievable profit level depends upon the problem's parameters. Economists call this function the firm's *indirect profit function.* For our example it is the function $v : \Re^3_{++} \times \{(\beta_1, \beta_2) \mid \beta_1 > 0, \ \beta_2 > 0, \ 0 < \beta_1 + \beta_2 < 1\} \mapsto \Re$ that is

$$
\begin{aligned}
&v(p, w_1, w_2, \beta_1, \beta_2) \\
&= py^*(p, w_1, w_2, \beta_1, \beta_2) - w_1 x_1^*(p, w_1, w_2, \beta_1, \beta_2) - w_2 x_2^*(p, w_1, w_2, \beta_1, \beta_2)) \\
&= (1 - \beta_1 - \beta_2) \left(\frac{p \beta_1^{\beta_1} \beta_2^{\beta_2}}{w_1^{\beta_1} w_2^{\beta_2}} \right)^{1/(1-\beta_1-\beta_2)}
\end{aligned}
\tag{11.7}
$$

once we substitute from (11.5a), (11.5b), and (11.5c), and simplify the resulting expression.

11.3 Existence of an Optimal Solution

Not every constrained optimization problem has an optimal solution. An example is the problem $\max_x f(x) = x$ subject to the constraint $x < 1$. Then there are other optimization problems that have optimal solutions for some values of their parameter vectors γ and have no optimal solutions for other values of the parameter vectors. For an example, think of the problem $\max_x f(x) = ax^2 + 2x + 3$, where the parameter a can be any real number. If $a < 0$, then the problem has the optimal solution $x^*(a) = 1/a$. But if $a \geq 0$, then the problem has no optimal solution. If, for a particular parameter vector γ, an optimization problem has no optimal solution, then the value of the optimal solution correspondence is the empty set; $X^*(\gamma) = \emptyset$. Other problems have many, even an infinity, of optimal solutions; *e.g.* $\max_x f(x) \equiv 2$ for $0 \leq x \leq 1$ is a constrained optimization problem with an infinity of optimal solutions. For which types of constrained optimization problems can we be sure that there is always at least one optimal solution? Are there problems in which there is always a unique optimal solution?

The good news is that almost all of the constrained optimization problems encountered by economists have an optimal solution. If the feasible set of the problem is nonempty, closed, and bounded with respect to the Euclidean metric topology on E^n, and if the problem's objective function is upper-semi-continuous over the feasible set, then there exists at least one global maximizing solution to the problem. If the objective function is instead lower-semi-continuous over the feasible set, then there exists at least one global minimizing solution to the problem. In many cases we will not be interested in both types of solutions. For example, most firms want to avoid profit-minimizing production plans.

Theorem 11.1 (Weierstrass's Theorem for Upper-Semi-Continuous Functions). *Let $\mathcal{C}$ be a nonempty subset of $\Re^n$ that is compact with respect to E^n. Let $f : \mathcal{C} \mapsto \Re$ be a function that is upper-semi-continuous on $\mathcal{C}$. Then there exists $\overline{x} \in \mathcal{C}$ such that $f(\overline{x}) \geq f(x)$ for every $x \in \mathcal{C}$.*

An example of the content of this theorem is displayed in Figure 11.1. The upper-semi-continuous function f displayed there must attain a global maximum on the compact set that is the interval $[a, b]$. It is possible that an upper-semi-continuous function also attains local maxima, local minima, and a global minimum, but it is only the existence of the global maximum that is assured.

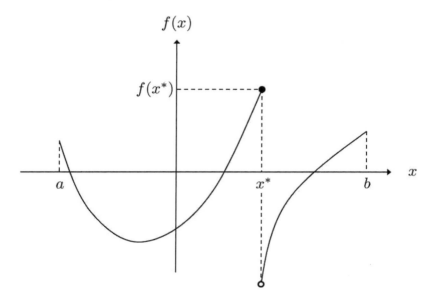

Figure 11.1: On the compact interval $[a, b]$, the upper-semi-continuous function f attains a global maximum at $x = x^*$, attains a local minimum, and does not attain a global minimum.

Proof of Theorem 11.1. Let $\overline{f} = \sup_{x \in \mathcal{C}} f(x)$. It must be shown that there is a value $\overline{x} \in \mathcal{C}$ for which the corresponding value of f is $\overline{f}$.

Since $\overline{f} = \sup_{x \in \mathcal{C}} f(x)$, there exists in $\mathcal{C}$ a sequence $\{x_n\}_{n=1}^{\infty}$ such that

$$f(x_n) \to \overline{f}. \tag{11.8}$$

Since $\mathcal{C}$ is compact, this sequence must contain a convergent subsequence $\{x_{n_k}\}_{k=1}^{\infty}$. Let $\overline{x} = \lim_{k \to \infty} x_{n_k}$. $\overline{x} \in \mathcal{C}$ because $\mathcal{C}$ is a closed set.

Since f is upper-semi-continuous on $\mathcal{C}$,

$$\lim_{k \to \infty} f(x_{n_k}) \leq f(\overline{x}). \tag{11.9}$$

The sequences $\{f(x_n)\}_{n=1}^{\infty}$ and $\{f(x_{n_k})\}_{k=1}^{\infty}$ must converge to the same value, so it follows from (11.8) and (11.9) that $\overline{f} \leq f(\overline{x})$. But, by definition, $\overline{f} \geq f(x)$ for every $x \in \mathcal{C}$, so it must be that $\overline{f} = f(\overline{x})$. $\qquad \square$

Theorem 11.2 (Weierstrass's Theorem for Lower-Semi-Continuous Functions). *Let $\mathcal{C}$ be a nonempty subset of $\Re^n$ that is compact with respect to E^n. Let $f : \mathcal{C} \mapsto \Re$ be a function that is lower-semi-continuous on $\mathcal{C}$. Then there exists $\underline{x} \in \mathcal{C}$ such that $f(\underline{x}) \leq f(x)$ for every $x \in \mathcal{C}$.*

The proof is very similar to that of Theorem 11.1, so take some time to understand the proof of Theorem 11.1 and then prove Theorem 11.2 for yourself – this is problem 11.2.

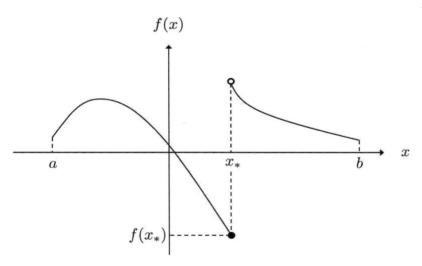

Figure 11.2: On the compact interval $[a, b]$, the lower-semi-continuous function f attains a global minimum at $x = x_*$, attains a local maximum, and does not attain a global maximum.

An example of the content of Theorem 11.2 is displayed in Figure 11.2. The lower-semi-continuous function f displayed there must attain a global minimum on the compact set that is the interval $[a, b]$. It is possible that a lower-semi-continuous function also attains local maxima, local minima, and a global maximum, but it is only the existence of the global minimum that is assured.

The most commonly employed existence result is the theorem that one obtains when the constrained optimization problem's objective function is continuous, and so is both lower-semi-continuous and upper-semi-continuous on the problem's feasible set $\mathcal{C}$. Combining Theorems 11.1 and 11.2 gives the following result.

Theorem 11.3 (Weierstrass's Theorem for Continuous Functions). *Let $\mathcal{C}$ be a non-empty subset of $\Re^n$ that is compact with respect to E^n. Let $f : \mathcal{C} \mapsto \Re$ be a function that is continuous on $\mathcal{C}$. Then there exists $\bar{x} \in \mathcal{C}$ such that $f(\bar{x}) \geq f(x)$ for every $x \in \mathcal{C}$ and, also, there exists $\underline{x} \in \mathcal{C}$ such that $f(\underline{x}) \leq f(x)$ for every $x \in \mathcal{C}$.*

The content of Weierstrass's Theorem is displayed in Figure 11.3. Notice that Weierstrass's Theorem implies neither a *unique* global maximizing solution nor a unique global minimizing solution.

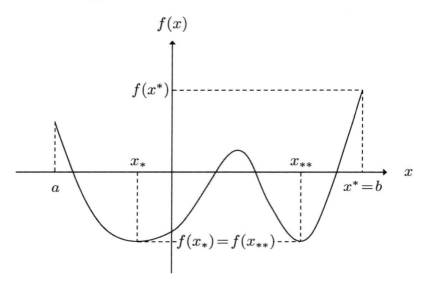

Figure 11.3: On the compact set $[a, b]$, the continuous function $f(x)$ attains a global maximum at $x = x^*$, and attains a global minimum at both $x = x_*$ and $x = x_{**}$.

The above theorems are sufficiency statements. It is possible that a lower-semi-continuous function can attain a global maximum and that an upper-semi-continuous function can attain a global minimum. It is also possible that a lower-semi-continuous function defined on a compact set does not attain even a local maximum and that an upper-semi-continuous function defined on a compact set does not attain even a local minimum, as the following two examples demonstrate. Let $\mathcal{C} = [0, 4]$. The function

$$v(x) = \begin{cases} x, & 0 \leq x \leq 2 \\ 5 - x, & 2 < x \leq 4 \end{cases}$$

is lower-semi-continuous on $[0, 4]$ and does not attain even a local maximum on $[0, 4]$. Again let $\mathcal{C} = [0, 4]$. The function

$$t(x) = \begin{cases} 5 - x, & 0 \leq x \leq 2 \\ x, & 2 < x \leq 4 \end{cases}$$

is upper-semi-continuous on $[0, 4]$ and does not attain even a local minimum on $[0, 4]$.

Now let us turn to discovering some of the properties that can be possessed by an optimal solution correspondence.

11.4 Theorem of the Maximum

Let's start with an example. Consider the budget allocation problem in which a consumer wants to maximize his utility from consumption of quantities x_1 and x_2 of commodities 1 and 2. Commodity 2 is the numeraire commodity, so $p_2 = 1$. The consumer regards the two commodities as perfect substitutes, so his direct utility function is $U(x_1, x_2) = x_1 + x_2$. The consumer's problem is

$$\max_{x_1, x_2} U(x_1, x_2) = x_1 + x_2 \text{ subject to } x_1 \geq 0, \ x_2 \geq 0 \text{ and } p_1 x_1 + x_2 \leq y. \quad (11.10)$$

The optimal solution correspondence is

$$X^*(p_1, y) = \begin{cases} \left(\dfrac{y}{p_1}, 0 \right) & , \ p_1 < 1 \\ \{(x_1, x_2) \mid x_1 \geq 0, x_2 \geq 0, x_1 + x_2 = y\} & , \ p_1 = 1 \\ (0, y) & , \ p_1 > 1. \end{cases} \quad (11.11)$$

This optimal solution correspondence, which maps to $\Re_+^2$, is upper-hemi-continuous with respect to p_1 and is displayed in Figure 11.4. It says that when commodity 1 is the less expensive (*i.e.* $p_1 < p_2 = 1$) the consumer purchases only commodity 1. When commodity 2 is the less expensive (*i.e.* $p_1 > p_2 = 1$) the consumer purchases

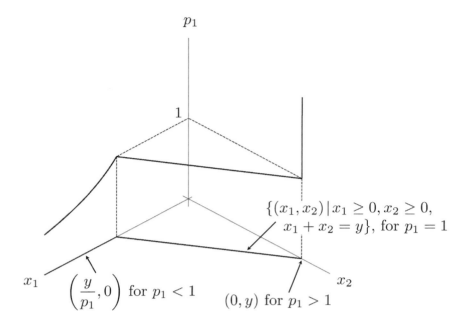

Figure 11.4:   The ordinary demand correspondence $X^*(p_1, y)$ is upper-hemi-continuous with respect to p_1.

only commodity 2. When the commodities are equally expensive (*i.e.* $p_1 = p_2 = 1$) the consumer cares only about the total number of commodity units he acquires.

For $p_1 = 1$, the consumer does not care which commodity he purchases, so the image of the optimal solution correspondence for $p_1 = 1$ is the set $X^*(p_1 = 1, y) = \{(x_1, x_2) \mid x_1 \geq 0, \ x_2 \geq 0, \ x_1 + x_2 = y\}$. The correspondence is thus not single-valued everywhere and so is not a function.

If $p_1 > 1$, then the consumer purchases only commodity 2, so $X^*(p_1, y) = (0, y)$ for all $p_1 > 1$. Therefore the limit of the images of the optimal solution correspondence as p_1 approaches unity from above is

$$\lim_{p_1 \to 1^+} X^*(p_1, y) = \lim_{p_1 \to 1^+} (0, y)$$

$$= (0, y) \in \{(x_1, x_2) \mid x_1 \geq 0, \ x_2 \geq 0, \ x_1 + x_2 = y\} = X^*(1, y).$$

The limit $\lim_{p_1 \to 1^+} X^*(p_1, y)$ is a member of the set $X^*(p_1 = 1, y)$.

If $p_1 < 1$, then the consumer purchases only commodity 1, so $X^*(p_1, y) = (y/p_1, 0)$ for all $0 < p_1 < 1$. Therefore the limit of the images of the optimal solution correspondence as p_1 approaches unity from below is

$$\lim_{p_1 \to 1^-} X^*(p_1, y) = \lim_{p_1 \to 1^-} \left(\frac{y}{p_1}, 0\right)$$
$$= (y, 0) \in \{(x_1, x_2) \mid x_1 \geq 0, \ x_2 \geq 0, \ x_1 + x_2 = y\} = X^*(1, y).$$

The limit $\lim_{p_1 \to 1^-} X^*(p_1, y)$ is also a member of the set $X^*(p_1 = 1, y)$.

Since $\lim_{p_1 \to 1^-} X^*(p_1, y) \in X^*(p_1 = 1, y)$ and $\lim_{p_1 \to 1^+} X^*(p_1, y) \in X^*(p_1 = 1, y)$, X^* is upper-hemi-continuous at $p_1 = 1$. X^* is a continuous function for all $p_1 > 0$ other than $p_1 = 1$ and so is upper-hemi-continuous for all $p_1 > 0$.

It turns out that there is a large class of constrained optimization problems of interest to economists for which the optimal solution correspondence is upper-hemi-continuous. This very useful information is provided by the *Theorem of the Maximum*, a result proved in 1959 by Claude Berge. At first sight the statement of this important result appears daunting and confusing. But don't worry – we will examine it part by part and will discover that it is not too complicated after all.

Theorem 11.4 (Berge's Theorem of the Maximum). *Consider problem* (11.3). *The problem's feasible set correspondence is* $\mathcal{C} : \times_{j=1}^m B_j \times \boldsymbol{b} \to X$, *where*

$$\mathcal{C}(\beta, b) = \{x \in X \mid g_j(x; \beta_j) \leq b_j \ \forall \ j = 1, \ldots, m\}.$$

The problem's optimal solution correspondence is $X^* : A \times_{j=1}^m B_j \times \boldsymbol{b} \to X$, *where*

$$X^*(\alpha, \beta, b) = \{x^* \in \mathcal{C}(\beta, b) \mid f(x^*; \alpha) \geq f(x; \alpha) \ \forall \ x \in \mathcal{C}(\beta, b)\}.$$

The problem's maximum-value function is $v : A \times_{j=1}^m B_j \times \boldsymbol{b} \to \Re$, *where*

$$v(\alpha, \beta, b) = f(x^*; \alpha) \ \forall \ x^* \in X^*(\alpha, \beta, b).$$

If f is jointly continuous with respect to (x, α) and if $\mathcal{C}$ is nonempty-valued, compact-valued, and continuous with respect to (β, b), then X^* is nonempty-valued and is upper-hemi-continuous with respect to (α, β, b), and v is continuous with respect to (α, β, b).

An example will help to make sense of the statement of the theorem, so let us think of a small generalization to problem (11.10). Consider the problem

$$\max_{x_1, x_2} f(x_1, x_2; \alpha) = \alpha x_1 + x_2 \text{ subject to } x_1 \geq 0, \ x_2 \geq 0, \text{ and } p_1 x_1 + x_2 \leq y. \quad (11.12)$$

We again take commodity 2 to be the numeraire, meaning that $p_2 = 1$. Observe that the problem's objective function is jointly continuous in (x_1, x_2, α) (joint continuity is more demanding than is continuity in each of x_1, x_2, and α individually – see Section 5.6). The problem's feasible solution correspondence is

$$\mathcal{C}(p_1, y) = \{(x_1, x_2) \mid x_1 \geq 0, \ x_2 \geq 0 \text{ and } p_1 x_1 + x_2 \leq y\}.$$

For given values for $p_1 > 0$ and $y \geq 0$, the problem's feasible set is a nonempty and compact subset of $\Re^2_+$. Thus $\mathcal{C}$ is a nonempty-valued and compact-valued correspondence. Notice that the feasible set's boundaries move smoothly (*i.e.* continuously) as the values of either p_1 or y are changed. This is what we mean by the statement that $\mathcal{C}(p_1, y)$ is a correspondence that is continuous with respect to (p_1, y).

The optimal solution (ordinary demand) correspondence is

$$X^*(\alpha, p_1, y) = \begin{cases} \left(\dfrac{y}{p_1}, 0\right) & , \ p_1 < \alpha \\ \{(x_1, x_2) \mid x_1 \geq 0, x_2 \geq 0, \alpha x_1 + x_2 = y\} & , \ p_1 = \alpha \\ (0, y) & , \ p_1 > \alpha. \end{cases}$$

Figure 11.4 displays the optimal solution correspondence for $\alpha = 1$. The important feature to notice is that the correspondence is upper-hemi-continuous with respect to $p_1 > 0$ and $\alpha > 0$, and is fully continuous (thus upper-hemi-continuous) with respect to $y \geq 0$.

The problem's maximum-value (indirect utility) function is

$$v(\alpha, p_1, p_2, y) = \max\left\{\dfrac{\alpha}{p_1}, 1\right\} y.$$

This is a continuous function of the problem's parameters $\alpha > 0$, $p_1 > 0$ and $y \geq 0$.

Proof of the Theorem of the Maximum. The proof is a somewhat lengthy sequence of steps, but only two involve serious thought. To make it easier to follow, I have placed titles at the start of each new part of the proof. For notational brevity we will once again use γ to denote the parameter vector (α, β, b) and use Γ to denote the parameter space $A \times^m_{j=1} B_j \times \boldsymbol{b}$.

(i) Show X^* is not empty-valued. What do we know about the feasible set? We are given that, for any $\gamma \in \Gamma$ (actually, for any given β and b), the feasible set $\mathcal{C}(\beta, b)$ is not empty and is a compact set. What do we know about the objective function? For any $\gamma \in \Gamma$ (actually, for any given α), we know that the objective function

$f(x; \alpha)$ is continuous with respect to x. It follows from Weierstrass's Theorem 11.3 that there is at least one $x^* \in \mathcal{C}(\beta, b)$ that achieves a maximum for $f(x; \alpha)$ over $\mathcal{C}(\beta, b)$; *i.e.* $X^*(\gamma) \neq \emptyset$. Since this is true for every $\gamma \in \Gamma$, X^* is a nonempty-valued correspondence.

(ii) Show $X^*(\gamma)$ is a bounded set. The set of solutions that are optimal given γ is a subset of the set of solutions that are feasible given γ; *i.e.* $X^*(\alpha, \beta, b) \subseteq \mathcal{C}(\beta, b)$. $\mathcal{C}$ is a compact-valued correspondence, so for any given $\gamma \in \Gamma$ the feasible set $\mathcal{C}(\beta, b)$ is a bounded set. Hence its subset $X^*(\gamma)$ is also a bounded set.

(iii) Show $X^*(\gamma)$ is a closed set. We need to show that the limit of any convergent sequence of elements in $X^*(\gamma)$ is an element of $X^*(\gamma)$, so we start by taking a sequence $\{x_n^*\}_{n=1}^\infty$ of elements with $x_n^* \in X^*(\gamma)$ for every $n \geq 1$ that converges to some point x_0; *i.e.* $x_n^* \to x_0$. The first thing we need to do is to show that x_0 is a feasible solution; *i.e.* $x_0 \in \mathcal{C}(\beta, b)$. Then we need to show that x_0 is optimal; *i.e.* $x_0 \in X^*(\gamma)$.

Let's show that $x_0 \in \mathcal{C}(\beta, b)$. Each of the optimal solutions x_n^* must be a feasible solution: $x_n^* \in \mathcal{C}(\beta, b)$ for every $n \geq 1$. But then $x_0 \in \mathcal{C}(\beta, b)$ because $x_n^* \to x_0$ and $\mathcal{C}(\beta, b)$ is a closed set.

Now we need to show that $x_0 \in X^*(\gamma)$. For the given value of α, the objective function $f(x; \alpha)$ is continuous with respect to x, so

$$\lim_{n \to \infty} f(x_n^*; \alpha) = f(\lim_{n \to \infty} x_n^*; \alpha) = f(x_0; \alpha). \tag{11.13}$$

All of the optimal solutions x_n^* provide the same maximum value; denote it by $\overline{v}$. That is, $f(x_n^*; \alpha) = \overline{v}$ for all $n \geq 1$. Therefore (11.13) is the statement that

$$\overline{v} = f(x_0; \alpha). \tag{11.14}$$

That is, x_0 provides the maximum value $\overline{v}$ so x_0 is an optimal solution: $x_0 \in X^*(\gamma)$. Therefore $X^*(\gamma)$ is a closed set.

(iv) Show $X^*(\gamma)$ is a compact set. $X^*(\gamma)$ is both closed and bounded, so the set is compact with respect to E^n.

(v) Show X^* is upper-hemi-continuous on Γ. What is it that we need to prove here? Have a look at Figure 11.5. We need to consider a sequence $\{\gamma_n\}_{n=1}^\infty$ of parameter vectors in Γ that converges to a vector that we will denote by γ_0; $\gamma_n \to \gamma_0$. For each value γ_n, there is a set of solutions $X^*(\gamma_n)$ that are optimal when $\gamma = \gamma_n$. From each of the sets $X^*(\gamma_1), X^*(\gamma_2), \ldots$, we take arbitrarily one element and so form a sequence x_n^*, where $x_n^* \in X^*(\gamma_n)$ for each $n \geq 1$. We need to show that this sequence possesses a convergent subsequence (let's call the limit x_0^*), and then we need to show that x_0^* is a solution that is optimal when $\gamma = \gamma_0$; *i.e.* we need to show that $x_0^* \in X^*(\gamma_0)$.

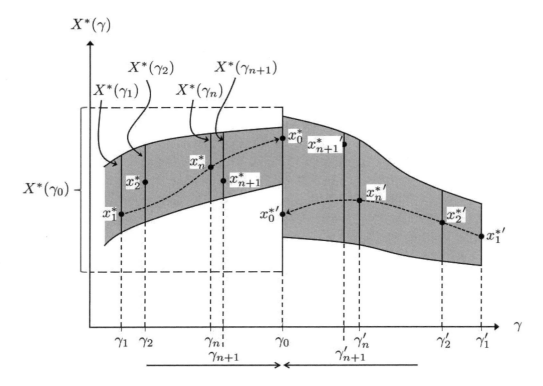

Figure 11.5: $X^*(\gamma)$ is upper-hemi-continuous at $\gamma = \gamma_0$.

We start with the sequence $\{\gamma_n\}_{n=1}^{\infty}$ with $\gamma_n \to \gamma_0$ and the associated sequence of optimal solution sets $\{X^*(\gamma_n)\}_{n=1}^{\infty}$, from each of which a single element has been selected arbitrarily to form the sequence $\{x_n^*\}_{n=1}^{\infty}$. The sequence $\{x_n^*\}_{n=1}^{\infty}$ need not be convergent. However, it must contain at least one convergent subsequence. Why so? Well, again note that any optimal solution is a feasible solution, so $x_n^* \in \mathcal{C}(\beta_n, b_n)$ (the set of feasible solutions when $\gamma = \gamma_n$) for each $n \geq 1$. We are given that $\mathcal{C}$ is a correspondence that is continuous, and thus is upper-hemi-continuous, with respect to (β, b). Therefore the sequence $\{x_n^*\}_{n=1}^{\infty}$ of feasible solutions must possess a subsequence $\{x_{n_k}^*\}_{k=1}^{\infty}$ that converges to a value that we denote by x_0^* and, moreover, $x_0^* \in \mathcal{C}(\beta_0, b_0)$; *i.e.* x_0^* is a feasible solution when $\gamma = \gamma_0$.

Now we need to show that x_0^* is an optimal solution when $\gamma = \gamma_0$; *i.e.* we need to show that

$$f(x_0^*; \alpha_0) \geq f(z_0; \alpha_0) \ \forall \ z_0 \in \mathcal{C}(\beta_0, b_0). \tag{11.15}$$

Choose any $z_0 \in \mathcal{C}(\beta_0, b_0)$. Since $\mathcal{C}$ is a continuous correspondence with respect to (β, b), it is lower-hemi-continuous and so there must exist a sequence $\{z_n\}_{n=1}^{\infty}$ with

$z_n \in \mathcal{C}(\beta_n, b_n)$ for all $n \geq 1$ that converges to z_0. Now let's create the subsequence $\{z_{n_k}\}_{k=1}^{\infty}$ by selecting the elements from the $\{z_n\}_{n=1}^{\infty}$ sequence that correspond to the $\{x_{n_k}^*\}_{k=1}^{\infty}$ subsequence. Any subsequence of a convergent subsequence is convergent, so $z_{n_k} \to z_0$. Now let's remember that

$$f(x_{n_k}^*; \alpha_{n_k}) \geq f(z_{n_k}; \alpha_{n_k}) \ \forall \ k \geq 1, \tag{11.16}$$

because $x_{n_k}^*$ is optimal when $\gamma = \gamma_{n_k}$, while z_{n_k} is merely feasible when $\gamma = \gamma_{n_k}$. f is jointly continuous in (x, α), so it follows from (11.16) that

$$f\big(\lim_{k \to \infty} x_{n_k}^*; \lim_{k \to \infty} \alpha_{n_k}\big) = f(x_0^*; \alpha_0) \geq f\big(\lim_{k \to \infty} z_{n_k}; \lim_{k \to \infty} \alpha_{n_k}\big) = f(z_0; \alpha_0). \tag{11.17}$$

Thus x_0^* is optimal when $\gamma = \gamma_0$; *i.e.* $x_0^* \in X^*(\gamma_0)$, establishing that X^* is upper-hemi-continuous at γ_0. But γ_0 is an arbitrary choice from Γ, so X^* is upper-hemi-continuous on Γ.

We have now completed the part of the theorem that deals with the properties of the optimal solution correspondence X^*. The rest of the proof establishes the claimed properties of the maximum-value function.

(vi) Show v exists and is a function. By definition, $v(\gamma) = f(x^*(\gamma); \alpha)$. Since $X^*(\gamma) \neq \emptyset$, the image set $v(\gamma) \neq \emptyset$. Suppose that, for some $\tilde{\gamma} \in \Gamma$, the set $v(\tilde{\gamma})$ is not a singleton. Then $v(\tilde{\gamma})$ must contain at least two different values, say, v' and v''. Without loss of generality, suppose that $v' < v''$. But then v' is not a maximum value. Contradiction. Thus $v(\gamma)$ must be a singleton for each $\gamma \in \Gamma$; *i.e.* v is a function.

(vii) Show v is continuous on Γ. We must show that $v(\gamma_n) \to v(\gamma_0)$ for any sequence $\{\gamma_n\}_{n=1}^{\infty}$ that converges to γ_0. So we start by taking any sequence $\{\gamma_n\}_{n=1}^{\infty}$ that converges to some limit γ_0. Then we look at the accompanying sequence of maximum values $\{v(\gamma_n)\}_{n=1}^{\infty}$. This sequence must be bounded, both above and below, so the sequence has a least upper bound (the limit superior of the sequence; see Definition 4.6) and, therefore, contains a subsequence $\{v(\gamma_{n_k})\}_{k=1}^{\infty}$ that converges to this least upper bound: $v(\gamma_{n_k}) \to \limsup v(\gamma_n)$. The accompanying subsequence $\{\gamma_{n_k}\}_{k=1}^{\infty}$ must converge to γ_0 because it is drawn from the sequence $\{\gamma_n\}_{n=1}^{\infty}$ and $\gamma_n \to \gamma_0$. For each $k \geq 1$, there is an optimal solution $x^*(\gamma_{n_k}) \in X^*(\gamma_{n_k})$ providing the maximum value $v(\gamma_{n_k})$. Construct a sequence $\{x_{n_k}^*\}_{k=1}^{\infty}$ of these optimal solutions by arbitrarily selecting one element from each of the sets $X^*(\gamma_{n_k})$. Since the optimal solution correspondence X^* is upper-hemi-continuous with respect to γ, the sequence $\{x_{n_k}^*\}_{k=1}^{\infty}$ must contain a subsequence that converges to some $x_0^* \in X^*(\gamma_0)$. Denote this subsequence by $\{x_{n_{k_j}}^*\}_{j=1}^{\infty}$; $x_{n_{k_j}}^* \to x_0^*$. From the joint continuity of f with respect

to (x, α),

$$\lim_{j \to \infty} v(\gamma_{n_{k_j}}) = \lim_{j \to \infty} f(x^*_{n_{k_j}}; \alpha_{n_{k_j}}) = f(\lim_{j \to \infty} x^*_{n_{k_j}}; \lim_{j \to \infty} \alpha_{n_{k_j}}) = f(x^*_0; \alpha_0) = v(\gamma_0).$$
(11.18)

Thus

$$v(\gamma_0) = \limsup v(\gamma_n). \tag{11.19}$$

The bounded sequence $\{v(\gamma_n)\}_{n=1}^{\infty}$ must also have a greatest lower bound (the limit inferior of the sequence; see Definition 4.6) and so must contain a subsequence $\{v(\gamma_{n_t})\}_{t=1}^{\infty}$ that converges to this greatest lower bound: $v(\gamma_{n_t}) \to \liminf v(\gamma_n)$. Repeating the above argument for this subsequence shows that

$$v(\gamma_0) = \liminf v(\gamma_n). \tag{11.20}$$

(11.19) and (11.20) together show that the sequence $\{v(\gamma_n)\}_{n=1}^{\infty}$ does converge and that its limit is $v(\gamma_0)$, so we have established that v is continuous at $\gamma = \gamma_0$. But γ_0 is an arbitrary choice from Γ, so v is continuous everywhere on Γ. $\qquad \square$

11.5 Comparative Statics Analysis

Economists are usually interested in the directions of change caused to economic variables when some other quantity, a policy variable perhaps, changes. Will an increase in a tax rate cause an increase in tax revenue, for example? These questions concern how the optimal solutions to, and maximum-value functions of, constrained optimization problems change as the parameters of the problems are changed. In this chapter we have not been able to address such questions because insufficient information is provided about the ways in which the objective and constraint functions are altered by changes to parameters. The following two chapters develop *comparative statics analysis*, a name given to any method that determines how optimal solutions or maximum values are altered by changes to parameters. These two chapters explain differential comparative statics analysis methods only. Another method, called monotone comparative statics analysis, which does not rely upon differentiability, is not presented in this book because of the amount of preparation needed to comprehend it.

Differentiable comparative statics analyses can be divided into two types. A comparative statics analysis that determines only the directions in which optimal solutions or maximum values change when a parameter changes is called "qualitative." Such an analysis might predict that the quantity demanded of coffee decreases when the price of coffee rises, but it would not say how quickly. A comparative statics analysis that determines the values of rates of change of optimal solutions or maximum values with respect to changes to a parameter is called "quantitative." Clearly a quantitative analysis is more informative than is a qualitative analysis, but undertaking a quantitative analysis requires a lot more information than does a qualitative analysis. Whether this additional information is available to you will in large part determine which type of analysis you are able to undertake. Chapter 12 explains how to undertake quantitative analyses. Chapter 13 explains how, under less demanding conditions, to conduct qualitative analyses.

11.6   Problems

Problem 11.1. Provide an example of an upper-semi-continuous function that is not continuous and that attains both a global maximum and a global minimum. Then provide an example of a lower-semi-continuous function that is not continuous and attains both a global maximum and a global minimum. Why is it that these examples do not contradict Theorems 11.1 and 11.2?

Problem 11.2. Have another look at the proof provided for Weierstrass's Theorem for upper-semi-continuous functions (Theorem 11.1). Then prove Weierstrass's Theorem for lower-semi-continuous functions (Theorem 11.2).

Problem 11.3. Consider a consumer with nonconvex preferences that are represented by the direct utility function $U(x_1, x_2) = x_1^2 + x_2^2$. The consumer faces given per unit prices $p_1 > 0$ and $p_2 = 1$ for commodities 1 and 2, and has a budget of \$$y > 0$ to spend.
(i) What is the consumer's ordinary demand correspondence?
(ii) Prove that the ordinary demand correspondence is upper-hemi-continuous with respect to p_1.
(iii) Derive the consumer's maximum-value (*i.e.* indirect utility) function $v(p_1, y)$. Show that this function is continuous with respect to p_1. Is this maximum-value function also differentiable with respect to p_1?

Problem 11.4. Consider the constrained optimization problem

$$\max_{x \in \Re^n} f(x; \alpha) \text{ subject to } g_j(x; \beta_j) \leq b_j \text{ for } j = 1, \ldots, m,$$

where $\alpha \in A$, $\beta_1 \in B_1, \ldots, \beta_m \in B_m$, and $b_j \in \Re$ for $j = 1, \ldots, m$. The objective function $f : \Re^n \times A \to \Re$ is jointly continuous with respect to (x, α). Each constraint function $g_j : \Re^n \times B_j \to \Re$ is jointly continuous with respect to (x, β_j), for $j = 1, \ldots, m$. Let $\beta = (\beta_1, \ldots, \beta_m)^{\mathrm{T}}$, let $b = (b_1, \ldots, b_m)^{\mathrm{T}}$, and let $\gamma = (\alpha : \beta : b)^{\mathrm{T}}$. Let $B = B_1 \times \cdots \times B_m$ and let $\Gamma = A \times B \times \Re^m$. The feasible-set correspondence $\mathcal{C} : B \times \Re^m \mapsto \Re^n$ is

$$\mathcal{C}(\beta, b) = \{x \in \Re^n \mid g_1(x; \beta_1) \leq b_1, \ldots, g_m(x; \beta_m) \leq b_m\}.$$

For all $(\beta, b) \in B \times \Re^m$, suppose that $\mathcal{C}(\beta, b)$ is a bounded subset of $\Re^n$ with a nonempty interior. The optimal solution correspondence $X^* : \Gamma \mapsto \Re^n$ is

$$X^*(\gamma) = \{x^* \in \Re^n \mid f(x^*; \alpha) \geq f(x; \alpha) \ \forall \ x \in C(\beta, b)\}.$$

(i) Must $X^*(\gamma) \neq \emptyset$ for every $\gamma \in \Gamma$? Prove your answer.

(ii) Suppose, additionally, that every one of the constraint functions g_j is quasi-convex with respect to $x \in \Re^n$ and that the objective function f is quasi-strictly-concave with respect to $x \in \Re^n$. For any given $\gamma \in \Gamma$, what is the cardinality of the set $X^*(\gamma)$; *i.e.* how many elements are there in the set $X^*(\gamma)$? Prove your answer.

(iii) Suppose that every one of the constraint functions g_j is quasi-convex with respect to $x \in \Re^n$ and that the objective function f is quasi-strictly-concave with respect to $x \in \Re^n$. Is the optimal solution correspondence X^* a continuous function on Γ? Prove your answer.

Problem 11.5. Consider the equality constrained optimization problem

$$\max_{x \in \Re^n} f(x; \alpha) \text{ subject to } h(x; \beta, b) \equiv b - g(x; \beta) = 0.$$

Write $\gamma = (\alpha, \beta, b) \in A \times B \times \Re = \Gamma$. Suppose that f is jointly concave in $(x, \alpha) \in \Re^n \times A$ and that $h(x; \beta, b)$ is jointly concave in $(x, \beta, b) \in X \times B \times \Re$. Prove that the problem's maximum-value function $v(\gamma)$ is concave on Γ.

Problem 11.6. Most readers will have had some experience with basic game theory. The usual games discussed are Nash games, so-called because the notion of equilibrium used in these games was developed by John Nash. Nash proved that at least one Nash equilibrium exists for any game consisting of a finite number of players, each with von Neumann-Morgenstern preferences (*i.e.* preferences represented by expected utility functions), and in which each player possesses a finite number of pure actions. The argument that Nash gave has two major parts to it. The first part is a demonstration that each player's "best-response correspondence" is upper-hemi-continuous with respect to the (typically mixed) actions chosen by all of the other players. The second part, which we will not discuss here, is an application of Kakutani's Fixed-Point Theorem. Nash games are now a standard part of modeling strategic economic environments, so it is useful to understand why it is that each Nash player's best-response correspondence is upper-hemi-continuous with respect to the actions chosen by the other players. You might think that this is going to be difficult, but it is not. The argument consists of a sequence of quite simple steps, and the problem is broken up into parts, one part for each step.

We will start with a description of the game. There are $n \geq 2$ players. Let's think about Player 1's problem. Player 1 can choose from m_1 *pure* actions $a_1^1, \ldots, a_{m_1}^1$. These might be actions such as "sulk," "tantrum," "throw something," and so on. Let's use A^1 to denote the set of pure actions: $A^1 = \{a_1^1, \ldots, a_{m_1}^1\}$. Player 1 is allowed

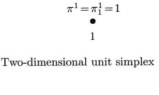

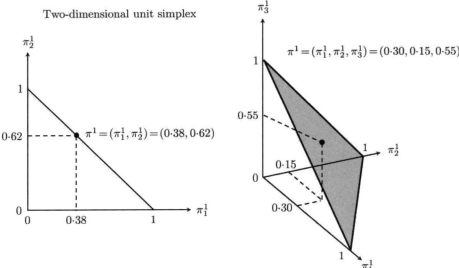

Figure 11.6: The unit simplices of dimensions one, two, and three, and some examples of mixed actions.

to make randomized choices over the pure actions available to her so, for example, she might choose "sulk" with probability 3/4, "tantrum" with probability zero, and "throw something" with probability 1/4. Such a randomization over Player 1's pure actions is a *mixed* action for Player 1.   It is a probability distribution over all of the m_1 pure actions available for Player 1 to choose from. So, for Player 1, a mixed action is a discrete probability distribution

$$\pi^1 = (\pi_1^1, \ldots, \pi_{m_1}^1), \text{ where } \pi_1^1 \geq 0, \ldots, \pi_{m_1}^1 \geq 0 \text{ and } \pi_1^1 + \cdots + \pi_{m_1}^1 = 1,$$

where π_i^1 is the probability that she will select her i^{th} pure action a_i^1. The collection of all mixed actions available to Player 1 is her *mixed action set*

$$\Sigma^1 = \left\{ \left(\pi_1^1, \ldots, \pi_{m_1}^1\right) \mid \pi_1^1 \geq 0, \ldots, \pi_{m_1}^1 \geq 0 \text{ and } \pi_1^1 + \cdots + \pi_{m_1}^1 = 1 \right\}.$$

This set is the m_1-dimensional unit simplex. The one, two, and three-dimensional unit simplices are displayed in Figure 11.6. A pure action a_i^1 is the probabilistically degenerate mixed action in which $\pi_i^1 = 1$ and $\pi_j^i = 0$ for all $j = 1, \ldots, m_i$; $j \neq i$.

Player 1's payoff depends upon the *pure* actions that end up being chosen by all of the players in the game. Let's use a to denote a complete list of these pure actions, so $a = (a^1, \ldots, a^n)$ is an ordered list of the pure actions chosen by Players 1 to n. We can also write this list as $a = (a^1, a^{-1})$, where $a^{-1} = (a^2, \ldots, a^n)$ is the list of the pure actions chosen by all of the players other than Player 1; *i.e.* the superscript "-1" means "excluding Player 1". Player 1's payoff function is $g^1(a)$.

In a Nash game, each Player i selects a strategy using the belief (this belief is called the *Nash conjecture*) that whatever action is chosen by Player i does not cause any of the other players to change the actions already selected by them. So, for example, Player 1 believes that she can alter her choice of pure action from "tantrum" to "throw something" without causing any of Players 2 to n to alter their chosen actions. In other words, Player 1 treats the list of actions taken by the other players as parametric; *i.e.* fixed and given.

We will use $\pi^{-1} = (\pi^2, \ldots, \pi^n)$ to denote the ordered list of the mixed actions chosen by all of the other Players 2 to n. For a given list π^{-1}, and a given mixed action choice π^1 by Player 1, what is Player 1's expected payoff? Consider a given list of strategies $\pi^1, \pi^2, \ldots, \pi^n$. Then the probability that Player 1 chooses pure action $a^1_{j_1}$ is $\pi^1_{j_1}$, the probability that Player 2 chooses pure action $a^2_{j_2}$ is $\pi^2_{j_2}$, and so on. Thus the probability that the particular list of pure actions chosen by the players is $a^1_{j_1}, a^2_{j_2}, \ldots, a^n_{j_n}$ is

$$\Pr\left(a^1_{j_1}, a^2_{j_2}, \ldots, a^n_{j_n}\right) = \pi^1_{j_1} \times \pi^2_{j_2} \times \cdots \times \pi^n_{j_n}.$$

This is the probability that Player 1's payoff is $g^1\left(a^1_{j_1}, a^2_{j_2}, \ldots, a^n_{j_n}\right)$, so the payoff expected by Player 1 when the list of strategies for the players is $\pi^1, \pi^2, \ldots, \pi^n$ is

$$f^1(\pi^1; \pi^{-1}) = \sum_{j_1=1}^{m_1} \sum_{j_2=1}^{m_2} \cdots \sum_{j_n=1}^{m_n} g^1(a^1_i, a^2_{j_2}, \ldots, a^n_{j_n}) \times \pi^1_{j_1} \times \pi^2_{j_2} \times \cdots \times \pi^n_{j_n}$$

$$= \sum_{j_1=1}^{m_1} \underbrace{\left\{ \sum_{j_2=1}^{m_2} \cdots \sum_{j_n=1}^{m_n} g^1(a^1_i, a^2_{j_2}, \ldots, a^n_{j_n}) \times \pi^2_{j_2} \times \cdots \times \pi^n_{j_n} \right\}}_{\text{independent of } \pi^1_1, \ldots, \pi^1_{m_1}} \times \pi^1_{j_1}. \quad (11.21)$$

Player 1 treats the other players' strategies as fixed and given, and so believes the quantities in the { } braces to be given numbers. Thus Player 1 believes that her expected payoff function (11.21) is linear with respect to each of $\pi^1, \ldots, \pi^1_{m_1}$.

Player 1 chooses her action π^1 so as to maximize her expected payoff given π^{-1}; *i.e.* Player 1's problem is:

$$\max_{\pi^1_1, \ldots, \pi^1_{m_1} \in \Sigma^1} f^1(\pi^1; \pi^{-1}).$$

The optimal solution to this problem is $\pi^{*1}(\pi^{-1})$, the set of mixed actions (probability distributions) that each maximize Player 1's expected payoff given the (parametric, she believes) list π^{-1} of the other players' actions. This optimal solution is Player 1's *best-response correspondence*.

(i) Prove that $\pi^{*1}(\pi^{-1}) \neq \emptyset$, for any list π^{-1} of the other players' (mixed) actions.

(ii) Prove that π^{*1} is an upper-hemi-continuous correspondence of π^{-1}.

Problem 11.7. The 2×2 table below is the payoff matrix for a Nash game that is played by two firms. One firm, the incumbent, is initially the only firm present in a market. The other firm, the entrant, decides between entering the market (action "Enter") and not entering (action "Stay Out"). The incumbent chooses between the actions of "Fight"ing entry and "Yield"ing to entry. The first element in each payoff pair is the entrant's payoff. The second is the incumbent's payoff.

(i) Compute the best-response correspondences for the two firms.

Incumbent

		Fight	Yield
	Enter	(-1, -1)	(1, 1)
Entrant	Stay Out	(0, 4)	(0, 4)

(ii) Are the best-response correspondences upper-hemi-continuous? Are they convex-valued? What are the domains and ranges of the correspondences?

(iii) What is the game's best-response correspondence? What is its domain and range? What is its graph? Explain why its graph is closed. With respect to which space is the graph closed?

11.7   Answers

Answer to Problem 11.1. The function

$$f(x) = \begin{cases} 3 - (x - 1)^2 & , \text{ if } 0 \leq x \leq 2 \\ (x - 3)^2 & , \text{ if } 2 < x \leq 4 \end{cases}$$

is displayed in Figure 11.7. f is discontinuous at $x = 2$, is upper-semi-continuous on the interval $[0, 4]$, attains a global maximum at $x = 1$, and attains a global minimum at $x = 3$.

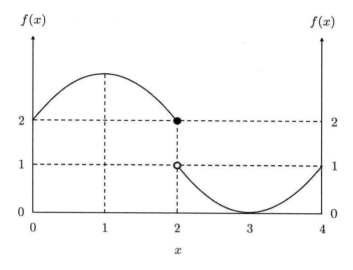

Figure 11.7: Graph of $f(x)$ for problem 11.1.

The function $-f(x)$ is discontinuous at $x = 2$, is lower-semi-continuous on the interval $[0, 4]$, attains a global minimum at $x = 1$, and attains a global maximum at $x = 3$.

Theorem 11.1 states that an upper-semi-continuous function with a domain that is a compact set must attain a global maximum. The theorem does not say that such a function cannot also attain a global minimum. Similarly, Theorem 11.2 states that an lower-semi-continuous function with a domain that is a compact set must attain a global minimum. The theorem does not say that such a function cannot also attain a global maximum.   □

Answer to Problem 11.2.

Proof of Theorem 11.2. Let $\underline{f} = \inf_{x \in C} f(x)$. It must be shown that there is a value $\underline{x} \in C$ for which the corresponding value of f is $\underline{f}$.

Since $\underline{f} = \inf_{x \in C} f(x)$, there exists in C a sequence $\{x_n\}_{n=1}^{\infty}$ such that

$$f(x_n) \to \underline{f}. \tag{11.22}$$

Since C is compact, this sequence must contain a convergent subsequence $\{x_{n_k}\}_{k=1}^{\infty}$. Let $\underline{x} = \lim_{k \to \infty} x_{n_k}$. $\underline{x} \in C$ because C is a closed set.

Since f is lower-semi-continuous on $\mathcal{C}$,

$$\lim_{k \to \infty} f(x_{n_k}) \geq f(\underline{x}). \tag{11.23}$$

The sequences $\{f(x_n)\}_{n=1}^{\infty}$ and $\{f(x_{n_k})\}_{k=1}^{\infty}$ must converge to the same value, so it follows from (11.22) and (11.23) that $\underline{f} \geq f(\underline{x})$. But, by definition, $\underline{f} \leq f(x)$ for every $x \in \mathcal{C}$, so it must be that $\underline{f} = f(\underline{x})$. □

Answer to Problem 11.3.

(i) The consumer's ordinary demand correspondence is

$$X^*(p_1, y) = \begin{cases} \left(\dfrac{y}{p_1}, 0\right) & \text{, if } 0 < p_1 < 1 \\[2mm] \{(y, 0), (0, y)\} & \text{, if } p_1 = 1 \\[2mm] (0, y) & \text{, if } 1 < p_1. \end{cases} \tag{11.24}$$

(ii) For $0 < p_1 < 1$ and $1 < p_1$, the demand correspondence is single-valued and continuous, and thus is upper-hemi-continuous for $p_1 \neq 1$. The demand correspondence is not continuous at $p_1 = 1$.

Take any sequence $\{p_n\}_{n=1}^{\infty}$ with $p_n \geq 1$ for all $n \geq 1$ and $p_n \to 1$. The corresponding sequence of ordinary demands is $\{(0, y)\}_{n=1}^{\infty}$, which is convergent to $(0, y) \in X^*(p_1 = 1, y)$. Now take any sequence $\{p_n\}_{n=1}^{\infty}$ with $0 < p_n < 1$ for all $n \geq 1$ and $p_n \to 1$. Then the corresponding sequence of ordinary demands is $\{(y/p_1, 0)\}_{n=1}^{\infty}$, which converges to $(y, 0) \in X^*(p_1 = 1, y)$. Thus $X^*(p_1, y)$ is upper-hemi-continuous at $p_1 = 1$. This, together with the above paragraph, establishes that $X^*(p_1, y)$ is upper-hemi-continuous with respect to p_1 for $p_1 > 0$.

(iii) The consumer's indirect utility is

$$v(p_1, y) = \begin{cases} \left(\dfrac{y}{p_1}\right)^2 & \text{, if } 0 < p_1 < 1 \\[2mm] y^2 & \text{, if } p_1 = 1 \\[2mm] y^2 & \text{, if } 1 < p_1 \end{cases} = \begin{cases} \left(\dfrac{y}{p_1}\right)^2 & \text{, if } 0 < p_1 < 1 \\[2mm] y^2 & \text{, if } 1 \leq p_1. \end{cases}$$

As $p_1 \to 1^-$, $(y/p_1)^2 \to y^2$, so $v(p_1, y)$ is continuous for all $p_1 > 0$.

v is not differentiable at $p_1 = 1$. Why? For $p_1 > 1$, the value of $\partial v/\partial p_1$ is zero. For $0 < p_1 < 1$, the value of $\partial v/\partial p_1 = -2y^2/p_1^3$, so, as $p_1 \to 1^-$, $\partial v/\partial p_1 \to -2y^2 \neq 0$. Thus v is not differentiable with respect to p_1 at $p_1 = 1$. This example makes the point, that while the Theorem of the Maximum gives conditions that are sufficient for a maximum-value function to be continuous, these same conditions are generally not sufficient for the maximum-value function to be differentiable. □

Answer to Problem 11.4.

(i) Proof. Yes. Take any $\gamma \in \Gamma$. The feasible set $\mathcal{C}(\beta, b) \neq \emptyset$. Also,

$$\mathcal{C}(\beta, b) = \{x \in \Re^n \mid g_1(x; \beta_1) \leq b_1, \ldots, g_m(x; \beta_m) \leq b_m\}$$
$$= \bigcap_{j=1}^{m} \{x \in \Re^n \mid g_j(x; \beta_j) \leq b_j\}.$$

Since each constraint function g_j is continuous jointly with respect to (x, β_j), it is continuous with respect to x alone for fixed β_j. Therefore g_j is lower-semi-continuous on $\Re^n$ for any given β_j, and so the sets $\{x \in \Re^n \mid g_j(x; \beta_j) \leq b_j\}$ are all closed in E^n. Hence $\mathcal{C}(\beta, b)$ is the intersection of a finite number of sets that are closed in E^n, and so it too is a closed subset of E^n. Since it is given above that any feasible set is not empty and is bounded in E^n, it follows that $\mathcal{C}(\beta, b)$ is a compact and nonempty subset of E^n.

The objective function f is jointly continuous with respect to (x, α), and so is continuous with respect to x alone for any fixed value of α. Hence, for any given $\gamma' \in \Gamma$, the constrained optimization problem is to maximize a function $f(x; \alpha')$ that is continuous with respect to x on a nonempty and compact subset $\mathcal{C}(\beta', b')$ of $\Re^n$. Weierstrass's Theorem asserts that there is at least one maximizing (optimal) solution to this problem; *i.e.* $X^*(\gamma') \neq \emptyset$. Since γ' is an arbitrary choice from Γ, $X^*(\gamma) \neq \emptyset$ for every $\gamma \in \Gamma$. □

(ii) $X^*(\gamma)$ is a singleton; *i.e.* $\#X^*(\gamma) \equiv 1$ on Γ.

Proof. Take any $\gamma \in \Gamma$. Since $g_j(x; \beta_j)$ is quasi-convex with respect to x, the lower-contour set $\{x \in \Re \mid g_j(x; \beta_j) \leq b_j\}$ is a convex subset of $\Re^n$. Hence $\mathcal{C}(\beta, b)$ is the intersection of convex sets, and so is a convex subset of $\Re^n$.

Since $f(x; \alpha)$ is quasi-strictly-concave with respect to $x \in \Re^n$, the upper-contour set $\{x \in \Re^n \mid f(x; \alpha) \geq k\}$ is a strictly convex subset of $\Re^n$ if it has a nonempty interior, or is weakly convex if it is a singleton or is empty.

It has been established that $X^*(\gamma) \neq \emptyset$, so $\#X^*(\gamma) \geq 1$. Suppose $\#X^*(\gamma) > 1$. Then there exist at least two optimal solutions $x', x'' \in X^*(\gamma)$ with $x' \neq x''$. Denote the maximum value provided by these solutions by

$$\bar{v} = f(x'; \alpha) = f(x''; \alpha).$$

Since x' and x'' are optimal solutions, they are also feasible solutions, meaning that $x', x'' \in \mathcal{C}(\beta, b)$, a convex set. So, for any $\mu \in [0, 1]$, $x(\mu) = \mu x' + (1 - \mu)x'' \in \mathcal{C}(\gamma)$;

i.e. $x(\mu)$ is a feasible solution. But, since f is quasi-strictly-concave with respect to x, the objective function value provided by $x(\mu)$ is

$$f(\mu x' + (1 - \mu)x''; \alpha) > f(x'; \alpha) = f(x''; \alpha) = \overline{v}.$$

This contradicts the optimality of x' and x'', so $\#X^*(\gamma) \not> 1$. Hence $\#X^*(\gamma) = 1$. □

(iii) Proof. Yes. Since $\#X^*(\gamma) \equiv 1$ on Γ, X^* is a function. Since X^* is upper-hemi-continuous on Γ, it is a continuous function. □

Answer to Problem 11.5. Choose $\gamma', \gamma'' \in \Gamma$ with $\gamma' \neq \gamma''$. Use $x^*(\gamma')$ to denote a solution that is optimal for $\gamma' = (\alpha', \beta', b')$ and use $x^*(\gamma'')$ to denote a solution that is optimal for $\gamma'' = (\alpha'', \beta'', b'')$. Then

$$v(\gamma') = f(x^*(\gamma'); \alpha') \text{ and } h(x^*(\gamma'); \beta', b') \geq 0, \tag{11.25}$$

$$\text{and} \quad v(\gamma'') = f(x^*(\gamma''); \alpha'') \text{ and } h(x^*(\gamma''); \beta'', b'') \geq 0. \tag{11.26}$$

Since h is jointly concave in (x, β, b), for any $\mu \in [0, 1]$,

$$\begin{aligned} &h(\mu x^*(\gamma') + (1 - \mu)x^*(\gamma''), \mu\beta' + (1 - \mu)\beta'', \mu b' + (1 - \mu)b'') \\ &\geq \mu h(x^*(\gamma'); \beta', b') + (1 - \mu)h(x^*(\gamma''); \beta'', b'') \geq 0 \end{aligned} \tag{11.27}$$

by (11.25) and (11.26). Hence $\mu x^*(\gamma') + (1 - \mu)x^*(\gamma'')$ is a feasible point when $\gamma = \mu\gamma' + (1 - \mu)\gamma''$. Then

$$\begin{aligned} v(\mu\gamma' + (1 - \mu)\gamma'') &= f(x^*(\mu\gamma' + (1 - \mu)\gamma''); \mu\alpha' + (1 - \mu)\alpha'') \\ &\geq f(\mu x^*(\gamma') + (1 - \mu)x^*(\gamma''); \mu\alpha' + (1 - \mu)\alpha'') \tag{11.28} \\ &\geq \mu f(x^*(\gamma'); \alpha') + (1 - \mu)f(x^*(\gamma''); \alpha'') \tag{11.29} \\ &= \mu v(\gamma') + (1 - \mu)v(\gamma''), \end{aligned}$$

where (11.28) follows from the fact that $x = \mu x^*(\gamma') + (1 - \mu)x^*(\gamma'')$ need not be optimal for $\gamma = \mu\gamma' + (1 - \mu)\gamma''$, and where (11.29) follows from the joint concavity of f with respect to (x, α). □

Answer to Problem 11.6. Player 1's problem

$$\max_{\pi^1 \in \Sigma^1} f^1(\pi^1; \pi^{-1}).$$

is to select a mixed action π^1 from her set Σ^1 of available mixed actions so as to maximize her expected payoff, given the list π^{-1} of the other players' chosen mixed actions.

(i) The problem's feasible set is the unit simplex

$$\Sigma^1 = \left\{ \left(\pi_1^1, \ldots \pi_{m_1}^1 \right) \mid \pi_1^1 \geq 0, \ \ldots, \ \pi_{m_1}^1 \geq 0, \ \pi_1^1 + \cdots + \pi_{m_1}^1 = 1 \right\}.$$

This set is not empty, is convex, and is compact with respect to E^{m_1}. The problem's objective function $f^1(\pi^1; \pi^{-1})$ is linear, and therefore continuous, with respect to each of $\pi_1^1, \ldots, \pi_{m_1}^1$. Weierstrass's Theorem asserts that there is a mixed action $\pi^{*1} \in \Sigma^1$ that maximizes Player 1's expected payoff given the list π^{-1} of the mixed actions chosen by Players 2 to n; *i.e.* $\pi^{*1}\left(\pi^{-1} \right) \neq \emptyset$.

(ii) Does Player 1's choice problem satisfy the conditions of Berge's Theorem of the Maximum? The problem's objective function (11.21) is jointly continuous with respect to each of $\pi_1^1, \ldots, \pi_{m_1}^1$, each of $\pi_1^2, \ldots, \pi_{m_2}^2$, and so on, up to each of $\pi_1^n, \ldots, \pi_{m_n}^n$. The value of the problem's feasible set correspondence is constant at Σ^1 because, by assumption, in a Nash game the pure actions available to any player cannot be changed by any other player(s). In this trivial sense, then, the problem's feasible set correspondence is continuous with respect to the parameter (from Player 1's perspective) vector π^{-1}. As well, the set Σ^1 is not empty, and is compact with respect to E^{m_1}. Thus, Berge's Theorem may be applied to Player 1's problem, establishing that the problem's optimal solution correspondence π^{*1} is upper-hemi-continuous on the set $\Sigma^2 \times \cdots \times \Sigma^n$ that contains all of the possible lists of mixed actions for Players 2 to n. $\qquad \square$

Answer to Problem 11.7. Let p_y denote the probability that the incumbent will choose action "Yield." Then $1 - p_y$ is the probability that the incumbent will choose action "Fight." Let p_e denote the probability that the potential entrant will choose action "Enter." Then $1 - p_e$ is the probability that the potential entrant will choose action "Stay Out." In other words, the incumbent's mixed strategy is $\sigma^I = (p_y, 1 - p_y)$ and the potential entrant's mixed strategy is $\sigma^E = (p_e, 1 - p_e)$.

(i) Given the incumbent's strategy, the expected value to the potential entrant, E, of choosing action "Enter" is

$$\text{EV}_{\text{Enter}}^E = 1 \times p_y + (-1) \times (1 - p_y) = 2p_y - 1.$$

The expected value to the potential entrant of choosing action "Stay Out" in response to the incumbent's strategy is

$$\text{EV}_{\text{Stay Out}}^E = 0.$$

So the potential entrant's best-response correspondence is

$$\sigma^{*E} = (p_e^*, 1 - p_e^*) = \begin{cases} (0,1) & \text{, if } 0 \le p_y < 1/2 \\ (\alpha, 1-\alpha) \text{ for any } \alpha \in [0,1] & \text{, if } p_y = 1/2 \\ (1,0) & \text{, if } 1/2 < p_y \le 1. \end{cases} \qquad (11.30)$$

Similarly, the incumbent's best-response correspondence is

$$\sigma^{*I} = (p_y^*, 1 - p_y^*) = \begin{cases} (\beta, 1-\beta) \text{ for any } \beta \in [0,1] & \text{, if } p_e = 0 \\ (1,0) & \text{, if } 0 < p_e \le 1. \end{cases} \qquad (11.31)$$

Figure 11.8 displays the graphs of the best-response correspondences.

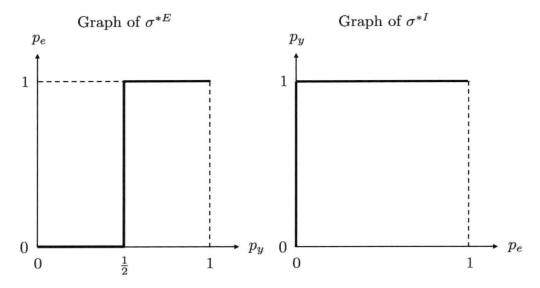

Figure 11.8: The entrant's and incumbent's best-response correspondences.

(ii) σ^{*E} maps from the strategy space of the incumbent into the strategy space of the potential entrant. That is, $\sigma^{*E} : S \mapsto S$, where $S = \{(p, 1-p) \mid 0 \le p \le 1\}$ is the unit simplex in $\Re^2$. Similarly, σ^{*I} maps from the strategy space of the potential entrant into the strategy space of the incumbent. That is, $\sigma^{*E} : S \mapsto S$.

When $0 \le p_y < 1/2$, $\sigma^{*E}((p_y, 1-p_y))$ is the singleton set containing only the vertex $(0,1)$ of the simplex S. This is a compact and weakly convex subset of $\Re^2$. When $1/2 < p_y \le 1$, $\sigma^{*E}((p_y, 1-p_y))$ is the singleton set containing only the vertex $(1,0)$ of the simplex S. This too is a compact and weakly convex subset of $\Re^2$. When $p_y = 1/2$, $\sigma^{*E}((p_y, 1-p_y))$ is the interval that is the edge of the simplex S between the vertex $(0, 1)$ and the vertex $(1, 0)$. This is a compact and weakly convex subset of $\Re^2$. Since the image of σ^{*E} is always a compact and convex subset of $\Re^2$, σ^{*E} is a compact-valued and convex-valued correspondence. Similarly, σ^{*I} is a convex-valued, compact-valued correspondence also.

Both σ^{*E} and σ^{*I} are upper-hemi-continuous correspondences. There are two ways to demonstrate this. First, we can use Berge's Theorem of the Maximum. Second, we can use the Closed Graph Theorem. To apply Berge's Theorem, notice that the incumbent's problem is to maximize an expected value function that is continuous in the probabilities p_e and p_y. Next, the incumbent's choice set is the unit simplex in $\Re^2$, which is a compact set. Last, this unit simplex choice set is independent of the potential entrant's strategic choice, so, in this trivial sense, the incumbent's choice set is a compact-valued and continuous correspondence of the potential entrant's strategy choice. Berge's Theorem now applies and we conclude that the incumbent's best-response correspondence is upper-hemi-continuous on the potential entrant's strategy space.

To apply the Closed Graph Theorem, notice from (11.30) that the union of all of the images of σ^{*E} is just the one-dimensional unit simplex, which is compact in $\Re^2$. The graph of σ^{*E} is the set

$$\text{graph}\left(\sigma^{*E}\right) = \{(p_e^*, 1 - p_e^*, p_y) \mid p_e^* = 0 \text{ for } 0 \leq p_y < 1/2, \ p_e^* \in [0, 1] \text{ for } p_y = 1/2,$$
$$\text{and } p_e^* = 1 \text{ for } 1/2 < p_y \leq 1\}.$$

This set is closed in $\Re^3$ so the Closed Graph Theorem informs us that the potential entrant's best-response correspondence is upper-hemi-continuous on the unit simplex that is the incumbent's strategy space. Similarly, the incumbent's best-response correspondence is upper-hemi-continuous on the unit simplex that is the entrant's strategy space.

(iii) The game's best-response correspondence σ^* lists the individual players' best-response correspondences; *i.e.* $\sigma^* = (\sigma^{*E}, \sigma^{*I})$. σ^* maps from the game's strategy space, which is the direct product of the two players' strategy spaces, to the same space; *i.e.* $\sigma^* : S^2 \mapsto S^2$. Written out in detail, σ^* is

$\sigma^*((p_e, 1 - p_e), (p_y, 1 - p_y)) =$

$$\begin{cases} (0,1), (\beta, 1-\beta) \ \forall \ \beta \in [0,1] & \text{, if } 0 \leq p_y < 1/2 \text{ and } p_e = 0 \\ (0,1), (1,0) & \text{, if } 0 \leq p_y < 1/2 \text{ and } 0 < p_e \leq 1 \\ (\alpha, 1-\alpha) \ \forall \ \alpha \in [0,1], (\beta, 1-\beta) \ \forall \ \beta \in [0,1] & \text{, if } p_y = 1/2 \text{ and } p_e = 0 \\ (\alpha, 1-\alpha) \ \forall \ \alpha \in [0,1], (1,0) & \text{, if } p_y = 1/2 \text{ and } 0 < p_e \leq 1 \\ (1,0), (\beta, 1-\beta) \ \forall \ \beta \in [0,1] & \text{, if } 1/2 < p_y \leq 1 \text{ and } p_e = 0 \\ (1,0), (1,0) & \text{, if } 1/2 < p_y \leq 1 \text{ and } 0 < p_e \leq 1. \end{cases}$$

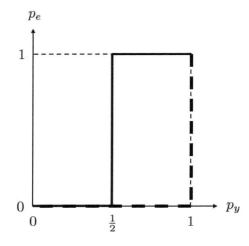

Figure 11.9: The entry game's best-response correspondence.

The graph of this correspondence is closed in $\Re^4$. A lower-dimensional drawing of the game's best-response correspondence can be constructed in (p_e, p_y)-space, which is $[0,1]^2$; see Figure 11.9. It is constructed by superimposing on each other the above diagrams for (11.30) and (11.31) (see Figure 11.8 – one of the diagrams has to be rotated by 90° to have both diagrams on the same axes). $\qquad \square$

Chapter 12

Comparative Statics Analysis, Part 1

12.1   What Is Comparative Statics Analysis?

Comparative statics analysis is the comparison of the values taken by the optimal solution correspondence to a static optimization problem for different parameter values. Understand that comparative statics analysis has nothing to do with the study of dynamic problems. When we talk of changes in a dynamic problem or its solution, we are speaking of changes that occur through time. Time does not exist in a static problem.

$$\max_{x \in \Re^n} f(x; \alpha) \text{ subject to } g_j(x; \beta_j) \leq b_j \text{ for all } j = 1, \ldots, m. \qquad (12.1)$$

If you have not already done so, then you should read Section 11.2 to understand the notation being used in (12.1). The feasible set correspondence, the optimal solution correspondence, and the maximum-value function for the problem are

$$\mathcal{C}(\beta, b) \equiv \{x \in \Re^n \mid g_j(x; \beta_j) \leq b_j \; \forall \; j = 1, \ldots, m\},$$
$$X^*(\gamma) = X^*(\alpha, \beta, b) \equiv \{x^* \in \mathcal{C}(\beta, b) \mid f(x^*; \alpha) \geq f(x; \alpha) \; \forall \; x \in \mathcal{C}(\beta, b)\},$$
$$\text{and} \quad v(\gamma) \equiv f(x^*; \alpha) \text{ where } x^* \in X^*(\alpha, \beta, b).$$

In the example that is problem (11.4), the parameters not assigned numerical values are the elements of the parameter vector $\gamma = (p, w_1, w_2, \beta_1, \beta_2)$. These are the parameters that are of interest for comparative statics analyses of the problem. The typical *comparative statics experiment* is where one of a problem's parameters is varied. The experimenter then observes the changes caused to the problem's optimal solution(s). For example, if in problem (11.4) the value of the firm's product's price p is altered, then the experimenter observes the consequences of a slight change to p. These will be changes to the quantity of product supplied by the firm, changes to the quantities used of the firm's inputs, changes to the values of the multipliers of the constraints that bind at the profit-maximizing solution to the firm's problem, and a change to the firm's maximum profit level. Similarly, the experimenter could slightly alter the price w_1 of input 1 and observe the consequences. Using such experiments to analyze the properties of the firm's profit-maximizing production plan is a *comparative statics analysis* of the firm's problem.

More generally, two different values γ' and γ'' of the parameter vector γ define two parametrically different versions of problem (12.1), and typically cause two different values $X^*(\gamma')$ and $X^*(\gamma'')$ of the optimal solution correspondence and two different values $v(\gamma')$ and $v(\gamma'')$ of the maximum-value function. Comparing these two optimal solution values and the two maximized values of the objective function helps us to determine the properties of both the optimal solution correspondence and the maximum-value function. Sometimes this is easily done. In problem (11.4), for example, we were able to discover explicit algebraic equations for the problem's optimal solution; see (11.5). These equations directly tell us everything there is to know about the properties of the optimal solution to problem (11.4). For example, we observe from (11.5a) that the quantity y^* that the firm supplies of its product falls as the price w_2 of input 2 increases. This is a *qualitative* comparative statics result. Again from (11.5a), by differentiation we can determine the *value* of the rate at which the firm's quantity supplied decreases as w_2 increases. This is a *quantitative* comparative statics result. So comparative statics analyses can be divided into two types, qualitative and quantitative. In a qualitative analysis, we are interested only in the directions of change of the parts of the optimal solution as values of the problem's parameters are changed. In a quantitative analysis we want to know as well the numerical magnitudes of the changes or rates of change. In this chapter we will consider how to obtain quantitative comparative statics results. In the following chapter we will confine ourselves to obtaining qualitative comparative statics results.

12.2 Quantitative Comparative Statics Analysis

Let us begin with a simple example. Consider the problem

$$\max_{x} f(x; \alpha_1, \alpha_2, \alpha_3) = -\alpha_1 x^2 + \alpha_2 x + \alpha_3 \text{ with } \alpha_1 > 0. \tag{12.2}$$

The necessary first-order optimality condition is

$$
\frac{\mathrm{d}f(x; \alpha_1, \alpha_2, \alpha_3)}{\mathrm{d}x}\Big|_{x=x^*(\alpha_1,\alpha_2,\alpha_3)} = -2\alpha_1 x^*(\alpha_1, \alpha_2, \alpha_3) + \alpha_2 = 0
$$
$$
\Rightarrow \quad x^*(\alpha_1, \alpha_2, \alpha_3) = \frac{\alpha_2}{2\alpha_1}.
$$
(12.3)

Because we have an explicit equation for the problem's optimal solution, it is easy to discover all of the properties of the optimal solution. For instance, the optimal solution decreases as α_1 increases, increases as α_2 increases, and is independent of α_3.

More commonly, however, there will not exist an algebraically explicit optimal solution. What can we learn in such a case? Consider the problem

$$
\max_{x \geq 0} f(x; \gamma) = x(1 - \ln(\gamma + x)).
$$
(12.4)

We will restrict the parameter γ to values from zero to unity: $\gamma \in [0, 1]$. The necessary first-order optimality condition is

$$
0 = \frac{\mathrm{d}f(x; \gamma)}{\mathrm{d}x} = 1 - \ln(\gamma + x) - \frac{x}{\gamma + x} \quad \text{at } x = x^*(\gamma).
$$
(12.5)

It is not possible to rewrite this equation so that the optimal solution mapping $x^*(\gamma)$ is stated as an explicit function of γ. Yet, for any given value for $\gamma \in [0, 1]$, there is an optimizing value $x^*(\gamma)$ for x; see Figure 12.1. In this case, then, the optimal solution to the problem is defined only implicitly by the first-order maximization condition. For such cases the Implicit Function Theorem (stated below) is often used to obtain differential quantitative comparative statics results. The procedure is straightforward. The key is to realize that, for any given value of γ, at the corresponding optimal value $x^*(\gamma)$ for x, the first-order maximization condition (12.5) *necessarily* has the value zero. Therefore, *when evaluated only at optimal values of x, the first-order maximization condition* (12.5) *is identically* zero:

$$
0 \equiv 1 - \ln(\gamma + x^*(\gamma)) - \frac{x^*(\gamma)}{\gamma + x^*(\gamma)} \quad \forall \, \gamma \in [0, 1].
$$
(12.6)

The right-hand side of (12.6) is a function only of γ (because $x^*(\gamma)$ is a function of γ), so, in recognition of this, let us write (12.6) as

$$
I(\gamma) \equiv 1 - \ln(\gamma + x^*(\gamma)) - \frac{x^*(\gamma)}{\gamma + x^*(\gamma)} \equiv 0 \,\, \forall \, \gamma \in [0, 1].
$$
(12.7)

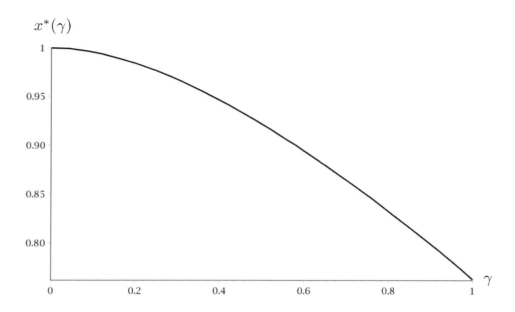

Figure 12.1: The graph of the implicit optimal solution $x^*(\gamma)$ to problem (12.4).

The identity mapping $I(\gamma)$ is constant-valued (at zero) so its rate of change with respect to γ must be zero. Accordingly, using the Chain Rule to differentiate (12.7) with respect to γ gives

$$\frac{\mathrm{d}I(\gamma)}{\mathrm{d}\gamma} = -\,\frac{\gamma + (2\gamma + x^*(\gamma))\,\dfrac{\mathrm{d}x^*(\gamma)}{\mathrm{d}\gamma}}{(\gamma + x^*(\gamma))^2} = 0. \tag{12.8}$$

The numerator of (12.8) necessarily is zero, which tells us that the rate of change with respect to γ of the value of the implicit optimal solution $x^*(\gamma)$ is

$$\frac{\mathrm{d}x^*(\gamma)}{\mathrm{d}\gamma} = -\,\frac{\gamma}{2\gamma + x^*(\gamma)}\,. \tag{12.9}$$

So what have we discovered? We have an expression for the rate at which the optimal solution to problem (12.4) changes as the problem's parameter γ changes. But since we do not have an algebraic equation for the optimal solution $x^*(\gamma)$, we do not have an algebraic equation for this rate of change. Have we, then, learned anything new at all? Well, yes – actually we have learned a great deal. First, notice from (12.7), that if $\gamma = 0$, then we can easily determine that the value of the optimal solution is

Table 12.1: $x^*(\gamma)$ and its order 2 Taylor's series approximation.

γ	0	0·001	0·01	0·1	0·2
$\Delta\gamma$	0	0·001	0·01	0·1	0·2
$x^*(\gamma)$	1	0·9999995	0·99995	0·9956	0·984
$1 - \dfrac{(\Delta\gamma)^2}{2}$	1	0·9999900	0·99990	0·9900	0·960

unity: $x^*(0) = 1$. So then, from (12.9), we know that the rate of change for $x^*(\gamma)$ with respect to γ is zero at $\gamma = 0$ (check that this is so in Figure 12.1). And if we differentiate (12.9), then we obtain

$$\frac{\mathrm{d}^2 x^*(\gamma)}{\mathrm{d}\gamma^2} = \frac{\gamma \dfrac{\mathrm{d}x^*(\gamma)}{\mathrm{d}\gamma} - x^*(\gamma)}{(2\gamma + x^*(\gamma))^2} = -\frac{(\gamma + x^*(\gamma))^2}{(2\gamma + x^*(\gamma))^3} \tag{12.10}$$

after substitution from (12.9). Since $x^*(0) = 1$ we have that, at $\gamma = 0$, the value of the second derivative of $x^*(\gamma)$ at $\gamma = 0$ is -1. Now we can use an order-2 Taylor's series to assert that, for values of $\gamma = 0 + \Delta\gamma$ that are close to $\gamma = 0$, the value of the optimal solution $x^*(\gamma)$ is close to

$$x^*(0 + \Delta\gamma) \approx x^*(0) + \frac{\mathrm{d}x^*(\gamma)}{\mathrm{d}\gamma}\Big|_{\gamma=0}\Delta\gamma + \frac{1}{2}\frac{\mathrm{d}^2 x^*(\gamma)}{\mathrm{d}\gamma^2}\Big|_{\gamma=0}(\Delta\gamma)^2 = 1 - \frac{(\Delta\gamma)^2}{2}.$$

Table 12.1 lists numerically computed values of $x^*(\gamma)$ and of the approximation $1 - (\Delta\gamma)^2/2$ for various values of $\Delta\gamma$. The table shows that the approximation for $x^*(\gamma)$ is quite accurate for small values of $\Delta\gamma$. All of this is achieved without having a formula for the optimal solution $x^*(\gamma)$ – that's quite impressive.

12.3 Implicit Function Theorems

The argument we used in going from (12.7) to (12.8) and then to (12.9) is an explanation of the use of the Implicit Function Theorem for a single equation. The theorem is a result often used by economists when undertaking comparative statics analyses.

Theorem 12.1 (Implicit Function Theorem for a Single Equation). *Let $I(x, \gamma_1, \ldots, \gamma_k)$ be a C^1 function defined in a neighborhood about a point $(x', \gamma_1', \ldots, \gamma_k')$. Let c denote the value of I at the point $(x', \gamma_1', \ldots, \gamma_k')$; i.e. $I(x', \gamma_1', \ldots, \gamma_k') = c$. If*

$$\frac{\partial I(x, \gamma_1, \ldots, \gamma_k)}{\partial x} \neq 0 \ at \ (x', \gamma_1', \ldots, \gamma_k'),$$

then there exists an $\varepsilon > 0$ and a C^1 function $x = g(\gamma_1, \ldots, \gamma_k)$ defined over the ball $B_{d_E}\left((\gamma_1', \ldots, \gamma_k'), \varepsilon\right)$, such that
(i) $I(g(\gamma_1, \ldots, \gamma_k), \gamma_1, \ldots, \gamma_k) \equiv c$ on $B_{d_E}\left((\gamma_1', \ldots, \gamma_k'), \varepsilon\right)$,
(ii) $x' = g(\gamma_1', \ldots, \gamma_k')$, and
(iii) for $j = 1, \ldots, k$, the rate of change of g with respect to γ_j at $(\gamma_1', \ldots, \gamma_k')$ is

$$\frac{\partial g(\gamma_1, \ldots, \gamma_k)}{\partial \gamma_j}\Big|_{\substack{\gamma_1 = \gamma_1' \\ \vdots \\ \gamma_k = \gamma_k'}} = -\frac{\partial I(x, \gamma_1, \ldots, \gamma_k)/\partial \gamma_j}{\partial I(x, \gamma_1, \ldots, \gamma_k)/\partial x}\Big|_{\substack{x = x' \\ \gamma_1 = \gamma_1' \\ \vdots \\ \gamma_k = \gamma_k'}}.$$

Let's take careful note of some features of this result. First, the function I is *continuously* differentiable, not just differentiable, to order 1 with respect to each of $x, \gamma_1, \ldots, \gamma_k$. In our example above, the function is $I(x, \gamma) = 1 - \ln(\gamma + x) - \gamma/(\gamma + x)$ (see (12.5)). The first-order derivatives of $I(x, \gamma)$ are

$$\frac{\partial I(x, \gamma)}{\partial \gamma} = -\frac{\gamma}{(\gamma + x)^2} \quad \text{and} \quad \frac{\partial I(x, \gamma)}{\partial x} = -\frac{2\gamma + x}{(\gamma + x)^2}.$$

Both of these derivative functions are continuous in a neighborhood about $(x, \gamma) = (1, 0)$, so I is continuously differentiable to order 1 over the neighborhood. Moreover the value at $(x, \gamma) = (1, 0)$ of $\partial I/\partial x = -1 \neq 0$. The theorem then assures us that, in some (possibly small) neighborhood centered on $(x, \gamma) = (1, 0)$, there exists a continuously differentiable to order 1 implicit function $x = g(\gamma)$, such that $I(\gamma) \equiv I(g(\gamma), \gamma) \equiv 0$ over the neighborhood and the rate of change of $g(\gamma)$ at $\gamma = 0$ is

$$\frac{\mathrm{d}g(\gamma)}{\mathrm{d}\gamma}\Big|_{\gamma=0} = -\frac{\partial I(x, \gamma)/\partial \gamma}{\partial I(x, \gamma)/\partial x}\Big|_{\substack{x=1 \\ \gamma=0}} = -\frac{0}{-1} = 0,$$

just as we determined from (12.9).

In most of the problems that interest economists, there are several choice variables $x_1, \ldots, x_n$ to be solved for in terms of several parameters $\gamma_1, \ldots, \gamma_k$. The Implicit Function Theorem extends to these more general cases. I'll state this version of the theorem and then explain what it says. The theorem looks a bit ugly but don't be deterred. It is just talking about when we can solve linear equation systems, a topic we considered in Section 2.3.

Theorem 12.2 (Implicit Function Theorem for an Equation System).
Let $I_1(x_1, \ldots, x_n, \gamma_1, \ldots, \gamma_k), \ldots, I_n(x_1, \ldots, x_n, \gamma_1, \ldots, \gamma_k)$ be C^1 functions defined in a neighborhood about a point $(x'_1, \ldots, x'_n, \gamma'_1, \ldots, \gamma'_k)$. Let c_i denote the value of I_i at the point $(x'_1, \ldots, x'_n, \gamma'_1, \ldots, \gamma'_k)$; i.e. $I_i(x'_1, \ldots, x'_n, \gamma'_1, \ldots, \gamma'_k) = c_i$ for $i = 1, \ldots, n$. Let $\det J_I(x', \gamma')$ denote the value at $(x'_1, \ldots, x'_n, \gamma'_1, \ldots, \gamma'_k)$ of the determinant of the Jacobian matrix

$$J_I(x, \gamma) = \begin{pmatrix} \dfrac{\partial I_1}{\partial x_1} & \cdots & \dfrac{\partial I_1}{\partial x_n} \\ \vdots & \ddots & \vdots \\ \dfrac{\partial I_n}{\partial x_1} & \cdots & \dfrac{\partial I_n}{\partial x_n} \end{pmatrix}.$$

If $\det J_I(x', \gamma') \neq 0$, then, there exists an $\varepsilon > 0$, and C^1 functions

$$x_1 = g_1(\gamma_1, \ldots, \gamma_k), \ldots, x_n = g_n(\gamma_1, \ldots, \gamma_k)$$

defined over the ball $B_{d_E}\left((\gamma'_1, \ldots, \gamma'_k), \varepsilon\right)$, such that
(i) $I_i(g_1(\gamma_1, \ldots, \gamma_k), \ldots, g_n(\gamma_1, \ldots, \gamma_k), \gamma_1, \ldots, \gamma_k) \equiv c_i$ on $B_{d_E}\left((\gamma'_1, \ldots, \gamma'_k), \varepsilon\right)$ for each $i = 1, \ldots, n$,
(ii) $x'_i = g_i(\gamma'_1, \ldots, \gamma'_k)$ for $i = 1, \ldots, n$, and
(iii) for each $j = 1, \ldots, k$, the values of the rates of change of x_i with respect to γ_j at $(\gamma'_1, \ldots, \gamma'_k)$ are the solution to

$$J_I(x', \gamma') \begin{pmatrix} \dfrac{\partial x_1}{\partial \gamma_j} \\ \vdots \\ \dfrac{\partial x_n}{\partial \gamma_j} \end{pmatrix} = - \begin{pmatrix} \dfrac{\partial I_1}{\partial \gamma_j} \\ \vdots \\ \dfrac{\partial I_n}{\partial \gamma_j} \end{pmatrix} \Bigg|_{\substack{x_1 = x'_1 \\ \vdots \\ x_n = x'_n \\ \gamma_1 = \gamma'_1 \\ \vdots \\ \gamma_k = \gamma'_k}}.$$

Let's look at a simple example in which we must solve for two choice variable values. Consider the problem

$$\max_{x_1, x_2} f(x_1, x_2; \gamma) = -(x_1 - \gamma)(x_2 - 2\gamma) = -x_1 x_2 + 2\gamma x_1 + \gamma x_2 - 2\gamma^2.$$

The optimal solution is $(x_1^*(\gamma), x_2^*(\gamma)) = (\gamma, 2\gamma)$. The comparative-statics results are $dx_1^*(\gamma)/d\gamma = 1$ and $dx_2^*(\gamma)/d\gamma = 2$. How do we obtain these results using the above theorem? The first-order conditions, necessarily true at the optimal solution, are

$$\frac{\partial f(x_1, x_2; \gamma)}{\partial x_1} = -x_2 + 2\gamma = 0 \text{ and } \frac{\partial f(x_1, x_2; \gamma)}{\partial x_2} = -x_1 + \gamma = 0$$

at $(x_1, x_2) = (x_1^*(\gamma), x_2^*(\gamma))$. Let's change our notation to match that used in the above theorem. Then we have that, at the point $(x_1, x_2, \gamma) = (x_1^*(\gamma), x_2^*(\gamma), \gamma)$, necessarily

$$I_1(x_1, x_2, \gamma) \equiv -x_2 + 2\gamma = c_1 = 0 \quad \text{and} \quad I_2(x_1, x_2, \gamma) \equiv -x_1 + \gamma = c_2 = 0.$$

The Jacobian matrix of this equation system is

$$J_I(x_1, x_2, \gamma) = \begin{pmatrix} \dfrac{\partial I_1}{\partial x_1} & \dfrac{\partial I_1}{\partial x_2} \\ \dfrac{\partial I_2}{\partial x_1} & \dfrac{\partial I_2}{\partial x_2} \end{pmatrix} = \begin{pmatrix} 0 & -1 \\ -1 & 0 \end{pmatrix}.$$

The vector

$$\begin{pmatrix} \dfrac{\partial I_1}{\partial \gamma} \\ \dfrac{\partial I_2}{\partial \gamma} \end{pmatrix} = \begin{pmatrix} 2 \\ 1 \end{pmatrix}.$$

The value of the determinant of the Jacobian matrix is $-1 \neq 0$, so the Implicit Function Theorem says that the comparative statics quantities $\mathrm{d}x_1^*(\gamma)/\mathrm{d}\gamma$ and $\mathrm{d}x_2^*(\gamma)/\mathrm{d}\gamma$ are the solution to

$$J_I(x_1, x_2, \gamma) \begin{pmatrix} \dfrac{\mathrm{d}x_1^*(\gamma)}{\mathrm{d}\gamma} \\ \dfrac{\mathrm{d}x_2^*(\gamma)}{\mathrm{d}\gamma} \end{pmatrix} = \begin{pmatrix} 0 & -1 \\ -1 & 0 \end{pmatrix} \begin{pmatrix} \dfrac{\mathrm{d}x_1^*(\gamma)}{\mathrm{d}\gamma} \\ \dfrac{\mathrm{d}x_2^*(\gamma)}{\mathrm{d}\gamma} \end{pmatrix} = -\begin{pmatrix} 2 \\ 1 \end{pmatrix}. \qquad (12.11)$$

The solution is as we discovered earlier: $\mathrm{d}x_1^*(\gamma)/\mathrm{d}\gamma = 1$ and $\mathrm{d}x_2^*(\gamma)/\mathrm{d}\gamma = 2$. Why? What's going on here? It's simple. We know that, if we substitute into the first-order conditions the optimizing values $x_1^*(\gamma)$ and $x_2^*(\gamma)$ for x_1 and x_2, then the values of the first-order condition *have* to be zeros; *i.e.* the first-order conditions become zero-valued identities,

$$I_1(x_1^*(\gamma), x_2^*(\gamma), \gamma) = -x_2^*(\gamma) + 2\gamma \equiv 0 \quad \text{and} \quad I_2(x_1^*(\gamma), x_2^*(\gamma), \gamma) = -x_1^* + \gamma \equiv 0.$$

Both are *constant* (at zero) so their rates of change with respect to γ must be zero; *i.e.* the values of the derivatives of these identities with respect to γ must both be zero. Using the Chain Rule, then, we get

$$\frac{\partial I_1}{\partial x_1} \times \frac{\mathrm{d}x_1^*(\gamma)}{\mathrm{d}\gamma} + \frac{\partial I_1}{\partial x_2} \times \frac{\mathrm{d}x_2^*(\gamma)}{\mathrm{d}\gamma} + \frac{\partial I_1}{\partial \gamma} = 0 \times \frac{\mathrm{d}x_1^*(\gamma)}{\mathrm{d}\gamma} + (-1) \times \frac{\mathrm{d}x_2^*(\gamma)}{\mathrm{d}\gamma} + 2 = 0$$

and $\quad \dfrac{\partial I_2}{\partial x_1} \times \dfrac{\mathrm{d}x_1^*(\gamma)}{\mathrm{d}\gamma} + \dfrac{\partial I_2}{\partial x_2} \times \dfrac{\mathrm{d}x_2^*(\gamma)}{\mathrm{d}\gamma} + \dfrac{\partial I_2}{\partial \gamma} = (-1) \times \dfrac{\mathrm{d}x_1^*(\gamma)}{\mathrm{d}\gamma} + 0 \times \dfrac{\mathrm{d}x_2^*(\gamma)}{\mathrm{d}\gamma} + 1 = 0.$

These are exactly the same as their matrix version, (12.11). The nonzero value of the determinant of the Jacobian matrix is an insistence that the n first-order conditions, one with respect to each of $x_1, \ldots, x_n$, yield n linearly independent equations in the n comparative statics quantities $\partial x_1^*(\gamma)/\partial\gamma, \ldots, \partial x_n^*(\gamma)/\partial\gamma$ for which we wish to solve.

The discussion in this section is intended only as an explanation of how the Implicit Function Theorem may be used to compute the values of comparative statics quantities. Nothing here is a proof.

12.4 Starting Points

Generally, the goal of a differential comparative statics analysis is to obtain values, for a particular given value of the parameter vector γ, of the derivatives $\partial x_i^*/\partial\gamma_k$ and $\partial\lambda_j^*/\partial\gamma_k$ that measure quantitatively the rate of change of the optimal value x_i^* of the ith choice variable and the rate of change of the value λ_j^* of the jth constraint's multiplier as the value of the kth parameter γ_k changes. The good news is that the procedure used to obtain these results is not difficult. It is, in fact, just the procedure used above in our last example. The bad news is that often the algebra required is lengthy and tedious.

There are two starting points for obtaining quantitative differential comparative statics results for a constrained optimization problem. These are the problem's first-order necessary optimality conditions and the problem's maximum-value function. These two starting points provide different types of comparative statics results, as we shall see. In Section 12.6 we will see what types of results we can obtain from the problem's first-order conditions. In Section 12.7 we will see the types of results that we can obtain from the problem's maximum-value function.

12.5 Assumptions

To undertake *differentiable* comparative statics analyses of problem (12.1), we impose conditions sufficient for the problem's optimal solution correspondence to be a vector of differentiable functions.

Assumption 1 (Unique Solution). $X^*(\gamma)$ is a singleton for every $\gamma \in \Gamma$. In recognition of this the optimal solution function will be written as $x^* : \Gamma \mapsto \Re^n$, where

$$f(x^*(\gamma); \alpha) > f(x; \alpha) \ \forall \ x \in \mathcal{C}(\beta, b), \ x \neq x^*(\gamma).$$

Assumption 2 (Constraint Qualification). For every $\gamma \in \Gamma$, the optimal solution $x^*(\gamma)$ is a regular point in $\mathcal{C}(\beta, b)$.

Assumption 3 (Twice-Continuous Differentiability). $f, g_1, \ldots, g_m$ are all twice-continuously differentiable with respect to each choice variable x_i and with respect to each parameter γ_k.

These assumptions are collectively sufficient for the optimal solution $(x^*(\gamma), \lambda^*(\gamma))$ to be the unique, continuously differentiable solution to the first-order optimality conditions for problem (12.1). That is, there exist functions $x_i^* : \Gamma \to \Re$ for $i = 1, \ldots, n$ and $\lambda_j^* : \Gamma \mapsto \Re_+$ for $j = 1, \ldots, m$, such that, for any given $\gamma \in \Gamma$, the values $(x_1^*(\gamma), \ldots, x_n^*(\gamma), \lambda_1^*(\gamma), \ldots, \lambda_m^*(\gamma))$ uniquely solve

$$\frac{\partial f(x; \alpha)}{\partial x_i}\Big|_{x=x^*(\gamma)} = \sum_{j=1}^{m} \lambda_j^*(\gamma) \frac{\partial g_j(x; \beta_j)}{\partial x_i}\Big|_{x=x^*(\gamma)} \ \forall \ i = 1, \ldots, n, \qquad (12.12)$$

$$\lambda_j^*(\gamma)(b_j - g_j(x^*(\gamma); \beta_j)) = 0 \ \forall \ j = 1, \ldots, m, \qquad (12.13)$$

with $\quad \lambda_j^*(\gamma) \geq 0 \ \forall \ j = 1, \ldots, m, \qquad (12.14)$

and $\quad g_j(x^*) \leq b_j \ \forall \ j = 1, \ldots, m. \qquad (12.15)$

The maximum-value function $v : \Gamma \to \Re$ for the constrained optimization problem is

$$v(\gamma) \equiv f(x^*(\gamma); \alpha) + \sum_{j=1}^{m} \lambda_j^*(\gamma)(b_j - g_j(x^*(\gamma); \beta_j)). \qquad (12.16)$$

Since each $x_i^*(\gamma)$ and each $\lambda_j^*(\gamma)$ is a function that is continuously differentiable with respect to each parameter γ_k, the maximum-value function v is also a continuously differentiable function of each γ_k.

12.6   Using the First-Order Conditions

We start by writing down the necessary first-order optimality conditions for the given problem. Then we note that these equations hold as identities when evaluated at the optimal solution $(x_1^*(\gamma), \ldots, x_n^*(\gamma), \lambda_1^*(\gamma), \ldots, \lambda_m^*(\gamma))$. Next we differentiate each of these identities with respect to whichever one of the parameters γ_k that is of interest to us. This gives us $n + m$ linear equations in the $n + m$ unknowns that are the comparative statics quantities $\partial x_1^*(\gamma)/\partial \gamma_k, \ldots, \partial \lambda_m^*(\gamma)/\partial \gamma_k$. So long as these $n + m$ equations are linearly independent, we can compute the values of these derivatives at the optimal solution to the problem. That is all there is to it. Let's have a more detailed look at the procedure.

Our constrained optimization problem is (12.1). For a given value of the parameter vector γ, the optimal solution is $(x^*(\gamma), \lambda^*(\gamma)) = (x_1^*(\gamma), \ldots, x_n^*(\gamma), \lambda_1^*(\gamma), \ldots, \lambda_m^*(\gamma))$. Slack constraints are of no interest, so, without loss of generality, suppose that the binding (both strictly binding and just-binding) constraints are those indexed by $j = 1, \ldots, \ell$, where $1 \leq \ell \leq m$. Consequently $\lambda_1^*(\gamma) \geq 0, \ldots, \lambda_\ell^*(\gamma) \geq 0$ (> 0 for each strictly binding constraint and $= 0$ for each just-binding constraint) and $\lambda_{\ell+1}^*(\gamma) = \cdots = \lambda_m^*(\gamma) = 0$. The necessary first-order optimality conditions are the n Karush-Kuhn-Tucker conditions

$$\frac{\partial f(x; \alpha)}{\partial x_1} - \lambda_1 \frac{\partial g_1(x; \beta_1)}{\partial x_1} - \cdots - \lambda_\ell \frac{\partial g_\ell(x; \beta_\ell)}{\partial x_1} = 0$$

$$\vdots \qquad\qquad\qquad \vdots \qquad\qquad (12.17)$$

$$\frac{\partial f(x; \alpha)}{\partial x_n} - \lambda_1 \frac{\partial g_1(x; \beta_1)}{\partial x_n} - \cdots - \lambda_\ell \frac{\partial g_\ell(x; \beta_\ell)}{\partial x_n} = 0$$

and the ℓ complementary slackness conditions

$$\lambda_1(b_1 - g_1(x; \beta_1)) = 0, \ldots, \lambda_\ell(b_\ell - g_\ell(x; \beta_\ell)) = 0. \qquad (12.18)$$

These $n + \ell$ equations are functions of $x_1, \ldots, x_n$, $\lambda_1, \ldots, \lambda_\ell$ and of the parameters listed in γ. The optimal solution $(x_1^*(\gamma), \ldots, \lambda_\ell^*(\gamma))$ is a list of functions of only the parameters in γ, so when we substitute the optimal solution into (12.17) and (12.18), we obtain the following $n + \ell$ equations that are functions of *only the parameters*:

$$\frac{\partial f(x; \alpha)}{\partial x_1}\Big|_{x=x^*(\gamma)} - \lambda_1^*(\gamma)\frac{\partial g_1(x; \beta_1)}{\partial x_1}\Big|_{x=x^*(\gamma)} - \cdots - \lambda_\ell^*(\gamma)\frac{\partial g_\ell(x; \beta_\ell)}{\partial x_1}\Big|_{x=x^*(\gamma)} = 0,$$

$$\vdots \qquad\qquad\qquad\qquad \vdots \qquad\qquad (12.19)$$

$$\frac{\partial f(x; \alpha)}{\partial x_n}\Big|_{x=x^*(\gamma)} - \lambda_1^*(\gamma)\frac{\partial g_1(x; \beta_1)}{\partial x_n}\Big|_{x=x^*(\gamma)} - \cdots - \lambda_\ell^*(\gamma)\frac{\partial g_\ell(x; \beta_\ell)}{\partial x_n}\Big|_{x=x^*(\gamma)} = 0,$$

and $\lambda_1^*(\gamma)(b_1 - g_1(x^*(\gamma); \beta_1)) = 0, \ldots, \lambda_\ell^*(\gamma)(b_\ell - g_\ell(x^*(\gamma); \beta_\ell)) = 0.$

Necessarily, each of these $n + \ell$ equations is *always zero*, so let us write them as

$$I_1(\gamma) \equiv \frac{\partial f(x; \alpha)}{\partial x_1}\Big|_{x=x^*(\gamma)} - \lambda_1^*(\gamma)\frac{\partial g_1(x; \beta_1)}{\partial x_1}\Big|_{x=x^*(\gamma)} - \cdots - \lambda_\ell^*(\gamma)\frac{\partial g_\ell(x; \beta_\ell)}{\partial x_1}\Big|_{x=x^*(\gamma)} \equiv 0,$$

$$\vdots \qquad\qquad \vdots \qquad\qquad (12.20)$$

$$I_n(\gamma) \equiv \frac{\partial f(x; \alpha)}{\partial x_n}\Big|_{x=x^*(\gamma)} - \lambda_1^*(\gamma)\frac{\partial g_1(x; \beta_1)}{\partial x_n}\Big|_{x=x^*(\gamma)} - \cdots - \lambda_\ell^*(\gamma)\frac{\partial g_\ell(x; \beta_\ell)}{\partial x_n}\Big|_{x=x^*(\gamma)} \equiv 0,$$

$$I_{n+1}(\gamma) \equiv \lambda_1^*(\gamma)(b_1 - g_1(x^*(\gamma); \beta_1)) \equiv 0, \ldots, I_{n+\ell}(\gamma) \equiv \lambda_\ell^*(\gamma)(b_\ell - g_\ell(x^*(\gamma); \beta_\ell)) \equiv 0.$$

The $n + \ell$ comparative statics quantities $\partial x_1^*(\gamma)/\partial \gamma_k, \ldots, \partial \lambda_\ell^*(\gamma)/\partial \gamma_k$ are obtained by differentiating this system of zero-valued identities with respect to γ_k, and then solve the resulting $n + \ell$ linear equations in these quantities.

Consider the identity $I_1(\gamma) \equiv 0$. Its value is constant, so its rate of change with respect to any parameter γ_k is always zero: $\partial I_1(\gamma)/\partial \gamma_k = 0$ for all possible values of γ. From (12.20), differentiating $I_1(\gamma) \equiv 0$ with respect to γ_k gives

$$\begin{aligned}
0 &= \frac{\partial I_1(\gamma)}{\partial \gamma_k} \\
&= \frac{\partial^2 f(x; \alpha)}{\partial x_1^2}\Big|_{x=x^*(\gamma)}\frac{\partial x_1^*(\gamma)}{\partial \gamma_k} + \cdots + \frac{\partial^2 f(x; \alpha)}{\partial x_1 \partial x_n}\Big|_{x=x^*(\gamma)}\frac{\partial x_n^*(\gamma)}{\partial \gamma_k} + \frac{\partial^2 f(x; \alpha)}{\partial x_1 \partial \gamma_k}\Big|_{x=x^*(\gamma)} \\
&\quad - \lambda_1^*(\gamma)\left(\frac{\partial^2 g_1(x; \beta_1)}{\partial x_1^2}\Big|_{x=x^*(\gamma)}\frac{\partial x_1^*(\gamma)}{\partial \gamma_k} + \cdots + \frac{\partial^2 g_1(x; \beta_1)}{\partial x_1 \partial x_n}\Big|_{x=x^*(\gamma)}\frac{\partial x_n^*(\gamma)}{\partial \gamma_k}\right) \\
&\qquad\qquad\qquad \vdots \qquad\qquad\qquad\qquad \vdots \qquad\qquad\qquad (12.21) \\
&\quad - \lambda_\ell^*(\gamma)\left(\frac{\partial^2 g_\ell(x; \beta_\ell)}{\partial x_1^2}\Big|_{x=x^*(\gamma)}\frac{\partial x_1^*(\gamma)}{\partial \gamma_k} + \cdots + \frac{\partial^2 g_\ell(x; \beta_\ell)}{\partial x_1 \partial x_n}\Big|_{x=x^*(\gamma)}\frac{\partial x_n^*(\gamma)}{\partial \gamma_k}\right) \\
&\quad - \lambda_1^*(\gamma)\frac{\partial^2 g_1(x; \beta_1)}{\partial x_1 \partial \gamma_k}\Big|_{x=x^*(\gamma)} - \cdots - \lambda_\ell^*(\gamma)\frac{\partial^2 g_\ell(x; \beta_\ell)}{\partial x_1 \partial \gamma_k}\Big|_{x=x^*(\gamma)} \\
&\quad - \frac{\partial \lambda_1^*(\gamma)}{\partial \gamma_k}\frac{\partial g_1(x; \beta_1)}{\partial x_1}\Big|_{x=x^*(\gamma)} - \cdots - \frac{\partial \lambda_\ell^*(\gamma)}{\partial \gamma_k}\frac{\partial g_\ell(x; \beta_\ell)}{\partial x_1}\Big|_{x=x^*(\gamma)}.
\end{aligned}$$

Let's tidy up (12.21). Collect the terms with $\partial x_1^*(\gamma)/\partial \gamma_k$, then collect the terms with

$\partial x_2^*(\gamma)/\partial\gamma_k$, and so on down to collecting the terms with $\partial\lambda_\ell^*(\gamma)/\partial\gamma_k$. This gives

$$
\begin{aligned}
0 = {}& \left(\frac{\partial^2 f(x;\alpha)}{\partial x_1^2} - \lambda_1^*(\gamma)\frac{\partial^2 g_1(x;\beta_1)}{\partial x_1^2} - \cdots - \lambda_\ell^*(\gamma)\frac{\partial^2 g_\ell(x;\beta_\ell)}{\partial x_1^2}\right)\bigg|_{x=x^*(\gamma)}\frac{\partial x_1^*(\gamma)}{\partial\gamma_k} \\
& \qquad\qquad \vdots \qquad\qquad\qquad\qquad \vdots \\
+{}& \left(\frac{\partial^2 f(x;\alpha)}{\partial x_n\partial x_1} - \lambda_1^*(\gamma)\frac{\partial^2 g_1(x;\beta_1)}{\partial x_n\partial x_1} - \cdots - \lambda_\ell^*(\gamma)\frac{\partial^2 g_\ell(x;\beta_\ell)}{\partial x_n\partial x_1}\right)\bigg|_{x=x^*(\gamma)}\frac{\partial x_n^*(\gamma)}{\partial\gamma_k} \\
+{}& \frac{\partial^2 f(x;\alpha)}{\partial x_1\partial\gamma_k}\bigg|_{x=x^*(\gamma)} - \lambda_1^*(\gamma)\frac{\partial^2 g_1(x;\beta_1)}{\partial x_1\partial\gamma_k}\bigg|_{x=x^*(\gamma)} - \cdots - \lambda_\ell^*(\gamma)\frac{\partial^2 g_\ell(x;\beta_\ell)}{\partial x_1\partial\gamma_k}\bigg|_{x=x^*(\gamma)} \\
-{}& \frac{\partial g_1(x;\beta_1)}{\partial x_1}\bigg|_{x=x^*(\gamma)}\frac{\partial\lambda_1^*(\gamma)}{\partial\gamma_k} - \cdots - \frac{\partial g_\ell(x;\beta_\ell)}{\partial x_1}\bigg|_{x=x^*(\gamma)}\frac{\partial\lambda_\ell^*(\gamma)}{\partial\gamma_k}\ . \qquad (12.22)
\end{aligned}
$$

This still looks like an ugly expression, but in fact it is very simple. Remember that all of the derivatives of f and g are being evaluated at the point $x = x^*(\gamma)$, so they are just numbers, as are the values $\lambda_j^*(\gamma)$. So (12.22) is actually a linear equation

$$
0 = a_{11}\frac{\partial x_1^*(\gamma)}{\partial\gamma_k} + \cdots + a_{1n}\frac{\partial x_n^*(\gamma)}{\partial\gamma_k} + c_1 + a_{1,n+1}\frac{\partial\lambda_1^*(\gamma)}{\partial\gamma_k} + \cdots + a_{1,n+\ell}\frac{\partial\lambda_\ell^*(\gamma)}{\partial\gamma_k} \quad (12.23)
$$

with *numerical* coefficients

$$
a_{11} = \left(\frac{\partial^2 f(x;\alpha)}{\partial x_1^2} - \lambda_1^*(\gamma)\frac{\partial^2 g_1(x;\beta_1)}{\partial x_1^2} - \cdots - \lambda_\ell^*(\gamma)\frac{\partial^2 g_\ell(x;\beta_\ell)}{\partial x_1^2}\right)\bigg|_{x=x^*(\gamma)}
$$

$$
\vdots \qquad\qquad\qquad\qquad \vdots
$$

$$
a_{1n} = \left(\frac{\partial^2 f(x;\alpha)}{\partial x_n\partial x_1} - \lambda_1^*(\gamma)\frac{\partial^2 g_1(x;\beta_1)}{\partial x_n\partial x_1} - \cdots - \lambda_\ell^*(\gamma)\frac{\partial^2 g_\ell(x;\beta_\ell)}{\partial x_n\partial x_1}\right)\bigg|_{x=x^*(\gamma)}
$$

$$
c_1 = \left(\frac{\partial^2 f(x;\alpha)}{\partial x_1\partial\gamma_k} - \lambda_1^*(\gamma)\frac{\partial^2 g_1(x;\beta_1)}{\partial x_1\partial\gamma_k} - \cdots - \lambda_\ell^*(\gamma)\frac{\partial^2 g_\ell(x;\beta_\ell)}{\partial x_1\partial\gamma_k}\right)\bigg|_{x=x^*(\gamma)}
$$

$$
a_{1,n+1} = -\frac{\partial g_1(x;\beta_1)}{\partial x_1}\bigg|_{x=x^*(\gamma)}, \ldots, a_{1,n+\ell} = -\frac{\partial g_\ell(x;\beta_\ell)}{\partial x_1}\bigg|_{x=x^*(\gamma)}
$$

and unknowns $\partial x_1^*(\gamma)/\partial\gamma_k, \ldots, \partial\lambda_\ell^*(\gamma)/\partial\gamma_k$.

We repeat this process for the identity $I_2(\gamma) \equiv 0$, and obtain another linear equation

$$
0 = a_{21}\frac{\partial x_1^*(\gamma)}{\partial\gamma_k} + \cdots + a_{2n}\frac{\partial x_n^*(\gamma)}{\partial\gamma_k} + c_2 + a_{2,n+1}\frac{\partial\lambda_1^*(\gamma)}{\partial\gamma_k} + \cdots + a_{2,n+\ell}\frac{\partial\lambda_\ell^*(\gamma)}{\partial\gamma_k} \quad (12.24)
$$

in which the numerical coefficients are

$$a_{21} = \left(\frac{\partial^2 f(x;\alpha)}{\partial x_1 \partial x_2} - \lambda_1^*(\gamma) \frac{\partial^2 g_1(x;\beta_1)}{\partial x_1 \partial x_2} - \cdots - \lambda_\ell^*(\gamma) \frac{\partial^2 g_\ell(x;\beta_\ell)}{\partial x_1 \partial x_2} \right) \Big|_{x=x^*(\gamma)}$$

$$\vdots \qquad\qquad\qquad \vdots$$

$$a_{2n} = \left(\frac{\partial^2 f(x;\alpha)}{\partial x_n \partial x_2} - \lambda_1^*(\gamma) \frac{\partial^2 g_1(x;\beta_1)}{\partial x_n \partial x_2} - \cdots - \lambda_\ell^*(\gamma) \frac{\partial^2 g_\ell(x;\beta_\ell)}{\partial x_n \partial x_2} \right) \Big|_{x=x^*(\gamma)}$$

$$c_2 = \left(\frac{\partial^2 f(x;\alpha)}{\partial x_2 \partial \gamma_k} - \lambda_1^*(\gamma) \frac{\partial^2 g_1(x;\beta_1)}{\partial x_2 \partial \gamma_k} - \cdots - \lambda_\ell^*(\gamma) \frac{\partial^2 g_\ell(x;\beta_\ell)}{\partial x_2 \partial \gamma_k} \right) \Big|_{x=x^*(\gamma)}$$

$$a_{2,n+1} = -\frac{\partial g_1(x;\beta_1)}{\partial x_2}\Big|_{x=x^*(\gamma)}, \ldots, a_{2,n+\ell} = -\frac{\partial g_\ell(x;\beta_\ell)}{\partial x_2}\Big|_{x=x^*(\gamma)}$$

and the unknowns are again $\partial x_1^*(\gamma)/\partial \gamma_k, \ldots, \partial \lambda_\ell^*(\gamma)/\partial \gamma_k$. We continue this process for each of the identities $I_3(\gamma) \equiv 0$ to $I_n(\gamma) \equiv 0$. Each differentiation of an identity gives us another linear equation similar to (12.23) and (12.24).

Now we differentiate $I_{n+1}(\gamma) \equiv 0$ with respect to γ_k, knowing that the value of this derivative must be zero, and so obtain that

$$0 = \frac{\partial \lambda_1^*(\gamma)}{\partial \gamma_k} (b_1 - g_1(x^*(\gamma); \beta_1)) + \lambda_1^*(\gamma) \frac{\partial b_1}{\partial \gamma_k}$$
$$- \lambda_1^*(\gamma) \left(\frac{\partial g_1(x;\beta_1)}{\partial x_1}\Big|_{x=x^*(\gamma)} \frac{\partial x_1^*(\gamma)}{\partial \gamma_k} + \cdots + \frac{\partial g_1(x;\beta_1)}{\partial x_n}\Big|_{x=x^*(\gamma)} \frac{\partial x_n^*(\gamma)}{\partial \gamma_k} \right) \quad (12.25)$$
$$- \lambda_1^*(\gamma) \frac{\partial g_1(x;\beta_1)}{\gamma_k}\Big|_{x=x^*(\gamma)}.$$

The first term on the right-hand side of (12.25) is zero because the first constraint binds at $x = x^*(\gamma)$. Thus (12.25) reduces to

$$0 = \lambda_1^*(\gamma) \left(\frac{\partial g_1(x;\beta_1)}{\partial x_1}\Big|_{x=x^*(\gamma)} \frac{\partial x_1^*(\gamma)}{\partial \gamma_k} + \cdots + \frac{\partial g_1(x;\beta_1)}{\partial x_n}\Big|_{x=x^*(\gamma)} \frac{\partial x_n^*(\gamma)}{\partial \gamma_k} \right)$$
$$+ \lambda_1^*(\gamma) \frac{\partial g_1(x;\beta_1)}{\gamma_k}\Big|_{x=x^*(\gamma)} - \lambda_1^*(\gamma) \frac{\partial b_1}{\partial \gamma_k}. \quad (12.26)$$

$\partial b_1 / \partial \gamma_k = 0$ unless γ_k is b_1, in which case $\partial b_1 / \partial \gamma_k = 1$. $\partial g_1(x;\beta_1)/\partial \gamma_k$ is zero unless γ_k is one of the parameters listed in the vector β_1. (12.26) is a linear equation

$$a_{n+1,1} \frac{\partial x_1^*(\gamma)}{\partial \gamma_k} + \cdots + a_{n+1,n} \frac{\partial x_n^*(\gamma)}{\partial \gamma_k} = c_{n+1} \quad (12.27)$$

in which the numerical coefficients are

$$a_{n+1,1} = \lambda_1^*(\gamma)\frac{\partial g_1(x;\beta_1)}{\partial x_1}\Big|_{x=x^*(\gamma)}, \ldots, a_{n+1,n} = \lambda_1^*(\gamma)\frac{\partial g_1(x;\beta_1)}{\partial x_n}\Big|_{x=x^*(\gamma)}$$

$$\text{and} \quad c_{n+1} = -\lambda_1^*(\gamma)\frac{\partial g_1(x;\beta_1)}{\partial \gamma_k}\Big|_{x=x^*(\gamma)} + \lambda_1^*(\gamma)\frac{\partial b_1}{\partial \gamma_k}.$$

Now we repeat this process for each in turn of the identities $I_{n+2}(\gamma) \equiv 0$ to $I_{n+\ell}(\gamma) \equiv 0$. For example, differentiating the identity $I_{n+\ell}(\gamma) \equiv 0$ yields the linear equation

$$a_{n+\ell,1}\frac{\partial x_1^*(\gamma)}{\partial \gamma_k} + \cdots + a_{n+\ell,n}\frac{\partial x_n^*(\gamma)}{\partial \gamma_k} = c_{n+\ell} \tag{12.28}$$

in which the numerical coefficients are

$$a_{n+\ell,1} = \lambda_\ell^*(\gamma)\frac{\partial g_\ell(x;\beta_\ell)}{\partial x_1}\Big|_{x=x^*(\gamma)}, \ldots, a_{n+\ell,n} = \lambda_\ell^*(\gamma)\frac{\partial g_\ell(x;\beta_\ell)}{\partial x_n}\Big|_{x=x^*(\gamma)}$$

$$\text{and} \quad c_{n+\ell} = -\lambda_\ell^*(\gamma)\frac{\partial g_\ell(x;\beta_\ell)}{\partial \gamma_k}\Big|_{x=x^*(\gamma)} + \lambda_\ell^*(\gamma)\frac{\partial b_\ell}{\partial \gamma_k}.$$

Together, these differentiations create the linear simultaneous equation system

$$\begin{pmatrix} a_{11} & \cdots & a_{1n} & a_{1,n+1} & \cdots & a_{1,n+\ell} \\ \vdots & \ddots & \vdots & \vdots & & \vdots \\ a_{n1} & \cdots & a_{nn} & a_{n,n+1} & \cdots & a_{n,n+\ell} \\ a_{n+1,1} & \cdots & a_{n+1,n} & a_{n+1,n+1} & \cdots & a_{n+1,n+\ell} \\ \vdots & & \vdots & \vdots & \ddots & \vdots \\ a_{n+\ell,1} & \cdots & a_{n+\ell,n} & a_{n+\ell,n+1} & \cdots & a_{n+\ell,n+\ell} \end{pmatrix} \begin{pmatrix} \partial x_1^*(\gamma)/\partial \gamma_k \\ \vdots \\ \partial x_n^*(\gamma)/\partial \gamma_k \\ \partial \lambda_1^*(\gamma)/\partial \gamma_k \\ \vdots \\ \partial \lambda_\ell^*(\gamma)/\partial \gamma_k \end{pmatrix} = \begin{pmatrix} c_1 \\ \vdots \\ c_n \\ c_{n+1} \\ \vdots \\ c_{n+\ell} \end{pmatrix}.$$

$$\tag{12.29}$$

Every one of the coefficients a_{ij} is a number. Every one of the coefficients c_i is a number (many of them will be zeros). So long as the rows of the matrix (a_{ij}) are all linearly independent of each other, you now can use whatever is your favorite method for solving linear simultaneous equation systems to discover the value at the optimal solution to problem (12.1) of the comparative statics quantities $\partial x_1^*(\gamma)/\partial \gamma_k, \ldots, \partial \lambda_\ell^*(\gamma)/\partial \gamma_k$. That is all there is to this method of conducting a quantitative comparative statics analysis of the optimal solution to problem (12.1). The process may be tedious but it is not difficult.

We will proceed to an example in a moment, but, before doing so, there is a really important point for you to realize. What exactly do we need in order to compute the numerical values of the coefficients in the (a_{ij})-matrix on the left-hand side of (12.29)?

We are given the functions $f, g_1, \ldots, g_\ell$ and the values of all of the parameters in the vector γ. We are also given the values $x_1^*(\gamma), \ldots, \lambda_\ell^*(\gamma)$ of the optimal solution for the given parameter values. This is all we need to compute the numerical value of every one of the a_{ij} coefficients. So what *don't* we need? Particularly, we do not need to know the formulae (if they even exist, since they may be only implicitly defined) for the optimal solution functions $x_1^*(\gamma), \ldots, \lambda_\ell^*(\gamma)$. This is a huge advantage. It lets us compute the values of all of the rates of change $\partial x_i^*(\gamma)/\partial \gamma_k$ and $\partial \lambda_j^*(\gamma)/\partial \gamma_k$ without having equations for $x_1^*(\gamma), \ldots, \lambda_\ell^*(\gamma)$.

For an example we will use the problem faced by a price-taking and production-cost-minimizing firm that uses two variable inputs and must produce at least a specified quantity $y \geq 0$ of its product. The firm's production function is $g(x_1, x_2) = x_1^{1/2} x_2^{1/2}$, so the firm's problem is

$$\min_{x_1, x_2} w_1 x_1 + w_2 x_2 \text{ subject to } x_1 \geq 0, \ x_2 \geq 0, \text{ and } x_1^{1/2} x_2^{1/2} \geq y, \qquad (12.30)$$

where w_1 and w_2 are the given per unit prices of the firm's inputs. The parameter vector for the problem is

$$\gamma = \begin{pmatrix} w_1 \\ w_2 \\ y \end{pmatrix}.$$

The problem has three constraints. At the optimal solution

$$(x_1^*(w_1, w_2, y), x_2^*(w_1, w_2, y), \lambda_1^*(w_1, w_2, y), \lambda_2^*(w_1, w_2, y), \lambda_3^*(w_1, w_2, y)),$$

the first and second constraints are slack. Thus $\lambda_1^*(w_1, w_2, y) = \lambda_2^*(w_1, w_2, y) = 0$, and we consider only the third constraint during our comparative statics analysis of the problem's optimal solution. The comparative statics quantities that we wish to evaluate are

$$\frac{\partial x_1^*(w_1, w_2, y)}{\partial \gamma_k}, \ \frac{\partial x_2^*(w_1, w_2, y)}{\partial \gamma_k}, \text{ and } \frac{\partial \lambda_3^*(w_1, w_2, y)}{\partial \gamma_k},$$

where γ_k is any one of the parameters w_1, w_2, or y. Let's say that we want to see how the optimal solution changes as the price of input 2 changes. Then we select $\gamma_k = w_2$ and proceed to evaluate the comparative statics quantities

$$\frac{\partial x_1^*(w_1, w_2, y)}{\partial w_2}, \ \frac{\partial x_2^*(w_1, w_2, y)}{\partial w_2}, \text{ and } \frac{\partial \lambda_3^*(w_1, w_2, y)}{\partial w_2}.$$

We start by rewriting problem (12.30) so that it is in the format of problem (12.1). That is, we rewrite problem (12.30) so that it is a maximization problem and has constraints of the form $g(x) \leq b$. To convert the problem from a minimization problem into a maximization problem, simply multiply the objective function by negative one. To convert a $\geq$ constraint into a $\leq$ constraint, multiply it by negative one. This gives us the problem

$$\max_{x_1, x_2} -w_1 x_1 - w_2 x_2 \text{ subject to } -x_1 \leq 0, \; -x_2 \leq 0, \text{ and } y - x_1^{1/2} x_2^{1/2} \leq 0. \quad (12.31)$$

We write down the problem's necessary first-order optimality conditions. These are

$$-w_1 = -\frac{\lambda_3}{2} x_1^{-1/2} x_2^{1/2}, \quad -w_2 = -\frac{\lambda_3}{2} x_1^{1/2} x_2^{-1/2}, \quad \text{and} \quad 0 = \lambda_3 \left(-y + x_1^{1/2} x_2^{1/2}\right).$$

Now we note that, for *all* parameter values $w_1 > 0$, $w_2 > 0$, and $y > 0$, these equations are true when evaluated at the optimal solution $x_1^*(w_1, w_2, y)$, $x_2^*(w_1, w_2, y)$, and $\lambda_3^*(w_1, w_2, y)$. This allows us to write the identities

$$I_1(w_1, w_2, y) \equiv -w_1 + \frac{\lambda_3^*(w_1, w_2, y)}{2} x_1^*(w_1, w_2, y)^{-1/2} \, x_2^*(w_1, w_2, y)^{1/2} \equiv 0,$$
$$(12.32)$$

$$I_2(w_1, w_2, y) \equiv -w_2 + \frac{\lambda_3^*(w_1, w_2, y)}{2} x_1^*(w_1, w_2, y)^{1/2} \, x_2^*(w_1, w_2, y)^{-1/2} \equiv 0,$$
$$(12.33)$$

and $I_3(w_1, w_2, y) \equiv \lambda_3^*(w_1, w_2, y) \left(-y + x_1^*(w_1, w_2, y)^{1/2} x_2^*(w_1, w_2, y)^{1/2}\right) \equiv 0.$
$$(12.34)$$

Each identity is a function of only the parameters w_1, w_2, and y. Since each identity's value is constant, at zero, for any values $w_1 > 0$, $w_2 > 0$, and $y > 0$, we know that

$$\frac{\partial I_1(w_1, w_2, y)}{\partial w_2} = 0, \quad \frac{\partial I_2(w_1, w_2, y)}{\partial w_2} = 0, \text{ and } \frac{\partial I_3(w_1, w_2, y)}{\partial w_2} = 0.$$

So, from (12.32), (12.33), and (12.34), we obtain

$$\frac{\partial I_1(w_1, w_2, y)}{\partial w_2} = 0 = \frac{1}{2} \frac{\partial \lambda_3^*(\cdot)}{\partial w_2} x_1^*(\cdot)^{-1/2} x_2^*(\cdot)^{1/2} - \frac{\lambda_3^*(\cdot)}{4} x_1^*(\cdot)^{-3/2} x_2^*(\cdot)^{1/2} \frac{\partial x_1^*(\cdot)}{\partial w_2}$$

$$+ \frac{\lambda_3^*(\cdot)}{4} x_1^*(\cdot)^{-1/2} x_2^*(\cdot)^{-1/2} \frac{\partial x_2^*(\cdot)}{\partial w_2}, \tag{12.35}$$

$$\frac{\partial I_2(w_1, w_2, y)}{\partial w_2} = 0 = -1 + \frac{1}{2} \frac{\partial \lambda_3^*(\cdot)}{\partial w_2} x_1^*(\cdot)^{1/2} x_2^*(\cdot)^{-1/2} + \frac{\lambda_3^*(\cdot)}{4} x_1^*(\cdot)^{-1/2} x_2^*(\cdot)^{-1/2} \frac{\partial x_1^*(\cdot)}{\partial w_2}$$

$$- \frac{\lambda_3^*(\cdot)}{4} x_1^*(\cdot)^{1/2} x_2^*(\cdot)^{-3/2} \frac{\partial x_2^*(\cdot)}{\partial w_2}, \text{ and} \tag{12.36}$$

$$\frac{\partial I_3(w_1, w_2, y)}{\partial w_2} = 0 = \frac{\partial \lambda_3^*(\cdot)}{\partial w_2} \left(-y + x_1^*(\cdot)^{1/2} x_2^*(\cdot)^{1/2} \right) + \frac{\lambda_3^*(\cdot)}{2} x_1^*(\cdot)^{-1/2} x_2^*(\cdot)^{1/2} \frac{\partial x_1^*(\cdot)}{\partial w_2}$$

$$+ \frac{\lambda_3^*(\cdot)}{2} x_1^*(\cdot)^{1/2} x_2^*(\cdot)^{-1/2} \frac{\partial x_2^*(\cdot)}{\partial w_2}. \tag{12.37}$$

It will be easier to solve these equations for $\partial x_1^*(\cdot)/\partial w_2$, $\partial x_2^*(\cdot)/\partial w_2$, and $\partial \lambda_3^*(\cdot)/\partial w_2$ if we first tidy up the equations. Multiply (12.35) by $4x_1^*(\cdot)^{3/2} x_2^*(\cdot)^{1/2}$ and rearrange the result to

$$-\lambda_3^*(\cdot) x_2^*(\cdot) \frac{\partial x_1^*(\cdot)}{\partial w_2} + \lambda_3^*(\cdot) x_1^*(\cdot) \frac{\partial x_2^*(\cdot)}{\partial w_2} + 2x_1^*(\cdot) x_2^*(\cdot) \frac{\partial \lambda_3^*(\cdot)}{\partial w_2} = 0. \tag{12.38}$$

Then multiply (12.36) by $4x_1^*(\cdot)^{1/2} x_2^*(\cdot)^{3/2}$ and rearrange the result to

$$\lambda_3^*(\cdot) x_2^*(\cdot) \frac{\partial x_1^*(\cdot)}{\partial w_2} - \lambda_3^*(\cdot) x_1^*(\cdot) \frac{\partial x_2^*(\cdot)}{\partial w_2} + 2x_1^*(\cdot) x_2^*(\cdot) \frac{\partial \lambda_3^*(\cdot)}{\partial w_2} = 4x_1^*(\cdot)^{1/2} x_2^*(\cdot)^{3/2}. \tag{12.39}$$

Last, note that the first term on the right-hand side of (12.37) is zero (because the constraint binds at the optimal solution). Multiply the other two terms on the right-hand side of (12.37) by $2x_1^*(\cdot)^{1/2} x_2^*(\cdot)^{1/2}$, divide by $\lambda_3^*(\cdot)$ (you can do this because $\lambda_3^*(\cdot) > 0$), and rearrange the result to

$$x_2^*(\cdot) \frac{\partial x_1^*(\cdot)}{\partial w_2} + x_1^*(\cdot) \frac{\partial x_2^*(\cdot)}{\partial w_2} = 0. \tag{12.40}$$

(12.38), (12.39), and (12.40) are three linear equations in the three unknowns that are the comparative statics quantities we wish to evaluate. So all that remains is to solve these equations. You can verify for yourself that the solution is

$$\frac{\partial x_1^*(w_1, w_2, y)}{\partial w_2} = \frac{y}{\lambda_3^*(w_1, w_2, y)}, \tag{12.41}$$

$$\frac{\partial x_2^*(w_1, w_2, y)}{\partial w_2} = -\frac{x_2^*(w_1, w_2, y)^{3/2}}{x_1^*(w_1, w_2, y)^{1/2}\lambda_3^*(w_1, w_2, y)}, \tag{12.42}$$

and
$$\frac{\partial \lambda_3^*(w_1, w_2, y)}{\partial w_2} = \left(\frac{x_2^*(w_1, w_2, y)}{x_1^*(w_1, w_2, y)}\right)^{1/2}. \tag{12.43}$$

To evaluate these comparative statics quantities, all we need to know are the values of $x_1^*(w_1, w_2, y)$, $x_2^*(w_1, w_2, y)$, and $\lambda_3^*(w_1, w_2, y)$ for the given values of w_1, w_2, and y. Particularly, we do not need to have equations for any of $x_1^*(w_1, w_2, y)$, $x_2^*(w_1, w_2, y)$, and $\lambda_3^*(w_1, w_2, y)$ to obtain the numerical values of all three comparative statics quantities.

What of economic interest do we learn from (12.41), (12.42), and (12.43)? It is that a firm that wishes to keep its production costs of producing y units of its product as small as possible responds to a higher per unit price w_2 for input 2 by increasing its quantity demanded of input 1 at the rate that is the value of (12.41) and by reducing its quantity demanded of input 2 at the rate that is the value of (12.42). The higher input price w_2 also increases $\lambda_3^*(\cdot)$, the firm's marginal production cost, at the rate that is the value of (12.43).

As an exercise, why don't you repeat the analysis of the firm's cost-minimization problem for the comparative statics experiment in which only the required production level y is altered? Remember to provide an economic interpretation of these results.

12.7 Using the Maximum-Value Function

In the previous section we used the first-order optimality conditions together with the Implicit Function Theorem to obtain quantitative results about the rates of change of the optimal solution components $x_1^*(\gamma), \ldots, \lambda_m^*(\gamma)$. In this section we use a different information source to create a different type of comparative statics result. The new information source is the maximum-value function of the constrained optimization problem. The technique that we use to obtain these results employs a rather wonderful tool called the *First-Order Envelope Theorem*.

Our discussion will be made a little easier if we slightly alter the notation that we have used so far for the constraints. From here onwards I would like to write

$$h_j(x; \beta_j, b_j) \equiv b_j - g_j(x; \beta_j) \geq 0 \text{ for } j = 1, \ldots, m,$$

and, consequently, write our constrained optimization problem as

$$\max_{x \in \Re^n} f(x; \alpha) \text{ subject to } h_j(x; \beta_j, b_j) \geq 0 \text{ for } j = 1, \ldots, m. \tag{12.44}$$

This notational change does not alter our problem at all and makes it easier to write down some of the expressions that you will see shortly.

Let's get started by recalling what is meant by the *maximum-value function* of our constrained optimization problem.

Definition 12.1 (Maximum-Value Function). *The* maximum-value function *for the constrained optimization problem* (12.44) *is*

$$v(\gamma) \equiv \max_{x \in \Re^n} f(x; \alpha) \text{ subject to } h_j(x; \beta_j, b_j) \geq 0 \text{ for } j = 1, \ldots, m \tag{12.45}$$

$$\equiv f(x^*(\gamma); \alpha) \tag{12.46}$$

$$\equiv f(x^*(\gamma); \alpha) + \sum_{j=1}^{m} \lambda_j^*(\gamma) h_j(x^*(\gamma); \beta_j, b_j). \tag{12.47}$$

Notice that each of (12.45), (12.46), and (12.47) is *identical* to the other two expressions. (12.45) and (12.46) are identical by the definition of an optimal solution. (12.46) is identical to (12.47) because, at an optimal solution to the problem, each complementary slackness term $\lambda_j^*(\gamma) h_j(x^*(\gamma); \beta_j, b_j)$ necessarily is zero. (12.47) reveals to us that the problem's maximum-value function is exactly the same as the problem's Lagrange function evaluated at the problem's optimal solution.

Two examples of maximum-value functions that we have already encountered are the indirect utility function (11.6) and the indirect profit function (11.7).

The properties possessed by a maximum-value function depend upon the properties of the constrained optimization problem to which it belongs. This chapter considers problems for which the maximum-value function is differentiable on the parameter space Γ.

The First-Order Envelope Theorem is often called "the Envelope Theorem," but there is more than one envelope theorem, so for clarity let's call the theorem by its full name.

Theorem 12.3 (First-Order Envelope Theorem). *Consider a problem* (12.44) *for which the optimal solution correspondence* $(x^*, \lambda^*) : \Gamma \mapsto \Re^n \times \Re_+^m$ *is a function that is differentiable on* Γ *and for which the maximum-value function* (12.45) *is also* *differentiable on* Γ. *Let* $I(x^*(\gamma))$ *be the set of indices of the constraints that bind at* $x = x^*(\gamma)$. *Then*

$$\frac{\partial v(\gamma)}{\partial \gamma_k} = \frac{\partial f(x; \alpha)}{\partial \gamma_k}\Big|_{x=x^*(\gamma)} + \sum_{j \in I(x^*(\gamma))} \lambda_j^*(\gamma) \frac{\partial h_j(x; \beta_j, b_j)}{\partial \gamma_k}\Big|_{x=x^*(\gamma)}. \qquad (12.48)$$

Let's be sure to read this result correctly. It says that the rate of change of the maximum value with respect to a parameter γ_k can be computed in the following way. We are given a constrained optimization problem that is defined in part by a given parameter vector γ. First, we write down the problem's Lagrange function. Second, in the Lagrange function, we *fix the value of each* x_i at $x_i^*(\gamma)$ and also *fix the value of each* λ_j at $\lambda_j^*(\gamma)$. Each x_i^* and each λ_j^* is just a number, so this second step creates a restricted Lagrange function of only the parameter vector γ. Especially important is that this function depends upon the parameters γ_k only *directly*, meaning that the dependency of the restricted Lagrange function upon γ_k is only through γ_k's effect directly upon whichever of the functions $f, g_1, \ldots, g_m$ directly depend upon γ_k. Particularly, the restricted Lagrange function does not depend upon γ_k through the x_i^*'s and λ_j^*'s (these are called the *indirect effects on v through x^* and λ^**) because we have *fixed* their values. Last, we differentiate the restricted Lagrange function with respect to γ_k.

It is easy to misunderstand what I have said in the preceding paragraph, so let's again use the firm's profit-maximization problem (11.4) as an example. Suppose $\beta_1 = \beta_2 = \frac{1}{3}$, $p = 3$, and $w_1 = w_2 = 1$. From (11.5) the profit-maximizing solution is $(y^*, x_1^*, x_2^*, \lambda_1^*, \lambda_2^*, \lambda_3^*, \lambda_4^*) = (1, 1, 1, 0, 0, 0, 3)$. The first step is to write down the problem's Lagrange function, which is

$$L(y, x_1, x_2, \lambda_1, \lambda_2, \lambda_3, \lambda_4; p, w_1, w_2, \beta_1, \beta_2)$$
$$= py - w_1 x_1 - w_2 x_2 - \lambda_1 y - \lambda_2 x_1 - \lambda_3 x_2 + \lambda_4 (x_1^{\beta_1} x_2^{\beta_2} - y).$$

The second step is to substitute the numerical values of the solution that is optimal for the parameter vector $(p, w_1, w_2, \beta_1, \beta_2) = \left(3, 1, 1, \frac{1}{3}, \frac{1}{3}\right)$. Note: We do not substitute the numerical values of the parameters. This gives us the restricted Lagrange function of p, w_1, w_2, β_1, and β_2 that is

$$L^r(p, w_1, w_2, \beta_1, \beta_2) = p \times 1 - w_1 \times 1 - w_2 \times 1 - 0 \times 1 - 0 \times 1 - 0 \times 1 + 3\left(1^{\beta_1} \times 1^{\beta_2} - 1\right)$$
$$= p - w_1 - w_2. \qquad (12.49)$$

The important point is that this function's value at the particular parameter vector value $(p, w_1, w_1) = (3, 1, 1)$ is the firm's maximum achievable profit for these prices.

This maximum profit value is $3 - 1 - 1 = 1$. Really? Let's check by using (11.7). For $(p, w_1, w_2, \beta_1, \beta_2) = \left(3, 1, 1, \frac{1}{3}, \frac{1}{3}\right)$, the value of the indirect profit function is

$$v(p, w_1, w_2, \beta_1, \beta_2) = (1 - \beta_1 - \beta_2)\left(\frac{p\beta_1^{\beta_1}\beta_2^{\beta_2}}{w_1^{\beta_1}w_2^{\beta_2}}\right)^{1/(1-\beta_1-\beta_2)} = \frac{1}{3}\left(\frac{3 \times \frac{1}{3}^{1/3} \times \frac{1}{3}^{1/3}}{1^{1/3} \times 1^{1/3}}\right)^3 = 1,$$
$$(12.50)$$

so (12.49) is indeed reporting the maximum profit that the firm can achieve for the parameter values $(p, w_1, w_2, \beta_1, \beta_2) = \left(3, 1, 1, \frac{1}{3}, \frac{1}{3}\right)$. When applied to our example, the First-Order Envelope Theorem claims that the rates of change of the firm's maximum profit level with respect to p, w_1, and w_2 are the values at $(p, w_1, w_2, \beta_1, \beta_2) = \left(3, 1, 1, \frac{1}{3}, \frac{1}{3}\right)$ of the partial derivatives of (12.49) with respect to each of p, w_1, and w_2. These are

$$\frac{\partial L^r(p, w_1, w_2, \beta_1, \beta_2)}{\partial p}\Big|_{\substack{(p,w_1,w_2,\beta_1,\beta_2) \\ =\left(3,1,1,\frac{1}{3},\frac{1}{3}\right)}} = 1, \quad \frac{\partial L^r(p, w_1, w_2, \beta_1, \beta_2)}{\partial w_1}\Big|_{\substack{(p,w_1,w_2,\beta_1,\beta_2) \\ =\left(3,1,1,\frac{1}{3},\frac{1}{3}\right)}} = -1,$$

and $\quad \dfrac{\partial L^r(p, w_1, w_2, \beta_1, \beta_2)}{\partial w_2}\Big|_{\substack{(p,w_1,w_2,\beta_1,\beta_2) \\ =\left(3,1,1,\frac{1}{3},\frac{1}{3}\right)}} = -1.$ $\qquad\qquad(12.51)$

We can check this by computing the partial derivatives of (12.50) with respect to p, w_1, and w_2, and evaluating them at $(p, w_1, w_2, \beta_1, \beta_2) = \left(3, 1, 1, \frac{1}{3}, \frac{1}{3}\right)$. These values are

$$\frac{\partial v(p_1, w_1, w_2, \beta_1, \beta_2)}{\partial p}\Big|_{\substack{(p,w_1,w_2,\beta_1,\beta_2) \\ =\left(3,1,1,\frac{1}{3},\frac{1}{3}\right)}} = \left(\frac{p^{\beta_1+\beta_2}\beta_1^{\beta_1}\beta_2^{\beta_2}}{w_1^{\beta_1}w_2^{\beta_2}}\right)^{1/(1-\beta_1-\beta_2)}\Big|_{\substack{(p,w_1,w_2,\beta_1,\beta_2) \\ =\left(3,1,1,\frac{1}{3},\frac{1}{3}\right)}}$$

$$= 1 = \frac{\partial L^r(p, w_1, w_2, \beta_1, \beta_2)}{\partial p}\Big|_{\substack{(p,w_1,w_2,\beta_1,\beta_2), \\ =\left(3,1,1,\frac{1}{3},\frac{1}{3}\right)}}$$

$$\frac{\partial v(p_1, w_1, w_2, \beta_1, \beta_2)}{\partial w_1}\Big|_{\substack{(p,w_1,w_2,\beta_1,\beta_2) \\ =\left(3,1,1,\frac{1}{3},\frac{1}{3}\right)}} = -\beta_1\left(\frac{p\beta_1^{\beta_1}\beta_2^{\beta_2}}{w_1^{1-\beta_2}w_2^{\beta_2}}\right)^{1/(1-\beta_1-\beta_2)}\Big|_{\substack{(p,w_1,w_2,\beta_1,\beta_2) \\ =\left(3,1,1,\frac{1}{3},\frac{1}{3}\right)}}$$

$$= -1 = \frac{\partial L^r(p, w_1, w_2, \beta_1, \beta_2)}{\partial w_1}\Big|_{\substack{(p,w_1,w_2,\beta_1,\beta_2), \\ =\left(3,1,1,\frac{1}{3},\frac{1}{3}\right)}}$$

and $\quad \dfrac{\partial v(p_1, w_1, w_2, \beta_1, \beta_2)}{\partial w_2}\Big|_{\substack{(p,w_1,w_2,\beta_1,\beta_2) \\ =\left(3,1,1,\frac{1}{3},\frac{1}{3}\right)}} = -\beta_2\left(\dfrac{p\beta_1^{\beta_1}\beta_2^{\beta_2}}{w_1^{\beta_1}w_2^{1-\beta_1}}\right)^{1/(1-\beta_1-\beta_2)}\Big|_{\substack{(p,w_1,w_2,\beta_1,\beta_2) \\ =\left(3,1,1,\frac{1}{3},\frac{1}{3}\right)}}$

$$= -1 = \frac{\partial L^r(p, w_1, w_2, \beta_1, \beta_2)}{\partial w_2}\Big|_{\substack{(p,w_1,w_2,\beta_1,\beta_2). \\ =\left(3,1,1,\frac{1}{3},\frac{1}{3}\right)}}$$

So, for our example at least, the First-Order Envelope Theorem seems to work. Notice that it is much easier to differentiate (12.49) than it is to differentiate (12.50). One of the great advantages of the theorem is that it typically saves us from grinding through a lot of tedious algebra.

This algebraic simplification is due to our not having to compute the (indirect) effects caused by a change to a parameter changing the problem's optimal solution $x_1^*(\gamma), \ldots, \lambda_m^*(\gamma)$ and thereby changing the value of the problem's maximum value. Why is this so? Why don't we have to consider the changes caused to the maximum value $v(\gamma)$ by changes to the optimal solution $(x^*(\gamma), \lambda^*(\gamma))$ when computing the rate of change of the maximum value? Because, as you will see in the proof of the theorem, all of the indirect effects cancel each other out – they sum to zero. This results in a huge simplification. Before we work through the proof, it will be helpful to see an example of exactly how the theorem allows us to ignore the indirect effects, so, for one more time, let's go back to our example of the profit-maximizing firm.

The Lagrange function for (11.4) is

$$L(y, x_1, x_2, \lambda_1, \lambda_2, \lambda_3, \lambda_4; p, w_1, w_2, \beta_1, \beta_2)$$
$$= py - w_1 x_1 - w_2 x_2 + \lambda_1 y + \lambda_2 x_1 + \lambda_3 x_2 + \lambda_4 (x_1^{\beta_1} x_2^{\beta_2} - y).$$

For brevity, we will use only y^*, x_1^*, x_2^*, λ_1^*, λ_2^*, λ_3^*, and λ_4^* to denote the optimal values, rather than go to the bother of substituting in complicated equations such as those on the right-hand sides of (11.5). Be clear that, for a *given* parameter vector $(p, w_1, w_2, \beta_1, \beta_2)$, the quantities $y^*, \ldots, \lambda_4^*$ are *fixed values*. The maximum-value function is

$$\pi^*(p, w_1, w_2, \beta_1, \beta_2)$$
$$\equiv py^* - w_1 x_1^* - w_2 x_2^* + \lambda_1^* y^* + \lambda_2^* x_1^* + \lambda_3^* x_2^* + \lambda_4^* \left((x_1^*)^{\beta_1} (x_2^*)^{\beta_2} - y^* \right). \quad (12.52)$$

According to the First-Order Envelope Theorem, to compute the rate of change of the firm's maximum profit with respect to, say, the parameter p, all we need to do is to compute the derivative of the right-hand side of (12.52) with respect to p (remembering that $y^*, \ldots, \lambda_4^*$ are numbers, and thus are constants). This easily gives us that

$$\frac{\partial \pi^*(p, \cdot)}{\partial p} = y^*(p, w_1, w_2, \beta_1, \beta_2). \quad (12.53)$$

If, instead, you insist upon doing things the hard way by applying the chain rule of differentiation to (12.52), then you obtain

$$
\begin{aligned}
\frac{\partial \pi^*(p, \cdot)}{\partial p} =\ & y^*(p, \cdot) + p \frac{\partial y^*(p, \cdot)}{\partial p} - w_1 \frac{\partial x_1^*(p, \cdot)}{\partial p} - w_2 \frac{\partial x_2^*(p, \cdot)}{\partial p} \\
& + \frac{\partial \lambda_1^*(p, \cdot)}{\partial p} y^*(p, \cdot) + \lambda_1^*(p, \cdot) \frac{\partial y^*(p, \cdot)}{\partial p} + \frac{\partial \lambda_2^*(p, \cdot)}{\partial p} x_1^*(p, \cdot) \\
& + \lambda_2^*(p, \cdot) \frac{\partial x_1^*(p, \cdot)}{\partial p} + \frac{\partial \lambda_3^*(p, \cdot)}{\partial p} x_2^*(p, \cdot) + \lambda_3^*(p, \cdot) \frac{\partial x_2^*(p, \cdot)}{\partial p} \qquad (12.54) \\
& + \frac{\partial \lambda_4^*(p, \cdot)}{\partial p} \left(x_1^*(p, \cdot)^{\beta_1} x_2^*(p, \cdot)^{\beta_2} - y^*(p, \cdot) \right) \\
& + \lambda_4^*(p, \cdot) \Bigg(\beta_1 x_1^*(p, \cdot)^{\beta_1 - 1} x_2^*(p, \cdot)^{\beta_2} \frac{\partial x_1^*(p, \cdot)}{\partial p} \\
& \qquad\qquad + \beta_2 x_1^*(p, \cdot)^{\beta_1} x_2^*(p, \cdot)^{\beta_2 - 1} \frac{\partial x_2^*(p, \cdot)}{\partial p} - \frac{\partial y^*(p, \cdot)}{\partial p} \Bigg).
\end{aligned}
$$

What a mess! But (12.53) and (12.54) are the same thing, so all of the indirect effect terms that contain quantities such as $\partial x^*/\partial p$, $\partial y^*/\partial p$ and $\partial \lambda^*/\partial p$) in (12.54) must sum to zero. How can this be? Let's group the terms in (12.54) together as follows:

$$
\begin{aligned}
\frac{\partial \pi^*(p, \cdot)}{\partial p} =\ & y^*(p, \cdot) + \left(p + \lambda_1^*(p, \cdot) - \lambda_4^*(p, \cdot) \right) \frac{\partial y^*(p, \cdot)}{\partial p} \\
& - \left(w_1 - \lambda_2^*(p, \cdot) - \lambda_4^*(p, \cdot) \beta_1 x_1^*(p, \cdot)^{\beta_1 - 1} x_2^*(p, \cdot)^{\beta_2} \right) \frac{\partial x_1^*(p, \cdot)}{\partial p} \\
& - \left(w_2 - \lambda_3^*(p, \cdot) - \lambda_4^*(p, \cdot) \beta_2 x_1^*(p, \cdot)^{\beta_1} x_2^*(p, \cdot)^{\beta_2 - 1} \right) \frac{\partial x_2^*(p, \cdot)}{\partial p} \\
& + \frac{\partial \lambda_1^*(p, \cdot)}{\partial p} y^*(p, \cdot) + \frac{\partial \lambda_2^*(p, \cdot)}{\partial p} x_1^*(p, \cdot) + \frac{\partial \lambda_3^*(p, \cdot)}{\partial p} x_2^*(p, \cdot) \qquad (12.55) \\
& + \frac{\partial \lambda_4^*(p, \cdot)}{\partial p} \left(x_1^*(p, \cdot)^{\beta_1} x_2^*(p, \cdot)^{\beta_2} - y^*(p, \cdot) \right).
\end{aligned}
$$

The maximum value for the problem for a given parameter vector γ is the objective function's value at the problem's *optimal* solution $(x^*(\gamma), \lambda^*(\gamma))$, where necessarily the Karush-Kuhn-Tucker and the complementary slackness conditions are satisfied;

i.e.

$$\begin{pmatrix} p \\ -w_1 \\ -w_2 \end{pmatrix} = \lambda_1^*(p, \cdot) \begin{pmatrix} -1 \\ 0 \\ 0 \end{pmatrix} + \lambda_2^*(p, \cdot) \begin{pmatrix} 0 \\ -1 \\ 0 \end{pmatrix} + \lambda_3^*(p, \cdot) \begin{pmatrix} 0 \\ 0 \\ -1 \end{pmatrix}$$

$$+ \lambda_4^*(p, \cdot) \begin{pmatrix} 1 \\ -\beta_1 x_1^*(p, \cdot)^{\beta_1 - 1} x_2^*(p, \cdot)^{\beta_2} \\ -\beta_2 x_1^*(p, \cdot)^{\beta_1} x_2^*(p, \cdot)^{\beta_2 - 1} \end{pmatrix}, \tag{12.56}$$

$$0 = \lambda_1^*(p, \cdot) y^*(p, \cdot), \tag{12.57}$$

$$0 = \lambda_2^*(p, \cdot) x_1^*(p, \cdot), \tag{12.58}$$

$$0 = \lambda_3^*(p, \cdot) x_2^*(p, \cdot), \tag{12.59}$$

$$\text{and} \quad 0 = \lambda_4^*(p, \cdot) \left(y^*(p, \cdot) - (x_1^*(p, \cdot))^{\beta_1} (x_2^*(p, \cdot))^{\beta_2} \right). \tag{12.60}$$

(12.56) says that the second, third, and fourth terms on the right-hand side of (12.55) are necessarily zero. (12.57) says that necessarily either $\lambda_1^*(p, \cdot) = 0$, in which case $\partial \lambda_1^*(\gamma)/\partial p = 0$, or else $y^*(p, \cdot) = 0$. Either way, the fifth term on the right-hand side of (12.55) is necessarily zero. Similarly, (12.58), (12.59), and (12.60), respectively, inform us that necessarily the sixth, seventh, and last terms on the right-hand side of (12.55) are each zero. Thus all the indirect effect terms can be ignored, and we have the conclusion provided earlier by the First-Order Envelope Theorem that

$$\frac{\partial \pi^*(p, \cdot)}{\partial p} = y^*(p, \cdot).$$

The proof of the First-Order Envelope Theorem is merely a restatement of the argument we have just completed, albeit in a more general setting. Here it is.

Proof of the First-Order Envelope Theorem. Given γ, the primal problem's optimizing solution is $x^*(\gamma) = (x_1^*(\gamma), \ldots, x_n^*(\gamma))$ and the associated vector of Lagrange multipliers is $\lambda^*(\gamma) = (\lambda_1^*(\gamma), \ldots, \lambda_m^*(\gamma))$. From (12.46),

$$\frac{\partial v(\gamma)}{\partial \gamma_k} = \frac{\partial f(x; \alpha)}{\partial \gamma_k}\Big|_{x = x^*(\gamma)} + \sum_{i=1}^{n} \frac{\partial f(x; \alpha)}{\partial x_i}\Big|_{x = x^*(\gamma)} \times \frac{\partial x_i^*(\gamma)}{\partial \gamma_k}. \tag{12.61}$$

Since $x = x^*(\gamma)$ is an optimal solution, the Karush-Kuhn-Tucker condition must be satisfied at $x = x^*(\gamma)$; *i.e.*

$$\frac{\partial f(x; \alpha)}{\partial x_i}\Big|_{x = x^*(\gamma)} = -\sum_{j=1}^{m} \lambda_j^*(\gamma) \frac{\partial h_j(x; \beta_j, b_j)}{\partial x_i}\Big|_{x = x^*(\gamma)} \forall\, i = 1, \ldots, n. \tag{12.62}$$

Substitution of (12.62) into (12.61) gives

$$
\begin{aligned}
\frac{\partial v(\gamma)}{\partial \gamma_k} &= \frac{\partial f(x; \alpha)}{\partial \gamma_k}\Big|_{x=x^*(\gamma)} - \sum_{i=1}^{n}\left(\sum_{j=1}^{m} \lambda_j^*(\gamma)\frac{\partial h_j(x; \beta_j, b_j)}{\partial x_i}\Big|_{x=x^*(\gamma)}\right)\frac{\partial x_i^*(\gamma)}{\partial \gamma_k} \\
&= \frac{\partial f(x; \alpha)}{\partial \gamma_k}\Big|_{x=x^*(\gamma)} - \sum_{j=1}^{m} \lambda_j^*(\gamma)\left(\sum_{i=1}^{n} \frac{\partial h_j(x; \beta_j, b_j)}{\partial x_i}\Big|_{x=x^*(\gamma)}\frac{\partial x_i^*(\gamma)}{\partial \gamma_k}\right). \quad (12.63)
\end{aligned}
$$

Also necessarily satisfied at $x^*(\gamma)$ are the complementary slackness conditions

$$
\lambda_j^*(\gamma)h_j(x^*(\gamma); \beta_j, b_j) \equiv 0 \text{ for each } j = 1, \ldots, m.
$$

Consequently, for each $j = 1, \ldots, m$,

$$
\begin{aligned}
0 = &\frac{\partial \lambda_j^*(\gamma)}{\partial \gamma_k}h_j(x^*(\gamma); \beta_j, b_j) + \lambda_j^*(\gamma)\frac{\partial h_j(x; \beta_j, b_j)}{\partial \gamma_k}\Big|_{x=x^*(\gamma)} \\
&+ \lambda_j^*(\gamma)\sum_{i=1}^{n} \frac{\partial h_j(x; \beta_j, b_j)}{\partial x_i}\Big|_{x=x^*(\gamma)}\frac{\partial x_i^*(\gamma)}{\partial \gamma_k}.
\end{aligned}
\qquad (12.64)
$$

If the jth constraint is slack, then $\lambda_j^*(\gamma) = 0$ and $\partial \lambda^*(\gamma)/\partial \gamma_k = 0$. If the jth constraint binds, then $h_j(x^*(\gamma); \beta_j, b_j) = 0$. Therefore, the first term of the right-hand side of (12.64) is zero for every $j = 1, \ldots, m$. Consequently, for each $j = 1, \ldots, m$,

$$
\lambda_j^*(\gamma)\frac{\partial h_j(x; \beta_j, b_j)}{\partial \gamma_k}\Big|_{x=x^*(\gamma)} = -\lambda_j^*(\gamma)\sum_{i=1}^{n} \frac{\partial h_j(x; \beta_j, b_j)}{\partial x_i}\Big|_{x=x^*(\gamma)}\frac{x_i^*(\gamma)}{\partial \gamma_k}. \qquad (12.65)
$$

Substitution from (12.65) into (12.63) gives

$$
\frac{\partial v(\gamma)}{\partial \gamma_k} = \frac{\partial f(x; \alpha)}{\partial \gamma_k}\Big|_{x=x^*(\gamma)} + \sum_{j=1}^{m} \lambda_j^*(\gamma)\frac{\partial h_j(x; \beta_j, b_j)}{\partial \gamma_k}\Big|_{x=x^*(\gamma)}. \qquad (12.66)
$$

$I(x^*(\gamma))$ is the set of indices of the constraints that bind at $x = x^*(\gamma)$, so $\lambda_j^*(\gamma) = 0$ for each $j \notin I(x^*(\gamma))$ and (12.66) is

$$
\frac{\partial v(\gamma)}{\partial \gamma_k} = \frac{\partial f(x; \alpha)}{\partial \gamma_k}\Big|_{x=x^*(\gamma)} + \sum_{j \in I(x^*(\gamma))} \lambda_j^*(\gamma)\frac{\partial h_j(x; \beta_j, b_j)}{\partial \gamma_k}\Big|_{x=x^*(\gamma)}. \qquad \square
$$

Now let's get a clear understanding of the geometry of the First-Order Envelope Theorem. Figure 12.2 displays three curves labeled $v^r(\gamma; x)$ for three *fixed* values x',

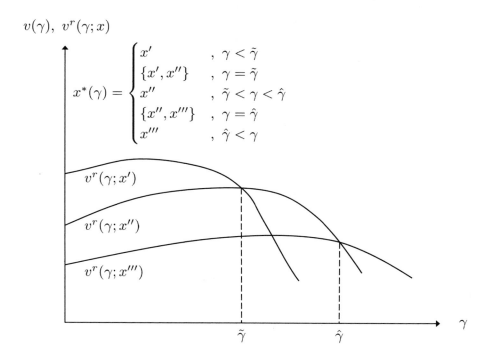

$$v(\gamma), \ v^r(\gamma; x)$$

$$x^*(\gamma) = \begin{cases} x' & , \ \gamma < \tilde{\gamma} \\ \{x', x''\} & , \ \gamma = \tilde{\gamma} \\ x'' & , \ \tilde{\gamma} < \gamma < \hat{\gamma} \\ \{x'', x'''\} & , \ \gamma = \hat{\gamma} \\ x''' & , \ \hat{\gamma} < \gamma \end{cases}$$

Figure 12.2: The restricted functions $v^r(\gamma; x')$, $v^r(\gamma; x'')$, and $v^r(\gamma; x''')$.

x'', and x''' of x. The superscript "r" denotes "restricted." For example, $v^r(\gamma; x')$ is the function $v(\gamma, x)$ restricted by fixing x at the value x'. There is one restricted function $v^r(\gamma; x)$ for each of the three allowed values of x.

Take any value of $\gamma < \tilde{\gamma}$ in Figure 12.2. Observe that the values of the three restricted functions are then $v^r(\gamma; x') > v^r(\gamma; x'') > v^r(\gamma; x''')$. If your goal is to attain the highest of these values, then which value for x would you choose? Well, that would be $x = x'$. We have that the optimal solution to the problem

$$\max_x v^r(x; \gamma) \text{ subject to } x \in \{x', x'', x'''\}$$

is $x^*(\gamma) = x'$ for $\gamma < \tilde{\gamma}$.

Now take any value of γ satisfying $\tilde{\gamma} < \gamma < \hat{\gamma}$ in Figure 12.2. The largest of the values of the three restricted functions is now $v^r(\gamma; x'')$, so the optimal solution to the problem

$$\max_x v^r(x; \gamma) \text{ subject to } x \in \{x', x'', x'''\}$$

is $x^*(\gamma) = x''$ for $\tilde{\gamma} < \gamma < \hat{\gamma}$.

Last, for any value of $\gamma > \hat{\gamma}$, the largest of the values of the three restricted functions is $v^r(\gamma; x''')$ and the optimal solution to the problem

$$\max_x v^r(x; \gamma) \text{ subject to } x \in \{x', x'', x'''\}$$

is $x^*(\gamma) = x'''$ for $\gamma > \hat{\gamma}$.

Put the above three paragraphs together and we have discovered that the optimal solution for the problem $\max_x v^r(x; \gamma)$ subject to $x \in \{x', x'', x'''\}$ is

$$x^*(\gamma) = \begin{cases} x' & , \ \gamma < \tilde{\gamma} \\ \{x', x''\} & , \ \gamma = \tilde{\gamma} \\ x'' & , \ \tilde{\gamma} < \gamma < \hat{\gamma} \\ \{x'', x'''\} & , \ \gamma = \hat{\gamma} \\ x''' & , \ \hat{\gamma} < \gamma. \end{cases}$$

The maximum-value function for the problem is

$$v(\gamma) = \begin{cases} v^r(\gamma; x') & , \ \text{for } \gamma < \tilde{\gamma} \\ v^r(\gamma; x') = v^r(\gamma; x'') & , \ \text{for } \gamma = \tilde{\gamma} \\ v^r(\gamma; x'') & , \ \text{for } \tilde{\gamma} < \gamma < \hat{\gamma} \\ v^r(\gamma; x'') = v^r(\gamma; x''') & , \ \text{for } \gamma = \hat{\gamma} \\ v^r(\gamma; x''') & , \ \text{for } \hat{\gamma} < \gamma. \end{cases}$$

In Figure 12.3 the graph of this maximum-value function is the thick black line that runs along the tops of the graphs of the three restricted value functions $v^r(\gamma; x')$, $v^r(\gamma; x'')$, and $v^r(\gamma; x''')$. This "upper-most" graph encloses from above, or "envelops" from above, the graphs of all of the restricted value functions $v^r(\gamma; x)$, which is why the graph of $v(\gamma)$ is called the "upper envelope" of the graphs of the three $v^r(\gamma; x)$ functions.

In many problems the allowed values for x lie in some interval I, so let's see how our above analysis extends to such a case. Look again at Figures 12.2 and 12.3, but now think of the three restricted value functions that are displayed as being just three of infinitely many such functions, one for each of the infinitely many values of $x \in I$ that are now allowed. Each one of these infinitely many restricted functions has its own graph, each similar to the three graphs that are displayed. Our problem remains the same. That is, for a given value of γ, we seek the value for $x \in I$ that makes the value function $v^r(x; \gamma)$ as large as is possible. This is the problem

$$\max_x v^r(x; \gamma) \text{ subject to } x \in I. \tag{12.67}$$

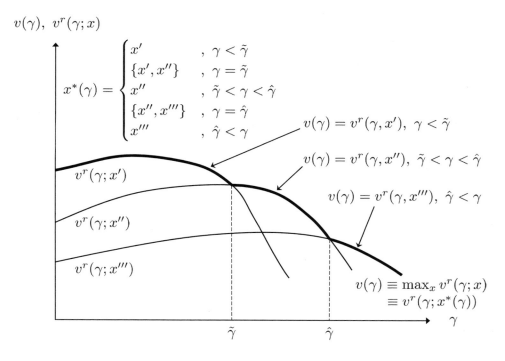

Figure 12.3: The upper envelope $v(\gamma)$ generated by the restricted functions $v^r(\gamma; x')$, $v^r(\gamma; x'')$, and $v^r(\gamma; x''')$.

In this problem γ's value is fixed. The solution to this problem is the value of x that is optimal for γ; *i.e.* $x^*(\gamma)$. The maximum value for problem (12.67) for the given value of γ is therefore

$$v(\gamma) = v^r(x^*(\gamma); \gamma). \tag{12.68}$$

If we now vary γ over the entire parameter space Γ (this is the comparative statics experiment), but for each possible value of γ we still treat γ as a parameter in problem (12.67), then we obtain both the entire optimal solution function $x^*(\gamma)$ defined on Γ and the entire maximum-value function for problem (12.67), which is

$$v(\gamma) \equiv v^r(x^*(\gamma); \gamma) \ \forall \ \gamma \in \Gamma. \tag{12.69}$$

The graph of this function is displayed in Figure 12.4 as the darker, uppermost of the four curves. This graph of the unrestricted maximum value $v(\gamma)$ is the upper envelope of all of the graphs of the family of the $v^r(\gamma; x)$ functions.

Now look again at Figure 12.4. Consider the particular value γ' for γ. Here is the crucial idea. As you can see from point A in the figure, for $\gamma = \gamma'$ the value $v(\gamma')$

$v(\gamma), \ v^r(\gamma; x)$

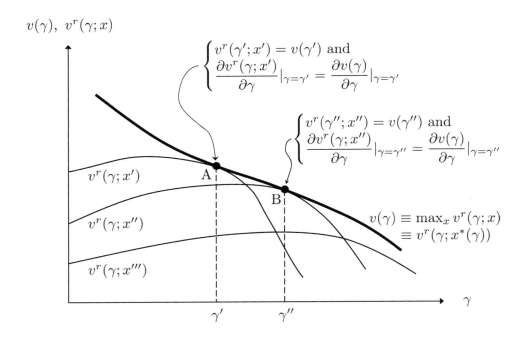

Figure 12.4: The upper envelope $v(\gamma)$ generated by the family of functions $v^r(\gamma; x)$.

of the (unrestricted) maximum-value function is the same as the value $v^r(\gamma'; x')$ of the restricted function $v^r(\gamma; x')$ at $\gamma = \gamma'$. Thus $x^*(\gamma') = x'$. This tells us that the restriction $x = x'$ is just-binding. Put another way, when $\gamma = \gamma'$, the unrestricted optimizing choice for x is $x = x'$, so the restriction that x must be the number x' is effectively not a restriction when $\gamma = \gamma'$.

Not only that, but, at $\gamma = \gamma'$, *the slope with respect to γ of the unrestricted maximum-value function $v(\gamma)$ is the same as the slope with respect to γ of the restricted value function $v^r(\gamma; x')$* (see point A). That is,

$$\frac{\partial v(\gamma)}{\partial \gamma}\Big|_{\gamma=\gamma'} = \frac{\partial v^r(\gamma; x')}{\partial \gamma}\Big|_{\substack{\gamma=\gamma' \\ x'=x^*(\gamma')}}. \tag{12.70}$$

Statement (12.70) is the First-Order Envelope Theorem. It says something remarkably simple and useful: if you want to know the rate at which a maximum value $v(\gamma)$ changes with respect to a parameter γ at a particular value γ' of γ, then all you need to do is the simpler task of computing the rate at which the restricted value $v^r(\gamma; x)$ changes with respect to γ at $\gamma = \gamma'$, when x is fixed at the value $x^*(\gamma')$. There are no "indirect effects" (*i.e.* terms that measure how $x^*(\gamma)$ changes as γ changes) because

x is *fixed* at the value $x^*(\gamma')$.

Similarly, at the particular value γ'' for γ, the value of x that makes the function $v(\gamma''; x)$ largest is $x = x''$, which is, therefore, the optimizing value of x when $\gamma = \gamma''$: $x'' = x^*(\gamma'')$. Consequently when $\gamma = \gamma''$ restricting x to the value x'' is a just-binding restriction. This causes (see point B in the figure) the value $v(\gamma'')$ of the (unrestricted) maximum-value function to be the same as the value $v^r(\gamma''; x'')$ of the restricted function $v^r(\gamma; x'')$ at $\gamma = \gamma''$. It also causes at $\gamma = \gamma''$, the rate of change with respect to γ of the unrestricted maximum value $v(\gamma)$ to be the same as the rate of change with respect to γ of the restricted value $v^r(\gamma; x'')$ (see point B); *i.e.*

$$\frac{\partial v(\gamma)}{\partial \gamma}\Big|_{\gamma=\gamma''} = \frac{\partial v^r(\gamma; x'')}{\partial \gamma}\Big|_{\substack{\gamma=\gamma'' \\ x''=x^*(\gamma'')}}.$$

Many applications of the First-Order Envelope Theorem are familiar to economists. Perhaps the best-known examples are Roy's Identity, Shephard's Lemma, and Hotelling's Lemma. It is very helpful to visualize how the First-Order Envelope Theorem provides these results, so let's examine how Hotelling's Lemma is derived from the theorem.

Theorem 12.4 (Hotelling's Lemma). *Consider a profit-maximizing, price-taking firm with a direct profit function*

$$\pi(y, x_1, \ldots, x_n; p, w_1, \ldots, w_n) = py - w_1 x_1 - \cdots - w_n x_n,$$

where $p > 0$ and $w_i > 0$ for $i = 1, \ldots, n$, and with a technology described by a twice-continuously differentiable and strictly concave production function $y = g(x_1, \ldots, x_n)$. Denote the firm's profit-maximizing plan by $(y^*(p, w), x_1^*(p, w), \ldots, x_n^*(p, w))$, where $w = (w_1, \ldots, w_n)$. Denote the firm's indirect profit function by

$$\pi^*(p, w) \equiv py^*(p, w) - w_1 x_1^*(p, w) - \cdots - w_n x_n^*(p, w).$$

Then

$$\frac{\partial \pi^*(p, w)}{\partial p} = y^*(p, w) \tag{12.71}$$

$$and \quad \frac{\partial \pi^*(p, w)}{\partial w_i} = -x_i^*(p, w) \text{ for } i = 1, \ldots, n. \tag{12.72}$$

To understand this result and how it is derived from the First-Order Envelope Theorem, start by thinking of the following restricted version of the firm's problem (you might recognize this restricted problem as a particular "short-run" problem that is often described in microeconomics textbooks):

$$\max_{y, x_2, \ldots, x_n} \pi^r(y, x_2, \ldots, x_n; \overline{x}_1, p, w) = py - w_1\overline{x}_1 - w_2 x_2 - \cdots - w_n x_n$$

$$\text{subject to } y \geq 0, \ x_2 \geq 0, \ \ldots, \ x_n \geq 0, \text{ and } g(\overline{x}_1, x_2, \ldots, x_n) - y \geq 0, \qquad (12.73)$$

where the quantity used of input 1, x_1, is fixed at $\overline{x}_1 > 0$. The solution is the restricted (short-run) production plan $(y^r(p, w; \overline{x}_1), \overline{x}_1, x_2^r(p, w; \overline{x}_1), \ldots, x_n^r(p, w; \overline{x}_1))$. Denote the firm's restricted indirect profit function by

$$\pi^r(p, w; \overline{x}_1) \equiv py^r(p, w; \overline{x}_1) - w_1\overline{x}_1 - w_2 x_2^r(p, w; \overline{x}_1) - \cdots - w_n x_n^r(p, w; \overline{x}_1). \quad (12.74)$$

There is one such function for each possible value $\overline{x}_1$, so we may speak of the *family* (*i.e.* the complete collection) of all of these restricted, or short-run, maximum-profit functions. Now realize that the firm's unrestricted indirect profit function

$$\pi^*(p, w) \equiv \max_{\overline{x}_1 \geq 0} \pi^r(p, w; \overline{x}_1). \qquad (12.75)$$

This is a statement that *the unrestricted indirect profit function $\pi^*(p, w)$ is the upper envelope of the family of restricted indirect profit functions $\pi^r(p, w; \overline{x}_1)$*. The idea is illustrated in Figure 12.5 for just the (w_1, π)-plane. In this plane the graph of each restricted profit function $\pi^r(p, w; \overline{x}_1)$ is a straight line with a slope $-\overline{x}_1$ with respect to w_1 (see (12.74)). Three such restricted profit functions' graphs are displayed, one for x_1 fixed at the value $\overline{x}_1'$, another for x_1 fixed at the value $\overline{x}_1''$, and the last for x_1 fixed at the value $\overline{x}_1'''$. Also displayed is the graph of the unrestricted profit function $\pi^*(p, w_1, w_2)$. Consider the point $(w_1', \pi^*(p, w_1', \cdot)) = (w_1', \pi^r(p, w_1', \cdot; \overline{x}_1'))$ (labeled A in the figure). At this point the restriction $x_1 = \overline{x}_1'$ only just-binds since, when $w_1 = w_1'$, the firm chooses $x_1 = \overline{x}_1'$ even if it is not restricted to do so; *i.e.* $x_1^*(p, w_1', \cdot) = \overline{x}_1'$. So, if $w_1 = w_1'$, then the firm's unrestricted maximum profit level and the firm's maximum profit level when it is restricted to $\overline{x}_1'$ units of input 1 are the same. As well, the rates of change of these profit levels with respect to w_1 are the same; this is statement (12.72). As an exercise to test your understanding of this reasoning, you should draw a picture similar to Figure 12.5 and examine why (12.71) is true. Start by considering the restricted version of the firm's problem that is

$$\max_{x_1, \ldots, x_n} \pi^r(x_2, \ldots, x_n; \overline{y}, p, w) = p\overline{y} - w_1 x_1 - w_2 x_2 - \cdots - w_n x_n$$

$$\text{subject to } x_1 \geq 0, \ \ldots, \ x_n \geq 0, \text{ and } \overline{y} \leq g(x_1, x_2, \ldots, x_n), \qquad (12.76)$$

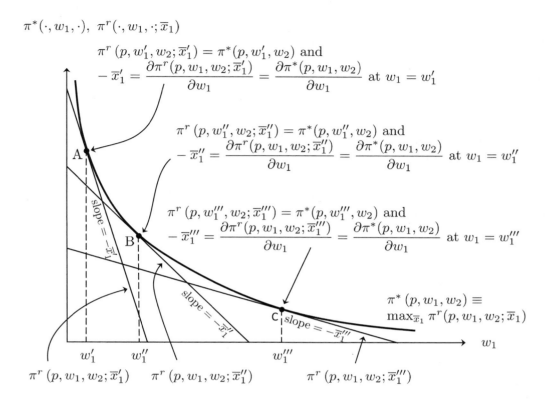

Figure 12.5: Hotelling's result that $\partial \pi^*(p,w)/\partial w_1 = -x_1^*(p,w)$.

where the firm's quantity supplied, y, is fixed at some value $\overline{y} > 0$.

Here we have used the First-Order Envelope Theorem to obtain some select quantitative comparative statics results. This technique complements the Implicit Function method that we used in the previous section. Which method should you use? That depends upon the type of quantitative comparative statics result you wish to obtain. The First-Order Envelope Theorem provides results of the type $\partial v(\gamma)/\partial \gamma_k$. The Implicit Function Theorem provides results of the types $\partial x_i^*(\gamma)/\partial \gamma_k$ and $\partial \lambda_j^*(\gamma)/\partial \gamma_k$.

12.8 Qualitative *vs.* Quantitative Analyses

This chapter has explained two techniques commonly used for quantitative comparative statics analyses. The Implicit Function Theorem approach is particularly demanding in that to use it you must have a lot of information about the objective and constraint functions of the constrained optimization problem that is being analyzed. But what if you don't? Well, you could assume the missing information and provide quantitative comparative statics results that are conditional upon your assumptions being true. This is quite often done. If you do not like this idea, then you will have to settle for qualitative comparative statics results. Qualitative analyses are less informative but they require much less information. Which approach is appropriate for you will depend upon what questions you want answered and upon what you know about the properties of the objective and constraint functions of the problem you wish to analyze.

Chapter 13 explains an elegant method of deriving qualitative comparative-statics results from the information provided by the second-order necessary optimization condition.

12.9 Problems

This problem set is presented in two parts. The first part presents problems that use the first-order optimality conditions and the Implicit Function Theorem. The second part presents problems that use the maximum-value function and the First-Order Envelope Theorem.

Part 1: Problems that use the first-order optimality conditions and the Implicit Function Theorem.

Problem 12.1. At the start of this chapter, we considered the problem

$$\max_x f(x; \alpha_1, \alpha_2, \alpha_3) = \alpha_1 x^2 + \alpha_2 x + \alpha_3,$$

where the parameter $\alpha_1 < 0$. We solved the problem by computing the first-order derivative of f with respect to x and then noting that, at the optimal solution x^*, this derivative necessarily has the value zero. That is, we solved

$$\frac{\mathrm{d} f(x; \alpha_1, \alpha_2, \alpha_3)}{\mathrm{d}x} = 2\alpha_1 x + \alpha_2 = 0 \qquad (12.77)$$

and obtained that the optimal solution is the algebraically explicit function

$$x^*(\alpha_1, \alpha_2) = -\frac{\alpha_2}{2\alpha_1}. \qquad (12.78)$$

Having this function makes it easy to deduce the comparative statics quantities

$$\frac{\partial x^*(\alpha_1, \alpha_2)}{\partial \alpha_1} = \frac{\alpha_2}{2\alpha_1^2}, \ \frac{\partial x^*(\alpha_1, \alpha_2)}{\partial \alpha_2} = -\frac{1}{2\alpha_1}, \ \text{and} \ \frac{\partial x^*(\alpha_1, \alpha_2)}{\partial \alpha_3} = 0. \qquad (12.79)$$

Suppose that you are not able to derive (12.78). Use the Implicit Function Theorem to derive the comparative statics quantities listed in (12.79).

Problem 12.2. Consider the consumer demand problem

$$\max_{x_1, x_2} U(x_1, x_2) = x_1 x_2 \text{ subject to } x_1 \geq 0, \ x_2 \geq 0, \text{ and } p_1 x_1 + p_2 x_2 \leq y.$$

You probably already know that the optimal solution is

$$x_1^*(p_1, p_2, y) = \frac{y}{2p_1}, \ x_2^*(p_1, p_2, y) = \frac{y}{2p_2}, \text{ and } \lambda^*(p_1, p_2, y) = \frac{2p_1 p_2}{y},$$

but suppose that this algebraically explicit solution is not known to you. Use the Implicit Function to obtain the comparative statics quantities

$$\frac{\partial x_1^*}{\partial p_1}, \ \frac{\partial x_2^*}{\partial p_1}, \ \text{and} \ \frac{\partial \lambda^*}{\partial p_1}.$$

Problem 12.3. It is not difficult to discover the algebraically explicit optimal solution $(x_1^*(p_1, p_2, y), x_2^*(p_1, p_2, y), \lambda^*(p_1, p_2, y))$ to the consumer demand problem

$$\max_{x_1, x_2} U(x_1, x_2) = \sqrt{x_1} + \sqrt{x_2}$$

$$\text{subject to } x_1 \geq 0, \ x_2 \geq 0, \ \text{and } g(x_1, x_2) = p_1 x_1 + p_2 x_2 \leq y, \tag{12.80}$$

but suppose that you are unable to compute the equations of this optimal solution. You want to know the rates of change of the values of x_1^*, x_2^*, and the budget constraint's multiplier λ^* as p_1 changes; *i.e.* you wish to evaluate $\partial x_1^*/\partial p_1$, $\partial x_2^*/\partial p_1$, and $\partial \lambda^*/\partial p_1$. Use the Implicit Function Theorem to derive these quantities.

Part 2: Problems that use the maximum-value function and the First-Order Envelope Theorem.

Consider a family of functions $\psi : X \times \Gamma \mapsto \Re$, where $X \subseteq R^n$ is the space of choice variables and $\Gamma \subseteq \Re^s$ is the parameter space.

Definition: If for every $\gamma \in \Gamma$ there exists an $x^*(\gamma) \in X$ such that

$$\Theta^*(\gamma) \equiv \psi(x^*(\gamma), \gamma) \geq \psi(x, \gamma) \ \forall \ x \in X,$$

then the function $\Theta^* : \Gamma \to \Re$ is the *upper envelope* of the family of functions ψ.

Definition: If for every $\gamma \in \Gamma$ there exists an $x_*(\gamma) \in X$ such that

$$\Theta_*(\gamma) \equiv \psi(x_*(\gamma), \gamma) \leq \psi(x, \gamma) \ \forall \ x \in X,$$

then the function $\Theta_* : \Gamma \to \Re$ is the *lower envelope* of the family of functions ψ.

Problem 12.4. Consider the family of functions $f : X \times \Gamma \to \Re$, where $X = \Re$, $\Gamma = [0, 8]$, and $f(x, \gamma) = -x^2 + \gamma x + 2$.
(i) What is the optimal solution $x^*(\gamma)$ to the problem $\max_x f^r(x; \gamma) = -x^2 + \gamma x + 2$, in which $\gamma \in [0, 8]$ is a parameter? The maximum-value function for this problem is $v(\gamma) \equiv f^r(x^*(\gamma); \gamma) = -x^*(\gamma)^2 + \gamma x^*(\gamma) + 2$. Derive the function $v(\gamma)$.
(ii) For each of the particular values $x = 1, 2, 3$, write down the function $f^r(\gamma; x)$ in which x is parametric and γ is variable. Then, on the same diagram, plot the graphs of these three functions for $\gamma \in [0, 8]$.
(iii) Now add to your diagram the graph of the maximum-value function $v(\gamma)$. Confirm that $v(\gamma) \geq f^r(\gamma; x)$ for $\gamma \in [0, 8]$ with = for $x = x^*(1)$, $x = x^*(2)$, and $x = x^*(3)$.

Problem 12.5. Consider the family of functions $f : X \times \Gamma \to \Re$, where $X = \Re$, $\Gamma = \Re_{++}$, and $f(x, \gamma) = \gamma^2 x^2 - \gamma x + 2$.

(i) What is the optimal solution $x_*(\gamma)$ to the problem $\min_x f^r(x; \gamma) = \gamma^2 x^2 - \gamma x + 2$ in which $\gamma > 0$ is parametric? The minimum-value function is $v(\gamma) \equiv f^r(x_*(\gamma); \gamma) = \gamma^2 x_*(\gamma)^2 - \gamma x_*(\gamma) + 2$. Derive the function $v(\gamma)$.

(ii) For each of the particular values $x = \frac{1}{6}, \frac{1}{4}, \frac{1}{2}$, write down the function $f^r(\gamma; x)$ in which x is parametric and γ is variable. Then, on the same diagram, plot the graphs of these three functions for $\gamma \in (0, 5]$.

(iii) Now add to your diagram the graph of the minimum-value function $v(\gamma)$. Confirm that $v(\gamma) \leq f^r(\gamma; x)$ with $=$ for $x = x^*\left(\frac{1}{6}\right)$, $x = x^*\left(\frac{1}{4}\right)$, and $x = x^*\left(\frac{1}{2}\right)$.

The First-Order Upper-Envelope Theorem. Let $X \subseteq \Re^n$ be open with respect to E^n. Let $\Gamma \subseteq \Re^m$ be open with respect to E^m. Let $\psi : X \times \Gamma \mapsto \Re$ be a function that is continuously differentiable with respect to $(x, \gamma) \in X \times \Gamma$. If, for every $\gamma \in \Gamma$, there exists $x^*(\gamma) \in X$ such that

$$\psi(x^*(\gamma), \gamma) \geq \psi(x, \gamma) \ \forall \ x \in X,$$

then define the maximum-value mapping $\Theta^* : \Gamma \mapsto \Re$ by

$$\Theta^*(\gamma) = \psi(x^*(\gamma), \gamma) \ \forall \ \gamma \in \Gamma.$$

Then Θ^* is a continuously differentiable function on Γ and

$$\frac{\partial \Theta^*(\gamma)}{\partial \gamma_k} = \frac{\partial \psi(x, \gamma)}{\partial \gamma_k}\Big|_{x = x^*(\gamma)}.$$

The First-Order Lower-Envelope Theorem. Let $X \subseteq \Re^n$ be open with respect to E^n. Let $\Gamma \subseteq \Re^m$ be open with respect to E^m. Let $\psi : X \times \Gamma \mapsto \Re$ be a function that is continuously differentiable with respect to $(x, \gamma) \in X \times \Gamma$. If, for every $\gamma \in \Gamma$, there exists an $x_*(\gamma) \in X$ such that

$$\psi(x_*(\gamma), \gamma) \leq \psi(x, \gamma) \ \forall \ x \in X,$$

then define the minimum-value mapping $\Theta_* : \Gamma \mapsto \Re$ by

$$\Theta_*(\gamma) = \psi(x_*(\gamma), \gamma) \ \forall \ \gamma \in \Gamma.$$

Then Θ_* is a continuously differentiable function on Γ and

$$\frac{\partial \Theta_*(\gamma)}{\partial \gamma_k} = \frac{\partial \psi(x, \gamma)}{\partial \gamma_k}\Big|_{x = x_*(\gamma)}.$$

Problem 12.6.
(i) Draw a simple diagram that illustrates the content of the First-Order Upper-Envelope Theorem and state in simple words the meaning of the result.
(ii) Prove the First-Order Upper-Envelope Theorem.

Problem 12.7.
(i) Draw a simple diagram that illustrates the content of the First-Order Lower-Envelope Theorem and state in simple words the meaning of the result.
(ii) Prove the First-Order Lower-Envelope Theorem.

Problem 12.8. Consider again the family of functions described in problem 12.4.
(i) Use the diagram that you constructed when answering parts (ii) and (iii) of problem 12.4 to help you determine what information is provided by applying the First-Order Upper-Envelope Theorem to the envelope that is the maximum-value function derived in part (iii) of problem 12.4.
(ii) Suppose that $\gamma = \frac{5}{2}$. Use the First-Order Upper-Envelope Theorem to discover $x^*\left(\frac{5}{2}\right)$, the optimal value for x when $\gamma = \frac{5}{2}$. Once you have done so, return to the diagram constructed for your answers to parts (ii) and (iii) of problem 12.4, and confirm visually that you have correctly determined the value $x^*\left(\frac{5}{2}\right)$.
(iii) Repeat part (ii), but with $\gamma = \frac{3}{2}$.

Problem 12.9. Consider again the family of functions described in problem 12.5.
(i) Use the diagram that you constructed when answering parts (ii) and (iii) of problem 12.5 to help you determine what information is provided by applying the First-Order Lower-Envelope Theorem to the envelope that is the minimum-value function derived in part (iii) of problem 12.5.
(ii) Suppose that $\gamma = \frac{2}{5}$. Use the First-Order Lower-Envelope Theorem to discover $x_*\left(\frac{2}{5}\right)$, the optimal value for x when $\gamma = \frac{2}{5}$. Once you have done so, return to the diagram constructed for your answers to parts (ii) and (iii) of problem 12.5, and confirm visually that you have correctly determined the value $x_*\left(\frac{2}{5}\right)$.
(iii) Repeat part (ii), but with $\gamma = \frac{2}{3}$.

Problem 12.10. The versions of the First-Order Envelope Theorems stated above are particular to constrained optimization problems in which the maximum-value functions are differentiable, both with respect to the choice variables x_i and the parameters γ_k. This question explores envelopes and their properties more generally.
(i) Prove that the maximum-value and minimum-value mappings Θ^* and Θ_* stated above are functions.

(ii) Provide a counterexample to the assertion that, if $\psi(x, \gamma)$ is differentiable with respect to $(x, \gamma) \in X \times \Gamma$, then Θ^* and Θ_* must be differentiable with respect to $\gamma \in \Gamma$.

(iii) Prove that, if $\psi(x, \gamma)$ is convex with respect to $\gamma \in \Gamma$, then $\Theta^*(\gamma)$ is convex with respect to $\gamma \in \Gamma$.

(iv) Provide a counterexample to the assertion that, if $\psi(x, \gamma)$ is convex with respect to $\gamma \in \Gamma$ for given $x \in X$, then $\Theta_*(\gamma)$ is convex with respect to $\gamma \in \Gamma$.

(v) Prove that, if $\psi(x, \gamma)$ is concave with respect to $\gamma \in \Gamma$, then $\Theta_*(\gamma)$ is concave with respect to $\gamma \in \Gamma$.

(vi) Provide a counterexample to the assertion that, if $\psi(x, \gamma)$ is concave with respect to $\gamma \in \Gamma$ for given $x \in X$, then $\Theta^*(\gamma)$ is concave with respect to $\gamma \in \Gamma$.

Problem 12.11. A perfectly competitive firm's "long-run" profit-maximization problem is

$$\max_{y, x_1, x_2} py - w_1 x_1 - w_2 x_2 \text{ subject to } y \leq \psi(x_1, x_2).$$

ψ is the firm's production function. y is the output level. x_1 and x_2 are the quantities used of inputs 1 and 2. p is the given per unit price of the firm's product. w_1 and w_2 are the given per unit prices of inputs 1 and 2. Assume that there is a unique profit-maximizing plan $(y^l(p, w_1, w_2), x_1^l(p, w_1, w_2), x_2^l(p, w_1, w_2))$ for any given $(p, w_1, w_2) \gg (0, 0, 0)$. Denote the multiplier for the production constraint by $\lambda^l(p, w_1, w_2)$. The problem's maximum-value function is the firm's long-run indirect profit function

$$
\begin{aligned}
\pi^l(p, w_1, w_2) &\equiv py^l(p, w_1, w_2) - w_1 x_1^l(p, w_1, w_2) - w_2 x_2^l(p, w_1, w_2) \\
&\quad + \lambda^l(p, w_1, w_2) \left[\psi(x_1^l(p, w_1, w_2), x_2^l(p, w_1, w_2)) - y^l(p, w_1, w_2) \right].
\end{aligned}
$$

(i) Use the First-Order Upper-Envelope Theorem to derive Harold Hotelling's result that

$$\frac{\partial \pi^l(p, w_1, w_2)}{\partial p} = y^l(p, w_1, w_2).$$

(ii) Draw a carefully labeled diagram that explains Hotelling's result. Give a simple, accurate verbal explanation of the result.

(iii) Prove that the firm's long-run indirect profit function is a convex function of p.

Problem 12.12. A perfectly competitive firm's "long-run" cost-minimization problem is

$$\min_{x_1, x_2} w_1 x_1 + w_2 x_2 \text{ subject to } y \leq \psi(x_1, x_2).$$

ψ is the firm's production function. $y > 0$ is a given output level. x_1 and x_2 are the quantities used of inputs 1 and 2. w_1 and w_2 are the given per unit prices of inputs 1 and 2. Assume that, for any given $(w_1, w_2) \gg (0, 0)$, there is a unique cost-minimizing input bundle $(x_1^l(w_1, w_2, y), x_2^l(w_1, w_2, y))$. Denote the multiplier for the production constraint by $\mu^l(w_1, w_2, y)$. The problem's minimum-value function is the firm's long-run cost function

$$c^l(w_1, w_2, y) \equiv w_1 x_1^l(w_1, w_2, y) + w_2 x_2^l(w_1, w_2, y)$$
$$+ \mu^l(w_1, w_2, y) \left[\psi(x_1^l(w_1, w_2, y), x_2^l(w_1, w_2, y)) - y \right].$$

(i) Use the First-Order Lower-Envelope Theorem to derive Shephard's result that

$$\frac{\partial c^l(w_1, w_2, y)}{\partial w_i} = x^l(w_1, w_2, y) \text{ for } i = 1, 2.$$

(ii) Draw a carefully labeled diagram that explains Shephard's result. Give a simple, accurate verbal explanation of the result.

(iii) Prove that the firm's long-run cost function is a concave function of w_1.

Problem 12.13. A consumer's budget allocation problem is

$$\max_{x_1, x_2} U(x_1, x_2) \text{ subject to } p_1 x_1 + p_2 x_2 \leq y,$$

where U is the consumer's direct utility function, $y > 0$ is the consumer's budget, x_1 and x_2 are the consumption levels of commodities 1 and 2, and p_1 and p_2 are the given per unit prices of commodities 1 and 2. Assume that, for any given $(p_1, p_2, y) \gg (0, 0, 0)$, there is a unique utility-maximizing consumption bundle $(x_1^*(p_1, p_2, y), x_2^*(p_1, p_2, y))$. The problem's maximum-value function is the consumer's indirect utility function

$$v(p_1, p_2, y) \equiv U(x_1^*(p_1, p_2, y), x_2^*(p_1, p_2, y))$$
$$+ \lambda^*(p_1, p_2, y)[y - p_1 x_1^*(p_1, p_2, y) - p_2 x_2^*(p_1, p_2, y)].$$

(i) Use the First-Order Upper-Envelope Theorem to derive that

$$\frac{\partial v(p_1, p_2, y)}{\partial p_i} = -\lambda^*(p_1, p_2, y)x_i^*(p_1, p_2, y) \text{ for } i = 1, 2, \quad (12.81)$$

$$\text{and} \quad \frac{\partial v(p_1, p_2, y)}{\partial y} = \lambda^*(p_1, p_2, y), \quad (12.82)$$

$$\text{and hence that} \quad \frac{\partial v(p_1, p_2, y)/\partial p_i}{\partial v(p_1, p_2, y)/\partial y} = -x_i^*(p_1, p_2, y) \text{ for } i = 1, 2. \quad (12.83)$$

(12.83) is known as Roy's Identity, named after the French economist René Roy.
(ii) Draw a carefully labeled diagram that explains (12.81) and (12.82). Give a simple, accurate verbal explanation of these results.

Problem 12.14. $U(x_1, \ldots, x_n)$ is a consumer's direct utility function. The consumer faces given positive prices $p_1, \ldots, p_n$ for commodities 1 to n. The consumer's budget is $y > 0$. Assume that the consumer's preferences are strictly monotonic and strictly convex. Use $e(p_1, \ldots, p_n, u)$ to denote the consumer's expenditure function, use $h_i(p_1, \ldots, p_n, u)$ to denote the consumer's Hicksian demand for commodity i, and use $x_i^*(p_1, \ldots, p_n, y)$ to denote the consumer's ordinary demand for commodity i ; $i = 1, \ldots, n$. For given $p_1, \ldots, p_n$, and y, Slutsky's equation is

$$\frac{\partial x_i^*}{\partial p_j} = \frac{\partial h_i}{\partial p_j} - x_j^* \frac{\partial x_i^*}{\partial y} \text{ for } i, j = 1, \ldots, n.$$

Derive Slutsky's equation.

12.10   Answers

Answer to Problem 12.1. We start by noting that the first-order maximization condition (12.77) holds as a zero-valued identity if we evaluate (12.77) only at the problem's optimal solution $x^*(\alpha_1, \alpha_2, \alpha_3)$. Thus we write

$$I(\alpha_1, \alpha_2, \alpha_3) \equiv 2\alpha_1 x^*(\alpha_1, \alpha_2, \alpha_3) + \alpha_2 \equiv 0. \tag{12.84}$$

Differentiation of this identity with respect to α_1 yields

$$0 = 2x^*(\alpha_1, \alpha_2, \alpha_3) + 2\alpha_1 \frac{\partial x^*(\alpha_1, \alpha_2, \alpha_3)}{\partial \alpha_1} \Rightarrow \frac{\partial x^*(\alpha_1, \alpha_2, \alpha_3)}{\partial \alpha_1} = -\frac{x^*(\alpha_1, \alpha_2, \alpha_3)}{\alpha_1} . \tag{12.85}$$

Similarly, differentiation of (12.84) with respect to α_2 yields

$$0 = 2\alpha_1 \frac{\partial x^*(\alpha_1, \alpha_2, \alpha_3)}{\partial \alpha_2} + 1 \Rightarrow \frac{\partial x^*(\alpha_1, \alpha_2, \alpha_3)}{\partial \alpha_2} = -\frac{1}{2\alpha_1} . \tag{12.86}$$

Last, differentiation of (12.84) with respect to α_3 yields

$$0 = 2\alpha_1 \frac{\partial x^*(\alpha_1, \alpha_2, \alpha_3)}{\partial \alpha_3}, \quad \text{so} \quad \frac{\partial x^*(\alpha_1, \alpha_2, \alpha_3)}{\partial \alpha_3} = 0 \tag{12.87}$$

because $\alpha_1 \neq 0$. You should use (12.79) to verify (12.85), (12.86), and (12.87).   □

Answer to Problem 12.2. Consumption bundles with $x_1 = 0$ or $x_2 = 0$ can never be optimal, so the first-order optimality conditions are

$$\left(\frac{\partial U(x_1, x_2)}{\partial x_1}, \frac{\partial U(x_1, x_2)}{\partial x_2}\right)\bigg|_{\substack{x_1 = x_1^*(p_1, p_2, y) \\ x_2 = x_2^*(p_1, p_2, y)}} = (x_2^*(p_1, p_2, y), x_1^*(p_1, p_2, y)) = \lambda^*(p_1, p_2, y)(p_1, p_2)$$

and $\qquad \lambda^*(p_1, p_2, y)(y - p_1 x_1^*(p_1, p_2, y) - p_2 x_2^*(p_1, p_2, y)) = 0,$

yielding the identities

$$I_1(p_1, p_2, y) \equiv x_2^*(p_1, p_2, y) - \lambda^*(p_1, p_2, y)p_1 \equiv 0, \tag{12.88}$$

$$I_2(p_1, p_2, y) \equiv x_1^*(p_1, p_2, y) - \lambda^*(p_1, p_2, y)p_2 \equiv 0, \tag{12.89}$$

$$\text{and} \quad I_3(p_1, p_2, y) \equiv \lambda^*(p_1, p_2, y)(y - p_1 x_1^*(p_1, p_2, y) - p_2 x_2^*(p_1, p_2, y)) \equiv 0. \tag{12.90}$$

Differentiation with respect to p_1 gives

$$0 = \frac{\partial x_2^*(\cdot)}{\partial p_1} - \frac{\partial \lambda^*(\cdot)}{\partial p_1}p_1 - \lambda^*(\cdot), \tag{12.91}$$

$$0 = \frac{\partial x_1^*(\cdot)}{\partial p_1} - \frac{\partial \lambda^*(\cdot)}{\partial p_1}p_2, \text{ and} \tag{12.92}$$

$$0 = \frac{\partial \lambda^*(\cdot)}{\partial p_1}(y - p_1 x_1^*(\cdot) - p_2 x_2^*(\cdot)) - \lambda^*(\cdot)\left(x_1^*(\cdot) + p_1\frac{\partial x_1^*(\cdot)}{\partial p_1} + p_2\frac{\partial x_2^*(\cdot)}{\partial p_1}\right). \tag{12.93}$$

The first term on the right-hand side of (12.93) is zero, so we have

$$\frac{\partial x_2^*(\cdot)}{\partial p_1} \qquad - p_1\frac{\partial \lambda^*(\cdot)}{\partial p_1} = \lambda^*(\cdot), \tag{12.94}$$

$$\frac{\partial x_1^*(\cdot)}{\partial p_1} \qquad - p_2\frac{\partial \lambda^*(\cdot)}{\partial p_1} = 0, \tag{12.95}$$

$$\text{and} \quad \lambda^*(\cdot)p_1\frac{\partial x_1^*(\cdot)}{\partial p_1} + \lambda^*(\cdot)p_2\frac{\partial x_2^*(\cdot)}{\partial p_1} = -\lambda^*(\cdot)x_1^*(\cdot). \tag{12.96}$$

The solution to these linear equations is

$$\frac{\partial x_1^*(p_1, p_2, y)}{\partial p_1} = -\frac{p_2\lambda^* + x_1^*}{2p_1}, \quad \frac{\partial x_2^*(p_1, p_2, y)}{\partial p_1} = \frac{p_2\lambda^* - x_1^*}{2p_2},$$

$$\text{and} \quad \frac{\partial \lambda^*(p_1, p_2, y)}{\partial p_1} = -\frac{p_2\lambda^* + x_1^*}{2p_1 p_2}. \tag{12.97}$$

Using the first-order condition (12.89) simplifies (12.97) to

$$\frac{\partial x_1^*(p_1, p_2, y)}{\partial p_1} = -\frac{p_2\lambda^*}{p_1} < 0, \quad \frac{\partial x_2^*(p_1, p_2, y)}{\partial p_1} = 0, \quad \text{and} \quad \frac{\partial \lambda^*(p_1, p_2, y)}{\partial p_1} = -\frac{\lambda^*}{p_1} < 0.$$

An increase to p_1 results in a lower quantity demanded of commodity 1, no change to the quantity demanded of commodity 2, and a lower value for the consumer's marginal utility of expenditure. You should use the algebraically explicit optimal solution stated in the problem to verify these results. $\square$

Answer to Problem 12.3. The problem's first-order optimality conditions are that there exists a $\lambda^*(\cdot) \geq 0$ such that

$$\left(\frac{\partial U(x_1, x_2)}{\partial x_1}, \frac{\partial U(x_1, x_2)}{\partial x_2} \right) \Bigg|_{\substack{x_1 = x_1^*(p_1, p_2, y) \\ x_2 = x_2^*(p_1, p_2, y)}} = \left(\frac{1}{2\sqrt{x_1^*(p_1, p_2, y)}}, \frac{1}{2\sqrt{x_2^*(p_1, p_2, y)}} \right)$$

$$= \lambda^*(p_1, p_2, y) (p_1, p_2)$$

and $\quad \lambda^*(p_1, p_2, y) (y - p_1 x_1^*(p_1, p_2, y) - p_1 x_2^*(p_1, p_2, y)) = 0,$

yielding the identities

$$I_1(p_1, p_2, y) \equiv \frac{1}{2\sqrt{x_1^*(p_1, p_2, y)}} - \lambda^*(p_1, p_2, y)p_1 \equiv 0, \tag{12.98}$$

$$I_2(p_1, p_2, y) \equiv \frac{1}{2\sqrt{x_2^*(p_1, p_2, y)}} - \lambda^*(p_1, p_2, y)p_2 \equiv 0, \tag{12.99}$$

and $\quad I_3(p_1, p_2, y) \equiv \lambda^*(p_1, p_2, y) (y - p_1 x_1^*(p_1, p_2, y) - p_2 x_2^*(p_1, p_2, y)) \equiv 0. \tag{12.100}$

These are constant-valued identities, so

$$\frac{\partial I_1(p_1, p_2, y)}{\partial \gamma} = 0, \frac{\partial I_2(p_1, p_2, y)}{\partial \gamma} = 0, \quad \text{and} \quad \frac{\partial I_3(p_1, p_2, y)}{\partial \gamma} = 0,$$

where γ is any one of the parameters p_1, p_2 or y. We are asked to set $\gamma = p_1$. Differentiating each of (12.98), (12.99), and (12.100) with respect to p_1 gives

$$0 = -\frac{1}{4} x_1^*(\cdot)^{-3/2} \frac{\partial x_1^*(\cdot)}{\partial p_1} - \frac{\partial \lambda^*(\cdot)}{\partial p_1} p_1 - \lambda^*(\cdot), \tag{12.101}$$

$$0 = -\frac{1}{4} x_2^*(\cdot)^{-3/2} \frac{\partial x_2^*(\cdot)}{\partial p_1} - \frac{\partial \lambda^*(\cdot)}{\partial p_1} p_2, \quad \text{and} \tag{12.102}$$

$$0 = \frac{\partial \lambda^*(\cdot)}{\partial p_1} (y - p_1 x_1^*(\cdot) - p_2 x_2^*(\cdot)) - \lambda^*(\cdot) \left(x_1^*(\cdot) + p_1 \frac{\partial x_1^*(\cdot)}{\partial p_1} + p_2 \frac{\partial x_2^*(\cdot)}{\partial p_1} \right). \tag{12.103}$$

The first term on the right-hand side of (12.103) is zero because the budget constraint binds. A little tidying up of (12.101), (12.102), and (12.103) gives

$$\frac{1}{4} x_1^*(\cdot)^{-3/2} \frac{\partial x_1^*(\cdot)}{\partial p_1} + p_1 \frac{\partial \lambda^*(\cdot)}{\partial p_1} = -\lambda^*(\cdot), \tag{12.104}$$

$$\frac{1}{4} x_2^*(\cdot)^{-3/2} \frac{\partial x_2^*(\cdot)}{\partial p_1} + p_2 \frac{\partial \lambda^*(\cdot)}{\partial p_1} = 0, \tag{12.105}$$

$$\text{and} \quad \lambda^*(\cdot) p_1 \frac{\partial x_1^*(\cdot)}{\partial p_1} + \lambda^*(\cdot) p_2 \frac{\partial x_2^*(\cdot)}{\partial p_1} = -\lambda^*(\cdot) x_1^*(\cdot). \tag{12.106}$$

$\lambda^*(\cdot) > 0$ because the budget constraint is strictly binding. This lets us divide (12.106) by $\lambda^*(\cdot)$ and we end up with

$$\frac{1}{4} x_1^*(\cdot)^{-3/2} \frac{\partial x_1^*(\cdot)}{\partial p_1} \qquad\qquad\qquad + p_1 \frac{\partial \lambda^*(\cdot)}{\partial p_1} = -\lambda^*(\cdot), \tag{12.107}$$

$$\frac{1}{4} x_2^*(\cdot)^{-3/2} \frac{\partial x_2^*(\cdot)}{\partial p_1} \qquad + p_2 \frac{\partial \lambda^*(\cdot)}{\partial p_1} = 0, \tag{12.108}$$

$$\text{and} \quad p_1 \frac{\partial x_1^*(\cdot)}{\partial p_1} \qquad\qquad + p_2 \frac{\partial x_2^*(\cdot)}{\partial p_1} \qquad\qquad = -x_1^*(\cdot). \tag{12.109}$$

The solution is

$$\frac{\partial x_1^*(p_1, p_2, y)}{\partial p_1} = -\frac{\dfrac{p_1 x_1^*}{4(x_2^*)^{3/2}} + p_2^2 \lambda^*}{\dfrac{p_2^2}{4(x_1^*)^{3/2}} + \dfrac{p_1^2}{4(x_2^*)^{3/2}}}, \tag{12.110}$$

$$\frac{\partial x_2^*(p_1, p_2, y)}{\partial p_1} = -\frac{p_2 \left(\dfrac{1}{4(x_1^*)^{1/2}} - p_1 \lambda^* \right)}{\dfrac{p_2^2}{4(x_1^*)^{3/2}} + \dfrac{p_1^2}{4(x_2^*)^{3/2}}}, \tag{12.111}$$

$$\text{and} \quad \frac{\partial \lambda^*(p_1, p_2, y)}{\partial p_1} = \frac{\dfrac{1}{4(x_2^*)^{3/2}} \left(\dfrac{1}{4(x_1^*)^{1/2}} - p_1 \lambda^* \right)}{\dfrac{p_2^2}{4(x_1^*)^{3/2}} + \dfrac{p_1^2}{4(x_2^*)^{3/2}}}. \tag{12.112}$$

These expressions can be simplified. Squaring and cubing (12.98) gives

$$\frac{1}{4x_1^*} = \lambda^{*2} p_1^2 \implies x_1^* = \frac{1}{4p_1^2 \lambda^{*2}} \quad \text{and} \quad \frac{1}{8x_1^{*3/2}} = \lambda^{*3} p_1^3 \implies \frac{1}{4x_1^{*3/2}} = 2\lambda^{*3} p_1^3. \tag{12.113}$$

Substituting from (12.113) into (12.110), (12.111), and (12.112) gives

$$\frac{\partial x_1^*(p_1, p_2, y)}{\partial p_1} = -\frac{(2p_1 + p_2)x_1^*}{p_1(p_1 + p_2)} < 0, \quad \frac{\partial x_2^*(p_1, p_2, y)}{\partial p_1} = \frac{p_1 x_1^*}{p_2(p_1 + p_2)} > 0,$$

and $\quad \dfrac{\partial \lambda^*(p_1, p_2, y)}{\partial p_1} = -\dfrac{p_2 \lambda^*}{2p_1(p_1 + p_2)} < 0.$

Without knowing the explicit equations for x_1^*, x_2^*, and λ^*, we have discovered that an increase to p_1 results in a lower quantity demanded of commodity 1, an increase to the quantity demanded for commodity 2, and a lower value for the consumer's marginal utility of expenditure. □

Answer to Problem 12.4.

(i) The optimal solution to the problem $\max_x f^r(x; \gamma) = -x^2 + \gamma x + 2$, in which γ is parametric, necessarily satisfies the first-order maximization condition

$$0 = \frac{df^r(x; \gamma)}{dx}\Big|_{x=x^*(\gamma)} = -2x^*(\gamma) + \gamma \quad \Rightarrow \quad x^*(\gamma) = \frac{\gamma}{2}.$$

The second-order condition confirms that $x^*(\gamma)$ is a local maximum for $f^r(x; \gamma)$. Since this is the function's only critical point, the point is a global maximum for $f^r(x; \gamma)$. Consequently the maximum-value function for the problem is

$$v(\gamma) \equiv f^r(x^*(\gamma); \gamma) = -x^*(\gamma)^2 + \gamma x^*(\gamma) + 2 = \frac{\gamma^2}{4} + 2.$$

(ii) and (iii). See Figure 12.6.

$x = 1$ is an optimal solution if and only if $x^*(\gamma) = 1$; *i.e.* if and only if $\gamma/2 = 1$. So $x = 1 = x^*(\gamma)$ if and only if $\gamma = 2$. The value of the function $f^r(x; \gamma)$ when $x = 1$ and $\gamma = 2$ is $f^r(1; 2) = -1^2 + 2 \times 1 + 2 = 3$. The value of the envelope function $v(\gamma)$ when $\gamma = 2$ is $v(2) = 2^2/4 + 2 = 3$. Thus the restricted function $f^r(\gamma; x = 1)$ is a part (just a point) of the envelope at $\gamma = 2$.

$x = 2$ is an optimal solution if and only if $x^*(\gamma) = 2$; *i.e.* if and only if $\gamma/2 = 2$. So $x = 2 = x^*(\gamma)$ if and only if $\gamma = 4$. The value of the function $f^r(x; \gamma)$ when $x = 2$ and $\gamma = 4$ is $f^r(2; 4) = -2^2 + 4 \times 2 + 2 = 6$. The value of the envelope function $v(\gamma)$ when $\gamma = 2$ is $v(2) = 4^2/4 + 2 = 6$. Thus the restricted function $f^r(\gamma; x = 2)$ is a part of the envelope at $\gamma = 4$.

$x = 3$ is an optimal solution if and only if $x^*(\gamma) = 3$; *i.e.* if and only if $\gamma/2 = 3$. So $x = 3 = x^*(\gamma)$ if and only if $\gamma = 6$. The value of the function $f^r(x; \gamma)$ when $x = 3$ and $\gamma = 6$ is $f^r(3; 6) = -3^2 + 6 \times 3 + 2 = 11$. The value of the envelope function $v(\gamma)$

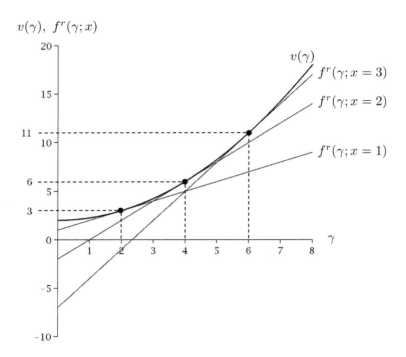

Figure 12.6: The upper envelope for problem 12.4.

when $\gamma = 6$ is $v(2) = 6^2/4 + 2 = 11$. Thus the restricted function $f^r(\gamma; x = 3)$ is a part of the envelope at $\gamma = 6$.   □

Answer to Problem 12.5.

(i) The optimal solution to the problem $\min_x f^r(x; \gamma) = \gamma^2 x^2 - \gamma x + 2$, in which $\gamma > 0$ is parametric, necessarily satisfies the first-order minimization condition

$$0 = \frac{\mathrm{d}f^r(x; \gamma)}{\mathrm{d}x}\Big|_{x=x_*(\gamma)} = 2\gamma^2 x_*(\gamma) - \gamma \quad \Rightarrow \quad x_*(\gamma) = \frac{1}{2\gamma}.$$

The second-order condition confirms that $x_*(\gamma)$ is a local minimum for $f^r(x; \gamma)$. Since this is the function's only critical point, the point is a global minimum for $f^r(x; \gamma)$ and so the problem's minimum-value function is

$$v(\gamma) \equiv f^r(x_*(\gamma); \gamma) = \gamma^2 x_*(\gamma)^2 - \gamma x_*(\gamma) + 2 \equiv \frac{7}{4}.$$

(ii) and (iii). See Figure 12.7.

$x = 1/6$ is an optimal solution if and only if $x_*(\gamma) = 1/6$; *i.e.* if and only if $1/2\gamma = 1/6$. So $x = 1/6 = x_*(\gamma)$ if and only if $\gamma = 3$. The value of the function

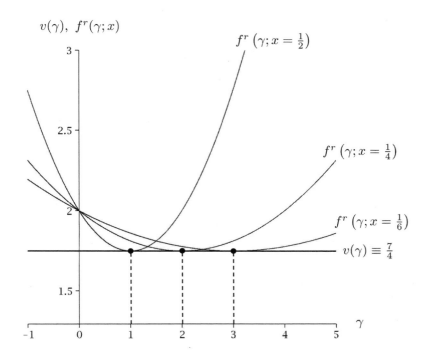

Figure 12.7: The lower envelope for problem 12.5.

$f^r(x; \gamma)$ when $x = 1/6$ and $\gamma = 3$ is $f^r(1/6; 3) = 3^2 \times (1/6)^2 - 3 \times 1/6 + 2 = 7/4 = v(3)$. Thus the restricted function $f^r(\gamma; x = 1/6)$ is a part of the envelope at $\gamma = 3$.

$x = 1/4$ is an optimal solution if and only if $x_*(\gamma) = 1/4$; *i.e.* if and only if $1/2\gamma = 1/4$. So $x = 1/4 = x_*(\gamma)$ if and only if $\gamma = 2$. The value of $f^r(x; \gamma)$ when $x = 1/4$ and $\gamma = 2$ is $f^r(1/4; 2) = 7/4 = v(2)$. Thus the restricted function $f^r(\gamma; x = 1/4)$ is a part of the envelope at $\gamma = 2$.

$x = 1/2$ is an optimal solution if and only if $x_*(\gamma) = 1/2$; *i.e.* if and only if $1/2\gamma = 1/2$. So $x = 1/2 = x_*(\gamma)$ if and only if $\gamma = 1$. The value of $f^r(x; \gamma)$ when $x = 1/2$ and $\gamma = 1$ is $f^r(1/2; 1) = 7/4 = v(1)$. Thus the restricted function $f^r(\gamma; x = 1/2)$ is a part of the envelope at $\gamma = 1$. $\qquad \square$

Answer to Problem 12.6.

(i) The diagram should be drawn with the horizontal axis measuring the values of a parameter γ_k and the vertical axis measuring the value of a maximum-value function $\Theta^*(\gamma_k)$. A few values, say, x', x'', and x''', should be taken from the choice set X. For each *fixed* value of x, a graph of $\psi(x, \gamma_k)$ should be drawn. In this example there will be three such graphs, one for each of x', x'', and x'''. The upper-envelope of these three graphs consists of the segments of these graphs that are highest; *i.e.*

$$\Theta^*(\gamma_k) = \max\{\psi(x', \gamma_k), \psi(x'', \gamma_k), \psi(x''', \gamma_k)\}.$$

Now notice that, wherever the envelope Θ^* coincides with a particular $\psi(x, \gamma_k)$, the slope with respect to γ_k of the envelope $\Theta^*(\gamma_k)$ is the same as the slope with respect to γ_k of the $\psi(x, \gamma_k)$ curve with the value of x *fixed*. This is the content of the theorem.
(ii) Proof. For any $\gamma \in \Gamma$, there exists an $x^*(\gamma) \in X$ for which

$$\psi(x^*(\gamma), \gamma) \geq \psi(x, \gamma) \ \forall \ x \in X.$$

Since ψ is continuously differentiable on $X \times \Gamma$, necessarily

$$\frac{\partial \psi(x, \gamma)}{\partial x_i}\Big|_{x=x^*(\gamma)} = 0 \ \forall \ i = 1, \dots, n. \tag{12.114}$$

Since (12.114) is always evaluated at the maximizing solution $x^*(\gamma)$, (12.114) holds as an identity. Since ψ is continuously differentiable on $X \times \Gamma$, the Implicit Function Theorem asserts that $x^*(\gamma)$ is a continuously differentiable function on Γ. Therefore

$$\frac{\partial \Theta^*(\gamma)}{\partial \gamma_k} = \frac{\partial \psi(x, \gamma)}{\partial \gamma_k}\Big|_{x=x^*(\gamma)} + \sum_{i=1}^{n} \frac{\partial \psi(x, \gamma)}{\partial x_i}\Big|_{x=x^*(\gamma)} \times \frac{\partial x_i^*(\gamma)}{\partial \gamma_k}$$

$$= \frac{\partial \psi(x, \gamma)}{\partial \gamma_k}\Big|_{x=x^*(\gamma)} \text{ by (12.114).} \qquad \square$$

Answer to Problem 12.7.
(i) The diagram should be drawn with the horizontal axis measuring the values of a parameter γ_k and the vertical axis measuring the value of a minimum-value function $\Theta_*(\gamma_k)$. A few values, say x', x'', and x''', should be taken from the choice set X. For each *fixed* value of x, a graph of $\psi(x, \gamma_k)$ should be drawn. In this example there will be three such graphs, one for each of x', x'', and x'''. The lower-envelope of these three graphs consists of the segments of these graphs that are lowest; *i.e.*

$$\Theta_*(\gamma_k) = \min\{\psi(x', \gamma_k), \psi(x'', \gamma_k), \psi(x''', \gamma_k)\}.$$

Now notice that, wherever the envelope Θ_* coincides with a particular $\psi(x, \gamma_k)$, the slope with respect to γ_k of the envelope $\Theta_*(\gamma_k)$ is the same as the slope with respect to γ_k of the $\psi(x, \gamma_k)$ curve with the value of x *fixed*. This is the content of the theorem.
(ii) Proof. For any $\gamma \in \Gamma$, there exists an $x_*(\gamma) \in X$ for which

$$\psi(x_*(\gamma), \gamma) \leq \psi(x, \gamma) \ \forall \ x \in X.$$

Since ψ is continuously differentiable on $X \times \Gamma$, necessarily

$$\frac{\partial \psi(x, \gamma)}{\partial x_i}\Big|_{x=x_*(\gamma)} = 0 \ \forall \ i = 1, \ldots, n. \tag{12.115}$$

Since (12.115) is always evaluated at the minimizing solution $x_*(\gamma)$, (12.115) holds as an identity. Since ψ is continuously differentiable on $X \times \Gamma$, the Implicit Function Theorem asserts that $x_*(\gamma)$ is a continuously differentiable function on Γ. Therefore

$$\begin{aligned}
\frac{\partial \Theta_*(\gamma)}{\partial \gamma_k} &= \frac{\partial \psi(x, \gamma)}{\partial \gamma_k}\Big|_{x=x_*(\gamma)} + \sum_{i=1}^{n} \frac{\partial \psi(x, \gamma)}{\partial x_i}\Big|_{x=x_*(\gamma)} \times \frac{\partial x_{*i}(\gamma)}{\partial \gamma_k} \\
&= \frac{\partial \psi(x, \gamma)}{\partial \gamma_k}\Big|_{x=x_*(\gamma)} \text{ by (12.115).} \qquad \square
\end{aligned}$$

Answer to Problem 12.8. For the problem $\max_x f^r(x; \gamma) = -x^2 + \gamma x + 2$, in which γ is parametric, the maximum value is

$$v(\gamma) \equiv f^r(x^*(\gamma); \gamma) = -x^*(\gamma)^2 + \gamma x^*(\gamma) + 2.$$

(i) The First-Order Upper-Envelope Theorem states that the two-step process that derives the value of the rate of change of the maximum value $v(\gamma)$ with respect to γ at a particular value γ' of γ is, first, to fix the value of x at the number $x' = x^*(\gamma')$ and, second, to differentiate the resulting function with respect to γ. The first step gives us the function of only γ (since x is fixed at the number x') that is

$$f^r(\gamma; x') = -\left(x'\right)^2 + \gamma x' + 2.$$

The value at $\gamma = \gamma'$ of the derivative of this function with respect to γ is

$$\frac{\mathrm{d}f^r(\gamma; x')}{\mathrm{d}\gamma}\Big|_{\gamma=\gamma'} = x'.$$

The First-Order Upper-Envelope Theorem informs us that this is the value at $\gamma = \gamma'$ of the rate of change with respect to γ of the maximum value $v(\gamma)$; *i.e.*

$$\frac{\mathrm{d}v(\gamma)}{\mathrm{d}\gamma}\Big|_{\gamma=\gamma'} = \frac{\mathrm{d}f^r(\gamma; x')}{\mathrm{d}\gamma}\Big|_{\gamma=\gamma'} = x' = x^*(\gamma').$$

Since the maximum-value function is $v(\gamma) = \gamma^2/4 + 2$, we have that

$$x^*(\gamma') = \frac{\mathrm{d}}{\mathrm{d}\gamma}\left(\frac{\gamma^2}{4} + 2\right)\Big|_{\gamma=\gamma'} = \frac{\gamma'}{2}.$$

This is the optimality result obtained in part (i) of problem 12.4. The point is that the same result can be obtained directly from a knowledge of only the maximum-value function and the family of (restricted) functions that generate the envelope that is the maximum-value function.

(ii) If $\gamma = \frac{5}{2}$, then the corresponding optimal value for x is $x^*\left(\frac{5}{2}\right) = \frac{5/2}{2} = \frac{5}{4}$. The restricted function in which the value of x is fixed at $\frac{5}{4}$ is $f^r\left(\gamma; x = \frac{5}{4}\right) = -\left(\frac{5}{4}\right)^2 + \frac{5}{4}\gamma + 2 = \frac{7}{16} + \frac{5}{4}\gamma$. At $\gamma = \frac{5}{2}$, the value of this restricted function is $f^r\left(\frac{5}{2}; \frac{5}{4}\right) = \frac{7}{16} + \frac{5}{4} \times \frac{5}{2} = \frac{57}{16}$, which is the maximum value for $\gamma = \frac{5}{2}$. So the envelope and the restricted function are the one and the same for $\gamma = \frac{5}{2}$. Therefore the slopes of these two functions are the same for $\gamma = \frac{5}{2}$, and this common slope is $x^*\left(\frac{5}{2}\right) = \frac{5}{4}$. Add the graph of $\frac{7}{16} + \frac{5}{4}\gamma$ to your diagram for parts (ii) and (iii) of problem 12.4, and you will observe a tangency with the graph of the maximum-value function at $\gamma = \frac{5}{2}$. The slope at the tangency is $\frac{5}{4}$.

(iii) If $\gamma = \frac{3}{2}$, then the corresponding optimal value for x is $x^*\left(\frac{3}{2}\right) = \frac{3/2}{2} = \frac{3}{4}$. The restricted function in which the value of x is fixed at $\frac{3}{4}$ is $f^r\left(\gamma; x = \frac{3}{4}\right) = -\left(\frac{3}{4}\right)^2 + \frac{3}{4}\gamma + 2 = \frac{23}{16} + \frac{3}{4}\gamma$. At $\gamma = \frac{3}{2}$, the value of this restricted function is $f^r\left(\frac{3}{2}; \frac{3}{4}\right) = \frac{41}{16}$, which is the maximum value for $\gamma = \frac{3}{2}$. So the envelope and the restricted function are the same for $\gamma = \frac{3}{2}$. Therefore the slopes of these two functions are the same for $\gamma = \frac{3}{2}$, and this common slope is $x^*\left(\frac{3}{2}\right) = \frac{3}{4}$. Add the graph of $\frac{23}{16} + \frac{3}{4}\gamma$ to your diagram for parts (ii) and (iii) of problem 12.4, and you will observe a tangency with the graph of the maximum-value function at $\gamma = \frac{3}{2}$. The slope at the tangency is $\frac{3}{4}$. $\square$

Answer to Problem 12.9. For the problem $\min_x f(x; \gamma) = \gamma^2 x^2 - \gamma x + 2$, in which γ is parametric, the minimum-value function is $v(\gamma) \equiv \frac{7}{4}$.

(i) To apply the First-Order Lower-Envelope Theorem, we first select some value γ' for γ. Next we fix the value of x at whatever is the number $x' = x_*(\gamma')$. This gives us the function

$$f^r(\gamma; x') = \gamma^2 (x')^2 - \gamma x' + 2.$$

We differentiate this function of only γ and evaluate the derivative at $\gamma = \gamma'$, obtaining

$$\frac{\mathrm{d} f^r(\gamma; x')}{\mathrm{d}\gamma}\Big|_{\gamma=\gamma'} = 2\gamma' (x')^2 - x'.$$

The First-Order Lower-Envelope Theorem informs us that this is the value at $\gamma = \gamma'$ of the rate of change with respect to γ of the minimum value $v(\gamma)$; *i.e.*

$$\frac{\mathrm{d}v(\gamma)}{\mathrm{d}\gamma}\Big|_{\gamma=\gamma'} = \frac{\mathrm{d} f^r(\gamma; x')}{\mathrm{d}\gamma}\Big|_{\gamma=\gamma'} = 2\gamma' (x')^2 - x' = 2\gamma' x_*(\gamma')^2 - x_*(\gamma').$$

Since the minimum-value function is $v(\gamma) \equiv \frac{7}{4}$ we have that

$$2\gamma' x_*(\gamma')^2 - x_*(\gamma') = \frac{\mathrm{d}}{\mathrm{d}\gamma}\left(\frac{7}{4}\right)\big|_{\gamma=\gamma'} = 0 \quad \Rightarrow \quad x_*(\gamma') = \frac{1}{2\gamma'}.$$

This is the optimality result obtained in part (i) of problem 12.5.

(ii) If $\gamma = \frac{2}{5}$, then the corresponding optimal value for x is $x_*\left(\frac{2}{5}\right) = \frac{5}{4}$. The restricted function in which the value of x is fixed at $\frac{5}{4}$ is $f^r\left(\gamma; x = \frac{5}{4}\right) = \frac{25}{16}\gamma^2 - \frac{5}{4}\gamma + 2$. At $\gamma = \frac{2}{5}$, the value of this restricted function is $f^r\left(\frac{2}{5}; \frac{5}{4}\right) = \frac{7}{4}$, which is the minimum value for $\gamma = \frac{2}{5}$. So the envelope and the restricted function are the same for $\gamma = \frac{2}{5}$. Therefore the slopes of these two functions are the same for $\gamma = \frac{2}{5}$, and this common slope is $2 \times \frac{2}{5} \times x_*\left(\frac{2}{5}\right)^2 - x_*\left(\frac{2}{5}\right) = \frac{4}{5} \times \frac{25}{16} - \frac{5}{4} = 0$. Add the graph of $\frac{25}{16}\gamma^2 - \frac{5}{4}\gamma + 2$ to your diagram for parts (ii) and (iii) of problem 12.5, and you will observe a tangency with the graph of the minimum-value function at $\gamma = \frac{2}{5}$. The slope at the tangency is zero.

(iii) If $\gamma = \frac{2}{3}$, then the corresponding optimal value for x is $x_*\left(\frac{2}{3}\right) = \frac{3}{4}$. The restricted function in which the value of x is fixed at $\frac{3}{4}$ is $f^r\left(\gamma; x = \frac{3}{4}\right) = \frac{9}{16}\gamma^2 - \frac{3}{4}\gamma + 2$. At $\gamma = \frac{2}{3}$, the value of this restricted function is $f^r\left(\frac{2}{3}; \frac{3}{4}\right) = \frac{7}{4}$, which is the minimum value for $\gamma = \frac{2}{3}$. So the envelope and the restricted function are the same for $\gamma = \frac{2}{3}$. Therefore the slopes of these two functions are the same for $\gamma = \frac{2}{3}$, and this common slope is $2 \times \frac{2}{3} \times x_*\left(\frac{2}{3}\right)^2 - x_*\left(\frac{2}{3}\right) = \frac{4}{3} \times \frac{9}{16} - \frac{3}{4} = 0$. Add the graph of $\frac{9}{16}\gamma^2 - \frac{3}{4}\gamma + 2$ to your diagram for parts (ii) and (iii) of problem 12.5, and you will observe a tangency with the graph of the minimum-value function at $\gamma = \frac{2}{3}$. The slope at the tangency is zero. $\qquad\square$

Answer to Problem 12.10.

(i) Proof. Suppose that Θ^* is not a function on Γ. Then there exists at least one value $\gamma' \in \Gamma$ such that there are at least two distinct values $\hat{\theta}, \tilde{\theta} \in \Theta(\gamma')$. Either $\hat{\theta} > \tilde{\theta}$ or *vice versa*. Suppose $\hat{\theta} > \tilde{\theta}$. But then $\tilde{\theta}$ is not a maximum value for γ'. Contradiction. Hence Θ^* is a function on Γ.

A similar argument establishes that Θ_* is also a function on Γ. $\qquad\square$

(ii) Consider the family of functions $\psi : [-1, 1] \times [-1, 1] \to [-1, 1]$, where

$$\psi(x, \gamma) = \gamma x \text{ for } x \in [-1, 1] \text{ and } \gamma \in [-1, 1].$$

Every function in this family is continuously differentiable to any order. The family's upper and lower envelopes are

$$\Theta^*(\gamma) = \max_{-1 \leq x \leq 1} \gamma x = \begin{cases} -\gamma & ;-1 \leq \gamma < 0 \\ +\gamma & ;0 \leq \gamma \leq 1 \end{cases} \text{ and } \Theta_*(\gamma) = \min_{-1 \leq x \leq 1} \gamma x = \begin{cases} +\gamma & ;-1 \leq \gamma < 0 \\ -\gamma & ;0 \leq \gamma \leq 1. \end{cases}$$

Neither Θ^* nor Θ_* is differentiable at $\gamma = 0$.

(iii) Proof. Take $\gamma', \gamma'' \in \Gamma$ with $\gamma' \neq \gamma''$. Then, for any $\mu \in [0, 1]$,

$$\Theta^*(\mu\gamma' + (1 - \mu)\gamma'') = \psi(x^*(\mu\gamma' + (1 - \mu)\gamma''), \mu\gamma' + (1 - \mu)\gamma'')$$
$$\leq \mu\psi(x^*(\mu\gamma' + (1 - \mu)\gamma''), \gamma') + (1 - \mu)\psi(x^*(\mu\gamma' + (1 - \mu)\gamma''), \gamma''),$$

because $\psi(x, \gamma)$ is convex with respect to γ. $x^*(\mu\gamma' + (1 - \mu)\gamma'')$ is not necessarily a maximizing value for x when $\gamma = \gamma'$, and $x^*(\mu\gamma' + (1 - \mu)\gamma'')$ is not necessarily a maximizing value for x when $\gamma = \gamma''$; *i.e.*

$$\psi(x^*(\mu\gamma' + (1 - \mu)\gamma''), \gamma') \leq \psi(x^*(\gamma'), \gamma') \text{ and } \psi(x^*(\mu\gamma' + (1 - \mu)\gamma''), \gamma'') \leq \psi(x^*(\gamma''), \gamma'').$$

Therefore

$$\Theta^*(\mu\gamma' + (1 - \mu)\gamma') \leq \mu\psi(x^*(\gamma'), \gamma') + (1 - \mu)\psi(x^*(\gamma''), \gamma'') = \mu\Theta^*(\gamma') + (1 - \mu)\Theta^*(\gamma''). \quad \square$$

(iv) The example given as an answer to part (ii) is a counterexample.

(v) Proof. Take $\gamma', \gamma'' \in \Gamma$ with $\gamma' \neq \gamma''$. Then, for any $\mu \in [0, 1]$,

$$\Theta_*(\mu\gamma' + (1 - \mu)\gamma'') = \psi(x_*(\mu\gamma' + (1 - \mu)\gamma''), \mu\gamma' + (1 - \mu)\gamma'')$$
$$\geq \mu\psi(x_*(\mu\gamma' + (1 - \mu)\gamma''), \gamma') + (1 - \mu)\psi(x_*(\mu\gamma' + (1 - \mu)\gamma''), \gamma''),$$

because $\psi(x, \gamma)$ is concave with respect to γ. $x_*(\mu\gamma' + (1 - \mu)\gamma'')$ is not necessarily a minimizing value for x when $\gamma = \gamma'$, and $x_*(\mu\gamma' + (1 - \mu)\gamma'')$ is not necessarily a minimizing value for x when $\gamma = \gamma''$; *i.e.*

$$\psi(x_*(\mu\gamma' + (1 - \mu)\gamma''), \gamma') \geq \psi(x_*(\gamma'), \gamma') \text{ and } \psi(x_*(\mu\gamma' + (1 - \mu)\gamma''), \gamma'') \geq \psi(x_*(\gamma''), \gamma'').$$

Therefore

$$\Theta_*(\mu\gamma' + (1 - \mu)\gamma'') \geq \mu\psi(x_*(\gamma'), \gamma') + (1 - \mu)\psi(x_*(\gamma''), \gamma'') = \mu\Theta_*(\gamma') + (1 - \mu)\Theta_*(\gamma''). \quad \square$$

(vi) The example given as an answer to part (ii) is a counterexample. $\quad \square$

Answer to Problem 12.11.

(i) Applying the First-Order Upper-Envelope Theorem to the firm's long-run indirect profit function proves the result directly.

(ii) See Figure 12.8. The diagram's horizontal axis measures the per unit price p of the firm's product. The vertical axis measures the firm's profit.

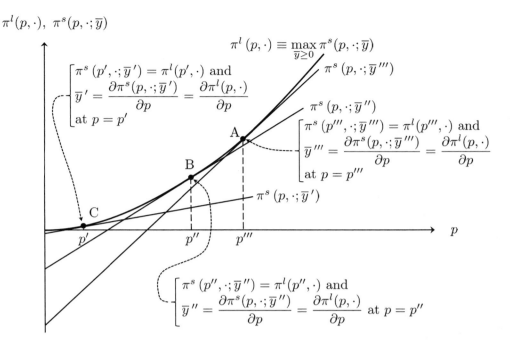

$\pi^l(p, \cdot), \ \pi^s(p, \cdot; \overline{y})$

$\pi^l(p, \cdot) \equiv \max_{\overline{y} \geq 0} \pi^s(p, \cdot; \overline{y})$

$\pi^s(p, \cdot; \overline{y}''')$

$\begin{bmatrix} \pi^s(p', \cdot; \overline{y}') = \pi^l(p', \cdot) \text{ and} \\ \overline{y}' = \dfrac{\partial \pi^s(p, \cdot; \overline{y}')}{\partial p} = \dfrac{\partial \pi^l(p, \cdot)}{\partial p} \\ \text{at } p = p' \end{bmatrix}$

$\pi^s(p, \cdot; \overline{y}'')$

$\begin{bmatrix} \pi^s(p''', \cdot; \overline{y}''') = \pi^l(p''', \cdot) \text{ and} \\ \overline{y}''' = \dfrac{\partial \pi^s(p, \cdot; \overline{y}''')}{\partial p} = \dfrac{\partial \pi^l(p, \cdot)}{\partial p} \\ \text{at } p = p''' \end{bmatrix}$

A

B

$\pi^s(p, \cdot; \overline{y}')$

C

p' p'' p''' p

$\begin{bmatrix} \pi^s(p'', \cdot; \overline{y}'') = \pi^l(p'', \cdot) \text{ and} \\ \overline{y}'' = \dfrac{\partial \pi^s(p, \cdot; \overline{y}'')}{\partial p} = \dfrac{\partial \pi^l(p, \cdot)}{\partial p} \text{ at } p = p'' \end{bmatrix}$

Figure 12.8: Hotelling's result that $\partial \pi^*(p, \cdot)/\partial p = y^*(p, \cdot)$.

Consider the firm's profit problem in which the firm is restricted to producing a given quantity $\overline{y} \geq 0$ of its product. This "short-run" problem is

$$\max_{x_1, x_2} p\overline{y} - w_1 x_1 - w_2 x_2 \text{ subject to } - \psi(x_1, x_2) \leq -\overline{y}.$$

This is the problem of locating an input bundle that minimizes the cost of producing $\overline{y}$ units of the firm's product, but we will continue to consider this problem as one of maximizing profit. The solution will be denoted by $(x_1^s(p, w_1, w_2; \overline{y}), x_2^s(p, w_1, w_2; \overline{y}))$. The multiplier for the production constraint will be denoted by $\lambda^s(p, w_1, w_2; \overline{y})$. The maximum-value function for this restricted problem is the "short-run" indirect profit function

$$\pi^s(p, w_1, w_2; \overline{y}) \equiv p\overline{y} - w_1 x_1^s(p, w_1, w_2; \overline{y}) - w_2 x_2^s(p, w_1, w_2; \overline{y})$$
$$+ \lambda^s(p, w_1, w_2; \overline{y})[-\overline{y} + \psi(x_1^s(p, w_1, w_2; \overline{y}), x_2^s(p, w_1, w_2; \overline{y}))].$$

Notice that this function is affine with respect to p, because $\overline{y}$ is a given constant.

Select, say, three values p', p'', and p''' for p, with $p' < p'' < p'''$. Use $\overline{y}'$ to denote the value for y that is long-run profit-maximizing when $p = p'$; i.e. $\overline{y}' = y^l(p', w_1, w_2)$.

Similarly, use $\overline{y}''$ and $\overline{y}'''$ to denote the values for y that are long-run profit-maximizing for $p = p''$ and $p = p'''$, respectively; $\overline{y}' < \overline{y}'' = y^l(p'', w_1, w_2) < \overline{y}''' = y^l(p''', w_1, w_2)$.

Plot the short-run profit function $\pi^s(p, w_1, w_2; \overline{y}')$ on the diagram. The graph is a straight line with a positive slope of $\overline{y}'$ profit dollars per unit increase in p. The graph's intercept is the value of the short-run indirect profit when $p = 0$. This is

$$\pi^s(0, w_1, w_2; \overline{y}') = -w_1 x_1^s(0, w_1, w_2; \overline{y}') - w_2 x_2^s(0, w_1, w_2; \overline{y}').$$

The graph of $\pi^s(p, w_1, w_2; \overline{y}'')$ is a straight line with a slope of $\overline{y}''$ and a vertical intercept of

$$\pi^s(0, w_1, w_2; \overline{y}'') = -w_1 x_1^s(0, w_1, w_2; \overline{y}'') - w_2 x_2^s(0, w_1, w_2; \overline{y}'')$$
$$< -w_1 x_1^s(0, w_1, w_2; \overline{y}') - w_2 x_2^s(0, w_1, w_2; \overline{y}'),$$

since $\overline{y}'' > \overline{y}'$. Thus the graph of $\pi^s(p, w_1, w_2; \overline{y}'')$ commences at a lower vertical intercept than does the graph of $\pi^s(p, w_1, w_2; \overline{y}')$, and increases at a greater constant positive slope. Similarly, the graph of $\pi^s(p, w_1, w_2; \overline{y}''')$ commences at a still lower vertical intercept, and increases at the even greater constant positive slope $\overline{y}'''$.

The graph of the long-run indirect profit function is the upper envelope of affine graphs such as the three described above. Therefore the long-run indirect profit function's slope with respect to p is the same as the slope of the short-run indirect profit function that is part of the envelope at that point. Thus, for the value p' of p, the slope $\partial \pi^l(p, w_1, w_2)/\partial p$ evaluated at p' is the same as the slope $\partial \pi^s(p, w_1, w_2; \overline{y}')/\partial p$ evaluated at p', because $\overline{y}'$ is the long-run profit-maximizing choice for y when $p = p'$, meaning that the short-run profit function $\pi^s(p, w_1, w_2; \overline{y}')$ *is* the envelope $\pi^l(p, w_1, w_2)$ when $p = p'$. Therefore, at $p = p'$, the slope with respect to p of the envelope $\pi^l(p, w_1, w_2)$ is the slope with respect to p of the short-run profit function $\pi^s(p, w_1, w_2; \overline{y}')$. That is, $\partial \pi^l(p, w_1, w_2)/\partial p = \overline{y}' = \partial \pi^s(p, w_1, w_2; \overline{y}')/\partial p$ at $p = p'$. The same statements may be made for $p = p''$ and for $p = p'''$.

(iii) Proof. The firm's Lagrange function

$$L(y, x_1, x_2, \lambda; p, w_1, w_2) = py - w_1 x_1 - w_2 x_2 + \lambda(-y + \psi(x_1, x_2))$$

is jointly convex in (p, y). Applying the result stated in part (iii) of problem 12.10 gives that the firm's long-run indirect profit function is a convex function of p. $\square$

Answer to Problem 12.12.

(i) Applying the First-Order Lower-Envelope Theorem to the firm's long-run cost function immediately yields the result.

(ii) See Figure 12.9. Consider the short-run circumstance in which the firm has a fixed input. Suppose this is input 1. Denote the level at which it is fixed by $\overline{x}_1$. Input 2 remains variable. The firm's short-run total cost function is then

$$c^s(w_1, w_2, y; \overline{x}_1) = w_1\overline{x}_1 + w_2x_2 + \lambda^s(w_1, w_2, y; \overline{x}_1)(y - \psi(x_2; \overline{x}_1)).$$

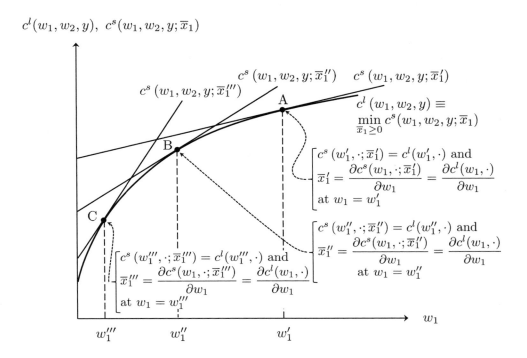

Figure 12.9: Shephard's result that $\partial c^l(w_1, w_2, y)/\partial w_1 = x_1^l(w_1, w_2, y)$.

Figure 12.9 displays three short-run cost functions, one for x_1 fixed at $\overline{x}_1'$, another for x_1 fixed at $\overline{x}_1''$, and the other for x_1 fixed at $\overline{x}_1'''$, where $\overline{x}_1' < \overline{x}_1'' < \overline{x}_1'''$. Each short-run cost function is affine with respect to w_1, and has a slope of $\overline{x}_1$ when plotted with w_1 measured on the horizontal axis and cost measured on the vertical axis.

The graph of the short-run cost function $c^s(w_1, w_2, y; \overline{x}_1')$ is a straight line with a positive slope of $\overline{x}_1'$ cost dollars per unit increase in w_1. The graph's vertical intercept is the value of the short-run variable input 2 cost when $w_1 = 0$. This variable input cost is w_2x_2', where $y = \psi(\overline{x}_1', x_2')$; *i.e.* x_2' is the quantity of the variable input 2 that, combined with the fixed $\overline{x}_1'$ units of input 1, provides y output units. This variable input 2 requirement, and its cost, both decrease as the fixed quantity $\overline{x}_1$ of input 1 increases.

The graph of $c^s(w_1, w_2, y; \overline{x}_1'')$ is a straight line with a greater slope of $\overline{x}_1''$ and a lesser vertical intercept of $w_2 x_2''$, where $y = \psi(\overline{x}_1'', x_2'')$ and $x_2'' < x_2'$ because $\overline{x}_1'' > \overline{x}_1'$. Similarly, the graph of $c^s(w_1, w_2, y; \overline{x}_1''')$ is a straight line with a still greater slope of $\overline{x}_1'''$ and a still lesser vertical intercept of $w_2 x_2'''$, where $y = \psi(\overline{x}_1''', x_2''')$. The graph of the long-run cost function is the lower envelope of affine graphs such as the three described above. Therefore the long-run cost function's slope with respect to w_1 is the same as the slope of the short-run cost function that is part of the envelope at that point. Thus, for the value w_1' of w_1, the slope $\partial c^l(w_1, w_2, y)/\partial w_1$ evaluated at w_1' is the same as the slope $\partial c^s(w_1, w_2, y; \overline{x}_1')/\partial w_1$ evaluated at w_1', because $\overline{x}_1'$ is the long-run cost-minimizing choice for x_1 when $w_1 = w_1'$, meaning that the short-run cost function $c^s(w_1, w_2, y; \overline{x}_1')$ *is* the envelope $c^l(w_1, w_2, y)$ when $w_1 = w_1'$. Therefore, at $w_1 = w_1'$, the slope with respect to w_1 of the envelope $c^l(w_1, w_2, y)$ is the slope with respect to w_1 of the short-run cost function $c^s(w_1, w_2, y; \overline{x}_1')$. That is, $\partial c^l(w_1, w_2, y)/\partial w_1 = \overline{x}_1' = \partial c^s(w_1, w_2, y; \overline{x}_1')/\partial w_1$ at $w_1 = w_1'$. The same statements may be made for $w_1 = w_1''$ and for $w_1 = w_1'''$.

(iii) Proof. The firm's Lagrange function

$$L(x_1, x_2, \lambda; w_1, w_2, y) = w_1 x_1 + w_2 x_2 + \lambda(y - \psi(x_1, x_2))$$

is concave with respect to w_1. Applying the result stated in part (v) of problem 12.10 gives that the firm's long-run cost function is a concave function of w_1. $\square$

Answer to Problem 12.13.

(i) Applying the First-Order Upper-Envelope Theorem to the indirect utility function by differentiating with respect to p_i gives (12.81) immediately. (12.82) is obtained immediately by applying the First-Order Upper-Envelope Theorem to the indirect utility function and differentiating with respect to y.

(ii) We will begin with an explanation of (12.81), for $i = 1$. Consider the consumer's budget allocation problem modified by the restriction that the quantity consumed of commodity 1 is fixed at $\overline{x}_1 > 0$. Use $(\overline{x}_1, x_2^c(p_1, p_2, y; \overline{x}_1), \lambda^c(p_1, p_2, y; \overline{x}_1))$ to denote the optimal solution to this problem. The maximum-value function for the problem is the quantity-constrained indirect utility function

$$v^c(p_1, p_2, y; \overline{x}_1) \equiv U(\overline{x}_1, x_2^c(p_1, p_2, y; \overline{x}_1)) + \lambda^c(p_1, p_2, y; \overline{x}_1)(y - p_1 \overline{x}_1 - p_2 x_2^c(p_1, p_2, y; \overline{x}_1)).$$

Note that v^c is affine with respect to p_1, with a slope of $-\lambda^c(p_1, p_2, y; \overline{x}_1) \overline{x}_1$. The usual argument now applies. The upper envelope of all of the quantity-constrained indirect utility functions v^c is the indirect utility function v. Any point on the graph of this upper-envelope must be a point on the graph of one of the quantity-constrained indirect utility functions, and so the slopes, at this point, of both curves are the same. The slope of the indirect utility function is $\partial v / \partial p_1$ for some value p_1' of p_1. The slope of the quantity-constrained indirect utility function that coincides with the indirect utility function at $p_1 = p_1'$ is $-\lambda(p_1', p_2, y; \overline{x}_1') \, \overline{x}_1'$, where $\overline{x}_1'$ is the same as the value $x_1^*(p_1', p_2, y)$ that is the consumer's rational (with x_1 free) choice of the quantity demanded of commodity 1 when $p_1 = p_1'$. This explains (12.81).

The explanation for (12.82) is analogous to the explanation of (12.81) once the constraint on the consumer is changed from a fixed level of x_1 to a fixed income level y. Try it. $\square$

Answer to Problem 12.14. Let $v(p_1, \ldots, p_n, y)$ denote the consumer's indirect utility function. For given values of $p_1, \ldots, p_n$, and y, the consumer's ordinary demand for commodity i is $x_i^*(p_1, \ldots, p_n, y)$. The consumer's Hicksian demand for commodity i is $h_i(p_1, \ldots, p_n, u)$, where $u = v(p_1, \ldots, p_n, y)$, and $x_i^*(p_1, \ldots, p_n, y) = h_i(p_1, \ldots, p_n, u)$. Since the consumer's (minimum-value) expenditure function is

$$e(p_1, \ldots, p_n, u) \equiv p_1 h_1(p_1, \ldots, p_n, u) + \cdots + p_n h_n(p_1, \ldots, p_n)$$
$$+ \lambda^*(p_1, \ldots, p_n, u)(u - U(h_1(p_1, \ldots, p_n, u), \ldots, h_n(p_1, \ldots, p_n, u))),$$

it follows from the First-Order Lower-Envelope Theorem that

$$\frac{\partial e}{\partial p_i} = h_i(p_1, \ldots, p_n, u); \ \ i = 1, \ldots, n. \tag{12.116}$$

$u \equiv v(p_1, \ldots, p_n, e(p_1, \ldots, p_n, u))$, so

$$0 = \frac{\partial v}{\partial p_i} + \frac{\partial v}{\partial y} \times \frac{\partial e}{\partial p_i}$$

which, from (12.116) and Roy's Identity, asserts that, for $y = e(p_1, \ldots, p_n, u)$,

$$0 = -x_i^*(p, y) \times \frac{\partial v}{\partial y} + \frac{\partial v}{\partial y} \times h_i(p, u). \tag{12.117}$$

The consumer's marginal utility of expenditure $\partial v / \partial y$ is positive (thus, not zero) because the consumer's preferences are strictly monotonic, so (12.117) simplifies to

$$h_i(p, u) = x_i^*(p, y) \text{ when } y = e(p, u), \tag{12.118}$$

where $p = (p_1, \ldots, p_n)$. That is,

$$h_i(p, u) \equiv x_i^*(p, e(p, u)) \text{ for } i = 1, \ldots, n.$$

Since this is an identity, the rates of change of the left and right sides are the same;

$$\frac{\partial h_i(p, u)}{\partial p_j} = \frac{\partial x_i^*(p, y)}{\partial p_j}\Big|_{y=e(p,u)} + \frac{\partial x_i^*(p, y)}{\partial y}\Big|_{y=e(p,u)} \times \frac{\partial e(p, u)}{\partial p_j}. \tag{12.119}$$

Using (12.116) and (12.118) in (12.119) gives Slutsky's equation:

$$\frac{\partial h_i(p, u)}{\partial p_j} = \frac{\partial x_i^*(p, y)}{\partial p_j}\Big|_{y=e(p,u)} + x_j^*(p, y)\Big|_{y=e(p,u)} \times \frac{\partial x_i^*(p, y)}{\partial y}\Big|_{y=e(p,u)}. \qquad \square$$

Chapter 13

Differentiable Comparative Statics, Part 2

13.1 Qualitative Comparative Statics Analysis

The method explained in this chapter was devised by Eugene Silberberg in a paper entitled *A Revision of Comparative Statics Methodology in Economics, or, How to Do Comparative Statics on the Back of an Envelope* (see Silberberg 1974). Once you have read and understood this chapter, you will realize that the title of Silberberg's paper is an amusing double entendre.

The goal is to discover only the *signs* of the differential comparative statics quantities $\partial x_i^*/\partial \gamma_k$ and $\partial \lambda_j^*(\gamma)/\partial \gamma_k$.

Silberberg's method relies upon a comparison of two types of constrained optimization problems: *primal* and *primal-dual* problems. Primal problems are the problems we have talked about so far in this book. Primal-dual problems are new and are built in a rather clever way from families of primal problems. What this means is explained in the next section. Once we have understood what primal-dual problems are, we will examine their optimal solutions. It turns out that the first-order optimality conditions to a primal-dual problem give us much of what we have already discussed. Particularly, we are given both the first-order optimality conditions for primal problems and the results of applying the First-Order Envelope Theorem to primal problems. Not only that, but this is all done in a very easy manner. Of course we already have these results, even if we will now be able to obtain them in a different way. So what do we get from Silberberg's approach that is new? Well, we use something old to get something new. The old thing is the necessary second-order optimality condition, but for the primal-dual problem. Rather amazingly, this condition gives us every qualitative comparative statics result there is for the primal problems used to construct the primal-dual problem, and it does it in a relatively easy way.

So here is the plan. We start in the next section with an explanation of a primal-dual problem. In the following section, we will examine the first-order optimality conditions for a primal-dual problem. The section after that gets to the heart of the matter by examining the necessary second-order optimality condition for the primal-dual problem.

There is more. Many times in economics you see statements such as, "When the price of a firm's product changes the firm adjusts the quantity that it supplies of its product by more in the long-run than in a short-run." Translated into more standard English this statement is, "When the price of a firm's product changes the firm adjusts the quantity that it supplies of its product by more when the firm is subject to fewer constraints upon its choices of production plans." Introductory textbooks often paraphrase this with statements like, "the slope of the firm's supply curve is flatter in the long-run than in a short-run" (remember, economists do this weird thing of plotting supply curves with the product price p measured on the vertical axis). Statements like these are about *comparisons of comparative statics results*. If the slopes of the firm's long-run and short-run supply functions are $\partial y^\ell / \partial p$ and $\partial y^s / \partial p$, then the assertion is that $\partial y^s / \partial p < \partial y^\ell / \partial p$. Such comparisons of comparative statics results nowadays are often called Le Chatelier phenomena, after the person who first brought them to the attention of scientists. In the last part of this chapter, we will see how to obtain them by using a different type of envelope theorem, the Second-Order Envelope Theorem. Don't worry. It's quite a simple and obvious result.

13.2   Primal and Primal-Dual Problems

Consider again the *primal* constrained optimization problem

$$\max_{x_1,\dots,x_n} f(x_1,\dots,x_n;\alpha) \text{ subject to } h_j(x_1,\dots,x_n;\beta_j,b_j) \geq 0 \text{ for } j=1,\dots,m. \quad (13.1)$$

For the purposes of this chapter, the crucial feature of a primal problem is that it has choice *variables* $x_1,\dots,x_n$, and *fixed quantities*, the parameters $\gamma_1,\dots,\gamma_r$. Let us denote the number of parameters for this problem by r, so $\gamma = (\gamma_1,\dots,\gamma_r)$ and the problem's parameter space $\Gamma \subset \Re^r$. Suppose that all of the functions $f, h_1, \dots, h_m$

are twice-continuously differentiable and that the solution correspondence is a function; *i.e.* for any $\gamma \in \Gamma$, the optimal solution $(x^*(\gamma), \lambda^*(\gamma))$ to the primal problem is unique. The maximum-value function for the primal problem is the problem's objective function evaluated at $x^*(\gamma)$. This is the function $v : \Gamma \mapsto \Re$, defined by

$$v(\gamma) \equiv f(x^*(\gamma); \alpha). \tag{13.2}$$

From the primal problem, Silberberg constructs another constrained optimization problem that he calls *primal-dual*. It is

$$\max_{x \in \Re^n, \gamma \in \Gamma} \theta(\gamma, x) \equiv f(x, \alpha) - v(\gamma) \tag{13.3}$$

subject to $h_j(x, \beta_j, b_j) \geq 0$ for $j = 1, \ldots, m$.

The semicolons in f and in each of $h_1, \ldots, h_m$ for the primal problem (13.1) have, in the primal-dual problem, been replaced with commas, indicating that in the primal-dual problem, all of the r quantities in the vectors α, β and b are variables, not fixed parameters. The primal-dual problem thus has $n + r$ choice variables; $x_1, \ldots, x_n, \gamma_1, \ldots, \gamma_r$.

It appears at a casual glance that the primal and primal-dual problems have the same constraints, but this is not so. Yes, the equations of the constraints are the same for both problems, but even so, the constraints for the primal problem are "more constraining" than are the constraints for the primal-dual problem. Why? Suppose that the primal problem has just one constraint, say, $h(x_1, x_2; \beta, b) = b - x_1 - \beta x_2 \geq 0$ (notice the semi-colon in h), where $\beta > 0$ and $b \geq 0$. The set of feasible choices (x_1, x_2) for this primal problem is $\mathcal{C}^p(\beta, b) = \{(x_1, x_2) \mid x_1 + \beta x_2 \leq b\}$ for *particular fixed and given values* for β and b, say, $\beta = 2$ and $b = 3$. The primal problem's constraint is thus a restriction on choices of only x_1 and x_2 for given particular values of β and b. $\mathcal{C}^p(2, 3) = \{(x_1, x_2) \mid x_1 + 2x_2 \leq 3\}$ is a particular example of a primal problem's feasible set. The primal-dual problem's version of this constraint is $h(x_1, x_2, \beta, b) = b - x_1 - \beta x_2 \geq 0$ (notice that the semi-colon in h is replaced by a comma), meaning that the constraint is jointly on choices of all of x_1, x_2, β, and b. The primal-dual's feasible set is thus

$$\mathcal{C}^{pd} = \{(x_1, x_2, \beta, b) \mid x_1 + \beta x_2 \leq b, \ \beta > 0, \ b \geq 0\}.$$

The complete set of values of x_1 and x_2 that, for one or more values of β and b, are feasible for the primal-dual problem, is therefore

$$\bigcup_{\substack{\beta > 0 \\ b \geq 0}} \mathcal{C}^p(\beta, b).$$

This typically is a much larger set than a feasible set, such as $\mathcal{C}^p(2,3)$, for the primal problem with particular and fixed values for β and b.

Another interesting feature of the primal-dual problem is that it has no parameters. This may seem odd since we are so used to dealing with problems in which some quantities have fixed values (*i.e.* are parameters). But a moment's thought should make this idea appear less strange. Consider, for example, the primal problem

$$\min_x (x - b)^2. \tag{13.4}$$

This problem has one choice variable, x, and one parameter, b. For any given value of b, the unique minimizing solution is $x^*(b) = b$. There are many primal problems, each defined by a different given value of b, and with one optimal solution, $x^*(b) = b$. Now consider the primal-dual problem

$$\min_{x,b} (x - b)^2,$$

in which both x and b are choice variables. There are no parameters for this problem and, consequently, there is just one primal-dual problem. This one problem possesses an infinity of optimal solutions (x^*, b^*), in each of which $x^* = b^*$. Notice also that this one primal-dual problem corresponds to infinitely many primal problems (13.4), one for each possible value of the (primal) parameter b. This is true in general. A fixed value for the parameter vector γ in problem (13.1) defines a particular primal problem. There is one such primal problem for each possible value of γ. In the primal-dual problem (13.3) the vector γ is allowed to vary (it's not parametric) over all values admissible for it. Hence there is just one primal-dual problem.

This is a good moment for you to pause before reading further. It is very easy to misunderstand what a primal-dual problem really is and how it is created from an entire family of primal problems. So before you plunge into reading about solving a primal-dual problem, I recommend that you review this section to make sure you understand both the similarities and the differences between any family of primal problems and the primal-dual problem created from that family.

13.3 Primal-Dual First-Order Conditions

For any particular $\gamma \in \Gamma$ (thus, for any particular primal problem), $v(\gamma) \geq f(x;\gamma)$ for every $x \in \mathcal{C}(\beta, b)$, the primal problem's feasible set. Therefore the primal-dual objective function $\theta(\gamma, x)$ never takes a positive value. What is the greatest value that the primal-dual objective function can take? Think about it before proceeding to the next paragraph.

The answer is zero. Why? Well, what does an optimal solution to the primal-dual problem look like? Take any value allowed in the primal-dual problem for the *choice* vector γ; *i.e.* take any $\gamma \in \Gamma$. Then solve the primal problem using γ as a fixed parameter vector. Now we have the point in $\Re^{n+m+r}$ that is $(x^*(\gamma), \lambda^*(\gamma), \gamma)$. This point is an optimal solution to the primal-dual problem because, at this point, the value of the primal-dual problem's objective function is

$$\theta(\gamma, x^*(\gamma)) = f(x^*(\gamma); \alpha) - v(\gamma) = f(x^*(\gamma); \alpha) - f(x^*(\gamma); \alpha) = 0.$$

So, how many optimal solutions does the primal-dual problem have? Think about it before reading further.

There is one optimal solution $(x^*(\gamma), \lambda^*(\gamma), \gamma)$ for every $\gamma \in \Gamma$. Since we have assumed that the functions in the primal-dual problem are differentiable with respect to γ there are infinitely many values in Γ and, for each one, an optimal solution to the primal-dual problem.

The necessary first-order optimization conditions must hold at any optimal solution to the primal-dual problem. From (13.3), the Karush-Kuhn-Tucker component of the first-order optimality conditions is that, at a primal-dual optimal solution $(x^*(\gamma), \lambda^*(\gamma), \gamma)$, necessarily the scalars $\lambda_1^*(\gamma), \ldots, \lambda_m^*(\gamma)$ are all nonnegative, not all zero, and such that the gradient vector of the objective function θ is

$$\nabla_{\gamma,x}\theta(\gamma, x)\big|_{x=x^*(\gamma)} = -\sum_{j=1}^{m} \lambda_j^*(\gamma)\nabla_{\gamma,x}h_j(x, \beta_j, b_j)\big|_{x=x^*(\gamma)}. \tag{13.5}$$

$\nabla_{\gamma,x}$ denotes the gradient vector in which the gradients are measured in each one of the directions of the primal-dual problem's variables $\gamma_1, \ldots, \gamma_r$ and $x_1, \ldots, x_n$, and in that order, so the gradient vector of θ is

$$\begin{aligned}
\nabla_{\gamma,x}\theta(\gamma, x) &= \left(\frac{\partial\theta(\gamma, x)}{\partial\gamma_1}, \ldots, \frac{\partial\theta(\gamma, x)}{\partial\gamma_r}, \frac{\partial\theta(\gamma, x)}{\partial x_1}, \ldots, \frac{\partial\theta(\gamma, x)}{\partial x_n}\right) \\
&= \left(\frac{\partial f(x, \alpha)}{\partial\gamma_1} - \frac{\partial v(\gamma)}{\partial\gamma_1}, \ldots, \frac{\partial f(x, \alpha)}{\partial\gamma_r} - \frac{\partial v(\gamma)}{\partial\gamma_r}, \frac{\partial f(x, \alpha)}{\partial x_1}, \ldots, \frac{\partial f(x, \alpha)}{\partial x_n}\right) \\
&= (\nabla_\gamma\theta(\gamma, x), \nabla_x\theta(\gamma, x)),
\end{aligned}$$

where the gradient of $\theta(\gamma, x) = f(x, \alpha) - v(\gamma)$ in the directions of $\gamma_1, \ldots, \gamma_r$ only is

$$\nabla_\gamma\theta(\gamma, x) = \left(\frac{\partial f(x, \alpha)}{\partial\gamma_1} - \frac{\partial v(\gamma)}{\partial\gamma_1}, \ldots, \frac{\partial f(x, \alpha)}{\partial\gamma_r} - \frac{\partial v(\gamma)}{\partial\gamma_r}\right)$$

and the gradient of $\theta(\gamma, x) = f(x, \alpha) - v(\gamma)$ in the directions of $x_1, \ldots, x_n$ only is

$$\nabla_x \theta(\gamma, x) = \left(\frac{\partial f(x, \alpha)}{\partial x_1}, \ldots, \frac{\partial f(x, \alpha)}{\partial x_n} \right).$$

The gradient vectors of $h_1, \ldots, h_m$ similarly are $r + n$ dimensional row vectors. Expanded, the Karush-Kuhn-Tucker condition (13.5) for the primal-dual problem is (13.6) and (13.7). Then we add the other necessary first-order conditions that are the m complementary slackness conditions (13.8), so, in all, the first-order optimality conditions for the primal-dual problem consist of

$$\frac{\partial \theta(x, \gamma)}{\partial x_i}\Big|_{x=x^*(\gamma)} = \frac{\partial f(x, \alpha)}{\partial x_i}\Big|_{x=x^*(\gamma)} = -\lambda_1^*(\gamma) \frac{\partial h_1(x, \beta_1, b_1)}{\partial x_i}\Big|_{x=x^*(\gamma)} - \cdots$$

$$- \lambda_m^*(\gamma) \frac{\partial h_m(x, \beta_m, b_m)}{\partial x_i}\Big|_{x=x^*(\gamma)} \ \forall \ i = 1, \ldots, n, \qquad (13.6)$$

$$\frac{\partial \theta(x, \gamma)}{\partial \gamma_k}\Big|_{x=x^*(\gamma)} = \frac{\partial f(x, \alpha)}{\partial \gamma_k}\Big|_{x=x^*(\gamma)} - \frac{\partial v(\gamma)}{\partial \gamma_k} = -\lambda_1^*(\gamma) \frac{\partial h_1(x, \beta_1, b_1)}{\partial \gamma_k}\Big|_{x=x^*(\gamma)} - \cdots$$

$$- \lambda_m^*(\gamma) \frac{\partial h_m(x, \beta_m, b_m)}{\partial \gamma_k}\Big|_{x=x^*(\gamma)} \ \forall \ k = 1, \ldots, r, \qquad (13.7)$$

$$0 = \lambda_j^*(\gamma) h_j(x^*(\gamma), \beta_j, b_j) \ \forall \ j = 1, \ldots, m, \qquad (13.8)$$

$$\text{and} \quad h_j(x^*(\gamma), \beta_j, b_j) \geq 0 \ \forall \ j = 1, \ldots, m. \qquad (13.9)$$

The Karush-Kuhn-Tucker and complementary slackness conditions for x and λ for the primal-dual problem, (13.6) and (13.8), are exactly the same as the Karush-Kuhn-Tucker and complementary slackness conditions for x and λ for the primal problem for a given value of γ. If you think about it for a moment, you will realize that this must be so. After all, for any *given* parameter vector $\gamma \in \Gamma$, the primal problem's optimal solution $(x^*(\gamma), \lambda^*(\gamma))$ must also be the optimal solution to the primal-dual problem for the same value of γ, and thus must be a solution to the primal-dual problem's necessary first-order conditions for x and λ for that given value of γ. Perhaps the point will be clearer if you realize that, for a fixed value, say, γ', of γ, the maximum value $v(\gamma')$ is a fixed number and the primal-dual problem is, for γ fixed at γ',

$$\max_x f(x; \alpha') - v(\gamma') \text{ subject to } h_j(x; \beta_j', b_j') \geq 0 \text{ for } j = 1, \ldots, m.$$

This is exactly the primal problem parameterized by $\gamma = \gamma'$, other than that the constant $v(\gamma')$ is subtracted from the objective function, so the first-order necessary conditions with respect to x for this primal problem have to be the same as the first-order necessary conditions with respect to x for the primal-dual problem with $\gamma = \gamma'$.

Did you notice that (13.7) is a restatement of the First-Order Envelope Theorem? Why is the theorem a necessary implication of any optimal solution to the primal-dual problem? Pick some value of γ, say, γ'. What (13.7) says is that, if we hold the value of x fixed at $x^*(\gamma')$ then, when $\gamma = \gamma'$, an optimal solution $(x^*(\gamma'), \lambda^*(\gamma'), \gamma')$ to the primal-dual problem has been reached, so $v(\gamma') = f(x^*(\gamma'); \gamma')$; the primal problem's objective function's maximized value when $\gamma = \gamma'$ is the same as the value at $\gamma = \gamma'$ of the envelope $v(\gamma)$. Consequently the slopes with respect to γ_k of the envelope $v(\gamma)$ and of the restricted function $f^r(\gamma; x = x^*(\gamma'))$ must be the same at $\gamma_k = \gamma'_k$. This, the statement of the First-Order Envelope Theorem, is the part of the primal-dual problem's Karush-Kuhn-Tucker condition for the γ_k choice variable. There is no such condition in the primal problem because therein the vector γ is not variable.

13.4   The Primal-Dual Second-Order Condition

Silberberg's method concentrates upon the primal-dual problem's necessary second-order maximization condition because it is the source of the qualitative comparative statics results for the primal problems. The condition is that the Hessian matrix of the Lagrange function for the primal-dual problem must, when evaluated at a primal-dual optimal solution $(x^*(\gamma'), \lambda^*(\gamma'), \gamma')$, be negative-semi-definite for all small perturbations $(\Delta x, \Delta \gamma)$ from $(x^*(\gamma'), \gamma')$ that keep binding all of the constraints that bind at $(x^*(\gamma'), \gamma')$.

Let's be clear about the meaning of a "small" perturbation $(\Delta x, \Delta \gamma)$ from a point $(x^*(\gamma'), \gamma')$. The Δx part of the perturbation $(\Delta x, \Delta \gamma)$ means that we consider points $(x_1^*(\gamma') + \Delta x_1, \ldots, x_n^*(\gamma') + \Delta x_n)$ that are "close" to the point $(x_1^*(\gamma'), \ldots, x_n^*(\gamma'))$. Let's say that for the objective function the list of parameters is $(\alpha_1, \ldots, \alpha_a)$ and that for the jth constraint function the list of parameters is $\beta_{j1}, \ldots, \beta_{jn_j}$, for $j = 1, \ldots, m$. Then the $\Delta \gamma$ part of the perturbation $(\Delta x, \Delta \gamma)$ means that we consider points

$$(\alpha'_1 + \Delta \alpha_1, \ldots, \alpha'_a + \Delta \alpha_a, \beta'_{11} + \Delta \beta_{11}, \ldots, \beta'_{1n_1} + \Delta \beta_{1n_1}, \beta'_{21} + \Delta \beta_{21}, \ldots, \beta'_{2n_2} + \Delta \beta_{n_2},$$
$$\ldots, \beta'_{m1} + \Delta \beta_{m1}, \ldots, \beta'_{mn_m} + \Delta \beta_{mn_m}, b'_1 + \Delta b_1, \ldots, b'_m + \Delta b_m)$$

that are "close" to $\gamma' = (\alpha'_1, \ldots, \alpha'_a, \beta'_{11}, \ldots, \beta'_{1n_1}, \ldots, \beta'_{m1}, \ldots, \beta'_{mn_m}, b'_1, \ldots, b'_m)$.

The Lagrange function for the primal-dual problem is

$$L^{pd}(x, \gamma, \lambda) = f(x, \alpha) - v(\gamma) + \lambda_1 h_1(x, \beta_1, b_1) + \cdots + \lambda_m h_m(x, \beta_m, b_m). \quad (13.10)$$

Let $\Delta(\beta_j, b_j)$ denote a perturbation of the vector (β_j, b_j) of variables other than $x_1, \ldots, x_n$ in the jth constraint. Then the primal-dual problem's second-order necessary maximization condition is that, there is an $\varepsilon > 0$ for which

$$(\Delta x, \Delta \gamma) H_{L^{pd}}(x^*(\gamma'), \lambda^*(\gamma'), \gamma') \begin{pmatrix} \Delta x \\ \Delta \gamma \end{pmatrix} \leq 0 \; \forall \; (\Delta x, \Delta \gamma) \text{ such that} \tag{13.11}$$

$$(x^*(\gamma') + \Delta x, \gamma' + \Delta \gamma) \in B_{d_E}\left((x^*(\gamma'), \gamma'), \varepsilon\right), \text{ and} \tag{13.12}$$

$$\left(\nabla_x h_j(x, \beta_j, b_j), \nabla_{(\beta_j, b_j)} h_j(x, \beta_j, b_j)\right)\Big|_{\substack{(x,\gamma)= \\ (x^*(\gamma'),\gamma')}} \cdot \begin{pmatrix} \Delta x \\ \Delta(\beta_j, b_j) \end{pmatrix} = 0 \; \forall \; j \in I(x^*(\gamma'), \gamma'), \tag{13.13}$$

where $I(x^*(\gamma'), \gamma')$ is the set of indices of the constraints that bind at $(x, \gamma) = (x^*(\gamma'), \gamma')$, and where the Lagrange function's Hessian matrix with respect to the primal-dual problem's choice variables x and γ is the symmetric order-$(n+r)$ matrix

$$H_{L^{pd}}(x, \lambda, \gamma) = \begin{pmatrix} \dfrac{\partial^2 L^{pd}}{\partial x_1^2} & \cdots & \dfrac{\partial^2 L^{pd}}{\partial x_1 \partial x_n} & \dfrac{\partial^2 L^{pd}}{\partial x_1 \partial \gamma_1} & \cdots & \dfrac{\partial^2 L^{pd}}{\partial x_1 \partial \gamma_r} \\ \vdots & \ddots & \vdots & \vdots & & \vdots \\ \dfrac{\partial^2 L^{pd}}{\partial x_n \partial x_1} & \cdots & \dfrac{\partial^2 L^{pd}}{\partial x_n^2} & \dfrac{\partial^2 L^{pd}}{\partial x_n \partial \gamma_1} & \cdots & \dfrac{\partial^2 L^{pd}}{\partial x_n \partial \gamma_r} \\ \dfrac{\partial^2 L^{pd}}{\partial \gamma_1 \partial x_1} & \cdots & \dfrac{\partial^2 L^{pd}}{\partial \gamma_1 \partial x_n} & \dfrac{\partial^2 L^{pd}}{\partial \gamma_1^2} & \cdots & \dfrac{\partial^2 L^{pd}}{\partial \gamma_1 \partial \gamma_r} \\ \vdots & & \vdots & \vdots & \ddots & \vdots \\ \dfrac{\partial^2 L^{pd}}{\partial \gamma_r \partial x_1} & \cdots & \dfrac{\partial^2 L^{pd}}{\partial \gamma_r \partial x_n} & \dfrac{\partial^2 L^{pd}}{\partial \gamma_r \partial \gamma_1} & \cdots & \dfrac{\partial^2 L^{pd}}{\partial \gamma_r^2} \end{pmatrix}. \tag{13.14}$$

We can write this sometimes large matrix more briefly in its *block form*, which is

$$H_{L^{pd}}(x, \lambda, \gamma) = \begin{pmatrix} \nabla^2_{xx} L^{pd} & \nabla^2_{x\gamma} L^{pd} \\ \nabla^2_{\gamma x} L^{pd} & \nabla^2_{\gamma\gamma} L^{pd} \end{pmatrix}. \tag{13.15}$$

$\nabla^2_{xx} L^{pd}$ denotes the $n \times n$ upper-left block of terms $\partial^2 L^{pd}/\partial x_i \partial x_j$ for $i, j = 1, \ldots, n$ in the Hessian. $\nabla^2_{x\gamma} L^{pd}$ denotes the $n \times r$ upper-right block of terms $\partial^2 L^{pd}/\partial x_i \partial \gamma_k$ for $i = 1, \ldots, n$ and $k = 1, \ldots, r$. $\nabla^2_{\gamma x} L^{pd}$ denotes the $r \times n$ lower-left block of terms $\partial^2 L^{pd}/\partial \gamma_k \partial x_i$ for $k = 1, \ldots, r$ and $i = 1, \ldots, n$. $\nabla^2_{\gamma\gamma} L^{pd}$ denotes the $r \times r$ lower-right block of terms $\partial^2 L^{pd}/\partial \gamma_j \partial \gamma_k$ for $j, k = 1, \ldots, r$.

The necessary second-order maximization condition, then, is that the matrix (13.15), evaluated at $(x, \lambda, \gamma) = (x^*(\gamma'), \lambda^*(\gamma'), \gamma')$, must be negative-semi-definite for all small perturbations $(\Delta x, \Delta \gamma)$ from $(x^*(\gamma'), \gamma')$ that keep binding all of the constraints that bind at $(x^*(\gamma'), \gamma')$. That is, necessarily,

$$(\Delta x, \Delta \gamma) \begin{pmatrix} \nabla^2_{xx} L^{pd} & \nabla^2_{x\gamma} L^{pd} \\ \nabla^2_{\gamma x} L^{pd} & \nabla^2_{\gamma\gamma} L^{pd} \end{pmatrix} \Bigg|_{\substack{(x,\lambda,\gamma)= \\ (x^*(\gamma'),\lambda^*(\gamma'),\gamma')}} \begin{pmatrix} \Delta x \\ \Delta \gamma \end{pmatrix} \leq 0 \qquad (13.16)$$

for all small perturbations $(\Delta x, \Delta \gamma)$ from $(x^*(\gamma'), \gamma')$ such that

$$\left(\nabla_x h_j(x, \beta_j, b_j), \nabla_{(\beta_j, b_j)} h_j(x, \beta_j, b_j) \right) \Big|_{\substack{(x,\gamma)= \\ (x^*(\gamma'),\gamma')}} \begin{pmatrix} \Delta x \\ \Delta(\beta_j, b_j) \end{pmatrix} = 0 \ \forall \ j \in I(x^*(\gamma'), \gamma').$$
$$(13.17)$$

Silberberg then remarks that, in a comparative statics experiment, the only perturbations made are to the primal problem's parameters, listed in the vector γ. That is, for any comparative statics experiment, we set the "x-part" of the perturbation vector to zero. Then, from (13.16) and (13.17) with $\Delta x = \underline{0}_n$, it is necessarily true for comparative statics experiments that

$$\Delta \gamma^{\mathrm{T}} \left(\nabla^2_{\gamma\gamma} L^{pd} \right) \Big|_{\substack{(x,\lambda,\gamma)= \\ (x^*(\gamma'),\lambda^*(\gamma'),\gamma')}} \Delta \gamma \leq 0 \qquad (13.18)$$

for all small perturbations $\Delta \gamma$ from γ' such that

$$\nabla_{(\beta_j, b_j)} h_j(x, \beta_j, b_j) \Big|_{\substack{(x,\gamma)= \\ (x^*(\gamma'),\gamma')}} \cdot \Delta(\beta_j, b_j) = 0 \ \forall \ j \in I(x^*(\gamma'), \gamma'). \qquad (13.19)$$

The statement that is (13.18) and (13.19) combined is necessarily true as a consequence of the point $(x^*(\gamma'), \lambda^*(\gamma'), \gamma')$ being an optimal solution to the primal-dual problem (13.3). It is this statement that provides us with the qualitative comparative statics properties of the optimal solution to the primal problem (13.1). Let's see how to extract these results.

13.5   Qualitative Comparative Statics Results

Have a close look at the matrix $\nabla^2_{\gamma\gamma} L^{pd}$ in (13.18). It is

$$
\nabla^2_{\gamma\gamma} L^{pd} = \begin{pmatrix} \dfrac{\partial^2 L^{pd}}{\partial \gamma_1^2} & \cdots & \dfrac{\partial^2 L^{pd}}{\partial \gamma_1 \partial \gamma_r} \\ \vdots & \ddots & \vdots \\ \dfrac{\partial^2 L^{pd}}{\partial \gamma_r \partial \gamma_1} & \cdots & \dfrac{\partial^2 L^{pd}}{\partial \gamma_r^2} \end{pmatrix} \Bigg|_{\substack{(x,\lambda,\gamma)= \\ (x^*(\gamma'),\lambda^*(\gamma'),\gamma')}} . \tag{13.20}
$$

What does a typical element of this matrix look like? From (13.10),

$$
\frac{\partial L^{pd}}{\partial \gamma_k} = \frac{\partial f(x,\alpha)}{\partial \gamma_k} - \frac{\partial v(\gamma)}{\partial \gamma_k} + \lambda_1 \frac{\partial h_1(x,\beta_1,b_1)}{\partial \gamma_k} + \cdots + \lambda_m \frac{\partial h_m(x,\beta_m,b_m)}{\partial \gamma_m} , \tag{13.21}
$$

so

$$
\frac{\partial^2 L^{pd}}{\partial \gamma_j \partial \gamma_k} = \frac{\partial^2 f(x,\alpha)}{\partial \gamma_j \partial \gamma_k} - \frac{\partial^2 v(\gamma)}{\partial \gamma_j \partial \gamma_k} + \lambda_1 \frac{\partial^2 h_1(x,\beta_1,b_1)}{\partial \gamma_j \partial \gamma_k} + \cdots + \lambda_m \frac{\partial^2 h_m(x,\beta_m,b_m)}{\partial \gamma_j \partial \gamma_k} . \tag{13.22}
$$

The jk^{th}-element of the matrix (13.20) is the value of (13.22) at the primal-dual optimal solution $(x^*(\gamma'), \lambda^*(\gamma'), \gamma')$. This is

$$
\frac{\partial^2 L^{pd}}{\partial \gamma_j \partial \gamma_k}\Big|_{\substack{x=x^*(\gamma') \\ \lambda=\lambda^*(\gamma') \\ \gamma=\gamma'}} = \frac{\partial^2 f(x,\alpha)}{\partial \gamma_j \partial \gamma_k}\Big|_{\substack{x=x^*(\gamma') \\ \alpha=\alpha'}} - \frac{\partial^2 v(\gamma)}{\partial \gamma_j \partial \gamma_k}\Big|_{\gamma=\gamma'} + \lambda_1^*(\gamma') \frac{\partial^2 h_1(x,\beta_1,b_1)}{\partial \gamma_j \partial \gamma_k}\Big|_{\substack{x=x^*(\gamma') \\ (\beta_1,b_1)=(\beta_1',b_1')}}
$$

$$
+ \cdots + \lambda_m^*(\gamma') \frac{\partial^2 h_m(x,\beta_m,b_m)}{\partial \gamma_j \partial \gamma_k}\Big|_{\substack{x=x^*(\gamma') \\ (\beta_m,b_m)=(\beta_m',b_m')}} . \tag{13.23}
$$

Now recall that, when evaluated at only primal-dual optimal solutions, the first-order necessary conditions (13.6), (13.7), and (13.8) are identically zero, so, from (13.7),

$$
\frac{\partial v(\gamma)}{\partial \gamma_k} \equiv \frac{\partial f(x,\alpha)}{\partial \gamma_k}\Big|_{x=x^*(\gamma)} + \lambda_1^*(\gamma) \frac{\partial h_1(x,\beta_1,b_1)}{\partial \gamma_k}\Big|_{x=x^*(\gamma)} + \cdots + \lambda_m^*(\gamma) \frac{\partial h_m(x,\beta_m,b_m)}{\partial \gamma_k}\Big|_{x=x^*(\gamma)} .
$$

Differentiating this identity with respect to γ_j gives

$$
\frac{\partial^2 v(\gamma)}{\partial \gamma_j \partial \gamma_k} = \sum_{i=1}^{n} \frac{\partial^2 f(x,\alpha)}{\partial x_i \partial \gamma_k}\Big|_{x=x^*(\gamma)} \times \frac{\partial x_i^*(\gamma)}{\partial \gamma_j} + \frac{\partial^2 f(x,\alpha)}{\partial \gamma_j \partial \gamma_k}\Big|_{x=x^*(\gamma)} +
$$

$$
\sum_{t=1}^{m} \frac{\partial \lambda_t^*(\gamma)}{\partial \gamma_j} \times \frac{\partial h_t(x,\beta_t,b_t)}{\partial \gamma_k}\Big|_{x=x^*(\gamma)} + \tag{13.24}
$$

$$
\sum_{t=1}^{m} \lambda_t^*(\gamma) \left[\frac{\partial^2 h_t(x,\beta_t,b_t)}{\partial \gamma_j \partial \gamma_k}\Big|_{x=x^*(\gamma)} + \sum_{i=1}^{n} \frac{\partial^2 h_t(x,\beta_t,b_t)}{\partial x_i \partial \gamma_k}\Big|_{\substack{x=x^*(\gamma') \\ (\beta_t,b_t)=(\beta_t',b_t')}} \times \frac{\partial x_i^*(\gamma)}{\partial \gamma_j}\Big|_{\gamma=\gamma'} \right] .
$$

Evaluating (13.24) at $\gamma = \gamma'$ and then using (13.24) to substitute for $\partial^2 v(\gamma)/\partial\gamma_j\partial\gamma_k$ in (13.23) shows that value of the jk^{th}-element of the matrix (13.20) is

$$\frac{\partial^2 L^{pd}}{\partial\gamma_j\partial\gamma_k}\Big|_{\substack{x=x^*(\gamma')\\\lambda=\lambda^*(\gamma')\\\gamma=\gamma'}} = -\sum_{i=1}^{n}\left[\frac{\partial^2 f(x,\alpha)}{\partial x_i\partial\gamma_k} + \sum_{t=1}^{m}\lambda_t^*(\gamma')\frac{\partial^2 h_t(x,\beta_t,b_t)}{\partial x_i\partial\gamma_k}\right]\Bigg|_{\substack{x=x^*(\gamma')\\\gamma=\gamma'}} \times \frac{\partial x_i^*(\gamma)}{\partial\gamma_j}$$

$$-\sum_{t=1}^{m}\frac{\partial\lambda_t^*(\gamma)}{\partial\gamma_j} \times \frac{\partial h_t(x,\beta_t,b_t)}{\partial\gamma_k}\Bigg|_{\substack{x=x^*(\gamma')\\\gamma=\gamma'}}. \qquad (13.25)$$

(13.25) states that every element in (13.20) is a linear combination of the values at $x = x^*(\gamma')$ and $\gamma = \gamma'$ of the comparative statics quantities $\partial x_1^*(\gamma)/\partial\gamma_j, \ldots, \partial x_n^*(\gamma)/\partial\gamma_j$ and $\partial\lambda_1^*(\gamma)/\partial\gamma_j, \ldots, \partial\lambda_m^*(\gamma)/\partial\gamma_j$. Information about the signs of the elements in the matrix (13.20) therefore gives us information about the signs of the comparative statics quantities. What information is available to us?

First, a matrix is negative-semi-definite only if its main diagonal elements are all nonpositive;

$$\frac{\partial^2 L^{pd}}{\partial\gamma_k^2} \leq 0 \text{ for all } k = 1, \ldots, r. \qquad (13.26)$$

Second, the matrix is symmetric (because all of the functions $f, g_1, \ldots, g_m$ are twice-continuously differentiable);

$$\frac{\partial^2 L^{pd}}{\partial\gamma_j\partial\gamma_k} = \frac{\partial^2 L^{pd}}{\partial\gamma_k\partial\gamma_j} \text{ for all } j, k = 1, \ldots, r; \; j \neq k. \qquad (13.27)$$

If the constraints that bind at the particular optimal solution $(x^*(\gamma), \lambda^*(\gamma), \gamma)$ to the primal-dual problem are affine with respect to $\gamma_1, \ldots, \gamma_r$ (not necessarily affine with respect to $x_1, \ldots, x_n$), then we have a third way of extracting comparative statics results. If the binding constraints are all affine with respect to $\gamma_1, \ldots, \gamma_r$, then the combination of (13.18) and (13.19) is true if and only if the bordered principal minors of the bordered Hessian constructed from the Hessian (13.20) and the gradients, with respect to $\gamma_1, \ldots, \gamma_r$, of the constraints that bind at the optimal solution $(x^*(\gamma), \lambda^*(\gamma), \gamma)$ have the properties described in Theorem 10.2.

Let's examine this bordered Hessian. Without loss of generality, suppose that the constraints that bind at $(x^*(\gamma'), \lambda^*(\gamma'), \gamma')$ are indexed by $j = 1, \ldots, \ell$. Then the bordered Hessian, evaluated at $(x^*(\gamma'), \lambda^*(\gamma'), \gamma')$, is the symmetric order-$(\ell + r)$

matrix

$$
\overline{H}_{L^{pd}}(x^*(\gamma'), \lambda^*(\gamma'), \gamma') = \left. \begin{pmatrix} 0 & \cdots & 0 & \dfrac{\partial h_1}{\partial \gamma_1} & \cdots & \dfrac{\partial h_1}{\partial \gamma_r} \\ \vdots & \ddots & \vdots & \vdots & & \vdots \\ 0 & \cdots & 0 & \dfrac{\partial h_\ell}{\partial \gamma_1} & \cdots & \dfrac{\partial h_\ell}{\partial \gamma_r} \\ \dfrac{\partial h_1}{\partial \gamma_1} & \cdots & \dfrac{\partial h_\ell}{\partial \gamma_1} & \dfrac{\partial^2 L^{pd}}{\partial \gamma_1^2} & \cdots & \dfrac{\partial^2 L^{pd}}{\partial \gamma_1 \partial \gamma_r} \\ \vdots & & \vdots & \vdots & \ddots & \vdots \\ \dfrac{\partial h_1}{\partial \gamma_r} & \cdots & \dfrac{\partial h_\ell}{\partial \gamma_r} & \dfrac{\partial^2 L^{pd}}{\partial \gamma_r \partial \gamma_1} & \cdots & \dfrac{\partial^2 L^{pd}}{\partial \gamma_r^2} \end{pmatrix} \right|_{\substack{(x,\lambda,\gamma)= \\ (x^*(\gamma),\lambda^*(\gamma),\gamma)}} .
$$

$$(13.28)$$

Theorem 10.2 states that, if all of the constraints $j = 1, \ldots, \ell$ are affine with respect to $\gamma_1, \ldots, \gamma_r$, then (13.18) and (13.19) together are equivalent to the requirement that the bordered principal minors of the bordered Hessian (13.28) that are of orders $i = 2\ell + 1, \ldots, r$ are either zero or have the same sign as $(-1)^i$. This information provides still more comparative statics results.

13.6   An Example

Let's apply Silberberg's method of obtaining qualitative comparative-statics results to our primal problem example (11.4) of a price-taking, profit-maximizing firm. The maximum-value function for the problem is the firm's indirect profit function

$$
\begin{aligned}
&\pi^*(p, w_1, w_2, \beta_1, \beta_2) \\
&= p y^*(p, w_1, w_2, \beta_1, \beta_2) - w_1 x_1^*(p, w_1, w_2, \beta_1, \beta_2) - w_2 x_2^*(p, w_1, w_2, \beta_1, \beta_2),
\end{aligned}
$$

so the primal-dual problem's objective function is

$$
\theta(y, x_1, x_2, p, w_1, w_2, \beta_1, \beta_2) = p y - w_1 x_1 - w_2 x_2 - \pi^*(p, w_1, w_2, \beta_1, \beta_2)
$$

and the primal-dual problem itself is

$$
\max_{p, w_1, w_2, \beta_1, \beta_2, y, x_1, x_2} \theta(p, w_1, w_2, \beta_1, \beta_2, y, x_1, x_2) = p y - w_1 x_1 - w_2 x_2 - \pi^*(p, w_1, w_2, \beta_1, \beta_2)
$$

subject to $y \geq 0$, $x_1 \geq 0$, $x_2 \geq 0$, and $x_1^{\beta_1} x_2^{\beta_2} \geq y$.   (13.29)

The primal-dual problem's Lagrange function is

$$
L^{pd}(y, x_1, x_2, p, w_1, w_2, \beta_1, \beta_2, \lambda_1, \lambda_2, \lambda_3, \lambda_4)
$$
$$
= py - w_1 x_1 - w_2 x_2 - \pi^*(p, w_1, w_2, \beta_1, \beta_2) + \lambda_1 y + \lambda_2 x_1 + \lambda_3 x_2 + \lambda_4(x_1^{\beta_1} x_2^{\beta_2} - y).
$$

All of y, x_1, x_2, p, w_1, w_2, β_1, β_2, λ_1, λ_2, λ_3, and λ_4 are variables. The first-order derivatives of L^{pd} with respect to the primal-dual variables p, w_1, w_2, β_1, and β_2 that are parameters in the primal problem are

$$
\frac{\partial L^{pd}}{\partial p} = y - \frac{\partial \pi^*(p, \cdot)}{\partial p}, \quad \frac{\partial L^{pd}}{\partial w_i} = -x_i - \frac{\partial \pi^*(\cdot, w_i, \cdot)}{\partial w_i} \quad \text{for } i = 1, 2, \quad (13.30)
$$

and

$$
\frac{\partial L^{pd}}{\partial \beta_i} = -\frac{\partial \pi^*(\cdot, \beta_i)}{\partial \beta_i} + \lambda_4 \frac{\partial\left(x_1^{\beta_1} x_2^{\beta_2}\right)}{\partial \beta_i} \quad \text{for } i = 1, 2. \quad (13.31)
$$

Each of these necessarily is zero when evaluated at any optimal solution to the primal-dual problem. (13.30) therefore gives us Hotelling's Lemma:

$$
y^*(p, w_1, w_2, \beta_1, \beta_2) = \frac{\partial \pi^*(p, \cdot)}{\partial p} \quad \text{and} \quad x_i^*(p, w_1, w_2, \beta_1, \beta_2) = -\frac{\partial \pi^*(\cdot, w_1, \cdot)}{\partial w_i} \quad \text{for } i = 1, 2.
$$

(13.31) gives us the new result

$$
\frac{\partial \pi^*(\cdot, \beta_i)}{\partial \beta_i} = \lambda_4^*(\gamma) \frac{\partial\left(x_1^{\beta_1} x_2^{\beta_2}\right)}{\partial \beta_i}\Big|_{x = x^*(\gamma)} = p \frac{\partial\left(x_1^{\beta_1} x_2^{\beta_2}\right)}{\partial \beta_i}\Big|_{x = x^*(\gamma)} \quad \text{for } i = 1, 2. \quad (13.32)
$$

An increase to β_i increases the productivity of input i. (13.32) states that the rate at which the firm's maximum profit increases as β_i increases is the rate at which extra revenue is provided due to higher production caused by the enhanced productivity of input i. (13.32) is thus the firm's marginal valuation of the technology parameter β_i.

In what follows I'm going to hold β_2 fixed so we have to work with only 4×4 matrices. Using (13.25) shows that the Hessian matrix of L^{pd} with respect to the primal-dual problem choice variables $p, w_1, w_2,$ and β_1 is

$$
\left(\nabla^2_{\gamma\gamma} L^{pd}\right) = \begin{pmatrix} -\dfrac{\partial y^*}{\partial p} & \dfrac{\partial x_1^*}{\partial p} & \dfrac{\partial x_2^*}{\partial p} & -p\sum_{i=1}^2\left(g_{x_i\,\beta_1}\times\dfrac{\partial x_i^*}{\partial p}\right)-g_{\beta_1} \\[4mm] -\dfrac{\partial y^*}{\partial w_1} & \dfrac{\partial x_1^*}{\partial w_1} & \dfrac{\partial x_2^*}{\partial w_1} & -p\sum_{i=1}^2\left(g_{x_i\,\beta_1}\times\dfrac{\partial x_i^*}{\partial w_1}\right) \\[4mm] -\dfrac{\partial y^*}{\partial w_2} & \dfrac{\partial x_1^*}{\partial w_2} & \dfrac{\partial x_2^*}{\partial w_2} & -p\sum_{i=1}^2\left(g_{x_i\,\beta_1}\times\dfrac{\partial x_i^*}{\partial w_2}\right) \\[4mm] -\dfrac{\partial y^*}{\partial \beta_1} & \dfrac{\partial x_1^*}{\partial \beta_1} & \dfrac{\partial x_2^*}{\partial \beta_1} & -p\sum_{i=1}^2\left(g_{x_i\,\beta_1}\times\dfrac{\partial x_i^*}{\partial \beta_1}\right) \end{pmatrix}, \tag{13.33}
$$

where $g_{\beta_1} = \partial\left(x_1^{\beta_1}x_2^{\beta_2}\right)/\partial\beta_1 = x_1^{\beta_1}x_2^{\beta_2}\ln x_1$, $g_{x_1\,\beta_1} = \partial^2\left(x_1^{\beta_1}x_2^{\beta_2}\right)/\partial x_1\partial\beta_1 = x_1^{\beta_1-1}x_2^{\beta_2}(\beta_1\ln x_1 + 1)$, and $g_{x_2\,\beta_1} = \partial^2\left(x_1^{\beta_1}x_2^{\beta_2}\right)/\partial x_2\partial\beta_1 = x_1^{\beta_1}x_2^{\beta_2-1}(\beta_2\ln x_2 + 1)$.

(13.33) is a negative-semi-definite matrix only if each of its main diagonal elements is nonpositive, so

$$
\frac{\partial y^*(p, w_1, w_2, \beta_1, \beta_2)}{\partial p} \geq 0, \quad \frac{\partial x_i^*(p, w_1, w_2, \beta_1, \beta_2)}{\partial w_i} \leq 0 \text{ for } i = 1, 2, \tag{13.34}
$$

and $\quad p\left[\dfrac{\partial^2\left(x_1^{\beta_1}x_2^{\beta_2}\right)}{\partial x_1\partial\beta_1}\times\dfrac{\partial x_1^*(\cdot)}{\partial\beta_1} + \dfrac{\partial^2\left(x_1^{\beta_1}x_2^{\beta_2}\right)}{\partial x_2\partial\beta_1}\times\dfrac{\partial x_2^*(\cdot)}{\partial\beta_1}\right]\Bigg|_{\substack{x_1=x_1^*\\x_2=x_2^*}} \geq 0. \tag{13.35}$

(13.34) states the well-known results that the quantity supplied by the firm is a nondecreasing function of the price of the firm's product and that the firm's quantity demanded of an input is a nonincreasing function of the price of that input. (13.35) is not a well-known result. It says that the marginal value of the technology parameter β_1 is nondecreasing with respect to β_1; *i.e.* the value to the firm of its technology parameter β_1 is a convex function of β_1.

The Hessian matrix is symmetric, so we learn also that

$$\frac{\partial y^*(p, w_1, w_2, \beta_1, \beta_2)}{\partial w_i} = -\frac{\partial x_i^*(p, w_1, w_2, \beta_1, \beta_2)}{\partial p} \text{ for } i = 1, 2, \tag{13.36}$$

$$\frac{\partial x_1^*(p, w_1, w_2, \beta_1, \beta_2)}{\partial w_2} = \frac{\partial x_2^*(p, w_1, w_2, \beta_1, \beta_2)}{\partial w_1}, \text{ and} \tag{13.37}$$

$$\frac{\partial y^*(p, w_1, w_2, \beta_1, \beta_2)}{\partial \beta_1} = p \sum_{i=1}^{2} \left(\frac{\partial^2 \left(x_1^{\beta_1} x_2^{\beta_2} \right)}{\partial x_i \partial \beta_1} \Big|_{\substack{x_1 = x_1^* \\ x_2 = x_2^*}} \times \frac{\partial x_i^*}{\partial p} \right) + \frac{\partial \left(x_1^{\beta_1} x_2^{\beta_2} \right)}{\partial \beta_1} \Big|_{\substack{x_1 = x_1^* \\ x_2 = x_2^*}}. \tag{13.38}$$

(13.36) states that the rate at which the firm's quantity supplied decreases as the price of input i rises necessarily is the same as the rate at which the firm's quantity demanded of input i rises as the price of the firm's product rises. Did you know that? (13.37) states that the rate at which the firm's quantity demanded of input i increases as the price of input j rises is necessarily the same as the rate at which the firm's quantity demanded of input j rises as the price of input i rises. Understanding (13.38) requires a bit more work. The quantity of product supplied by the firm is

$$y^*(p, w_1, w_2, \beta_1; \beta_2) = x_1^*(p, w_1, w_2, \beta_1; \beta_2)^{\beta_1} x_2^*(p, w_1, w_2, \beta_1; \beta_2)^{\beta_2},$$

so

$$\frac{\partial y^*(\cdot)}{\partial \beta_1} = \frac{\partial \left(x_1^{\beta_1} x_2^{\beta_2} \right)}{\partial x_1} \Big|_{\substack{x_1 = x_1^*(\cdot) \\ x_2 = x_2^*(\cdot)}} \times \frac{\partial x_1^*(\cdot)}{\partial \beta_1} + \frac{\partial \left(x_1^{\beta_1} x_2^{\beta_2} \right)}{\partial x_2} \Big|_{\substack{x_1 = x_1^*(\cdot) \\ x_2 = x_2^*(\cdot)}} \times \frac{\partial x_2^*(\cdot)}{\partial \beta_1}$$
$$+ \frac{\partial \left(x_1^{\beta_1} x_2^{\beta_2} \right)}{\partial \beta_1} \Big|_{\substack{x_1 = x_1^*(\cdot) \\ x_2 = x_2^*(\cdot)}}. \tag{13.39}$$

The sum of the first two terms on the right side of (13.39) is the indirect effect of changing β_1, through changes caused to the profit-maximizing quantities used of inputs 1 and 2, on the firm's quantity supplied. The last term in the right side of (13.39) is the direct effect on quantity supplied of changing β_1. Setting the right sides of (13.38) and (13.39) equal to each other gives us that

$$\frac{\partial \left(x_1^{\beta_1} x_2^{\beta_2} \right)}{\partial x_1} \Big|_{\substack{x_1 = x_1^*(\cdot) \\ x_2 = x_2^*(\cdot)}} \times \frac{\partial x_1^*(\cdot)}{\partial \beta_1} + \frac{\partial \left(x_1^{\beta_1} x_2^{\beta_2} \right)}{\partial x_2} \Big|_{\substack{x_1 = x_1^*(\cdot) \\ x_2 = x_2^*(\cdot)}} \times \frac{\partial x_2^*(\cdot)}{\partial \beta_1}$$
$$= p \frac{\partial^2 \left(x_1^{\beta_1} x_2^{\beta_2} \right)}{\partial x_1 \partial \beta_1} \Big|_{\substack{x_1 = x_1^*(\cdot) \\ x_2 = x_2^*(\cdot)}} \times \frac{\partial x_1^*(\cdot)}{\partial p} + p \frac{\partial^2 \left(x_1^{\beta_1} x_2^{\beta_2} \right)}{\partial x_2 \partial \beta_1} \Big|_{\substack{x_1 = x_1^*(\cdot) \\ x_2 = x_2^*(\cdot)}} \times \frac{\partial x_2^*(\cdot)}{\partial p}. \tag{13.40}$$

The right side of (13.40) is the sum of the indirect effects of changing the product price p, through changes caused to the profit-maximizing quantities used of inputs 1 and 2, on the firm's marginal revenue product of the technology variable β_1. This, necessarily, is the same as the indirect effect of changing β_1 on the firm's quantity supplied. You may question if this is a useful result. Whether or not this is so depends upon the questions you want answered. The first point you should take from this example is that it demonstrates how Silberberg's method allows for the extraction of comparative statics results that are not obvious. The second point is that (13.40) is a simple linear equation in the unknowns $\partial x_1^*/\partial \beta_1$, $\partial x_2^*/\partial \beta_1$, $\partial x_1^*/\partial p$ and $\partial x_2^*/\partial p$. Why? Because all of the derivatives of $x_1^{\beta_1} x_2^{\beta_2}$ in (13.40) are *evaluated* at (x_1^*, x_2^*); *i.e.* they are just numbers. (13.40) is a linear restriction that gives us information about the signs possible for the four comparative statics quantities.

Can we use Theorem 10.2 to extract further comparative-statics results? Look once again at the primal-dual problem (13.29). What constraints bind at an optimal solution to this problem? For any interesting solution we will have $y > 0$, $x_1 > 0$, and $x_2 > 0$, so the only binding constraint is the technology constraint: $x_1^{\beta_1} x_2^{\beta_2} - y = 0$. This depends on none of the parameters p, w_1, and w_2. And, although the constraint does depend upon the parameters β_1 and β_2, these dependencies are not affine. So we cannot apply Theorem 10.2 to this particular problem.

13.7   Second-Order Envelope Theorem

The First-Order Envelope Theorem tells us about maximum-value functions' first-order derivatives. The Second-Order Envelope Theorem informs us about a *comparison of the second-order derivatives of two related maximum-value functions*. To discuss this theorem with clarity, we must once again adjust the notation we use.

The primal constrained optimization problem that we are considering is

$$\max_{x \in \Re^n} f(x; \alpha) \text{ subject to } h_j(x; \beta_j, b_j) \geq 0 \text{ for } j = 1, \dots, m. \qquad (13.41)$$

Denote the parameter vector for this m-constraint problem by $^m\gamma = (\alpha, {}^m\beta, {}^m b)$. Now choose a particular value for $^m\gamma$. This selects the particular version of (13.41) that is defined by that particular parameter vector $^m\gamma$. The optimal solution for this particular problem will be denoted by $(^m x^*(^m\gamma), {}^m\lambda^*(^m\gamma))$. Use $I(^m x^*(^m\gamma))$ to denote the set of indices of the constraints that bind at $x = {}^m x^*(^m\gamma)$. Without loss of generality, suppose that the indices in $I(^m x^*(^m\gamma))$ are $j = 1, \dots, \ell$, where $1 \leq \ell \leq m$. Then, given $^m\gamma$, the optimal solution to (13.41) is the same as the optimal solution to the *equality-constrained* primal problem

$$\max_{x \in \Re^n} f(x; \alpha) \text{ subject to } h_1(x; \beta_1, b_1) = 0, \ldots, h_\ell(x; \beta_\ell, b_\ell) = 0. \tag{13.42}$$

(13.42) is the *ℓ-constraint problem* with the parameter vector ${}^\ell\gamma = (\alpha, {}^\ell\beta, {}^\ell b)$. Denote the set of all possible values of ${}^\ell\gamma$ by ${}^\ell\Gamma$. Denote the optimal solution to the problem, for given ${}^\ell\gamma$, by $({}^\ell x^*({}^\ell\gamma), {}^\ell\lambda^*({}^\ell\gamma))$, where ${}^\ell x^*({}^\ell\gamma) = ({}^\ell x_1^*({}^\ell\gamma), \ldots, {}^\ell x_n^*({}^\ell\gamma))$ and ${}^\ell\lambda^*({}^\ell\gamma) = ({}^\ell\lambda_1^*({}^\ell\gamma), \ldots, {}^\ell\lambda_\ell^*({}^\ell\gamma))$. The problem's maximum-value function is

$$^\ell v(^\ell\gamma) \equiv f(^\ell x^*(^\ell\gamma); \alpha) + \sum_{j=1}^{\ell} {}^\ell\lambda_j^*(^\ell\gamma) h_j(^\ell x^*(^\ell\gamma); \beta_j, b_j). \tag{13.43}$$

Now we add to (13.42) a new *equality* constraint, $h_{\ell+1}(x; \beta_{\ell+1}, b_{\ell+1}) = 0$. This gives us the new, more constrained, primal problem

$$\max_{x \in \Re^n} f(x; \alpha) \text{ subject to } h_1(x; \beta_1, b_1) = 0, \ldots, h_\ell(x; \beta_\ell, b_\ell) = 0$$
$$\text{and} \quad h_{\ell+1}(x; \beta_{\ell+1}, b_{\ell+1}) = 0. \tag{13.44}$$

We will call (13.44) the $(\ell + 1)$-*constraint problem* with the parameter vector ${}^{\ell+1}\gamma = ({}^\ell\gamma : \beta_{\ell+1}, b_{\ell+1}) \equiv (\alpha : {}^\ell\beta, \beta_{\ell+1} : {}^\ell b, b_{\ell+1})$. ${}^{\ell+1}\lambda_{\ell+1}^*({}^{\ell+1}\gamma)$ is the value of the multiplier associated with the new constraint at the optimal solution $({}^{\ell+1}x^*({}^{\ell+1}\gamma), {}^{\ell+1}\lambda^*({}^{\ell+1}\gamma))$ to problem (13.44). Be clear that the parameter vector for the $(\ell+1)$-constraint problem is the same as the parameter vector for the ℓ-constraint problem but concatenated with (augmented by) the parameters $\beta_{\ell+1}$ and $b_{\ell+1}$ from the new constraint.

The ideas presented in what follows are not difficult, but because the notation is somewhat intricate, it will be helpful to use an example as we proceed. The example is again problem (11.4), but simplified by setting $\beta_1 = \beta_2 = \frac{1}{3}$. We have already noted that, at any interesting optimal solution to this problem, the technology constraint binds and all of the nonnegativity constraints are slack, so $\ell = 1$ and the optimal solution to the inequality constrained problem (11.4) is the same as the optimal solution to the 1-constraint equality constrained problem

$$\max_{y, x_1, x_2} py - w_1 x_1 - w_2 x_2 \text{ subject to } h_1(y, x_1, x_2) = x_1^{1/3} x_2^{1/3} - y = 0.$$

In terms of the notation introduced above, the parameter vector for this problem is

$^1\gamma = (p, w_1, w_2)$, the optimal solution function is (see (11.5))

$$
\begin{pmatrix} {}^1y^*(p, w_1, w_2) \\ {}^1x_1^*(p, w_1, w_2) \\ {}^1x_2^*(p, w_1, w_2) \\ {}^1\lambda^*(p, w_1, w_2) \end{pmatrix} = \begin{pmatrix} p^2/9w_1 w_2 \\ p^3/27w_1^2 w_2 \\ p^3/27w_1 w_2^2 \\ p \end{pmatrix},
$$

and the maximum-value function is (see (11.7) with $\beta_1 = \beta_2 = \frac{1}{3}$) the indirect profit function

$$
{}^1v({}^1\gamma) = {}^1v(p, w_1, w_2) = \frac{p^3}{27w_1 w_2}.
$$

Before we can proceed further, we have to understand the crucial idea of a *just-binding constraint*. Think of a simple inequality constrained optimization problem

$$
\max_{x \in \Re} f(x) \text{ subject to } g(x) \leq \bar{b}.
$$

The optimal solution is $(x, \lambda) = (x^*(\bar{b}), \lambda^*(\bar{b}))$. We say that the inequality constraint $g(x) \leq \bar{b}$ is *nonbinding* (or slack, ineffective, or not active) at $x = x^*(\bar{b})$ if $g(x^*(\bar{b})) < \bar{b}$, and that the constraint is *binding* (or tight, effective, or active) at $x = x^*(\bar{b})$ if $g(x^*(\bar{b})) = \bar{b}$. Recall that $\lambda^*(b)$ is the rate of change of the problem's maximum value with respect to the level b of the constraint: $\lambda^*(b) = \partial v(b)/\partial b$. When the constraint is slack, b can be changed over a small interval $(\bar{b}-\varepsilon, \bar{b}+\varepsilon)$ with the constraint remaining slack, so $\lambda^*(b) \equiv 0$ on this interval, and it is as if the constraint is not present in the problem. When a constraint is binding for $x = x^*(\bar{b})$, there are two possibilities. One is that, for a small enough $\varepsilon > 0$, $\lambda^*(b) > 0$ for all values $b \in (\bar{b} - \varepsilon, \bar{b} + \varepsilon)$, in which case the constraint is *strictly binding* for $b = \bar{b}$; tightening the constraint by reducing b to slightly below $\bar{b}$ lowers the problem's maximum value and relaxing the constraint by increasing the value of b to slightly above $\bar{b}$ raises the problem's maximum value. The other possibility is that $g(x^*(\bar{b})) = \bar{b}$ with $\lambda^*(\bar{b}) = 0$, and $g(x^*(b)) = b$ for $b < \bar{b}$ with $\lambda^*(b) > 0$ for $b < \bar{b}$. This second possibility is the *just-binding* for $b = \bar{b}$ case. What does it mean? When $b = \bar{b}$, the rate of change of the problem's maximum value is zero, stating that raising the constraint's level (*i.e.* relaxing the constraint) above $b = \bar{b}$ will make the constraint nonbinding. But any decrease in the constraint's level (*i.e.* tightening the constraint) causes a lower maximum value for the problem. Thus, for both $b = \bar{b}$ and $b > \bar{b}$, it is as if the constraint is not present in the problem, but, for any $b < \bar{b}$, the constraint is strictly binding and the problem's maximum value is reduced.

Here is an example. Consider the problem $\max_x f(x) = 4 - x^2$ subject to the constraint that $x \leq b$ (draw the problem). If $b < 0$, then the constraint strictly binds, the optimal solution is $x^*(b) = b$, the Lagrange multiplier is $\lambda^*(b) = -2b > 0$, and the maximum value is $v(b) = 4 - b^2 < 4$. If $b > 0$, then the constraint is nonbinding, the optimal solution is $x^*(b) = 0$, the Lagrange multiplier is $\lambda^*(b) = 0$, and the maximum value is $v(b) = 4$. If $b = 0$, then the optimal solution is $x^*(b = 0) = 0$, the constraint binds since $x^*(b = 0) = b = 0$, the Lagrange multiplier is $\lambda^*(b = 0) = -2b = 0$, the maximum value is $v(b = 0) = 4$, and any small tightening of the constraint (*i.e.* any decrease in b to below zero) results in the constraint becoming strictly binding. Thus the constraint $x \leq b$ is just-binding for $b = 0$.

What if the problem is equality constrained? Consider the problem

$$\max_{x \in \Re} f(x) \text{ subject to } g(x) = \bar{b}.$$

The optimal solution is $(x, \lambda) = \left(x^*(\bar{b}), \lambda^*(\bar{b})\right)$. The constraint is never slack because it is an equality constraint. The constraint is therefore always binding, either just-binding or strictly binding. The constraint is just-binding at $b = \bar{b}$ if $\lambda^*(\bar{b}) = 0$ and $\lambda^*(b) \neq 0$ for $b \neq \bar{b}$. That is, if $b = \bar{b}$, then even though the constraint binds, because $g(x^*(\bar{b})) = \bar{b}$, it is as if the constraint is not present, because the maximum value is the same as for the unconstrained problem $\max_{x \in \Re} f(x)$. But if $b \neq \bar{b}$, then the constraint strictly binds, and a change to the level b of the constraint changes both the optimal solution and the maximum value compared to when the constraint is absent. Consider the problem $\max_x f(x) = 4 - x^2$ subject to the equality constraint that $x = b$. The only feasible, and thus optimal, solution is $x^*(b) = b$. If $b \neq 0$, then the constraint is strictly binding. If $b = 0$, then the constraint is just-binding because the optimal solution $x^*(b = 0) = 0$ is the same as the solution to the unconstrained problem $\max_{x \in \Re} f(x) = 4 - x^2$, which is $x^{**} = 0$. Thus, when $b = 0$, it is as if the constraint is not there, even though the constraint $x = b = 0$ holds with equality; *i.e.* the constraint just-binds when $b = 0$.

Definition 13.1 (Just-Binding Equality Constraint). *If the $(\ell + 1)^{\text{th}}$ constraint in problem (13.44)*

$$h_{\ell+1}\left({}^{\ell+1}x^*\left({}^{\ell}\gamma^0 : \beta^0_{\ell+1}, b^0_{\ell+1}\right); \beta^0_{\ell+1}, b^0_{\ell+1}\right) = 0 \text{ and } {}^{\ell+1}\lambda^*_{\ell+1}\left({}^{\ell}\gamma^0 : \beta^0_{\ell+1}, b^0_{\ell+1}\right) = 0 \tag{13.45}$$

and, for every $\varepsilon > 0$, the neighborhood $B_{d_E}\left({}^{\ell}\gamma^0, \varepsilon\right)$ contains an ${}^{\ell}\gamma$ such that

$$h_{\ell+1}\left({}^{\ell+1}x^*\left({}^{\ell}\gamma : \beta^0_{\ell+1}, b^0_{\ell+1}\right); \beta^0_{\ell+1}, b^0_{\ell+1}\right) = 0 \text{ and } {}^{\ell+1}\lambda^*_{\ell+1}\left({}^{\ell}\gamma : \beta^0_{\ell+1}, b^0_{\ell+1}\right) \neq 0,$$
(13.46)

then the $(\ell+1)^{\text{th}}$ constraint is just-binding for ${}^{\ell+1}\gamma^0 = \left({}^{\ell}\gamma^0 : \beta^0_{\ell+1}, b^0_{\ell+1}\right)$.

The values $\beta^0_{\ell+1}$ and $b^0_{\ell+1}$ that parameterize the extra constraint will not alter in what follows, so we can simplify our notation a little by stating that the $(\ell+1)^{\text{th}}$-constraint just binds for ${}^{\ell}\gamma = {}^{\ell}\gamma^0$ and strictly binds for an ${}^{\ell}\gamma \neq {}^{\ell}\gamma^0$ that is near to ${}^{\ell}\gamma^0$.

(13.45) says that, when ${}^{\ell}\gamma = {}^{\ell}\gamma^0$, the extra constraint holds as an equality but has no effect on the problem's maximum value. (13.46) says that there is at least one value of ${}^{\ell}\gamma$ arbitrarily close to ${}^{\ell}\gamma^0$ for which the extra constraint strictly binds and changes the problem's maximum value.

Be clear that, for ${}^{\ell}\gamma \neq {}^{\ell}\gamma^0$, it is typically the case that the optimal solution ${}^{\ell}x^*\left({}^{\ell}\gamma\right)$ to the ℓ-constraint problem differs from the optimal solution ${}^{\ell+1}x^*\left({}^{\ell}\gamma : \beta^0_{\ell+1}, b^0_{\ell+1}\right)$ to the $(\ell+1)$-constraint problem. When ${}^{\ell}\gamma = {}^{\ell}\gamma^0$ the two optimal solutions are the same: ${}^{\ell}x^*\left({}^{\ell}\gamma^0\right) = {}^{\ell+1}x^*\left({}^{\ell}\gamma^0 : \beta^0_{\ell+1}, b^0_{\ell+1}\right)$.

The maximum-value function for the $(\ell+1)$-constraint problem is

$$
\begin{aligned}
{}^{\ell+1}v\left({}^{\ell}\gamma; \beta^0_{\ell+1}, b^0_{\ell+1}\right) &\equiv f\left({}^{\ell+1}x^*\left({}^{\ell}\gamma : \beta^0_{\ell+1}, b^0_{\ell+1}\right); \alpha\right) \\
&+ \sum_{j=1}^{\ell} {}^{\ell+1}\lambda^*_j\left({}^{\ell}\gamma : \beta^0_{\ell+1}, b^0_{\ell+1}\right) h_j\left({}^{\ell+1}x^*({}^{\ell}\gamma : \beta^0_{\ell+1}, b^0_{\ell+1}); \beta_j, b_j\right) \\
&+ {}^{\ell+1}\lambda^*_{\ell+1}\left({}^{\ell}\gamma : \beta^0_{\ell+1}, b^0_{\ell+1}\right) h_{\ell+1}\left({}^{\ell+1}x^*({}^{\ell}\gamma : \beta^0_{\ell+1}, b^0_{\ell+1}); \beta^0_{\ell+1}, b^0_{\ell+1}\right).
\end{aligned}
$$
(13.47)

Compare (13.43) and (13.47) before proceeding further.

For a given value of ${}^{\ell}\gamma^0$, the maximum value achieved in the $(\ell+1)$-constraint problem is never larger than the maximum value achieved in the ℓ-constraint problem (right?), but (13.45) and (13.46) say more. Particularly, (13.45) says that the maximum values of the ℓ-constraint and $(\ell+1)$-constraint problems are the same when ${}^{\ell}\gamma = {}^{\ell+1}\gamma^0$; *i.e.*

$$
{}^{\ell}v\left({}^{\ell}\gamma^0\right) = {}^{\ell+1}v\left({}^{\ell}\gamma^0 : \beta^0_{\ell+1}, b^0_{\ell+1}\right),
$$
(13.48)

and (13.46) says that there is at least one value ${}^{\ell}\gamma$ arbitrarily close to ${}^{\ell}\gamma^0$ for which the maximum value of the ℓ-constraint problem is strictly greater than the maximum value of the $(\ell+1)$-constraint problem; *i.e.* there is an $\varepsilon > 0$ for which

$$
{}^{\ell}v\left({}^{\ell}\gamma\right) > {}^{\ell+1}v\left({}^{\ell}\gamma : \beta^0_{\ell+1}, b^0_{\ell+1}\right) \text{ for at least one } {}^{\ell}\gamma \in B_{d_E}\left({}^{\ell}\gamma^0, \varepsilon\right); \; {}^{\ell}\gamma \neq {}^{\ell}\gamma^0. \quad (13.49)
$$

Why is this so? If an additional constraint is imposed upon a problem and this extra constraint is just-binding at the problem's optimal solution for some value ${}^{\ell}\gamma^0$ of the parameter vector ${}^{\ell}\gamma$, then for ${}^{\ell}\gamma = {}^{\ell}\gamma^0$ it is as if the additional constraint is not present. Consequently the two problems have the same feasible set and so have the same optimal solution and maximum value. But when, for some nearby parameter vector value ${}^{\ell}\gamma \neq {}^{\ell}\gamma^0$, the additional constraint strictly binds, the more constrained problem's feasible set is a strict subset of the less constrained problem's feasible set and does not contain the less constrained problem's optimal solution. Consequently the maximum value achieved in the more constrained problem is less than the maximum value achieved in the less constrained problem. The significant implication of this statement is that the function ${}^{\ell}v\left({}^{\ell}\gamma\right) - {}^{\ell+1}v\left({}^{\ell}\gamma : \beta_{\ell+1}^0, b_{\ell+1}^0\right)$ *must be strictly convex with respect to ${}^{\ell}\gamma$ for values of ${}^{\ell}\gamma$ that are close to ${}^{\ell}\gamma^0$.* Put more formally, if the extra constraint is just-binding for ${}^{\ell}\gamma = {}^{\ell}\gamma^0$, then, necessarily, (the First-Order Envelope Theorem)

$$ {}^{\ell}v\left({}^{\ell}\gamma^0\right) = {}^{\ell+1}v\left({}^{\ell}\gamma^0; \beta_{\ell+1}^0, b_{\ell+1}^0\right) $$
$$ \text{and } \nabla_{{}^{\ell}\gamma}{}^{\ell}v\left({}^{\ell}\gamma\right)|_{{}^{\ell}\gamma={}^{\ell}\gamma^0} = \nabla_{{}^{\ell}\gamma}{}^{\ell+1}v\left({}^{\ell}\gamma; \beta_{\ell+1}^0, b_{\ell+1}^0\right)|_{{}^{\ell}\gamma={}^{\ell}\gamma^0} $$

and also necessarily (the Second-Order Envelope Theorem), there exists $\varepsilon > 0$ such that the function ${}^{\ell}v\left({}^{\ell}\gamma\right) - {}^{\ell+1}v\left({}^{\ell}\gamma : \beta_{\ell+1}^0, b_{\ell+1}^0\right)$ is strictly convex with respect to ${}^{\ell}\gamma$ on the neighborhood $B_{d_E}\left({}^{\ell}\gamma^0, \varepsilon\right)$.

Figure 13.1 displays the two statements in both of its panels. The panels display graphs of ${}^{\ell}v\left(\cdot, \gamma_k\right)$ and ${}^{\ell+1}v\left(\cdot, \gamma_k : \beta_{\ell+1}^0, b_{\ell+1}^0\right)$, where γ_k is one of the elements of the vector ${}^{\ell}\gamma$. For $\gamma_k = \gamma_k^0$, the extra constraint is just-binding, so the maximum-value functions have the same value, ${}^{\ell}v\left(\cdot, \gamma_k^0\right) = {}^{\ell+1}v\left(\cdot, \gamma_k^0 : \beta_{\ell+1}^0, b_{\ell+1}^0\right)$, and the same slope, $\partial {}^{\ell}v\left(\cdot, \gamma_k\right)/\partial\gamma_k = \partial {}^{\ell+1}v\left(\cdot, \gamma_k : \beta_{\ell+1}^0, b_{\ell+1}^0\right)/\partial\gamma_k$, at $\gamma_k = \gamma_k^0$; see points A and B in Figure 13.1. For $\gamma_k \neq \gamma_k^0$, the extra constraint is strictly binding, so over the interval $(\gamma_k^0 - \varepsilon, \gamma_k^0 + \varepsilon)$ the upper-envelope function ${}^{\ell}v\left(\cdot, \gamma_k\right)$ must be strictly less concave (hence, strictly more convex) with respect to γ_k than is the function ${}^{\ell+1}v\left(\cdot, \gamma_k : \beta_{\ell+1}^0, b_{\ell+1}^0\right)$. So over this interval the function ${}^{\ell}v\left(\cdot, \gamma_k\right) - {}^{\ell+1}v\left(\cdot, \gamma_k : \beta_{\ell+1}^0, b_{\ell+1}^0\right)$ must be strictly convex with respect to γ_k.

Let's return to our example. Think of given values ${}^1\gamma^0 = (p^0, w_1^0, w_2^0)$ for the parameters of the firm's 1-constraint equality constrained problem. The optimal solution value for x_1 for these parameter values is ${}^1x_1^*(p^0, w_1^0, w_2^0) = p_0^3/27(w_1^0)^2 w_2^0$. Now impose the additional constraint that $x_1 = {}^1x_1^*\left({}^1\gamma^0\right) = {}^1x_1^*(p^0, w_1^0, w_2^0) = p_0^3/27(w_1^0)^2 w_2^0$.

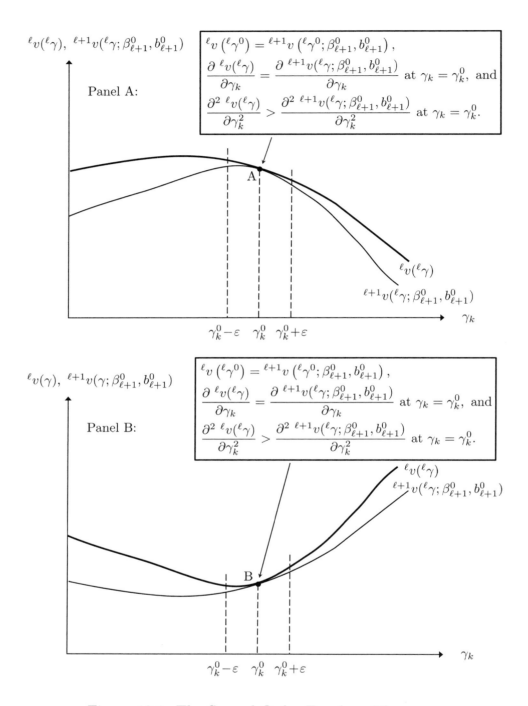

Figure 13.1: The Second-Order Envelope Theorem.

This gives the 2-constraint equality constrained problem

$$\max_{y,\,x_1,\,x_2} py - w_1 x_1 - w_2 x_2 \text{ subject to } h_1(y, x_1, x_2) = x_1^{1/3} x_2^{1/3} - y = 0$$

$$\text{and } h_2\left(x_1; {}^1x_1^*\left({}^1\gamma^0\right)\right) = {}^1x_1^*\left({}^1\gamma^0\right) - x_1 = \frac{p_0^3}{27\left(w_1^0\right)^2 w_2^0} - x_1 = 0.$$

This problem's parameter vector is ${}^2\gamma = \left({}^1\gamma : b_2\right) = \left({}^1\gamma : {}^1x_1^*\left({}^1\gamma^0\right)\right)$. The optimal solution is $\left({}^2y^*\left({}^2\gamma\right), {}^1x_1^*\left({}^1\gamma^0\right), {}^2x_2^*\left({}^2\gamma\right)\right)$. The additional constraint just-binds for ${}^1\gamma = {}^1\gamma^0 = (p^0, w_1^0, w_2^0)$ and strictly binds for ${}^1\gamma \neq {}^1\gamma^0$. The optimal solution is

$$\begin{pmatrix} {}^2y^*\left({}^1\gamma; {}^1x_1^*\left({}^1\gamma^0\right)\right) \\ {}^2x_1^*\left({}^1\gamma; {}^1x_1^*\left({}^1\gamma^0\right)\right) \\ {}^2x_2^*\left({}^1\gamma; {}^1x_1^*\left({}^1\gamma^0\right)\right) \\ {}^2\lambda_1^*\left({}^1\gamma; {}^1x_1^*\left({}^1\gamma^0\right)\right) \\ {}^2\lambda_2^*\left({}^1\gamma; {}^1x_1^*\left({}^1\gamma^0\right)\right) \end{pmatrix} = \begin{pmatrix} {}^2y^*\left(p, w_1, w_2; {}^1x_1^*\left({}^1\gamma^0\right)\right) \\ {}^2x_1^*\left(p, w_1, w_2; {}^1x_1^*\left({}^1\gamma^0\right)\right) \\ {}^2x_2^*\left(p, w_1, w_2; {}^1x_1^*\left({}^1\gamma^0\right)\right) \\ {}^2\lambda_1^*\left(p, w_1, w_2; {}^1x_1^*\left({}^1\gamma^0\right)\right) \\ {}^2\lambda_2^*\left(p, w_1, w_2; {}^1x_1^*\left({}^1\gamma^0\right)\right) \end{pmatrix} = \begin{pmatrix} \left(\dfrac{p\,{}^1x_1^*\left({}^1\gamma^0\right)}{3w_2}\right)^{1/2} \\ {}^1x_1^*\left({}^1\gamma^0\right) \\ \left(\dfrac{p^3\,{}^1x_1^*\left({}^1\gamma^0\right)}{27w_2^3}\right)^{1/2} \\ p \\ \left(\dfrac{p^3}{27w_2\,{}^1x_1^*\left({}^1\gamma^0\right)}\right)^{1/2} - w_1 \end{pmatrix}$$

and the maximum-value function is (see (13.47))

$$\begin{aligned} {}^2v\left({}^1\gamma : {}^1x_1^*\left({}^1\gamma^0\right)\right) &= {}^2v\left(p, w_1, w_2 : {}^1x_1^*\left({}^1\gamma^0\right)\right) \\ &= p\,{}^2y^*\left({}^1\gamma : {}^1x_1^*\left({}^1\gamma^0\right)\right) - w_1\,{}^1x_1^*\left({}^1\gamma^0\right) - w_2\,{}^2x_2^*\left({}^1\gamma : {}^1x_1^*\left({}^1\gamma^0\right)\right) \\ &\quad + {}^2\lambda_1^*\left({}^1\gamma : {}^1x_1^*\left({}^1\gamma^0\right)\right)\left({}^1x_1^*\left({}^1\gamma^0\right)^{1/3} \times {}^2x_2^*\left({}^1\gamma : {}^1x_1^*\left({}^1\gamma^0\right)\right)^{1/3} - {}^2y^*\left({}^1\gamma : {}^1x_1^*\left({}^1\gamma^0\right)\right)\right) \\ &\quad + {}^2\lambda_2^*\left({}^1\gamma : {}^1x_1^*\left({}^1\gamma^0\right)\right)\left({}^1x_1^*\left({}^1\gamma^0\right) - {}^2x_1^*\left({}^1\gamma : {}^1x_1^*\left({}^1\gamma^0\right)\right)\right) \\ &= \frac{2}{3}\left(\frac{p^3\,{}^1x_1^*\left({}^1\gamma^0\right)}{3w_2}\right)^{1/2} - w_1\,{}^1x_1^*\left({}^1\gamma\right). \end{aligned}$$

Notice that, for ${}^1\gamma = {}^1\gamma^0$, the value ${}^2\lambda_2^*\left(p, w_1, w_2; {}^1x_1^*\left({}^1\gamma^0\right)\right)$ of the multiplier of the additional constraint is

$$ {}^2\lambda_2^*\left(p^0, w_1^0, w_2^0; {}^1x_1^*\left({}^1\gamma^0\right)\right) = \left(\frac{p_0^3}{27w_2^0} \times \frac{27\left(w_1^0\right)^2 w_2^0}{p_0^3}\right)^{1/2} - w_1^0 = 0$$

and that ${}^2\lambda_2^*\left(p, w_1, w_2; {}^1x_1^*\left({}^1\gamma^0\right)\right) \neq 0$ for ${}^1\gamma \neq {}^1\gamma^0$.

Theorem 13.1 (The Second-Order Envelope Theorem). *Consider a primal optimization problem with ℓ equality constraints. If $\ell = 0$, then the problem is*

$$\max_{x \in \Re^n} f(x; \alpha).$$

If $\ell \geq 1$, then the problem is

$$\max_{x \in \Re^n} f(x; \alpha) \text{ subject to } h_j(x; \beta_j, b_j) = 0 \text{ for } j = 1, \ldots, \ell.$$

Denote the parameter vector for the ℓ-constraint problem by ${}^\ell\gamma \in {}^\ell\Gamma$. Consider only problems for which the optimal solution is a real-valued function $\left({}^\ell x^* \left({}^\ell\gamma\right), {}^\ell\lambda^* \left({}^\ell\gamma\right)\right)$ that is continuously differentiable on ${}^\ell\Gamma$. The maximum-value function for the ℓ-constraint problem is

$$ {}^\ell v \left({}^\ell\gamma\right) \equiv f \left({}^\ell x^* \left({}^\ell\gamma\right); \alpha\right) + \sum_{j=1}^{\ell} {}^\ell\lambda_j^* \left({}^\ell\gamma\right) h_j \left({}^\ell x^* \left({}^\ell\gamma\right); \beta_j, b_j\right). $$

The $(\ell + 1)$-constraint problem is the ℓ-constraint problem with one additional constraint $h_{\ell+1} \left(x; \beta_{\ell+1}, b_{\ell+1}\right) = 0$ that just-binds when ${}^\ell\gamma = {}^\ell\gamma^0$, and for which the optimal solution is a real-valued function $\left({}^{\ell+1} x^* \left({}^\ell\gamma : \beta_{\ell+1}^0, b_{\ell+1}^0\right), {}^{\ell+1}\lambda^* \left({}^\ell\gamma : \beta_{\ell+1}^0, b_{\ell+1}^0\right)\right)$ that is continuously differentiable on ${}^\ell\Gamma$. The maximum-value function for the $(\ell+1)$-constraint problem is

$$ {}^{\ell+1} v \left({}^\ell\gamma : \beta_{\ell+1}^0, b_{\ell+1}^0\right) \equiv f \left({}^{\ell+1} x^* \left({}^\ell\gamma : \beta_{\ell+1}^0, b_{\ell+1}^0\right); \alpha\right) $$
$$ + \sum_{j=1}^{\ell+1} {}^{\ell+1}\lambda_j^* \left({}^\ell\gamma : \beta_{\ell+1}^0, b_{\ell+1}^0\right) h_j \left({}^{\ell+1} x^* \left({}^\ell\gamma : \beta_{\ell+1}^0, b_{\ell+1}^0\right); \beta_j, b_j\right). $$

Then there is an $\varepsilon > 0$ for which the function ${}^\ell v \left({}^\ell\gamma\right) - {}^{\ell+1} v \left({}^\ell\gamma : \beta_{\ell+1}^0, b_{\ell+1}^0\right)$ is strictly convex with respect to ${}^\ell\gamma$ over the neighborhood $B_{d_E} \left({}^\ell\gamma^0, \varepsilon\right)$.

Proof. For small enough perturbations $\Delta^\ell\gamma$, a second-order Taylor's series expansion of ${}^\ell v \left({}^\ell\gamma\right)$ at ${}^\ell\gamma = {}^\ell\gamma^0$ gives

$$ {}^\ell v \left({}^\ell\gamma^0 + \Delta^\ell\gamma\right) = {}^\ell v \left({}^\ell\gamma^0\right) + \nabla_{{}^\ell\gamma} {}^\ell v \left({}^\ell\gamma\right) |_{\substack{{}^\ell\gamma \\ = {}^\ell\gamma^0}} \cdot \Delta^\ell\gamma + \frac{1}{2} \Delta^\ell\gamma^{\mathrm{T}} \nabla^2_{{}^\ell\gamma {}^\ell\gamma} {}^\ell v \left({}^\ell\gamma\right) |_{\substack{{}^\ell\gamma \\ = {}^\ell\gamma^0}} \Delta^\ell\gamma. $$

$$(13.50)$$

Similarly

$$
\begin{aligned}
{}^{\ell+1}v\left({}^{\ell}\gamma^0 + \Delta^{\ell}\gamma : \beta_{\ell+1}^0, b_{\ell+1}^0\right) \\
= {}^{\ell+1}v\left({}^{\ell}\gamma^0 : \beta_{\ell+1}^0, b_{\ell+1}^0\right) + \nabla_{\ell\gamma}\,{}^{\ell+1}v\left({}^{\ell}\gamma : \beta_{\ell+1}^0, b_{\ell+1}^0\right)\Big|_{{}^{\ell}\gamma \atop = {}^{\ell}\gamma^0} \cdot \Delta^{\ell}\gamma \\
+ \frac{1}{2}\Delta^{\ell}\gamma^{\mathrm{T}}\nabla^2_{\ell\gamma\ell\gamma}\,{}^{\ell+1}v\left({}^{\ell}\gamma : \beta_{\ell+1}^0, b_{\ell+1}^0\right)\Big|_{{}^{\ell}\gamma \atop = {}^{\ell}\gamma^0}\Delta^{\ell}\gamma.
\end{aligned}
\tag{13.51}
$$

Since the $(\ell+1)$th-constraint is just-binding for ${}^{\ell}\gamma = {}^{\ell}\gamma^0$,

$$
{}^{\ell}v\left({}^{\ell}\gamma^0\right) = {}^{\ell+1}v\left({}^{\ell}\gamma^0 : \beta_{\ell+1}^0, b_{\ell+1}^0\right)
\tag{13.52}
$$

$$
\text{and}\quad {}^{\ell}v\left({}^{\ell}\gamma^0 + \Delta^{\ell}\gamma\right) > {}^{\ell+1}v\left({}^{\ell}\gamma^0 + \Delta^{\ell}\gamma : \beta_{\ell+1}^0, b_{\ell+1}^0\right)
\tag{13.53}
$$

for all small enough $\Delta^{\ell}\gamma \neq \underline{0}$. By the First-Order Envelope Theorem,

$$
\nabla_{\ell\gamma}\,{}^{\ell}v\left({}^{\ell}\gamma\right)\Big|_{{}^{\ell}\gamma \atop = {}^{\ell}\gamma^0} = \nabla_{\ell\gamma}\,{}^{\ell+1}v\left({}^{\ell}\gamma : \beta_{\ell+1}^0, b_{\ell+1}^0\right)\Big|_{{}^{\ell}\gamma \atop = {}^{\ell}\gamma^0}.
\tag{13.54}
$$

Using (13.52), (13.53), and (13.54) in (13.50) and (13.51) gives

$$
\Delta^{\ell}\gamma^{\mathrm{T}}\left(\nabla^2_{\ell\gamma\ell\gamma}\,{}^{\ell}v\left({}^{\ell}\gamma\right) - \nabla^2_{\ell\gamma\ell\gamma}\,{}^{\ell+1}v\left({}^{\ell}\gamma : \beta_{\ell+1}^0, b_{\ell+1}^0\right)\right)\Big|_{{}^{\ell}\gamma \atop = {}^{\ell}\gamma^0}\Delta^{\ell}\gamma > 0
\tag{13.55}
$$

for small enough $\Delta^{\ell}\gamma$. That is, there is an $\varepsilon > 0$ for which ${}^{\ell}v\left({}^{\ell}\gamma\right) - {}^{\ell+1}v\left({}^{\ell}\gamma : \beta_{\ell+1}^0, b_{\ell+1}^0\right)$ is strictly convex with respect to ${}^{\ell}\gamma$ for all ${}^{\ell}\gamma \in B_{d_E}\left({}^{\ell}\gamma^0, \varepsilon\right)$. $\qquad\square$

For our example,

$$
{}^{1}v(p, w_1, w_2) - {}^{2}v\left(p, w_1, w_2; {}^{1}x_1^*\left({}^{1}\gamma^0\right)\right) = \frac{p^3}{27w_1w_2} - \frac{2}{3}\left(\frac{p^3\,{}^{1}x_1^*\left({}^{1}\gamma^0\right)}{3w_2}\right)^{1/2} + w_1\,{}^{1}x_1^*\left({}^{1}\gamma^0\right).
\tag{13.56}
$$

Choose any one of the parameters p, w_1, or w_2. I will pick p. You can try what follows for w_1 and w_2. The second partial derivative of (13.56) with respect to p is

$$
\frac{\partial^2\left({}^{1}v(p, \cdot) - {}^{2}v(p, \cdot)\right)}{\partial p^2} = \frac{2p}{9w_1w_2} - \frac{1}{2}\left(\frac{{}^{1}x_1^*\left({}^{1}\gamma^0\right)}{3pw_2}\right)^{1/2}.
\tag{13.57}
$$

At $(p, w_1, w_2) = (p^0, w_1^0, w_2^0)$ the value of (13.57) is

$$
\frac{\partial^2\left({}^{1}v(p, \cdot) - {}^{2}v(p, \cdot)\right)}{\partial p^2}\bigg|_{{}^{1}\gamma = \left(p^0, w_1^0, w_2^0\right)} = \frac{p^0}{6w_1^0w_2^0} > 0,
$$

establishing that (13.56) is strictly convex with respect to p at and near to $^1\gamma = {}^1\gamma^0 = (p^0, w_1^0, w_2^0)$. An evaluation at $^1\gamma^0$ of the Hessian matrix of (13.56) shows that (13.56) is jointly strictly convex with respect to p, w_1, and w_2 for values of (p, w_1, w_2) near to (p^0, w_1^0, w_2^0).

It is a simple matter to use the Second-Order Envelope Theorem to compare the comparative statics results of a constrained optimization problem to the results of a more constrained version of that problem. We will see how to do this in the next section.

13.8　Le Chatelier's Principle

Henri-Louis Le Chatelier (1850-1936) was a highly regarded French industrial chemist who made an observation that applies to a huge variety of circumstances. The most frustrating aspect of his principle is that, although it is a simple idea, it is not easy to state it accurately in just a few words. Le Chatelier's first published statement in 1884 of his principle was a lengthy and confusing paragraph in the research journal of the French Academy of Sciences. Four years later he gave a much simpler restatement. A translation into English of his restatement is:

> Every change of one of the factors of an equilibrium occasions a rearrangement of the system in such a direction that the factor in question experiences a change in a sense opposite to the original change.

Perhaps you do not find even his restatement to be immediately comprehensible?

Le Chatelier's main concern was with changes to the equilibria of chemical systems, but others have since tried to construct more useful statements of the principle and to make it applicable to the social sciences, including economics. Such a restatement is found in Milgrom and Roberts 1996. Put into words, it states that we are to consider two optimization problems that are the same except that one is subject to an extra equality constraint. We start with an optimal solution (an equilibrium, in Le Chatelier's terminology) to the more restricted problem at which the extra constraint is just-binding, so this is also an optimal solution to the less restricted problem. Now we perturb a little the vector of the parameters that are common to the two problems. Le Chatelier's Principle states that the changes caused to the optimal solution of the less restricted problem are at least as large as the changes caused to the optimal solution of the more restricted problem. An economic example often used to illustrate the idea is that the changes that a profit-maximizing competitive firm makes to its quantity supplied and input quantities demanded in response to a change to, say, the price of its product are at least as large in the (less-restricted) "long-run" as in any (more restricted) "short-run." We will examine this application in a moment. The tool that we will use is the Second-Order Envelope Theorem.

The theorem states that, if the $(\ell+1)^{\text{th}}$-constraint just-binds when $^\ell\gamma = {}^\ell\gamma^0$, then the Hessian matrix of the function $^\ell v \left({}^\ell\gamma \right) - {}^{\ell+1}v \left({}^\ell\gamma : \beta^0_{\ell+1}, b^0_{\ell+1} \right)$ with respect to the parameter vector $^\ell\gamma$ of the ℓ-constrained problem necessarily is positive-definite (not merely positive-semi-definite) at $^\ell\gamma^0$ for all small enough perturbations $\Delta^\ell\gamma$ from $^\ell\gamma^0$. That is,

$$\Delta^\ell\gamma^T \left(\nabla^2_{\ell\gamma\ell\gamma} \left({}^\ell v \left({}^\ell\gamma \right) - {}^{\ell+1}v \left({}^\ell\gamma : \beta^0_{\ell+1}, b^0_{\ell+1} \right) \right) \right) |_{\ell\gamma= \atop \ell\gamma^0} \Delta^\ell\gamma > 0 \qquad (13.58)$$

for all small enough perturbations $\Delta^\ell\gamma$ from $^1\gamma^0$. What do we learn from this?

The typical element in the Hessian matrix in (13.58) is

$$\frac{\partial^2\, {}^\ell v \left({}^\ell\gamma \right)}{\partial\gamma_i \partial\gamma_j} - \frac{\partial^2\, {}^{\ell+1} v \left({}^\ell\gamma : \beta^0_{\ell+1}, b^0_{\ell+1} \right)}{\partial\gamma_i \partial\gamma_j} \quad \text{for } i, j = 1, \ldots, r. \qquad (13.59)$$

A matrix is positive-definite only if all of its main diagonal elements are strictly positive, so, from (13.59),

$$\frac{\partial^2\, {}^\ell v \left({}^\ell\gamma \right)}{\partial\gamma_i^2} > \frac{\partial^2\, {}^{\ell+1} v \left({}^\ell\gamma : \beta^0_{\ell+1}, b^0_{\ell+1} \right)}{\partial\gamma_i^2} \quad \text{for } i = 1, \ldots, r. \qquad (13.60)$$

To see how to use this information, let's return to our example of a profit-maximizing firm. The original 1-constraint equality constrained problem is

$$\max_{y, x_1, x_2} py - w_1 x_1 - w_2 x_2 \text{ subject to } h_1(y, x_1, x_2) = x_1^{1/3} x_2^{1/3} - y = 0.$$

The 2-constraint equality constrained problem is

$$\max_{y, x_1, x_2} py - w_1 x_1 - w_2 x_2 \text{ subject to } h_1(y, x_1, x_2) = x_1^{1/3} x_2^{1/3} - y = 0$$
$$\text{and} \quad h_2 \left(x_1; {}^1x_1^* \left(p^0, w_1^0, w_2^0 \right) \right) = {}^1x_1^* \left(p^0, w_1^0, w_2^0 \right) - x_1 = 0,$$

where $^1x_1^* \left(p^0, w_1^0, w_2^0 \right)$ is the optimal value for x_1 in the 1-constraint problem when $(p, w_1, w_2) = (p^0, w_1^0, w_2^0)$. We have already discovered from Hotelling's Lemma (see

Theorem 12.4) that

$$\frac{\partial^2 \left({}^1v(p, w_1, w_2) \right)}{\partial p^2} = \frac{\partial \left({}^1y^*(p, w_1, w_2) \right)}{\partial p} \quad \text{and}$$

$$\frac{\partial^2 \left({}^2v \left(p, w_1, w_2 : {}^1x_1^* \left(p^0, w_1^0, w_2^0 \right) \right) \right)}{\partial p^2} = \frac{\partial \left({}^2y^* \left(p, w_1, w_2 : {}^1x_1^* \left(p^0, w_1^0, w_2^0 \right) \right) \right)}{\partial p},$$

that

$$\frac{\partial^2 \left({}^1v \left(p, w_1, w_2 \right) \right)}{\partial w_1^2} = - \frac{\partial \left({}^1x_1^* \left(p, w_1, w_2 \right) \right)}{\partial w_1} \quad \text{and}$$

$$\frac{\partial^2 \left({}^2v \left(p, w_1, w_2 : {}^1x_1^* \left(p^0, w_1^0, w_2^0 \right) \right) \right)}{\partial w_1^2} = - \frac{\partial \left({}^2x_1^* \left(p, w_1, w_2 : {}^1x_1^* \left(p^0, w_1^0, w_2^0 \right) \right) \right)}{\partial w_1} = 0,$$

and that

$$\frac{\partial^2 \left({}^1v \left(p, w_1, w_2 \right) \right)}{\partial w_2^2} = - \frac{\partial \left({}^1x_2^* \left(p, w_1, w_2 \right) \right)}{\partial w_2} \quad \text{and}$$

$$\frac{\partial^2 \left({}^2v \left(p, w_1, w_2 : {}^1x_1^* \left(p^0, w_1^0, w_2^0 \right) \right) \right)}{\partial w_2^2} = - \frac{\partial \left({}^2x_2^* \left(p, w_1, w_2 : {}^1x_1^* \left(p^0, w_1^0, w_2^0 \right) \right) \right)}{\partial w_2}.$$

Therefore, from (13.60),

$$\frac{\partial \left({}^1y^* \left(p, w_1, w_2 \right) \right)}{\partial p} > \frac{\partial \left({}^2y^* \left(p, w_1, w_2 : {}^1x_1^* \left(p^0, w_1^0, w_2^0 \right) \right) \right)}{\partial p}, \tag{13.61}$$

$$\frac{\partial \left({}^1x_1^* \left(p, w_1, w_2 \right) \right)}{\partial w_1} < \frac{\partial \left({}^2x_1^* \left(p, w_1, w_2 : {}^1x_1^* \left(p^0, w_1^0, w_2^0 \right) \right) \right)}{\partial w_1} = 0, \tag{13.62}$$

$$\text{and} \quad \frac{\partial \left({}^1x_2^* \left(p, w_1, w_2 \right) \right)}{\partial w_2} < \frac{\partial \left({}^2x_2^* \left(p, w_1, w_2 : {}^1x_1^* \left(p^0, w_1^0, w_2^0 \right) \right) \right)}{\partial w_2}. \tag{13.63}$$

These are familiar comparisons of comparative statics results. (13.61) informs us that rate-of-change of the quantity of product supplied by a competitive firm is strictly larger in the "long-run" than it is in the "short-run" in which one of the firm's input levels is fixed. (13.62) and (13.63) inform us that the rate-of-change of the quantity demanded of a variable input by a competitive firm is strictly more negative in the long-run than it is in the short-run in which one of the firm's input levels is fixed. In Le Chatelier's parlance, the long-run problem's equilibrium adjusts by more so as to better overcome, or exploit, the consequences of parameter value changes. In our parlance, the principle is that the rate at which any component of an optimal solution changes with respect to a parameter common to a less constrained and a more constrained problem is larger in size for the less constrained problem than for more constrained problem. The principle is a *necessary* consequence of the additional constraint reducing the ways in which a problem's choice variables can be adjusted to offset the adverse (maximum-value reducing) consequences of the additional constraint.

13.9   More Comparisons of Comparative Statics

Le Chatelier-type results are not the only type of comparative statics results provided by the Second-Order Envelope Theorem.

The Hessian matrix in (13.58) is symmetric, so

$$\frac{\partial^2 {}^\ell v\left({}^\ell\gamma\right)}{\partial\gamma_j\partial\gamma_k} - \frac{\partial^2 {}^{\ell+1}v\left({}^\ell\gamma:\beta^0_{\ell+1}, b^0_{\ell+1}\right)}{\partial\gamma_j\partial\gamma_k} = \frac{\partial^2 {}^\ell v\left({}^\ell\gamma\right)}{\partial\gamma_k\partial\gamma_j} - \frac{\partial^2 {}^{\ell+1}v\left({}^\ell\gamma:\beta^0_{\ell+1}, b^0_{\ell+1}\right)}{\partial\gamma_k\partial\gamma_j}$$

for $j, k = 1, \ldots, r$; $j \neq k$. In the context of our example, this gives us results such as

$$\frac{\partial\left({}^1 y^*(p, w_1, w_2)\right)}{\partial w_1} - \frac{\partial\left({}^2 y^*\left(p, w_1, w_2 : {}^1 x_1^*\left(p^0, w_1^0, w_2^0\right)\right)\right)}{\partial w_1} = -\frac{\partial\left({}^1 x_1^*(p, w_1, w_2)\right)}{\partial p},$$

as well as

$$\frac{\partial\left({}^1 y^*(p, w_1, w_2)\right)}{\partial w_2} - \frac{\partial\left({}^2 y^*\left(p, w_1, w_2 : {}^1 x_1^*\left(p^0, w_1^0, w_2^0\right)\right)\right)}{\partial w_2}$$

$$= -\frac{\partial\left({}^1 x_2^*(p, w_1, w_2)\right)}{\partial p} + \frac{\partial\left({}^2 x_2^*\left(p, w_1, w_2 : {}^1 x_1^*\left(p^0, w_1^0, w_2^0\right)\right)\right)}{\partial p} \quad \text{and}$$

$$\frac{\partial\left({}^1 x_1^*(p, w_1, w_2)\right)}{\partial w_2}$$

$$= -\frac{\partial\left({}^1 x_2^*(p, w_1, w_2)\right)}{\partial w_1} + \frac{\partial\left({}^2 x_2^*\left(p, w_1, w_2 : {}^1 x_1^*\left(p^0, w_1^0, w_2^0\right)\right)\right)}{\partial w_1}.$$

Whether or not these particular results are useful is debatable. All I wish to point out to you is that they are necessarily true and are easily obtained.

A symmetric matrix is positive-definite if and only if all of its successive principal minors are strictly positive. This provides still more comparison of comparative statics results from the Hessian matrix $\left(\nabla^2_{{}^1\gamma {}^1\gamma} {}^1 v\left({}^1\gamma\right) - \nabla^2_{{}^1\gamma {}^1\gamma} {}^2 v\left({}^1\gamma:\beta^0_{\ell+1}, b^0_{\ell+1}\right)\right)\big|_{{}^1\gamma = {}^1\gamma^0}$. These results have even more obscure economic interpretations than those above, so I will not present them, but you might like to derive some of them just to see what they look like.

13.10   Problems

Problem 13.1. A firm uses quantities x_1, x_2, and x_3 of three inputs to produce a single output. The positive per-unit prices of the inputs are w_1, w_2, and w_3. The firm's production function is $g(x_1, x_2, x_3)$. The firm's cost-minimization problem is

$$\max_{x_1, x_2, x_3} \ -w_1 x_1 - w_2 x_2 - w_3 x_3 \ \text{ subject to}$$

$$h_1(x_1) = x_1 \geq 0, \ h_2(x_2) = x_2 \geq 0, \ h_3(x_3) = x_3 \geq 0, \tag{13.64}$$

$$\text{and} \quad h_4(x_1, x_2, x_3; y) = g(x_1, x_2, x_3) - y \geq 0$$

for given values of w_1, w_2, w_3, and y. Assume that g is twice-continuously differentiable and that g's properties cause the nonnegativity constraints on x_1, x_2, and x_3 to be slack at an optimal solution when $y > 0$. That is, the cost-minimizing bundle $(x_1^*(w_1, w_2, w_3, y), x_2^*(w_1, w_2, w_3, y), x_3^*(w_1, w_2, w_3, y))$ of the firm's conditional input demands contains only positive values when $y > 0$. Assume also that g's properties cause the Karush-Kuhn-Tucker condition to be well-defined at any optimal solution to the primal problem (13.64).

(i) There is a different primal problem (13.64) for each different value of the parameter vector (w_1, w_2, w_3, y). What is the primal-dual problem that is generated by this family of primal problems?

(ii) Are any of the constraints in the primal-dual problem different from the constraints in the primal problems? Explain.

(iii) Write down the first-order necessary maximization conditions for any one of the primal problems.

(iv) Write down the first-order necessary maximization conditions for the primal-dual problem. Compare these conditions to the necessary first-order maximization conditions for any of the primal problems.

(v) Derive the necessary second-order local maximization condition for any one of the primal problems (13.64).

(vi) Derive the primal-dual problem's necessary second-order maximization condition.

(vii) Use your answer to part (vi) to derive some comparative statics properties of the firm's conditional input demand functions and its marginal cost of production function.

Problem 13.2. Slutsky's equation is the major quantitative comparative statics result of neoclassical consumer demand theory. It is a quantitative result because it allows numerical computation of the rates-of-change of ordinary demand functions,

Hicksian demand functions, and income effects. However, one wonders what *qualitative* comparative statics results might be implied by this theory of demand. The answer to this inquiry is obtained by applying Silberberg's methodology to the consumer's expenditure minimization problem. Set up the appropriate primal-dual problem and use its necessary optimization conditions to discover the implied qualitative comparative statics results.

Problem 13.3. The standard consumer expenditure minimization problem is

$$\min_{x_1,\ldots,x_n} p_1 x_1 + \cdots + p_n x_n \text{ subject to } x_1 \geq 0, \ldots, x_n \geq 0 \text{ and } U(x_1,\ldots,x_n) \geq u.$$

The parameters of this problem are $p_1,\ldots,p_n$, and u. Let $p = (p_1,\ldots,p_n)$ and let (p^0, u^0) denote an initial value for the parameter vector (p, u). $h(p^0, u^0)$ is the implied initial value of the expenditure-minimizing (Hicksian compensated demand) consumption vector, so, in particular, $h_1^0 = h_1(p^0, y^0)$ is the quantity of commodity 1 that is initially demanded when the consumer faces the initial price vector p^0 and achieves the utility level u^0.

Use the Second-Order Envelope Theorem to compare the comparative statics results for the consumer for small perturbations from (p^0, y^0) when the consumer is, and is not, subject to the extra constraint that $x_1 = h_1^0$.

13.11   Answers

Answer to Problem 13.1.
(i) The maximum-value function for the family of primal problems (13.64) is the negative of the firm's (long-run) cost of production function

$$-c^\ell(w_1, w_2, w_3, y) = -w_1 x_1^*(w_1, w_2, w_3, y) - w_2 x_2^*(w_1, w_2, w_3, y) - w_3 x_3^*(w_1, w_2, w_3, y),$$

so the primal-dual problem that is generated by the family of primal problems is

$$\max_{x_1, x_2, x_3, w_1, w_2, w_3, y} c^\ell(w_1, w_2, w_3, y) - w_1 x_1 - w_2 x_2 - w_3 x_3$$
$$\text{subject to} \quad h_1(x_1) = x_1 \geq 0, \quad h_2(x_2) = x_2 \geq 0, \quad h_3(x_3) = x_3 \geq 0, \qquad (13.65)$$
$$\text{and} \quad h_4(x_1, x_2, x_3, y) = g(x_1, x_2, x_3) - y \geq 0.$$

(ii) The first, second, and third constraints of the primal-dual problem are the same as the first, second, and third constraints of any of the primal problems. The fourth constraint in the primal-dual problem differs from the fourth constraint in any of the primal problems. Why? In the fourth constraint of any of the primal problems, the value of y is fixed, so this constraint confines choices of x_1, x_2, and x_3 to the set $S^p(y) = \{(x_1, x_2, x_3) \mid g(x_1, x_2, x_3) \geq y\}$. y is a choice variable in the primal-dual problem's fourth constraint, so the constraint confines choices of x_1, x_2, x_3, *and* y to the set $S^{pd} = \{(x_1, x_2, x_3, y) \mid g(x_1, x_2, x_3) - y \geq 0\}$. For any given value of $y > 0$, the set $S^p(y)$ is only a subset of S^{pd}.

(iii) The Karush-Kuhn-Tucker condition for the primal problem (13.64) is

$$(-w_1, -w_2, -w_3) = -\lambda_1^p(1, 0, 0) - \lambda_2^p(0, 1, 0) - \lambda_3^p(0, 0, 1) - \lambda_4^p \left(\frac{\partial g(\cdot)}{\partial x_1}, \frac{\partial g(\cdot)}{\partial x_2}, \frac{\partial g(\cdot)}{\partial x_3} \right)$$
(13.66)

evaluated at $(x_1, x_2, x_3) = (x_1^*(w_1, w_2, w_3, y), x_2^*(w_1, w_2, w_3, y), x_3^*(w_1, w_2, w_3, y))$. We are told that, at this maximizing solution, the first, second, and third constraints are slack, so $\lambda_1^p = \lambda_2^p = \lambda_3^p = 0$, making the Karush-Kuhn-Tucker condition

$$(w_1, w_2, w_3) = \lambda_4^{*p}(w_1, w_2, w_3, y) \left(\frac{\partial g(\cdot)}{\partial x_1}, \frac{\partial g(\cdot)}{\partial x_2}, \frac{\partial g(\cdot)}{\partial x_3} \right) \Bigg|_{\substack{x_1 = x_1^*(w_1, w_2, w_3, y) \\ x_2 = x_2^*(w_1, w_2, w_3, y) \\ x_3 = x_3^*(w_1, w_2, w_3, y)}}$$
(13.67)

with $\lambda_4^{*p}(w_1, w_2, w_3, y) > 0$. The only useful complementary slackness condition is

$$g(x_1^*(w_1, w_2, w_3, y), x_2^*(w_1, w_2, w_3, y), x_3^*(w_1, w_2, w_3, y)) = y.$$
(13.68)

(iv) The Karush-Kuhn-Tucker condition for the primal-dual problem (13.65) is

$$\left(-w_1, -w_2, -w_3, \frac{\partial c^\ell(\cdot)}{\partial w_1} - x_1^*(\cdot), \frac{\partial c^\ell(\cdot)}{\partial w_2} - x_2^*(\cdot), \frac{\partial c^\ell(\cdot)}{\partial w_3} - x_3^*(\cdot), \frac{\partial c^\ell(\cdot)}{\partial y} \right)$$
$$= -\lambda_1^{pd}(1, 0, 0, 0, 0, 0, 0) - \lambda_2^{pd}(0, 1, 0, 0, 0, 0, 0) - \lambda_3^{pd}(0, 0, 1, 0, 0, 0, 0)$$
$$- \lambda_4^{pd} \left(\frac{\partial g(\cdot)}{\partial x_1}, \frac{\partial g(\cdot)}{\partial x_2}, \frac{\partial g(\cdot)}{\partial x_3}, 0, 0, 0, -1 \right) \Bigg|_{\substack{x_1 = x_1^*(w_1, w_2, w_3, y) \\ x_2 = x_2^*(w_1, w_2, w_3, y) \\ x_3 = x_3^*(w_1, w_2, w_3, y)}} \cdot$$
(13.69)

The first three components of (13.69) are the primal problem's necessary maximization conditions (13.67). Why? Because any primal-dual problem optimal solution $(x_1^*(w_1, w_2, w_3, y), x_2^*(w_1, w_2, w_3, y), x_3^*(w_1, w_2, w_3, y), w_1, w_2, w_3, y)$ must, for the same but *fixed* values of w_1, w_2, w_3, and y, imply the same optimal solution values $x_1^*(w_1, w_2, w_3, y)$, $x_2^*(w_1, w_2, w_3, y)$, and $x_3^*(w_1, w_2, w_3, y)$ for the primal problem that is parameterized by these particular values for w_1, w_2, w_3, and y. Since the non-negativity constraints are slack at an optimal solution, $\lambda_1^{*pd} = \lambda_2^{*pd} = \lambda_3^{*pd} = 0$ and

$\lambda_4^{*pd}(w_1, w_2, w_3, y) > 0$, so the primal-dual problem's Karush-Kuhn-Tucker condition is

$$\left(-w_1, -w_2, -w_3, \frac{\partial c^\ell(\cdot)}{\partial w_1} - x_1^*(\cdot), \frac{\partial c^\ell(\cdot)}{\partial w_2} - x_2^*(\cdot), \frac{\partial c^\ell(\cdot)}{\partial w_3} - x_3^*(\cdot), \frac{\partial c^\ell(\cdot)}{\partial y} \right)$$
$$= -\lambda_4^{*pd}(\cdot) \left(\frac{\partial g(\cdot)}{\partial x_1}, \frac{\partial g(\cdot)}{\partial x_2}, \frac{\partial g(\cdot)}{\partial x_3}, 0, 0, 0, -1 \right) \Big|_{\substack{x_1 = x_1^*(w_1, w_2, w_3, y) \\ x_2 = x_2^*(w_1, w_2, w_3, y) \\ x_3 = x_3^*(w_1, w_2, w_3, y)}}. \qquad (13.70)$$

The primal-dual problem's Karush-Kuhn-Tucker condition contains a component for each of the primal-dual choice variables w_1, w_2, w_3, and y. These do not appear in the primal problems' Karush-Kuhn-Tucker conditions since these quantities have fixed values in any primal problem. These components

$$\frac{\partial c^\ell(w_1, w_2, w_3, y)}{\partial y} = \lambda_4^{*pd}(w_1, w_2, w_3, y) \text{ and } \frac{\partial c^\ell(w_1, w_2, w_3, y)}{\partial w_i} = x_i^*(w_1, w_2, w_3, y) \qquad (13.71)$$

for $i = 1, 2, 3$ reveal the First-Order Envelope Theorem result that is Shephard's Lemma, and also that the multiplier for the strictly binding production function constraint is the firm's marginal cost of production function.

(v) The primal problem's restricted Lagrange function is

$$L^{pr}(x_1, x_2, x_3; \lambda_1 = 0, \lambda_2 = 0, \lambda_3 = 0, \lambda_4 = \lambda_4^{*p}(w_1, w_2, w_3, y))$$
$$= -w_1 x_1 - w_2 x_2 - w_3 x_3 + \lambda_4^{*p}(w_1, w_2, w_3, y)(g(x_1, x_2, x_3) - y). \qquad (13.72)$$

The necessary second-order local maximization condition for a primal problem is that, there is an $\varepsilon > 0$ such that

$$(\Delta x_1, \Delta x_2, \Delta x_3) \begin{pmatrix} \frac{\partial^2 L^{pr}}{\partial x_1^2} & \frac{\partial^2 L^{pr}}{\partial x_1 \partial x_2} & \frac{\partial^2 L^{pr}}{\partial x_1 \partial x_3} \\ \frac{\partial^2 L^{pr}}{\partial x_2 \partial x_1} & \frac{\partial^2 L^{pr}}{\partial x_2^2} & \frac{\partial^2 L^{pr}}{\partial x_2 \partial x_3} \\ \frac{\partial^2 L^{pr}}{\partial x_3 \partial x_1} & \frac{\partial^2 L^{pr}}{\partial x_3 \partial x_2} & \frac{\partial^2 L^{pr}}{\partial x_3^2} \end{pmatrix} \Bigg|_{\substack{x_1 = x_1^*(\cdot) \\ x_2 = x_2^*(\cdot) \\ x_3 = x_3^*(\cdot)}} \begin{pmatrix} \Delta x_1 \\ \Delta x_2 \\ \Delta x_3 \end{pmatrix} = \qquad (13.73)$$

$$\lambda_4^{*p}(\cdot)(\Delta x_1, \Delta x_2, \Delta x_3) \begin{pmatrix} \frac{\partial^2 g}{\partial x_1^2} & \frac{\partial^2 g}{\partial x_1 \partial x_2} & \frac{\partial^2 g}{\partial x_1 \partial x_3} \\ \frac{\partial^2 g}{\partial x_2 \partial x_1} & \frac{\partial^2 g}{\partial x_2^2} & \frac{\partial^2 g}{\partial x_2 \partial x_3} \\ \frac{\partial^2 g}{\partial x_3 \partial x_1} & \frac{\partial^2 g}{\partial x_3 \partial x_2} & \frac{\partial^2 g}{\partial x_3^2} \end{pmatrix} \Bigg|_{\substack{x_1 = x_1^*(\cdot) \\ x_2 = x_2^*(\cdot) \\ x_3 = x_3^*(\cdot)}} \begin{pmatrix} \Delta x_1 \\ \Delta x_2 \\ \Delta x_3 \end{pmatrix} \leq 0$$

for all $(\Delta x_1, \Delta x_2, \Delta x_3)$ satisfying both $g(x_1^*(\cdot) + \Delta x_1, x_2^*(\cdot) + \Delta x_2, x_3^*(\cdot) + \Delta x_3) = y$ and $(x_1^*(\cdot) + \Delta x_1, x_2^*(\cdot) + \Delta x_2, x_3^*(\cdot) + \Delta x_3) \in B_{d_E}((x_1^*(\cdot), x_2^*(\cdot), x_3^*(\cdot)), \varepsilon)$. This is a statement that, over a set of values of (x_1, x_2, x_3) that are "close" to the optimal solution to a primal problem (13.64) and satisfy the binding constraint $g(x_1, x_2, x_3) = y$, the production function g is necessarily at least weakly concave.

(vi) The primal-dual problem's restricted Lagrange function is

$$L^{pdr}(x_1, x_2, x_3, w_1, w_2, w_3, y; \lambda_1 = 0, \lambda_2 = 0, \lambda_3 = 0, \lambda_4 = \lambda_4^{*pd}(w_1, w_2, w_3, y)) = \quad (13.74)$$

$$c^\ell(w_1, w_2, w_3, y) - w_1 x_1 - w_2 x_2 - w_3 x_3 + \lambda_4^{*pd}(w_1, w_2, w_3, y)(g(x_1, x_2, x_3) - y).$$

Let $(\Delta x, \Delta \gamma) = (\Delta x_1, \Delta x_2, \Delta x_3, \Delta w_1, \Delta w_2, \Delta w_3, \Delta y)$. Then the primal-dual problem's necessary second-order local maximization condition is that, there is an $\varepsilon > 0$ such that

$$(\Delta x, \Delta \gamma) \begin{pmatrix} \dfrac{\partial^2 L^{pdr}}{\partial x_1^2} & \dfrac{\partial^2 L^{pdr}}{\partial x_1 \partial x_2} & \dfrac{\partial^2 L^{pdr}}{\partial x_1 \partial x_3} & \dfrac{\partial^2 L^{pdr}}{\partial x_1 \partial w_1} & \dfrac{\partial^2 L^{pdr}}{\partial x_1 \partial w_2} & \dfrac{\partial^2 L^{pdr}}{\partial x_1 \partial w_3} & \dfrac{\partial^2 L^{pdr}}{\partial x_1 \partial y} \\[2mm] \dfrac{\partial^2 L^{pdr}}{\partial x_2 \partial x_1} & \dfrac{\partial^2 L^{pdr}}{\partial x_2^2} & \dfrac{\partial^2 L^{pdr}}{\partial x_2 \partial x_3} & \dfrac{\partial^2 L^{pdr}}{\partial x_2 \partial w_1} & \dfrac{\partial^2 L^{pdr}}{\partial x_2 \partial w_2} & \dfrac{\partial^2 L^{pdr}}{\partial x_2 \partial w_3} & \dfrac{\partial^2 L^{pdr}}{\partial x_2 \partial y} \\[2mm] \dfrac{\partial^2 L^{pdr}}{\partial x_3 \partial x_1} & \dfrac{\partial^2 L^{pdr}}{\partial x_3 \partial x_2} & \dfrac{\partial^2 L^{pdr}}{\partial x_3^2} & \dfrac{\partial^2 L^{pdr}}{\partial x_3 \partial w_1} & \dfrac{\partial^2 L^{pdr}}{\partial x_3 \partial w_2} & \dfrac{\partial^2 L^{pdr}}{\partial x_3 \partial w_3} & \dfrac{\partial^2 L^{pdr}}{\partial x_3 \partial y} \\[2mm] \dfrac{\partial^2 L^{pdr}}{\partial w_1 \partial x_1} & \dfrac{\partial^2 L^{pdr}}{\partial w_1 \partial x_2} & \dfrac{\partial^2 L^{pdr}}{\partial w_1 \partial x_3} & \dfrac{\partial^2 L^{pdr}}{\partial w_1^2} & \dfrac{\partial^2 L^{pdr}}{\partial w_1 \partial w_2} & \dfrac{\partial^2 L^{pdr}}{\partial w_1 \partial w_3} & \dfrac{\partial^2 L^{pdr}}{\partial w_1 \partial y} \\[2mm] \dfrac{\partial^2 L^{pdr}}{\partial w_2 \partial x_1} & \dfrac{\partial^2 L^{pdr}}{\partial w_2 \partial x_2} & \dfrac{\partial^2 L^{pdr}}{\partial w_2 \partial x_3} & \dfrac{\partial^2 L^{pdr}}{\partial w_2 \partial w_1} & \dfrac{\partial^2 L^{pdr}}{\partial w_2^2} & \dfrac{\partial^2 L^{pdr}}{\partial w_2 \partial w_3} & \dfrac{\partial^2 L^{pdr}}{\partial w_2 \partial y} \\[2mm] \dfrac{\partial^2 L^{pdr}}{\partial w_3 \partial x_1} & \dfrac{\partial^2 L^{pdr}}{\partial w_3 \partial x_2} & \dfrac{\partial^2 L^{pdr}}{\partial w_3 \partial x_3} & \dfrac{\partial^2 L^{pdr}}{\partial w_3 \partial w_1} & \dfrac{\partial^2 L^{pdr}}{\partial w_3 \partial w_2} & \dfrac{\partial^2 L^{pdr}}{\partial w_3^2} & \dfrac{\partial^2 L^{pdr}}{\partial w_3 \partial y} \\[2mm] \dfrac{\partial^2 L^{pdr}}{\partial y \partial x_1} & \dfrac{\partial^2 L^{pdr}}{\partial y \partial x_2} & \dfrac{\partial^2 L^{pdr}}{\partial y \partial x_3} & \dfrac{\partial^2 L^{pdr}}{\partial y \partial w_1} & \dfrac{\partial^2 L^{pdr}}{\partial y \partial w_2} & \dfrac{\partial^2 L^{pdr}}{\partial y \partial w_3} & \dfrac{\partial^2 L^{pdr}}{\partial y^2} \end{pmatrix} \begin{pmatrix} \Delta x \\ \Delta \gamma \end{pmatrix}$$

$$= (\Delta x, \Delta \gamma) \begin{pmatrix} \nabla^2_{x,x} L^{pdr} & \nabla^2_{x,w,y} L^{pdr} \\ \nabla^2_{w,y,x} L^{pdr} & \nabla^2_{w,y} L^{pdr} \end{pmatrix} \begin{pmatrix} \Delta x \\ \Delta \gamma \end{pmatrix} \leq 0 \qquad (13.75)$$

for all $(\Delta x_1, \Delta x_2, \Delta x_3, \Delta w_1, \Delta w_2, \Delta w_3, \Delta y)$ satisfying both

$$g(x_1^*(\cdot) + \Delta x_1, x_2^*(\cdot) + \Delta x_2, x_3^*(\cdot) + \Delta x_3) = y + \Delta y \quad \text{and}$$
$$(x_1^*(\cdot) + \Delta x_1, x_2^*(\cdot) + \Delta x_2, x_3^*(\cdot) + \Delta x_3, \Delta w_1, \Delta w_2, \Delta w_3, \Delta y)$$
$$\in B_{d_E}((x_1^*(\cdot), x_2^*(\cdot), x_3^*(\cdot), w_1, w_2, w_3, y), \varepsilon),$$

where

$$\nabla^2_{x,x} L^{pdr} = \lambda^{*pd}_4(\cdot) \begin{pmatrix} \dfrac{\partial^2 g}{\partial x_1^2} & \dfrac{\partial^2 g}{\partial x_1 \partial x_2} & \dfrac{\partial^2 g}{\partial x_1 \partial x_3} \\[2mm] \dfrac{\partial^2 g}{\partial x_2 \partial x_1} & \dfrac{\partial^2 g}{\partial x_2^2} & \dfrac{\partial^2 g}{\partial x_2 \partial x_3} \\[2mm] \dfrac{\partial^2 g}{\partial x_3 \partial x_1} & \dfrac{\partial^2 g}{\partial x_3 \partial x_2} & \dfrac{\partial^2 g}{\partial x_3^2} \end{pmatrix},$$

$$\nabla^2_{x,w,y} L^{pdr} = \begin{pmatrix} -1 & 0 & 0 & 0 \\ 0 & -1 & 0 & 0 \\ 0 & 0 & -1 & 0 \end{pmatrix}, \quad \nabla^2_{w,y,x} L^{pdr} = \begin{pmatrix} -1 & 0 & 0 \\ 0 & -1 & 0 \\ 0 & 0 & -1 \\ 0 & 0 & 0 \end{pmatrix},$$

and

$$\nabla^2_{w,y} L^{pdr} = \begin{pmatrix} \dfrac{\partial^2 c^\ell}{\partial w_1^2} & \dfrac{\partial^2 c^\ell}{\partial w_1 \partial w_2} & \dfrac{\partial^2 c^\ell}{\partial w_1 \partial w_3} & \dfrac{\partial^2 c^\ell}{\partial w_1 \partial y} \\[2mm] \dfrac{\partial^2 c^\ell}{\partial w_2 \partial w_1} & \dfrac{\partial^2 c^\ell}{\partial w_2^2} & \dfrac{\partial^2 c^\ell}{\partial w_2 \partial w_3} & \dfrac{\partial^2 c^\ell}{\partial w_2 \partial y} \\[2mm] \dfrac{\partial^2 c^\ell}{\partial w_3 \partial w_1} & \dfrac{\partial^2 c^\ell}{\partial w_3 \partial w_2} & \dfrac{\partial^2 c^\ell}{\partial w_3^2} & \dfrac{\partial^2 c^\ell}{\partial w_3 \partial y} \\[2mm] \dfrac{\partial^2 c^\ell}{\partial y \partial w_1} & \dfrac{\partial^2 c^\ell}{\partial y \partial w_2} & \dfrac{\partial^2 c^\ell}{\partial y \partial w_3} & \dfrac{\partial \lambda^{*pd}_4}{\partial y} \end{pmatrix}.$$

(vii) If $\Delta\gamma = (\Delta w_1, \Delta w_2, \Delta w_3, \Delta y) = (0,0,0,0)$, then the primal-dual problem's necessary second-order maximization condition is the same as for a primal problem. If we wish to conduct a comparative statics experiment, then we set $\Delta x = (\Delta x_1, \Delta x_2, \Delta x_3) = (0,0,0)$ and obtain from the primal-dual problem's necessary second-order maximization condition that, necessarily, there is an $\varepsilon > 0$ such that

$$(\Delta w_1, \Delta w_2, \Delta w_3, \Delta y)\, \nabla^2_{w,y} L^{pdr} \begin{pmatrix} \Delta w_1 \\ \Delta w_2 \\ \Delta w_3 \\ \Delta y \end{pmatrix} \leq 0$$

for all $(\Delta w_1, \Delta w_2, \Delta w_3, \Delta y) \in B_{d_E}((0,0,0,0), \varepsilon)$. From (13.71), this condition is

$$
(\Delta w_1, \Delta w_2, \Delta w_3, \Delta y)
\begin{pmatrix}
\dfrac{\partial x_1^*}{\partial w_1} & \dfrac{\partial x_1^*}{\partial w_2} & \dfrac{\partial x_1^*}{\partial w_3} & \dfrac{\partial x_1^*}{\partial y} \\[2mm]
\dfrac{\partial x_2^*}{\partial w_1} & \dfrac{\partial x_2^*}{\partial w_2} & \dfrac{\partial x_2^*}{\partial w_3} & \dfrac{\partial x_2^*}{\partial y} \\[2mm]
\dfrac{\partial x_3^*}{\partial w_1} & \dfrac{\partial x_3^*}{\partial w_2} & \dfrac{\partial x_3^*}{\partial w_3} & \dfrac{\partial x_3^*}{\partial y} \\[2mm]
\dfrac{\partial \lambda_4^{*pd}}{\partial w_1} & \dfrac{\partial \lambda_4^{*pd}}{\partial w_2} & \dfrac{\partial \lambda_4^{*pd}}{\partial w_3} & \dfrac{\partial \lambda_4^{*pd}}{\partial y}
\end{pmatrix}
\begin{pmatrix}
\Delta w_1 \\ \Delta w_2 \\ \Delta w_3 \\ \Delta y
\end{pmatrix}
\leq 0,
$$

revealing that, necessarily,

$$
\frac{\partial x_i^*}{\partial w_i} \leq 0 \text{ and } \frac{\partial x_i^*}{\partial y} = \frac{\partial \lambda_4^{*pd}}{\partial w_i} \text{ for } i = 1, 2, 3, \text{ and } \frac{\partial x_i^*}{\partial w_j} = \frac{\partial x_j^*}{\partial w_i} \text{ for } i, j = 1, 2, 3; i \neq j. \quad \square
$$

Answer to Problem 13.2. Use p to denote the price vector $(p_1, \ldots, p_n)$ and use x to denote the consumption bundle $(x_1, \ldots, x_n)$. Given p and a utility level u, the consumer's expenditure minimization problem is to choose x to minimize $p{\cdot}x$ subject to $U(x) \geq u$ or, equivalently, to

$$
\max_x -p{\cdot}x \text{ subject to } U(x) \geq u, \tag{13.76}
$$

where U is strictly increasing. This primal problem's Lagrange function is

$$
L^p(x, \lambda^p) = -p{\cdot}x + \lambda^p(U(x) - u). \tag{13.77}
$$

For given (p, u) the optimal solution is the Hicksian demand vector $h(p, u)$. The consumer's expenditure function is the minimum value function

$$
e(p, u) = p{\cdot}h(p, u) + \lambda^*(p, u)(U(h(p, u)) - u). \tag{13.78}
$$

Because the expenditure function is a minimum value function,

$$
e(p, u) - p{\cdot}x \leq 0 \text{ for all } x \text{ satisfying } U(x) \geq u.
$$

Therefore the primal-dual problem is

$$
\max_{x, p, y} e(p, u) - p{\cdot}x \text{ subject to } U(x) \geq u \tag{13.79}
$$

and its Lagrange function is

$$L^{pd}(x, p, u, \lambda^{pd}) = e(p, u) - p \cdot x + \lambda^{pd}(U(x) - u). \tag{13.80}$$

The first-order conditions for the primal-dual problem are

$$\frac{\partial L^{pd}}{\partial x_i} = -p_i + \lambda^{pd} \frac{\partial U}{\partial x_i} = 0; \quad i = 1, \ldots, n, \tag{13.81}$$

$$\frac{\partial L^{pd}}{\partial p_i} = \frac{\partial e}{\partial p_i} - x_i = 0; \quad i = 1, \ldots, n, \tag{13.82}$$

$$\frac{\partial L^{pd}}{\partial u} = \frac{\partial e}{\partial u} - \lambda^{pd} = 0, \quad \text{and} \tag{13.83}$$

$$U(x) = u. \tag{13.84}$$

(13.81) and (13.84) are the first-order conditions for the primal problem (13.76). (13.82) and (13.83) are applications of the First-Order Envelope Theorem to (13.78); their ratio establishes Roy's Identity. (13.83) shows that the value $\lambda^{*pd}(p, u) > 0$ of the multiplier of the utility constraint is the reciprocal of the consumer's marginal utility of expenditure. These results are not new. What is new arises from the fact that the Hessian of L^{pd} is necessarily negative-semi-definite for feasibility-preserving perturbations of (x, p, u). For perturbations just of (p, u), then, the submatrix of the Hessian of L^{pd} consisting only of the second-order partial derivatives of L^{pd} with respect to (p, u),

$$H^{pd}_{p,u} = \begin{pmatrix} \dfrac{\partial^2 L^{pd}}{\partial p_1^2} & \dfrac{\partial^2 L^{pd}}{\partial p_2 \partial p_1} & \cdots & \dfrac{\partial^2 L^{pd}}{\partial p_n \partial p_1} & \dfrac{\partial^2 L^{pd}}{\partial u \partial p_1} \\ \dfrac{\partial^2 L^{pd}}{\partial p_1 \partial p_2} & \dfrac{\partial^2 L^{pd}}{\partial p_2^2} & \cdots & \dfrac{\partial^2 L^{pd}}{\partial p_n \partial p_2} & \dfrac{\partial^2 L^{pd}}{\partial u \partial p_2} \\ \vdots & \vdots & \ddots & \vdots & \vdots \\ \dfrac{\partial^2 L^{pd}}{\partial p_1 \partial p_n} & \dfrac{\partial^2 L^{pd}}{\partial p_2 \partial p_n} & \cdots & \dfrac{\partial^2 L^{pd}}{\partial p_n^2} & \dfrac{\partial^2 L^{pd}}{\partial u \partial p_n} \\ \dfrac{\partial^2 L^{pd}}{\partial p_1 \partial u} & \dfrac{\partial^2 L^{pd}}{\partial p_2 \partial u} & \cdots & \dfrac{\partial^2 L^{pd}}{\partial p_n \partial u} & \dfrac{\partial^2 L^{pd}}{\partial u^2} \end{pmatrix}$$

is necessarily negative-semi-definite with respect to small feasibility-preserving perturbations of (p, u) when it is evaluated at an optimal solution to the primal-dual problem. $\partial e(p, u)/\partial p_i = h_i(p, u)$, so, from (13.81), (13.82), and (13.83), the Hessian's value is

$$H^{pd}_{p,u} = \begin{pmatrix} \dfrac{\partial h_1}{\partial p_1} & \dfrac{\partial h_1}{\partial p_2} & \cdots & \dfrac{\partial h_1}{\partial p_n} & \dfrac{\partial h_1}{\partial u} \\[2mm] \dfrac{\partial h_2}{\partial p_1} & \dfrac{\partial h_2}{\partial p_2} & \cdots & \dfrac{\partial h_2}{\partial p_n} & \dfrac{\partial h_2}{\partial u} \\[2mm] \vdots & \vdots & \ddots & \vdots & \vdots \\[2mm] \dfrac{\partial h_n}{\partial p_1} & \dfrac{\partial h_n}{\partial p_2} & \cdots & \dfrac{\partial h_n}{\partial p_n} & \dfrac{\partial h_n}{\partial u} \\[2mm] \dfrac{\partial \lambda^{*pd}}{\partial p_1} & \dfrac{\partial \lambda^{*pd}}{\partial p_2} & \cdots & \dfrac{\partial \lambda^{*pd}}{\partial p_n} & \dfrac{\partial \lambda^{*pd}}{\partial u} \end{pmatrix}. \tag{13.85}$$

Because this matrix is necessarily negative-semi-definite, the main diagonal elements are all nonpositive, informing us that

$$\frac{\partial h_i(p, u)}{\partial p_i} \leq 0 \text{ for all } i = 1, \ldots, n. \tag{13.86}$$

That is, any compensated demand curve slopes downwards or, equivalently, all pure own-price substitution effects are nonpositive.

If the consumer's expenditure function is twice-continuously differentiable, then the matrix $H^{pd}_{p,u}$ is symmetric:

$$\frac{\partial h_i(p, u)}{\partial p_j} = \frac{\partial h_j(p, u)}{\partial p_i} \text{ for all } i, j = 1, \ldots, n; \ i \neq j. \tag{13.87}$$

This is a statement that the rates of cross-price pure-substitution effects between commodities i and j are the same. Symmetry also shows that the rate of change with respect to p_i of the rate of change of the consumer's minimum expenditure with respect to u is the same as the rate of change with respect to u of the consumer's Hicksian demand for commodity i:

$$\frac{\partial}{\partial p_i} \left(\frac{\partial e(p, u)}{\partial u} \right) = \frac{\partial h_i}{\partial u} \text{ for } i = 1, \ldots, n.$$

The *Slutsky matrix* is the matrix of second-order partial derivatives with respect to prices of the consumer's expenditure function:

$$S(p,u) = \left(\frac{\partial^2 e(p,u)}{\partial p_i \partial p_j} \right) = \begin{pmatrix} \dfrac{\partial h_1}{\partial p_1} & \dfrac{\partial h_1}{\partial p_2} & \cdots & \dfrac{\partial h_1}{\partial p_n} \\[2mm] \dfrac{\partial h_2}{\partial p_1} & \dfrac{\partial h_2}{\partial p_2} & \cdots & \dfrac{\partial h_2}{\partial p_n} \\[2mm] \vdots & \vdots & \ddots & \vdots \\[2mm] \dfrac{\partial h_n}{\partial p_1} & \dfrac{\partial h_n}{\partial p_2} & \cdots & \dfrac{\partial h_n}{\partial p_n} \end{pmatrix}. \tag{13.88}$$

It is the matrix of the rates of change with respect to prices of Hicksian (compensated) quantities demanded. These are the slopes $\partial h_i / \partial p_i$ of Hicksian demand curves and the rates of pure-substitution effects $\partial h_i / \partial p_j$ for $i \neq j$. The famous comparative statics result that the Slutsky matrix is negative-semi-definite for small feasibility-preserving perturbations of p is easily obtained from (13.85), since $H^{pd}_{p,u}$ is negative-semi-definite. $\qquad \square$

Answer to Problem 13.3. The original problem is

$$\min_{x \in \Re^n} p \cdot x \text{ subject to } U(x) \geq u.$$

The optimal solution is the compensated demand vector $(h_1(p,u), \ldots, h_n(p,u))$. The minimum-value function for the problem is the consumer's expenditure function

$$e(p,u) \equiv p_1 h_1(p,u) + \cdots + p_n h_n(p,u) + \lambda^*(p,u)(U(h(p,u)) - u). \tag{13.89}$$

Choose a price vector $p^0 \gg \underline{0}$ and a utility level u^0. Then the expenditure-minimizing consumption bundle is $(h_1(p^0, u^0), \ldots, h_n(p^0, u^0))$. Let h_1^0 denote the numerical value $h_1(p^0, u^0)$. The new problem is the original with the additional constraint $x_1 = h_1^0$; *i.e.*

$$\min_{x \in \Re^n} p \cdot x \text{ subject to } U(x) \geq x \text{ and } x_1 = h_1^0.$$

The additional constraint is just-binding when $(p_1, \ldots, p_n) = (p_1^0, \ldots, p_n^0)$, and $u = u^0$. The solution is the compensated demand vector $h^r(p,u) = (h_1^r(p,u), \ldots, h_n^r(p,u))$, where the superscript r denotes the presence of the extra restriction. The minimum-value function for the new problem is the expenditure function

$$\begin{aligned} e^r(p,u;h_1^0) &\equiv p_1 h_1^r(p,u) + p_2 h_2^r(p,u) + \cdots + p_n h_n^r(p,u) \\ &\quad + \lambda^{*r}(p,u)(U(h^r(p,y)) - u) + \mu^r(p,u)(h_1^r(p,u) - h_1^0). \end{aligned} \tag{13.90}$$

The crucial facts are that

$$e(p^0, u^0) = e^r(p^0, u^0; h_1^0) \text{ and } e(p, u) < e^r(p, u; h_1^0) \text{ for } (p, u) \neq (p^0, u^0). \quad (13.91)$$

That is, $e(p, u)$ is the lower envelope formed from the family of functions $e^r(p, u; h_1^0)$ by minimizing $e^r(p, u; h_1^0)$ with respect to h_1^0.

For small enough ϵ and any $(p, u) \in B_{d_e}((p^0, u^0), \varepsilon)$, an order-2 Taylor's series can be used to write

$$e(p, u) = e(p^0, u^0) + \nabla e(p^0, u^0) \cdot (p - p^0, u - u^0)$$
$$+ \frac{1}{2}(p - p^0, u - u^0) H_{p,u}(p^0, u^0) \begin{pmatrix} p - p^0 \\ u - u^0 \end{pmatrix}, \quad (13.92)$$

where $H_{p,u}(p^0, u^0)$ is the value of the Hessian matrix for e at $(p, u) = (p^0, u^0)$. Similarly,

$$e^r(p, u) = e^r(p^0, u^0) + \nabla e^r(p^0, u^0) \cdot (p - p^0, u - u^0)$$
$$+ \frac{1}{2}(p - p^0, u - u^0) H_{p,u}^r(p^0, u^0) \begin{pmatrix} p - p^0 \\ u - u^0 \end{pmatrix}, \quad (13.93)$$

where $H_{p,u}^r(p^0, u^0)$ is the value of the Hessian matrix for e^r at $(p, u) = (p^0, u^0)$.

Combining (13.91), (13.89), and (13.93) shows that, necessarily,

$$\nabla e(p^0, u^0) \cdot (p - p^0, u - u^0) + \frac{1}{2}(p - p^0, u - u^0) H_{p,u}(p^0, u^0) \begin{pmatrix} p - p^0 \\ u - u^0 \end{pmatrix}$$
$$< \nabla e^r(p^0, u^0) \cdot (p - p^0, u - u^0) + \frac{1}{2}(p - p^0, u - u^0) H_{p,u}^r(p^0, u^0) \begin{pmatrix} p - p^0 \\ u - u^0 \end{pmatrix} \quad (13.94)$$

for any $(p, u) \in B_{d_E}((p^0, u^0), \varepsilon)$.

The kth element of the gradient vector of e is the partial derivative of e with respect to p_k. From (13.89) and the First-Order Envelope Theorem, this is

$$\frac{\partial e(p, u)}{\partial p_k} = h_k(p, u). \quad (13.95)$$

The last element of the gradient vector of e is the partial derivative of e with respect to u. From (13.89) and the First-Order Envelope Theorem, this is

$$\frac{\partial e(p, u)}{\partial u} = \lambda^*(p, u). \quad (13.96)$$

The kth element of the gradient vector of e^r is the partial derivative of e^r with respect to p_k. From (13.89) and the First-Order Envelope Theorem, this is

$$\frac{\partial e^r(p, u)}{\partial p_k} = h_k^r(p, u). \tag{13.97}$$

The last element of the gradient vector of e^r is the partial derivative of e^r with respect to u. From (13.89) and the First-Order Envelope Theorem, this is

$$\frac{\partial e^r(p, u)}{\partial u} = \lambda^{*r}(p, u). \tag{13.98}$$

When $(p, u) = (p^0, u^0)$, the constraint $x_1 = h_1^0$ is only just binding, so $\mu^{*r}(p^0, u^0) = 0$ and, particularly, $\lambda^*(p^0, u^0) = \lambda^{*r}(p^0, u^0)$ and $h(p^0, u^0) = h^r(p^0, u^0)$. Thus, from (13.93), (13.96), (13.97), and (13.98),

$$\nabla e(p, u) = \nabla e^r(p, u) \text{ at } (p, u) = (p^0, u^0) \tag{13.99}$$

and so, from (13.94) and (13.99), necessarily

$$(p - p^0, u - u^0) H_{p,u}(p^0, u^0) \begin{pmatrix} p - p^0 \\ u - u^0 \end{pmatrix} < (p - p^0, u - u^0) H_{p,u}^r(p^0, u^0) \begin{pmatrix} p - p^0 \\ u - u^0 \end{pmatrix}.$$

Rearranged, this is

$$(p - p^0, u - u^0) \left(H_{p,u}(p^0, u^0) - H_{p,u}^r(p^0, u^0) \right) \begin{pmatrix} p - p^0 \\ u - u^0 \end{pmatrix} < 0 \tag{13.100}$$

for $(p, u) \in B_{d_E}((p^0, u^0), \varepsilon)$; i.e. the matrix $H_{p,u}(p^0, u^0) - H_{p,u}^r(p^0, u^0)$ necessarily is negative-definite (not merely semi-definite).

The Hessian matrix of e is

$$H_{p,u} = \begin{pmatrix} \dfrac{\partial^2 e}{\partial p_1^2} & \cdots & \dfrac{\partial^2 e}{\partial p_1 \partial p_n} & \dfrac{\partial^2 e}{\partial p_1 \partial u} \\ \vdots & \ddots & \vdots & \vdots \\ \dfrac{\partial^2 e}{\partial p_n \partial p_1} & \cdots & \dfrac{\partial^2 e}{\partial p_n^2} & \dfrac{\partial^2 e}{\partial p_n \partial u} \\ \dfrac{\partial^2 e}{\partial u \partial p_1} & \cdots & \dfrac{\partial^2 e}{\partial u \partial p_n} & \dfrac{\partial^2 e}{\partial u^2} \end{pmatrix} = \begin{pmatrix} \dfrac{\partial h_1}{\partial p_1} & \cdots & \dfrac{\partial h_1}{\partial p_n} & \dfrac{\partial h_1}{\partial u} \\ \vdots & \ddots & \vdots & \vdots \\ \dfrac{\partial h_n}{\partial p_1} & \cdots & \dfrac{\partial h_n}{\partial p_n} & \dfrac{\partial h_n}{\partial u} \\ \dfrac{\partial \lambda^*}{\partial p_1} & \cdots & \dfrac{\partial \lambda^*}{\partial p_n} & \dfrac{\partial \lambda^*}{\partial u} \end{pmatrix} \tag{13.101}$$

from (13.95) and (13.96). Similarly, the Hessian matrix of e^r is

$$
H_{p,u}^r = \begin{pmatrix} \dfrac{\partial^2 e^r}{\partial p_1^2} & \cdots & \dfrac{\partial^2 e^r}{\partial p_1 \partial p_n} & \dfrac{\partial^2 e^r}{\partial p_1 \partial u} \\ \vdots & \ddots & \vdots & \vdots \\ \dfrac{\partial^2 e^r}{\partial p_n \partial p_1} & \cdots & \dfrac{\partial^2 e^r}{\partial p_n^2} & \dfrac{\partial^2 e^r}{\partial p_n \partial u} \\ \dfrac{\partial^2 e^r}{\partial u \partial p_1} & \cdots & \dfrac{\partial^2 e^r}{\partial u \partial p_n} & \dfrac{\partial^2 e^r}{\partial u^2} \end{pmatrix} = \begin{pmatrix} \dfrac{\partial h_1^r}{\partial p_1} & \cdots & \dfrac{\partial h_1^r}{\partial p_n} & \dfrac{\partial h_1^r}{\partial u} \\ \vdots & \ddots & \vdots & \vdots \\ \dfrac{\partial h_n^r}{\partial p_1} & \cdots & \dfrac{\partial h_n^r}{\partial p_n} & \dfrac{\partial h_n^r}{\partial u} \\ \dfrac{\partial \lambda^{*r}}{\partial p_1} & \cdots & \dfrac{\partial \lambda^{*r}}{\partial p_n} & \dfrac{\partial \lambda^{*r}}{\partial u} \end{pmatrix} \quad (13.102)
$$

from (13.97) and (13.98). From (13.101) and (13.102),

$$
H_{p,u}(p^0, u^0) - H_{p,u}^r(p^0, u^0) = \begin{pmatrix} \dfrac{\partial h_1}{\partial p_1} - \dfrac{\partial h_1^r}{\partial p_1} & \cdots & \dfrac{\partial h_1}{\partial p_n} - \dfrac{\partial h_1^r}{\partial p_n} & \dfrac{\partial h_1}{\partial u} - \dfrac{\partial h_1^r}{\partial u} \\ \vdots & \ddots & \vdots & \vdots \\ \dfrac{\partial h_n}{\partial p_1} - \dfrac{\partial h_n^r}{\partial p_1} & \cdots & \dfrac{\partial h_n}{\partial p_n} - \dfrac{\partial h_n^r}{\partial p_n} & \dfrac{\partial h_n}{\partial u} - \dfrac{\partial h_n^r}{\partial u} \\ \dfrac{\partial \lambda^*}{\partial p_1} - \dfrac{\partial \lambda^{*r}}{\partial p_1} & \cdots & \dfrac{\partial \lambda^*}{\partial p_n} - \dfrac{\partial \lambda^{*r}}{\partial p_n} & \dfrac{\partial \lambda^*}{\partial u} - \dfrac{\partial \lambda^{*r}}{\partial u} \end{pmatrix},
$$

$$(13.103)$$

where every term in the matrix is evaluated at (p^0, u^0).

The main diagonal elements of this matrix are necessarily *strictly* negative, so, necessarily,

$$
\frac{\partial h_i}{\partial p_i}\Big|_{(p,u)=(p^0,u^0)} < \frac{\partial h_i^r}{\partial p_i}\Big|_{(p,u)=(p^0,u^0)} \text{ for } i = 1, \ldots, n \quad (13.104)
$$

and
$$
\frac{\partial \lambda^*}{\partial u}\Big|_{(p,u)=(p^0,u^0)} < \frac{\partial \lambda^{*r}}{\partial u}\Big|_{(p,u)=(p^0,u^0)}. \quad (13.105)
$$

(13.104) states that the rate at which the consumer changes her Hicksian quantity demanded of commodity i as p_i rises is more negative when the consumer is not subject to the additional restriction $h_1 \equiv h_1^0$. Simply put, when the consumer is less restricted in her choices of consumption bundles, she is better able to reduce the adverse (higher expenditure) consequence of a larger p_i, and does so by making strictly greater (Hicksian) substitutions compared to when she is subject to the extra restriction of consuming a fixed quantity of commodity 1. This is what Le Chatelier would have predicted.

What does (13.105) say? The quantities $\partial\lambda^*/\partial u$ and $\partial\lambda^{*r}/\partial u$ are the reciprocals of the rates of change of the consumer's marginal utilities of expenditure with respect to the utility level achieved. These are both positive quantities, so (13.105) states that the consumer's marginal utility of expenditure increases at a slower rate, or, more likely, decreases at a faster rate when the consumer is subject to the additional restriction. This should be intuitively clear. If the consumer is more restricted in how she can use an extra dollar of disposable income, then that extra dollar will not provide her as much extra utility. This too is what Le Chatelier would have predicted.

If the two expenditure functions e and e^r are twice-continuously differentiable, then the matrices $H_{p,u}$ and $H^r_{p,u}$ are symmetric and so is the matrix $H_{p,u} - H^r_{p,u}$. Hence

$$\frac{\partial h_i}{\partial p_j} - \frac{\partial h^r_i}{\partial p_j} = \frac{\partial h_j}{\partial p_i} - \frac{\partial h^r_j}{\partial p_i} \text{ for all } i, j = 1, \ldots, n; \ i \neq j. \tag{13.106}$$

This states that, necessarily, the difference in the rates of the less and more restricted cross-price pure-substitution effects for commodity i with respect to p_j is the same as the difference in the rates of the less and more restricted cross-price pure-substitution effects for commodity j with respect to p_i. Similarly, for what it is worth, necessarily,

$$\frac{\partial h_i}{\partial u} - \frac{\partial h^r_i}{\partial u} = \frac{\partial \lambda^*}{\partial p_i} - \frac{\partial \lambda^{*r}}{\partial p_i} \text{ for } i = 1, \ldots, n. \tag{13.107}$$

Bibliography

Arrow, K., and A. Enthoven. 1961. "Quasi-Concave Programming." *Econometrica* 29 (4): 779–800.

Chiang, A., and K. Wainwright. 2005. *Fundamental Methods of Mathematical Economics.* McGraw-Hill.

Debreu, G. 1952. "Definite and Semidefinite Quadratic Forms." *Econometrica* 20 (2): 295–300.

Franklin, J. 2002. *Methods of Mathematical Economics: Linear and Nonlinear Programming, Fixed-Point Theorems.* Society for Industrial and Applied Mathematics.

Hoy, M., J. Livernois, C. McKenna, R. Rees, and T. Stengos. 2011. *Mathematics for Economics.* MIT Press.

John, F. 1948. "Extremum Problems with Inequalities as Subsidiary Conditions." In *Studies and Essays, Courant Anniversary Volume,* 187–204. Wiley Interscience New York.

Karush, W. 1939. "Minima of Functions of Several Variables with Inequalities as Side Constraints." M.Sc. Thesis, Department of Mathematics, University of Chicago.

Kuhn, H., and A. Tucker. 1951. "Nonlinear Programming." In *Proceedings of 2nd Berkeley Symposium on Mathematical Statistics and Probability,* edited by J. Neyman, 481–492. University of California Press, Berkeley.

Milgrom, P., and J. Roberts. 1996. "The Le Chatelier Principle." *American Economic Review* 86 (1): 173–179.

Silberberg, E. 1974. "A Revision of Comparative Statics Methodology in Economics, or, How to Do Comparative Statics on the Back of an Envelope." *Journal of Economic Theory* 7:159–172.

Simon, C., and L. Blume. 1994. *Mathematics for Economists.* W. W. Norton and Co.

Index